PROFESSOR OF APOCALYPSE

Professor of Apocalypse

THE MANY LIVES OF
JACOB TAUBES

Jerry Z. Muller

PRINCETON UNIVERSITY PRESS

PRINCETON & OXFORD

Published by Princeton University Press
41 William Street, Princeton, New Jersey 08540
99 Banbury Road, Oxford OX2 6JX

press.princeton.edu

All Rights Reserved
First paperback printing, 2024
Paperback ISBN 9780691259307

The Library of Congress has cataloged the cloth edition as follows:

Names: Muller, Jerry Z., 1954– author.
Title: Professor of apocalypse : the many lives of Jacob Taubes / Jerry Z. Muller.
Description: Princeton : Princeton University Press, [2022] | Includes
    bibliographical references and index.
Identifiers: LCCN 2021052969 (print) | LCCN 2021052970 (ebook) |
    ISBN 9780691170596 (hardback) | ISBN 9780691231600 (ebook)
Subjects: LCSH: Taubes, Jacob. | Jewish philosophers—Germany—Biography. |
    Jewish philosophers—United States—Biography. | Philosophy—History—20th century.
Classification: LCC B3346.T284 M86 2022 (print) | LCC B3346.T284 (ebook) |
    DDC 149/.94–dc23/eng/20211115
LC record available at https://lccn.loc.gov/2021052969
LC ebook record available at https://lccn.loc.gov/2021052970

British Library Cataloging-in-Publication Data is available

Editorial: Fred Appel and James Collier
Production Editorial: Kathleen Cioffi
Jacket/Cover Design: Lauren Smith
Production: Erin Suydam
Publicity: Kate Hensley and Kathryn Stevens
Copyeditor: Hank Southgate

Jacket/Cover image: Panel discussion in the Freie Universität (FU) Berlin with Richard Lowenthal, Jacob Taubes, Herbert Marcuse, Alexander Schwan, and Dieter Claessens, July 12, 1967. Ullstein bild—Jung / Granger. All rights reserved

This book has been composed in Miller

Printed in the United States of America

For Noam Zion, kin and kindred spirit

CONTENTS

PROFESSOR OF APOCALYPSE

Why Taubes?

Scenes from the Life and Afterlife of Jacob Taubes

Vienna, March 1936. The bar mitzvah of Jacob Taubes in the synagogue on the Pazmanitengasse, one of the largest in Vienna, where his father is the rabbi. Jacob reads from the Torah and the Haftorah (the Pentateuch and the Prophets). His father addresses him, first in German and then in a Hebrew richly inflected with Biblical and Talmudic allusions. He reminds Jacob that he is the scion of a family of great distinction, going back centuries, with ancestors who include great masters of rabbinic law and Hasidic rebbes.

Sankt Gallen, Switzerland, December 1944. The radically anti-Zionist, ultra-Orthodox Rebbe of Satmar arrives from Nazi-occupied Hungary on a train carrying a handful of Jews, the beneficiary of negotiations between a Zionist official and the Nazis. As the Rebbe speaks none of Switzerland's official languages, young Jacob Taubes acts as his assistant.

New York, January 1949. Having recently received his rabbinic ordination and doctorate of philosophy in Zurich, Jacob is now being groomed at the Jewish Theological Seminary to become a major Jewish theologian. The seminary pays the philosopher Leo Strauss to tutor Jacob on the great medieval Jewish thinker Moses Maimonides. Jacob, in turn, runs a seminar on Maimonides attended by a small group of up-and-coming young Jewish intellectuals—including Daniel Bell, Nathan Glazer, Gertrude Himmelfarb, and Irving Kristol—who will go on to become major figures in American academic and public life. He conveys to them, among other insights, Strauss's interpretation of the political functions of religion. That summer, they attend Jacob's wedding to Susan Feldmann.

Berlin, June 1967. The speakers' platform of the Auditorium Maximum of the Free University in Berlin where, having taught at Harvard, Princeton, and Columbia universities, Jacob is now on the faculty. Three thousand students crowd into the auditorium to hear Jacob's friend, Herbert Marcuse, lecture on "The End of Utopia." There on the platform with Marcuse is the star of the student left, Rudi Dutschke, and its leading faculty mentor, Jacob Taubes.

Plettenberg, September 1978. The small Rhineland town, home to Carl Schmitt, to which Taubes has traveled to meet face to face with the aged political theorist. Once one of the most prominent academics in Germany, Schmitt has come to be vilified among democrats and liberals for his active support of the Hitler regime. But Taubes has long been fascinated with him. Among the topics Schmitt and Taubes discuss is the proper interpretation of the passages related to the Jews in Paul's Epistle to the Romans.

Jerusalem, August 1981. The podium of the World Congress of Jewish Studies at the Hebrew University. Jacob Taubes draws a large crowd of scholars of Judaica who come to hear his critique of Gershom Scholem, the great scholar of Jewish mysticism and messianism, Taubes's erstwhile mentor, long turned enemy.

Heidelberg, February 1987. A Protestant educational institute, where Taubes, dying of cancer, offers a series of improvised lectures on the historical significance of the Apostle Paul. When he dies on March 21, he has not published a book since his doctoral dissertation in 1947, a work long out of print and barely read.

2022. A bookstore in Germany, France, or the United States. Four books by Taubes are now on the shelves: his republished doctoral dissertation, a collection of his essays, a booklet on Carl Schmitt, and an edited version of his lectures on the political theology of the Apostle Paul. Taubes's books have been translated into a dozen languages. His *Political Theology of Paul* has legitimated Paul as a radical figure, and a slew of European intellectuals, searching for new sources of inspiration after the discrediting of communism, take up the theme.

How did the ordained scion of a rabbinic family become an influential interpreter of Saint Paul? What was there about Taubes that led him to figures as diverse as Irving Kristol and Rudi Dutschke, Leo Strauss and Herbert Marcuse, Gershom Scholem and Carl Schmitt? And why were such a range of intellectual luminaries attracted to Jacob Taubes at one time or another?

Those are among the questions that this book tries to answer.

The life of Jacob Taubes covers a wide swath of the intellectual history of the twentieth century. Fate, cultural affinities, and an inner restlessness took him from interwar Vienna, to wartime Switzerland, to postwar New York, then to Israel in the years after the founding of the Jewish state, to several great American universities, and finally to the Free University in West Berlin, where he spent the largest portion of his adult life, with frequent visits to Paris, London, and Jerusalem. His was a restless existence, full of tension and contradictions. But those personal tensions and contradictions mirrored many larger issues: of religious belief versus scholarship; of allegiance to one's origins and the urge to escape them; of institutional membership and radical criticism; and above all, of the relationship between religion and politics.

It was Taubes's powerful mind and dramatic persona that seem to have attracted so remarkable a range of twentieth-century intellectuals in German-speaking Europe, the United States, France, and Israel. He was a repository of knowledge about the high culture of the West, both religious and secular—but also a storehouse of gossip about academics and intellectuals on three continents. He had a wide-ranging mind and was constantly on the lookout for large historical patterns. He was multilingual, fluent in German, English, French, Hebrew, and Yiddish, with a reading knowledge of Latin and Greek. He was, in some moods at least, a remarkable conversationalist, his talk full of energy, learning, and biting wit.

Yet, in interviewing scores of people who knew Jacob Taubes, I found the word most frequently used to describe him was "demonic"—a description used not only by his enemies, but by his friends. That designation is not entirely censorious, for in Plato it also connotes a semidivine source of creativity. Another adjective applied to Taubes was "Mephistophelian," with a similarly dual connotation of danger and inspiration. And then, there were those who opted for the more unequivocal "Satanic." Jacob Taubes exuded the fascination of the liminal and the paradoxical. For his was an existence on the border between Judaism and Christianity, between skepticism and belief, between scholarly distance and religious fervor. He was a man given to abstraction on the one hand, and carnality on the other. His was an erotic life in the many senses of the word.

During his lifetime and after, those who knew Jacob Taubes debated the depth, accuracy, and originality of his ideas. To some he seemed a genius, to others a charlatan, to yet others, "a con, but not a fraud."[1] As we will see, there are plausible grounds for all of these judgments.

To those who knew him, Jacob Taubes could be a source of joy and mirth, but he was both tormented and capable of tormenting others. He thrived on disorder and created disorder around him. He could elevate lives and wreck them. That is why Jacob Taubes was the object of love, fascination, fear, and antipathy—often by the same individual in successive phases of encounter.

But this book is not only about Jacob Taubes the man. It uses his biography to reconstruct a series of intellectual milieus in which Taubes operated. Those include the interactions between Christian and Jewish theologians in the shadow of the Holocaust; the New York Jewish intellectuals in the postwar decade; the Hebrew University in the late 1940s and early 1950s; the establishment of the academic study of religion in the United States in the 1950s; the creation of Jewish studies in West Germany; and the radicalization and deradicalization of German academic life from the 1960s to the 1980s.

Taubes is of particular interest as an intellectual conduit and a merchant of ideas between the American and German intellectual contexts from the 1940s through the 1980s, roles rarely explored in the writing of modern intellectual history. Ideas do not move across national and linguistic boundaries by their own force. Their transfer depends on the ability of individuals to stimulate others to take particular ideas seriously. That includes those who act as advisors and editors at journals and publishing houses, or who bring together intellectuals from a variety of disciplines or nations in academic conferences. Taubes played all of those roles. He was a self-appointed spotter and promoter of talent.

Taubes's published output was modest. But that is by no means an accurate measure of his influence, which often took the form of suggestions to others about unexpected lines of inquiry—or of experience—that they might pursue. He was influential behind the scenes, a secret agent in the academic world. The thinkers who get the most attention from historians tend to be those who exert influence through systematic and coherent research and inquiry. But then there are figures like Taubes—less easily documented, but not necessarily less significant in intellectual life—whose impact takes more diffuse forms.

Though Jacob Taubes may not have been among the most profound intellectuals of the twentieth century, his life is among the most interesting. He traversed different religious camps, political orientations, and national contexts. The intellectual and spiritual dilemmas he confronted were among the most pressing and widely shared of the age.

For many of those who encountered him as a teacher, Taubes embodied intellectualism as a way of life: a person who not only thought about ideas, but could impart them with verve. His breadth of knowledge, brilliance of insight, and sharpness of wit could dazzle. Though he spent most of his life in academic settings and taught at some of the most distinguished universities in the world, he was anything but a typical professor—nor did he seek to be. He aspired to be less a scholar than a seer. His self-appointed role was that of a gnostic, apocalypticist, or revolutionist—a man who fed on crisis, constantly on the lookout for signs of the impending destruction and transformation of a world perceived as evil or corrupted. To some that made him inspiring, to others frightening, to some a treasure, to others a purveyor of fool's gold.

This book combines several genres. It is a biography of a colorful, dramatic, and enigmatic personality, portraying his struggles, inner and outer conflicts, his achievements and disappointments. Because it is the biography of an intellectual, it is perforce a study of the ideas with which he wrestled and what he did with them. And because its protagonist was in conversation with so many of the leading intellectuals in Europe, Israel, and the United States, it is also a mosaic of twentieth-century intellectual life and an intellectual Baedeker, that is, a guide to key figures, schools, ideas, and controversies. As such, it tries to provide readers unacquainted with one or another thinker or milieu with enough information to make sense of the matters at hand. Since there are few readers who will be equally familiar with Christian "crisis theology," the Frankfurt School of critical theorists, the radical Hasidic sect of Toldot Aharon, and debates over "political theology," my hope is that readers already conversant with one or another of these will keep in mind that other readers will find these subjects terra incognita. My intention is that readers will find themselves learning about new intellectual worlds and the surprising ways in which Jacob Taubes managed to travel among them, as a facilitator, promoter, and connecting node.

My interest in Taubes was motivated in the first instance by two concerns. One was intellectual: to explore a chapter in the relationship between religion and politics, between religious belief and the historical and philosophical critique of religion, and religious critiques of modern liberal society—a twentieth-century chapter in a story that begins in the seventeenth century with Hobbes and Spinoza.

The second was the challenge of trying to explain the life of an enigmatic thinker and to discover why so many twentieth-century intellectuals found him of interest. In December 2003, I met up with Irving Kristol and his wife, Gertrude Himmelfarb, after a public lecture on Leo Strauss, during which the speaker had discussed Strauss's analysis of Maimonides in *Persecution and the Art of Writing*. I asked the couple whether they remembered a seminar I had heard about on Maimonides with Jacob Taubes, in which they had participated more than half a century earlier. Irving's eyes lit up: Remember? Of course he did, for Jacob Taubes was unforgettable, "the only really charismatic intellectual" he had met. "Someone should write something about him," Irving averred. I took up the challenge of trying to reconstruct and recapture the life of a charismatic intellectual.

A Note on Sources and on Psychology

The most important vector of influence for most intellectuals is through their publications. But not for Taubes, who, as we will see, had trouble writing for publication. Taubes actually wrote a great deal, but in the form of letters to colleagues, friends, and occasionally, enemies. Thus in reconstructing his life, I have made extensive use of his letters—scattered in archives and repositories in Europe, Israel, and the United States. Once I embarked on this project, over a decade ago, it became clear to me that one of the most important sources for understanding his life and influence was through those who had known him, and that, given the limits of human longevity, some of his peers would not be around much longer. I therefore made a point of interviewing as many people as possible who knew Taubes at various stages of his life, from his bar mitzvah in Vienna through his death in Berlin. That has involved over one hundred interviews, some by telephone, many in person. Most of those I approached were eager to talk about Taubes; but not a few refused, sometimes with comments like "Jacob Taubes was an evil man whose memory should be blotted out."

Memories, of course, must be treated with caution, for they are always partial and often reflect retrospective judgments. I have used them primarily in conjunction with archival or published sources, and wherever possible have tried to rely on multiple interviews to establish the facts. But Jacob Taubes was a person about whom many tales were told, both by others and by Taubes himself. These tales are themselves part of his story.

I have found indispensable the novel *Divorcing*, published in 1969 by Jacob's former wife, Susan Taubes. Though a work of fiction and hence of the creative imagination, it draws very heavily on the actual lives of Jacob and Susan Taubes, which are portrayed through a variety of lenses, some comic, some surrealistic. Nevertheless, there are times when the novel points to events that help illuminate archival sources. Used with caution, it provides yet another source from which to reconstruct the extraordinary life and times of Jacob Taubes.

When he was in his early fifties, Taubes suffered from a major episode of clinical depression, which was diagnosed as bipolar disorder, a condition characterized by periods of euphoria and high energy, alternating with periods of despair and lassitude. After treatment, he continued to cycle through manic and depressive phases of varying intensity. But like many who experience his form of the illness (what diagnosticians term "Bipolar II"), its symptoms appeared much earlier, in the milder form of hypomania. That is a moderately manic condition, characterized by a profusion of ideas and fluency in associating ideas with one another.[2]

Hypomanics frequently exhibit enhanced liveliness, interpersonal charm, and a high degree of perceptiveness, together with a sometimes uncanny ability to find vulnerable spots in others and to make use of them.[3] When in the hypomanic state, they are prone to "excessive involvement in pleasurable activities that have a high potential for painful consequences."[4] While manic depression is debilitating, the condition, especially in its milder form of hypomania, can also be a source of intellectual energy, creativity, and personal effervescence. It is part of what made Jacob Taubes both charismatic and puzzling. It would be reductive to explain Jacob Taubes's character as a symptom of an underlying biological condition, but to ignore the role of biology in accounting for personality would be equally fallacious.

A Note on Names

Jacob and his family functioned in a variety of languages—German, Hebrew, Yiddish, and English—and the spelling of their names varied accordingly. To spare the reader from unnecessary complications, I have tried to employ a single spelling for each name. For the first twenty-three years of his life, Jacob's name was spelled "Jakob," in the German fashion. When he first moved to the United States, he changed it to "Jacob," the spelling he retained thereafter. Jacob's father spelled his name "Zwi," pronounced "Tzvi." Jacob's sister's name was Mirjam, pronounced "Miriam."

FIGURE 0.1. Jacob Taubes, Bar Mitzvah, Vienna, 1936. (Ethan and Tania Taubes Collection.)

CHAPTER ONE

Yichus

JACOB TAUBES WAS descended from rabbinic nobility, in a culture in which distinguished lineage—*yichus*—meant a great deal. When Jacob entered the world in Vienna in 1923, he became the first member of his family born beyond the borders of Eastern Europe. He was raised in a family that spanned the cultures of Yiddish-speaking Eastern European Jewry and German-speaking, central European Jewry, as well as the intellectual worlds of traditional Jewish piety and modern European scholarship. To understand Jacob Taubes, then, we must begin with those cultures and intellectual worlds.

From Galicia to Vienna

Until shortly before Jacob's birth, his family had lived in Galicia. That region is no longer found on the map, a victim of the political transformations of the twentieth century. But Galicia was once a center of Jewish life, a heartland of the pietistic movement of Hasidism, and the birthplace of twentieth-century intellectual luminaries including the religious thinker Martin Buber, the novelist Shmuel Yosef Agnon, and the historian Salo Baron. For the century from the conclusion of the Napoleonic wars to the end of the Austro-Hungarian Empire, Galicia was the largest province in the Austrian half of the empire. In 1867, as the German-speaking house of Habsburg tried to accommodate rising ethnic nationalist sentiment, Galicia was placed under the administration of its Polish nobility, and Polish became its official language. With the dissolution of the empire in the wake of the First World War, Galicia was incorporated into the newly founded state of Poland. After the Second World War, the eastern half of Galicia became part of the Ukrainian Soviet Republic, and with the demise of the Soviet Union, part of Ukraine.

Among the more traditional Jews of eastern Galicia, from which the Taubes family sprang, the Galician dialect of Yiddish was the language of everyday conversation. Knowledge of Polish would have been more rare. But as a leader of the Jewish community in the town of Czernelica, Jacob's grandfather, Zechariah Edelstein, would have needed a command of Polish, and this seems to be the language he spoke to his grandson Jacob in the 1920s and 1930s.[1]

In the last decades of the nineteenth century and the first decades of the twentieth, Jews poured westward out of Galicia. Hoping to escape the poverty of their homeland, Galician Jews streamed into the United States, into Germany and Hungary, and into Vienna, whose burgeoning Jewish population was increasingly comprised of immigrants from Galicia.

By virtue of its geography, politics, and culture, Galicia was at the boundary between East and West.

The German-speaking Jews of Germany and of the Habsburg Empire often referred to the Yiddish-speaking Jews from Eastern Europe and Russia as *Ostjuden*—"Eastern Jews." The distinction was not only one of geography: it also referred to a cultural, social, and economic gradient that descended as one moved eastward. Western Jews characterized themselves by their manners and respectability, which included Western styles of dress and deportment; by their attachment to Western high culture; and by their movement beyond "traditional" Jewish occupations, such as peddling, characteristic of a more backward economy, into shopkeeping, banking, journalism, and the learned professions. The distinction was also reflected in their conceptions of Jewish identity. That the Jews were both a nation and a religious group was taken for granted in the East, while in the West there were movements of religious reform that jettisoned the national element of Judaism and expunged references to it from the prayerbook.[2] Religious services in the East were frequent, disorderly, and emotional. In the West, they were rarer, more orderly, and somber. But the distinction between Eastern and Western Jews was evanescent. Western Jews were often Eastern Jews who had moved westward a generation or two earlier and had assimilated to their new circumstances. The adoption of European culture and of languages other than Yiddish went on within the communities of Eastern Europe as well. If the distinctions between Western and Eastern Jews were fleeting, the evaluation of what it meant to be Eastern was also shifting. The style of life deemed backward could also come to be regarded as authentic, while, in turn, the adoption of Western culture and manners could be deemed artificial and inauthentic.[3]

Jacob Taubes had a foot in each of these worlds.

Jacob's Ancestry

Jacob Taubes descended from the Taubes, Eichenstein, and Edelstein families. They lived in a string of towns bounded by the Dniester River in the east and the Carpathian Mountains in the west, along a fifty-mile stretch from Stanislawow (now called Ivano-Frankivsk in Ukrainian) in the north, to Czernowitz (Chernivtsi) in the south. Jacob's father came from Czernelica, a town in the region of Stanislawow. Were one to place the point of a compass in Czernelica and trace out a radius of one hundred miles, to the southeast, one would hit Iasi, a major center of Jewish life in Romania, where several generations of Taubeses served as rabbis. In the southwest, one would hit Sighet (the hometown of Eli Wiesel) and Satu Mare, the Hungarian home of the Satmar dynasty of anti-Zionist Hasidic rabbis, who would exert a strong if intermittent attraction upon Jacob Taubes.

For Jews living in an age before the nation-state became the dominant political form in East-Central Europe, such political designations were by no means decisive. Their cultural horizons were only partially shaped by the shifting political borders of the multinational empires in which they lived. The Taubes, Eichenstein, and Edelstein family connections reached out beyond Galicia into Bukovina, Romania, and Hungary.

While there was no Jewish nobility in the sense of landowners of military origin, there was an aristocracy of the intellect and of the spirit: as one contemporary observer put it, "The post of rabbi functions as a letter of nobility."[4] Lineage (*yichus*) played a large role, and the Taubeses (like many rabbinic clans) traced their descent back to Rashi, the greatest of the medieval Jewish exegetes.[5] The names Taubes, Edelstein, and Eichenstein all signaled ancestry in the rabbinic nobility.

The surnames themselves, however, were relatively new. They had been imposed by the budding bureaucratic state in order to keep track of the Jews as subjects, and as potential objects of taxation and conscription. In 1777, the Habsburg emperor Joseph II decreed that the Jews of Galicia and Bukovina would be given fixed, hereditary surnames. These new names were often determined by the emperor's decidedly non-Jewish bureaucrats. Not infrequently, the names assigned were downright malicious. Jacob Taubes's mother, Fanny, for example, was surnamed "Blind."

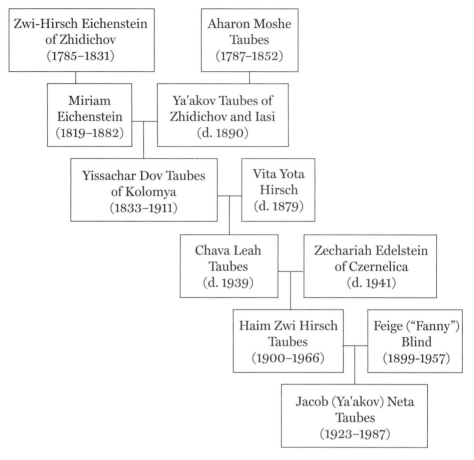

FIGURE 1.1. Jacob Taubes's Immediate Ancestors.

The origins of the name "Taubes" are ambiguous. It might have been derived from the German *taub*, meaning deaf. But more likely it was based upon the Yiddish feminine given name, "Toybe," derived from the Yiddish word for dove, *toyb*.[6] Yiddish orthography was not standardized in the nineteenth century, and the name was spelled in a variety of ways. Jews had traditionally referred to themselves by their given names and patronymic, and—in cases of distinction—by their towns of origin. Their given names were typically those of revered ancestors, and recurred frequently across generations. Such was the case of Jacob Taubes, born Jacob Neta Taubes, or in Hebrew "Yaakov."

It was on his grandmother's side that Jacob's ancestry was particularly illustrious. His eighteenth-century progenitors included Yaakov Taubes of Lvov, who sired several generations of scholars. Yaakov's son, Aharon Moshe Taubes of Sniatyn and Iasi (1787–1852)—Jacob's great-great-great-grandfather—was a luminary of Talmudic scholarship. His glosses on the Talmud and its commentators, *Karnei Re'em*, were incorporated into the *Vilna Shas*, which became the standard edition for the modern study of the Talmud. The notes of his son, Shmuel Shmelke Taubes, also made it into the *Vilna Shas*.

Nineteenth-century Galicia was a center of Hasidism, and one of Jacob's ancestors, Zwi-Hirsch Eichenstein of Zhidichov (1785–1831), was an early Hasidic wonder-rabbi, the founder of a minor Hasidic dynasty. Zwi-Hirsch was a *tzaddik*, a charismatic holy man. By virtue of his piety and lineage, the *tzaddik* was believed by his followers (Hasidim) to be able to intercede with God on their behalf. The sick, the blind, and the lame came to him in search of cures; childless wives in search of fertility; and businessmen in search of good fortune. Often there were formal pilgrimages to the rebbe, especially between Rosh Hashanah and Yom Kippur.[7]

Though Hasidism had about it an element of revolt against the perceived aridity of Talmudic learning, Zwi-Hirsch developed a particularly intellectualist brand of Hasidism. His best-known book, *Ateret Zwi*, was a commentary on the central text of Jewish mysticism, the *Zohar*, as well as on the great medieval kabbalist, Isaac Luria. But to say that Zwi-Hirsch was learned does not mean that he valued all learning. He was a fervid opponent of the *Maskilim*, Jews who favored the integration of traditional Jewish learning with modern enlightenment, and in 1822 he excommunicated the *Maskilim* of the city of Tarnopol.

Zwi-Hirsch founded a Hasidic court that attracted followers from Galicia, Slovakia, and Hungary. On the eleventh day of the Hebrew month of Tammuz, the anniversary of his death, Zwi-Hirsch's disciples and admirers celebrated their master with an annual pilgrimage to his grave.[8]

Jacob Taubes was named after his paternal great-grandfather, Natan Neta Ya'akov Edelstein, the rabbi of the small town of Czernelica. When he died, his place as town rabbi was taken by his son, Zechariah Edelstein (our Jacob's grandfather). He would marry a girl from the far more distinguished Taubes and Eichenstein families, Chava Leah Taubes.[9]

Here's how it happened. The daughter of the Hasidic wonder-rabbi and kabbalist, the Zhidichover Rav, Zwi-Hirsch Eichenstein, married Yaakov Taubes, a son of Aharon Moshe Taubes, the great Talmudist. This Ya'akov Taubes served as head of the rabbinical court (*av bet din*), first in Zhidichov and then in Iasi until his death in 1890. The son of Chava Leah and Yaakov, Yissachar Dov Taubes (1833–1911) became the rabbi of nearby Kolomya.[10] His wife, Vita Yota Hirsch (d. 1879), gave birth to a daughter, Chava Leah Taubes (d. 1939), who went on to marry Zechariah Edelstein, the rabbi of Czernelica. Chava Leah gave birth to twelve children, of whom seven survived into adulthood.[11]

Jacob's father, Haim Zwi Hirsch, was born in Czernelica in 1900. There was a Jewish school in the town, founded a decade earlier though the largess of Baron Maurice de Hirsch, who had created a foundation to provide Western-style education to the Jews of Galicia and Bukovina, with education in German, Polish, and Hebrew.[12] Haim Zwi may have been among the ninety students enrolled in the school.[13]

Haim Zwi Hirsch Taubes[14] was named for his distinguished ancestor Zwi-Hirsch Eichenstein. He studied with his father and also with his older brother, Rabbi Neta Ya'akov, who died as a young man in the influenza epidemic that followed the First World War.[15] If he attended the Hirsch school, Zwi Hirsch would have been the first generation in his family to receive a Western-style education, in addition to a traditional Talmudic education at the feet of his father and of his brother. Zwi was known by his mother's surname (Taubes) rather than his father's (Edelstein). This reflected the fact that because of the legal and financial costs, Zwi Hirsch's parents, like many Galician Jews, did not get a civil marriage, and siblings were often registered under different surnames.[16]

During the First World War, Galicia became a battleground between the contending armies of Russia and Austria-Hungary. The family of Jacob's grandfather, Zechariah Edelstein, like tens of thousands of Galician Jews, found safe haven in Vienna.[17] Like many fellow Jewish refugees, the Edelsteins remained in Vienna after the war. Though few Jews had been permitted to reside in Vienna until 1848, there was a steady flow of Jews into the city in the seven decades thereafter, many of them from more economically backward areas of the empire, such as eastern Galicia. Numbering over 200,000 souls, Jews comprised more than 10 percent of the population of the city.

Zwi Hirsch went on to study at the Rabbinical Seminary in Vienna and at the University of Vienna, and by 1930 was the rabbi of one of the largest synagogues in Vienna, in the Pazmanitengasse. Zwi's native town of Czernelica in eastern Galicia lay some 450 miles from the erstwhile imperial capital.[18] From Czernelica to the Pazmanitengasse was a long way—geographically, religiously, socially, and economically. The home in which Jacob was raised bore the residues of that journey.

Zwi Taubes's Intellectual Milieu:
Wissenschaft des Judentums

Jacob's father, Zwi Taubes, was a new sort of Orthodox rabbi, the first in his family to attend university and to graduate from a modern rabbinical seminary.

In Eastern Europe, advanced Jewish education traditionally took place in a yeshiva, where the curriculum was focused on the study of the Talmud and its commentators. Its students would typically have spent their early years in a cheder (primary school). There they would have learned Hebrew indirectly, as it were, not through the study of grammar, but in the course of learning to read the prayerbook, the siddur, and studying the Five Books of Moses, the Torah. In the upper levels of the cheder (at about the age of ten or twelve), boys would also begin the study of Talmud. Those with the intellectual and financial wherewithal would then proceed to the yeshiva, where education was focused on the study of the Talmud, the great compendium of debates on Jewish law and its applications to everyday life, together with many fanciful expansions of the narrative of the Biblical texts and philosophical reflections on their import—Aggadah. Upon completing their yeshiva education, some young men would apply for rabbinic status. Rabbinic ordination was granted not by the institution, but by an individual rabbi who orally examined the applicant on his knowledge of Jewish law.

Beginning in the second half of the nineteenth century, this traditional pathway of Jewish learning was challenged by new ideological and pedagogical currents. In the last decades of the century, Eastern European Zionists sought to make Hebrew the language not only of learned discourse, but of everyday life. They founded the *cheder metukkan* (reformed cheder), which taught both Jewish and non-Jewish subjects, and where the language of instruction was Hebrew. Growing up in Vienna, Jacob Taubes would attend a school influenced by this movement.

Higher Jewish education was also transformed. As Jews made their way into universities, some sought to bring modern European modes of learning to bear upon their understanding of Judaism. They tried to make use of the pedagogical methods and scholarly techniques of the modern university to create a corps of Jewish scholars who would apply the rigor of modern methods to traditional texts. This approach came to be known in German as *Wissenschaft des Judentums* or by the Hebrew term *Chochmat Yisrael*—best translated as "the academic study of Judaism."[19]

Traditional Jewish learning had tended to be ahistorical in its assumptions, intratextual in method, and associative in style. Its working premise was that the Five Books of Moses were a result of divine revelation. The body of debates about how to apply the laws laid out in the Bible to daily affairs were regarded as "the oral law" (*torah sheba'al peh*), whose origin was assumed to lie in the revelation at Sinai. Though post-Biblical Jews had produced poetry, philosophy, and historical narrative, none of these were part of the standard yeshiva curriculum. Higher Jewish learning was instead focused on the many commentaries on the Bible and on the Talmud. These were treated as if they were all part of a continuous and simultaneous discussion, without regard to the historical periods in which they had been composed. Historical anachronism abounded. The biblical patriarch, Jacob, for example, was said by the rabbis to have been a pupil in a house of study (*Bet Midrash*) established by Shem and Eber, the son and grandson of Noah. That is to say, Jacob studied a body of law purportedly revealed to Moses several hundred years later, at an institution established many centuries after Moses's death. On the assumption that the Bible was the product of a single, coherent revelation, its text was sometimes expounded by means of fanciful etymologies, and phrases from diverse sources within the Bible were juxtaposed to provide prooftexts. The characteristic mode of exposition was commentary on an existing text. As a result, discussion was often episodic, moving from one topic to another as it appeared in the original text, rather than laying out arguments systematically and conceptually.[20]

The new Jewish scholarship proceeded quite differently, according to the models of understanding that informed Western academic practice. Texts—even holy texts—had to be understood in their historical settings. It was important to establish the historical context in which they were written in order to comprehend their references and allusions. It was necessary to understand the language in which they were written. That meant not just the study of Hebrew grammar, but of other ancient languages that might help explain the roots of words and hence their original meanings. In accounting for inconsistencies or puzzling passages in a text, one had to consider the possibility (anathema to the traditional Jewish mind) that the text had been garbled in transmission, and may have been the product of multiple authors. And one aspired to present the ideas in the text philosophically, based on conceptual analysis and systematic exposition.

Moreover, rather than presuming that ideas, narratives, stories, and rituals were true because they were part of a holy tradition with its origin in divine revelation, the new brand of Jewish scholar began with a quest for objectivity. Though often breached in practice, in theory the findings of scholarship were to be valid regardless of the faith of the scholar or his readers. Catholics, Protestants, Jews, and atheists all ought to agree on the validity of the result of research, based on the objectivity of the methods by which those results were obtained. The dispassion of modern scholarship was to replace the passion of religious discourse. Modern historical method, it was hoped, would vanquish inherited theological animus.[21]

Most scholars of Judaism entered the field in order to better comprehend the tradition. But the assumptions of modern scholarship had an inevitable impact on the mind of the scholar and on his relationship with tradition. For the scholar—as opposed to the believer—answers could not be known in advance. Historical claims were to be decided by the weight of evidence, not the holiness of tradition. If, for the Psalmist, the beginning of wisdom is the fear of the Lord, for the historically minded scholar, the beginning of wisdom is the fear of error.[22] While more modernized Jews prized the new, university- and seminary-educated rabbi, the more traditional sectors of Orthodox Jewry were fiercely opposed to the very idea,[23] fearing (rightly) that new modes of teaching and scholarship might lead to new ideas as well.

If *Wissenschaft des Judentums* was seen as a threat by some Orthodox Jews, it also made many Christian scholars uncomfortable. For the canons of objectivity meant the tacit abandonment of the two premises of Protestant scholarship. Its first premise was that Christianity represented a theological, spiritual, and intellectual advance over Judaism (just as Protestantism represented an advance over Catholicism). The second was that the significant spiritual history of Judaism ended with the coming of Jesus of Nazareth.[24] Thus, while elements of the Jewish past were explored by Christian academics, it was rare for Jews to be allowed to teach such subjects at universities, which were dominated by Christian (usually Protestant) faculty.

Largely excluded from the university, the main home of the new Jewish scholarship was in a handful of rabbinical seminaries. The first of these was the Jüdisches-Theologisches Seminar (Jewish Theological Seminary), founded in Breslau in 1854. It was the spiritual center of Positive-Historical Judaism, which had developed out of a rejection of both Eastern European-style Orthodoxy and radical German Reform Judaism. The Reform seminary, the Hochschule für die Wissenschaft des Judentums, was founded in 1872 in Berlin. In the 1930s, its faculty included Leo Baeck, the best-known Reform rabbi in Germany, and the author of an influential interpretive work, *The Essence of Judaism* (1905), who would later attest to the young Jacob Taubes's Judaic knowledge. Orthodoxy as a formal religious ideology actually arose as a response to both Reform and Positive-Historical Judaism. It rejected the notion that historical development required changes in doctrine or practice, and it refused to recognize the authenticity of either the Reform or Positive-Historical (Conservative) movements or the legitimacy of their rabbis. But under the influence of its great theoretician, Samson Raphael Hirsch, German Orthodoxy embraced the principle of "Torah im Derekh Eretz"—of combining traditional observance and doctrine with the best of modern Western culture. The rabbinical institute of German Orthodoxy was the Seminar für das orthodoxe Judentum, founded in Berlin in 1883. Its faculty in the 1930s included Jehiel Jacob Weinberg, who a decade later would also affirm Jacob Taubes's credentials as a Jewish scholar.[25] The more liberal seminaries tended to disdain the scholarship of the more Orthodox academicians, who were chastised for their lack of scholarly impartiality, and the limits placed upon applying the tools of historical scholarship to the study of the Bible and of Jewish law.[26] For their part, the more Orthodox regarded the seminaries to their "left" as schools of heresy: Samson Raphael Hirsch even cast doubts on the orthodoxy of the Berlin Seminary for Orthodox Judaism.[27] And to the ultra-Orthodox in Eastern and Central Europe, all such institutions were hotbeds of unbelief.

One of the most important outposts of modern Jewish scholarship in the interwar era was the Israelitisch-Theologische Lehranstalt (Jewish Theological Seminary), founded in Vienna in 1893.[28] It was here that Zwi Taubes studied and received his ordination and doctorate. An understanding of its institutional culture provides us with a window into the Jewish life of the household in which Jacob Taubes was raised.

Zwi's doctoral advisor at the seminary was Adolf Schwarz (1846–1931), professor of Talmud, halachic literature, and homiletics, and the first rector of the institution. The teaching of homiletics—the art of giving a sermon—was an innovation characteristic of modern seminaries. For rabbis were now expected to give sermons, like Protestant pastors, rather than the traditional *drasha*, an exploration of legal and theological matters sometimes inspired by the Torah portion of the week. The title of one of Schwarz's publications—"The Developmental History of the School of Hillel"—captures the characteristic approaches of the Jewish scholarship of his day.[29]

Another of Zwi's teachers was Samuel Krauss (1866–1948).[30] He used the Talmud as a historical source to try to recapture Jewish social and political life at the time of its composition, and wrote several works exploring the links between the culture of the Jews and that of ancient Greece and Rome, as well as a book on the life of Jesus as reflected in Jewish sources.[31] Together with other professors at the Vienna Seminary, Krauss contributed to the first Bible commentary written in Hebrew that followed the tenets of modern Jewish scholarship.[32] A similar agenda, combining traditional learning with the characteristic concerns of modern scholarship, informed the work of another of Zwi's teachers at the seminary, Victor (Avigdor) Aptowitzer (1871–1942).[33] One of his books sought to clarify the literary nature of Aggadah (the nonlegal portions of the Talmud) by comparing it with the Apocrypha and with the homilies of the Church Fathers. Like Krauss, Aptowitzer was a committed Zionist, and both often lectured in Hebrew. Following in the footsteps of his teachers, Zwi Taubes would write about Biblical and Talmudic topics, using the tools he had learned from Schwarz, Krauss, and Aptowitzer. Jacob would develop a lifelong interest in the era of transition between Judaism and Christianity.

The Jewish Theological Seminary in Vienna was part of a network of institutions in which the modern scholarly study of Judaism was cultivated. Teachers and students often moved back and forth between this handful of establishments, located in Breslau, Berlin, Budapest, and Vienna, with lesser outposts in France, England, and Italy.[34] Those pursuing a rabbinical degree at such institutions were expected to study at the local university as well, graduating as "Rabbi Doctor." Even before the First World War, these seminaries served as the seedbed from which comparable institutions would be founded in the United States, and with the opening of the Hebrew University in 1925, in the Land of Israel as well. They formed a web in which Zwi Taubes felt most at home intellectually. Later on, those connections would help him find a position for his son, Jacob.

Perhaps the greatest influence on Zwi Taubes was Rabbi Zwi Peretz Chajes (1876–1927).[35] He too was born in Galicia to a distinguished rabbinic family, and acquired a traditional rabbinic education from his father and uncle before pursuing formal studies at the Jewish Theological Seminary and the University of Vienna. In 1918, he was appointed chief rabbi of Vienna, and in the decade that followed, he became the most influential Jewish personage in the city. Though much has been written about the contribution of marginal Jews or ex-Jews to the culture of Vienna, the existence of men like Chajes—highly educated, politically and socially active, yet deeply knowledgeable and committed Jews—goes unmentioned in most histories.[36] A charismatic and compelling speaker, his sermons attracted many young Jews who rarely found their way into a synagogue.

Inspired as a young man by his meeting with Theodore Herzl, Chajes was very active in the Zionist movement, presiding over the world Zionist conference in Vienna in 1925. His Zionism met with opposition from advocates of Jewish assimilation, especially among the wealthy Jews of Vienna. But it was also opposed by many Orthodox Jews, for whom the attempt to create a Jewish state by political means was a heretical affront to divine providence, which would restore the Jews to sovereignty in the Land of Israel in God's good time. When the Hebrew University was founded, Chajes aspired to a chair in Bible there, and was supported by the Zionist leader Chaim Weizmann. But Chajes's critical scholarly approach—his embrace of higher criticism, which called into question the divine authorship of the Biblical text—was anathema to some religious Zionists, who managed to torpedo the appointment.[37] So Chajes remained in Vienna, building up a network of Jewish institutions. When he died in December 1927 (at the age of fifty-one), fifty thousand Jews turned out for his funeral, so many that the police had to close off the city's main thoroughfare, the Ringstrasse, to allow the funeral procession to pass.[38]

Chajes created or rejuvenated a network of institutions in which Zwi Taubes, his future wife, Fanny Blind, and his son, Jacob, would be educated. He served as president of the Jewish Theological Seminary, from which Zwi received his rabbinical ordination, as did Zwi's slightly older classmate, Salo Baron, who went on to become a seminal figure in establishing Jewish studies in the United States. Chajes was active in the attached Seminary for Teachers and taught Bible in the Hebrew Teachers College (*Paedagogium*), where Fanny Blind was a student when she met Zwi Taubes. Chajes founded two elementary schools as well as a high school, which after his death was named in his memory. These schools combined Western education with the study of Jewish subjects, which, following a key principal of Zionist pedagogy, were taught in Hebrew.

The Taubes household in Vienna, and later in Zurich, was stamped in the cultural mold created by Chajes. It was a household that was Orthodox in observance, in which traditional rabbinic learning was valued. But so was modern German culture and modern Western scholarship. As part of his duties as a congregational rabbi in Vienna and later in Zurich, Zwi Taubes would be expected—and would expect of himself—to offer sermons that combined traditional Jewish sources with modern concerns. German was the language of familial discourse among the members of the Taubes family. But Zwi and his wife, Fanny, were committed to a synthesis of Zionism and Orthodoxy embodied in the Mizrachi movement, which Zwi would later head in Switzerland. Part of its agenda was the recovery of Hebrew as a spoken and written tongue, a language not only of prayer and study, but of communication as well. When their son, Jacob, reached adulthood, he was able to write and speak in Hebrew—a Hebrew steeped in Biblical and rabbinic tropes—before he set foot in Israel.

Zwi was a prize-winning student at the Rabbinical Seminary.[39] He wrote his doctoral dissertation at the University of Vienna on "Jesus and the Halakah."[40] While the topic might seem unconventional for an Orthodox rabbi, it was a characteristic subject of the *Wissenschaft des Judentums* of its day. For Jewish scholars in search of legitimation from colleagues in the Christian-dominated universities, placing Jesus into his original Jewish context offered a sort of market niche. For the Jewishly trained scholars had knowledge of rabbinic sources, which, with university training, they could combine with Greek and Latin sources to understand Jesus as a historical figure.[41]

For our purposes, Zwi's evidence and conclusions are less important than his approach to the texts of the Mishna (the earlier portion of the Talmud): his method was critical and historical, including the unorthodox assumption that the later generations of rabbis who contributed to the Talmud (amoraim) sometimes misunderstood the text of the Mishna. The dissertation attempted to relate Jesus's approach to several legal issues to the way those issues were framed in his day by the struggles between Pharisees and Sadducees. It demonstrated a deep knowledge of Talmudic sources, but also of modern scholarship on the topic, including the work of Abraham Geiger (the first Jewish scholar to write about Jesus), and the great Protestant biblical critic Julius Wellhausen.[42] Despite the title, much of the dissertation dealt with controversies among contending rabbinic factions. As Zwi saw it, Jesus observed all the commandments. His critiques of the Pharisees are best understood as representing the criticisms of one of the major rabbinic schools, the followers of Shammai, against the other major school, the followers of Hillel, the antecedents of the Pharisees. The Talmud, Zwi noted, is written from the perspective of the school of Hillel, and reflects its valuations, while offering a jaundiced view of the school of Shammai. In Zwi's reading of the sources, Jesus was a Shammaite, who rightly charged the Pharisees with instituting new practices that were not in the Bible and had only recently been introduced, such as the commandment to wash one's hands before eating.[43] Taubes also thought that some of Jesus's criticisms had influenced the development of Jewish law: he cited as an example the relaxation of the stringent laws of the Sabbath in order to save a life, which, he maintained, was instituted by the rabbis a hundred years after Jesus.[44] Jesus, then, was a Jew who advocated continuity of the law and of the Old Testament. Zwi suggested that statements attributed to Jesus in the synoptic Gospels that conflicted with existing Jewish law should be understood as later interpolations.[45]

Zwi's interest in and knowledge of Christianity prepared him for dialogue and outreach to Christian clergymen and theologians. His son, Jacob, grew up in a scholarly, Orthodox household, in which the issue of the relationship of the origins of Christianity to Judaism was a familiar topic.

Zwi never published the portions of his dissertation in which he set out this interpretation of Jesus's relationship to existing rabbinic traditions. But a few years later, in 1929, he published an article based in part on his doctoral research in the most prestigious journal of Jewish scholarship, the *Monatsschrift für Geschichte und Wissenschaft des Judentums*. The article, on the Talmudic laws of vow-taking, contended that one could trace a development within the Talmud from archaic taboos to laws that reflect more ethical considerations.[46]

Zwi, then, was headed for a career as a rabbi and as a scholar. A modern rabbi, to be sure, who could address his congregants with the authority of a deep knowledge of traditional Jewish sources as well as modern historical scholarship.

The Taubes Family in Vienna

In the interwar period, Vienna had the third-largest Jewish population in Europe (after Budapest and Warsaw). Jews made up 10 percent of the city's two million inhabitants. The term "Jews of Vienna" typically conjures up an image of highly assimilated Jews (some so assimilated they had converted to Christianity) such as Sigmund Freud, Arthur Schnitzler, or Gustav Mahler. But the Jewish community of Vienna was far more varied and internally divided. Especially after the influx of Jews from Galicia before and during the First World War, Vienna was also a center of Orthodoxy, or rather of a variety of Orthodoxies: the modern Orthodoxy of Chajes and Zwi Taubes, which sought to reconcile Judaism with modern culture, and the ultra-Orthodoxy of the Agudat Yisrael (which had its world headquarters in Vienna), which stood for uncompromising traditional Judaism with minimal concessions to modern culture and modes of comportment. In addition, a half dozen Hasidic dynasties had transferred from Galicia to Vienna. These included the various heirs of the Sadagora dynasty, to which the Taubeses were related.[47]

Committed Jews, both religious and secular, were also divided into Zionists and anti-Zionists. The Zionists believed that under modern conditions, in which ethnic national states were replacing the multi-ethnic empires of old, and nationalist movements were defining Jews as beyond the bounds of the national community, Jews needed a sovereign nation of their own, in the Land of Israel. There were many flavors of Zionism: religious, socialist, and liberal. What they had in common was a belief in the need for Jewish renewal, which they connected with the process of Jewish political self-assertion. Those who objected to the Zionist project did so on a variety of grounds. There were Jewish liberals who saw Zionism as a threat to Jewish integration into the nations in which they currently lived. There were socialists and communists who viewed particular ethnic commitments as retrograde. And there were the ultra-Orthodox Jews of Agudat Yisrael, who saw Zionism as a heretical secularist pretension that challenged the traditional Jewish belief that the Jews would be restored to sovereignty in their Land only in the messianic era, at a time of divine, not human, choosing. Viennese Jewry was split along these cultural, sectarian, and political lines.[48]

On January 29, 1922, while he was still studying for the rabbinate, Zwi married Feige Blind, known as "Fanny." The two could hardly have been better matched. They were close in age: she was born in 1899, he in 1900. Like Zwi, Fanny came from a rabbinic household, in Chodorow, another town in eastern Galicia. Like Zwi, she was at home in both traditional Jewish life and in modern scholarship. Her family was Hasidic, steeped in the heritage of the Zhidichov rabbinic dynasty. Her family, like Zwi's, moved to Vienna during the war. Fanny was educated at the Jewish Teachers Seminary in Vienna, the sister institution of the seminary that Zwi was attending, and they shared a number of teachers.[49]

The new couple lived not far from the Danube River, at Wehlistrasse 128, in the second district of Vienna, the Leopoldstadt, a part of the city with so high a concentration of Jews it was known as *Die Mazzesinsel* (Matzoh Island). It was here that most Orthodox Jews and recent immigrants from Galicia lived.[50] Storefronts sported signs in Yiddish.[51]

After getting married, they did what Jewish couples are obliged to do. Their first child, Jacob (in Hebrew, Neta Ya'akov), was born just over a year later, on February 25, 1923. A daughter, Mirjam, was born four years thereafter. Zwi and Feige had no more children after that, perhaps because Feige was unable to do so.[52] That meant an especially intense emotional investment in the children born. Jacob, as the sole male, was a particular object of parental solicitude and expectation. For he was not only the "kaddish"—the one expected to chant the prayer for the dead upon his parents' demise—he also bore the burden of carrying forward the family's heritage of Jewish learning.

Though Zwi and Feige lived and married in Vienna, and though their children were born there, none of them possessed Austrian citizenship. That was because with the demise of the Austro-Hungarian Empire after 1918, the towns in Galicia from which Zwi and Fanny hailed were no longer part of the same country as Vienna. Czernelica and Chodorow were now in independent Poland, Vienna, the capital of the rump state of Austria. According to the Treaty of St. Germain that concluded the war, Jews who were German speakers were to have the right to claim Austrian citizenship. But the new Austrian republic was not eager for additional Jewish citizens and made it difficult for people like the Taubeses to acquire citizenship.[53] As we will see, Switzerland, to which the Taubes moved in 1936, was even more reluctant to grant citizenship status to Jewish immigrants. As a result, Jacob would lack a national passport until decades later, when he became an American citizen.

Zwi's first pulpit was in the small Moravian city of Neu-Oderberg in what was then Czechoslovakia, where Jacob began to attend primary school. In September 1930, the family returned to Vienna, where Zwi was installed as the rabbi at one of the city's largest synagogues, congregation Aeschel Avrohom (The Tree of Abraham), located on the Pazmanitenstrasse, in the second district.[54] Its imposing structure, built shortly before the War as the Kaiser Franz Josephs-Huldigungstempel (Temple in Homage to Emperor Franz Joseph), could seat five hundred men on the ground floor of its sanctuary, and an additional four hundred people in the women's gallery.[55] The synagogue was a *Vereinstempel*, privately funded, but subsidized by the mainstream Jewish community (*Kultusgemeinde*). It was considered "liberal" in the Viennese context, but was in fact modern Orthodox. Men and women sat separately, and prayers were recited entirely in Hebrew. But unlike the scores of more traditional prayer chapels (*shtieblech*) characteristic of the ultra-Orthodox, the atmosphere in the Pazmanitenstrasse was decorous, and the sermon, delivered in German, was an important part of the service.[56] Zwi developed a reputation as a fine speaker, whose sermons blended traditional Jewish learning with modern concerns, expressed in impeccable German. His sermons were well attended, filling the large sanctuary.[57]

Jacob's School in Vienna

Between the ages of ten and fourteen, Jacob attended a unique and remarkable secondary school in the second district, the Chajes School, named after Zwi's mentor Rabbi Chajes. The only Jewish upper school

in Vienna, it was a *Realgymnasium*, which blended the traditional, classical curriculum with a more modern course of studies. Students studied
Latin, German, history, and mathematics, but also science and modern
languages (either French or English). The school tried to combine these
secular subjects with instruction in Hebrew, the Bible, and other Jewish
texts, which were taught in Hebrew. The school's orientation was Zionist and humanistic, with an appreciation of religion but without religious
dogmatism. Male students were allowed to wear a skullcap (*kippah*) when
studying Bible, but not during the rest of the school day. Classes were coed-
ucational, mixing boys and girls. Most of the students at the school were,
like Jacob, children of recent migrants from Galicia, who were regarded
by the state as *Ausländer* (foreign residents), not entitled to free school-
ing. Living in the heavily Jewish neighborhood and attending a school
that affirmed their religion and ethnicity, the students were spared the
antisemitism that Jews increasingly encountered in the public school system. Admission was by entrance exam, and the demanding curriculum—
expecting students (some of whom came from Yiddish-speaking homes)
to master German, Latin, Hebrew, and French or English—made for a
degree of self-selection of the student body.[58] The children knew that they
faced a future of antisemitic discrimination and therefore had to work
harder and prove themselves if they were to get ahead, and they displayed
a high level of motivation and achievement.[59] Six hours of instruction per
week were devoted to Hebrew subjects, and many students, like Jacob,
developed an active command of the language.

Within this intellectually demanding institution, young Jacob had
a reputation as a brilliant student, albeit a mischievous one. Impatient,
unable to sit still, and disruptive, he was frequently ejected from class.
Even as a youngster, it appears, Jacob had a problem with rules. It seems
fair to conclude that young Jacob was bored—and a dread of boredom
would continue to shape his view of the world for much of his life. He also
told tales on others—untrustworthy behavior that he would continue to
exhibit into adulthood. Jacob's mother was frequently called in to discuss
Jacob's problematic behavior with the school authorities. Zwi was too busy
with his rabbinical and scholarly activities to come along.[60]

Great Expectations: Jacob's Bar Mitzvah

But Zwi was certainly emotionally invested in his son, on whom so many
of his hopes rested. That was evident at Jacob's bar mitzvah, which took
place in his father's synagogue on March 7, 1936. Before the big day,

during the summer of 1935, Jacob was taken on a trip to Zhidichov in what had been Galicia, to the grave of his ancestor, the Zhidichover Rebbe. It was there that he acquired his *tflillin*, the phylacteries containing Biblical verses that Jewish men were commanded to wear during morning prayers.[61] Under his father's tutelage, Jacob composed a scholarly lecture on the blessings of the *tfillin*, which, as the cover page of the printed version notes, was edited by "his father, Rabbi Dr. Chaim Zwi Taubes," and was presumably distributed at the bar mitzvah.[62]

The bar mitzvah ceremony was an illustrious occasion, described in detail in the Jewish community newspaper, *Die Wahrheit*.[63] Attending were not only many family and friends, but the board members of the Vienna Jewish community and of the various scholarly and welfare organizations with which Rabbi Taubes was involved, not to speak of the full board of the synagogue itself.

Having been tutored by the synagogue's senior cantor, Jacob read the traditional *maftir* portion from the Torah and chanted the selection from the prophets, the *Haftorah*. It was the Sabbath before Purim, known in Hebrew as "Shabbat Zakhor" (the Sabbath of Remembrance), because the Torah portion that Jacob chanted includes the following verses:

> Remember what Amalek did to you on your journey, after you left Egypt—how, undeterred by fear of God, he surprised you on the march, when you were famished and weary, and cut down all the stragglers in your rear. Therefore, when the Lord your God grants you safety from all your enemies around you, in the land that the Lord your God is giving to you as a hereditary portion, you shall blot out the memory of Amalek from under heaven. Do not forget! (Deuteronomy 25:17–19)

In the *Haftorah* portion that was read next, from 1 Samuel 15, the prophet commands King Saul:

> Thus says the Lord of Hosts: I am exacting the penalty for what Amelek did to Israel, for the assault he made upon them on the road, on their way up from Egypt. Now go, attack Amalek, and proscribe all that belongs to him. Spare no one, but kill alike men and women, infants and sucklings.

The Jewish tradition drew a typological link between the inveterate enemies of the Jews in the times of Moses and of Samuel and their later enemies, as recounted in the Book of Esther, which is read on Purim. It was typically understood as a promise that God would destroy the enemies of his people.[64] But the radicalism of the commandment to the Children of Israel to destroy in their entirety the descendants of their erstwhile enemy had long troubled readers, especially because a few chapters earlier, in Deuteronomy 20:15-18, God demands a similar extirpation of the seven peoples of the Land of Israel, "lest they lead you into doing all the abhorrent things that they have done for their gods." Later in life, Jacob would claim that his bar mitzvah portion had sowed the seeds of his suspicion of the Law.[65]

Following Jacob's recitation, Rabbi Taubes addressed his son, first in German, and then in Hebrew. He reminded Jacob that he had been immersed since childhood in the study of Torah, and urged him to commit himself to ever greater efforts in the study and practice of Judaism. Zwi then read a letter he had written to his son in Hebrew—a Hebrew resonant with Biblical and Talmudic allusions—reminding him of his role as a link in the chain of generations. Jacob was descended from a family of great *yichus*, out of which had come many great sages (*gaonim*), holy men, and expounders of the oral law. Zwi cited YomTov Lippman-Heller (1578–1654), a great Talmudic scholar and author of the *Tosphot YomTov*, a commentary on the Mishnah; Joel Sirkis, the seventeenth-century author of the *Bayit Chadash*; and his grandson, Aharon Moshe Taubes, author of the *Karnei Rei'em* (a commentary on the *Shulchan Aruch*). There were also great spiritual leaders of Hasidism such as the Ba'al Shem Tov (the founder of Hasidism) and the Rebbe of Zhidichov. Zwi declared that he had tried to convey this legacy to Jacob to the best of his ability, and to fulfill the biblical injunction to teach one's sons, as had Jacob's mother, Feige. Now it was up to Jacob to carry on the tradition of learning and spiritual leadership. The letter was signed, "Your father, whose soul is bound up with yours" (*avicha shenafsho keshura benafshecha*), derived from the description of the biblical Jacob's existential tie his son (Genesis 44:30). Delivered in a quivering voice, it would be hard to find a message of greater paternal expectation and investment.

Then Jacob mounted the podium and, according to a reporter present, proceeded to fulfill those expectations. He delivered an "astonishingly fluid" learned talk, without notes, on the subject of his essay on the halacha of the commandment of *tfillin*, a talk that aroused a shout of congratulations from the congregation, for what the newspaper described as "this outstanding bar mitzvah boy with a stupendous knowledge of Judaism."

The next day, Sunday, was Purim, and after the reading of the Book of Esther, the family held a celebration at its home. The gathering was attended by the luminaries of Viennese Jewish life, including the chief rabbi and Samuel Krauss, the rector of the Rabbinical Seminary and Zwi's teacher. Jacob again spoke extemporaneously and unabashedly about the subject of his learned treatise, eliciting applause from the assembled guests. The chief rabbi praised Jacob's parents for the son they had reared, as well as Jacob himself, whom he pronounced an extraordinary person of great talents—not the first and not the last time that Jacob would be characterized in these terms. The chief rabbi expressed his hope that Jacob would follow in the footsteps of his dear parents, and through his expanding learning become a source of joy to them forevermore.[66]

From Vienna to Zurich

Half a year after Jacob's bar mitzvah, in September 1936, his father took up a new position, as the rabbi of the community synagogue in Zurich. Jacob and the rest of the family followed in 1937, presumably to give Jacob and his sister time to finish the school year. In March 1938, Austria was invaded by National Socialist Germany, and shortly thereafter annexed to the German Reich. The process of forced Jewish exclusion from social and economic life—a process that had taken five years in Germany—took a matter of months in Austria. In the war that followed, most Jews unable or unwilling to leave Vienna were deported to death camps in the East, including members of the Taubes family.

In retrospect, Zwi's decision to move his family from Vienna to Zurich seems remarkably prescient. But that is because we view these events with the wisdom of hindsight. At the time, they were still unimaginable.[67] And in fact Zwi's motivations were probably quite different. For him, the move to Zurich might well have seemed like a stepping-stone to an eventual return to Vienna, perhaps as chief rabbi—which is what many in Vienna anticipated.[68]

It was in Switzerland that Jacob would grow into adolescence and adulthood, and it was there, in the midst of the greatest catastrophe in the modern history of the Jewish people, that he would receive both a university and rabbinic education.

CHAPTER TWO

Coming of Age in Switzerland, 1936–47

RABBI TAUBES MOVED from Vienna to Zurich in the autumn of 1936, in time for Zwi to preside over High Holiday services at his new pulpit, and the rest of the family followed shortly thereafter. Zurich was the city in which Jacob attended high school and university, the site of his intellectual coming of age, and of his first great love affair. It provided an insecure gallery from which the Taubeses watched the increasing persecution and eventual extinction of most of European Jewry. But they were not passive spectators: during the course of the Second World War, Zwi—with some assistance from his son—would participate in a series of desperate attempts to save Jews from the maw of the Nazi juggernaut, activities that would bring Jacob into close contact with Christian activists and theologians. In the midst of the War, Jacob would pursue both his secular education and rabbinic course of study. And he would form a network of friends who would figure in his future. Zurich became the crucible in which most of Jacob Taubes's intellectual interests and political commitments were first distilled.

The Taubes Family in Zurich

The Taubeses lived in an apartment at Tödistrasse 66, not far from Zwi's synagogue on the Löwenstrasse. Though modest, it was a step up from their more austere quarters in Vienna. The apartment and the synagogue lay in the Enge district of Zurich, a largely Jewish part of the city, not far from the main commercial thoroughfare, the Bahnhofstrasse. Zwi and his wife, Fanny, became prominent figures in the world of Swiss Jewry.[1]

Like many rabbis of his generation, Zwi was a person of scholarly inclinations who became a congregational rabbi in part because there were so few academic venues open to him. As a rabbi he was more renowned for the quality of his sermons and lectures than for his pastoral touch. He exuded more intellect than warmth, and was more respected than loved. Within his family as well, he was an intellectual guide, rather oblivious to the emotional currents around him.

Fanny provided a contrast and complement to her husband. Where he was a man of the book, she was more people oriented. His formality was offset by her warmth and sense of humor. While he was active in the public world, she dominated the household. Those who visited the Taubes home described her as the quintessential traditional Jewish mother, nurturing and feeding her family as well as the many guests who dined at her table.[2] And while Zwi's was primarily a Judaism of the head, Fanny exuded a more traditional piety that reflected her Hasidic family background.[3] But Fanny was unusual for an Orthodox Jewish woman of her generation in that she was herself Jewishly learned. She often lectured, primarily to women's groups, not only on the Bible and traditional texts, but also on modern Hebrew literature, including the work of the great Hebrew poet, Haim Nachman Bialik, whom she knew personally.[4]

Though Zwi was a fine public speaker, his erudite sermons had a tendency to go over the heads of his congregants. It was said to be Fanny's editing that made them more accessible and more popular. Fanny was the complete rebbetzin (rabbi's wife): a helpmeet to her husband, and a formidable intellect to boot. In physical appearance too the Taubeses were a study in contrast. Zwi was an imposing man: thin, a natty dresser, with a perfectly groomed mustache and goatee. Fanny was short and stocky.

Between Zwi and Fanny there seems to have been a perfect meeting of the minds. They shared not only a common origin (in Galicia) and common education (in Vienna), but also a common vision for the Jewish future. That vision was one of religious Zionism, which saw the creation of a Jewish state as the completion of Judaism, and Zionism as a force for spiritual renewal within the Orthodox world, including a more active role for women within Jewish religious life.[5] Zwi became a leader in Switzerland of the religious Zionist movement, Mizrachi, a role that brought him into contact with leading figures of the movement in Europe and later in Israel.

Fostering Jewish life and learning was an uphill battle for the rabbi and rebbetzin. The congregation over which Zwi presided was that of the official synagogue of the Jewish community of Zurich, the *Israelitische*

Cultusgemeinde, which meant that its members were drawn from a wide swath of Jewish observance. Though the synagogue was officially Orthodox, most of its members were far from Orthodox in practice, and relatively few were Sabbath observant. When Zwi arrived from Vienna, one of his first acts was to remove the organ from the sanctuary, in keeping with traditional Jewish strictures against playing musical instruments on the Sabbath.[6] There were also a handful of more religious Jews in Zurich, with two synagogues of their own, but they tended to keep their distance from Zwi's congregation.

Beginning not long after his arrival and continuing through the decades of his rabbinate, Zwi, together with Fanny, organized a variety of courses and lectures to raise the level of Jewish education of their congregants. Though at one point the congregation included the great Jewish poetess Else Lasker-Schuler, such cultural luminaries were the exception. The Jews of Switzerland in general and of Zurich in particular were not oriented to intellectual pursuits. Their nineteenth-century ancestors had been cattle and horse dealers, and they were now moving upward as owners of shops and factories. University graduates were still the exception rather than the rule.[7] Among his congregants, Zwi's erudition was more admired than emulated. Though he eventually became the best-known rabbi in Switzerland, that made him a big fish in a small pond. His status probably never lived up to his aspirations.

Jacob was the older of the Taubes's two children, but their only male child, and one who gave early evidence of great intellectual gifts. Zwi and Fanny's expectations for him were greater than for their daughter, Mirjam, and they invested more in his education, both in terms of parental time and money. Mirjam shared her parents' high estimation of her big brother, and the relationship between the siblings seems to have been very close.[8] The relationship between Jacob and Zwi was one of admiration and intellectual exchange, increasingly accompanied by tension and sometimes conflict. When Jacob was a child and teenager, his father resorted to corporal punishment in a futile attempt to keep him in line, including spankings with a belt.[9] In time, the struggle between Zwi and Jacob would become a matter of notoriety within the Swiss-Jewish community. By contrast, Jacob was known to have an unusually strong attachment to his mother.[10] From that attachment he took a respect for and attraction to intellectual women, which would shape his marriages and his extramarital liaisons.

Though Zwi came to Zurich to serve as a rabbi and Jewish educator, the darkening fate of European Jewry would lead him into the wider world of political action and cooperation with Protestant and Catholic clergy. Accompanying him in these endeavors was his son, Jacob.

The Precarious Position of Swiss Jewry

The Jews of Switzerland in the 1930s were few in number and far less prominent in Swiss life than were their counterparts in Germany, Austria, or France—and the Swiss were committed to keeping it that way. Even in Zurich, where the largest concentration of Jews lived, they made up only 1.7 percent of the population, compared to 10 percent in cities like Berlin and Vienna.[11] Numbering about 20,000 across the country, Jews constituted less than ½ percent of the Swiss population. Of those, only half possessed Swiss citizenship, while the rest were classified as foreigners (*Ausländer*).[12] Switzerland, a federation of provinces with a strong republican and regionalist tradition, was sparing in granting citizenship rights, especially to Jews, and to Jews of Eastern European origin least of all. In 1894, the Swiss government had banned the kosher slaughter of meat, ostensibly on grounds of animal protection, but actually as a way of discouraging the ongoing migration of Jews into the country. In 1912, the canton of Zurich enacted regulations to block the granting of citizenship to Jews from Eastern Europe—the *Ostjuden*. These regulations were further tightened in 1920, and in 1926 they were extended to the Swiss Federation as a whole. By the 1930s, Jews were required to show residency in the country for twenty years before they could apply for citizenship, and the quota of Jews permitted to receive the status of citizen was set at twelve per annum for all of Switzerland.[13] These special regulations for *Ostjuden* were contested by the Jewish community and canceled after 1934, as such laws came to be identified with Nazism. But citizenship remained extremely difficult for Jews to obtain.

When Zwi Taubes moved his family to Zurich, he may have qualified for Swiss citizenship, though it remains unclear when, if ever, he received it. His wife and children were certainly not citizens. Their residence permits had to be renewed annually. When they traveled across national borders, it was with "Nansen passports." These were travel documents issued by the League of Nations to the hundreds of thousands of stateless individuals who had lost their citizenship when the political borders of Eastern and Central Europe were shifted at the end of the First World War.[14] They were named after the League's High Commissioner for Refugees, Fridtjof Nansen. That so many Jews in interwar Europe held only Nansen passports was testimony to the fact that they were unwanted by any existing nation-state and lacked the rights and security that only national governments were able to offer. For Jacob Taubes it meant that he had no real homeland: not Poland, listed on official records as his *Heimat* (homeland); nor Austria, in which he was born but never granted citizenship; nor Switzerland, in which he grew to adulthood.

Compared to their counterparts in Germany and Austria, the Jews of Switzerland lived in safety. But that safety was relative, and no one knew how long it would last. The fear of being overrun by foreigners (*Überfremdung*) was widespread among the Swiss population, and antisemitic, fascist groups such as the *Vaterländische Verband* (Patriotic Union) and the *Schweizerische Heimatwehr* (Swiss Home Guard) made some headway in the mid-1930s.[15] Incidents of antisemitic violence were rare, though one hit close to home, when a bomb damaged Zwi's synagogue in December 1936.[16]

One of the few forces in Swiss life that insisted that Jews were welcome was the Christian Socialist movement, headed by Leonhard Ragaz (1869–1945), which claimed to see in socialism the realization of God's Kingdom on Earth.[17] Jacob was acquainted with the movement, perhaps through Margarete Susman, a German-Jewish philosopher and literary critic who had moved to Zurich and was close to both Ragaz and the Taubes family.[18] The lonely voice of the Swiss Christian Socialists may have played a role in disposing Jacob to the political left, with which he came to identify.

From 1936 on, Swiss Jews didn't know whether they were safe in Switzerland or would have to go elsewhere. In 1938, after National Socialist Germany annexed neighboring Austria, many Swiss Jews feared that Switzerland would be next, and explored the possibilities of emigration.[19] Switzerland had a long tradition of welcoming political refugees. But as the flow of Jews out of the German Reich threatened to turn into a flood, the Swiss government urged the National Socialist regime to stamp the passports of German Jews with a red "J" (for *Jude*), to make it easier for Swiss authorities to track and bar their passage.[20] Swiss Jews were thus caught between solidarity with the victims of National Socialism and danger to their own position. Aware that the Swiss government did not want too many Jews, in order to keep the Swiss border open for asylum, Swiss Jews tried to ensure that the refugees would not stay, but rather transfer out of the country with help from international Jewish organizations.[21]

After the outbreak of war in September 1939, as the German army rolled over Poland, Holland, Belgium, and France, the situation of Swiss Jews became more precarious still. Terrified by the possibility of a German invasion, they would go to bed worried each night, and when they awoke, looked out their windows to see whether the Wehrmacht was in the streets. Zwi shared that dread. In May 1940, German maneuvers seemed to indicate that an attack on Switzerland was imminent, and the Swiss army was mobilized in response. Prominent Jews feared that they would be the first to be arrested in the event of German occupation, and some even prepared poison to take under such circumstances. Without informing his congregants, Zwi left Zurich, as did the synagogue's two teachers, who were also prayer leaders. That left the congregation without anyone to conduct the Sabbath prayers, and confounded about the fate of its rabbi. Zwi returned a few days later, explaining that he had been making arrangements for evacuating his family. There were murmurs among congregants who felt that the rabbi had left them in the lurch, and some members sought his resignation. But cooler heads prevailed, and Zwi retained his office.[22] Where he went that weekend remains unclear, but we do know that he obtained an American visa, and in early 1941 sent an appeal to the Chancellor of the Jewish Theological Seminary in New York, Louis Finkelstein. Writing in Hebrew, in a jagged handwriting that conveyed the psychic pressure he was under, Zwi informed Finkelstein of the deadly danger he faced from National Socialism, and of rumors that the situation was about to deteriorate. Zwi detailed his scholarly and rabbinic interests and achievements, and asked Finkelstein for help in finding him a position in the United States as either a rabbi or professor. He also provided information about his wife, his daughter, and his son Jacob, whom he described as already a "talmid chacham" (a learned Jew).[23]

Nothing seems to have come of this missive, at least in the short term. The Taubeses remained in Switzerland, where they survived the war. Many of Zwi's relatives were not so fortunate. His parents, Zechariah and Chava Leah Edelstein, had remained in Vienna, where they cared for Mottel, their mentally disturbed son. At about the time of *Kristallnacht*, in November 1938, the Gestapo arrested Zechariah and Mottel. A neighbor intervened on their behalf and soon had them released. But at the shock of their arrest, Chava Leah, who had a heart condition, dropped dead. Zwi's father managed to emigrate to Palestine and died in Tel Aviv in 1941. Zwi's sister Adel, who had remained in Vienna, was eventually deported to her death, together with her husband.[24]

Zwi, Jacob, and Paul

Though Jacob would eventually bridle at the expectations of his father, Zwi provided more of the impetus for Jacob's later interests and ideas than his son was wont to acknowledge.

On Saturday, February 10, 1940, Zwi Taubes gave a carefully prepared lecture on "What Judaism, Christianity and Islam Have in Common."[25] It was only months after Nazi Germany had dismembered Czechoslovakia and conquered Poland, and British troops were already in France preparing to defend against an expected German attack. In the present moment of crisis, Zwi proclaimed, in which the central conflict was between religion and Nazi racism, the existing religions needed to renew themselves. "The world is mired in an eschatological final struggle; only a new heroism born of religious intensity can lead beyond it," he declared.[26] To Zwi, the situation resembled that of two thousand years earlier: an old order was in decline, and there was a need to create a new one, as Paul had done with the founding of a new faith. Christianity, Zwi said, was an example of a religious renewal that had drawn upon Judaism. But though founded upon Jewish roots, Christianity had a tendency to gnaw away at them, in the form of anti-Judaism: "This inconsistency of Christianity, to struggle against a spiritual force whose creative power it had in a certain, transformed way adopted entirely, has long provided powerful ammunition for antisemitism, which has in turn eaten away at the fundamentals of Christianity."[27] That was not what Paul had intended when he founded the new faith, Zwi explained. Paul saw himself as an apostle to the gentiles, not to the Jews. Indeed Paulinism was nothing more than the attempt to give new form to the main religious motifs of the Jewish Ten Days of Atonement, and to spread them among the heathens.[28]

Jacob, then seventeen years of age, must have heard this lecture, and probably read it as well. He certainly took it to heart. The themes of eschatology (the end of days) and of movements of religiously inspired renewal would be the subject of his doctoral dissertation. And his interests were not purely historical, for Jacob aspired to become the philosopher of a spiritual revival that would draw upon Judaism but go beyond it. He came to identify himself with the Apostle Paul, who would take elements of Judaism and reformulate them for a larger audience. As Zwi had suggested, that would require reminding Christians of the Jewish roots of their faith, while cleansing Christianity of its anti-Judaism.

Worldly Activism

Zwi was drawn further away from Jewish scholarship by more tangible pressures. He devoted much of his energy first to the needs of Jewish refugees in Switzerland, and then to attempts to save the Jews of Hungary from the clutches of National Socialism. That effort ultimately contributed to the dispatch of the Swedish diplomat Raoul Wallenberg to Budapest and his rescue of thousands of Jews there.

The Swiss government did allow almost ten thousand Jewish refugees from National Socialism into the country (while turning back thousands more), on the condition that they not become an economic burden to the nation. The costs of maintaining these refugees were born by the Swiss-Jewish communities.[29] Thus during the War, the official Jewish community organization of Zurich, which numbered only 1,113 members, supported some 1,042 refugees and 837 other Jewish immigrants.[30] Many of these were housed in some seventy refugee homes and internment camps scattered about the city.[31] Zwi visited these refugees and sought to aid them.

Though officially neutral, the Swiss government took pains not to alienate the Germans in any way. That included strict controls over the Swiss media, to keep them from publicizing information that might embarrass the Third Reich. The official umbrella organization of Swiss Jewry, the Schweizerischer Israelitischer Gemeindebund (Union of Swiss Jewish Communities), was loath to offend the government, and therefore wary of publicizing information about murderous German actions in occupied Eastern Europe.[32] As news about the extent of the German campaign of mass murder reached Jews in Switzerland, the task of publicizing such information and of mobilizing world public opinion fell to persons and organizations beyond the Swiss administration and the Jewish establishment.

Zwi Taubes sought the aid of a Swiss Protestant pastor, Paul Vogt, who organized a conference of Swiss Protestant pastors on November 25, 1942, where Zwi gave a presentation about the dire situation of Eastern European Jewry and urged public protests. The assembled pastors decided on a more modest course, contending they could be most effective by combating antisemitism and fascism within Switzerland.

A year later, Zwi once again turned to the Swiss pastors, this time in the name of the Swiss Rabbinic Association (Schweizerischen Rabbiner-Verbandes), with an extensive report on the destruction of the Jews of Nazi-occupied Europe.[33] None of these attempts bore fruit, but they provided Zwi with a growing network of contacts among Swiss Protestant pastors and theologians. This network brought Zwi and then Jacob into contact with some of the leading figures in European Protestantism. And it set the stage for a more successful campaign to follow, a campaign to save the remnants of Hungarian Jewry from deportation to Auschwitz in 1944.

The impetus behind that crusade came from George Mantello, a Zionist of Romanian origin who had made his way to Switzerland. Mantello arranged to be appointed the consul of El Salvador in Geneva and struggled tirelessly and resourcefully to save as many European Jews as possible.

By the spring of 1944, it was becoming clear to most people that the war would end with an Allied victory. But how soon and under what circumstances was anyone's guess. The government of Hungary faced an uncertain future. Home to the largest intact Jewish population in Europe, Hungary was a German ally. But with the scales now weighted toward an Allied victory, the Hungarian government, headed by Admiral Horthy, put out feelers about changing sides. Then, in March 1944, to forestall Hungary leaving the Axis, the Germans occupied the country, installing a series of ever more pro-Nazi governments, still headed by Horthy. Partly under Nazi pressure and partly under the influence of the indigenous fascist movement, the Arrow Cross, the government cooperated with the Germans in plundering, ghettoizing, and deporting over four hundred thousand Hungarian Jews, mostly from the countryside, to the German killing centers in Poland. But another hundred thousand Jews remained in the capital, Budapest.

When the Nazis marched into Hungary, Mantello set into motion the Swiss Committee for Assistance to the Jews of Hungary (Schweizerische Hilfskomitee für die Juden in Ungarn), in which Zwi Taubes occupied a key position.[34]

On June 20, 1944, an emissary whom Mantello had dispatched to Budapest returned to Switzerland with the "Auschwitz Protocol." This was a report from two Slovakian Jews who had managed to escape from Auschwitz in April 1944 and make their way to Bratislava, where they provided a Jewish committee with detailed information about the precarious living conditions, the gas chambers, and the mass death at the notorious camp complex. Versions of the report reached Switzerland through several channels. The challenge was to publicize that information and to try to pressure the Hungarian government to halt further deportations to the death camps. Mantello sprang into action, translating the text of the protocol into a variety of languages, and sent copies to leading individuals and institutions.[35] On the Sabbath morning of June 24, Mantello stormed into Taubes's synagogue, interrupting the services, and demanding that Taubes accompany him immediately to appeal to Pastor Vogt. That very day, Vogt convened a meeting attended by Mantello, Zwi and Jacob Taubes, as well as Professor Alphons Koechlin, the president of the Swiss Council of Churches.[36] Together, they organized campaigns to mobilize public opinion. Vogt and Zwi Taubes arranged for the publication of the Auschwitz

Protocol, together with a letter affirming its validity and calling for immediate action, signed by Vogt and three of the most distinguished figures in European Protestantism: the Swiss theologians Karl Barth and Emil Brunner, and the Dutch theologian W. A. Visser't Hooft.[37] The result was a publicity campaign that included sermons in Calvinist churches, protest meetings, and publication in the Protestant and Catholic press of reports about the atrocities. Beyond the religious sphere, the Swiss Social Democratic Party also staged a protest rally condemning the murder of the Jews of Hungary.[38]

Jewish groups calculated that Sweden might be able to help save the remaining Jews of Hungary. For Sweden was a neutral nation, which represented Hungary's interests in the Allied countries where the Hungarians had no ambassadors. Zwi cabled the chief rabbi of Sweden, Marcus Ehrenpreis, with information about the mass deportations in Hungary, urging him to intervene with the Swedish monarch to send a delegate to aid the Jews of Budapest. Ehrenpreis passed on the cable from Taubes to the Swedish foreign minister, who in turn took it to the cabinet, which appealed to the king to send a message to Horthy urging him to protect the remaining Jews of Hungary. The king did so, and shortly thereafter the Swedish government dispatched an envoy to Budapest—Raoul Wallenberg.[39] Together with other Swedish diplomats in Budapest, he managed to save thousands of Jews by issuing them protective passes and providing safe houses.[40] The growing pressure of public opinion in Switzerland and Sweden, together with the urgings of the Swedish government, finally led Horthy to try to halt the deportations.

Zwi Taubes's exertions over several years thus played a small but significant role in publicizing the extermination of the Jews of Nazi-occupied Europe, and contributed to saving a small remnant. It also brought him—and Jacob—into contact with some of the leading lights of European Protestantism. Some of these figures, such as Karl Barth, were crucial for Jacob's intellectual development. And the experience of interreligious mobilization meant that, to a far greater extent than most Orthodox Jews, Jacob was well disposed toward Christians and to Christianity.

Toward Interfaith Dialogue: Rethinking the Roots of Christian Antisemitism

The challenge to normative Christianity posed by the radical antisemitism of National Socialism brought the beginnings of a change of attitude toward Jews and Judaism among Protestant and Catholic thinkers scattered across Europe. Protestant theologians began to echo Zwi's claim that the anti-Jewish strands in their tradition had contributed to Nazi antisemitism, which in turn was eroding Christianity itself. Protestant and Catholic intellectuals started to rethink the issue of their churches' relationship to the Jewish people, and began to reexamine and reinterpret their fundamental texts in ways that valued the Jews rather than denigrated them. Theologians would turn particularly to a new exegesis of chapters 9 to 11 of Paul's Epistle to the Romans.[41] There, Paul famously distinguishes between the children of Abraham "of the flesh" (the Jews) and the children of Abraham according to the "spirit," namely the followers of Christ, who are the authentic heirs of God's covenant. But he underscores his own Jewish origins, speaking in 9:3 of "my kindred according to the flesh," and declaring that "I myself am an Israelite, a descendant of Abraham, a member of the tribe of Benjamin" (11:1). The larger point of these chapters seems to be that there is a divine plan behind the Jewish rejection of Jesus as Messiah and savior, since it opened the way for God's covenant to reach all men, including those who were not the descendants of Abraham according to the flesh, that is, not Jews by ethnicity. Thus "through their [the Jews'] stumbling, salvation has come to the Gentiles" (11:11); "as regards the gospel they are enemies of God for your sake" (11:28). But the Jews too will eventually come to recognize the validity of Paul's message (11:11). Paul suggests that one purpose of his ministry as "apostle to the Gentiles" is "to make my own people jealous, and thus save some of them" (11:13–14). In the meantime, Christians should not regard themselves as superior to the Jews, who remain elect by virtue of their lineage (11:28). In the extended allegory of the olive tree, Paul characterizes the Jews as the "natural branches" of a tree that have been "broken off," while the Gentile followers of Christ are a "wild olive shoot" that have been grafted onto the root. Eventually the Jews too will be "grafted back" (11:17–24).

These portions of Paul's epistle contrast with other books of the New Testament, which convey a more unequivocally negative view of the Jewish people and which aver that God's covenant with the Jews was made obsolete by the coming of Christ. That was especially the case with the "Epistle to the Hebrews," a book traditionally attributed to Paul, but regarded by modern scholars as of later origin.[42]

Among the first theologians to reexamine Romans 9–11 was Erik Peterson, a German Protestant scholar who had converted to Catholicism, in his book, *The Church of Jews and Pagans*, published in 1934. Some of his themes were soon picked up by another Protestant-turned-Catholic,

Jacques Maritain.[43] Among Protestant theologians, the exploration of Romans 9–11 seems to have begun with a volume published by the Confessing Church (Bekennende Kirche), under the aegis of Karl Barth, in 1943.[44] Jacob Taubes knew Peterson's work well, and, as we will see, he too would make the interpretation of Roman 9–11 central to his interpretation of early Christianity. In the 1950s, Taubes would become close friends with the foremost postwar Protestant interpreter of Paul and his relationship to the Jews, Krister Stendahl.

In the aftermath of the war, Zwi became active in interfaith activities intended to end the scourge of Christian antisemitism. That began with meetings between Protestant, Catholic, and Jewish theologians in Switzerland, and then in a series of international conferences.[45] The first of these was held in Oxford in August 1946. Attended by both Zwi and his son, it provided an opportunity for Jacob to meet leading Protestant and Catholic figures from France and England. In the summer of 1947, Zwi was a participant in the International Emergency Conference on Antisemitism, which took place in the Swiss village of Seelisberg. Out of that conference emerged a program for combating antisemitism within the Christian churches, much of which was later incorporated into Catholic teaching during the Second Vatican Council with the promulgation of the declaration "Nostra Aetate" in 1965. The Seelisberg document emphasized the new interpretive weight placed on key passages of Paul's Epistle to the Romans.[46] Thus the seeming paradox that Jacob, the scion an Orthodox rabbinic family, would develop a lifelong fascination with the Apostle Paul can be explained in part as a continuation of his father's interests and activism in response to antisemitism.

The Montreux Yeshiva and the Satmar Rebbe

In the midst of these world-historical events, Jacob was also pursuing his education. From the time he moved to Zurich in 1937 through the spring of 1941, Jacob—or "Jacqui" as his friends and family knew him—received a dual education, secular and Jewish. He attended a *Gymnasium*, a high school intended to prepare students for a university education, where he acquired a background in the liberal arts, including history, Latin, some Greek, French, and English.[47] The education there also included an hour or two per week of religious instruction, during which an outside instructor would teach the Jewish students about their faith. A fellow Jewish student who attended these classes with Jacqui found him arrogant: clearly a person of great intellectual gifts, but disdainful of those who knew less. His haughtiness evoked laughter, and he had few friends.[48]

But Jacqui *did* know more than others. For not only was he a talented student in his secular studies at the *Gymnasium*, he was also engaged in an independent course of traditional Jewish learning. In addition to studies with his father, Jacob learned Talmud with Moshe Soloveitchik (1914–95), a tutor whom Zwi had found for him. A recent immigrant to Switzerland from a storied Eastern European rabbinic family associated with the anti-Hassidic tradition of the Volozhin yeshiva, Soloveitchik later became one of the guiding lights of European ultra-Orthodoxy, teaching first at the yeshiva in Montreux, and then founding a rival, anti-Zionist yeshiva in Lucerne. In Zurich, he was part of the ultra-Orthodox community, which tended to look down upon the less observant congregation over which Rabbi Taubes presided. While Rabbi Taubes was a Zionist, Soloveitchik was an opponent of Zionism. Thus, Jacob was exposed to both modern Orthodoxy and ultra-Orthodoxy, to religious Zionism and religious anti-Zionism.

After graduating from the *Gymnasium* and passing the university qualifying exam, the *Matura*, in the spring of 1941, Jacob began his academic education at the local University of Zurich. From 1942 to 1943, he took a year off from his university studies to pursue a traditional rabbinical education at the Etz Chaim Yeshiva in Montreux, where his teachers included his previous tutor, Moshe Soloveitchik.[49]

The Montreux Yeshiva was a unique institution. Located near Lausanne, at the former Villa Quisiana on a hillside overlooking Lake Geneva, it combined a traditional Jewish education with some of the amenities of a modern Swiss boarding school.[50] It was founded in 1927 by Rabbi Elijahu Botschko, who served as *Rosh Yeshiva*. Botschko had studied at the great Lithuanian yeshiva of Novardok, the center of the Musar movement, which had stressed moral and spiritual purity and self-examination.[51] But in contrast to his Musar teachers, who regarded the world outside the yeshiva as a source of spiritual contamination, Botschko thought of yeshiva education as a stage through which young men would pass before making their way into the working world. The students were between the ages of fourteen and twenty, and most were destined for careers in commerce or the professions rather than in the rabbinate. Thus, unlike many traditional yeshivot, the reigning assumption was that its students would go out into the larger world, and even acquire a university education, which Rabbi Botschko did not discourage.

Most of the day was devoted to the study of Talmud along with the commentaries of Rashi, the great eleventh-century commentator, and his grandsons, the *Ba'alei Tosfot*. There were prayers in the morning (shacharit) and in the late afternoon or early evening (minchah and maariv). Unusually for such an institution, students studied the Bible (Tanakh), and also some nonhalachic Jewish thought. The taken-for-granted assumption was that the study of Torah and Talmud was an exploration of revealed law, not a matter for the historical and critical approach characteristic of more liberal institutions. The approach was "critical" in the spirit of the Lithuanian tradition that honored a student's ability to pose questions about conceptual inconsistencies and propose novel solutions to contradictions. An unusual aspect of the yeshiva was that although it was affiliated with the ultra-Orthodox Agudat Yisrael movement, Botschko was a committed Zionist.[52] And although influenced by the ascetic Musar movement, Botschko came from and remained committed to Hasidism, with its more joyful and expressive style of Jewish spirituality.[53] Botschko lived out the Musar ideals of humility and modesty. Rather than drawing his income from the yeshiva, he supported himself by running a linen shop, together with his wife, and it was there he would write his articles and sermons.[54]

But by the time Jacob arrived at the yeshiva in 1942, the heartland of traditional Judaism in Eastern Europe was under Nazi domination, making Etz Chaim one of the few functioning yeshivot in all of Europe. It had a distinguished faculty, comprised in good part of refugees from the Telz Yeshiva, another outpost of the Musar movement. While the rabbi-teachers spoke Yiddish among themselves, the language of instruction was German.

Thus in his late teenage years, Jacob was immersed in at least two different worlds of learning—the world of the university and the world of the yeshiva. His knowledge of Talmud, already substantial when he arrived at Montreux, was deepened. He would continue to study Talmud daily in the years that followed, so that by 1946 he was able to attain a *heter hora'ah*, the traditional form of rabbinic ordination, conferred by a rabbinic sage after an oral examination.[55] Jacob received his ordination from Rabbi Jonathan Steif, who had been a senior rabbinic judge (*dayan*) in Budapest and escaped to Switzerland, and from Yisroel Yitzchak (Israel Isaac) Piekarski, a Lubavitch rabbi who later became a *Rosh Yeshiva* at Yeshiva Tomchei Temimin, a Lubavitch institution in Brooklyn.[56]

Despite its bucolic setting, the Montreux Yeshiva in 1942–43 was by no means an island cut off from the wider world. On the contrary. The destruction of European Jewry, and especially of the centers of traditional learning in Eastern Europe, dominated the consciousness of Botschko and those around him. Botschko's writings and sermons were replete with agonized lamentations for the great sages of the Orthodox world who were being murdered daily.[57] His friends Recha and Isaac Sternbuch, an ultra-Orthodox couple in Montreux, engaged first in attempts to smuggle Jewish refugees into Switzerland, and then in negotiations to rescue Jews from National Socialism.[58]

Just what impression the Montreux experience made on Jacob is difficult to ascertain. He was clearly deeply touched by the authentic piety and modesty of Rabbi Botschko, and by his son and successor, Moshe Botschko, who continued his father's tradition of earning his living as a shopkeeper. Jacob would remain in contact with the Botschko family for decades. At Montreux, Jacob was immersed in the world of Jewish texts that its students believed were of divine origin, at the very time when most students of those texts were being slaughtered by the hundreds of thousands. From this, a sensitive person might deduce the powerlessness of God. For to claim, as the Jewish tradition did, that the righteous shall prosper, seemed little short of absurd, not to say blasphemous. Or he might conclude that the world as we know it is saturated with evil, for which religion in general (or some form of Judaism in particular) offers a refuge and a perspective from which that world could be criticized. Jacob would eventually share all of these reactions.

But that took time. Jacob emerged from the yeshiva a paragon of piety and observance. Of this we have testimony from several sources. Margarete Susman remembers him at this stage as "a strictly Orthodox, deeply believing Jew, untroubled by doubt, who through his great intellect almost had the power to win over far older people to his convictions."[59] It was at this time that Jacob first reached out to Jean Bollack, a Jewish student of the classics living in Basel. When Jacob came to visit Bollack, his head was covered, and though the Bollack household kept kosher, Taubes was careful to bring his own food, lest the household not be kosher enough.[60]

A year after his return from the Montreux Yeshiva, Jacob had another intense encounter with a very different form of ultra-Orthodoxy, this time in the person of Rabbi Joel Teitelbaum, or "Reb Yoilish" as he was known to his disciples and admirers. Teitelbaum was the rebbe of a sect of Hasidim centered in Satmar, a town that in the interwar period had been within the borders of Romania but that in 1940 again became part of Hungary. Teitelbaum was a vehement anti-Zionist, who like most ultra-Orthodox Jews regarded the attempt to create a sovereign Jewish state by secular means as a sacrilege. He not only kept his distance from the Zionist movement, but also regarded it as sinful. (He would later interpret the Holocaust as God's punishment for Zionist transgressions.[61])

The Satmar Rebbe arrived in Switzerland in December 1944 under the most extraordinary circumstances. In the summer of that year, Jewish leaders in Hungary and abroad were desperately trying to find ways to save the remnants of Hungarian Jewry. A group of them, headed by the Zionist leader Rudolf Kasztner, engaged in protracted negotiations with some leading figures of the SS, who had suggested that up to one million Jews remaining in Eastern Europe might be traded for goods and money from the West. As a first step, and in exchange for large sums of money and forty trucks, some one thousand Jews were to be put on trains and transported first to the concentration camp at Bergen-Belsen, and then to the West. It was left to a small committee, headed by Kasztner, to select the Jews who would be saved. Kasztner deliberately chose leading figures from the full spectrum of Hungarian Jewry, including Teitelbaum and members of his court. The train—which ultimately carried 1,684 people—left Budapest on June 30 and reached Bergen-Belsen on July 8. There the transport was held up for six months while negotiations continued. In early December, a group of these Jews, including Teitelbaum, were permitted to cross the border into Switzerland.[62] Among those who waited to greet him after the train stopped in the town of Sankt Gallen was Jacob's teacher, Moshe Soloveitchik.[63] Teitelbaum went on to Montreux, Geneva, and other Swiss locales, before departing for Jerusalem in August 1945, and eventually for New York.

As the rebbe spoke neither German, French, nor English, he was in need of assistance in dealing with the Swiss authorities.[64] It was Jacob Taubes who acted as his aide, for which Reb Yoilish apparently felt a debt of gratitude. This was the beginning of a relationship between Jacob and the Satmar Rebbe and his followers that was to be periodically resumed over the decades that followed. Their contact would continue when both moved to New York City, and when Jacob prayed among the Satmars there, he was seated in a place of honor next to the rebbe.[65] For Jacob, the Satmars were paradigmatic of a wholesale rejection of the secular world—what his friend Herbert Marcuse, in another context, would call "the Great Refusal." Jacob's relationship with the anti-Zionist firebrand appalled his religious Zionist parents. His mother cautioned him not to become a follower of "Reb Yoilish": "He may be a *talmid chacham* [a man of learning]," she warned, "but he is obdurate and struck with blindness when it comes to matters concerning the Land of Israel."[66]

Intellectual Worlds

As a young adult in Zurich, Jacob impressed and was impressed by intellectuals of divergent and often conflicting orientations.

Perhaps the most idiosyncratic persona whom Jacob encountered was Oskar Goldberg (1885–1952). The center of a circle of followers in Berlin in the early decades of the twentieth century, Goldberg was a polymath, the author of learned and outrageous books, and a critic of modern liberal, technical civilization. Ritual, for Goldberg, was not a matter of symbolism: ritual acts, for those who engaged in them with the proper understanding, were ways of influencing God. In his *Die Wirklichkeit der Hebräer* (*The Reality of the Hebrews*) (1925), Goldberg maintained that the relations between God and the Jewish people described in the Bible were not mere myths, but conveyed a historical reality in which ritual actions had real influence on the divine, because each people, as a biological entity, had a link with their god, whose sway extended over a particular territory. That link had subsequently been lost by the Jews, but might be regained through a reinvigoration of ritual motivated by a belief in its actual efficacy. Goldberg and his disciples dabbled in esoteric doctrines and practices.

Jacob met Goldberg when the older man visited Zurich in 1938, and then read two of Goldberg's books. Asked at the age of nineteen to write an article on Jewish mysticism for an academic journal, Taubes borrowed at length from Goldberg's exposition of key kabbalistic ideas in his 1935 book on Maimonides—whom Goldberg faulted for being unable to appreciate mysticism because of his rationalistic philosophy.[67] For a while, Jacob was excited by Goldberg, exploring his work in a small seminar. Though he later outgrew that fascination, he would write about Goldberg in the 1950s for the magazine *Partisan Review*.

In the fall of 1946, as he was completing his doctoral dissertation, Jacob came to know Rabbi Leo Baeck, a guest from London visiting the Taubes household during the High Holidays. At the time, Baeck was the most renowned liberal Jewish theologian in Europe. Jacob seems to have been deeply impressed by Baeck, and Baeck was sufficiently impressed by Jacob to provide a letter of reference about him to the Jewish Theological Seminary in New York. At the same time, Jacob remained part of the Orthodox milieu around the Montreux Yeshiva, attending the funeral of Rabbi Botshko's son-in-law, Rabbi Saul Weingort, and carrying on conversations with Rabbi Yehiel Weinberg, the most distinguished Orthodox halachist (legal authority) to survive the war in Europe, who had been brought by Weingort to Montreux. Weinberg too would write a letter of recommendation on Jacob's behalf.[68]

But Jacob's intellectual contacts were by no means confined to Jewish circles. On his frequent visits to Basel, he discussed his plans for a new theology with the Catholic theologian Hans Urs von Balthasar. Balthasar's work on the secularization of religious apocalypticism would inspire Jacob's exploration of a similar theme in his doctoral dissertation.[69]

Nor were Jacob's intellectual contacts restricted to religious circles, Jewish or Christian. When Georg Lukács, the most prominent Communist philosopher in Europe, visited Zurich, Jacob spent several days talking to him and discussing his dissertation on occidental eschatology. Jacob's attitude toward Lukács was respectful, yet distanced and bemused. He read with admiration Lukács most famous work, *Geschichte und Klassenbewusstsein* (*History and Class Consciousness*) (1923) in which the Marxist theoretician had set out a philosophical defense of Leninism, emphasizing the role of intellectuals in guiding the working class to the desired, communist direction of history. Having laid the groundwork of intellectual Leninism, Lukács never deviated from his commitment to the Communist movement, emerging with the victory of the Red Army and the hegemony of Communism in his native Hungary as a high-profile intellectual spokesman for the movement.[70] In letters to his then girlfriend, Jacob characterized Lukács as "the demi-god of the Marxists. Lukács is the Church Father of the *ecclesia militans* and the *ecclesia triumphans* of Marxism"[71]—a characterization as erudite as it is amusing. For Jacob not only drew a parallel between Marxism and Christianity, but between the Communist movement and the Church. Lukács had been a prime participant in the movement not only when it was struggling, but when it was in power as well. "Lukács, the prime theorist of Marxism, is a smart fellow—that cannot be denied—but he is decidedly one-sided and constricts himself intellectually,"[72] Jacob concluded. Despite his reservations about Lukács, Jacob was pleased when the senior Marxist looked at his work and pronounced it important.

Friends

It was in Zurich that Jacob came to regard himself as a man of the left, committed to equality, in theory at least. In practice, he tended toward elitism—a pattern already visible in his high-school years—combined with a certain liberality. He was open to friendship with people of a wide range of religious and ideological orientations, if he thought they were particularly bright. During his university years, he befriended a number of men with whom he would remain in contact for decades, after he and they had left Switzerland to take up careers in Germany, France, and the United States.

The first of these was Lucien Goldmann, a young Marxist intellectual of Romanian Jewish origin, whom Zwi Taubes had first encountered at the internment camp in Gierenbad, near Zurich. Goldmann had once been a Communist but was increasingly having his doubts about the movement. When Zwi first met him, Goldmann had just been debating the legitimacy of Stalin's Moscow trials with Manès Sperber, another former Communist who had broken with the movement. Both men had spent the years before the war in Paris, and then fled from Nazi-occupied France into Switzerland. When Zwi appeared at the internment camp, he found Goldmann eager to discuss theological issues. Zwi dispatched his son Jacob to the camp to continue the discussion, and a friendship ensued. Zwi was able to use his influence to get Goldmann released from internment, and the Romanian refugee became a frequent guest in the Taubes household. Goldmann was a Marxist who was fascinated by religious issues, and eventually developed an interpretation of Pascal as a dialectical thinker: just as Pascal had wagered on the ultimate uncertainty of God, Marxists ought to wager on a future of socialist community that could not be scientifically proven.[73] The continuities between religion and modern radical movements would become a focus of interest of Jacob Taubes as well, and central to his doctoral dissertation. After the war, Goldmann moved back to France, where over time he developed a reputation as an independent Marxist thinker. In the 1960s, Jacob would bring him repeatedly to the Free University.

Another friend was François Bondy. Born in Berlin in 1915, the son of a German-Jewish theater director who moved to Italy in the 1920s, Bondy was raised in German, French, and Italian. He came to know antisemitism at first hand in a German-speaking *Gymnasium* in Davos in the 1930s, when some of his fellow students knocked out three of his teeth. 1936 found him in France, where, searching for an anti-fascist movement, he joined the French Communist Party, only to leave it in 1939 after the signing of the Hitler-Stalin pact. Following the fall of France, he was imprisoned for three months in a French internment camp in 1941, after which he left for Zurich. There he became a prominent journalist, editing the cultural weekly, *Die Weltwoche*. After the war, he too returned to Paris and in 1951 became the founding editor of *Preuves: une revue européenne à Paris*, the French magazine of the international Congress for Cultural

Freedom.[74] Bondy edited the highly influential journal through 1969. Like Goldmann, Bondy would become one of Jacob's links to Paris.

Three of Taubes's friends were students in Basel, a university town some forty miles from Zurich that he visited often while a student at the University of Zurich, and where he seems to have studied for a time as well. In 1943, not long after his studies in Montreux, Taubes sent a post-card to Jean Bollack, a young student of classics from a Jewish family that hailed from Strasbourg. Taubes reported that he had heard positive things about Bollack, and inquired whether the two might collaborate on founding a Jewish journal, one that would be distinguished by its quality. Shortly thereafter, the two met at Bollack's home in Basel, inaugurating a friendship that would continue for decades. Bollack was struck by Taubes's intellectual maturity, by his unusual combination of traditional Jewish education with that of the German *Gymnasium*, by his humor, and by his attractive, winning demeanor.[75] After the war, Bollack, like Goldmann and Bondy, made his way to France. There he continued his studies of the Greek classics, and developed an approach to texts that inquired into their conditions of production as well as the ways in which they had been read.[76] From 1955 to 1958, Bollack taught at the Free University of Berlin, and would play a role in attracting Jacob there.

Taubes had learned of Bollack through a mutual friend in Basel, Eugen Kullmann.[77] Born in Germany in 1915, Kullmann had studied at a yeshiva and at the Freies Jüdisches Lehrhaus, an independent institution of Jewish education in Frankfurt am Main, founded by the Jewish philosopher Franz Rosenzweig. After Hitler's accession to power, Kullmann moved to Switzerland, pursuing studies at the University of Basel in Greek philology, Semitics, philosophy, and a number of other subjects. He emerged as a scholar of remarkable erudition, whose friendship and learning Taubes soon came to value. After the war, Kullmann emigrated to the United States, where he held a series of academic posts, first in New York, and then at Kenyon College. Later, Taubes would try to get Kullmann to join him at the Free University in Berlin.

Goldmann, Bondy, Bollack, and Kullmann were all Jewish. What these disparate friends had in common was their multilingualism and a certain cosmopolitanism. They had come to Switzerland to escape National Socialism, and they departed when that menace subsided.

Not so Taubes's other lasting friend from these years, Armin Mohler. He was a native of Switzerland, who had been, if not quite a Nazi, then certainly a Nazi sympathizer. He too eventually left Switzerland, in part because of his engagement with the radical right.

Born in Basel in 1920, Mohler as a teenager had first been attracted to the antibourgeois left, but soon turned to the antiliberal, antibourgeois right.[78] The most prominent movement of the radical right was of course in the nearby German Reich. And so, in February 1942, Mohler crossed the border into Germany, with the intention of joining the Waffen-SS, motivated by his antiliberalism, but also by a trans-European enthusiasm. (Such was the appeal of this hypermasculine, anticommunist force that it attracted far more foreign volunteers than had the leftist International Brigades in the Spanish Civil War.) For reasons that remain uncertain, his intention was never realized. Instead, Mohler made his way to Berlin, and spent the rest of the year immersed in reading the works of German radical conservative thinkers, before returning to Switzerland in late 1942. There he was imprisoned for half a year for having crossed the border illegally and attempting to enroll in a foreign military. Since his real identification was with Germany, he regarded himself as a sort of "inner émigré" in Switzerland.[79]

The German intellectuals to whom Mohler was most attracted were Ernst Jünger and Carl Schmitt—both figures that soon came to interest Jacob Taubes as well. Jünger had volunteered for army service as a storm trooper during the First World War, and had written a series of books about battle as an experience that catapulted men out of the world of bourgeois safety. During the 1920s, Jünger became the most prominent exponent of a soldierly nationalism, asserting that the bourgeois liberal era was over, left behind by the state's increasing mobilization of society, and by "a grotesque, half-barbarian fetishism of the machine, a naive cult of technology."[80] In 1932, he published *Der Arbeiter*, which argued once again that the bourgeois world—characterized by liberalism, individuality, the search for security, and the victory of economic over political values—was about to be superseded by a new human type he called "The Worker."[81] Jünger found National Socialism too plebeian for his tastes and distanced himself from the movement even before it attained power. After the Second World War, he turned away from nationalism, heroic militarism, and politics. His skeptical attitude to technology was influenced by his brother, Friedrich Georg Jünger, who shortly after the Second World War published a book the thesis of which was encapsulated in the subtitle of its English translation, *The Failure of Technology: Perfection without Purpose*.[82]

After the war, Mohler wrote a doctoral dissertation that explored the range of radical right thought in late nineteenth- and twentieth-century Germany, *The Conservative Revolution in Germany, 1918–1932: An Outline of Its Worldviews.*[83] Published in 1950, the book was both scholarly and apologetic, intended to preserve and defend the reputation of thinkers and movements discredited by their association with Nazism, with an eye toward an eventual revival of their ideas. Mohler wrote his dissertation unsupervised by his nominal advisors. At his dissertation defense, one of his examiners, the liberal philosopher Karl Jaspers, told Mohler that "your work is a full-scale de-Nazification of these authors," which Jaspers was willing to approve only because Germany was no longer politically significant.[84]

Because of his politically suspect interests, Armin Mohler was something of a pariah in postwar Switzerland. Jacob Taubes, who had heard about Mohler from a mutual acquaintance, sought him out precisely because of those interests.[85] While writing his thesis, Mohler discussed the key points with Taubes. He used Taubes as something of a compass: Mohler adopted the positions on which they disagreed most.[86] Here we see an element of Taubes's character that would manifest itself throughout his life, and that helps to account for his wide range of intellectual acquaintances. He was open to people of conflicting views. Indeed, he sought them out. If those views were radical—whether from the left or right, whether based upon secular or religious premises—Taubes was all the happier to engage with them.

Taubes shared Mohler's interest in Jünger and the purported eclipse of traditional sources of meaning with the rise of technological civilization. In the summer of 1948, Mohler made a trip to Germany to bring material support to his intellectual heroes, Jünger and Schmitt. Jünger asked him to become his secretary, a chance that Mohler seized. But tension soon arose between master and disciple, for Mohler was still attracted to the political radicalism of the young Jünger, whereas Jünger himself, having drawn his conclusions from the disaster of National Socialism, was inclined toward political quietism.[87] In the years that followed, Mohler would serve as an intermediary between Taubes and Carl Schmitt, a figure who fascinated Jacob Taubes for reasons we will explore in the next chapter.

Late in his life, Jacob was accompanying some German friends around Paris, when he turned and abruptly informed them he was off to the synagogue. "Please excuse me," he said, "but I can't live in just one world."[88] Even as an adolescent and young man in Zurich, Jacob lived in multiple cultural and intellectual worlds. His parents were religious, Orthodox, and Zionist—and so, at least on the surface, was Jacob himself. But he had studied Talmud with the anti-Zionist Moshe Soloveitchik, and formed a bond with the anti-Zionist Rebbe of Satmar, both of whom were ultra-Orthodox. Jacob was exposed to contemporary Christianity, in both its Protestant and Catholics forms. Christian Socialism attracted him, and Marxism fascinated him. But so did the critique of modern, liberal society that emanated from figures on the German radical right, such as Jünger, Schmitt, and Martin Heidegger. All of these left their mark on Jacob's intellectual and scholarly development, to which we now turn.

CHAPTER THREE

Intellectual Roots, Grand Themes, 1941–46

THE PERIOD BETWEEN Jacob's graduation from high school (*Gymnasium*) in 1941 and his departure for the United States in November 1947 was one of intense study. It was in these years that he acquired a set of interests and a stock of erudition that would carry him through much of the rest of his life. With the exception of the months spent at the Montreux Yeshiva, Jacob lived and studied in Zurich, with frequent visits to nearby Basel. The War, the destruction of European Jewry, friendships, and love affairs all made calls upon his attention. But equipped with a solid grounding in Latin and Hebrew and a growing knowledge of Greek, French, and English, and unburdened by the need to earn a living, to teach, or to support a family, Jacob seems to have hit the books with a concentration he would never again repeat.

In later life, Jacob claimed that his father, Zwi, had expected him to become not only a rabbi and professor of philosophy, but a doctor and a rich man as well. As a result, he had enrolled in medical studies, but left after only five weeks, after confronting his first cadaver.[1] The story—like so many stories that Taubes told about himself—may be partly or wholly invented. But it conveys his awareness of his family's high expectations of him. By the time he left Zurich late in 1947, he had succeeded in acquiring a doctorate in philosophy as well as ordination as a rabbi. Of medicine and science he knew little; of money, less.

At the universities of Zurich and Basel, Jacob studied philosophy, history, sociology, and religion. It was the intersection of these fields that really interested him. As he explained in a conspectus of his intellectual development written shortly after he received his doctorate, his interest in the philosophy of history had been stimulated by contemporary events that raised the issue of the meaning of history. So too did his reading of Hegel's philosophy of history, and of Oswald Spengler's *Decline of the West* (*Untergang des Abendlandes*),[2] that grand work of historical speculation that moved a generation of interwar intellectuals in Europe and America. Taubes's doctoral exams at the University of Zurich were in three fields: philosophy, sociology, and German literature (*Germanistik*). His main focus was on religion. His studies of Judaism had taken place largely outside the university, at home, and at the Montreux Yeshiva. He studied Christianity with two of the most prominent Protestant theologians of his day, Emil Brunner and Karl Barth, and befriended Hans Urs von Balthasar, then a little-known chaplain at the University of Basel but soon to emerge as a major Catholic theologian. The emphasis of his sociological studies was the sociology of religion, especially that of Max Weber.

Before turning to the genesis and substance of his doctoral dissertation, *Abendländische Eschatologie*, we should scout the stars and constellations in his intellectual firmament as it took shape in Zurich.

Karl Barth: From Biblical Criticism to Neo-Orthodoxy

In the course of the nineteenth century—though the phenomenon had earlier roots—there was a quest by Protestant scholars, especially in German-speaking Europe, to use the techniques of modern humanistic scholarship to better understand their own faith. By the eve of World War I, that quest had a paradoxical outcome. The more Protestant scholars explored the Old and New Testaments in their historical contexts, the more they understood the linguistic nuances and puzzles of the biblical texts, the more they were able to identify the various strands and historical layers within those texts—the more elusive their prey became. Rather than illuminating a single message or even a single tradition, humanistic scholarship seemed to reveal a struggle of competing trends within the Christian tradition, a struggle that went back to the texts of the Gospels themselves. No distinct portrait of Jesus emerged, and insofar as one did, it was far removed from the Christ of faith, as Albert Schweitzer showed in a book of 1906 that Taubes knew well, *Von Reimarus zu Wrede: Eine Geschichte der Leben-Jesu-Forschung* (translated as *The Quest of the Historical Jesus*). Other scholars discovered that the earliest Christian community, as reflected in the New Testament, bore scant relation to the Church as it evolved over time. This problem had been recognized by John Henry Newman in his *Essay on the Development of Christian Doctrine*

(1845), who solved it by retroactive interpretation, based on faith, in which only those elements of the tradition that had survived into the present were deemed truly essential. But that approach, while comforting to the faithful, was fundamentally unhistorical. More radical, because more genuinely historical, was Franz Overbeck (1837–1905), a professor of theology at Basel and a scholar of the history of the early Church. Overbeck's studies led him conclude that there was no substantive continuity between the Christians of the New Testament, with their expectations of an imminent return of Christ, and the Church as it had developed in the Middle Ages and the modern era. Thus the spadework of scholarship ended up undermining the claims of faith. Taubes would later edit a volume of Overbeck's writings, along with an introductory essay entitled "Entzauberung der Theologie: Zu einem Porträt Overbecks" ("The Disenchantment of Theology: Toward a Portrait of Overbeck").[3] Overbeck's friend, Nietzsche, was descended from generations of Protestant pastors and was fascinated by contemporary developments in Biblical criticism. He incorporated them into his far-reaching critique of Christianity, an analysis that reached its apogee in his book, *The Antichrist* (1888), another work with which Taubes would become intimately acquainted.

As historical study of the Bible ate away at the fundaments of Christian orthodoxy, one response by Christian thinkers was to recast their faith in ever more rational terms, and to conceive of Jesus less as divine redemptor than as an exemplary human, as a sort of precursor of Goethe.[4] Especially among liberal Protestant theologians, there was a tendency to portray Christianity in general and Protestantism in particular as the root and origin of modern, liberal culture. Perhaps the most famous German exponent of this view was Adolf von Harnack (1851–1930), who was at one and the same time the most esteemed historian of Christianity in imperial Germany, an influential advisor to the Ministry of Education, and the Director of the Imperial Library, thus personifying the intertwining of Protestantism, culture, and national politics.[5] In July 1914, Harnack was ennobled for his efforts on behalf of German scholarship. When war broke out the month thereafter, he was among the most distinguished signatories of the "Manifest der 93," which defended Germany's declaration of war and accused the British of perfidy.

One response to the challenge posed by the critical, historical approach to religious faith was what came in the 1920s to be called "dialectical theology" or "crisis theology." The terms covered a range of thinkers, both Protestant and Jewish. What they had in common was a rejection of critical, historical approaches to the Bible, which they saw as linked to the project

of reconciling religion with the existing political and cultural establishment, an establishment they identified with the disaster of the Great War.
They insisted that interpretation of the Bible must begin not from historical science, but from faith. They thus adopted a strategy of simply ignoring
or bracketing out historical investigations of the Bible. Once one began
with the unproveable but unquestioned assumption of the validity of faith,
it became possible to critique contemporary society from that perspective.

The foremost Protestant practitioner of this intellectual move was the
Swiss theologian Karl Barth, with whom Taubes studied in Basel.[6] The
book that made his reputation was *The Epistle to the Romans*, written
during the war and first published at the end of 1918. Barth, who had
been a student of Harnack, was shocked by the war, by the support of the
war effort by liberal theologians such as his teacher, and by the identification of Protestantism with modern German culture. He came to reject
the liberal Protestant project in its entirety. Barth's book was an extended
interpretation of Paul's Epistle to the Romans, which it explored almost
verse by verse. Between the first and second, more famous, edition of his
book, Barth had encountered and been deeply influenced by Overbeck's
posthumously published, *Christentum und Kultur* (*Christendom and
Culture*) (1919), with its insistence on the absolute chasm between the
Gospel and modern, liberal, Protestant culture. Barth told his readers
that the Gospel sets "a question-mark against the whole course of this
world and its inevitability."[7] He insisted on the gap between faith, based
on grace, and the secular world, with its rationalist modes of understanding. He chastised his contemporaries for having made idols of the nation,
the state—and the church.[8] Here, then, was an attack on the political,
cultural, and religious status quo—all in the name of true faith. True faith
in God, Barth insisted, was only to be had by looking into the abyss, by
seeing the world in all its sinfulness, by despairing of a world so mani-
festly devoid of God's presence.[9]

As his critics soon pointed out, Barth's description of the secular world
as the realm of evil seemed to bring him close to what in the Christian
tradition was termed "Gnosticism"—and regarded as a heresy. This was
the idea of an absent God, or as he was known in Christian thought, *a
deus absconditus*.[10] In response, Barth contended that "Paulinism has
always stood on the brink of heresy." As for the radicalism of his position, he argued that it was wrong to disguise "the dangerous element of
Christianity."[11]

A decade later, Barth confronted a new challenge in the form of
National Socialism. Just as liberal Protestants had tried to reinterpret

Christianity in a manner compatible with liberalism, the rise of National Socialism led to attempts to transform German Protestantism along the lines of Nazi ideology. In September 1933, the dominant faction of the German Protestant Synod adopted an "Aryan clause," which forbade Jewish converts to Christianity from occupying clerical posts. Pastors who objected to the permeation of German Protestantism by such racist ideas soon formed a dissenting movement, the Confessing Church (Bekennende Kirche). Among their foremost spokesman was Barth, by then a professor of theology in Bonn. In 1935, he refused to take an oath of office to the Führer, and left for the University of Basel, where he would continue his opposition to National Socialism, and as we have seen, lend his voice to the campaign to save the Jews of Hungary.

Taubes was much taken by many of Barth's themes. That the world was an evil place seemed even more plausible after the destruction of European Jewry. Perhaps, as Barth suggested, the manifest absence of God's presence in the natural world could somehow be harnessed as evidence for the need of a supernatural God. And perhaps faith could provide a platform from which to chastise the secular world and its failings. Religion as most authentic when it was dangerous; Paul as a seminal figure who "stood on the edge of heresy"—Taubes would compose his own variations on these Barthian motifs in the decades ahead.

Emil Brunner

Although Barth is now regarded as among the most important theologians of the twentieth century, his international reputation was largely a product of the 1950s and 1960s. Better known in the 1930s and 1940s was Barth's theological ally and sometime intellectual sparring partner, Emil Brunner (1889–1966), professor of theology at the University of Zurich. Like Barth, Brunner abjured a critical, historical approach to faith. But he placed a higher valuation on the role of human reason in the perception of the divine.[12] Brunner rejected Barth's dichotomy between the church and the world and was influential in the development of German Christian Democracy. He was, in short, a more conciliatory thinker than Barth, and hence less attractive to Taubes. But many of Brunner's concerns in the mid-1940s clearly rubbed off on Jacob. Those themes included the problem of the meaning of history, the role of eschatology (i.e., theological speculation on the culmination of history and the end of days), and the present as an age of nihilism linked to the triumph of technique.[13] Brunner had spent time abroad in England and the United States, and his international renown would aid Taubes when he applied for jobs in the United States with a recommendation from Brunner in hand.

Martin Buber

Taubes's education was deeply influenced by his contact with Jewish, Protestant, and Catholic thinkers, including Balthasar, Barth, Botschko, and Brunner. To that list must be added the name of Martin Buber (1878–1965). From the 1920s until well into the second half of the twentieth century, Buber was the most prominent Jewish religious thinker among Western-educated Jews and Christians alike. His books on Hasidism manufactured an image of joyful, world-affirming, and wise pietists, a portrait at odds with much of learned opinion among educated Jews that the Hasidim were in fact benighted retrogrades in thrall to their obscurantist rebbes. Early in his career, in his *Three Lectures on Judaism* (*Drei Reden über das Judentum*) of 1911, Buber had championed the nonrational, non-Western elements of Judaism as a counter to the rationalism of the Occident. Many of the themes of Taubes's dissertation are adumbrated in this work: the struggle between the Jewish religious establishment and the "subterranean Judaism" (*untererdisches Judentum*) of those deemed heretics;[14] early Christianity (*Urchristentum*) as one of the most creative products of the Jewish spirit, which needed to be reintegrated into Jewish self-understandings;[15] and the centrality of time in Judaism, in the form of both memory and an orientation toward the future based on hope.[16] Buber's most famous book, *I and Thou* (*Ich und Du*) of 1923 had transformed the language of theology, conceiving of man's relation to God as the paradigm of authentic, noninstrumental relations in the human world as well, in which people would be treated as ends in themselves rather than as means. In *The Kingdom of God* (*Königtum Gottes*) of 1932, Buber turned to the political implications of Biblical theology, a theme that was to loom large in Taubes's dissertation. For Buber, Messianism was "Judaism's most profoundly original idea," transforming history into eschatology. Buber had left Germany for mandatory Palestine in 1938 to assume a chair at the Hebrew University. There he became a leading advocate of Jewish-Arab cooperation and of a binational state, rather than a Jewish one.

Martin Buber visited the Taubes home in Zurich in 1946, together with his granddaughter, Judith. He talked with Jacob at length and was much impressed by the young man.[17] Later on, their paths would cross again in Jerusalem and New York. For Taubes, as for many twentieth-century Jewish intellectuals (such as Gershom Scholem), Buber's work formed a sort of drawbridge, which was closed up after crossing. That is to say, Buber drew them into the world of Jewish scholarship on mysticism, Hasidism, and the political implications of the Bible. But once they had immersed themselves in their subjects, they often found Buber's work to be superficial or misleading.[18] Nevertheless, Taubes maintained contact with Buber until the older man's death in 1965, and would contribute a learned and highly critical essay on "Buber and Philosophy of History" to a volume on Buber's thought.[19]

Martin Heidegger

A more diffuse influence on the young Jacob Taubes was the work of Martin Heidegger. Heidegger had taken up some recurrent tropes of Christian theology and translated them into secular terms. That included "anxiety" (*Angst*) as the basic mode of human existence; the attempt to escape from that anxiety through the comforting embrace of common opinion; and the demand for more "authentic" forms of commitment. Though these themes had been adumbrated by Saint Paul in the Gospels and then by Augustine of Hippo, their foremost expositor in the modern period was the Danish Lutheran philosopher Søren Kierkegaard. When his works were translated into German in the first decades of the twentieth century, they had a profound impact on the young Heidegger, who though trained as a Catholic theologian, became increasingly drawn to Kierkegaard. In *Being and Time* (*Sein und Zeit*) (1927), these Christian themes were formalized, declared to be fundamental to the human condition, and stripped of their theological garb. But precisely because they echoed traditional religious concerns, they continued to have great appeal among theologians.[20] After *Being and Time*, Heidegger would turn to the notion that man only attains meaning by confronting the "nothingness" of the world (*das Nichts*), the lack of ultimate grounding for our existence—a contention that would, for a time, fascinate Taubes as well.[21]

Heidegger was among those influenced by Ernst Jünger's *Der Arbeiter*, and he drew upon its theme that technology was increasingly eclipsing older forms of life and meaning. For some years before and after 1933, Heidegger hoped that National Socialism would provide a vehicle for combining modern technology with collective purpose. When he became disillusioned with that possibility, he increasingly turned to a criticism of the technological attitude toward the world—the view of the world as nothing but material destined for human manipulation. He contended that the roots of this manipulative worldview were deeply rooted in the culture of the West, and had led to a forgetting of what, with great ambiguity, he called "Being."

That the present age was one in which technology replaced meaning and seriousness was another Heideggerian theme that appealed to Taubes. On the level of method, Taubes would try to replicate Heidegger's attempt to recapture the primary experience behind religious and philosophical texts, including breaking up familiar Greek and German terms to try to recover their original meanings and the experiences that lay behind them.

René König

Of Taubes's teachers in Zurich, none did more to foster his interests and his career than René König (1906–92). It was in König's courses that Jacob encountered the masters of German sociological thought, and especially the works of Max Weber, for whom religion and secularization were central themes. Taubes's doctoral dissertation first took shape in König's seminar, and it was ultimately published in a series that König edited.

König was a young German scholar whose opposition to National Socialism led him to emigrate to Switzerland in 1937. The next year he received his habilitation (license to teach at a university) and began to offer courses at the University of Zurich as a Privatdozent. That meant he drew no regular salary, but was paid out of student fees, which the multilingual König supplemented with work as an author, translator, and occasional book reviewer for François Bondy's *Die Weltwoche*. Despite his lack of a paid professorship, König counted himself fortunate, as he was one of the few intellectual émigrés able to get a university teaching position in Zurich. But he remained very much an outsider, regarded with suspicion by the academic establishment, both on political grounds, and because he wasn't a Swiss native.[22] König had met Zwi Taubes when both men were students at the University of Vienna in the mid-1920s. Single and unattached in Zurich, König was a frequent guest of the Taubes family there. They invited him for memorable High Holiday dinners, where he marveled at Fanny's gefilte fish.[23]

At the university, König offered lectures and seminars that dealt with the history of sociological thought and its relationship to philosophy, to intellectual history, and to social and economic history.[24] Jacob participated in König's seminar on work and vocation (*Beruf*), for which he wrote a paper on Jewish conceptions of work. Jacob also took König's lecture course on Karl Marx, and then a seminar, for which he wrote a paper that ultimately led to his doctoral dissertation.[25]

After the War, König returned to Germany as a professor of sociology at Cologne. He would become the leading figure in the German sociological profession, and in the 1960s, his path would once again cross with Jacob's.

Max Weber and Secularization

The theme that tied together Taubes's diverse interests was secularization, understood as the displacement of beliefs, hopes, concepts, and practices from the religious to the secular sphere.[26] The theme could take a variety of forms and could have diverse emphases. Stress could be placed on the fundamental *continuity* of contents as they moved from the erstwhile religious realm to the secular. Or it could be on the *loss* or *perversion* of substance as ideas, images, and practices were secularized. It could be on the valuable legacy of the religious past for the post-religious present or future, or, conversely, on the poisonous legacy of the religious past to the present. Or, in yet another variation, it could cast doubt upon the assumption that life in the modern age was really as devoid of religious premises as some maintained.

Jacob's dissertation on Western eschatology was, among other things, an extended exploration of the secularization of eschatological hopes. *Eschatology* denotes the doctrine of last things, or of God's reign on earth. Among Jews it was often linked to messianism, the coming of a collective savior, or of an age that would put an end to the Exile. In Christianity, it most often referred to the return of Jesus at the end of days. The continuity into the modern period of eschatological beliefs about a redemptive ending of history could be viewed in divergent ways. It could be seen as a burden: a continuity of illusions that were best abandoned as irrational and as holding out promises that could not possibly be met. Or it could be viewed as a source of hope—nonrational to be sure, but still desirable as providing the emotional energy for radical change. Taubes never confronted these alternative views head on, but his tacit view seemed to be that while eschatological belief was not *true*, it was highly *useful* in motivating historical actors to engage in radical, transformative action. The result would never match up to their expectations, but would provide a motor to move history forward.[27] "Secularization," "redemption," and "eschatology" are all terms that lend themselves to multiple meanings. The imprecision of the terms, together with their suggestiveness, makes it difficult to specify the claims entailed in their use. This allows for endless and ultimately unresolvable debates about their meaning and significance. That was true of many of the intellectual controversies in which Taubes would become involved.[28]

But since religion played so large a role in the lives of many of his inter-locutors and readers—whether as an active faith, a living memory, a long-ing, or as a feared antagonist—there was ongoing interest in the history and possible contemporary relevance of these themes.

These variations on the theme of secularization were all evident in the papers that Taubes wrote as a doctoral student, and in his dissertation.

One portion of Taubes's doctoral examinations was an essay prepared in advance (*Hausarbeit*) on "Transformations in the Theory of the Devel-opment of the Capitalist Ethos of Work since Max Weber," written for René König.[29] The essay provided a wide-ranging exploration of the reception of Weber's thesis about the links between Calvinism and the spirit of capitalism. It demonstrated an acquaintance with the controversy aroused by "the Weber thesis" among German social scientists in Weber's day, and subsequent discussions in France, England, and the United States. Though Weber did not use the term "secularization," his thesis about the transformation of an originally religious impulse—the search by believers in divine Predestination for signs of personal salvation in worldly activity—into a nonreligious valuation of secular work as an intrinsic good was a prime example of a secularization thesis. As Taubes noted in his essay, for Weber, as for Marx, this was a central question for understand-ing modernity as a whole. Taubes asserted that both Marx and Weber turned to the study of capitalism out of the common motive of wanting to understand modern, Faustian Man (a Spenglerian coinage). For Taubes, capitalism was a source of dehumanization. That was an assumption that Taubes never revisited, but took for granted.

Carl Schmitt and Political Theology

Another variation on the theme of secularization was what came to be called "political theology": the attempt to trace links between conceptions of God and of politics. Like the term secularization, it was ambiguous and could have divergent and even opposing connotations.

A key text in this debate was *Political Theology: Four Chapters on the Concept of Sovereignty* (*Politische Theologie: Vier Kapitel zur Lehre von der Souveränität*), first published in 1922 by the German legal theorist Carl Schmitt. Schmitt was writing in the aftermath of the First World War and the early years of the Weimar Republic, an era of crisis and instability in German political life. He was a legal scholar of unusual breadth, with a deep knowledge of the history of ideas, which he brought to bear in his legal analyses. Schmitt was led by inclination and experience toward a deep skepticism of liberalism, especially of the ability of liberal conceptions to provide an adequate framework for political stability under contemporary conditions. He was also steeped in Catholic critiques of the Enlightenment and of liberalism, though his own life course and intellectual development led him away from both the institutional Church and from Catholic doctrine. During the Weimar Republic, Schmitt's published interpretations of Article 48 of the Weimar Constitution—which allowed for presidential assumption of emergency powers when necessary—provided the rationale for the use of such powers, first by the Social Democrat, Friedrich Ebert, and then by the conservative president, Paul von Hindenburg.

As was often the case, Schmitt's antiliberalism was entwined with antisemitism, which he kept under wraps during the Weimar Republic, when he first emerged as a major figure on the German intellectual scene. After Hitler's ascension to power, Schmitt threw his support behind the new regime, and worked mightily to become its crown jurist. He not only wrote articles supporting the Hitler dictatorship, but organized a conference to rid German jurisprudence of its "Jewish" elements. He was thwarted in his goal by opposition from other Nazi jurists, who in 1936 opportunistically attacked him for his previous contacts with Jews and for his lack of full conformity to Nazi ideology. In the remaining years of the Third Reich, Schmitt penned a series of essays and short books on international affairs and international law, all of which served to legitimate a German-dominated Europe. The question of how a man of Schmitt's intellectual stature could have supported National Socialism would continue to trouble and fascinate Jacob Taubes.

Taubes first encountered Schmitt's *Political Theology* at age nineteen, in a seminar on religion and politics, taught by the historian Leonhard von Muralt. Taubes read the book without being aware of Schmitt's subsequent support of the Nazi regime, or of his antisemitic actions. Deeply impressed with the work, Taubes gave a forty-minute report about it to the seminar, only to have the book dismissed by the presiding professor as the work of an "evil man" (*bösen Mensch*).[30] Schmitt thought that liberalism had an overly benign, naive view of human affairs, overestimating the extent to which government could function based on rules and procedures alone, or politics on the basis of reasoned discussion. Life was too unruly for that, Schmitt thought, and liberalism, with its rationalist bias that all problems could be resolved by discussion and its emphasis upon adhering to the proper procedures at all costs, was therefore intellectually inadequate and politically faulty. It failed to account for the fact that there were exceptional situations in which sticking to existing laws and procedures might be fatal to the polity—as in the case of incipient civil war. It failed to recognize that on such occasions, there was a need for decisions that could not be reduced to following the approved procedures. And the most important decision that needed to be made was when such a state of emergency or exceptional situation actually existed. That, for Schmitt, was the real meaning of sovereignty—what individual or body was empowered to decide on the state of exception.[31]

Schmitt tied this political argument to a historical one that particularly interested Taubes. Schmitt claimed that "all significant concepts of the modern theory of the state are secularized theological concepts." He argued, for example, that there was an intrinsic connection between early modern deism and liberal constitutionalism. Just as deists believed that God created the world with its own laws that did not require further divine intervention in the form of miracles, so did liberals believe that government could be constituted by a set of rules and procedures alone. Just as deists denied the need for and possibility of miracles, Enlightenment thinkers and their liberal heirs believed that personal decision and the suspension of the legal rules had no place in a proper functioning state.[32] The obverse of this was that there was some sort of analogy (Schmitt was vague on this) between the religious belief in God's ability to perform miracles and the political sovereign's ability to suspend the normal constitutional rules.

As so often in the debates on secularization, Schmitt's arguments about the links between theological and political concepts were more suggestive than precise. That made them both stimulating and fodder for ongoing debate and discussion.

Like his teacher Max Weber, Schmitt was wont to conceive of modern politics as locked into the iron cage of economic and technical modes of thought, leading to a flaccid existence, devoid of intensity. Both Schmitt and Taubes were theologically interested and knowledgeable, and both felt compelled to maintain a link between politics and a theology in which they did not quite believe. They also shared a disdain for modern liberalism and for what they took to be the all-too-petty concerns of normal bourgeois life.

Hans Urs von Balthasar and the Secularization of Apocalypticism

Perhaps the most direct influence on Taubes's dissertation came from his older friend, the Jesuit theologian Hans Urs von Balthasar (1905–88). A man of patrician origins, Balthasar had dabbled in a variety of fields, from art and music to philosophy, before pursuing a doctorate in *Germanistik* and beginning his studies to enter the Jesuit order. The result was a book, *The History of the Eschatological Problems in Modern German Literature* (*Geschichte des eschatologischen Problems in der modernen deutschen Literatur*) (1930), which Balthasar spent much of the next decade expanding into a three-volume opus, published from 1937 to 1939, *Apocalypse of the German Soul: Studies toward a Theory of Ultimate Attitudes* (*Apocalypse der deutschen Seele: Studien zu einer Lehre von letzen Haltungen*). The book took the form of a series of in-depth studies of figures in German intellectual and cultural history from the eighteenth to the twentieth centuries, ending with Heidegger, Rilke, and Barth. In each case, Balthasar provided an analysis of their work from the perspective of their reflections on ultimate things, or man's final fate. The book traced the abandonment of the medieval assumption of man's transcendent relationship to God and ultimate salvation; its replacement in the eighteenth century by an ideology of historical progress, above all in German idealism; then the critique of that ideology in the nineteenth century; and finally, attempts to find alternatives to the progressive view of history in the twentieth century.[33] For Balthasar, the search for a this-worldly philosophy of history, whether in the form of an ideology of progress or in some other manner, marked a falling away from the medieval, Christian understanding of the Eschaton in transcendent, otherworldly terms, as the Kingdom of God. Since Balthasar assumed the medieval Christian view to be fundamentally correct, *Apocalypse der deutschen Seele* was a work of Catholic cultural criticism and apologetics. For Balathasar, in other words, the secularization of eschatology is presumptively illegitimate. Another of his interests was Gnosticism, which Balthasar understood as both an ancient heresy and a recurrent pattern in modern Western history, a phenomenon he judged to be fundamentally destructive.[34]

Taubes would adopt both Balthasar's fascination with the history of eschatological thinking and with Gnosticism. He would share Balthasar's interests, but not his valuations, some of which he would turn on their heads. Balthasar influenced the style of young Taubes as well. Balthasar was a nonlinear thinker, and his work often lacks argument, comprised instead by a stream of confident assertions.[35] Taubes picked up some of that as well.

When Taubes got to know him, Balthasar was a Catholic chaplain at the University of Basel, where he was close to Karl Barth, despite the latter's Protestantism. From early on in his career, Balthasar sought to break with what he saw as the desiccated theology of Neo-Scholasticism, and to recapture the drama of faith. Writing at first from a marginal position within the Catholic Church, his influence would wane and then wax. Excluded from the Second Vatican Council in 1962, he was about to be named a bishop by Pope John Paul II when he died in 1988.

Karl Löwith and the Secularization of Eschatology

Taubes's thinking about the transformation of religious contents into secular, political ones was deeply influenced by a book recommended to him by König, *From Hegel to Nietzsche: The Revolution in Nineteenth Century Thought* (*Von Hegel zu Nietzsche: Der revolutionäre Bruch im Denken des neunzehnten Jahrhunderts*) published in Zurich in 1941.[36] Its author was Karl Löwith, a German philosopher of Jewish "racial" origin—though he had been raised a Protestant—then living in Japanese exile. In the 1920s, Löwith had been a student of Martin Heidegger, as had Hans Jonas, Leo Strauss, Hannah Arendt, and Herbert Marcuse—all of Jewish origin, and all of whom would figure in Jacob Taubes's intellectual journey.

Löwith's book traced developments in German intellectual life in the course of the nineteenth century. It maintained that early in the century, Goethe and Hegel had each developed a sort of halfway house between Christianity and secularism, with Goethe practicing a kind of "Christian Paganism" and Hegel attempting to retain the symbols of Christianity while radically reinterpreting them. Löwith showed how Hegel had preserved elements of Christian eschatology—the belief in the redemptive ending of history—by translating them into a philosophy of world history as a story of increasing freedom and human self-realization, ending in the modern state and modern bourgeois society. Hegel, Löwith wrote, had tried to unite "antiquity and Christianity, God and the world, the internal and the external, being and existence."[37] But after him, the attempt at mediating between these alternatives fell apart. Much of the rest of German intellectual history in the nineteenth century could be understood as a series of reactions against Hegel's system, culminating on the one hand in Marx's radical materialist rejection of bourgeois society, and on the other in Søren Kierkegaard's radical rejection of any attempt to bridge the gap between Christian faith and the existing bourgeois world, and his insistence upon the necessity of deciding between these alternatives (a critique that influenced Karl Barth, Carl Schmitt, and Martin Heidegger). Löwith's book concluded with an examination of Nietzsche's radical critique of Christianity, and with Overbeck's scholarly undermining of the possibility of reconciling early Christianity with the modern world. In his doctoral dissertation and beyond, Taubes would draw heavily on Löwith's portraits of nineteenth-century German thought. Löwith, in turn, would draw upon Taubes's book on occidental eschatology in writing his subsequent book, *Meaning in History* (1949). But, as in the case of Balthasar, Taubes would borrow from Löwith's analysis while diverging from his conclusions. Löwith came to regard the legacy of eschatology as fundamentally pernicious. For even in secularized form it provided an illusory belief that history had a fundamental direction. Taubes, by contrast, would place a far more positive spin on the legacy of religious eschatology.

The Fascinations of Antinomianism: Bloch, Jonas, and Scholem

In formulating his dissertation, Taubes was deeply influenced by strands of interwar German intellectual life that explored heretical and antinomian trends within the Jewish and Christian traditions. He drew in particular upon three intellectuals with very different agendas.

The first of these was Ernst Bloch (1885–1977), an intellectual of Jewish origins but not of Jewish commitments. Bloch had been part of the circle around Max Weber, but his temperament was the opposite of Weber's own. While Weber was deeply interested in economic matters, and prided himself on a certain sobriety and realism, Bloch was poetic and deliberately utopian. Like some other young intellectuals shocked and repelled by the carnage of the First World War, Bloch had become first a radical pacifist, and then a communist, believing that it was capitalism that led to war. In a style more expressionistic than scholarly, he composed a series of works whose common theme was the way in which a utopian, non-alienated future might be envisioned. In an early work, *Geist der Utopie* (*The Spirit of Utopia*) (1923), Bloch cast Jewishness as a cultural ideal constituted by messianism, by an attitude of opposition to the existing order, and by the utopian impulse to create a just world.[38]

While Marx had rejected religion as the opium of the masses, Bloch was fascinated by religion as a source of utopian longing and hope, and of movements within Christianity that had sought a radical transformation to bring about the Kingdom of God on earth. That was the theme of his book *Thomas Münzer als Theologe der Revolution* (*Thomas Münzer as Theologian of Revolution*), published in 1921 (and dedicated to Margarete Susman, who would become a friend of the Taubes family). The book explored the ideas and actions of Münzer, a Reformation-era German preacher whose theology became increasingly egalitarian and radical

as he tried to realize biblical ideals, and who became an ideological supporter of the Peasants' War. Bloch's explicit aim in writing the book was
to provide a link between the history of Christian heretical and chiliastic movements and contemporary Marxism.[39] In a later work, *Heritage
of Our Times* (*Erbschaft dieser Zeit*) (1935), Bloch stressed the need for
Marxism to abandon its antireligious predilections, and in a demystified
fashion to integrate the religious aspirations that had historically nour-
ished demands for radical social change.[40] Taubes cited Bloch's book on
Münzer in his dissertation, and it provided a stimulus to his own work.

Bloch spent the years of the Second World War in the United States,
where, bereft of other sources of support, he washed dishes to make ends
meet. After the war, he made his way to communist East Germany, where
he became a chaired professor of philosophy. But communist reality was
no match for his utopian ideals, and in 1960 he moved to West Germany,
where he became a hero to the nascent New Left.

A seminal influence on Taubes's doctoral dissertation was a book published in 1934 by Hans Jonas, *Gnosticism and the Spirit of Late Antiquity*
(*Gnosis und Spätantiker Geist*). Jonas too had been a student of Martin
Heidegger, and brought certain Heideggerian modes of analysis to bear
in his work on Gnosticism. The term had a curious history and a variety
of meanings (which, again, made it grist for endless debate).[41] "Gnosis"
is Greek for "knowledge," and denoted some secret or esoteric knowledge about the world. Gnosticism turned the traditional Jewish notion
of a providential creation on its head. The world as most of us know it,
the Gnostics insisted, is indeed a creation: but it is a world of evil created by an evil deity. The possibility of a better world was open to those
who recognized the current one as saturated with evil. In the Christian
tradition, Gnosticism was regarded as a heresy, dating back to the second century. Indeed, it was regarded as so heretical that its literary works
were destroyed, so that much that was known about Gnosticism could
be gleaned only from the attacks on it by Christian theologians, such as
Irenaeus's *Against Heresies* (c. 180). In the nineteenth and early twentieth
centuries, there was an explosion of scholarship on Gnosticism. Scholars
disagreed as to whether it arose in the Greek world or in Persia, nor did
they agree on the extent to which parts of the Christian Gospels reflected
Gnostic influences.[42]

Jonas argued that Gnosticism arose in a number of societies around the
ancient Mediterranean at about the same time, and that it did so because
those societies faced a common experience that made Gnostic myths and
doctrines so appealing. His main innovation was to present what he called

a phenomenological account of Gnosticism, that is, an account that sought to recover the feelings, perceptions, and fundamental attitude toward the world (*Daseinshaltung*) of the adherents of Gnostic doctrines.[43] Not only did Jonas try to recapture Gnosticism using Heideggerian categories, his description of the Gnostic attitude bore a striking resemblance to elements of Heidegger's own view of the world, as expressed in his book *Being and Time*. Since, for the Gnostics, the world was evil and the creation of an evil deity, their fundamental experience (*Urerlebnis* or *Grunderlebnis*) was of being aliens in the world, of loneliness, anxiety, of not understanding the world and not being understood by it. The Gnostic also felt that without proper awareness, he could fall prey to forgetting his essential alienness, becoming assimilated into the world of evil, and alienated from his real origins, which lay in a better, transcendent realm. The first step toward real wisdom, the Gnostics believed, was to recognize one's own alienness, which was a sign of superiority. That went together with a longing (*Heim-weh*) for a higher, transcendent world.[44]

Gnosticism, Jonas wrote, was a revolutionary doctrine: not in the sense that it intended to overthrow the existing order of society and replace it with another, but in the sense of a wholesale devaluation of the world as it is, and its replacement by a counterworld, through an alternative interpretation of reality. God—the real God, not the gods embraced by society—is defined negatively, as entirely beyond this world, as an unknown God from whom redemption will come.[45] The result, Jonas wrote, is a sort of "cosmic nihilism" (*kosmische Nihilismus*), and allegiance to a deity who is a "Nothing" (*Nichts*), and a way of life that paradoxically derives its meaning through negation.[46] According to that interpretation, those possessed with a consciousness of the true spirit (pneuma) were able to break free of existing society and its norms. That resulted, at least in the first instance, in moral anarchism and libertinism, before possibly leading to new forms of self-denial (asceticism), or of religious community. Based on a purportedly higher knowledge, Gnosticism led to a disdain for the world and its "wisdom."[47] The pneumatics, in their own eyes at least, formed a privileged aristocracy, a new human type free of the obligations and standards of existing society. Indeed, the unrestrained use of this freedom was a positive injunction, leading to a sanctification of sacrilege. The pneumatic, as Jonas characterized him, glories in demonstrating his distinction from the rest of society through his actions. Libertinism, in its deliberate flouting of social conventions, is regarded as a sort of declaration of war against the world as it exists.[48]

A small coterie of German-speaking scholars read Jonas's book and recognized its brilliance and significance. But fate conspired to limit its impact. First because the book was subtitled "Part I," and some scholars understandably delayed their evaluation until the second part had appeared. But it did not appear for another two decades.[49] Further, as a Jew and a committed Zionist, Jonas felt compelled to leave Germany in 1933 and made his way to Jerusalem, in mandatory Palestine.

There, he was part of a circle of intellectuals around his friend Gershom Scholem. But opportunities to pursue a scholarly career in Jerusalem were few. There was only one university, the Hebrew University, which had been founded only a decade before, and it was still a small-scale operation. During the Second World War, Jonas fought in the Jewish Brigade of the British Army, and again in the Israeli War of Independence. Then, despairing of the possibility of finding an academic post in Israel, he took a position at Carleton University in Ottawa, Canada, before moving to the New School in New York City. There he made a second career as a philosopher, eventually writing a book, *The Principle of Responsibility* (1979), which would become a landmark in ecological thinking.

The reach of *Gnosis und Spätantiker Geist* was also limited by its style and structure. The book was written for specialized academics, beginning with a long survey of scholarly approaches to the subject, then offering Jonas's own existentialist approach, couched in language that was not easily accessible. Jonas's work on Gnosticism would achieve international impact only in the 1950s, when the book was reformulated in more accessible terms and published in English—in a series edited by Jacob Taubes.[50] But Taubes's interest in Gnosticism—at least, as Jonas had characterized it—was more than scholarly. He would adopt much of the Gnostic attitude toward the fallen world.

The relevance of Jonas's exploration of Gnosticism to Jewish history was demonstrated by his friend Gershom Scholem in his seminal essay of 1937, "Mitzvah habaah ba'averah" (later translated as "Redemption through Sin"), about the seventeenth-century Jewish false messiah, Sabbatai Zevi (the English spelling varies), and his eighteenth-century successor, Jacob Frank. Under pressure from the Ottoman authorities, Sabbatai Zevi converted to Islam, while Frank ultimately converted to Catholicism in Poland. In each case, their followers developed intricate theological rationales to explain the unanticipated fate of their messiah. And they engaged in deliberately transgressive behavior, on the grounds that the coming of the messiah liberated his followers from the yoke of the law, and that the world could only be redeemed from evil by exhausting the evil within it through acts of sacrilege. Following Jonas's lead, Scholem pointed out the connection between their sense of spiritual election and nihilism:

> To the pneumatic, the spiritual universe which he inhabits is of an entirely different order from the world of ordinary flesh and blood, whose opinion of the new laws he has chosen to live by is therefore irrelevant; insofar as he is above sin . . . he may do as the spirit dictates without needing to take into account the moral standards of the society around him. Indeed he is, if anything, duty-bound to violate and subvert this "ordinary" morality in the name of the higher principles that have been revealed to him.[51]

Though Scholem is not cited in Taubes's dissertation, shortly after finishing it Taubes seems to have thrown himself into reading Scholem's work.

As this conspectus of the stars in Taubes's intellectual firmament makes clear, while he was buffeted by diverse and sometimes conflicting intellectual trends, they were almost always *German* intellectual trends, including the influence of German-Jewish thinkers such as Buber and Scholem. German thought and culture were second nature to him.

Those influences and themes left their mark on his doctoral dissertation on occidental eschatology, his first—and only—published book.

CHAPTER FOUR

Occidental Eschatology and Beyond, 1946–47

IN THE YEARS after his stint at the yeshiva in Montreux, Jacob took seminars at the University of Zurich and worked on what would become his doctoral dissertation. The thesis grew out of his interests in Marxism and religion. Drawing upon a remarkable range of reading in a variety of fields, the dissertation, soon published as a book, created a useable past for contemporary radicals, and for religious folk inclined toward worldly radicalism. The themes of Gnosticism and apocalypticism, which were central to the book, were themes Taubes would continue to reflect upon throughout his career. Having completed his thesis, his mind turned to additional topics in the fields of philosophy, history, and Judaica, topics that came together in the work of Gershom Scholem, to whom Taubes turned before sailing to America to take up a fellowship at the Jewish Theological Seminary in New York.

The Genesis of Occidental Eschatology

The seed for Taubes's dissertation on occidental eschatology lay in a paper, "Karl Marx's Justification of Socialism" ("Die Begründung des Sozialismus durch Karl Marx"), which he wrote for König's seminar.[1] Taubes's main claim was that beneath its rationalistic conceptual structure, Marx's socialism had an irrational charge that helped explain its appeal.[2] Marx's contention that the coming of socialism was both historically inevitable and morally desirable was based ultimately on faith (*Glaube*). "The assumption that the discovery of the natural laws [of history] provide some sort of insight into a more desirable social order makes no sense, unless one assumes that there is a divine plan for the world leading to a pre-established harmony. Otherwise, it is incomprehensible why the triumph of the material process should not lead to the triumph of ultimate meaninglessness, or to slavery, or to anarchy."[3] Marxism, Taubes asserted, rests ultimately on a core of apocalyptic belief, on a search for certainty about when the end of the current world will arrive and the beginning of a new and better one will commence. Like other apocalyptics, Marx sees history as divided in two, between the evil realm of necessity and the realm of freedom and justice that communism will bring, a "Kingdom of God— without God [*Reich Gottes—ohne Gott*]."[4] "The pathos and the tremendous power of Marxist ideas rest upon a theory of human salvation and the messianic vocation of the proletariat," Jacob wrote.[5] The essay concludes that Marx, like every major thinker, has time-bound and timeless elements, and that Marx reflects his time in his emphasis on economics. "But amidst all of that there sounds a will, a hope, and a longing that is eternal," namely, "the eternal longing of fallen man for redemption."[6] This would remain one of the main contentions of *Abendländische Eschatologie* (*Occidental Eschatology*). (It is a line of analysis most recently embraced by Yuri Slezkine in his history of the first generation of Bolsheviks.[7])

Taubes's research then moved backward historically. A first sketch for the dissertation telegraphs its intention, conveyed in its original name, "Apocalyptic and Marxist Conceptions of History: Studies in Karl Marx's View of History" ("Apokalyptsche und Marx'sche Geschichtsanschauung. Studien zur Geschichtsanschauung von Karl Marx").[8] That draft already shows the influence of Balthasar's *Apocalypse der deutschen Seele*. Though Balthasar had not been particularly interested in Marx, Taubes borrowed ideas from Balthasar about the centrality of apocalypticism in the history of the Christian and post-Christian West, as well as the pivotal role of the twelfth-century monk and theologian Joachim of Fiore in the secularization of eschatological thinking. Taubes then seems to have read Löwith's book, which had a major impact upon him. For the new working title of the dissertation was to be "Logos und Telos: Studien zur Geschichte und System der abendländlschen Eschatologie von der Prophetie und Apokalyptik bis Hegel, Marx, und Kierkegaard" ("Logos and Telos: Studies on the History and System of Occidental Eschatology, from the Prophets and Apocalyptics to Hegel, Marx, and Kierkegaard").[9]

One person who had no discernable influence on Jacob or on his thesis was his nominal director, Hans Barth (1904–65). Barth had for many years been the cultural editor at the *Neue Zürcher Zeitung*, a highly respected liberal newspaper, and one that achieved particular prominence in the 1930s and 1940s, when formerly liberal newspapers in Germany and Austria had been ideologically "co-ordinated" by the Nazi regime. (In his many wanderings, it would remain Taubes's favorite newspaper, probably less for its liberalism than for its high intellectual standards.) In 1945, Barth published a book-length study and critique of ideological notions of truth, and in 1946, just before Taubes completed his dissertation, Barth was appointed to the first chair in political philosophy in Switzerland, at the University of Zurich.[10]

Taubes wrote the dissertation with very little academic guidance. That was not unusual at Swiss universities at the time, and his friend Armin Mohler had a similar experience in Basel. "How do you write a book?" Taubes asked Rudolf Zipkes, a friend of the family who had recently published a book of his own. The lack of professorial direction helps account for some of the book's idiosyncrasies.

Occidental Eschatology

Occidental Eschatology, Taubes's doctoral dissertation at the University of Zurich, was completed when he was twenty-three. It was the first and last of his books published during his lifetime. It is the work of a very bright, remarkably erudite, and intellectually ambitious young man, working hard to convey just how bright and erudite he is. Written under minimal supervision, it is also the book of an author trying to figure out how to write and changing intellectual register along the way. The book begins in the mode of 1920s existentialist expressionism, characterized by vatic pronouncements about human existence (á la Barth, Rosenzweig, and Heidegger). It then moves on to the more academic genres of the history of religion (*Religionsgeschichte*, a German school of scholarship that tried to interpret the Bible in its historical context) and the history of ideas (*Ideengeschichte*), before concluding with a vaguely religious admonition. It is the contribution of a precocious young man to a contemporary genre that might be called the spiritual history of mankind. Outstanding examples of that genre included the recent books by Balthasar and Löwith, upon which Taubes drew and which he tried to imitate. Digressive and abounding in casual overgeneralization, *Occidental Eschatology* is derivative for long stretches. Yet the book is also remarkable in its own way.

It would be an understatement to say that the book's opening reflects the influence of Martin Heidegger. For the first paragraph replicates the style and often the very wording of the opening of Heidegger's 1943 essay, "On the Essence of Truth" ("Vom Wesen der Wahrheit"). Here is Heidegger's opening paragraph, followed by Taubes's:

> Heidegger: The subject of inquiry is the essence of truth. The question regarding the essence of truth is not concerned with whether the truth is one of practical experience, or of economic calculation, the truth of some technical consideration or of political sagacity, or, in particular, the truth of some scientific research or of an artistic formation, or even the truth of thoughtful reflection or of some cultic belief. From all of these the question of essence turns away and attends to the one thing that distinguishes every truth as truth.[11]

> Taubes: The subject of inquiry is the essence of history. The question regarding the essence of history is not concerned with individual historical events, whether battles, victories, defeats, or treaties, whether political happenings, or economic complexities, or artistic or religious formations, or of the products of scientific knowledge. From all of these the question of essence turns away and attends only to this: how is history possible at all, what is the sufficient condition on which the very possibility of history rests?[12]

The book's first theme concerns the religious origins of the philosophy of history. In the ancient Orient and in classical antiquity, history was understood as cyclical. The notion that history has a linear direction, rather than a recurrent, nature-like pattern, is a product of the eschatological habit of mind, with its origins in the Hebrew Bible. For, so Taubes claims, it is the notion that history is headed to some end that makes it possible to view history as a meaningful process. If everything in history is of equal value, then it is all arbitrary: only the notion of an end point of history creates the possibility that history has a plot or a meaning.[13] The book traces the origins of this eschatological vision in the Hebrew Bible and the New Testament, then follows its medieval transformations, and its ultimate secularization in modern German philosophy and in Marxism.

Taubes borrowed the theme of the linkage of eschatology with the progressive philosophy of history from Karl Löwith. But while he agreed with Löwith's analysis, he reversed Löwith's evaluation. For Löwith, the continuity between religious eschatology and the modern philosophy of history demonstrated the irrationality of that philosophy. Taubes, by contrast, affirmed the conception of history as fundamentally a tale of human liberation, a conception that he saw as having religious roots.

The second theme, which comprises the greater part of the volume, treats the history of apocalypticism and of Gnosticism. Both share the belief that the existing order (or existing world) is evil and corrupt. Apocalyptics search for signs that the existing order is coming to an end, and they engage in action to bring about the Kingdom of God on earth. Gnostics convey knowledge (gnosis) about the fallenness of the world, and they claim to know of an alternative, more perfect order. Both are antinomian, that is, antipathetic to the law. But apocalypticism is more active and oriented to external transformation, while Gnostics are more inclined to the transformation of the self through their purported special knowledge. The book seeks to convey both the history of these recurrent propensities, and what Taubes calls "the revolutionary pathos of apocalypticism and Gnosis." That revolutionary pathos runs through much of the book—and through Taubes's subsequent work as well. Apocalyptic movements inevitably fail, at least by their own standards. But, Taubes asserts, they serve as the motor force of history, transforming old orders into new ones. Their failure leads to a new round of Gnosticism, which serves as a subterranean stream of discontent until the next round of apocalyptic enthusiasm and redemptive action.

Drawing from a diverse range of writers and scholars, Taubes tries to trace these themes through the history of the West, from the Book of Daniel, through the Zealots, early Christianity, the medieval monk Joachim of Fiore, the early modern Anabaptists and Puritans, and then through the secularization of eschatology, ultimately in Marxism. He also takes a stab—quite unusual at the time—at exploring parallels in the development of eschatological strains of Judaism alongside those of Christianity. The book concludes with an epilogue in which Heidegger's assertion that inauthentic man has strayed from contact with the mystery of Being by making himself the measure of all things is equated by Taubes with man's forgetting of God. Thus, a turn toward some new relationship to God seems to be the solution to the alienated world of technology evoked by Heidegger.[14]

While much of the learning on display is secondhand, Taubes was able to draw together themes from disparate scholars, including Martin Buber on Biblical theocracy; Hans Jonas on Gnosticism; Herbert Grundmann on Joachim; Ernst Benz on Franciscanism; Ernst Bloch on Thomas Münzer; Hans Urs von Balthasar on early modern German thought; and Löwith's *From Hegel to Nietzsche*, from which Taubes drew most of his interpretation of nineteenth-century thought. His bold attempt was to synthesize this diverse material into a coherent narrative and analytic framework.

Aspiration exceeds execution, for sometimes the material seems more cut and pasted than fully integrated. Thus the reader is likely to be intellectually stimulated and exasperated by turn. Despite the book's pastiche-like nature, aggravated by a plethora of tangents and aperçus, with some effort one can distill the main lines of argument.

Biblical Israel is the origin of revolutionary apocalypticism, Taubes maintains.[15] For the biblical hope was for divine sovereignty: Israel's theocratic ideal of religious community on earth poses "the religious preconditions of revolutionary pathos." The theocratic ideal of politics contains an anarchic element, for it expresses the desire not to be ruled by any human ruler, an idea that Taubes borrowed from Martin Buber. Eschatology arises from the contradiction between the reality of a godless world and the conception of a Kingdom of God on earth. And that eschatological hope would continue to reappear. Thus, among Christians, the Old Testament was the basis of recurrent religious-revolutionary movements: in the late Middle Ages, among the fifteenth-century Taborites (followers of Jan Hus) and the sixteenth-century Puritans. Since the era of Jewish emancipation in the nineteenth century, Taubes notes, Jews have played a prominent role in the revolutionary movement, from Marx to Trotsky.[16]

Borrowing extensively from the work of Hans Jonas, Taubes explores Gnosticism.[17] "The world stands in opposition to God, and God in opposition to the world. God is an unknown stranger to this world," Taubes writes, summarizing Jonas's argument.[18] According to Taubes, the sustained alienation expressed in Gnosticism is closely related to apocalypticism, the expectation that the current world—fallen, dark, and evil—will give way to a new world of goodness and light. Apocalypticism typically has a passive attitude toward the world, of waiting for the right time to arrive.[19] "Marx too sees in history higher powers at work that cannot be influenced by the individual, clothed in the mythological garb of his age as 'forces of production,'"[20] Taubes notes. Taubes characterizes Gnostic and apocalyptic thought as based on a dialectical technique that emphasizes "the power of the negative," a critical mode of thought that remained subterranean in medieval Aristotelian and Scholastic thought, only to reemerge with Hegel and Marx.[21]

Taubes sees reflections of this Gnostic sensibility in the Apostle Paul, a historical personage who played a minor role in *Occidental Eschatology*, but who would loom ever larger in Taubes's subsequent development. Taubes notes that "for Paul, just as in Gnostic literature, demonic powers are 'the rulers of this world' and the 'Prince of this world' is Satan."[22] This view of Paul as either a Gnostic, as influenced by Gnosticism, or as a proto-Gnostic was a recurrent theme of interwar scholarship on Gnosticism.[23]

Then Taubes turned to the history of apocalypticism. Its origins in the West were traced to the apocalyptic chapters of the Book of Daniel, which, drawing upon modern critical scholarship of the Bible, Taubes attributed to the Maccabean period of the second century BC. Then, again making use of critical Biblical scholarship, he contends that Jesus must be understood contextually, as part of a larger messianic wave in Israel, which itself was part of an apocalyptic wave in the broader Aramaic-Syrian world of his time. Jesus's message of a world turned upside down, in which the last were to be first, presented a challenge to the Roman Empire.[24]

Taubes portrays Christianity as an offshoot of Judaism that responded to the growth of individualism and self-consciousness in late antiquity and to the spiritual emptiness of the Roman Empire, with a new promise of community and otherworldly salvation. For the community created by Paul, Christ is a sort of anti-Caesar, the ultimate abnegation of the ethos of Rome.[25] (Here Taubes drew upon the interpretations offered by the young Hegel, by the nineteenth-century Hegelian biblical critic, Bruno Bauer, and by a now-forgotten 1935 work of the German young conservative writer Otto Petras, *Post Christentum*.) The founder of Christianity is not Jesus—who, together with his small group of Jewish followers expected the imminent coming of the messiah, the Son of Man—but Paul, who makes not the life and teachings of Jesus, but the death of Jesus into the center of the new faith. While the original circle around Jesus awaits his immanent return (Parousia), Paul preaches that as a result of Christ's sacrifice, the new era has already dawned, and the old world is passing away.[26] He thus marks a point of transition between apocalyptic expectations of the end of the world, and a new Gnostic knowledge of the transformative turn of history, the kairos. It is Paul who takes a Jewish messianic figure, Jesus, and interprets his death as of universal import.

The oppression of the early Christian communities by the Roman emperors leads to a recrudescence of Jewish apocalyptic motifs, as expressed in the twentieth chapter of the Book of Revelations, which, Taubes notes, became "the *Magna Carta* of chiliasm."[27] But from the second Christian century on, a transformation occurs, as the ever-awaited Parousia fails to occur, and what was once a scattering of Christian communities becomes a Church. Beginning with the Church Father Origen and reaching its culmination in Augustine, eschatology is turned inward. It is no longer an expectation of the imminent transformation of the external, historical world; instead it becomes an internal drama of the soul, of ascent from body to spirit. With the adoption of Christianity as the religion of the Empire under Constantine, eschatological hope is further domesticated in Christian theology. The Kingdom of God, once expected to mark a transformation of the external world, comes to be identified by Augustine with the Church itself, which exerts its influence on the city of man, thus accepting the reality of secular politics.[28] The revolutionary power of the apocalyptic ideal is sapped.

But it reemerges in a new and influential form, Taubes contends, in the twelfth-century monk Joachim of Fiore. Joachim offered a novel interpretation of history that endowed the present and future with radically new meaning. He distinguished three historical eras. The first, the Age of the Father, corresponded to the Old Testament; the second, the Age of the Son, began with the New Testament. But now, Joachim proclaimed, a new age was at hand, the Age of the Holy Spirit, in which the institutional Church would be superseded by a new spiritual church (*ecclesia spiritualis*).[29] According to Taubes, Joachim marks the beginning of the modern age. Here Taubes drew upon the work of Balthasar and perhaps (without noting it) on Ernst Bloch's *Heritage of Our Times*, which had called attention to the central role of Joachim's form of historical messianism.[30]

To orthodox Catholic theologians such as Thomas Aquinas, Joachim and his followers, the Joachimites, seemed incomprehensible, Taubes writes. This, Taubes observes, demonstrates a recurrent pattern in the history of occidental eschatology: each new wave of apocalypticism bursts apart the settled order, its norms and expectations. The newly interpreted ideal of the Kingdom of God then serves to erode and delegitimate the current order, and leads to an apocalyptic moment that seeks to realize that ideal on earth. "With each new apocalyptic wave a new syntax is created, and the breakdown of meaning in language makes people from the old age appear deranged to those of the new, and vice versa. . . . To the new men, the old man is a corpse, a has-been, as the [Bolshevik] Russians call the *emigrés*, while in the eyes of the old men, the new men are deranged."[31]

Taubes then traced recurrent waves of struggles to bring about the divine kingdom on earth, from the Reformation-era radical Thomas Münzer, whose revolutionary theology provided a warrant for violence, to the English Puritans and Fifth Monarchy men.[32] He noted parallel developments in the Jewish world, as the Gnostic ideas in the Zohar were radicalized in the kabbalistic teachings of Isaac Luria and then turned in an apocalyptic direction in the seventeenth century by the would-be messiah, Sabbatai Zevi.[33]

Finally, Taubes traces the secularization of the eschatological philosophy of history in German Idealism, from Lessing's *The Education of Mankind* (*Erziehung des Menschengeschlechts*) (1780), through Hegel. Hegel's philosophy is Joachimite, Taubes avers, in that it equates the history of spirit with world history: both have a dynamic, historical conception of spirit.[34] But while Hegel tried to reconcile Christianity with modern bourgeois liberalism, his synthesis broke down in the generations thereafter, Taubes claimed (borrowing extensively from Löwith).[35] Both Søren Kierkegaard and Karl Marx interpreted the world as an alienated place. Kierkegaard would reject the view of history as one of progress, and tried to recapture the rejection of the world characteristic of early Christianity, before its reconciliation with the existing historical world. Marx, by contrast, took eschatological ideas in a revolutionary direction. For him, history was a tale of human alienation, leading to ultimate redemption, but expressed in materialist terms. He was on the lookout for the possibility of an apocalyptic revolution.[36]

In an epilogue, the book, which begins on a Heideggerian note, ends on one as well.[37] Taubes concludes by asserting that the modern age has come to an end, and with it the history of the Western spirit. "A new epoch is beginning, which introduces a new aeon that is post-Christian in a more profound sense than that of the calendar."[38] (A sentence lifted partly from the Petras book.) The task was not to vilify the past nor to attempt to revive it, but amidst the meaningless present to keep oneself open to "the first signs of a new day."[39] With a nod toward Heidegger, Taubes contends that humanity has surrounded itself with an artificial technological shell that measures success by the ability to manipulate the world. But unlike Heidegger, Taubes draws a theological conclusion, namely the need to overcome the manipulative attitude toward the world, which pushes God into the realm of mystery, and rediscover our proper relationship to God—an echo of Oskar Goldberg.[40]

This religious peroration fits uncomfortably with the body of the book. For Taubes's analysis of the history of Judaism and of Christianity is based upon immersion in modern biblical criticism. That mode of understanding takes religion as the object of scholarly, historical inquiry, which means taking a position outside of any particular faith. As Otto Petras put it, "A religion that one understands is, for he who understands, no longer a religion. For by comprehending it, he stands above it; he surveys its conditions and possibilities, and to the extent that he does so he no longer feels like the unconditional object of religious demands. One can be possessed and awe-struck only as long as one does not understand how and why that occurs."[41] Taubes's book sought to recapture the antinomian and radical pathos of religious eschatology and the influence of such movements in history. But for the most part it seemed to do so from a stance *outside* of religious belief, only to return to a religious message in its final paragraphs.

Occidental Eschatology revealed many of the intellectual qualities that would distinguish Taubes's subsequent career. There was the search for breadth, for discovering the very meaning and direction of history. There was the ability to recognize (or construct) patterns across diverse historical and religious contexts. There was the willingness to read scholars against the grain of their own arguments, that is, to draw upon their analysis while reaching quite different conclusions. There was a tendency toward juxtaposition of insights, rather than systematic argumentation.

And there was a tendency to borrow from other writers, sometimes with acknowledgment and sometimes without. Several acquaintances— Rudolf Zipkes, Margarete Susman, and René König—would all claim that Taubes had borrowed from their writings without noting that he had done so.[42] Hans Jonas and Karl Löwith would later note extensive cribbing from their works. Yet one could argue that none of this mattered much, for to borrow ideas and even phrases from many authors matters less than the way in which those ideas are combined and the uses to which they are put. Or one could regard it as the first of many of Jacob Taubes's violations of academic norms. To some, it was part of his genius; to others, evidence of charlatanism.

The tensions between religious belief and scholarly distance, and between political commitment and scholarly skepticism ran not only through the book, but through its author. Not long after completing his dissertation, when Taubes met Judith Buber, he explained to her that he had been a Marxist but preferred a more authentic eschatology. He had therefore decided to live the life of a religious Jew, even if he knew the weaknesses of that position.[43]

Doctor Jacob Taubes

Jacob submitted his doctoral dissertation on October 1, 1946, and prepared to take his doctoral examinations. Before doing so, he required a certificate of good character (*Leumundszeugnis*) from the local police. The document noted that he was a citizen of Poland, listed Czernelica (in Poland) as his "home location" (*Heimatort*), and certified that he had lived in Zurich since September 1936. As his address, it listed his parents' home at Tödistrasse 66.

Taubes was evaluated on his thesis; on a sit-down examination (*Klausurarbeit*) in his primary field of philosophy with Hans Barth; on a take-home examination in his secondary field (*Nebenfach*) of sociology with René König; and, it seems, a purely verbal exam in his other secondary field of "The History of German Literature to Goethe" with Emil Staiger, a distinguished professor of literature with whom Taubes had developed a personal relationship.[44]

As the topic for his sit-down examination in philosophy he was assigned a question on the nineteenth-century German philosopher Arthur Schopenhauer. That was a subject about which he knew little. But his response demonstrated his remarkable ability to fake it, or to put it more charitably, to use his broad knowledge to compensate for particular gaps, and to give the impression that he knew more than was actually the case. Rather than focus on Schopenhauer, he wrote nineteen pages on the philosopher as a transitional figure from German Idealism to European nihilism.[45]

Taubes's examiners were deeply impressed by both his oral performance and by his written work. The dissertation, Hans Barth opined in his written evaluation, demonstrated an extraordinary range of knowledge. He noted that for Taubes it was a way station to the development of a nonconfessional theology. And though he found the beginning and ending portions speculative and too mystical to be subject to scholarly proof, he judged the work as a whole worthy of a "Summa."[46]

The thesis was published under the title *Abendländische Eschatologie* by Francke Verlag, a respectable publisher of scholarly books in Bern, in a series edited by René König. Its publication was made possible by financial subventions that Zwi arranged from Zurich's Jewish community. To save on publication costs, the book was published with a stripped-down scholarly apparatus.

First Great Love

For Jacob, the years immediately after the war were filled with religious, academic, and erotic enrichment—and turmoil.

Jacob's first great romance began when he was twenty-two years of age, working on his doctoral dissertation, and still, in observance at least, very much an Orthodox Jew. The object of his affections was Myrie Bloch, a member of one of the more eminent families of Swiss Jewry, the Bollags.[47]

To Jacob's parents, his sister Mirjam, and many others in the Jewish community of Zurich, the affair was scandalous. Born in 1893, Myrie was old enough to be Jacob's mother—in fact, she was six years *older* than Fanny, and the mother of two daughters who were about Jacob's age. Myrie was widowed as a result of an act of violence that had horrified the Jews of Switzerland. On April 16, 1942, her husband, Arthur, a cattle dealer in Bern, visited the village of Payerne. There, four young men under the influence of an antisemitic demagogue lured him into a stall, murdered him, and cut his body to pieces.[48]

Myrie's liaison with Jacob began several years later, in 1946. Far from hiding his affair with Myrie, Jacob flaunted it.[49] It must therefore have come as a relief to his parents when she left for New York later that year. That in turn gave rise to a stream of letters from the lovestruck Jacob, which reveal a good deal not only about his feelings toward Myrie but also about his spiritual and psychic development.

The letters from Jacob to Myrie are filled with drama and self-dramatization. In an undated letter written before Myrie's decision to depart for New York, Jacob addressed the disapproval that their relationship elicited in others, a reaction to which he feared that Myrie herself was beginning to succumb. He urged her to ignore the opinion of others and to embrace the extraordinary nature of their love. "It happened and can't be undone. We have unbolted a gate that is usually covered and disguised: that mother and son meet and close the rift, the double rift between the sexes—as man and woman, and as parent and child—this double rift around which the wounds of all people, the suffering of all sexes, circles. . . . [This is] an event that is inextinguishable, and nothing in the world can change it."[50] He entreated her in language drawn from Martin Buber's classic text: "Between us, every barrier between I and Thou has fallen away, we are one flesh, one body, one soul."[51]

These were missives from a young man still religiously observant, who had recently received rabbinic ordination.[52] Most began with the Hebrew letters bet-heh in the upper right corner, the religious acronym for *be-ezrat Hashem* (with God's help). Jacob remained scrupulous in his observance of the Sabbath.[53] Required to take his oral defense of his doctoral dissertation on Friday afternoon, he was eager to inform his family that he had received a "Summa"; but he ran home, rather than taking a tram, since the Sabbath was descending and he carried no money.[54]

Yet beneath the veneer of unbroken observance, Jacob's belief had begun to waver. "Matters are rather unsettled in the landscape of my soul," he wrote to Myrie. "The barriers of an Orthodox education are falling away, but gradually and not without pain; but so it must be, for I can't continue to maintain this double (or triple, or quadruple) spiritual book-keeping."[55] He found himself unsure of his overall direction, asking, "How much reality can a person tolerate, how much reality can he bear?"[56] He remained in search of God. Facing the prospect of leaving Switzerland and German-speaking Europe for either the Land of Israel or for the English-speaking world, he lamented, "All that can only be withstood out of a deep faith, which I don't possess, but which I seek: that man is rooted in God, and thus is always and everywhere at home and alien."[57]

In a pattern he was to repeat throughout his life, Jacob's letters to Myrie cast his personal and erotic longings in religious terms. He was fascinated by the erotics of the Kabbala, and its Neoplatonic image of the male and female elements of the divine fused before the creation of the world, separated at creation, to be eventually reunited.[58] He made use of such imagery, telling Myrie, "A relationship like ours can only be a blessing or a curse, it cannot be casual; it can descend to the depths of Jocasta and Oedipus, or can rise to the holy circumstances of the primeval age and the promise of things to come."[59]

But despite Jacob's continuing affirmations of the extraordinary nature of their love, the pressure—whether of society or of her conscience—was too much for Myrie. In the fall of 1946, while Jacob was working on his dissertation, she fled Switzerland to take up residence with her relatives in Forest Hills, New York (a neighborhood in Queens). But there was no escaping Jacob. When Myrie failed to respond to his importuning letters, Jacob dispatched a telegram: "Am sick without news from you. Cable immediately."[60] He sent her a postcard describing his melancholy. He visited her room in Zurich and recalls "the happy hours and afternoons that we spent together here, wound around one another, united without inhibition, in flesh and in soul. That is my only consolation."[61] He too would come to New York, he suggested, and after her younger daughter got married, Myrie and Jacob would be able to wed as well.[62] Distressed by the fact that Myrie wanted to break off their relationship, Jacob was plagued by headaches.[63]

Jacob chafed at the attempts of his parents to control his future. They invited a well-to-do young woman from London to visit, in the hope that Jacob would be enticed into marrying her. But he was not interested, and felt ever more constricted in his current surroundings.[64] For a moment, it all seemed to be too much for Jacob to bear. He could not live without Myrie and decided to end it all. "By the time these lines reach you, it will all be over," he wrote. "I'm resolved . . . and I hope that I succeed. I'm saying my farewell. . . . I'm deeply resolved to bring this life to an end."[65]

At that point Jacob disappeared from the view of his family. On March 10, 1947, his frantic father sent a telegram to Myrie in New York: "Jacob has vanished. Farewell letter says Myrie knows all."[66] But then, a day later, a second telegram from Zwi: "Jacob here. Taubes."[67]

It was not only his distress over Myrie's withdrawal that led Jacob to contemplate suicide. He was also torn internally between his identity as a Jew and his identification with German culture. Rather than confronting this dilemma directly, he explored it at a historical distance, in an essay on the German-Jewish poet Richard Beer-Hofmann. Writing about the meeting of Jews with German culture, of *Judentum* and *Deutschtum*, Jacob's conclusions were troubled and tentative. "The time has not yet come to be able to definitively pass judgment on this encounter. For we are still too close to the events of the last few years to be able to view the significance of this encounter in its entirety. He who thinks that the events of recent years are only an accident, after which one can begin as if nothing has happened, is a fool, and it is no better when one surrounds this opinion with clever-seeming explanations, be they psychological, sociological, or however defined. But he would also be overly hasty and jumping to conclusions who, referring triumphantly to the events of recent years, would instruct us: 'See, there is nothing common between Germans and Jews; tear out every memory—it was all crooked and warped and you see how it all ended.'"[68] At about the same time as he composed this essay, he wrote in his suicide note to Myrie of his inner disjunction. "Perhaps I'm divided in my very self, indeed I think the division lies deeper. The elements of my existence are discordant: the circles of my language and my spirits, the Jewish and the German, confront one another today as two enemy brothers, as enemies to life and death, in a war without mercy, without reconciliation, and the slash goes right through me, and because of this cut I'm bleeding to death."[69]

In Jacob's letters to Myrie and in other letters from this period, romantic and spiritual themes were played out over an ostinato of more practical, vocational concerns. It was clear to Jacob and his family that as a Jew in postwar Switzerland he had no academic job prospects. For he lacked Swiss citizenship, and the government did not grant work permits to foreign citizens like himself. Zwi seems to have taken it for granted that given his knowledge and talents, Jacob would pursue a career in Jewish scholarship, or if that turned out to be impossible, in the rabbinate—that is, that Jacob would replicate Zwi's own path, perhaps with greater success. Zwi extended his tendrils to his contacts in the United States, in hopes of finding a position for his son in the network of institutions in which academic

Jewish scholarship was pursued. Those contacts included Zwi's slightly older colleague, Salo Baron, now ensconced at Columbia University as the first chaired professor of Jewish history in the United States. Zwi reached out as well to scholars of his acquaintance at Yeshiva University, the citadel of American-Jewish Orthodoxy, including rabbis Abraham Wein and Leo Jung. But the most promising prospects seemed to be at the Jewish Theological Seminary (JTS), the rabbinical school of the Conservative movement, where Zwi had himself sought a position in 1941.[70] Now he wrote again to the chancellor of the Seminary, Louis Finkelstein, telling him of his brilliant son, who is Jewishly learned—a *talmid chacham*—has traditional rabbinic ordination (*hatarat hora'ah*), and knows a great deal of modern philosophy and history. But the situation of Jews in Europe was declining from year to year, Zwi wrote, whereas in America the spirit of Israel was beginning to ascend.[71]

That Jacob was headed for a career in Jewish scholarship was clearer to Zwi than to his son. Writing to Myrie on New Year's Eve of 1947, Jacob reflected on his successes of the year just past, during which he received rabbinic ordination and his doctorate. He does not want to become a congregational rabbi, but is open to teaching at a rabbinical seminary. But he might also be interested in psychoanalysis or psychiatry, or in teaching German literature in America.[72] And in other letters from the period, he asks Myrie to approach on his behalf not only scholars at Yeshiva University and the Jewish Theological Seminary, but also Paul Tillich, the German Protestant émigré theologian teaching at Union Theological Seminary, whose book *Die sozialistische Entscheidung* (*The Socialist Decision*) of 1933—an anti-Nazi work that pled the religious case for socialism—Jacob much admired.[73]

Jacob not only passed his doctoral exams summa cum laude, he received a grade of "Extraordinary" (*ausserordentlich*) on the dissertation itself, which, the dean told him had last been awarded a decade earlier.[74] His family was bursting with pride, their faith in Jacob's abilities confirmed.

Yet even with a celebrated doctorate, Jacob was unemployed and without serious prospects for an academic post in Switzerland. He spent the early months of 1947 as a substitute teacher at a local Jewish school, considering his future options, exploring possible topics for research and writing, and awaiting Myrie's return in March.[75]

Myrie did indeed return to Switzerland, and from the little evidence that remains, she and Jacob were reconciled, but they did not resume their romantic relationship. On July 24, Myrie wrote from her family's home in

Zurich to Jacob, who was visiting in St. Moritz: "Dear Jacob, tomorrow I must enter the hospital, and ask that if you can, you pray for me on Friday. I'm placing myself entirely in God's hands, and hope that things will go well. Otherwise, I wish you all the best, and ask you to make something meaningful of your life. Myrie."[76] But things did not go well. A letter from Myrie's relative reported that Myrie was getting worse, receiving injections of a narcotic and losing strength.[77] In November, Jacob's mother, Fanny, visited Myrie and gave her a copy of the *Neue Schweitzer Rundschau*, which contained an excerpt from Jacob's forthcoming book, which, Fanny reported, made Myrie very happy.[78] Finally, in December, when Jacob was already in New York, a telegram arrived from Myrie's daughter, conveying the sad news that Myrie had been released from her earthly bonds.[79] Jacob's mother attended the funeral.[80] Shortly after Myrie's death, her relative Sissy Bollag contacted Zwi Taubes about the sensitive matter of what to do with Jacob's letters to Myrie.[81] The letters were eventually sent to Jacob in New York, where he saved them in a box that remained in the family.

From the point of view of Jacob's parents and sister, the romance between Myrie and Jacob had been a disaster. Jacob had not only brought embarrassment upon his parents by consorting with a woman a generation older, but he had lost valuable time in the search for a proper spouse. "I have one fervent request, Jacob dear," wrote his mother Fanny. "Close the Bloch chapter of your life once and for all. You wasted three years on this, and now the last half year as well. . . . Let her rest in peace." [82] Jacob's sister, Mirjam, was equally direct. Consort with young people, she advised him. "No married women. Search out healthy relationships."[83]

Jacob's reaction was quite different. His liaison with Myrie gave him a taste of the delights of transgression. Having experienced the pleasures of a relationship with a mature woman closer to his mother's age than his own, he would soon pursue another such love affair in New York. Nor was Myrie his sole love interest during his student years at Zurich. There was at least one other of which we have some record, a graduate student of German studies, who was almost certainly not Jewish: another source of worry for Jacob's parents.[84]

A Fountain of Ideas

In the months between completing his doctorate in December 1946 and his departure from Zurich in the late autumn of 1947, Jacob continued to read voraciously and to try out new ideas for development. He also served as an assistant to Ferdinand Gonseth, a philosopher of mathematics at the

Zurich Polytechnical Institute (the later ETH) and an editor of the journal *Dialectica*, which published an excerpt from Jacob's dissertation.[85] Taubes later claimed that he had written a second thesis there on the philosophy of mathematics. But for that there is no evidence.

Some of the ideas that Jacob was trying to develop were laid out in his letters to Myrie Bloch and to Gonseth, others in a letter of application sent to an unnamed American religious institution (probably JTS), and yet others survive as fragments and outlines.

His plan was to create "the basis for a new theology beyond all confessional boundaries, but not the fizzy water of the superficial Enlightenment, but as a continuation of the work of Franz Rosenzweig and Rudolf Otto in historical relationship to Kierkegaard and Nietzsche."

He was beginning with a new commentary on the Song of Songs, which was to lead to an "ontology of gender" and ultimately a new anthropology.[86] He discussed the topic with Balthasar in Basel and gave a lecture there on it, only to find that many of his ideas had already been formulated by an obscure author, Otfried Eberz, in a work of 1931 entitled *On the Rise and Fall of the Masculine Era* (*Vom Aufgang und Niedergang des männlichen Weltalters*). That book maintained that the proper cultural ideal was one of androgyny (*Zweigeschlechterwesen*), and that history consisted of eras of matriarchy and patriarchy. The present, masculine age, characterized by technical civilization, was in a period of decline, and would be followed by a new, more female-centered age.[87] Taubes filled some pages with sketches of ideas for a book on the rise of the feminine principle, to be titled "The Rise of the Material, 1847–1947" ("Der Aufstand der Materie, 1847–1947"). Its central theme would have been that the current age was one of transition from an era of patriarchy to one of matriarchy. He toyed with the notion that the feminine principle might be more inclined toward matter and the tangible, while the masculine was more inclined toward spirit and abstraction. Perhaps Nazism and its destruction of the Jews (which he encapsulated in the word *Maidanek*) might represent a feminine attempt to break the domination of the abstract, masculine spirit represented by both the spirit of capitalism and Marxist socialism. Another idea was that Christianity, with its Trinity of the Father-Son-Holy Spirit, had lacked a feminine aspect, a lacuna that the Catholic Church filled with its emphasis on Mary. As part of these investigations, Taubes took an interest in the work of the nineteenth-century Swiss scholar Johann Jacob Bachofen, whose book *Mutterrecht* (*Mother Right*) of 1861 put forward the notion that a matriarchal age had preceded the current age of patriarchy.[88]

A second project was to be on "the law," not only in Judaism and Christianity, but also in nature and in jurisprudence. According to Taubes, both Judaism and Christianity see the world as a prison. Judaism holds out the hope of release through eschatology, while Christianity imagines that the prison has already been burst open (through Christ). The tension within the Jewish soul, Taubes asserted, was between recognition of the law on one hand, and a hope for redemption, including from the law itself.[89] As a characterization of Judaism as a whole, this contention is debatable—but it certainly applied to the soul of Jacob Taubes. Taubes hoped to explore this theme both analytically and historically, including the development of the idea of law in the Torah and halacha; then the idea of opposition to the law in Paul, Marcion (a second-century Christian Gnostic), Gnosticism, Luther, and Kant; and finally the problematics of the law in Spinoza, Freud, and Kafka. His inquiry, he noted, was open-ended. He had a topic, but no conclusion.

Yet another project was to deal with anthropology (i.e., the philosophy of human existence) in Jewish mysticism, as expressed in the theory of sex in the kabbalistic tradition, and in the theory of "Adam Kadmon" (the Primeval Man)—themes Taubes had touched upon in his first published article, on Kabbalah.[90] This was a field that he longed to learn, and he cited Gershom Scholem as its master.

As Jacob wrote in his application to the Jewish Theological Seminary in New York, he aspired to be more than a scholar—he wanted to be a theologian. He was convinced "that theology must overcome its confessional barriers, and that the institutions that do this should strive to create a new type of pastor, knowledgeable about psychology, psychotherapy and the religious needs of our generation."[91] In a letter to Ferdinand Gonseth, he put it this way: "Theology today is a title conferred upon a group of people who write for a distinct circle of believers, whose 'holy' scriptures they interpret. But as you know, for me, theology is something quite different, for the voice of God speaks not only through scriptures, but must be 'heard' in a quite different way, in order to be interrogated."[92]

All of this was as ambitious as it was vague. Jacob was after the big answers to the big questions: questions that Gonseth thought were too big to be answered.[93] "You seem to feel an impatience to know everything, all at once, without delay, to know all that counts, and the desire to tear the veil from the world to reveal its reality, I would say even a despair of not knowing or seeking the true and real. This impatience, I feel with you," Gonseth wrote. But he warned Taubes against what he saw as the attempt by Heidegger and others to create "a Jacob's ladder to the transcendental spheres. . . . In Jacob's dream, it is angels, and not men, who descend and ascend the countless steps. In short: everything leads me to believe that anyone who seeks to imitate them, commits the most irreparable error."[94]

Arguably a good deal of Jacob's subsequent career would be determined by the gap between these aspirations to respond to ultimate questions and the recognition that he did not have the answers to them. Perhaps that is because the questions were unanswerable. Perhaps because he was too versed in the history of theological and philosophical debate to be able to accept any particular answer as true. At the time, however, he still thought it possible to do so, from the perspective not of scholarship but of faith. As he put it to Gonseth, he would elucidate the issue of the Law and its relationship to freedom in what he called a "Pauline" manner, based on the assumption that one cannot only "observe" but also "believe."[95]

This reference to Paul was no passing fancy. For by his early twenties, Jacob was increasingly fascinated with the Apostle to the Gentiles, for whom he believed he had a deep affinity. The Pauline epistles, he seemed to feel, were particularly accessible to one steeped in rabbinic culture, which was necessary to understand many of the allusions in Paul's writings. According to Taubes's later account, when walking near the university with Emil Staiger, a professor of German literature and translator into German of Greek tragedies, Staiger exclaimed, "Taubes, yesterday I reread some Epistles of Paul. It's not Greek, it's Yiddish!" To which Taubes responded, "You're quite right, Herr Professor, but that's why I understand and love Paul, just as I love the Eastern European Jews, even when they stink of garlic. Paul would have stunk too."[96]

Two of the themes of Paul's letters seem to have had a deep resonance for Jacob. The first was the inevitability of sin and need for divine compassion (*Erbarmen*) and grace (*Gnade*).[97] The concept of divine compassion is both Jewish and Christian, but the theme of the inevitability of sin is a decidedly Pauline one. For Judaism, sin is due to a misdirection of the will, and repentance (*tshuvah*) is the reorientation of the will in the proper direction—a process that ultimately affirms man's will. For Paul, the will is bound to be sinful, while repentance is only possible through surrender or abnegation of the will.[98] Taubes found this latter view more congenial, since it accorded with his sense that his will was beyond his control.

The second concerned the Law. For Paul, the Law (halacha) was in itself a source of sin or at least of the consciousness of sin, for the existence of a prohibition evokes the sinful passion to violate it. The very existence of the Law tempts one to break it.[99] But, thanks to God's grace, man is set free of the Law—a message that Taubes found tempting.

In a letter to Margarete Susman written shortly before he left Switzerland, Jacob described his aspiration to do for Paul what Heidegger had done for Kierkegaard. "What Heidegger managed to do for Kierkegaard, namely to anchor Kierkegaard's categories universally in an ontology, to unchain those concepts from Kierkegaard's specific context—that is what I have in mind in regard to the apostle: just as the apostle unchained the content of Judaism into Christianity, so I want to unchain this Christian content into something universal, to make Paul's categories universal by anchoring them in an ontology. Paul himself has shown how to do this, the way of un-chaining." At this point in his life, Taubes thought that the essential content of Paul was to show that the way to God was through a recognition of the powerlessness of God in this world, his weakness, his seeming withdrawal from the world, his "nothingness" (*Nichts*). For the next four decades, Taubes would return time and again to this quest to take his interpretation of Paul's insights and translate them from a Christian context to a more universal theology.[100]

It was Paul who took what was a Jewish sect and transformed it with a message of trans-ethnic appeal. Not very far beneath Taubes's writings on Paul one detects an identification based on the hope that just as a first-century son of Pharisees, in an era of spiritual crisis, had come up with a way of repackaging his ancestral tradition for a broader audience, so too might his twentieth-century counterpart.

For Taubes, Paul is "an apostle *from the Jews* to the nations." If Jacob's identification with Paul led him to read Paul with more sympathy and empathy than most scholars, Christian or Jewish, it also led him to retroject his own sensibility upon his first-century model.

Zionism and Palestine

Jacob's pressing concerns were not only theological or personal. Raised in a religious Zionist household, and conversant in Hebrew, the fate of the Jewish national project was much on his mind.

In 1947, he was active in the Christlich-jüdische Arbeitsgemeinschaft in der Schweiz (Christian-Jewish Working Group in Switzerland), an interdenominational group of Protestants and Jews, founded a year earlier, that included Pastor Paul Vogt. At the Seelisberg Conference that summer, which Jacob attended with his father, Jacob passed on to William W. Simpson of the Council of Christians and Jews in London a memorandum on the future of Palestine that Jacob had drafted together

with Vogt and other members of the working group. This "Memorandum zur Palästinafrage" survives. (It should be noted that at the time the
term "Palestine" was widely used in Zionist circles; before it was closed
down by the Nazi regime, the Jewish Agency's office in Germany was the
Palästina-Amt.)

In May 1942, the leadership of the Zionist movement had called for
ending the British mandate over Palestine, and the establishment of a sovereign Jewish state that would allow for the free immigration of Jews. In
the years that followed, the fate of mandatory Palestine became a matter
of violent dispute between the Zionists determined to found a sovereign
state, and their Arab opponents, committed to preventing such a course.
Clashes between Jews and Arabs escalated. Meanwhile, hundreds of thousands of Jewish displaced persons in Europe awaited the possibility of
finding refuge. The British announced their intention to give up mandatory control, and in May 1947, the United Nations appointed a Special
Committee on Palestine.

The memorandum by Taubes and his colleagues began by noting
that the situation in Palestine was one of increasing violence and headed
toward catastrophe. It asserted that political solutions based upon partition were inadequate and improper. The creation of two small states
would leave national minorities in each, which would make them a neu-
ralgic point for the entire Middle East, and likely to become embroiled
in the conflict between East and West. It also overlooked the fact that
the land was holy for Christians as well, and therefore Muslims, Jews,
and Christians all had claims over the land as a whole. Therefore, the
memorandum reasoned, Palestine as a whole should be declared a holy
site. Christians, Muslims, and Jews should all be allowed to immigrate,
to the degree that this was economically feasible; indeed it should be
open to all oppressed people, regardless of religion or origin (*Abstam-
mung*). It should be founded as a *Freistaat*, which would be nonsover-
eign and demilitarized. Its security would be guaranteed by the Western
great powers, the United Nations, and by Muslim, Jewish, and Christian
councils. It would be governed by a political administration made up of
members of small neutral states, and by representatives of the Muslims,
Christians, and Jews living in it.[101]

This memorandum on Palestine was as ecumenical as it was unworldly:
the sort of plan that made sense to idealistic religious figures in neutral
Switzerland, but that overlooked the enmities on the ground and the
implausibility of international control. It was never published and had no

discernable influence on the events that followed. But it marks Jacob's first formal foray into the fate of the Zionist project, an issue that would engage him with varying degrees of intensity for the rest of his life. Yet before he made his way to the nascent Jewish state, he would spend two formative years in New York.

To America

As Jacob was finishing his dissertation in late 1946, a hunt began to find him a post abroad. The United States seemed to offer the greatest promise for an aspiring Jewish theologian or philosopher. Zwi wrote to colleagues in England (Alexander Altmann) and in the United States extolling the abilities and learning of young Jacob, and requested their help in finding a post for him.[102] Jacob also asked Myrie Bloch to make inquiries on his behalf with Louis Finkelstein of the Jewish Theological Seminary.[103] But none of these seem to have borne fruit until the spring of 1947, when Finkelstein received a visit from Reinhold Niebuhr, a professor at Union Theological Seminary, located just a few blocks from the JTS. Niebuhr, who was at the time the most famous religious thinker in the United States, had just returned from several months in Europe. He reported to Finkelstein that in Zurich he had met a remarkable young man, Jacob Taubes, who not only had studied with Barth and Brunner, but had rabbinical ordination, and recommended that Finkelstein reach out to him.[104] Jacob was offered a fellowship at JTS, though the precise status he would occupy remained murky.

Jacob thus *talked* his way into a position in America—as he would for almost all of his subsequent posts. His oral performance was clearly remarkable, impressing not only his doctoral examiners, but also some of the most distinguished rabbis, Protestant and Catholic theologians, and Marxist theoreticians in the world. That verbal display was the product of a well-stocked mind, to be sure. But it also reflected years of precocious participation in discussions with scholars who had passed through his parents' household. His relationship with his father, Zwi, had been complex, comprised of deep love and mutual respect, but also by Jacob's desires to transcend the Jewish world as he knew it, and by a certain pleasure in transgression that struck terror into the heart of his parents.

In October 1947, Jacob set out for the New World on the Cunard Line's ocean liner, the *R. M. S. Queen Elizabeth*.[105] Now, at the age of twenty-four, he was launched beyond Zurich, beyond the Old World and into the New.

First Encounter with Scholem

Even as Jacob embarked on his westward journey from Europe to America (where he would change the spelling of his name from "Jakob" to the more English "Jacob"), his heart was in the East—in Jerusalem. From on board the ship transporting him to America, he penned a letter (still headed with the devout "bet-heh") to Gershom Scholem, a man who was to awe, shadow, and haunt him for the rest of his days. Jacob initiated the fateful relationship with a long missive that combined respect, erudition, and chutzpah in equal measure.[106]

Taubes and Scholem were on life paths that converged from opposite directions. Born in Berlin in 1897 into a Jewish family, young Gerhard (as he was then called) Scholem had rebelled against the assimilationist liberalism of his bourgeois parents.[107] As a seventeen-year-old at the outbreak of World War I, he was revolted by the German patriotism of his parents and so many other German Jews; already a convinced Zionist, Scholem thought that the fate of the Jews should not be tied to that of the German Reich. In the years that followed, he deepened his knowledge of Hebrew and of Talmud. He threw himself into the study of Jewish mystical texts, a field then unknown in the academy, and foreign to virtually all rabbis in Germany as well.

While living in Germany, Scholem was close to a number of other young intellectuals whose paths would cross with Jacob Taubes, including fellow Zionists Hugo Bergmann, Hans Jonas, Ernst Simon, and Leo Strauss. His dearest companion, however, was Walter Benjamin, the cultural critic whose flirtation with theological motifs owed a good deal to his dialogues with Scholem.

In 1923, Scholem moved to Jerusalem, in what was then British mandatory Palestine. There he married Escha Burchhardt, whom he had met in Germany and who preceded him to Jerusalem. After the founding of the Hebrew University of Jerusalem in 1925, Scholem was appointed to teach Jewish mysticism, becoming a full professor in 1934. There, with the help of Bergmann, Simon, and others, he built up a program of Jewish studies that was central to the mission of the new university.

Scholem's scholarship of the 1920s to the 1940s served to establish the history of Jewish mysticism as an academic subject. He discovered hitherto unknown texts, used his philosophical acumen to read and explicate them, and placed them in the larger history of religion and of the Jewish people. He combined passion for his subject and a belief in its larger historical significance with the patience and industry to work through difficult and recondite texts.

Scholem's interests in the history of Jewish mysticism, messianism, and apocalypticism were not merely academic—they were closely linked to his post-assimilationist Zionism. From an early age he devoted himself to these subjects out of the conviction that they represented the vital, dynamic currents within the history of the Jewish people—currents that had been played down by nineteenth-century Jewish historians and theologians who, eager to present Judaism as acceptable to modern European culture, had focused on the rationalist and legal aspects of the Jewish past. Scholem, by contrast, explored the irrational and symbolic realms of Jewish mysticism, and movements that were stigmatized as heretical or atavistic. He combined a personality given to bourgeois order and industry with a taste for the anarchic and the subversive. He identified the legal and the rationalistic currents in Judaism with the staid and the stodgy. In short, his scholarship was a revolt against the dominant Central European trends—assimilatory, Reform, and Orthodox—in which he had been raised.[108]

Several of Scholem's writings are of particular importance for his relationship with Jacob Taubes. We have already noted his pathbreaking article on "Redemption through Sin" published in the Hebrew journal, *Knesset*, in 1937, which explored the ideas and influence of the seventeenth-century putative Messiah, Sabbatai Zevi, and a century later, of Jacob Frank, who once again proclaimed himself the redeemer before becoming an apostate by converting to Christianity, together with his followers. Frank developed a theology that proclaimed the need to violate Jewish law and to descend to the depths of sin in order to liberate the divine sparks from a fallen world, and he and his followers engaged in libertine practices.

The Sabbatian and Frankist movements had echoed across generations. But by the twentieth century, they were largely forgotten by most Jews, and regarded by historians of the *Wissenschaft des Judentums* as an aberration and an embarrassment. Scholem's approach was entirely different. For him, Sabbatianism was central to understanding Jewish history. It represented undercurrents of vitality and resistance to the unredeemed world of the Exile, and Zionism made it possible to sympathetically unpack its real significance.[109] Scholem insisted that

> we owe much to the experience of Zionism for enabling us to detect
> in Sabbatianism's throes those gropings toward a healthier national
> existence which must have seemed an undiluted nightmare to the

peaceable Jewish bourgeois of the nineteenth century. . . .[110] The
desire for total liberation which played so tragic a role in the development of Sabbatian nihilism was by no means a purely self-destructive
force; on the contrary, beneath the surface of lawlessness, antinomianism, and catastrophic negation, powerful constructive impulses
were at work. . . . [For] this nihilism, in turn, helped pave the way
for the *Haskalah* [Jewish Enlightenment] and the reform movement
of the nineteenth century, once its original religious impulse was
exhausted.[111]

Scholem drew a fleeting parallel between Sabbatianism and early
Christianity. In each case, the putative messiah had met a scandalous fate:
crucifixion in the case of Jesus, apostasy in the case of Sabbatai Zevi.[112]
He also pointed to the revival of Gnostic motifs among the more radical Sabbatians, and the belief that the proper response to an evil world
was to destroy it from within through descending into the abyss of impu-
rity.[113] For Scholem, the libidinal antinomianism of the Frankists recalled
the Gnostic pneumatics that Jonas had explored.[114] And he thought that
the pattern of inspired heresy eroding the inner core of orthodox religion
and leading to revolutionary developments was by no means confined to
Judaism. In a theme that Jacob Taubes seized upon, Scholem noted that
within Christianity, the conflict between ecstatic, pneumatic spiritual-
ists in the Middle Ages led to internal conflicts, and "the spiritualist sects
which it produced went on to play important roles in the development of
new social and religious institutions, often giving birth, albeit in religious
guise, to the most revolutionary ideas. To take but one example, historical research during the last several decades has clearly shown the direct
connection between Christian sectarianism in Europe and the growth of
the Enlightenment and the ideal of toleration in the seventeenth and eighteenth centuries."[115]

Scholem's contention in "Redemption through Sin" that Zionism had
made possible the appreciation and appropriation of a richer conception
of the Jewish past was more fully developed in an article published in the
Hebrew newspaper *Haaretz* in 1944, entitled "Reflections on the *Wissenschaft des Judentums.*" He charged that pre-Zionist nineteenth-century
German-Jewish scholarship was distorted by its apologetic purposes. In
search of ammunition to legitimate the quest for Jewish emancipation in
a hostile diasporic environment, Jewish scholars had portrayed the Jewish past to conform to the tenets of enlightenment rationalism by over-
emphasizing the rationalist elements of Judaism, while overlooking or

downplaying the irrationalist, messianic, and apocalyptic moments. It had thus banished "the demonic enthusiasm" from Jewish history, the very elements that gave Jewish history its vitality and creativity. The *Wissenschaft des Judentums*, Scholem declared, "became the mouthpiece of the [Jewish] bourgeoisie for whom the slogans of destruction and construction are equally infuriating because they want to go to sleep. This sleep is known as gradual progress, preservation of the status quo through reform." Zionism, by lifting the burden of apologetics, made possible the writing of a more rounded and accurate history, one that recognized the dialectics of historical processes.[116]

Scholem broke through to a modicum of international recognition with his magnum opus, *Major Trends in Jewish Mysticism*. The book grew out of a series of lectures at the Jewish Institute of Religion in New York in 1938, summarizing his research. It was published in Jerusalem in 1941 by the Schocken publishing house, and in a revised edition in 1946 by Schocken in New York. In the decades that followed, the book opened a window onto a Jewish world of wild imaginings that would capture the fancy of many educated readers in Europe and America. *Major Trends* explored themes to which Taubes was already attracted before he opened the book, and others that aroused his interest after reading it, including the mystical conception of God as "nothing," Jewish Gnosticism, Sabbatianism, and Hasidism.

Jacob's letter, mailed from New York, reached Scholem in Jerusalem in early December. After reading it, Scholem wrote to his friend in New York, Hannah Arendt, that he has just received "a long and quite peculiar letter about myself or my publications from a young man from Zurich, who is now studying at the Jewish Theological Seminary, and there's something to it. I don't know the man personally at all, his name is Dr. Jacob Taubes, but if you should meet him, I'd be grateful if you gave me your impression of him. He seems to have immersed himself in studying me."[117]

And a peculiar letter it was, expressing fascination, obsequiousness, and criticism.[118] Noting that Scholem had probably already heard about him from their mutual acquaintance, Margarete Susman, Jacob launched into a discussion of Scholem's work, including not only "Redemption through Sin," but more obscure writings, such as an open letter critiquing trends in German Zionism that Scholem had published decades earlier.[119]

Then Taubes began to make his pitch. "I came to your essay . . . from entirely different circumstances and an entirely different milieu . . . and in a peculiar manner our paths have crossed, though perhaps only for a while. My highest aspiration is to tread this portion of the path together with you." He wanted to begin by obtaining Scholem's permission to review *Major Trends* for some journal (a permission he had no need to acquire), though he made immediately clear that his review would not be a hymn of praise. He was skeptical, for example, that writing the history of Kabbalah from a nationalist standpoint represented progress; perhaps it distorted as much as illuminated. The sentiments oscillated from admiration to critique and back. "Professor Buber knows that it would be my highest desire to be able to become a student of yours. But for now, my path leads first to New York, where the Jewish Theological Seminary has provided me with a fellowship." Taubes promised to send Scholem a copy of *Abendländische Eschatologie*, but warned that the published version had had to be radically shortened due to the costs of publication (no longer version has yet come to light). He appealed to Scholem to provide him with guidance: from whom in New York could he learn about the subject matter of Scholem's work? He suggested that he might work with Scholem at a distance, perhaps writing articles for Scholem to comment upon, including a topic suggested to him by his reading of *Major Trends*, namely a comparison between Pauline and Sabbatian theology. After citing several mutual acquaintances—Susman, Buber, Leo Baeck, and others—Taubes concluded, "It almost seems as if I have failed to convey what is most essential, as if I haven't written what I most meant to say, that my criticism has gone too far—but the sea is rather stormy and it is hard to concentrate. But perhaps the good will to learn and to be instructed is obvious, and it would be the greatest pleasure for me if you would answer my questions and guide me."

Intrigued, Scholem responded with a lengthy letter of his own. "I'm exceedingly pleased to find someone who is so intensely occupied with topics that are close to my heart," he wrote, "and would be happy to offer you whatever support is possible from afar." A comparison of Pauline and Sabbatian theology would be fruitful, he noted, were one able to access the relevant sources on both sides of the comparison. Was Taubes interested in devoting himself to the mastery of difficult kabbalistic and Sabbatian sources? He also sent Taubes a copy of his "Reflections on the *Wissenschaft des Judentums*," noting that it too warned of the hazards of the nationalist historiography practiced by some of his colleagues.[120] Scholem also put Taubes in touch with one of his best students, Josef Weiss. Weiss sent Taubes a number of publications, including his own recent essay on Scholem, published in the German-language Tel Aviv daily *Yedioth Hayom,* on the occasion of Scholem's fiftieth birthday. Weiss suggested that between the lines of Scholem's scholarship there were esoteric messages available only to initiates—which only served to intensify Jacob's fascination with the scholarly master.[121] But it would take time for them to meet face to face.

CHAPTER FIVE

New York and the Jewish Theological Seminary, 1947–49

JACOB ARRIVED IN New York City in September of 1947, at the age of twenty-four. At 5′9″ he was of moderate height and slight build. His face was long and thin, with a boyish softness of features. A wild and disheveled shock of thick and wavy brown hair topped a high forehead. His brown eyes were deep set and narrowly spaced, and his chin sported a pronounced cleft. His preternatural pallor, elongated features, and penetrating gaze could be visually striking. His smile was sensuous, mischievous. His mellifluous voice was high, verging on the feminine. His manner of speaking was dramatic: when he was weaving an argument, his index finger would move upward and around, as if charting the ascension of his ideas.

Jacob would spend two formative years in New York City as a postgraduate student at the Jewish Theological Seminary (JTS), an institution that was an outpost of the scholarly study of Judaism as well as an academy for the training of Conservative rabbis. He left his family and the familiarity of German-speaking Europe for the disjunctive experience of urban America in the early years of its postwar boom. At JTS, he would experience anew the tensions between the scholarly study of religion and religious commitment, and between his commitment to Judaism and his antinomian propensities. He would deepen his knowledge of rabbinic Judaism, and of the relationship between theology and politics in medieval Jewish philosophy. He would begin to establish a reputation among intellectuals in the United States, including the web of intellectual émigrés from German-speaking Europe and a younger generation of American-Jewish intellectuals. And he would form romantic and erotic relationships with new women, including the one who would become his wife.

The Jewish Theological Seminary: The Inner Tensions

After a brief sojourn with the family of his uncle (Zwi's brother, Israel Edelstein) in New York, Jacob moved into the dormitory at JTS. The Seminary was located in the Morningside Heights section on the Upper West Side of Manhattan, at the corner of Broadway and 122nd Street. Across Broadway lay Union Theological Seminary—a citadel of liberal Protestantism—and a few blocks to the south, Columbia University. Most of the JTS, Union, and Columbia faculty lived in the area as well. It was in this stretch of Manhattan that Jacob would spend much of the next two decades.

JTS was one of four institutions of higher Jewish learning in the New York area. Its primary constituency was the Conservative movement. A more traditionalist alternative to Reform Judaism, Conservative Judaism was committed in theory to combining halacha with some degree of ritual innovation, though in practice there was a gulf between a small elite that maintained such practices and a larger base that was far less observant.[1] JTS aimed to combine a traditional but non-Orthodox Judaism with modern modes of scholarship. To the theological left of JTS, so to speak, was Hebrew Union College, a Reform rabbinical seminary. To its right was the Rabbi Isaac Elchanan Theological Seminary, an Orthodox institution connected to Yeshiva University. And beyond that in the spectrum of traditionalism were a number of small yeshivas including the Mesivta Chaim Berlin, a Lithuanian-style yeshiva located in Brooklyn, which taught a traditional Talmudic curriculum.[2]

JTS aspired to be both a center of Jewish scholarship—on the model of the *Wissenschaft des Judentums*—and of the training of rabbis and Jewishly educated and committed laymen. In Switzerland, Jacob had studied philosophy and Christianity within the university, but Judaism beyond the confines of the academy—at home, and at the Montreux Yeshiva. At JTS, he would encounter Judaism as an object of commitment as well as of objective scholarship. JTS was headed by Louis Finkelstein, an American-born rabbi and professor of Talmud, who was named president in 1940 (his title was later changed to chancellor). At a time when antisemitism was rife in the United States, and when many Jews were falling away from Jewish identification, Finkelstein sought to convince both Jews and Christians of the ongoing relevance of Judaism, and of its consonance with American liberal democracy.[3] In short, he "turned Jewish survival into an American good."[4] Indeed he believed that American Jews would only return to greater Jewish identification and observance once Judaism had attained legitimacy in the broader culture. To that purpose, he founded an Institute for Religious Studies and the Conference on Science, Philosophy, and Religion, to bring Jewish scholars together with their Christian and secular counterparts. It was in these precincts that the notion of "the Jewish-Christian tradition" was birthed, together with the idea that American democracy sprang from Judeo-Christian values.[5]

The older generation of faculty at JTS had typically combined a traditional yeshiva education with a Western academic one. Its most distinguished member was Louis Ginzberg. He had trained at the famed Telshe Yeshiva in Lithuania, then went on to study mathematics and Semitics at the University of Heidelberg. A good friend of Rabbi Zwi Chajes (Zwi Taubes's mentor), and part of the international network of scholars of the *Wissenschaft des Judentums*, Ginzberg was named professor of Talmud at the Jewish Theological Seminary, and served as one of the first visiting professors at the newly established Hebrew University.[6] (The extent of his learning is illustrated by the following anecdote. On one occasion, Albert Einstein attended a formal dinner at the Seminary and was seated beside Ginzberg. At the conclusion of the evening, Einstein asked the then president, Cyrus Adler, why he had a professor of mathematics on the faculty of the Seminary. Apparently, that was the subject they had spent the evening discussing![7]) Finkelstein was on the lookout for scholars who combined traditional learning with Western academic training. Such men were an increasingly rare commodity.[8] In 1945, Finkelstein had hired someone else who fit that description, Abraham Joshua Heschel, who came from a traditional Hasidic background and had obtained a doctorate from the University of Berlin. Jacob Taubes had all the signs of being such a catch.

Most rabbinical students at JTS came either from Orthodox backgrounds and had some yeshiva education, or had been educated in the network of Hebraist schools that then dotted the country. (Those who lacked such backgrounds were required to take preparatory courses.) They looked forward to bringing a traditional but Americanized style of Judaism to an increasingly middle-class constituency. During the first three decades of the twentieth century, American Jews of Eastern European origin, striving to gain a foothold in the United States, had turned away from Jewish affiliation. The 1940s and 1950s saw a reversal of that trend. Growing economic prosperity made the struggle for material existence less urgent, and left a space for more spiritual pursuits. At the same time, Jews were moving to the suburbs, where synagogues provided an anchor of community. The Conservative movement was the main beneficiary of these trends. The Seminary trained the new rabbis for these growing congregations of upwardly mobile Jews.[9]

There was an intrinsic tension at JTS between its commitments to the articles of traditional belief and the canons of academic scholarship as developed by the *Wissenschaft des Judentums*. Should the Bible, especially the Torah (the Five Books of Moses) be taught on the traditional premise that it was the product of a single, divinely inspired source, or should instruction reflect the conclusions of biblical criticism that it was the product of several hands? The Seminary was loath to openly espouse the critical position, but it did not think it could teach texts in a way that ignored modern scholarship. The paradoxical result was that its rabbinic school did not teach Torah at all! The other parts of the Bible, the Prophets and the Wisdom Literature, were taught, and with the use of modern critical scholarship. But the Pentateuch was relegated to an entrance exam, so that students were expected to study it before entering the rabbinical program.[10] Only in the 1950s would source criticism become part of the curriculum.[11]

On the modernist end of the JTS faculty was Mordecai Kaplan, who taught homiletics, a subject that required prospective rabbis to consider the relationship between the content of Judaism and the needs of their congregants. Trained as an Orthodox rabbi, Kaplan had gone further than any of his peers in trying to come to terms with modern scholarship and science, rejecting supernaturalism *tout court*. Influenced by the philosophical pragmatism of John Dewey, the naturalist religious hermeneutics of Matthew Arnold, the sociology of Emile Durkheim, and the cultural Zionism of Ahad Ha'am, Kaplan was arguably the boldest Jewish theologian of his day. In his book *Judaism as a Civilization* (1934) and many subsequent publications, Kaplan put forth a vision of Judaism grounded in peoplehood, an understanding in which social scientific appreciation of the function of Jewish identity and culture replaced a transcendent conception of the divine. God was characterized as "the power that makes for salvation." Kaplan laid out a program of institutional and ritual innovation, from the Jewish community center to a refined liturgy. Among his efforts at religious innovation was creating the institution of a bat mitzvah—a ceremonial coming of age for girls, parallel to the traditional male bar mitzvah. Another was the publication in 1945 of a new prayerbook that jettisoned doctrines that Kaplan thought untenable, including prayers for the restoration of the temple in Jerusalem, and all references to Jewish chosenness. His influence over rabbinical students was palpable, but not without opposition from other members of the faculty. The publication of his new prayerbook met with public condemnation by the more traditionalist members of the JTS faculty.[12] The ultra-Orthodox Union of Rabbis went further: they excommunicated Kaplan and burned his prayer book.

Zionism was another point of contention at JTS. The Seminary's board of directors was largely comprised of wealthy German Jews, such as the publisher of the *New York Times*, Arthur Hays Sulzberger, who were vehemently opposed to the Zionist movement and its quest for a Jewish state. Finkelstein—who had never visited Palestine—was a lukewarm Zionist, in favor of a Jewish homeland, but skeptical of the desirability of a Jewish polity. Like the American-born president of the Hebrew University, Judah Magnes, Finkelstein worried about squaring Zionist activity with religious principles, of the tension between politics and holiness. Many of the JTS faculty and student body, by contrast, were fervent supporters of the Zionist cause, and thought Finkelstein unworldly on the matter. Once the leadership of the Yishuv stated its intention to declare independence, however, Finkelstein found himself in the position of what one might call an anti-anti-Zionist, and sought to dissuade Jewish opponents of the new State of Israel from testifying against it at the United Nations.[13]

Jacob Taubes may have been among those so tempted. He was in contact with the anti-Zionist Rebbe of Satmar, who sought to enlist him in the anti-Zionist cause, which Jacob resisted.[14] Hannah Arendt, whom Taubes also got to know, asserted in the pages of the new Jewish magazine, *Commentary*, that the era of sovereign nation-states was over, and that the only viable way of preserving a Jewish homeland in Palestine was for an Arab-Jewish federation there—for which, she failed to note, there were no Arab interlocutors.[15] Jacob was in contact with a coterie of German-Jewish professors in Jerusalem who formed the core of the Ichud, a small Zionist organization devoted to Arab-Jewish cooperation that was suspicious of the feasibility and desirability of a sovereign Jewish state. Among its leading members were Martin Buber, Judah Magnes, and Ernst Simon, a philosopher of education at the Hebrew University, who was a visiting professor at JTS.[16]

The historic vote of November 29, 1947, in the United Nations General Assembly that called for the partition of mandatory Palestine into a Jewish and an Arab state was greeted with enthusiasm by most American Jews, including most of the faculty and students of JTS. A few months later, on January 28, 1948, Taubes wrote once again to Scholem, in yet another letter both learned and—from Scholem's point of view as a committed Zionist—problematic.

It seems that difficult times are afoot, that makes one feel like a coward for being in New York—for how can those who do not participate in the sufferings of Israel share its consolations? To be sure there are signs in the Jewish heaven that recall the storms of Sabbatianism—and it is not "pure" scholarship when you and those in your circle turn with such intensity to that chapter of history; there is something in the air. When in America one experiences the "victory" celebrations, the messianic intoxication of the Jewish masses, the chanting of *Hallel* in the synagogues, one can be haunted by visions of a frightening sort. It would be good if some shepherds of the people, masked as historians, retained their sobriety.[17]

Jacob's First Impressions of America

Jacob's experiences at JTS can be reconstructed from a handful of surviving letters in Jacob's own hand, from the memories of those who knew him at the time, and from a rich cache of letters written to Jacob by his father, mother, and sister from Zurich. Jacob's mother, Fanny, wrote mostly in German and occasionally in Hebrew; his sister, Mirjam, in German exclusively. The letters from Jacob's father, Zwi, are sometimes in German, but for the most part in Yiddish, the language of greater intimacy, except when he meant to be officious, for which he used Hebrew. But all three frequently mixed German, Hebrew, and Yiddish in their correspondence with Jacob.

There was a constant, weekly stream of correspondence. Clearly all three loved Jacob deeply. Most of Zwi's letters begin in Yiddish with "my beloved, precious child" (*Liebes, teyeres Kind*), though their content was almost entirely about professional matters, above all Jacob's academic career at JTS. When Jacob failed to write, his parents would respond with frantic entreaties for him to do so, and even at times with telegrams expressing their anxiety. The letters make clear the high hopes that Zwi, Fanny, and Mirjam shared for Jacob, and their expectations of his ultimate success. They were relieved that he had left Switzerland for what seemed like greener pastures.

But the letters also convey a streak of infantilization, and, on Jacob's part, a helplessness in mundane matters. His father assures him repeatedly that he will straighten out difficulties that have arisen between Jacob and his teachers at JTS. His mother worries about his wardrobe—including his undershirts—and sends him shirts from Zurich. She admonishes him repeatedly to pay attention to his hygiene, to take care with his clothing, to wash, and to shave.[18]

Mirjam, who adored Jacob but was well aware of his faults and his idiosyncrasies, offered advice that illuminates Jacob's character. She counseled him that living in the Jewish Theological Seminary necessitated that he take care in regard to women, and not bring them to spend the night with him in his room.[19] Jacob should take pains not to speak enthusiastically about Christianity in front of Jews, and should decorate the walls of his room with a map of Palestine—not pictures of the Madonna.[20] She too reminded him to pay some attention to his appearance, to dress neatly and keep his nails clean.[21]

Above all, Mirjam worried about two subjects: work and women. She repeatedly exhorted Jacob to live up to his great potential "and fulfill the wishes of the grandparents by becoming a Jewish luminary." "Don't be lazy, but rather work," she wrote, aware of Jacob's propensity to fritter his time away by loafing or endless casual conversation.[22] And she worried about Jacob finding the right woman. (She herself was married in August 1948, in what her mother described as "a fine match" to "a well-situated merchant, with fine Jewish parents."[23]) He should consort with young people, she wrote early in his sojourn: "No married women. Search out healthy relationships. Believe me, I know what I'm talking about."[24] And a few months later, "Look only for girls from the best families. Not used goods. Breeding plays a big role."[25]

Their concerns were indeed justified.

During his first year in New York, Jacob's mind seemed to be everywhere but on his studies at JTS. He visited a wide range of German intellectual émigrés in the city and beyond. He spent time with Paul Tillich at Union Theological Seminary;[26] visited the historian of religion Joachim Wach at the University of Chicago;[27] met frequently with his old companion Eugen Kullmann, who was living in Brooklyn; befriended the German-Israeli publisher Salman Schocken, and Hannah Arendt, who was then an editor at Schocken Books in New York. Then there was Erich Fromm, an erstwhile member of the Frankfurt Institute for Social Research, who had recently published a seminal interpretation of the rise of National Socialism, *Escape from Freedom* (1941).[28] During the spring of 1948, as he reported to his parents, Jacob visited with the Satmar rebbe Reb Yoilish, who had set up his court in the Williamsburg section of Brooklyn and tried to enlist Jacob in his crusade against the creation of a Jewish state.[29] That summer he spent a few weeks among ultra-Orthodox Jews at a modest resort in the Borscht Belt of the Catskill Mountains. There he encountered *yeshiva bochers* who had spent five years in Siberia and emerged with their faith intact. He found them refreshing, among the few who lived in America with higher aspirations than mere material betterment.[30]

But though he was not focused on his studies, Jacob's mind remained active—and anguished.

His early impressions of life in New York City were of America as a new Rome, powerful but ultimately lacking in culture—a recurrent trope among German intellectuals of his day. To Martin Buber in Jerusalem, Jacob wrote that "New York is like imperial Rome—broken soil, ripe for sowing any seeds. Paul would feel comfortable here. To be sure, no one has yet written an Epistle to the Romans to New York, but who knows?"[31]

From early on, Jacob perceived America as dominated by technology, money, and a hegemonic ideology that consigned all alternatives beyond the horizon of plausibility. As he wrote to Hans Ornstein, a Jewish writer and activist in Zurich, "Woe to a world that is ruled from the East, and woe to a world that is ruled from the West." The news from Russia was horrible. But in the West the "system of exploitation" (*System der Ausbeutung*) was preserved through bread and circuses, by which the people were deceived and made stupid through radio, the press, and the schools. "But the masses have their revenge without knowing it: the masses end up setting the standards."[32] The radio, he complained, was fit for an average nine-year-old; the movies were inferior, the books no more than average, and the publishers drawn to trash.

Jacob's critique applied to American Jews as well:

> The East European masses increasingly displace the small elite stratum of German Jews; in that sense the Jews are undergoing a process occurring in the non-Jewish world as well. The backbone of America—the Puritan strictness, the Calvinist seriousness, the man of the frontier—is almost as much of a museum piece as the Indians, except that no reservations have been created for them. Negroes, Italians, Mediterranean types in general set the standards of taste and the nature of the cityscape; the Jews understand best how to transform the achievements of the technological spirit into the small change of the street.... No word is used as often as "money," "to make a living," "how much does it mean in dollars and cents"—that is the vocabulary of young and old, rich and poor. The one alternative possibility is the cloister of the spirit, the cloister of scholarship—without any relationship to reality.... Every "reality"— university, the state, sisterhoods, companies—they are all a "business." Everything has the same ideology, known here as "common sense."... That there are some things that money can't buy is beyond the horizon of their imaginings. One can't speak, with Marx, of "self-alienation." For there is no real "self" to be alienated.

Jacob's jaundiced portrait of America, as expressed in these letters, was far from unique. He picked up a common theme among German intellectual refugees of various stripes—especially those who had studied with Martin Heidegger. In *Being and Time*, Heidegger had insisted that modern society was dominated by what he called *das Man*, by which he meant an existence that eschewed seriousness and authenticity. Heidegger hit upon the marvelously malleable term "Being" (*Sein*) to denote what had been lost from sight—where the vacuity of the term guaranteed endless room for interpretation about what he meant. For Heidegger, America was a wasteland of modernity, a technological Moloch lacking roots in tradition or history.[33]

The intellectuals associated with the Frankfurt School gave the notion of *das Man* a social and economic grounding. For Max Horkheimer, Theodor Adorno, and Herbert Marcuse, the masses were kept in thrall by a combination of growing affluence and the "culture industry"—those commercial means of entertainment and information that appealed to the instincts without allowing for more elevated, creative, and collective forms of expression. It is no wonder that when Jacob came into more direct contact with the members of the Frankfurt School, he found that their interpretation of Western capitalism resonated with his own predispositions.

Jacob's antipathy to capitalism was also reflected in his attitudes toward international affairs, which tended toward a "Third Way"-ism, suspicious of the Soviet Union, but critical of the influence of the United States as well. In early 1948, as the Cold War was heating up, he wrote to his friend Margarete Susman that although he had many doubts about Russia, and especially about Stalin, he still believed that "ex oriente lux"—the light shall come from the East. His analysis of domestic American politics was no more astute. He told Susman that in supporting the anti-Communist reaction, American Jews failed to realize that they were cutting off the branch on which they sat, "For after the defeat of communism, they will come after the Jews."[34]

To his distress and disdain for what he found in New York were added Jacob's spiritual storms and strains. Paul's letters spoke to him across the centuries that separated them. Though he never penned his own version of Paul's Epistle to the Romans, he did compose a letter to the Apostle Paul. Jacob's letter was never sent of course, but survives in draft form. Referring to his experience in America, he wrote, "If what is on offer here is the greatest in the world, then this world is really not worth the effort. So I sat at the feet of Gamaliel [a reference to Paul's words as reported in Acts 3:3, that he was 'educated at the feet of Gamaliel according to the strict manner of the law of our fathers'] and tried to make a go of it, but my heart is not in it, and so I have sunk and am sinking ever deeper into darkness and the works of darkness, jerked one way and then the other."[35] He quoted (in Greek) Paul's own ambivalent words in regard to the law: from Romans 4:15, "For law brings wrath," and later from Romans 7:7, "Is the law sin? By no means,"[36] lamenting that he was "jerked here and there between the law in my organs and the law of God" (a paraphrase of Romans 7:23), asking, with Paul, "Who will rescue me from this body of death?" Jacob admitted that he remained torn between being a Jew and his debt to German culture: "You know just how 'German' I fundamentally am." "For a long time I tried to avert my eyes from the events and hardly paid attention when the horrors (which unfortunately were all too true) were spoken of: what ostrich-like behavior," he lamented. That opened a wound and a chasm between Germans and Jews, a wound and a chasm that ran right through him. He hoped that he would somehow bridge the gap between Christians and Jews, because, like his avatar Paul, he combined "Israel according to the flesh" with "Israel according to the spirit." Just how he might do so remained a mystery, however.

In addition to being an observant Jew with a strong Pauline streak, Jacob also felt a strong pull toward Jerusalem. Writing to Martin Buber, Jacob conveyed his longing to go to Israel: "The further I move to the West, the more I'm drawn to the East. Today, one belongs in the Land [of Israel] especially at this moment, in the most difficult days of our history since Sabbatai Zevi; precisely because of one's forebodings and fears, one should not stay away. That keeps me from being happy here regarding the so-called 'opportunities.'"[37]

Louis Finkelstein and Saul Lieberman

Among Jacob's most important relationships was with the president of JTS, Louis Finkelstein. It was Finkelstein who had brought Jacob to JTS, with, it appears, the intention of grooming him as a Jewish theologian. Though an aloof man, Finkelstein was clearly taken with Jacob, with whom he discussed scholarly matters. In letters to her son, Fanny urged Jacob to look to Finkelstein for guidance, and to regard him as a father.[38] Jacob was a frequent guest for sabbath meals at the Finkelstein home, and befriended Finkelstein's children—especially his youngest daughter, Emunah, who was seventeen years of age when Jacob first arrived in their household. Erudite and obviously exceedingly bright, Jacob made a striking impression on the Finkelstein family, and not least on Emunah, who found him fascinating.[39] He wrote to his parents and sister about the Finkelsteins, and his sister urged him to ask Emunah out, which he proceeded to do.[40] It was custom at more traditional yeshivas for the favored pupil to marry the daughter of the *Rosh Yeshiva*, and Jacob may have had this model in mind. But no romance developed: Jacob seems to have acted in a way they regarded as "taking liberties" with the young girl, which put an end to any further courting, and cast a pall over Jacob's relationship to Emunah's father.[41]

There was another source of strain in the relationship between the president and young Jacob—Jacob's failure to concentrate on his studies. In a letter to her son of November 1947, Fanny agreed with Finkelstein's judgment that Jacob should spend his time working, not wasting his time visiting hither and yon.[42] In the spring of 1948, just after Passover, Jacob wrote a long letter to Finkelstein offering excuses for his failure to produce any scholarship of note, and asking for more time to prove his mettle. "You don't want to push me into a situation that will cut me off before my wings are strong enough to take flight," he wrote.[43] Jacob's propensities to open-ended speculation, to interest himself in everything but the scholarly subject at hand, and the lack of scholarly productivity that flowed from it, would remain the bane of his life.[44]

By June of 1948 there was another source of tension: Finkelstein seems to have wanted Jacob to take the rabbinical exam in order to obtain rabbinical ordination from JTS, which Jacob thought superfluous—he had, after all, submitted letters from prominent rabbis attesting to having acquired a traditional rabbinic ordination. His parents agreed with Finkelstein, arguing that the formal title could only be to Jacob's advantage.[45] In this case, Jacob won out. But his struggles with Finkelstein took a psychic toll on him. He told his parents that his nerves were shattered, and he considered returning to Europe.[46] Zwi was sufficiently alarmed that he wrote personally to Finkelstein to try to straighten matters out.[47] In the end, Jacob remained in New York.

Jacob came to JTS with a full quiver of vague ideas aimed at formulating a new theology. He told President Finkelstein of his plan to write about the relationship between *din* (law, or justice) and *chesed* (mercy). The constituent elements of Jewish theology, Taubes wrote to Finkelstein, had been rent asunder and driven into a variety of cultural realms.[48] "The measure of *din* and of mercy, of *chesed* and love have all been dressed up in art and belles lettres," he wrote. "The secret of unification and plurality, and of finite to the infinite, has found more appropriate expression in the realm of mathematics than of theology. The lord has been chased from the face of human beings into sociology and psychology, and god has been chased from the face of the natural sciences and has contracted into hidden places to the point of *ayin* [nothingness]. Theology needs to unite the nothingness of God with the being of the world, and to know that the *ayin* expresses not only existence, the *ayin* is existence." The notion that God had been chased from consciousness by the social and natural sciences was drawn directly (though without acknowledgment) from Gershom Scholem's Hebrew essay, "Franz Rosenzweig and His Book *The Star of Redemption*" (1930). The assertions about nothingness and existence combined ingredients from Kabbalah and existentialism into an opaque brew. Jacob would spend years trying to explain it—to himself first of all.

As we know from Jacob's letter to Scholem, he came to JTS hoping to study Kabbalah and engage in creative theology. But Finkelstein had other plans for him. Jewish mysticism was not deemed a proper object of study at JTS, and even the recently hired Abraham Joshua Heschel, who later acquired a reputation for his interpretation of Hasidism, was not permitted to teach it. Finkelstein wanted Jacob to study Talmud and medieval Jewish philosophy, and sent him to study Talmud with Saul Liebermann and Maimonides with Leo Strauss.[49] Jacob was resentful and wrote to his parents expressing his discontent. His mother told him that Finkelstein was right: Jacob did indeed have gaps in his Jewish knowledge, and he should be grateful for the opportunity to study with the likes of Lieberman and Strauss. He would find time for his own philosophical work and for the study of Kabbalah.[50] Despite his complaints and inner resistance to being forced to deepen his knowledge of such topics, the experience proved seminal, as it brought Jacob into contact with two of the most formidable scholars of his day.[51]

The first of these was Saul Lieberman, professor of Talmud.[52] Born in Lithuania in 1898, Lieberman had studied at a number of the great yeshivot and received his ordination at the age of eighteen. In 1927, he moved to Jerusalem, where he pursued the academic study of Talmud, as well as of Greek. Lieberman's approach was to bring to bear the history and literature of the extra-Jewish, Hellenistic environment in which the Talmud was written, and he pioneered the use of such sources for understanding the Jerusalem Talmud (that is, the Talmud developed in the Land of Israel, rather than the better-known Babylonian Talmud). His scholarly acumen was complemented by a remarkable, photographic memory: he seems to have known the entire Jerusalem Talmud by heart—and perhaps the much longer Babylonian Talmud as well![53] The Hebrew University, struggling economically, was unable to offer him a post, despite the high esteem in which he was held by colleagues such as Gershom Scholem. In 1940, Lieberman accepted a position as professor of Talmud at JTS, an appointment that Finkelstein considered his greatest coup. His admiration for Lieberman was unbounded, and he did everything in his power to provide Lieberman with the resources to pursue his own research. Within a short time of his arrival, Lieberman became Finkelstein's adviser on almost every aspect of Seminary policy. He also served as a liaison to scholars at Hebrew University, a succession of whom came to JTS as visiting faculty.

Yet despite his commitment to modern modes of scholarship, Lieberman remained entirely Orthodox in his practice, and to a considerable degree in his social connections as well. That was not difficult at JTS. Finkelstein had a broad conception of the institution's mission as serving all traditional Jews, not only the Conservative denomination. The synagogue at JTS—of which Lieberman served as rabbi—was Orthodox in its prayerbook and ritual, and men and women sat separately. Many of the students were of Orthodox background as well. Potential conflicts were minimized by the fact that Lieberman regarded himself as a scholar who taught and researched at JTS—not as a theologian who sought to influence the Conservative movement or be influenced by it.[54] Nor was he inclined to discuss his actual beliefs and how they comported with his scholarship.[55] The rabbinic students he taught were awed by his learning, but could not fail to notice the disdain Lieberman exhibited toward Conservative pulpit rabbis, whom he considered as little more than ill-learned social workers—a sentiment shared by not a few of the leading faculty at JTS.[56] It was said by wags that the Seminary was an Orthodox institution for the training of Conservative rabbis who served mostly Reform congregants.[57]

Finkelstein assigned Taubes to study directly with Lieberman—a mark of the high expectations Finkelstein had of the young man, for only the most promising students were permitted to study privately with the great Talmudist. Their text was *The Fathers according to Rabbi Nathan* (*Avot deRabi Natan*), an extracanonical alternative version of the Talmudic tractate *The Fathers* (*Avot*), dealing with ethical maxims as well as a range of theological reflections, including those of Elisha ben Abuyah, who subsequently became a heretic.

Lieberman seems to have been impressed by Taubes, at least at first. He invited him (and later, his wife Susan) to his Passover seder, and recommended him to his friend Scholem. We don't know what textual skills Taubes derived from his studies with Lieberman. But we do know that he concluded that despite Lieberman's remarkable erudition, he was theologically barren, with no appreciation for the (purported) spiritual or psychological depths of Gnosticism, nor answers to the larger religious questions posed by contemporary events.[58]

That, indeed, was Taubes's verdict on scholarship at JTS as whole. It was either learned but unwilling to confront genuine theological dilemmas, or insipid in its identification with liberal bourgeois democracy. There was something to this: Finkelstein's scholarly stars were adept at combining philological virtuosity with the taken-for-granted validity of rabbinic Judaism.[59]

The other scholar to whom Finkelstein steered Taubes had a more lasting impact upon his intellectual development. That was Leo Strauss. At the time, Strauss was a professor at the Graduate Faculty of the New School for Social Research in Greenwich Village, a faculty founded in 1933 as the "University in Exile" to provide a home to distinguished scholarly refugees from fascist-dominated Europe. A number of intellectuals from German-speaking Europe with whom Taubes was to associate taught there, including the German diplomat-turned-philosopher, Kurt Riezler, the philosopher Alfred Schutz, and the sociologist Albert Salomon. But none made as much of an impression as Strauss.

Strauss and the Maimonides Seminar

In Leo Strauss, Taubes would find a scholar who shared his interest in the relationship between politics and theology, but who approached the issue with very different premises and came to very different conclusions.

Strauss was born in a small town in Hesse in 1899. Like Hans Jonas and Hannah Arendt, he studied philosophy with Martin Heidegger in the early 1920s. After a stint at the Academy for Jewish Research in Berlin, in 1932 Strauss obtained a fellowship to study in Paris. When Hitler's rise to power precluded his return to Germany, he made his way to Cambridge University, and then to New York in 1937, where he finally found employment at the Graduate Faculty of the New School. But while the New School provided a haven, his job there was poorly paid, and working conditions were not those of a great university. To get by, he took a variety of additional jobs, including working with postdoctoral students from JTS and advising them on their research papers—for which he was paid six dollars per hour in 1945.[60]

Strauss's intellectual trajectory was influenced by his youthful commitment to political Zionism. Like his friends Gershom Scholem and Hans Jonas, Strauss was part of a generation of Jews who saw the attempt to assimilate entirely into German society as a failure, while remaining deeply imbued with elements of German academic culture. It was the

Zionist critique of progressive assumptions that led Strauss to a broader critique of liberalism.[61]

In his writings of the 1920s, Strauss emphasized that for Zionism to succeed as a political movement it needed to develop a sober, realistic view of politics. That meant avoiding multiple snares: an irrational faith in Orthodox Judaism, an unwarranted faith in liberal humanitarianism, and the unholy combination of the two that he saw as characteristic of "cultural Zionism." And it meant eschewing the tendency of so many Jews to substitute moralistic judgment for realistic analysis of human motivation and behavior. That led him on a quest for thinkers who explained the world as it really was. In the 1920s and early 1930s, he turned to studies of Hobbes and Spinoza, seventeenth-century thinkers who treated the question of the relationship between religion and politics as central.

Beginning with his book *Philosophy and Law* (*Philosophie und Gesetz*) of 1935 and continuing through the late 1940s when Taubes studied with him, Strauss's quest led him to a more encompassing critique of modern political thought and a recovery of the medieval appreciation of the political uses of religion.[62] His studies focused on what he dubbed "the theological-political predicament" or the "theological-political dilemma."[63] By this, Strauss meant a number of things.[64] The most important, perhaps, was that the members of a polity require rules that restrict and restrain their evil and base impulses. Most people are more likely to obey such rules if they believe that the rules are "laws" of divine origin, such that transgressing the laws will result in ultimate punishment, and obeying them will result in ultimate reward. But it is the nature of philosophy to call into question the divine origin (and hence validity) of such rules, and, in the quest for more reliable knowledge, to challenge the reigning opinion upon which ordered political life depends. So understood, the theological-political predicament entails the recognition of a tension between the philosopher's open-ended quest for knowledge and the normative demands of any polity for consensus, order, and restraint. The philosopher is an atheist, or at least a skeptic when it comes to received opinion. But (so Strauss asserted) a polity can only handle a limited amount of skepticism: demonstrate to most men the contingency of the rules by which they live, and they will either slip the yoke of decent behavior or set out for new, more radical, and potentially dictatorial sources of authority. Because not all truths are harmless, the challenge for the philosopher is to engage in the skeptical pursuit of philosophical truth without openly calling into question the truths that his society regards as "self-evident."

That led Strauss to an exploration of the phenomenon of esoteric writing: the various methods by which potentially dangerous messages can be conveyed to philosophically inquiring minds without destroying the normative basis of political order by undermining society's received truths. It is this sensibility, Strauss claimed, that distinguished what he called "the medieval Enlightenment" from its modern counterpart.[65] He developed that thesis most fully in a series of penetrating essays on Moses Maimonides, published in the years just before Taubes came to study with him: "The Literary Character of the Guide to the Perplexed" (1941); "Persecution and the Art of Writing" (1941); and "How to Study Medieval Philosophy" (1944).

The subject of those essays, the twelfth-century sage Moses Maimonides (Rabbi Moses ben Maimon, or Rambam in Hebrew acronym), was perhaps the greatest Jewish intellectual of the Middle Ages, renowned as a physician, community leader, philosopher, and legal authority.[66] His two most significant works were attempts to recast Jewish knowledge. The *Mishneh Torah* was an attempt to systematize Jewish law (halacha), presented in the form of a code, rather than through the debates characteristic of the Talmud. His *Guide to the Perplexed* was an attempt to explicate the Bible and the commandments drawing upon the legacy of Greek philosophy as it had been inherited within the Islamic world. In the *Guide*, Maimonides offered an uncompromising refutation of anthropomorphism, the tendency to conceive of God in human terms, including the conception of divine will. He interpreted biblical passages that seemed to do just that as metaphors rather than descriptions of divine action. He also explained the rational purposes of the laws, including their role in weaning the Israelites away from pagan practices.

Strauss's dramatic claim was that Maimonides's predominant concerns were twofold. He sought to present a defense of Judaism in the face of the challenge of rationalist philosophy, but to do so in a way that would both guide the philosophically adept to the truths of philosophy while leaving intact the belief among the multitude of the divine origin of the law (commandments) and hence its binding nature. That, Strauss maintained, was a belief that the philosopher knows to be a "likely tale" or even a "noble lie"—noble because it promotes the well-being of society. *The Guide to the Perplexed*, Strauss maintained, was deliberately written in an esoteric manner. It contained a double teaching, one for the wise few and another for the vulgar multitude. "An exoteric book contains then two teachings: a popular teaching of an edifying character, which is in the foreground; and a philosophic teaching concerning the most important subject, which is indicated only between the lines."[67] Through a series of techniques that Strauss enumerated, including allusion and deliberate self-contradiction, "Maimonides teaches the truth not plainly, but secretly; i.e. he reveals the truth to those learned men who are able to understand by themselves and at the same time he hides it from the vulgar."[68] In short, for Strauss, Maimonides's *Guide* was a *political* work, shot through with concerns about maintaining social order through preserving religious belief in the necessity of the law. These concerns were evident in Maimonides's other works as well, Strauss asserted, including the introductory book of the *Mishneh Torah, The Book of Knowledge (Sefer HaMadda).*[69]

In Strauss, Taubes was confronted by a scholar of remarkable historical range and acuity. Both Strauss and Taubes had been led (by Carl Schmitt among others) to an interest in the intersection of religion, philosophy, and politics. But while Taubes's interest was in religion as a source of drama and apocalyptic transformation, Strauss was interested in it as a source of social and political stability. While Taubes was inclined toward antinomianism, Strauss argued for the importance of compliance with the law as a control on the human passions. Moreover, Strauss wrote from a position of religious skepticism, while Taubes still maintained at least one foot in religious belief. While Taubes was attracted to antinomianism, he remained religiously observant; while Strauss affirmed the political value of religious belief, he was not.

Jacob studied with Strauss from the spring of 1948 until Strauss left for the University of Chicago in January 1949, and in the months that followed Jacob wrote to Strauss about once a month. In mid-February, Jacob assured Strauss that "the *Guide to the Perplexed* now accompanies me on my ways." By April he had concluded that in one respect at least, Scholem was mistaken: while Maimonides and Spinoza might lack the "drama" of the kabbalistic cosmic scheme, they had a greater element of the quest for truth.[70] Taubes reported to Strauss that he showed his plan of research to Finkelstein, who was disappointed. For Finkelstein wanted not more scholarly research in the manner of Strauss, but a "believing exegesis" (*gläubige Exegese*) that would make Maimonides accessible to the general Jewish reader, such as Elliot Cohen, the editor of *Commentary* magazine. He also wanted a quasi-official theology (perhaps as a more traditionalist alternative to Mordecai Kaplan's Reconstructionism), not the sort of innovative theology to which Taubes aspired. And that Taubes could not provide.[71]

Influenced by Strauss, and in search of a research topic that would suit his own interests and perhaps satisfy Finkelstein, Jacob turned to a project on "Law and Reason: A Chapter of Political Theology, Illustrated by

Maimonides' *Mishneh Torah*." While working on the project, he described its thesis as follows: that the *Mishneh Torah* is more "philosophical" than the ostensibly more philosophical *Moreh Nevuchim* (*Guide to the Perplexed*), where "philosophy" is understood not in the modern sense, but as Plato and Aristotle understood it. It is best compared to Plato's *Laws* (which deals with the best polity given the far-from-ideal realities of human nature), in that the existing Oral Law is placed within a framework of universal reason.[72] Here Taubes's thesis closely follows that of Strauss himself. Two months later, having completed his paper, he described the radical conclusions he had come to, in a letter to his Swiss friend Armin Mohler.

> I was shifted by the Seminary into the study of Maimonides (that is, medieval Jewish philosophy of religion) and have delivered a tentative manuscript. . . . [Maimonides] is revealed to be an atheist and a grand inquisitor on a grand scale, hence by no means harmless. . . . The "wisdom" of the "death of God" was only divulged by N. [Nietzsche]— already in the Middle Ages a few sought to live beyond the magic circles of religion, art, and politics in the naked depth of the "nothing." . . . Nihilism is the eternal secret history of the spirit. . . . To be sure, an iron distinction was maintained between the esoteric and exoteric.[73]

Taubes claimed to Scholem that the manuscript amounted to 150 pages.[74] It has never turned up. But Strauss told Lieberman how impressed he was by his student.[75]

Jacob put what he learned from Strauss about Maimonides to use in a small seminar that met through the winter and spring of 1949, made up of a handful of young Jewish intellectuals who would go on to become major players on the stage of American intellectual life. Known by some as the "young *Commentary* intellectuals," they referred to themselves tongue-in-cheek as the "Pseudo-Cabal." At Jacob's suggestion, they compiled a summary protocol of their weekly meetings—a procedure that Taubes would maintain for most of the seminars he taught thereafter, perhaps because it helped him to make later use of the ideas that occurred to him in the course of discussion. The surviving protocols provide a window into the way in which Taubes conveyed Strauss's ideas (together with some of his own), at a time when Strauss's own work was unknown to the *Commentary* intellectuals or to the larger intellectual public.

The regular participants in the seminar were Irving Kristol; his wife, Gertrude Himmelfarb; her brother, Milton Himmelfarb; Daniel Bell; Nathan Glazer and his wife, Ruth (who, after their divorce and her remarriage to the historian Peter Gay, became Ruth Gay); and Arthur A. Cohen. Bell's then girlfriend, Elaine Graham, attended some sessions as well.

In the decades that followed, Daniel Bell and Nathan Glazer would become two of the most distinguished sociologists in the United States. Irving Kristol would found and edit a variety of small but highly influential journals, and would eventually become the pivotal figure of what came to be known as "neoconservatism." His wife, Gertrude Himmelfarb (Bea Kristol to her friends) would become an acclaimed historian of Victorian thought and a public intellectual in her own right. (The Kristols were so much in spiritual tune with one another that intellectual influence flowed in both directions.) Her brother, Milton, became a leading authority on trends in American Jewry as director of research for the American Jewish Committee, and a probing essayist. Arthur A. Cohen, at twenty years of age the youngest of the group, became an influential publisher and a liberal theologian. Ruth Glazer would become a historian of modern German and Eastern European Jewry.

Many of the members of the "Pseudo-Cabal" went on to intellectual fame and political influence. But in 1949, they were a group of relatively unknown young men and women at transition points in their lives. All were Jewish, but most had no connections to major Jewish institutions and organizations.

In 1945, the American Jewish Committee decided to transform its staid journal, *The Contemporary Jewish Record*, into a magazine that would reach a broader audience. The AJC was decidedly non-Zionist, fearing that Jewish nationalism would cast doubt on the patriotism of American Jews. Its editor was Elliot Cohen, a Jewish intellectual from the South who was charged with creating a magazine that would have Jewish content but also appeal to a wide readership. Under Cohen's editorship, *Commentary* brought together German-Jewish refugees (such as Hannah Arendt), Ivy League professors, intellectuals associated with the avant-garde journal *Partisan Review*, and freelance writers, mostly drawn from the independent left. Glazer got a job there as an assistant editor, as did Irving Kristol in the fall of 1947. Glazer edited "The Study of Man," a section devoted to new developments in the social sciences. Kristol wrote primarily on philosophical, literary, and theological topics. He also served as the religion editor, which often meant rewriting articles by rabbis.

Kristol suggested to Glazer that since the two of them were now assistant editors of a Jewish magazine, it would behoove them to gain some knowledge of traditional Jewish texts. Meanwhile, Ernst Simon, a visiting professor at JTS from the Hebrew University in Jerusalem who had worked with Franz Rosenzweig in Frankfurt, asked his friend Leo Lowenthal how he could connect with young American Jewish intellectuals. Simon hoped to inspire in them an interest in Jewish learning of the sort that Rosenzweig had fostered at the *Lehrhaus* in Frankfurt in the 1920s. Lowenthal in turn asked Glazer, who together with Kristol assembled a small group of friends to meet with Simon.[76] Shortly thereafter, Simon returned to Jerusalem and recommended Jacob Taubes as a resource person.

Taubes proposed that the group study the first book of Maimonides's *Mishneh Torah*, the *Sefer ha-Madda* (*The Book of Knowledge*)—a book that he had just studied with Strauss. They used a recently published edition with Hebrew on one side (without vowels) and an English translation on the other.[77] Strauss had lately published a review in which he noted that the *Mishneh Torah*, since it was addressed to all men (and not only to the philosophically inclined), is "more exoteric than the *Guide*. . . . To see this, one only has to consider what secret teaching, according to Maimonides' principles, means. It means teaching the truth to those who are able to understand by themselves, while at the same time hiding it from the vulgar."[78] Jacob was certainly acquainted with Strauss's interpretation.

The group met together with Taubes at one of their homes every Sunday night for dinner and then, sitting around the table, a discussion of the *Mishneh Torah*. For some of them, it was a first exposure to the study of Jewish texts as a serious, adult enterprise. Bell and Glazer wrote a summary of each week's discussion.

"Taubes was a brilliant teacher," according to Irving Kristol, and from the protocols we get a sense of what he taught.[79]

Taubes began his explication of the first chapter of *The Book of Knowledge*, which deals with creation (*Ma-aseh bereshit*) by making explicit a point that is by no means obvious, but that was an important element of Strauss's interpretation. That is, that Maimonides does not actually endorse the proposition that God created the world "ex nihilo"—a key point of contention between the traditional Jewish understanding of the world, and that of Aristotelian philosophy—and thus implied that he did not believe in miracles or in miraculously revealed law.[80] "Rambam in refusing to accept *creatio ex nihilo* thus accepts the philosophical frame as the one in which the meaningful questions of the world may be asked. In this sense, he is a naturalist. Yet why does he then write a theological volume, the core of which is admonitions on the correct [way of] living according to revealed law?" Taubes offered two answers: that "Rambam, as a sociologist, is depicting the pattern of Jewish life by discussing the rules of Jewish living as they have been accepted in the past and present by the Jewish community." More importantly,

> Rambam is a political theologian who understands the need of law as a means of binding the community. Natural law, which seems to be reasonable, is not so. It has no compulsive sanction and force behind it. Such law is possible only from commandment. Thus Rambam accepts the fact of revelation in Torah as a means of commanding obedience to law through the authority of God's word. . . . The great fear of Rambam, as of the Talmud, as of Luther and Augustine, is atheism. Atheism implies anarchy, the loss of a sense of limit. The creaturehood of man is that he is able to understand his own limitations and accept them. . . . Man can live by curbing his appetites and accept reason. The implication of Rambam's doctrine is that man alone, without the rule of God's law, is incapable thus of realizing his humanity. Such a doctrine underlies the attack of Talmud, Luther and Augustine against Stoicism and Epicurianism, for while the latter essentially practice renunciation or moderation, their essential premise is the belief in man's self-sufficiency. While single individuals may so be able to live, Rambam's premise is the masses could not.
>
> The relation of Rambam's thought to a later political tradition, particularly Spinoza and Hobbes, becomes obvious. Rambam starts from revealed religion and works within its frame because the people of the day accept religion as the word of authority. By the time of Hobbes, religion has lost its authority. Hobbes in his social contract theory, in which the authority of the king is necessary for the protection of all, through law, is an attempt to create a civic religion whose utilitarian motive is obvious. Rambam works within tradition and through it seeks to rationalize a concept of order. Hobbes can only seek to create a new tradition.

This disquisition from Taubes raised a series of questions from the other members of the seminar to which he then responded:

> Question: "If Rambam wanted divine sanction for use in establishing the concept of law and authority, why not accept—in a manipulative fashion—the doctrine of *creatio ex nihilo* and thus avoid a host of problems?" Taubes: "If he did, he would have to accept miracles, which apparently he doesn't, and thus lose his own deep intellectual integrity. He could not and also fight an important enemy of his day, a growing tendency to accept anthropomorphism."

Question: "If he does not accept miracles, then what for him is revelation?" Taubes: "For him, revelation is an ultimate fiction."

Question: "Is the Messiah also a fiction?" Taubes: "Maimonides does not accept the Messiah as final judgment. For him the coming of the Messiah means the breaking of the subjection to other kingdoms."

In a later session, Taubes noted that Maimonides departs from his naturalistic, philosophic explanation only when dealing with Moses as a recipient of God's revelation. Maimonides was willing to resort to an explanation that was at odds with his larger propensities, Taubes explained, because "that is the philosopher's price which he must pay for purchasing the law. . . . From Maimonides' attack on anthropomorphism, it follows that the Bible is, for him, mythology, a 'dream,' or at best an allegory of the relations of philosophic concepts."[81]

All in all, the first session of the Pseudo-Cabal provided the *Commentary* intellectuals with a clear and concise summary of Strauss's understanding of Maimonides—without ever mentioning Strauss. In subsequent sessions, Taubes expounded upon other themes, many drawn from Strauss. Among them were the relationship between Aristotle's *Physics* and *Metaphysics* and *The Guide to the Perplexed*;[82] how a close reading of the text and its comparison with cited sources could yield clues to the author's esoteric intentions; and the importance of the absolute middle page of a text for the esoteric mode of writing.[83] Some of the ideas that Taubes conveyed came from other sources, or from Taubes himself, such as why Judaism lacks the conception of natural law so prominent in Christian theology.

The discussion of Maimonides's insistence upon God's unity and his absolute otherness, a function of his opposition to any form of idolatry, led to probing questions about the sustainability of Maimonidean religion, an issue that clearly resonated with at least some of the participants. One of them posed the question, "Did not Rambam, by making God so abstract, by rejecting all attributes, run the risk of idolatry? For by making God so unapproachable, you tempt the masses to vulgar and completely idolatrous conceptions."[84]

As he would so often, Taubes called attention to larger patterns. He noted that in contrast to the rabbis who emphasize the fear of God, Maimonides "emphasizes love; his fear is attenuated." "This emphasis on love, as opposed to the more orthodox fear, can lead equally to the post-rational mysticism of the Zohar or to Spinoza's *amor dei intellectualis* [rational love of God]." There were numerous aperçus, such as "the ultimate paradox of Torah as a system of revelation and *mitzvot* [commandments] is that in its revelation it conceals God, or at least removes Him to a distance." And sweeping observations:

> The great insight of orthodoxy is the recognition that all chiliasm [millenarianism] is premature, whether the secular chiliasm of socialism and science, or the Christian chiliasm of Christ, or the Jewish chiliasm of Zionism. This must necessarily be so, since history and the millennium are incompatible. . . . When the millennium arrives, there will be no more history, but eschatology. The fact that all chiliasm has so far been premature and the fact that we are still living in history do not mean that there will not eventually be a millennium; but it does give a sober justification to orthodoxy's underlying skepticism about all chiliasm.[85]

The most consistent topic of the seminar was the nature of law (in the sense of religious commandments, but more broadly as well) and the reasons for it, a central theme in Maimonides's writings. As the seminar progressed, Taubes's dominant role faded, and the other participants played a more active part in the proceedings, bringing to bear their own knowledge and conceptual acumen. In one such discussion, Taubes interjected an unexpected note—though one close to his own heart—on the significance of antinomianism, the deliberate violation of the law. Gertrude Himmelfarb observed that the law could be interpreted on several levels: utilitarian, sociological, or as more fundamental than any metaphysical interpretation of it, so that "the law corresponds to relations-of-production in Marx, and metaphysical interpretations to ideological superstructure." Taubes responded that the Talmud warns against giving reasons for the laws. He explained a link between wisdom and antinomianism: those who have greater insight into the law and understand its purposes can transcend it; or they may believe that the law is evil because it distracts from what is most real. Hence the argument of those who uphold the law that law itself is primary and that there is nothing beyond it.[86]

At least some of the participants found Taubes a wonder, and the protocols provide a sense of why.[87] In the course of the eight sessions for which we have protocols, Taubes not only elucidated the text of *The Book of Knowledge*, he expounded upon a remarkable range of topics: the fact that "at some point in its history, Judaism must have purged itself of Gnosticism, for our present sources, which are post-Bar Kochbah, have clearly been edited and emasculated";[88] Maimonides's misuse of Biblical and Talmudic quotations to argue against anthropomorphic conceptions of God; on Gnostic and kabbalistic conceptions of God; on medieval conceptions of Biblical criticism, as in the case of Hivi Ha-Balki, "whose ideas we know only from Saadia's refutation of them"; and upon the reasons for the rise of atheism in the nineteenth century.[89] He cited thinkers from Aristotle, to medieval Jewish philosophers, to modern Christian thinkers including Kierkegaard, Max Scheler, and Karl Barth.

After a while, Taubes suggested that they examine Carl Jung's theory of psychological types, and the group went on to read Jung.[90] Thus Taubes had failed to inspire in the participants a desire for more Jewish learning—Ernst Simon's original aim for the seminar. But they were deeply impressed with Taubes, who seemed sui generis.

Gertrude Himmelfarb, who had spent several years at JTS, found that its faculty included scholars but not intellectuals. Both she and her husband, Irving, found the JTS faculty parochial. Part of the attraction of Jacob Taubes was precisely because he seemed to be a real intellectual. He was younger than most of them (and looked younger still), yet had what seemed a remarkable grasp of Western thought and of the tradition of Jewish texts. (The other personality of this sort who befriended the *Commentary* intellectuals at this time was Emil Fackenheim. But Taubes was more traditional in background and practice.) And he seemed to have a sense of the broad sweep of history; not only where it had been, but the direction of the World Spirit (*Weltgeist*).[91] His youth, his erudition, his traditional observance combined with his antinomian sensibility created an air of mystery about him.[92]

Victor Gourevitch, a graduate student preparing for a career in philosophy by studying with Leo Strauss at the University of Chicago, also attended some sessions of the Maimonides seminar when he visited New York. Gourevitch, who had come to the United States as a teenager, stemmed from a cultured but highly assimilated German-Jewish family, who "could sing the *Internationale* in three languages," but knew not a word of Hebrew. Taubes struck him too as worldly and brilliant. He envied Taubes his traditional German *Gymnasium* education, which included Latin and Greek, as well as his training in Hebrew and Jewish sources. Taubes's knowledge of contemporary German philosophy, and especially of Heidegger, was as impressive as it was rare in postwar America. The two struck up a friendship that would be renewed in the years that followed.[93]

Taubes's relationship with the members of the seminar blossomed into friendship. When Daniel Bell married Elaine Graham in 1949, they asked Taubes to officiate.[94] The wedding took place at the home of her father, Benjamin Graham (born Grossbaum), the founder of securities analysis, and the head of the Wall Street firm Graham-Davis. (His protégé was Warren Buffett.) This seems to have been as close as Jacob Taubes ever got to a sympathetic analyst of capitalism. On the second night of Passover, the members of the Pseudo-Cabal attended a seder that Taubes conducted for them in his room at JTS. Later that spring, they were among the handful of guests at Taubes's wedding. He would maintain an episodic relationship with Daniel Bell, Arthur A. Cohen, and the Kristols for decades.

But what influence did the Rambam seminar have upon the *Commentary* intellectuals?

Kristol and Himmelfarb were already developing a more conservative sensibility when they began their study with Taubes. If anything, the seminar on Maimonides seems to have deepened their proclivities.

Up until the seminar, Kristol's intense interest in religious thought had been focused on the challenge presented by Judaism and Christianity to liberal, bourgeois rationalism, and he appears to have maintained his own belief in God till the end of his days. But after the seminar, he came to write less about theological topics, and his references to religion pertained more to its instrumental value in maintaining human decency than in its ultimate veracity—a Maimonidean theme, at least as interpreted by Leo Strauss and conveyed by Jacob Taubes.

It was through articles published shortly after the seminar by Irving Kristol and by Gertrude Himmelfarb that Leo Strauss came to the attention of a broader audience. In January of 1950, in the course of an article entitled "The Prophets of the New Conservatism: What Curbs for Presumptuous Democratic Man?" Himmelfarb provided a brief discussion of Strauss's book *On Tyranny* and the theme of "the existence of an esoteric truth which it would be dangerous or unwise to circulate in society. A truth, an objective truth of the nature of social reality, may become, when it escapes from the sanctum of philosophy, a political 'falsehood.'" This, she thought, was characteristic of many conservative thinkers, not least Edmund Burke. "The conservative suspects that the truth, which gives life and dignity—and power—to an aristocracy or elite, might bring catastrophe if allowed to permeate the lower layers of society."[95] Himmelfarb did not endorse this view, but neither did she dismiss it. Indeed, by presenting it with clarity, she suggested its plausibility to an overwhelmingly liberal audience not predisposed to take such views seriously—a rather Straussian maneuver. Shortly thereafter, Himmelfarb provided a more lengthy exposition in the pages of *Commentary* of Strauss's key theses about why and how to read the great political thinkers of the past, an article that showed her immersion in his recent work.[96]

Daniel Bell seems to have derived a different lesson from his participation in the Maimonides seminar. Studying the *Mishneh Torah*, for Bell, was an attempt to discover the plausibility of religious Judaism. It led him to conclude that philosophy (in broad sense of a scientific approach to the world) and religious faith were not reconcilable, that one had to choose one or the other. His decision was for the scientific approach. Though lacking religious faith, his sense of Jewish attachment remained.[97]

In May 1949, under the rubric "The Cedars of Lebanon," which published translations of traditional Jewish texts, *Commentary* ran a lengthy selection from the *Sefer ha-Madda*, entitled "Prophets and Prophecy," with a brief introduction by Taubes—his first publication in English. The next issue saw a long article on sociologists and religion, by Albert Salomon, an émigré sociologist at the New School. He offered a paragraph-long summary of *Abendländische Eschatologie*, which he deemed "a significant volume." Though the article was not particularly cogent, it did offer an insightful characterization of Taubes himself, a man known both to Salomon and to Kristol and Glazer, one of whom almost certainly edited and substantially rewrote the article. "Writing from his marginal position, Taubes can see religion from within and without," wrote Salomon. He classed Taubes as a "spiritual thinker," a type "who returns to and proceeds from the root religious experiences which he knows at first hand. He is, therefore, an uncompromising radical, for he knows not only the externals of ecclesiastical institutions, but their inner logic and necessity. Sharing the primal passion behind organized religion, he is capable of a thorough disrespect for religious institutions."[98] That captured what was so unusual about Jacob Taubes—he appeared to be both a believer and a scholar of religion, but one whose knowledge of Judaism and Christianity led him to a critical perspective on both.

Taubes's greatest impact was on the youngest member of the seminar, Arthur A. Cohen.[99] The precocious son of affluent and highly assimilated New York parents, Cohen had entered the University of Chicago at age sixteen. Famed for its emphasis on teaching the classics of Western thought, Chicago was the most intellectual and cerebral of American campuses. Recognizing that the Western culture into which he was being inculcated was a Christian culture—it was said of the University of Chicago that it was a place where Protestant students were taught Roman Catholic philosophy by Jewish instructors—Cohen contemplated converting to Christianity. Alarmed by that prospect, his parents sent him to study Judaism with Milton Steinberg, the erudite rabbi of Manhattan's Park Avenue Synagogue. Cohen began to learn Hebrew and to acquire the rudiments

of a Jewish education. After completing his BA and MA in philosophy
at Chicago, he came to study at JTS, and it is there that he encountered
Jacob Taubes. Taubes was tasked to serve as Cohen's tutor for the study of
Talmud,[100] and no doubt invited him to participate in the Maimonides
seminar as well. Cohen too found the atmosphere at JTS insular and
uninspiring, at least when it came to philosophy and theology—except
for Jacob Taubes. After studying at JTS, he left the academy and from
1951 to 1969 had a spectacular career as a publisher of serious nonfiction
books. In addition to his day job, he wrote and edited works of theology.
His best-known book was the collection *The Myth of the Judeo-Christian
Tradition*—a title that echoed Taubes's 1953 essay in *Commentary*, "The
Issue between Judaism and Christianity: Facing Up to the Unresolvable
Difference." Indeed Cohen thought so highly of Taubes's essay that he
republished it in his 1970 anthology, *Arguments and Doctrines: A Reader
of Jewish Thinking in the Aftermath of the Holocaust*. The publication
of that essay in the pages of *Commentary* would help Taubes to secure
a place in American academic life—yet another by-product of the Maimonides seminar.

Jacob and His Contemporaries

Jacob's relations with his peers at JTS were problematic. He lived in a
dorm room there, together with the rabbinical students. Some found him
fascinating, some alienating, and some unnerving—or all three in succession. Rooming next door were Wolfe Kelman, Morton Leifman, and Geoffrey Wigoder.[101]

Leifman and Kelman were drawn to Jacob by his learning and his charisma—at first, that is.[102] They were struck not only by Jacob's knowledge of Jewish philosophy and Talmud, but by a certain magic about him.
While sitting around one evening, Jacob said to Leifman, "tell me about
yourself," and then proceeded to show a depth of insight into his interlocutor that Leifman found frightening.[103]

The third member of the suite was Geoffrey Wigoder. Like Taubes, he
too stemmed from a rabbinical family, and came to JTS after obtaining a
doctorate in medieval Jewish history from Oxford. Learned and charming, he arrived expecting to teach, but Finkelstein made him a student,
and (unlike Taubes) Wigoder followed Finkelstein's direction and was
ordained as a rabbi. He then left for Jerusalem and a career as a journalist
and scholar, eventually becoming the editor of the *Encyclopedia Judaica*.
Wigoder had an allergic reaction to Taubes. He concluded early on that

Taubes was a phony: that he lied, bluffed about his knowledge in various fields, and had a cynicism about the texts he did know. "I won't speak to this man," he told Kelman and Leifman.[104]

In time, Leifman and Kelman too became alienated by Jacob's extreme behavior, which seemed to them on the border between the neurotic and the psychotic—behavior that was in keeping with some of the characteristic features of manic depressive illness in its milder, hypomanic form.[105] Jacob seemed to have no sense of boundaries, propriety, or private property. When his clothes got dirty, he would throw them into his closet. The smell permeated the room, and eventually the maid refused to enter because of the stench. When he ran out of socks, he simply appropriated them from others. He was also boastful about his sexual escapades, which he described in graphic terms that shocked the rabbinical students. And he combined this violation of sexual norms with elements of ongoing religious piety, explaining that he would not sleep with a woman unless she obeyed the laws of ritual purity, and recounted the fact that one such woman, not wanting to be seen in the ritual bath (*mikva*) as it would reveal her erotic relationship, went and immersed herself in the Hudson River for the occasion. Jacob conveyed the impression that he thought himself so smart that he could get away with anything.[106] His was a kind of Gnostic posture.

The fullest portrait of Taubes as he appeared to his peers at JTS comes from the memoir of Richard L. Rubenstein, a friend of Kelman at the time. Coming from a background of minimal Jewish knowledge, Rubenstein had enrolled at the Reform Hebrew Union College, but attracted to more traditional forms of Judaism, soon left to pursue a rabbinical degree at JTS. Since his knowledge of Bible and Talmud was inadequate, he was enrolled in the institution's preparatory program, the *mechinah*. Taubes befriended him, offered to tutor him in Talmud, and took him with on a visit to the Satmar Rebbe.[107] To Rubenstein, Taubes, "seemed to be a living link to the chain of Jewish tradition that had been almost totally obliterated by the Nazis. He was also a link with a European intellectual life I had learned to respect."[108]

Rubenstein's depiction of Taubes is so vivid that it is worth quoting at length. Taubes appears in Rubinstein's memoir under the pseudonym "Ezra Band."

> There was . . . something indefinably disturbing, one might almost say demonic, about the man. . . . Although his movements were quick and energetic, he did not seem very robust. On the contrary, his coloring suggested that his natural habitat was the sidewalk café, the

dingy hotel, and the library carrel, that he was a stranger to the world of nature. He was fascinating to a certain class of overly cultivated women who were perhaps more interested in exploring the hidden, the unusual, and the mysterious than in openly celebrating the uncomplicated joys of physical love. . . . When we first met, some of the seminary students called him the crown prince, because he seemed to be courting Emunah Finkelstein, the chancellor's daughter. He always wore the longest and the most ostentatious prayer shawl when he came, as he did frequently, to those services at the seminary synagogue that were presided over by Dr. Finkelstein. In spite of his display of piety, he talked a great deal about blasphemy, the holiness of sin, and mystical antinomianism. At one of our earliest meetings, he made the accurate prediction that I would soon find more meaning in the pagan gods of Canaan than in the Lord of Israel. . . .

I have vivid memories of his long digressions on Søren Kierkegaard, Paul of Tarsus, and Sabbatai Zevi. [His] theological strategy was to demonstrate the impossibility of all commitments devoid of religious faith. He sought to generate faith out of horror of the secular alternatives. He was, however, perhaps more skillful than any secular humanist I had ever met in arguing for the very world without God he called upon me to reject. . . .

I became fascinated with the more prominent forms of mystical antinomianism as they had surfaced in Jewish history. I saw Paul of Tarsus's proclamation that Christ is the "end of the Law" as the classical expression of mystical Jewish antinomianism. . . .

Between Talmudic discussions of an ox which gored a cow, Ezra and I discussed Paul's "antinomianism." On the surface Paul's proclamation of the "end of the Law" was an expression of the spiritual wasteland we had rejected. At another level, we were both fascinated with the rabbi who became Christendom's greatest and most perennially influential theologian. We were also intrigued by Sabbatai Zevi. . . .

Could I have been a crypto-Sabbatian? I hovered between love of God and dreams of sinful liberty. Ezra's personality heightened those tendencies. [Rubenstein's wife] Ellen and I were simultaneously attracted and repulsed by him. One day Ellen was preparing for a Bible lesson in an empty room in the seminary dormitory. I entered the room while she was engrossed in study. She did not notice me. I came up behind her, put my right hand on her breast and fondled it. She relaxed and became limp. We continued for a few minutes until I broke the erotic atmosphere by speaking.

"My God," she said, "I thought you were Band [Taubes]. I felt hypnotized and couldn't resist." Band had a seductive, disturbing effect on both of us.[109]

Because Taubes had only limited time to tutor him, Rubenstein decided to improve his knowledge of Talmud by studying part-time at the ultra-Orthodox yeshiva, Mesifta Chaim Berlin. Distressed by his internal pull toward antinomianism, he reacted by becoming increasingly attracted to Orthodoxy. After being admitted to the rabbinical school at JTS, he considered the possibility of transferring to the ultra-Orthodox yeshiva, despite the costs of time and emotion required to become an Orthodox rabbi. His friends at JTS tried to dissuade him—except for Taubes.

> Ezra Band was the only one who encouraged me to leave the seminary. . . . He warned me that, were I to remain at the seminary I would be worse than the most contemptible bourgeois because I understood what was spiritually at stake in choosing the compromises of Conservative Judaism. . . .
>
> Band was almost manic in his enthusiasm. He rolled his eyes and gesticulated energetically as he said, "Isn't it wonderful, he's going to leave this terrible place and go to Chaim Berlin!"
>
> "If it's so bad," Wolfe asked him, "why do you stay?"
>
> "I'll leave as soon as I can. I have to make my plans carefully," Band answered. "But think of the drama. A man with Rubenstein's background leaving all this corruption and compromise to go to the *Mesivta*!"
>
> "Whose drama," Wolfe calmly asked, "yours or his? You goad him into leaving while you stay. He's got a pregnant wife. He's made enough changes. Do you want to wreck him?"
>
> As Wolfe spoke, I began to see Ezra as a peculiar kind of Mephistopheles. . . . Band was seducing me with the promise of an impossible ideological purity, made all the more questionable by his own refusal to take the same path. . . .
>
> When Ezra saw that the drama was not going to take place, he cooled toward me immediately. He became extremely contemptuous.[110]

Here was Taubes in the role of tempter, suggesting new possibilities beyond the horizons of a settled life. After his rabbinic ordination at JTS, Rubenstein went on to study for a doctorate in philosophy at Harvard, where once again he would come into contact with Jacob Taubes. Whenever they met, Taubes "would reinforce my negative feelings about myself for having become a Conservative rabbi and for having contaminated myself by daily association with ordinary middle-class Jews."[111] But Taubes was right about Rubenstein's ultimate inclinations: contending that the experience of Auschwitz negated any traditional conception of God, Rubenstein embraced an atheistic form of Judaism, and much later went on to write a work of theological reflection entitled *Brother Paul*.[112]

Kelman, Leifman, Wigoder, and Rubenstein all came to see Taubes as a brilliant, perverted, demonic manipulator.[113] Here was an aspect of Jacob's personality that many others would discover over time. He had an almost animal-like instinct for human weakness and how to exploit it. Just as an animal knows the softest spot of its prey in which to sink its teeth, Taubes could quickly discern individual vulnerability and use it to his own purposes. These qualities correspond to some of the classic characteristics of manic depression in its milder, hypomanic phase: enhanced liveliness, interpersonal charm, the ability to find vulnerable spots in others and to make use of them, and unusual perceptiveness at the subconscious or unconscious level.[114]

Translating Paul with Milton Steinberg

Many of those who came to know Taubes during his years at JTS were aware of his fascination with the Apostle Paul. The interlocutor with whom he explored the topic most closely was Milton Steinberg.

Steinberg was at the time among the most famous rabbis in the country. Twenty years older than Taubes, who was about twenty-five when they met, Steinberg was the rabbi of the prestigious Park Avenue Synagogue, and an expositor of Judaism to a wider public, through his books *The Making of the Modern Jew* (1934) and *Basic Judaism* (1947), as well as his novel of ideas, *As a Driven Leaf* (1939), which explored the tensions between Judaism and philosophical rationalism. He had obtained his BA in classics, and had been ordained at JTS, where he was much influenced by Mordechai Kaplan's rationalistic brand of Judaism. But Steinberg's rationalist commitments were increasingly in tension with his own affirmation of faith in God as an ultimate reality.[115]

Taubes met Milton Steinberg in 1949, perhaps through Arthur A. Cohen, whom Steinberg had brought back to Judaism from his flirtation with Christianity. Steinberg was deeply impressed by Taubes, regarding him as a fascinating person of superior intellect. Jacob visited Steinberg several times, including two visits on the Sabbath when Jacob trekked from the Seminary to the Steinberg home on 145 E. 92nd Street. To Steinberg's teenage son, Jonathan, Taubes seemed menacing if not diabolical:

intense, dressed in black, and sweating profusely—perhaps because he was a heavy smoker who refrained from smoking on the Sabbath, though even then he clutched an unlit cigarette in his hand.[116]

The conversations between Taubes and Steinberg turned first to Mordechai Kaplan's thought, which Steinberg characterized as "insufficient" and Taubes as insignificant and pagan. Soon enough, Taubes brought up his perennial concern with Paul. Instead of discussing in the abstract whether or not Paul could be considered Jewish, Taubes made a concrete proposal. Since Steinberg's Greek was excellent while his Biblical Hebrew was weak, while Taubes's Greek was weak but his Hebrew was excellent, he and Steinberg should sit down and translate some portions of Paul's epistles from Greek into Hebrew to see what sounded "Jewish" and what was "impossible in the Jewish ear." The idea was to get a sense of how Paul's first, Jewish listeners would have perceived his message.[117] The project produced no tangible results—not least because it was cut short by Steinberg's wife, Edith. She was eager to guard the time of her husband, who had suffered a serious heart attack a few years earlier. She also loathed Taubes, perhaps because he seemed to stimulate the nonrationalist element of her husband's faith, for which she had no patience. Edith ejected Taubes from the Steinberg household, which led to a row between her and Milton, one of many in their rocky marriage.[118]

From *his* engagement with the Pauline texts, Steinberg concluded that Paul was the source of much of what was least plausible and palatable about Christian theology, of which Judaism was blessedly free: "All Christian religious thought is shot through with the feverish spirituality of Paul. It was he who imposed on it such vagaries as the corruption of the flesh, Original Sin, justification by faith alone, the incarnation, vicarious atonement and a salvation that is of individuals only. . . . Because of him these must constitute a large part of the program and raw materials of any Christian theology. Judaism has been spared by Paul's departure from it. It is free then to address itself to the real themes of religion, unadorned and undistorted: God, revelation, and redemption."[119] Taubes, by contrast, remained intrigued with Paul. Yet in his subsequent reflections on Paul, he tended to ignore most the elements of Paul's teaching that had so exercised Steinberg.

Second Great Love

In the many letters dispatched by Jacob's mother and sister during his time at JTS, the most recurrent theme was that he keep his eyes out for an appropriate wife—preferably someone who was Jewishly knowledgeable and committed, but also cultured and of good breeding. Jacob did not tell them that he had found a woman who matched those criteria—but that she was a widow, a mother, and his senior by fourteen years. Her name was Gerda Seligsohn (she later changed the spelling to Seligson).

Gerda's family history reflected an often-forgotten phenomenon among German Jews: the movement of men and women of Jewish ancestry back and forth across the confessional lines of Judaism and Christianity.[120] On the eve of the National Socialist rise to power, there were almost as many such "persons of Jewish origin" in Germany as those of Jewish faith.[121] Gerda's father, Richard Kroner, was a distinguished philosopher and interpreter of German Idealism, who came to teach at Union Theological Seminary in 1941.[122] Richard's paternal grandfather had been a rabbi; his maternal grandfather a wealthy merchant; his father a physician. They thus personified a pattern among German Jews: the transition from traditional learning and mercantile activity in the mid-nineteenth century, into the free professions at the century's end. Richard, born in 1884, took a step further on the typical German-Jewish path from *Besitz* (property) to *Bildung* (culture), by becoming a professor of philosophy in 1919. He took a step beyond Judaism as well, by converting to Protestantism. That too was not unusual: the chances of promotion from unsalaried privatdozent to remunerated professor were much greater for the converted than for the unconverted.[123] In the case of Richard Kroner, however, conversion was more than opportunistic: he converted while still a *Gymnasium* student, and later published works that interpreted Christianity in Hegelian terms.[124] After the Nazi rise to power, Kroner was forced out of his university post despite having been a veteran of the First World War, during which he had been awarded the Iron Cross for valor. He and his family left Germany in 1938, and after a stay in the United Kingdom, came to the United States in 1940.

Kroner's daughter Gerda was born in 1909, and in 1924—at about the age at which her father had converted from Judaism to Protestantism—she converted from Protestantism to Judaism, with Rabbi Leo Baeck. She went on to study classics and pedagogy at a series of German universities, and in 1935 married Rudolf Seligsohn, a young reform rabbi also trained in classics. In 1939 they too moved to England, where she received a BA. Rudolf died in 1943, not long after the birth of their only child, Elizabeth. In 1947, Gerda and Elizabeth moved to New York, living near Union Theological Seminary, where her father was teaching. The thirty-eight-year-old widow began teaching at the elite Brearley School in Manhattan. The widow of a rabbi and the daughter of a teacher at a leading Protestant seminary, she personified the coming together of Jewish commitment with classical Western culture.

Not long after arriving in New York, Gerda befriended Ernst Simon, and it was through him that she met Jacob Taubes. Recently arrived at JTS, the young scholar felt estranged from his new surroundings, and was still recovering emotionally from his ill-fated relationship with Myrie Bloch. We can trace Jacob's relationship with Gerda through a score of letters he sent to her, which she preserved to the end of her days.

In July of 1948, Jacob was still addressing her as "Frau Seligsohn"—a measure of a certain distance—as he assured her that had it not been for her friendship and that of Ernst Simon, he would have already returned to Europe.[125] By October, a Platonic friendship was turning into something more. The imminent departure of Ernst Simon would leave just the two of them, he wrote. "The circle of friendship and love between us is closing . . . perhaps has already closed? I almost hesitate to acknowledge it, yet we've known it for quite some time."[126]

Their relationship had a highly intellectual element, which included Gerda reading classical texts with Jacob, who was eager to improve his Greek, and Jacob's letters are replete with references to Greek figures, from Agamemnon to Aphrodite. As the latter reference indicates, their relationship was more than cerebral. In a letter addressed to "My most beloved Gerda," Jacob wrote, "A great orgy has overtaken us. Love can bear all and forgives all. . . . I sin only against myself, and matters proceed according to the dictum of my dear friend Paul: that which I will, I do not do; that which I would not do, I do."[127] Paul's declaration eased Jacob's sense of being unable to resist temptation, especially erotic temptation.

But at this stage of his life, there was still guilt and anxiety. On November 23, 1948, Gerda wrote to him (in a letter that probably remained unsent), "Since you have taken or at least eased the curse of widowhood that lies upon me, I'll pray for you tonight. I am thankful to you for what you felt and did for me. Don't feel you can only come to me as a lover. I think you are a good lover (though I am no expert) and I don't think I have the strength to refuse your love-making. But there is, alas, still too much rugged independence in me to forget that I tried all my life to stand for truth and the truth is that I owe you more than you owe me, at present." Jacob's propensity to dramatic despair is evident in the passage that follows: "I am terribly worried about you tonight, almost as much as about me. I am so worried that I swallowed my pride and phoned you only to get my worrying confirmed by your absence. Don't jump."[128]

He didn't. In the months that followed, Jacob proved to be a persistent and ardent lover. In a slew of brief letters—each beginning with the Hebrew letters bet-heh or bet-ayin-heh (*be-ezrat Hashem*, "with God's help"), a mark of his continuing piety—he let her know when he would appear at her residence ("We'll see one another tonight. Leave the door open"), where he would sometimes spend the night (and instructed her that there was no need to wash the shirt he had left in her top drawer). As in his letters to Myrie Bloch, religious and erotic imagery were often intertwined. He referred to Gerda as his *hierodule*—a holy slave or prostitute in ancient Greece. He addressed her (in letters at least) as *ishti* (my wife), established a loving relationship with her young daughter, Elizabeth, and speculated about having children with Gerda.[129]

Throughout the spring of 1949, when Jacob was increasingly involved with the much-younger Susan Feldmann, he continued his relationship with Gerda. After Jacob and Susan decided to marry, Jacob drew up a formal document in which he and Gerda pledged their lifelong devotion, "to love, honor, and be concerned with one another insofar as it does not disrupt other obligations."[130] He convinced Susan that Gerda and her daughter Elizabeth would be part of their "extended family" (*Grossfamilie*). After the wedding—at which Gerda served as matron of honor—he wrote to her that Susan was so terribly naive that she still has no idea about the intensity and sexual nature of the relationship between himself and Gerda, a sign of Susan's "blessed innocence" (*glückliche Unschuld*).[131] Eventually he did tell Susan about the nature of that relationship: far from being jealous, Susan became closer to Gerda than ever, and thanked Jacob for choosing her over Gerda.[132]

Like Myrie Bloch, Gerda Seligsohn was a good deal older than Jacob, and her relationship to Jacob had a maternal element. So would Jacob's relationship to many subsequent women: his need to be looked after was part of his attraction. But he was also supportive of the recently widowed Gerda, as he had been of Myrie Bloch, assuring Gerda of her uniqueness and desirability. Intellectuality and joint cultural pursuits were important elements of their relationship, as they would be for many of Jacob's partners. Like Myrie—and like many of his future female partners—Gerda was religious. So, in his own way, was Jacob. But he guided them into erotic relations that violated religious propriety. It was his own version of redemption through sin.

After Jacob's wedding, Gerda traveled to Europe, where, among other stops, she visited with Zwi and Fanny Taubes in Zurich. Jacob advised

Gerda on finding a suitable husband. She never did. She eventually moved to Ann Arbor, Michigan, where she taught Greek and Latin at the University of Michigan. She remained a committed Jew, and after moving to Ann Arbor, was active in her local congregation. Susan, who succeeded Gerda as Jacob's great love, was cut from very different cloth.

Susan Feldmann

From the time he met her in 1948 until his death in 1987, there was no woman who occupied so large a space in Jacob's soul as his first wife, Susan. Even late in life, he would keep a photo of her on his mantle and in his wallet, and would sometimes startle acquaintances by pointing to it and exclaiming, "This is my wife. She committed suicide."[133]

Susan was beautiful. Susan was very bright. Susan was spiritual. And unconventional. And Jewish, with *yichus* (distinguished lineage). Their relationship was one of extraordinary intensity, both when it waxed and when it waned.

They met not long after Susan moved to New York City in the summer of 1948. Jacob, who had been in New York for almost a year, met her at a soirée at the home of Ruth Nanda Anshen, a self-appointed intellectual impresario, whose daughter, Judith, was Susan's close friend.[134] According to those who knew her at the time, she was beautiful, charming, an "exquisite creature." She was otherworldly and naive. She had come to New York to work in the theater, which she viewed as a kind of sacred rite.[135] Impressed, Jacob invited her to attend Rosh Hashanah services at JTS—a novel experience for Susan, who had grown up in an antireligious household.[136]

Susan Feldmann, as she was then known, was five years younger than Jacob. Born in Budapest on January 12, 1928, she was twenty when they met, and twenty-one when they married. She stemmed from a Jewishly distinguished family: her grandfather, Moses Feldmann (1859–1927), was the chief rabbi (*Oberrabbiner*) of Budapest.[137] Yet she was raised in an entirely secular household. Susan's father, Dr. Sandor S. Feldmann, personified another variation of the Jewish encounter with modernity. The author of volumes in Hungarian on *Nervousness and Instincts: Studies in the Fields of Psychopathology and Sexual Pathology* and *Nervous Anxiety: And Other Chapters in the Field of Psychopathology*, Feldmann was a psychoanalyst, a strict Freudian of the first generation of disciples, for whom the books of Freud were as much a matter of orthodoxy as the Books of Moses had been for his ancestors, and for whom almost all human behavior could be rationally explained by reference to childhood experience. Though versed in Hebrew from the education of his youth, Feldmann was entirely estranged from Jewish religious practice. His wife, Marion, was no more interested in matters Jewish. Thus their only child, Susan, was raised in a decidedly secular, if still residually Jewish, home. The traditional sabbaths and Passover seders at the home of her grandmother were treated by her father as archaic, if quaint.[138]

Susan's family life was unconventional and fragmented. Susan was the apple of Sandor's eye—leaving little room for attention to his wife, Marion. Devoted to his work and to his daughter, Sandor encouraged his wife to see other men, which she did.[139] In 1939, with war on the horizon, Sandor emigrated to the United States with his daughter, then aged eleven. Shortly before, his wife had agreed to an amicable divorce, and declined to follow him to America. When Sandor and Susan first arrived in New York City, he stayed on to establish himself professionally in the new country, while Susan went to Philadelphia to live with relatives. They were reunited in 1941, when Sandor found a position as professor of psychiatry at the medical center of the University of Rochester. There, as one of the few psychoanalysts beyond New York City, he developed a private practice, earning enough to support himself, his daughter, and eventually, at times, her family as well.

It was in Rochester that Susan completed high school in 1945, already showing signs of her intellectual gifts. From 1945 through 1947, she studied at Bryn Mawr near Philadelphia, one of the elite "Seven Sisters" colleges, at a time when it was "the self-chosen destination of the most intellectual, intelligent, determined, and well-prepared young women in America."[140] Active in theater, she focused her studies on philosophy and literature. Showing a propensity to rebelliousness and extreme individualism, together with extraordinary intelligence, she bristled at the constraints of academic disciplines. An academic highlight of her experience was an advanced seminar on Man and Society taught by the philosopher Paul Weiss, who departed shortly thereafter to teach at Yale. In a letter of recommendation, the president of the college described her as "a dedicated intellectual" and "an individualist."[141]

Susan's mother survived the war in Budapest, but many of Susan's relatives did not. For that reason—though not for that reason alone—Susan's view of the world was grim. "Sometimes I almost pray that the world of man should be blown up; either that or that a miracle should happen and man grow up to his humanness," she wrote in the summer after her first year of college. "It is the waiting that is so terrible."[142] In the summer of 1947, she visited her mother in Budapest, seeing her for the first time in eight years. Though her mother immigrated to the United States in 1950, their relationship was strained. Susan had come of age in a motherless home, or rather a series of residences—in Budapest, Philadelphia, Rochester, Bryn Mawr—none of which seemed like her real home. She was homeless, in the many senses of the word.

After another trip to Europe in the summer of 1948, she decided to break off her studies at Bryn Mawr. Instead she moved to New York City, where, supported financially by her father, she took courses in theater at Columbia University, just down Broadway from JTS. It was then that she met Jacob Taubes and was invited by him to Rosh Hashanah services.

In the months that followed, the relationship between Jacob and Susan grew closer, despite the efforts of Gerda Seligsohn, who, understandably perhaps, tried to discourage it.[143] On the other hand, there was the stream of letters flowing across the Atlantic from his mother, Fanny, and his sister, Mirjam, reminding Jacob of the need to find an appropriate woman as his wife. But on March 3, 1949, Zwi too weighed in on the topic of a potential spouse. He asked Jacob whether he had found a girl, and encouraged him to look for one in "good circles," that is "circles of cultivated Jews, that synthesize Torah and culture."[144]

Jacob and Susan were united and separated by Jewishness. Both came from families for whom Jewishness was a fate. But Jacob and his family were so steeped in Orthodox Judaism that it provided the cultural air that they breathed and the ritual frame of their lives. A training in Hebrew, a familiarity with the prayerbook, the Bible, Talmud, modern Hebrew literature and Jewish scholarship, and not least, Zionism—these formed the taken-for-granted cultural referents of Jacob's life. Though Jacob took pleasure in rattling the cage of the Law, it was the cage that gave him an object to rattle. He was at home in the synagogue, though haunted by doubts about the plausibility of any traditional conception of God.

For Susan, by contrast, the world of traditional Jewish belief and practice was alien. Her first encounter with the Torah came in a college literature class.[145] Nor did she have much exposure to Christianity. She was, for all intents and purposes, a pagan, as Jacob put it. For Jacob, all of this was a source of concern—but also of attraction.[146]

Susan, who according to Jacob was "in confused revolt against the hollowness of the secular world,"[147] shared his Gnostic view of the world as fundamentally evil, not to speak of banal. Jacob talked to her at length about his characteristic concerns. About whether one could speak of the death of God, which might lead to nihilism. About the alternative, of believing in God despite—or perhaps precisely because of—the lack of evidence of God in this world. About believing precisely because it was absurd (*Credo quia absurdum*). About the role of the Law in creating the sanctification of life.[148] In short, he seems to have tried to talk her into sharing a life with him: a Jewish life, albeit one embraced with deep doubt, and a faith always on the edge of vanishing.

Having loaded the ammunition, Jacob pulled the trigger. On Wednesday, April 13, the first night of Passover, he brought Susan to a seder at the Lieberman household.[149] The second night was spent at a seder over which Jacob presided with his friends from the *Commentary* crowd. And then, on Easter Sunday, April 17, they made love, Susan for the first time, Jacob with plenty of experience. She did so with abandon, although Jacob warned her that she could get pregnant.[150] Afterwards, Jacob proposed marriage to her. Susan, to his astonishment, suggested they live together in free love.[151] Jacob was appalled at that prospect, and over the next six weeks made repeated attempts to convince her, until he wore her down and she consented.[152] They contacted her father in Rochester, and Jacob's parents in Zurich, who were delighted to learn that their only son had found a girl, a Jewish girl, and a beautiful Jewish girl at that. Jacob's sister Mirjam sent them fifty dollars, and his parents one hundred, to celebrate and aid the young couple to be.[153]

There was an engagement party, attended by their friends, including the members of the Pseudo-Cabal. Ruth Glazer brought along her friend, Annette Michelson, thinking that Annette would find Jacob interesting. She did, and became an ongoing friend of both Jacob and Susan. Among the others in attendance was Hannah Arendt.[154]

The wedding took place with lightning speed: Zwi and Fanny were informed in early May, and the wedding was set for Sunday, June 5. Zwi traveled to New York for the occasion, which took place in the synagogue of JTS.[155] Among those attending was Nahum Glatzer, an editor at the Schocken publishing house in New York, who was soon to become one of the most important figures in transporting the legacy of German-Jewish philosophy and literature to an American audience. Salo Baron, by now a professor of Jewish history at Columbia, sent a gift to the young couple. So did Jacob's friend Victor Gourevitch, who presented them with a rare edition of the Greek Presocratics. Jacob's friends from the Pseudo-Cabal were on hand as well.[156]

Officiating as *mesadrai kedushin* were three rabbis: and what three rabbis! Louis Finkelstein, Saul Lieberman, and Zwi Taubes—a rather extraordinary trio, given that Finkelstein and Lieberman usually eschewed

FIGURE 5.1. Susan Taubes, engagement photo. (Ethan and Tania Taubes Collection.)

such public roles, lest they be seen as favoring some students over others. But Susan was not impressed. Jacob had promised her a traditional Orthodox wedding, with fiddlers, dancing, and the ceremony of the bride walking around the groom seven times.[157] The reality did not live up to her aesthetic expectations. The wedding was a compromise affair, and the reception "a banal cocktail party with cheese sandwiches from a kosher caterer." The breaking of the glass at the end of the marriage ceremony

FIGURE 5.2. Susan and Jacob in 1949. (Ethan and Tania Taubes Collection.)

was preceded by an anthropological discourse from Simon Greenberg, the acting president of JTS (for Finkelstein was on leave), a talk that the couple found disappointing.

Toward Jerusalem?

By early 1949, it was becoming clear that Jacob's time at JTS would not extend beyond the current academic year. Finkelstein, Lieberman, and Simon Greenberg thought that there was no room in the Seminary's faculty for a person of his chief interests, which were in the history of philosophy, theology, and religion. That at least was the official explanation. Perhaps other considerations figured into their calculations: Jacob's lack of research productivity, the scattered nature of his reading, his conduct vis-à-vis Finkelstein's daughter, or other elements of his behavior. Jacob was not a good enough fit for the Seminary to keep, but its leadership thought his mind too valuable a commodity to waste.

A possible solution began to emerge with the visit of Gershom Scholem to JTS in late February and March. Scholem and Jacob had remained in contact by letter since Jacob first wrote to the master in the fall of 1947, and they seem to have hit it off well when they met in person.[158] Leo Strauss, who was impressed with Jacob's intellect but had doubts about his character, told his friend Scholem that Scholem was perhaps the only one who could instill discipline into Jacob and make something of him.[159] Lieberman and Scholem discussed the possibility of Jacob going to the Hebrew University to study, with a fellowship from JTS.[160]

In the meantime, with his future prospects uncertain, Jacob looked about for a job. An unexpected possibility arose when he received an inquiry in mid-March from a Liberal (i.e., Reform) congregation in Amsterdam, a congregation made up of the handful of German-Jewish families who had survived the Holocaust in Holland. They had learned about Jacob from his father and were very interested in hiring him as a rabbi.[161] But Jacob did not follow up the offer. In the meantime, another rabbinical post presented itself, at the Chodorower Synagogue, a small congregation on the Lower East Side of Manhattan. On April 11, Jacob actually signed a contract to serve as the rabbi of the congregation for two years.[162] But a congregational rabbi was the last thing that Jacob wanted to be. Instead he put out feelers to acquaintances at a number of academic institutions, including Joachim Wach at the University of Chicago, and the mathematician Hermann Weyl at the Institute for Advanced Study in Princeton. As scholars who could offer letters of recommendation, he listed Leo Baeck, Leo Strauss, Paul Tillich of Union Theological Seminary, and Paul Weiss, a philosopher of metaphysics with whom Susan had studied, who was now at Yale.[163] But none of these possibilities panned out, leaving Hebrew University as the alternative. Jacob was disappointed that Finkelstein had not offered him a professorial post, but he was very interested in going to Jerusalem.[164] The Executive Committee of the Seminary's Board of Directors agreed to fund his studies in Jerusalem for two years, beginning in September, with an annual fellowship of $2,000—a substantial sum at the time.

In May, just weeks before his wedding, the acting president of JTS, Simon Greenberg, wrote to Jacob to make clear both the reasons for the Seminary's generosity and the limits of its commitment, in a letter written "to avoid any possibility of future misunderstanding." The fellowship was intended "to enable you to continue your fruitful studies because we believe that the Jewish people will have in you a representative in the realms of Theology and Philosophy who will be a blessing to it." However, he made clear that Jacob should harbor no hopes of a job at JTS at the end of his fellowship, since "the field in which you have so brilliantly distinguished yourself thus far is one which up to the present time, has not been part of the Seminary curriculum."[165]

That summer, Jacob's mother, Fanny, wrote to him to say that Gershom Scholem—"your idol"—had just visited with them in Zurich. It was the first time that Scholem attended the Eranos conference in Ascona, Switzerland, an annual gathering of scholars of religion to which Scholem would return annually.[166] Scholem, Fanny said, spoke highly of Jacob, and assured them that he should go to Jerusalem, and that if he worked, he would grow. Zwi informed his son that Scholem looked forward to his arrival in Jerusalem, and even had a topic for him to work on in Scholem's seminar. But, Zwi noted after his conversation, Jacob should plan to spend much of his time studying not with Scholem, but with Julius Guttmann, whose specialty was Jewish philosophy.[167]

Shortly after their wedding, Jacob and Susan moved into an apartment just south of Columbia University, at 612 W. 112th St.[168] For Susan, married life was marked by erotic exhilaration and omens of spiritual troubles to come. On June 29, Jacob reported to Gerda (then visiting in England) that Susan was uncomfortable with the Jewish way of life, living instead in an unmoored world of abstractions. "Her views are hair-raising," Jacob averred, adding optimistically, "but I've learned . . . not to take people's metaphysical views too seriously."[169] A letter that Susan wrote to Jacob (but probably never mailed) shows just how estranged she was from the Jewish life that Jacob had imagined for them.

> I must follow the voice that speaks in my soul and not deceive myself by any talmudic or jesuitical rationalization that I can attach and commit myself to any mass belief and tradition. . . . I desire more than to worship in community and not in loneliness [but] I will suffer my loneliness rather than to give myself to hypocrisy and falsehood. I don't think you have a right to force me to repeat and repeat the same process of decision. . . . I want to build my own altar. It is awful, it is perhaps the most frightening thing not to be able to worship and live in the tradition of any people—it is truly death—but we must live this awfulness and not make sentiment[al] or political compromises. . . .
>
> And if your whole life and truth is the Torah and your whole aim to build a life and family according to its law you were unjust not to make your conditions clear to me before, because you will not be able to force me in this mold. I am just sick from it and you must admit that this was not the basis on which we married and I am simply terrified.[170]

If they did not have a full meeting of their minds, they seem to have made up for it through the meeting of their bodies. On July 23, Jacob wrote to Gerda with some big news: Susan was pregnant, and "You are (of course) the first to know about it." He assured her that he and Susan still regarded Gerda's daughter as their own, adding that Susan did not yet understand the nature of Jacob's relationship to Gerda, reporting that "pregnancy has allowed Susan to become more Dionysian. . . . But we have to be careful and not take things too fast."[171] In the same letter, Jacob reported that Susan had begun bleeding, and that day the doctor had told them that she needed to rest and remain in bed. But after ten days of sickness and bleeding, Susan miscarried. The doctor assured her she would be able to get pregnant again in a few months—though pregnancy does not seem to have been in their plans.[172]

Jacob and Susan had intended to leave for Jerusalem, with a stop in Zurich to meet the rest of Jacob's family, at the beginning of September. Jacob handed in his paper on Maimonides at the very last moment, on September 1. (He confessed to Gerda that among Susan's virtues was the fact that she got him to work. Fanny agreed, and complimented Susan for being a good influence on Jacob in that regard.[173]) But their departure was delayed by Jacob's visa problems. Lacking national citizenship, and as the holder of a Nansen passport, he needed a visa from every country

FIGURE 5.3. The new couple visits Zurich, 1949. L to R, Zwi Taubes, Armand Dreyfus, Mirjam Dreyfus, Fanny, Jacob, Susan Taubes. (Ethan and Tania Taubes Collection.)

he was to pass through. In order to be able to re-enter the United States in the future, he first traveled to Toronto, Ontario, where he got a new clerical visa that allowed him to return to the United States as Rabbi Taubes.[174]

And so, after a sojourn with the family in Zurich, in December 1949, Jacob and Susan departed for the Holy Land. He wrote to Hans Urs von Balthasar that he was happy to be leaving America for Israel.[175] Using the same stationery on which he had first written his letter of introduction to Scholem on his way to America two years earlier, Jacob sent Scholem a much shorter missive, saying that they were on their way and happy about "making *aliyah* [immigration, understood as ascension] to Israel, to the camels, the wildernesses, the starry heavens of Jerusalem, the landscape, and the people of the past and present."[176]

CHAPTER SIX

Jerusalem, 1949–52

TAUBES SPENT AN intense two and a half years in Jerusalem, from December 1949 to July 1952. For part of that time, Susan lived there with him, but alienated by her encounter with the new Jewish state, she spent the bulk of those years in the United States and in Paris.[1] A by-product of their frequent separations was a rich correspondence: hundreds of Susan's letters have survived, as have a handful of Jacob's, providing a window into their development, and the strains, intellectual and personal, between them.[2]

For Jacob, Jerusalem offered one of several plausible alternatives for pursuing a career as a Jewish intellectual. Jewish intellectual life had been all but wiped out in continental Europe by the destruction of almost all of its Jewish communities, and there were few remaining institutions of higher Jewish learning. The surviving human repositories of European Jewish culture had largely made their way to America. But Jacob's initial encounter with America had left him unimpressed with it as a place to make his life. That left the new State of Israel, the other node of Jewish learning, and especially Jerusalem, with its cohort of German-Jewish scholars.

Jacob's Jerusalem sojourn forced him to engage directly with the tensions between religious aspiration and political necessity, between particular commitments and universal claims, between faith and historical understanding, and between Jacob's identity as a Jew—however heretical—and Susan's decidedly non-Jewish, and increasingly anti-Jewish, propensities.

The couple arrived in Jerusalem and rented rooms in the suburb of Talpiot. In August 1950, they again visited Jacob's parents in Zurich, after which Jacob returned to Jerusalem. Susan travelled to the United States to complete the requirements for her BA at Bryn Mawr College, and to scout out job prospects for Jacob. Jacob lived for a time at the home of his

FIGURE 6.1. Photo from Jacob's Israeli identity certificate,
March 24, 1952. (Ethan and Tania Taubes Collection.)

friends, Joseph and Miriam Weiss—about whom we'll hear a good deal
later in this chapter—before moving in October 1950 into small quarters
in Meonot Ovdim, an urban cooperative housing complex on Gaza Road
in Rehavia, and then to some rooms in a house in the nearby Greek Colony
(Moshava Yevanit). The couple was reunited from late July to late October 1951, which they spent at the home of Susan's father in Rochester, New
York, a visit punctuated by a letter from Gershom Scholem heralding the
end of his mentorship of Jacob. Jacob returned to Jerusalem to teach and
to try to write, while Susan continued her studies at the Sorbonne in Paris
through the first half of 1952. In the summer of 1952, after another visit to
Zurich and brief stays in Paris and London, they moved back to Rochester,
jobless and desperate.

The Setting: Jerusalem

The Jerusalem to which Jacob and Susan arrived was a divided city in
transition. The city had been inhabited by Arabs (both Christian and
Muslim) and one hundred thousand Jews, both secular and religious,

who formed the majority. The British government's decision to relinquish control over its Palestine mandate was followed by the vote of the UN General Assembly in November 1947 to partition the territory into Jewish and Arab states, with Jerusalem as an international zone. When the plan was rejected by the Arabs, civil war broke out in Jerusalem, and after the declaration of a Jewish state in May 1948, a war between the new Jewish army and invading armies from the surrounding Arab states. The Jewish portions of Jerusalem came under siege, and their residents found their water supply and electricity cut off. When the fighting was ended by an armistice in April 1949, the eastern half of the city came under Jordanian control, and with it, the Old City with its ancient walls. That part of the city was ethnically cleansed of its Jewish inhabitants, its synagogues and cemeteries destroyed. The western part of the city came under the control of the new Jewish State of Israel, after many of its Arab inhabitants had fled or been driven out of their neighborhoods into the Jordanian zone and beyond. The hardships of the siege had left Jewish Jerusalem with a population of sixty-nine thousand.[3] A barbed-wire fence separated the two halves of the city. Occasionally Jordanian snipers would fire at the Jewish Jerusalemites on the west side of the divide.

Three of the major institutions of Jewish Jerusalem—the Hebrew University, the National Library, and the Hadassah Hospital—were located on Mount Scopus, a Jewish enclave within the Jordanian-held portion of the city. According to the armistice agreement, arrangements were to be made for their continuing operation. But that portion of the agreement remained a dead letter. The buildings could only be accessed by means of a small convoy that traveled to Mount Scopus every fortnight, under UN protection. The Hebrew University, bereft of its buildings and library, resumed operation at the Terra Sancta building, a former Franciscan college at the intersection of Gaza Road and Keren Hayesod streets.

Jewish Jerusalem, then, was a small city when the Taubeses arrived. But it was the location of the national government, the national radio broadcast network, Kol Yisrael, and the Hebrew University, the country's only university (aside from the Technion and the Weizmann Institute, institutions oriented to engineering and science), at which Jacob was to study and teach. The city included a remarkable range of social types—ultra-Orthodox Jews long resident in the Meah She'arim neighborhood and antipathetic to the Zionist project; modern Orthodox Zionists; secular Zionists; Jews who had migrated from Yemen, from Eastern Europe, and from German-speaking Europe; monks, and even a Nazarite—all of whom Jacob would encounter.

Jacob's Jerusalem was smaller still, stretching from the neighborhoods of Talpiot in the east to Rehavia in the west. Jacob and Susan moved into a small apartment in a villa in Talpiot,[4] a neighborhood founded in 1922 as a garden city. Its most illustrious inhabitant was Shai Agnon, already a famous author, and eventually a recipient of the Nobel Prize for Literature, whom Jacob and Susan befriended.[5] A few steps from their house one could see the Jordanian desert, the mountains of Moab, and the Dead Sea.[6] Terra Sancta was a half-hour walk westward. A few blocks more and one reached Rehavia, the neighborhood in which Gershom Scholem, Ernst Simon, Hugo Bergmann, and other luminaries of the Hebrew University dwelled.[7]

With the end of the British restrictions on Jewish immigration, a stream and then a torrent of Jews began arriving in the new State of Israel in 1949: European Jews from displaced persons camps in Germany and Cyprus, and Jews from Yemen, Tunisia, Turkey, and Libya—a quarter of a million in all. That was followed in 1950 by a mass migration of 120,000 Jews from Iraq, and a wave from Romania. Between 1949 and 1951, the Jewish population increased by more than 50 percent.[8] Housing was at a premium, as demand quickly swamped the supply. The housing shortage was partially eased by the availability of homes abandoned by their previous Arab inhabitants. Such houses became the property of a government agency, the Custodian of Abandoned Property, which was in charge of distributing or selling the now-vacant homes. In West Jerusalem, the well-heeled neighborhoods of Baka, the German Colony, and the Greek Colony, all adjoining Terra Sancta and Rehavia, were in that category. But in the rather chaotic conditions that followed the war, some houses were occupied by squatters, who thereafter had legally ambiguous claims to the homes they occupied—a potential hazard that would ensnare the Taubeses when they sought to buy a home.[9]

Material conditions in the city, as in the new country as a whole, were spartan. The government, led by Prime Minister David ben Gurion of the Mapai (Labor) Party, struggled to create administrative institutions while integrating waves of new immigrants. Imports of goods from abroad far exceeded exports, and foreign currency was limited, leading the government to enact a program of austerity (*tzena*) that lasted throughout the years that Jacob and Susan spent in the country. Foodstuffs, clothing, and footwear were rationed, giving birth to a thriving black market. Fuel was scarce and expensive, and even paper was in short supply.[10] Friends and relatives from abroad sent packages of food. Coming from the United States and accustomed to its more affluent standard of living, the absence in Jerusalem of commodities taken for granted in the United States weighed on Susan.[11]

Hebrew University

The Hebrew University, which had opened its doors in 1925, was staffed in good part by scholars trained in Germany, and it maintained the high academic standards of a German university.[12] Most departments at the university were small, and their borders were permeable. From early on, the university sought to become the foremost institution for the academic study of Judaism and Jewish history. At the center of that endeavor was Gershom Scholem.[13]

From 1949 to 1952, Scholem made a number of trips to Germany as a member of the committee on Jewish Cultural Reconstruction. It was their sad task to discover and evaluate the libraries of Jewish communities destroyed by the Nazis, and to distribute the books and manuscripts among Jewish institutions in Israel and America. In that capacity, Scholem cooperated closely with Hannah Arendt, with whom he had become acquainted before the war. It was from Arendt that Scholem had learned of the death of their mutual friend, Walter Benjamin, whose literary legacy both devoted themselves to preserving.[14] Scholem's student, Joseph Weiss, informed Taubes of Scholem's devotion to Benjamin, which no doubt led Taubes to read Benjamin's work at a time when it was little known beyond the circle of Benjamin's friends.[15]

Scholem was in the process of becoming the most internationally renowned academic at the Hebrew University. In the decades after the Second World War, Scholem's portrayal of the Kabbalah offered a conception of Judaism rich in symbolism and speculation, backed by massive scholarship, that provided nonreligious readers in America and Europe with an alternative to the dominant image of Judaism as a form of moral edification, or the legalistic conceptions characteristic of Orthodox Judaism.[16] His budding international reputation flowered with the publication in 1954 of a new edition of his *Major Trends in Jewish Mysticism*.[17]

Taubes had come to Jerusalem planning to study primarily with Julius Guttmann, the senior professor of Jewish philosophy. But in April 1950, not long after Taubes arrived in Israel, Guttmann suffered a heart attack in the midst of a conference at Hebrew University marking his seventieth birthday.[18] He passed away that May. That left Scholem as Taubes's scholarly mentor.

Scholem's university seminars on Jewish mysticism took place at Terra Sancta, where in 1949–50 he taught courses on the history of Sabbatianism and on the Zohar, as well as a seminar on the Safed Kabbalist, Moshe Cordovero.[19] Among the handful of students who attended were two American undergraduates, Arnold Band and Isadore Twersky—who were to be numbered among the founders of Jewish Studies in the United States, at UCLA and Harvard, respectively—and Rivka Goldschmidt (Horwitz), who later taught Jewish philosophy and mysticism at the Ben-Gurion University in Beersheba. Taubes sat in on the seminar, and, typically, did not hide his light under a bushel. As one participant remembers, "Whatever he knew was paraded before you." He stood out for his knowledge of Protestant theology and his frequent comparisons between Jewish and Christian history, a perspective quite foreign to the Zionist culture of the new state and to Scholem's style of scholarship, which focused on internal Jewish developments. In the setting of the new state of Israel, such perspectives seemed outlandish, indeed bizarre.[20]

Taubes also participated in another of Scholem's seminars, this one offered at Scholem's home, which at the time housed the best collection of books of and about Jewish mysticism in the city (and perhaps in the world.) That seminar included not only graduate students, but fellow professors, such as Hugo Bergmann, the historian Jacob Katz, the philosopher Natan Rotenstreich, and Jacob Fleischmann, a scholar of Jewish thought who later taught at the Sorbonne.[21] Scholem, in short, was the hub of the wheel of scholars of Jewish philosophy and history in Jerusalem.

Bergmann was another of Taubes's interlocutors and supporters. Born in Prague in 1883—and thus one of the most senior professors at the university—Bergmann had come to Jerusalem in 1920, where he headed the newly founded National Library, created by the World Zionist Organization. In 1928, he joined the philosophy department of the university, and from 1935 to 1938 served as its rector.[22] In 1945, together with Guttmann and Martin Buber, he founded the journal *Iyyun*, devoted in part to introducing the ideas of contemporary philosophy to a Hebrew-speaking readership. One of their aims was the translation of the great works of Western philosophy into Hebrew, a goal that Bergmann helped fulfill by translating Kant's three *Critiques*. At the time he befriended Jacob and Susan Taubes, Bergmann was the head of the Department of Philosophy, and, together with Scholem, carried a great deal of weight in the larger affairs of the university.

The relationship between Scholem and Bergmann was quite extraordinary. They were close friends, despite the fact that some years earlier, Scholem's wife, Escha, had transferred her allegiance to Bergmann, whom she married in 1936. Shortly thereafter, Scholem married Fania Freud, another highly intellectual woman who had been his student, and the two couples remained close.[23]

In addition to Scholem and Bergmann, Taubes's senior interlocutors in Jerusalem included Martin Buber and Akiva (Ernst) Simon. All were of German-Jewish origin, had become Zionists as young men, and had moved to the Land of Israel (Buber belatedly, in 1938). They had all believed that Zionism existed more to transform the Jews than to provide them with a sovereign state. Their goal was the spiritual revival of Judaism and the creation of a moral community in which that mission could be realized.[24] They varied in religious practice and belief. Simon had belonged to the Orthodox Zionist Mizrachi, though he was increasingly attracted to Conservative Judaism. Neither Buber nor Scholem were observant in any traditional sense. Buber was best known among Protestant theologians, and his most famous work, *I and Thou*, was decidedly nonsectarian. His political philosophy, such as it was, had affinities with anarchism: hardly the basis of a sovereign Jewish state. Bergmann's practice was more traditional, but his faith was nondogmatic; his journals reveal an ongoing struggle to articulate and establish his own relationship with God.[25] He believed there were multiple paths to the divine, did not ascribe superiority to Judaism or Christianity, and was scornful of Zionists who drew political conclusions from religious premises.[26]

In the 1930s, all four men had belonged to Brit Shalom (The Fellowship of Peace), a tiny organization devoted to Jewish-Arab comity, and all had supported a binational state. By the time Taubes arrived in Jerusalem, such visions were a dead letter. Brit Shalom and its successor organization, Ichud, found no Arab interlocutors in positions of influence who were interested in their plans.[27] A series of events they had not anticipated led them to rethink their positions: the experience of the Holocaust, the War of Independence (the members of Brit Shalom had feared that the outcome would be "the complete annihilation of the Jewish population of Palestine"), and the exigencies of absorbing the huge influx of immigrants from Europe and the Arab world led them to embrace the necessity of a Jewish state, but to maintain a certain ambivalence about the new Israeli reality.[28]

That ambivalence had multiple sources. It was grounded in part on guilt over the departure, partly due to expulsion, of a large portion of the Arab population. In part over the ongoing necessity of military preparation in light of the enmity of the neighboring Arab states. They struggled with the question of how the conception of the Jews as a holy people could be reconciled with the political and military realities of a Jewish sovereign state subject to most of the infirmities to which flesh is heir: a state, moreover with a predominantly secular populace, a socialist Zionist leadership, and a susceptibility to interpreting the new state in messianic terms—an interpretation that Scholem, Buber, Simon, and Bergmann all found dangerous.[29] Yet despite the gap between their youthful expectations and present realities, all four were connected critics, with a deep commitment to the Zionist project: as Simon later put it, "Critique without solidarity is rootless. Solidarity without critique lacks direction."[30]

Their students, who came from well beyond the small reservoir of immigrants from Central Europe, wrestled with the issues of how the historical legacies of Judaism were to be interpreted in the new state. Among them were Geula Cohen and Yosef Ben-Shlomo.

At the time, Geula Cohen was a student of both Scholem and Bergmann. From a traditional Yemenite and Turkish family, she was famous (or infamous) as the former voice on the underground radio station of Lechi (Freedom Fighters of Israel), a radical splinter group of the Revisionist Irgun Z'vai Leumi (National Military Organization). Its leader, Avraham Stern, was a Hebrew poet and a scholar of Greek and Latin who fused secular nationalist conceptions with religious images, and who adopted a strategy of terror to try to galvanize the Jewish masses and drive the British out of the country. His goal: the "establishment of the Kingdom of Israel in its historical borders."[31] In the mind of the young Geula Cohen, she and her comrades were fighting for a freedom that "was not simply a freedom from foreign rule, but one that would enable us to create a new, distinctively Hebraic way of life."[32] In 1946 she was arrested and imprisoned by the British, but escaped from prison in 1947. The conclusion of the War of Independence left her with a sense of dissatisfaction and unfulfilled hopes for a Jewish polity that ought to have stretched from the Nile to the Euphrates, and a life of "perpetual sacrifice on the fields of holiness and creation."[33] She came to study philosophy and Jewish studies at Hebrew University, while writing for a journal published by the Lechi circle.

Bergmann urged Taubes to meet Geula Cohen, and he did so. He went to her home, and together they walked the streets of Jerusalem until past midnight. They discussed the problem of tradition and how the longing for holiness could be fulfilled under the new historical circumstances of living in a sovereign Jewish state. Taubes was struck by the holy longings (*kisufai kodesh*) that lay behind Cohen's nationalist aspirations. But he urged her to consider whether the territorial maximalism of her political creed really corresponded to her religious quest. "What is the advantage of sovereignty, with borders to the River Prat [the Euphrates], if it's made up of human riff-raff [*im asafsuf enoshi*]? If it is a mitzvah to die for these borders, it is a double mitzvah to shape the image of man, the type of man who is appropriate for sovereignty. . . . Your lives and images have to be a faithful example, your lives have to be filled with holiness." Otherwise, he warned, she and her comrades faced the hazard of becoming a Golem, a nationalist body devoid of spirit.[34] No doubt to try to shock her, when they passed by Terra Sancta, Taubes took her into the library, pulled off the shelf a book by a German author, and began translating the writer's nationalist sentiments to her. Cohen found them moving. At which point, Taubes informed her that it was written by a Nazi thinker (probably Carl Schmitt).[35] While Taubes found Cohen quite fascinating, he seems to have had no influence on her political or intellectual development.

Yosef Ben-Shlomo attended two of Taubes's lecture courses at Hebrew University in 1951–52, one on Modern Philosophy from Descartes to Spinoza, the other on Marxism.[36] Born in Poland in 1930 into a religious family, he had come to mandatory Palestine as a child. He served in the Haganah and then the new Israeli army, before beginning his university studies. By then he had given up religious observance and become a man of the socialist left. He began as a student of philosophy, but his encounter with Gershom Scholem led him to a dual focus on philosophy and Jewish thought.

Ben-Shlomo found the course on Marxism especially memorable. Taubes was an enthusiastic and captivating lecturer, and his course attracted thirty students—a large class by the standards of Hebrew University at that time. Taubes began by exploring the tensions arising from the French Revolution, between liberty, equality, and fraternity, and went on to discuss the dialectic between man and citizen.[37] At the time there were Marxist students of many varieties at the university, and Taubes taught Marxism in a way that would disturb their materialist dogmatism. Unusually, he focused on Marx's *Eighteenth Brumaire*, the most un-Marxist of his major works, in that its analysis departs radically from any purely materialist account of politics.[38] Taubes's course on early modern philosophy seems to have had an even greater impact on Ben-Shlomo, who became, in addition to a scholar of Kabbalah, a scholar of Spinoza, whose works he translated into Hebrew.

Ben-Shlomo found Taubes brilliant, sharp, and arrogant. He was an ambiguous figure, impossible for students to figure out. For he wore a *kippah* when he ate (in Orthodox fashion), but he spoke sympathetically about Christianity, and flirted with female students. Taubes, Ben-Shlomo saw, was clearly drawn to the antinomian strains in Judaism, but unlike Scholem, his interest was more than purely intellectual.[39] After Taubes's departure, Ben-Shlomo would go on to become a professor of philosophy at Tel Aviv University. His path would cross Taubes's again decades later, when Taubes returned to Jerusalem.[40]

In addition to the courses he offered in the Department of Philosophy, Taubes taught a course (in the fall of 1950) on modern religious thought, focused on Moses Mendelssohn's *Jerusalem*, a seminal work of Enlightenment Jewish thought—testimony to the fact that he straddled the academic disciplines of philosophy and Jewish thought.[41] Not only was Taubes a popular university lecturer, he also broadcast to a wider audience on the national radio station, Kol Yisrael, which saw itself as having a national, pedagogic mission.[42] In the spring of 1951, he gave a series of brief lectures on the weekly program *Haskalah La'am* (*Education for the People*) on the topic of Faith and Heresy in the Nineteenth-Century, dealing with Dostoyevsky, Nietzsche, and the German Romantic author, Jean Paul, as well as a lecture on Heidegger. (Lamentably, there are no recordings or transcripts.[43])

On the whole, Taubes was at home in the culture of Jerusalem. He celebrated the Passover seder at the home of Agnon. (Taubes reported to Bergmann that Agnon recited the traditional imprecation upon the oppressors of the Jewish people, "Pour out Thy wrath upon the nations who know ye not," seven times; a demonstration, no doubt, of how a traditional ritual could be imbued with additional weight in the aftermath of the Holocaust.[44]) Jerusalem also provided contact with a fascinating variety of Jews and Christians. He visited in the ultra-Orthodox neighborhood of Meah She'arim.[45] He met David Cohen, an ascetic, German-speaking Zionist messianist. Cohen was known as "the Nazarite," having taken a vow to abstain from drink and from cutting his hair. He visited a monastery on Mount Zion and was deeply impressed by its abbot.[46]

If, as we will see, Taubes had his doubts about the direction of Israeli society or its failure to live up to his vague ideals, those were doubts he shared with many of his interlocutors at Hebrew University, including Simon, Bergmann, Buber, and Scholem. He does not seem to have shared their sense of intense involvement with the project of building a Jewish state and society. Yet were it up to Jacob, he may well have stayed and made his career in Jerusalem.

Religious Dilemmas: Judaism and the Jewish State

Taubes had come to Jerusalem intending to wrestle with his own issues of faith. His most intensive intellectual experience at JTS had been his encounter with Leo Strauss, for whom authentic philosophy was atheistic. In the spring of 1949, when he had decided to come to Israel, Taubes wrote to Ernst Simon about the religious doubt that Strauss had instilled in him, and his hope that his faith might be rekindled in Jerusalem. "For me, Leo Strauss is more than an interpreter of Maimonides, he is really a guide in the spiritual desert. Therefore, it is good to go to *Eretz Yisrael* and to test whether the ice of atheism and the cold aura that emanates from it will melt under the sun and fire of God's word. That will really be a test!"[47]

Taubes also had his doubts about the fate of Judaism in the new state. A month into his stay, he wrote to Chancellor Finkelstein of JTS that

> there is in general no interest in religion, and the relation (religio= relation!) of man to God sinks into oblivion. The old *Yishuv* lives in a ghetto [i.e., Meah She'arim] and a small Orthodox circle is interested to keep a monopoly over the religious service. One can see the devil gloating over the strange unity of interest of a group seeking religious monopoly and a population so indifferent to religion that it offers no resistance and gives a free sway to this dark clerical will to power. Any ways and attempts of a new religious expression are subject for ridicule and contempt on the one side and apathy on the other side.[48]

Shortly thereafter, on Purim 1950, Taubes wrote to Simon Greenberg of JTS about his fears that Zionism would prove to be merely a form of mass, voluntary liquidation of the heritage of Judaism. Secular Israelis seemed to him too bent upon the normalization of the Jewish people; the religious life of Meah She'arim seemed holy but implausible, at least for modern people like him; the willingness of Israeli Orthodoxy to employ the coercive power of government struck him as pernicious.[49]

Taubes was already deeply antipathetic to any redemptive or messianic conception of the new Jewish state when he arrived there.[50] Yet, while he was willing to deflate Geula Cohen's attempts to renew Judaism through radical Zionism, he was deeply uncertain about his own relationship to Judaism or to the new society being created in Israel. As he explained to Bergmann in 1951, he was attracted to universalist ideologies like Catholicism and communism, but accepted neither, though he saw both as the offspring of the Jewish people. Zionism was too particularist an ideology to satisfy him. His real hope was that the Jewish people would create a new ideology with universal reach, as they had in the past created Christianity and Marxism. And he thought that might develop in Israel.

> Jerusalem seems to be a not inappropriate place for this: not in the slavish repetition of the prophets (or the Talmud) as the word of God, not as an opportunity to finally develop a state with all the forms of domination, in order to catch up on what we have "ignored" for almost

two thousand years, but rather in the hope that the seed of Israel will produce no evil fruit for the fate of man as man. . . . That the Jewish people is a people that ever seeks to reach beyond itself . . . a *Volk* that is also a non-*Volk* (what a blessing!), a *Volk* that does not make a demon of its peoplehood—though it is more prone than other people to make an idol of its own peoplehood, which is just what we've been doing recently. (Susan now sees only the demonized form of this, as does Simone Weil; a demon that has its roots in the Pentateuch, but also the willingness to sacrifice for something beyond the *Volk* has its roots in some words of the prophets [as does the discovery of the individual in Ezekiel 18]). . . . The Jewish *Volk* as such a non-*Volk* perhaps still has the chance to reach and influence beyond itself (despite nationalist waves). I think we should concern ourselves not so much with the pres-ervation of the Jews (Juden<u>tums</u>) or the Jewish nation . . . but of that which was once experienced as the "Kingdom of God."[51]

In short, Taubes aspired to become one of those Jewish thinkers who would contribute to the creation of a new, universalist message—precisely the terms in which he thought of Paul. He wanted to combine the rational and the irrational, to create a myth appropriate to the modern age.[52] He rejected Jewish particularism while hoping to renew the religious core of Judaism—all of which he thought as possible in Israel as anywhere. And he identified the core of Jewishness as the generation of new critical worldviews that would upend existing human relations. All of this was vague, utopian, and steeped in a Buberian vocabulary.

If Taubes had his doubts about the direction of Israeli society or its failure to live up to his ideals—well, he shared that with Simon, Berg-mann, Buber, and Scholem, all of whom lived satisfying lives in Jerusalem, despite their discontents.

Carl Schmitt Viewed from Jerusalem

Another ongoing and unresolved tension for Taubes was his relationship to German thought and culture, and especially to thinkers he admired who had supported the Nazi regime. Most prominent among those were Martin Heidegger and Carl Schmitt, whose work on "political theology" had so deeply impressed him when he was writing his dissertation.

The fact that Heidegger and Schmitt had actively supported a regime that had devoted itself to the mass murder of the Jews was, for Taubes, a conundrum. He was less interested in condemning them (the reaction of most of those around him in Jerusalem) than in understanding how men who were so intellectually penetrating could have made such political choices. For Taubes, Schmitt was not a distant figure, for the two were linked by Taubes's friend, Armin Mohler.

In January 1952, Jacob wrote to Susan that Israel was in an uproar over Prime Minister Ben Gurion's negotiations with the government of West Germany for reparations. "Pictures of concentration camps are shown and one experiences how deep the wound is. I think we'll all have to consider this when we travel on the 'heights' of German philosophy. The deeds of National Socialism are part of the cross of our age, and speak to us as well. I stand without the shadow of an answer—my entire compass is destroyed, for the rift between 'Europe' and my people is a rift that cuts right through me."[53] His thinking about the subject had not changed in the years since he had left Zurich.

Yet that did not keep Taubes from entreating his friend Mohler to send him the latest works by Schmitt, Jünger, and other intellectuals on the German radical right. And just weeks after his writing to Susan about his lack of a compass, Jacob dispatched a letter to Mohler about Schmitt, a missive that he must have suspected would be passed on to Schmitt himself—as indeed it was.[54]

Because he was among the most prominent intellectuals to support the Nazi regime, Schmitt was regarded as beyond the pale of respectable opinion in the mainstream political culture of West Germany. Yet Schmitt was not without influence. In the decades after the founding of the Federal Republic in 1949, Schmitt not only maintained his relationships with leading right-wing German intellectuals of his generation; he also built up a wide-ranging network of intellectual contacts among the younger generation, primarily but by no means exclusively on the intellectual right, and extending well beyond the borders of Germany. These younger men (there were no women) were attracted to Schmitt by the scope of his erudition in history, philosophy, literature, and law; by his talent for suggestive conceptual formulations; and for some at least, by the frisson of contact with an intellectual outlaw. Through participation in seminars with sympathetic colleagues, face-to-face meetings at his home in the village of Plettenberg, and a wide-ranging correspondence, Schmitt labored to rebuild his reputation and extend his influence despite his official disgrace.[55] This was the context in which Schmitt came to read Taubes's letter to Mohler.

Taubes began by declaring that

> Carl Schmitt is the most intellectually powerful figure (along with Heidegger), standing head and shoulders above the scribbling of

other intellectuals. Of that there can be no doubt. . . . That both Carl Schmitt and Martin Heidegger welcomed the National Socialist revolution, indeed 'co-operated,' is still a problem for me that I can't resolve with clichés like base or swinish. Here in front of me is a notice about Schmitt's article "The Führer Protects the Law," (*Deutsche Juristen Zeitung* 1934) [in which Schmitt defended Hitler's murder of some of his political antagonists on the "Night of the Long Knives"] and I have no way of coming to terms with it. Where did the 'seduction' of National Socialism lie? Did the fact that the liberal-humanistic world was out of joint provide sufficient reason to fall into the arms of these lemurs?[56]

Taubes reported that he had recently gotten his hands on the sole copy in Jerusalem of Schmitt's recently published apologia, *On Deliverance from Captivity* (*Ex Captivitate Salus*) (1950), which took the form of reflections written in 1945–47 while Schmitt was imprisoned by the American occupation authorities. While others had characterized the book as a fleeing of responsibility and a failure to acknowledge guilt, Taubes thought it a deeply moving account, which, if it did not clarify all, provided a window into the author's soul. If only Heidegger had had the courage to write something similar, Taubes remarked. Yet having looked at Schmitt's latest book on international law, *The Nomos of the Earth in the International Law of the European Public Law* (*Der Nomos der Erde im Völkerrecht des Jus Publicum Europaeum*) (1950), he criticized Schmitt for failing to confront the issue of the moral and legal ramifications of the Nazi regime: "Should it be left to foreigners to gather material about the concentration camps and gas chambers, or is that not the proper task of those inside Germany who are concerned about it, for once to look directly at what was done in the name of the German *Volk*; and to explain, if possible, what happened and why?"[57]

In the midst of this letter, which was both flattering and admonitory, Taubes recounted a curious anecdote—the significance of which Mohler would magnify. Seeking to develop a constitution for the new state, the Israeli minister of justice (the German-born and -educated Pinchas Rosen, born Felix Rosenblüth), had put in an urgent request to the Hebrew University library for Schmitt's 1928 book *Constitutional Theory* (*Verfassungslehre*). Since the book was in the library's collection housed in the enclave on Mount Scopus, it had to be retrieved by the convoy of soldiers who made the fortnightly trip under the protection of United Nations forces.[58]

As Taubes had anticipated, Mohler sent the letter to Schmitt, along with a cover letter asking Schmitt for his response to this letter from "my rabbi friend in Jerusalem" (*meines Rabbinerfreundes aus Jerusalem*), adding,

"What do you say to the fact that you've become the midwife to the Israeli constitution?" (In the event, as Taubes revealed decades later, the justice minister did not keep the book out for very long: probably just long enough to consult the book's explication of the various meanings of the term "basic law," at a time when the Knesset was adopting the notion of a "Basic Law" that would precede the promulgation of a full-fledged constitution.[59])

Schmitt did not reply to Taubes, though in a letter to Mohler he called Taubes's letter a "quite remarkable, grand document."[60] But Schmitt had copies of the letter made and sent to some thirty-three of his friends and acquaintances.[61] For Schmitt, what seems to have counted was not Taubes's criticisms but the encomium from this impeccably Jewish source. He disseminated Taubes's letter, thinking it would serve to further bolster his damaged reputation. Thus began a relationship that would slowly intensify over the decades to come.

Between Philosophy and Theology

Taubes's deepest aspiration was to try to discover how modern science, philosophy, and theology might be dialectically combined into some new synthesis: to do, in other words, what Hegel had tried to do in the early nineteenth century. In addition, in both his letters and his publications, he was groping with the question of whether one could create a theology premised not on God's presence in the world but on God's absence from it.

The few articles that Taubes published in this period circled around a number of key themes. He continued to be interested in the continuities and discontinuities between Judaism, Christianity, and modern European philosophy. Related to this was the effect of modern historicist consciousness upon religious self-understandings. Then there was the theme of law and its deliberate violation (antinomianism), a theme related, Taubes claimed, to the apocalyptic, eschatological, and messianic trends he had traced in his doctoral dissertation. His articles rarely made a straightforward argument, but circled around the issues that exercised him—a quality that continued to mark his published works and even his letters.

Even when he was living in Jerusalem and studying with Scholem, much of Taubes's intellectual energy was directed toward engaging the philosophy of Heidegger. In a sense, that was unremarkable: many of the intellectuals Jacob admired had been Jewish students of Heidegger— Hans Jonas, Karl Löwith, Leo Strauss, Hannah Arendt, and Herbert Marcuse (whom he had yet to meet, but whose work he had read)—and were themselves engaged in coming to terms with their teacher.[62] But Taubes's engagement with Heidegger was unusual in the context of Jerusalem, less than a decade after the murder of the Jews by the regime that Heidegger had endorsed.

While still in New York at the Jewish Theological Seminary, Taubes published an article in the *Review of Metaphysics*, a new journal of philosophy edited by Susan's undergraduate teacher, Paul Weiss, entitled "Notes on an Ontological Interpretation of Theology." The article was abstruse to the point of obscurity. (It was also something of a pastiche of ideas from a variety of thinkers including Heidegger and Leo Strauss.) He argued that modern philosophy, in the wake of the atheistic Enlightenment, regards its faith in scientific knowledge as capable of making the world intelligible without reference to God. It is therefore based on the premise that "God is not." But the notion that "God is not," Taubes claims, also comports with theology, at least with that strand of (Maimonidean) theology that defined God as entirely different from anything in the world: in that sense, theology agrees with atheism.[63] Theology, Taubes suggested, should build on the notion that God is "nothing." Here he latched onto an obscure assertion by Heidegger that "the nothing" is that which is prior to every thing and every one. Heidegger's ontology (theory of being), Taubes claimed, was a way of treating traditional theological questions "in an exact and neutral way without recourse to myth."[64] This sort of thinking, Taubes claimed, mirrored the medieval idea that God created the world out of nothing (*creatio ex nihilo*) but also out of himself (a kabbalistic idea), so that God himself must in some sense be nothing.[65] This "theological atheism," he concluded, belongs to "the most extreme modes of thinking and existence" where "disbelief and faith coincide."[66] It was part of an attempt, as he wrote Armin Mohler, to make something out of "nothing" (*das Nichts*).[67] The article was far from convincing, evincing more overlapping wordplay than conceptual clarity.[68]

Once in Jerusalem, Taubes began to publish in *Iyyun*, the new Hebrew-language journal of philosophy. In its third volume, published in January 1952, he reviewed a new German philosophical annual, *Symposion: Jahrbuch für Philosophie*, published by Catholic-oriented students of Heidegger in Freiburg, and dedicated to Heidegger on the occasion of his fiftieth birthday. Taubes complained that the conservative contributors to *Symposion* were unwilling to follow the decidedly non-Christian implications of Heidegger's thought. For Heidegger's was a response to a real crisis of Western thought, which historically was intimately bound up with Christianity and with the figure of Jesus. Following Karl Löwith, Taubes contended that Hegel had been the last philosopher who attempted to reconcile philosophy and religion, two realms separated in the generation after him, fragmenting in various directions in the thought of Feuerbach, Marx, and Kierkegaard, and leading to Nietzsche's contention that God is dead. We therefore live in a post-Christian era, Taubes asserted, in which there is an irrevocable gap between philosophy and Christianity. In *Being and Time*, Taubes noted, Heidegger had aimed to eliminate the residues of Christian theology from the realm of ontology, by reinterpreting Christian contents in atheistic terms, such as *Angst* (anxiety). Rather than trying to preserve the status quo, he advised, Heidegger's followers should learn from the master that there are times that require the abandonment of an old tradition and the creation of a new one.[69]

By the end of his stay in Israel, Taubes was less enamored of Heidegger, as evidenced in "The Development of the Ontological Question in Recent German Philosophy," an article written in his final year in Jerusalem and published upon his return to the United States in the *Review of Metaphysics*. The article appeared under the rubric of "Notes and Observations," an indication that, like his earlier article, it was a set of loosely connected observations rather than a coherent argument. Like his earlier article, this one demonstrated a broad knowledge of the history of philosophy (especially late nineteenth- and early twentieth-century German schools) and some detailed knowledge about Heidegger's background and development (such as his debt to neo-Kantianism) that would have been terra incognita to most American readers. But Taubes now characterized Heidegger's notion of the "noughting of nothing" (*das Nichten des Nichts*) as a myth, and "Heidegger's meditation on anxiety" as "a mythical description" of the human "experience of frailty."[70] As we will see, Jacob's growing disenchantment with Heidegger betrayed the influence of Susan upon his own intellectual development.

Faith, Reason, and Historical Understanding—and Spinoza

Jacob Taubes's scholarship reflected the quandaries with which he struggled.

His only substantial publication in Hebrew was a chapter on "Beliefs and Ideas in Nineteenth Century Theology," published in a 1952 collection, *Aspects of Judaism: A Volume of Essays*, a volume dedicated to the memory of Julius Guttmann, comprised of lectures by his colleagues and students.[71] Taubes's Hebrew essay (as well as his earlier review in *Iyyun*) reflected the concerns of the German-Jewish intellectuals of Rehavia with whom he consorted: Bergmann, Simon, Scholem, and Buber. Stylistically, they are striking for combining the translation of philosophy (especially modern German philosophy) into modern Hebrew, but with frequent recourse to tropes drawn from Biblical, Talmudic, and liturgical Hebrew. They flowed from the pen of an academic philosopher steeped in traditional Jewish sources.

Taubes's topic was the struggle within Judaism of faith after the Enlightenment, and he drew upon the work of Löwith, Leo Strauss, Scholem, and Guttmann, while adding interpretations and insights of his own.

He began on a Straussian note: what distinguished the modern Enlightenment from the earlier Hellenistic and medieval enlightenments was that while earlier enlightened philosophers addressed themselves to a select few, the modern Enlightenment aspired to enlighten the masses. The fundamental ideas of the modern Enlightenment were destructive of the principles of faith. He then explored a variety of Jewish responses to that challenge.

It was in this context that Taubes placed the Hasidic master, Nachman of Breslov (1782–1810) (the subject of his friend Joseph Weiss's dissertation). Aspects of Nachman's thought show the penetration of Enlightenment-inspired doubt into faith itself, Taubes contended. Drawing upon Nachman's *Collected Teachings* (*Likkutei Moharan*), Taubes showed how Nachman interprets the doubt deriving from autonomous reason into the language and symbols of the Lurianic Kabbalah. He takes the kabbalistic notion of God's self-imposed withdrawal (*zimzum*), which according to Lurianic Kabbalah makes possible the creation of the world and therefore the existence of evil, and turns it from a cosmological image into a process within man himself. *Zimzum* becomes a divine concealment within human reason, such that doubt about God is part of God's creation. Doubt and heresy are the natural way of human reason. Reason and faith are thus truly irreconcilable—but faith is necessary as an antidote to despair.[72]

Taubes traced the response of the leading theologians of Reform Judaism, such as Abraham Geiger and Zachariah Frankel (the theorist of positive-historical Judaism, later adopted by Conservative Judaism), who insisted that Judaism was a historical and developing religion. Unlike the previous notion of tradition as received through an act of divine revelation, Reform thinkers regarded tradition as a continuous process, in need of renewal.

Another thinker who tried to incorporate historicist understandings into Judaism was Nachman Krochmal (1785–1840), a Galician autodidact and author of *The Guide to the Perplexed of Our Times*, who, Taubes wrote, like Hegel tried to reconcile reason and faith. He developed a historicist account of Judaism that combined elements of Maimonides, Kabbalah, and modern philosophy. Like Hegel, Krochmal tried to transform religious images into conceptual terms. Like Hegel, Krochmal had a dialectical conception of history, but Krochmal preserved the notion of God's law as absolute while stressing that man's *understanding* of that law was relative and subject to historical development.

Taubes then turned to a theme that had only the loosest connection to the nominal subject of his essay, but one that was close to his heart. That was the messianic critique of Law within the Jewish tradition. He pointed to a tension within Judaism, between the notion of the Law as eternal and what Taubes called a messianic/historical claim that the Law would be suspended at the end of days. He noted that Paul used this interpretation to delimit the ongoing validity of halacha, and that this antinomian critique reappeared in later messianic movements in Judaism, as in the case of Nathan of Gaza (the Paul to Sabbatai Zevi's Jesus, as it were). They all claimed that halacha had been valid until the present, but with the coming of redemption, it was no longer in force. This messianic polemic *within* Judaism, Taubes wrote, has a polemical dependence on the Law: that is to say, it defined itself over and against the Law—an inclination evident in Jacob himself. The modern, rationalist critique of Judaism dissolves this dependence: it robs the Law of its validity, but in a manner that no longer understands itself as part of the Jewish tradition.

At the origin of the modern, historicist understanding of the Bible was Spinoza, who, in the seventh chapter of his *Theological-Political Treatise* (1670), "Of the Interpretation of Scripture," set out canons for the interpretation of Biblical texts that remain the hallmark of modern Biblical scholarship. The first of these is the assumption that the Bible is to be treated like any other book, and to be analyzed using the rules of evidence that we bring to any other work written long ago and far away. Rather than reading later concepts, doctrines, and concerns into the text—including our own—we must strive to understand the text on its own terms. That means that we need to master the original language, to understand its grammar, and to grasp its characteristic literary figures of speech. It means that we need to compare the usage of words within the text to determine their meaning. So too, we ought to compare all the pronouncements on any given matter to see whether the text conveys a single understanding, or many, perhaps conflicting views. Attention must be paid to the speaker, his audience, and the occasion for his statement. It means that we ought to look first at internal, textual evidence, and to any reliable external facts, to see what we can determine about the authorship of the work in question. In judging the veracity of the events reported, we ought as nearly as possible to reconstruct the mindset of the author, his cultural assumptions, and even personal psychological dispositions. Last but not least, we should try to reconstruct the history of the text itself, to determine where and how it was redacted and canonized, and whether spurious insertions have been added.

Spinoza occupied a special status in the self-understandings of modern Jews. For some, he was an arch-heretic, having been excommunicated by the Jewish authorities of his native Amsterdam, and having lived thereafter beyond the bounds of the Jewish community. Others saw him as a pioneer of Jewish rationalism or post-Jewish secularism.

Spinoza had a particular place in the Zionist imagination, not only as a radical Jew, but as one who could be claimed as a forerunner of Zionism. That claim, however ill-founded, was based on a few lines of the *Theological-Political Treatise*. There, Spinoza had offered an interpretation of the Law as promulgated by Moses as an eminently *political* code, which had, for a while at least, succeeded in creating a secure and prosperous state for the Jews. Then, after attributing their continuity in the Diaspora to their self-isolation through peculiar rituals (above all, circumcision), Spinoza went on to offer a sort of thought experiment: "Were it not that the fundamental principles of their religion discourages manliness, I would not hesitate to believe that they will one day, given the opportunity—such is the mutability of human affairs—establish once more their independent state, and that God will again choose them."[73] The last phrase was clearly ironic, for Spinoza did not believe in the sort of God who could "choose" anyone.

Nevertheless, this passage was seized upon by some Zionists, including the prime minister of Israel, David Ben-Gurion, as a sort of rationalist prophecy of Jewish national resurgence. In his address to the international Zionist congress in Jerusalem in 1951 (the first such gathering in the State of Israel), Ben-Gurion cited what he regarded as Spinoza's prophecy of a restoration of Jewish sovereignty.[74]

It was therefore an occasion of potential significance when Jacob Taubes was tasked with translating the original Latin text of the *Theological-Political Treatise* into Hebrew. It was part of a project to translate all of Spinoza's works, an effort spearheaded by Ben-Gurion himself, who, with the help of his minister of education, the historian Ben-Zion Dinur, sought out financial support, publishers, and translators for the project.[75] How precisely they hit upon Jacob Taubes for the task of translating what they regarded as Spinoza's most significant work remains uncertain. But there was logic to the choice. Taubes had been teaching a course on early modern philosophy from Descartes to Spinoza.[76] He had the requisite languages, Latin and Hebrew, and a knowledge of the Biblical texts that Spinoza cited with frequency. After leaving Israel, Taubes continued to work on the translation for a while.[77] Writing to a friend, he complained that Spinoza's Latin was wooden and stiff, but that his attitude to the Apostle Paul was praiseworthy.[78]

In the end, the Hebrew translation of the *Theological-Political Treatise* became one of Jacob's many uncompleted projects. (It was ultimately translated by Chaim Wirszubski and published in 1961.[79])

Susan and Jacob: The Pagan versus the Heretic

When Susan first encountered Jacob in New York, she aspired to a career in the theater. Much later, in her autobiographical novel, *Divorcing*, she claimed that it was Jacob who convinced her to pursue a dissertation in philosophy.[80] And, indeed, in the early years of their marriage, Jacob does seem to have tried to mold his young wife—still an undergraduate—in his own intellectual image. He encouraged her to write an honors thesis on "Logos and Mythos" in Heidegger, and then a doctoral dissertation on Gnostic themes in Heidegger's work. At first Susan complied, grateful for Jacob's tutorship, and immersed herself in the texts Jacob recommended, mimicking their abstruse vocabulary. When others in Jerusalem sought to discuss the subject of her research with her, she said that she was not comfortable discussing Heidegger without her husband. To Joseph Agassi, a young philosopher who knew the couple, it seemed that her views on Heidegger were more or less dictated by Jacob.[81] "The 'ideas' I have only pass through me from you and all I have to say in my thesis is what I know through you," she confessed in a letter to her husband.[82] Her later description in *Divorcing* comports with this, but hints at a more dynamic intellectual relationship. "Mostly Ezra [the Jacob figure] spoke for her. When he expressed her view in company, she thought it was just as well he did. She would never express herself in such a way, certainly not as artfully or persuasively as Ezra. . . . When Ezra made statements for her or about her, he put them together from their conversations, her remarks on the books he had her read."[83]

Jacob, for his part, regarded his young bride as a treasure,[84] a prize he had won (or perhaps earned): a woman intelligent, beautiful, and of exquisite sensitivity, whose critical sensibilities matched his own. On the occasion of Susan's twenty-third birthday, he wrote to her, "You were blessed with great gifts of beauty and spirit and most all: you were granted that all your gifts are 'rooted' in the holy order and in the holy chaos and so you are a deeply essential creature. I wish you to grow into both dimensions, into the holy order and into the holy chaos deeper and deeper."[85] His self-appointed role was to guide her deeper into order—and chaos.

They began from divergent but overlapping points of departure. Susan, as we have seen, was raised in a household in which her father, her only resident parent, had abjured Jewish belief and practice. Her knowledge of Judaism as religion or of the Hebrew language was close to nonexistent.[86] Jacob, by contrast, was steeped in Jewish knowledge, already fluent in Hebrew, and was living a life of Jewish ritual observance. But he bridled at the yoke of the Law, and was attracted by the universalism of Christianity. The ramparts of his faith had been sapped by his exposure to the philosophical atheism of Leo Strauss. Susan seems to have had no sense of commitment to the Jewish people as an ethnic community. Jacob had a taken-for-granted sense of belonging. Jacob's language and worldview were deeply rooted in modern German culture, and his key philosophical concerns owed much to Hegel and Heidegger and their (sometimes wayward) successors. Susan was as yet much less formed. Her first language was Hungarian, a culture she had been forced to abandon as a child. She had come of age in the United States, yet had no affinity for the country or for any particular place within it. Both were rootless—and conscious of that fact. Both saw the world as an alienating place.

There are those for whom the absence of God is a fact, accepted with reluctance or with resignation, or proclaimed with defiance or with joy (think of Nietzsche, or Bertrand Russell). For others, the absence of God's presence is felt as a lack, a source of bewilderment or of pain. At times, that is how Jacob and Susan felt. As he put it in a letter written from Jerusalem to Chancellor Finkelstein of JTS, "It seems to me that 'the root question of theology'" is "to forge in the smithy of our soul the syllabus of the human answer to the divine silence."[87] In the early years of their marriage, both Jacob and Susan were attracted to thinkers who suggested—paradoxically, and perhaps absurdly—that recognizing the absence of God from the world was a step toward faith (as in the case of Simone Weil),[88] or that doubt was at the heart of faith (as in the case of Nachman of Breslov). As we've seen, Jacob was fascinated by the Gnostic conception of the world as a fallen realm, and by the echoes of that conception in Heidegger's description of contemporary life as marked by inauthenticity—all of which Jacob conveyed to his young wife.

Though Jacob hailed from a family steeped in religious observance, and Susan from a family devoid of it, they shared a sensitivity to the role of ritual in providing a symbolic structure to human communities. Upon moving to Israel, as a sort of lowest common denominator, they developed if not a religion of their own, then a consciously created cult, comprised of ritual elements and symbols borrowed from various traditions, and meant to reinforce the only community of which they could be sure—their own dyad. In her letters, Susan addresses Jacob as her "priest," "my holy animal, my most trusted one, with whom I, a whorish pagan woman, made my eternal covenant."[89] (As their relationship progressed, she came to address him as "my scheming one, my demonic one."[90]) They composed a document outlining their plans to live a "sacramental way of life."[91] That document has not survived, but there are references scattered through Susan's letters of 1950–51 to various elements of what she called "cult," which included rituals to be performed at night, and before sex, clearly intended to make the sexual act a religious one as well. They included lighting candles ("the serpent's fire"), ritual washing (especially important because of Jacob's tendency to overlook hygiene), and symbols such as the serpent (meant to have a phallic resonance) and the octopus—a Gnostic symbol that adorned some of her letters to Jacob.[92] The idea seems to have been to inaugurate the cult with just the two of them, and then expand it outward to a circle of initiates. A male companion with whom Susan lived for a while in New York City was the first of these; their relationship moved from platonic to "cultic" to sexual, and back.[93] But the "cult" turned out to be a dead end, and was soon abandoned.

While for Jacob Jerusalem provided a vital environment in which he could pursue his scholarly interests and explore his own religious and philosophical dilemmas, Susan's experience there was one of alienation. That was in part because of her lack of knowledge of Hebrew and of Judaism, in part because of her lack of any emotional attachment to a sense of Jewish peoplehood. Her disaffection was exacerbated by material difficulties and disappointments, beginning with housing. Precisely what happened remains unclear. But it seems that the Taubeses first had a conflict with their landlords in Talpiot, perhaps because of a lack of adequate heating.[94] Their greatest trauma revolved around their attempt to establish a foothold in Jerusalem. Here too, the details are sketchy, but it is clear that they invested most of their savings—some $1,000—in buying a house, only to discover from the Custodian of Abandoned Properties that the seller's ownership rights were legally dubious, so that Susan and Jacob lost their money as well as their hope of owning a home.[95] In addition, they were ensnared in a legal case (probably involving the disputed property). Jacob was called as a witness, and he urged Susan to put off her return to Jerusalem until after the hearing, to spare her being called as well.[96] This exposure to financial corruption seems to have shaken them both, reminding Jacob of how far life in Jerusalem was from holiness, and intensifying Susan's estrangement from the country.

When she returned to New York City in the fall of 1950, Susan lived briefly with her mother (with whom she had a strained relationship), partly with Jacob's former lover, Gerda Seligsohn, with whom she developed a close friendship, and for a time with the above-mentioned male companion. In addition to writing her thesis, she conferred with Saul Lieberman, Louis Finkelstein, and other senior acquaintances about where Jacob might find a job in the United States. One of her priorities was for the stateless Jacob to acquire American citizenship, and thus an American passport.[97]

She consulted with Susan Langer, a philosopher at Columbia University, about the possibility of writing a thesis there. Susan outlined her ideas for a dissertation about an ontological approach to myth and to logos, and how they emerged out of Being. But for Langer (as for most academic philosophers in the English-speaking world at that time), "Being" was "an empty, mystical, and 'literary' term" and not a fit subject for philosophy. Langer advised Susan that she was no philosopher and should turn her attention to other pursuits.[98] Susan and Jacob did indeed live much of their mental lives in a world of ill-defined terms—*Geist*, Being, Nothingness—terms alien to those schooled in Anglo-American analytic or empiricist philosophy. But such terms remained resonant to those steeped in continental European philosophy, which preserved the legacy of religious longings, the expressions of which were inevitably ill-defined.

In March 1951, Susan returned to Jerusalem to work on her honors thesis, living in the Greek Colony with Jacob in two rooms within a home that had been divided up into small rental units.[99] By then, Susan had begun to show signs of revolt against Jacob's tutelage, which was starting to feel like an assertion of his superiority.[100] At the end of the year, she went to Paris, in part "because I resented and revolted against the Israeli-decision" (that is, Jacob's decision to remain in Israel),[101] in part to pursue her philosophical interests at the Sorbonne. When not in lectures or studying, she attended the theater, often several times a week. She met frequently with Jacob's old friend, Lucien Goldmann, who was at work on his book on Pascal, which combined Marxist and existentialist lines of analysis. She consorted and consulted with a range of thinkers, from professors of philosophy (Jean Wahl, Eric Weil) to Albert Camus, whose recently published book, *L'homme révolté* (*The Rebel*), affected her deeply, as did her reading of Nietzsche. She wrote a review of Camus's book, which, translated into Hebrew, was published by Bergmann in the journal *Iyyun*.[102] The upshot, for Susan, was a deepening critique of both Judaism and Christianity. By the spring of 1952, Susan was increasingly disillusioned with Heidegger and skeptical of the fruitfulness of tracing Gnostic motifs in his work.[103]

As her interest in Heidegger waned, her reading of Simone Weil's *L'enracinement* (1949) (translated as *The Need for Roots*) increased her interest in that French thinker. Influenced by Gnosticism, Weil had developed a radical critique of modern life.[104] Born into a Jewish family, Weil had embraced Catholicism, but remained unwilling to formally convert because she regarded the Church as corrupted by its Jewish elements (a decidedly Gnostic critique). Weil's nightmarish view of the world resonated with Susan's own. "The world looks like a more or less well organized concentration camp, where nobody is sure who are the rulers, or who are the privileged," she wrote to Jacob.[105] Interest in Weil was on the rise in France, and the philosopher Jean Wahl suggested that Susan shift the topic of her thesis from Heidegger to Weil,[106] advice that she was eventually to follow.

Susan's letters to Jacob were for the most part highly cerebral, though intermixed with expressions of eroticism and passion. They included frequent references to the fact that she was almost constantly assailed by propositions from men, who importuned her for sex or with marriage proposals—a reminder to Jacob of her desirability.[107] Finally she concluded that this too had its costs. "I am anxious to leave Paris," she wrote. "Life is becoming unbearable; I don't know anybody who is not in love with me with the result that I don't have a single friend, only scenes and complications. I am not a playful woman and I suffer."[108]

Susan's letters alternated between encouragement of Jacob and attestations to his brilliance on the one hand, with anxiety about Jacob's nonproductive style of work on the other. She complained that rather than reading deeply in texts and analyzing them, he was given to "dreaming up things on the basis of what 'comes to one's ear' about Plato-Kant."[109] As she worked on translating his dense article on "The Development of the Ontological Question in Recent German Philosophy" from German into English, she expressed occasional concern about his tendency to get lost in abstractions. She seems to have suspected that his work habits combined with his propensity for vague and abstract formulations were leading to a dead end.

For his part, by early 1952, Jacob was wracked with anxiety about his difficulty in applying himself and his lack of productivity. Paul's statement in Romans 7:19, "The good that I will, I do not do," resonated deeply with him.[110] On the eve of Passover (which Jacob spent in Jerusalem, and Susan with Jacob's family in Zurich), it was clear to him that his attempt to formulate a "transcendental ontology" that would combine religion and philosophy was going nowhere.[111] While he had aspired, in Susan's words, "to be the Hegel of the twentieth century," he was hardly up to the task.[112]

Underlying and overlaying these stresses were the increasing conflicts between Susan and Jacob, conflicts about religion, belonging, and how they were to live their lives together. At the center of these were the ever more severe conflicts about Judaism, and Jacob's aspiration to be the new Paul.

Traditionally, Judaism has been both a religion and an ethnicity, based on religious belief or practice as well as a shared sense of peoplehood. Zionism insisted that under modern conditions, Jewish continuity (physical and spiritual) was best served by the creation of a sovereign Jewish national state. Susan was opposed to all of these. In common with many universalistic intellectuals, she was disdainful of nationalism, and in common with Christian understandings, she regarded the whole notion of a particularist faith as retrograde. Jacob's identification with the past and future of the Jewish people, and his worries about the Jewish state, struck her as fundamentally irrelevant. "The center of the 'crisis' is not in the 'Jewish problem,'" she wrote, "the question is not posed, nor can it be solved within Judaism. Retreat into the clan, into national enthusiasm, preoccupation with national problems, is an evasion, because we were not only the 'victims' but the accomplices as well of European history." Living in Israel struck her as no more than "tribalism,"[113] and Jacob's concern for Judaism and the fate of the Jews as "belly-button-worship."[114] She was particularly fearful of the consequences of combining religious and national identity: "The existence of the Jewish state may improve the status of the Jews all over the world, personally it makes me feel ill at ease. Unless, the state means the renunciation of the jew's religious pretensions as a group. But it doesn't mean that."[115] As for Zionism: "The experiment may succeed, but can the people worship any other god than the one that created them as a people, can they do otherwise than to deify their success? They will be like all the other peoples, only more proud and pretentious."[116] That was a fear shared by Zionists such as Ernst Simon and Martin Buber—but for them, unlike for Susan, the potential hazards of the Zionist project did not negate that project itself.

When Susan married Jacob and decided to explore Judaism, she did so largely by reading the Bible, in English, since she had almost no knowledge of Hebrew. Susan's image of Judaism was drawn from that reading, as filtered through interpreters such as Simone Weil. Thus she characterized Judaism as the worship of a "tyrant god" or a "Moloch-God."[117]

Jacob repeatedly tried to explain to Susan the meaning and value of Jewish practices, but for her, their virtues were negated by what she saw as Judaism's "glorification of the jewish people and its condemnation of others."[118] Jewish philosophers with whom she discussed her views, including Hugo Bergmann in Jerusalem and Emmanuel Levinas in Paris, told her that she was ignorant about Judaism and overlooked its more universal elements.[119] Jacob told her that as an outsider to Judaism she misunderstood its laws as nothing more than arbitrary decrees. A cult cannot be created by an act of will, he contended, and religious practice made most sense within a historical religion.[120] Susan, by contrast, was only interested in a form of spirituality unlinked to history, to revelation, or to any particular historical group.[121] When Jacob argued the need for connection to a people and to its past, she rejected the claims of historical fidelity, which, she thought, destroys the possibility of a new beginning. "Faithfulness to the memory of the dead" was no basis of identity, she responded.[122]

Purporting to speak for both of them, Susan told Goldmann that "although we know that a life without dedication is dust, the sheer nostalgia for self-sacrifice without a deep conviction is not a sufficient reason for throwing one's self in the fire of any cause, marxism, zionism, catholicism."[123] In short, she was in search of a cause to which to commit herself, but none seemed compelling.

Over time, Susan convinced Jacob—or rather, half-convinced him. Despite his doubts about the accuracy of what he called her "pagan antisemitism" (*paganischen Antisemitismus*),[124] by April 1952 he conceded that his obligations to the Jewish people were limited, and that perhaps he was too attracted by the romanticism of the emphasis on blood, soil, language, and homeland (*Blut, Boden, Sprache, Heimat*) characteristic of both German culture and Zionism.[125] Yet in his very next letter he declared that the State of Israel was worth defending, and that were it up to him, he'd be willing to stay on in Jerusalem.[126]

Susan, however, was more adamant than ever: she insisted not only that Jacob leave Israel, but that she did not want Judaism to play a role in their home.[127] "Whatever sacrifice it entails we must remain in the 'avant-garde' and not fall back into 'jewish community projects' . . . I warn you: the moment there is a danger of 'backsliding' I 'convert': if we are looking for comfort and integration, I am more comfortable and integrated in the protestant community. But the whole thing is too nauseating. A new world cannot be created without sacrifice. The jewish protest against Christianity is not enough."[128]

Since Susan rejected any historically based conception of religion and lacked a sense of attachment to either historical Judaism or Christianity, the relationship between the two faiths was of no great interest to her. Thus, she did not share Jacob's interests in the nexus between Judaism and Christianity, or in Paul as the founder of a more antinomian and more universal form of Judaism. Since she did not believe in the possibility of revealed law, the Pauline revolt against the law was of no interest to her either.[129] Jacob was haunted by the problem of sin (*Schuld*): but since Susan did not accept the theological premise of sin, she saw it as a pseudoproblem.[130]

In a striking formulation, she characterized Paul's apostolate as "a plan for 'international religion'—by making the whole world a little jewish and the jews a little less jewish."[131] She found Paul's obsession with "the law" (and Jacob's) to be infantile and a distraction from the real world: "Paul (I mean all Pauls) was too engrossed in masturbation to see the wonder of the phallus. The world of the 'law' is also an infantile world. It is for the child that every object is associated with a 'may and may not.' The adult comes directly in contact with things."[132] In short, she found Paul "a successful charlatan."[133] And the more she read, the more critical she was of Jacob's fascination with eschatology. "The 'eschatologischer Geist' [eschatological spirit] in all its forms is a sickness of the spirit, a puerility, a not-coming-to-terms with human life such as it is."[134]

Jacob had come to regard himself as a theological heretic,[135] what in the Jewish tradition is known as an apikores. As a waggish scholar has noted, "The *apikores* is always leaving."[136] That is to say, his very identity as a heretic links him inextricably to the tradition against which he defines himself. So, too, the antinomian[137]—another term that Jacob used to characterize himself—who is largely defined by the law he defies. But Susan was something quite different: a genuine pagan. To an outsider, the distance between a self-defined antinomian heretic and a pagan might not seem large. But for Jacob and Susan, it was vast.

Tensions with Scholem

The ultimate breach between Scholem and Taubes was overdetermined. That is to say, it was a product of many factors. As we've seen, in his letters to Scholem from New York, Taubes had portrayed himself as Scholem's disciple (though not Scholem's alone), and it was Scholem who arranged with Saul Lieberman to have JTS pay for Taubes to pursue further studies at the Hebrew University. When Taubes moved to Jerusalem, Scholem was at first pleased, writing to Finkelstein that Taubes showed signs of promise (*simanai beracha*), and that he hoped Taubes would write a serious piece of scholarship on the border of Kabbalah and philosophy.[138] In June 1951, a year and a half after Jacob had arrived, Scholem wrote again to Finkelstein, with the positive news that Scholem and his colleagues at the University had decided to award Jacob with a Warburg Fellowship for the next two years, a sign of their confidence and hopes for the young scholar. "We've all found that he is greatly talented and has a lot to contribute to scholarship if he can focus seriously on his work. I haven't been satisfied in this regard with the progress of the work he is supposed to be dealing with. But on the other hand, I can't ignore the fact that this is a special young man . . . and hence we feel our responsibility for his development."[139] Finkelstein was pleased, and informed Scholem that JTS had decided to provide Taubes with support for the coming year.

But over time, Scholem became ever more skeptical and then downright disenchanted. There had been evidence of tension in February 1951, when Taubes gave a lecture at the Philosophical Society, which was attended by the Olympians of the Hebrew University, with Bergmann in the chair. Scholem regarded Taubes as his student and expected him to speak on a subject related to Scholem's own scholarly interests. Instead, Taubes spoke on "Heidegger and The Question," at a time when Heidegger's erstwhile support of Hitler made discussion of his work unpopular in Jerusalem. The talk was followed by questions, one of which was from a young graduate student, Taubes's friend (and Buber's son-in-law), Joseph (Joshka) Agassi. Bergmann took all the questions and comments, many of them skeptical, then turned to Taubes for the traditional response. Taubes was very theatrical: he took his time, rose, and said, "I've heard a lot of garbage here tonight, but the one good question was from Joshka," which elicited a roar of laughter. But at the end of the evening, Scholem was appalled and began to remonstrate openly with Taubes about his choice of topic. Writing to Susan, Jacob lamented that Scholem and others in the audience had not understood his lecture. Susan wondered whether it was too "abstract." (For his part, Agassi, a philosopher of science, regarded the lecture as "pretentious rubbish."[140])

Scholem's greatest source of dissatisfaction with Taubes, however, was the younger man's lack of scholarly productivity, which Scholem attributed to his lack of personal and intellectual self-discipline. As Scholem later explained to a mutual friend, "Gescheit sind wir alle; Sitzleder muß man haben"—"We're all smart, but there's no substitute for scholarly endurance"—the discipline to stay seated, pour over texts, and write.[141] That, indeed, was Jacob's Achilles Heel, as many who knew him were to testify throughout his life. Susan's letters to Jacob were studded with admonitions to apply himself, and Susan even wrote to Scholem urging him to "please make Jacob work."[142] But no one could get Jacob to engage in systematic research and writing. Jacob was not lacking in ideas—if anything, he had too many of them. But most of those ideas found expression in lectures, in conversation, and in his letters. Those that made it into publishable articles were often stimulating, but rarely fleshed out coherently and systematically.

Scholem took pleasure in sitting in his study and working his way through difficult texts (often in manuscript), hour after hour, day after day, year after year. He was an industrious, meticulous, and exacting scholar.[143] Though he had rebelled against his bourgeois, German origins, Scholem's style of life was in many respects Prussian and proper. Just as Scholem's scholarship reflected his personality, Jacob's flights of speculation and lack of disciplined scholarship reflected his. In that respect, the two were polar opposites. And the contrast in their personalities extended further. Scholem's scholarship on Kabbalah and Sabbatianism revealed a fascination with the transgressive and the erotic—but for Scholem, eroticism and transgression were matters of the head, the subject of scholarly inquiry. Neither his marriage nor his relationships were markedly erotic. (After his death, his wife would confess that Scholem's only great love had been his friend, Walter Benjamin.[144])

Jacob and Susan Taubes, by contrast, were bohemian, certainly by the standards of their day. Susan wore bareback dresses that were jarring in the staid milieu of Jerusalem in the era of austerity.[145] Scholem was scandalized by aspects of their behavior. He claimed, for example, that Susan had walked around Jerusalem in a trench coat, with nothing underneath. And he characterized Jacob's erotic adventurism as "moral insanity."[146]

Joseph Weiss and the Break with Scholem

It was the triangular relations between Taubes, Scholem, and Joseph Weiss that led to the traumatic sundering of the connection between Taubes and Scholem.

Weiss was among Scholem's closest students.[147] Born in Hungary in 1918 to a Neologue (the Hungarian variety of Liberal Judaism) family, he

had attended the Budapest rabbinical seminary before coming to Jerusalem in 1940. At Hebrew University, he studied Jewish history, philosophy,
and Kabbalah, and worked as an assistant to Scholem. His interests ran
to Gnosticism and its influence on Kabbalah, and to the links between
Sabbatianism and the early history of Hasidism.[148] He was more interested than Scholem in the psychological basis of mysticism, and like Jacob
Taubes, was drawn to existentialist thought, especially that of Kierkegaard.
In 1947, Joseph married Miriam, herself a student of Jewish philosophy
and Kabbalah at Hebrew University, and the next year he was awarded the
university's Warburg Fellowship. That fellowship was intended to allow
him to concentrate on his doctoral thesis, on the dialectics of faith and
doubt in the thought of Nachman of Breslov. Like Nachman, Weiss was
a conflicted soul: he passed through periods of Jewish ritual observance
and nonobservance; he was critical of Orthodoxy, but at the same time
had a strong sympathy for the ultra-Orthodox and anti-Zionist *Neturei
Karta*—all propensities that Taubes would share.[149] Weiss was psychologically troubled, and given to paranoia.

Scholem had put Taubes into contact with Weiss, and upon Jacob's
arrival in Jerusalem, their epistolary relationship soon developed into a
friendship, or rather into a complex of relationships between the Taubeses
and the Weisses. Joseph Weiss and Susan Taubes were native Hungarian
speakers and conversed in that tongue. Miriam's first language was Polish,
which Jacob knew from his grandparents. When Susan left Jerusalem for
New York in September 1950J, Jacob moved in briefly with the Weisses.[150]
It was at that point, probably, that Jacob and Miriam Weiss developed a
relationship that, unbeknownst to Joseph, went beyond the platonic.[151]

The pressures of life in Jerusalem—and of living in Scholem's shadow—
led Weiss to search for opportunities abroad. In November 1950, in the closing stages of completing his dissertation, and after a bitter argument with
Scholem, Joseph and Miriam left abruptly for Leeds in England (where
he took a job as a teacher in a Hebrew school) without talking to Scholem.
Weiss left a note for his teacher, explaining that for psychological reasons
he had to leave, but that he intended to return at the end of the year to
make any changes to the dissertation that Scholem thought necessary.[152]

Hearing nothing from Scholem for several months, Weiss was wracked
with self-doubt. But by March 13, 1951, having learned secondhand that
Scholem had nominated him for a fellowship at the Jewish Theological
Seminary in New York, he felt more self-assured, and planned to return
to Jerusalem shortly.[153] A week later, some four months after his sudden departure from Jerusalem, during which he had heard nothing from
Scholem, Weiss wrote to his advisor asking plaintively whether Scholem

had yet had an opportunity to read his dissertation.[154] Scholem responded almost immediately, in a letter in which he informed Weiss that while the first three chapters of the dissertation were acceptable (though in need of revision), the final, crowning chapter, was not. According to Scholem, that chapter, "The Paradoxical Essence of Faith," which combined historical with philosophical categories drawn from Kierkegaard and Heidegger, was based in part on faulty scholarship and on rampant speculation, or what he called "the pursuit of fantastic nonsense" (*ridifah acharai divrai hevel fantastiyim*). The problems were greater than could be handled through correspondence, Scholem wrote, and unless Weiss was prepared to return to Jerusalem to review the sources and make the necessary corrections, Scholem saw no alternative but to return Weiss's work to him.[155]

Two months later, on June 23, 1951, Scholem received a letter from Yonina Gerber Talmon, a young Israeli sociologist who was studying in Leeds together with her husband, Shmaryahu Talmon, a scholar of the Bible. As the Talmons and the Weisses were the only Israelis in Leeds, Joseph Weiss and Shmaryahu Talmon soon became acquainted. Since Yonina was on good terms with Scholem, it was she who wrote to him with some distressing news.[156]

Someone in Jerusalem, Talmon reported, had sent a letter to Weiss saying that Scholem had found signs of insanity in Joseph's dissertation and washed his hands of him. That had set off a bout of depression in both Joseph and Miriam. Miriam showed signs of insanity, and, afraid she would commit suicide, Joseph had her hospitalized: she had received insulin and shock therapy, but neither were effective, and she was confined to bed. Joseph was deeply depressed, and told Shmaryahu repeatedly that Scholem's lack of faith in him was undermining the very foundations of his existence. Yonina suggested to Scholem that a strong recommendation from Scholem of Weiss for a position as a lecturer at the University of Leeds for the next academic year might help restore Weiss's mental equilibrium.[157] In all of this there was not yet a mention of Jacob Taubes.

In late June, Jacob and Susan returned to the United States and spent the summer in Rochester, with plans for Jacob to return to Jerusalem in the fall. Jacob opened a registered letter from Scholem that sent him into a panic:

28 Abarbanel Road, Jerusalem, October 7, 1951
Dear Herr Dr. Taubes,

I beg your forgiveness for writing a letter so critical to our relationship shortly before your return and, so to speak, out of the blue. But with great pain and regret I am compelled by my own conscience to do so. I would have written sooner had the information I am about to convey been known to me earlier.

Not long ago a certain Mr. Talmon, a graduate of our university, returned from Leeds in England. Prior to his stay there, he never heard your name and had never met you. He spent last year as a lecturer at the University of Leeds. I learned from him that in late winter or early spring he read a number of your letters to Josef Weiss, which were shown to him by Weiss. Mr. Talmon knew nothing about your relationship to Weiss or about mine to you, but was most shocked by the letters' contents. I was all the more dismayed to learn two things from his account.

First, you revealed things that you and I had said to each other in the strictest confidence, even though you made all kinds of declarations that you would pass nothing on. Apparently, you conveyed them in writing to Mr. Weiss, the person in the world they were least intended for. To my great horror, Mr. Talmon cited from your letters statements concerning Weiss himself as well as certain parts of his dissertation—things I had said to you during an evening conversation which I allowed myself to get dragged into, and things I now regret (for instance, that I'd learned Weiss was undergoing psychoanalytic treatment and that I claimed to have found signs of mental illness in the last sections of his dissertation).

Second, you repeatedly counseled him in your letters to avoid contacting me and to avoid writing to anyone in Jerusalem, least of all to me (because, you said, his prospects here are now hopeless, and because I persecute him, etc.), despite the fact that after various inquiries you knew I had not written to Weiss after his nighttime departure because I was waiting to see if he would get in touch with me—as should be expected, given the distressing way in which he unfortunately left the country. I can only attribute it to the active intervention of Mr. Talmon and his wife that Weiss, notwithstanding all of your advice, finally got in touch with me.

While I could perhaps somehow explain the second point as a misunderstanding which, however difficult to explain, does not constitute a breach of confidence, the first point has profoundly hurt me. Of course, I am ready and duty-bound to hear your explanation, if you have one. Tell me: How can you imagine any kind of continued relationship with me after such an extreme breach of trust? Given Mr. Talmon's all too persuasive account concerning the content of your letters, I have to assume that an indiscretion actually occurred. If you indeed committed a breach of trust—and I write after discussing it with professor Bergmann and with his full knowledge—you should anticipate what is for me the most severe outcome: namely, the need for me to sever all contact with you. For without trust my relationship with you cannot continue, and this case has shown that the absolutely necessary condition of personal trust is lacking. For you, there are no less severe consequences. Technically, of course, you can return and deliver your lectures as a research fellow without continuing to regard yourself as one of my students. In this case I would ask you to cease attending my seminars. But you should think about whether, *rebus sic stantibus* [things not having substantially changed], it wouldn't be better to reconsider both your return here and your stay in America. Perhaps it would be wiser for you not to return, but instead use the help your father-in-law would surely give you and build yourself an academic career over there. . . . [158]

Should you believe that the circumstances are not such that you could convince me that my assumptions are in error—namely the fact of your breach of my trust—my advice to you (and Bergmann agrees with me on this) would be that it would be better not to return [to Jerusalem]. For however extraordinary I have regarded your intellectual potential, I'm convinced that nothing good can come from an association in which the moral impetus would be so glaringly lacking.

Expressing once again my regret that I have had to write this letter, I wish you and your wife a good year and a good life.

Yours truly,
G. Scholem

Jacob responded immediately, in distress. He had not broken Scholem's trust, he wrote to Scholem. His goal had been to spare Weiss from more errors. The information he provided to Weiss about Scholem's judgments were conveyed only after they had become public knowledge in the circle of Scholem's students. He had told Weiss not to write to Scholem only at the moment of Scholem's greatest anger at his student, and the moment that anger subsided he had advised Weiss to write to Scholem forthwith. He had found himself caught between his deep regard for both Scholem and Weiss.[159]

Shortly thereafter Jacob received a letter from Hugo Bergmann, who advised him that if he wanted to return to Jerusalem, he had two alternatives: he could come back and try to convince Scholem that the problem was a misunderstanding, or he could concede Scholem's point and ask for forgiveness.[160] Jacob did so almost immediately. In a second letter, written a week after the first, he begged Scholem for forgiveness and reconciliation. "I can only say: mea culpa, truly mea maxima culpa and for me it will be an ever-open wound that will live on and on. Whatever you decide: your disappointment is my greatest humiliation."[161] In a letter to Bergmann, Taubes wrote that if Bergmann and Scholem were to see reconciliation as impossible, Susan would return to Jerusalem to close down their household. Perhaps the Warburg fellowship for 1952–53 could be paid to him in Rochester, he suggested. The alternative—depending once again on Susan's father for financial support—would make them "lose all self-respect."[162]

Scholem had many reasons to be disappointed with his erstwhile protégé. Jacob seemed to have turned from Jewish scholarship to general philosophy. He showed no signs of scholarly productivity. The unfortunate events around Joseph Weiss, and what Scholem saw as a breach of trust revealing a deeply flawed character, thus served more as the straw that broke the camel's back of their relationship, rather than its ultimate cause.

In the event, Jacob did return to Jerusalem—despite Susan's urging that he not do so[163]—where he taught during the first semester of 1951–52. His decision to leave Jerusalem was determined not by Scholem, but by Susan.

Despite the threats in his letter to Taubes, Scholem did not break off relations entirely. When Taubes returned to Jerusalem, he seems to have attended Scholem's seminar on Kabbalah.[164] But relations were strained and never healed while Jacob was in Jerusalem.[165]

In the spring of 1952, Taubes decided that he would return to the United States to try his hand in the academic world there. He made his decision despite the fact that he was promised a continuation of his fellowship if he remained in Jerusalem, and was informed he could continue to lecture in the Department of Philosophy. He told Bergmann that the material hardships of living in Jerusalem had put a strain on his marriage to Susan, and that the experience of living in Israel had sapped their faith. But while Jacob felt that he had found a homeland but no house, Susan had found neither a house nor a homeland.[166] He told friends and family that were it not for Susan, he would have remained in Jerusalem.[167]

In March 1952, Taubes asked Hebrew University for permission to be absent during 1952–53 in order to return to the United States for a year, and suggested faculty members who could take over his courses.[168] In mid-March, the executive vice-president of the university, Werner Senator, met separately with Taubes and with Scholem. Taubes expressed his desire to remain in Jerusalem, but told Senator that Susan's willingness was uncertain, and that much would depend on whether the university would help them to acquire an apartment. For its part, Senator noted in a memo on the topic, the faculty was uncertain about whether or not to offer Taubes a permanent post in the Department of Philosophy, as it was "not clear whether he will develop into a successful scholar."[169] Bergmann hoped that he would stay on. Scholem, by contrast, was disappointed with Taubes. He was prepared to pause the Warburg Fellowship while Taubes was abroad, but not to give it to him if he left the country.[170]

Scholem was relieved by Taubes's departure. "After 2 ½ years of observing him close up, I am unfortunately deeply disappointed with Taubes," he wrote to Leo Strauss. "He makes use of his undoubtedly great talents to engage in philosophical games that I regard as wholly unserious, rather than working with self-discipline and self-renunciation. [The result is] Rhapsodies on themes of others and hugely pretentious twaddle, lacking solidity. I haven't been able to change this young man."[171]

Jacob tried to keep open the possibility of reconciliation. Writing to Scholem from Rochester in September 1952, on the eve of the Jewish New Year, he noted that the past year had been one of anger and suffering (*Zorn und Leid*), and he lamented Scholem's unwillingness to put the "incident" behind them. He reiterated his apology. If only Scholem would forgive him and reconcile, it would be a huge relief to him.[172] But Scholem would have none of it. "Schluss!!!" he wrote on the margin of the letter—an end to this. And later, presumably when he put his correspondence in order for future scholars, he wrote, in Hebrew, "I saw no reason to respond to this letter."

It is said that time heals. But not, as we will see, for Scholem when it came to Taubes. And not for Taubes, when it came to Scholem.

European Interlude

En route from Israel to the United States, Jacob met up with Susan in Europe. They spent some weeks in Paris, where Jacob held conversations with a colorful bouquet of intellectuals, including Ernst Jünger, the poet W. H. Auden, and the Catholic theologian, Jacques Maritain (a convert from Protestantism), and his wife, Räisa (a convert from Judaism).[173]

First, though, Jacob returned briefly to Zurich, to see his family. While there, he gave a public lecture on "The Religious Situation in Israel." In the audience was Rudolf Zipkes, a Jewish lawyer and civil servant in Zurich, who had known Taubes since he was a teenager, and who had the extraordinary habit of maintaining a daily diary for over half a century. He noted that Taubes "respects the *Neturei Karta*, who radically reject the state, as well as the Marxists, who are atheistic socialists, though not beholden to Russia. . . . The Orthodox he demonizes. . . . He hates the Orthodox. His hatred sharpens his perception." As for Jacob's persona, Zipkes observed, "He has a fascinating way of presenting himself, is a fine speaker and debater, though there are elements of conceit, refinement, and pretension." Zipkes wondered what would become of Taubes. Would he devote himself to vanquishing Orthodoxy? Or would he embrace some new orthodoxy, as a communist, or a Catholic, or an Agudist, espousing the *Neturei Karta* position? Or would his propensity to stand above the fray and negate all existing positions win out?[174]

Jacob did not know either.

CHAPTER SEVEN

Making It? 1952–56

IN THE YEARS from 1952 to 1956, Taubes struggled to establish himself professionally. He published articles and reviews in both specialized professional journals and magazines associated with the "New York intellectuals" and oriented to a broadly educated audience. He held lectureships and visiting positions at two of the most prestigious universities in the United States, Harvard and Princeton. He expanded the range of his academic contacts, especially among scholars who were refugees from Germany. He delved for the first time into the world of commercial publishing, by editing a series for the Beacon Press. And throughout, he exhibited the traits that marked him as charismatic and brilliant, but also unreliable and even treacherous. In the end, after years of what he called a gypsy life, he landed a more permanent perch at Columbia University.

Rochester

During the spring of 1952, when Susan was still in Europe and her husband in Jerusalem, Susan's letters to Jacob expressed ever greater anguish and despair. She urged Jacob to join her as soon as possible: "I need you terribly, and each day is an agony,"[1] she wrote. "My soul is full of noise, come to me and silence the voices."[2] By the time they reached London in August, Susan seemed suicidal. The couple were en route to live in her father's house in Rochester, without a job and without resources beyond what Dr. Feldmann would provide. Jacob had a solution to Susan's suicidal gloom: a baby to root her in life. So it was that their first child was conceived.[3] Born in May 1953, they named him Ethan Josiah—his middle name in honor of the Josiah Royce fellowship that Susan had just received from Radcliffe College to do graduate work at Harvard.[4] Susan renamed

FIGURE 7.1. Jacob with his son, Ethan, Rochester, 1953. (Ethan and Tania Taubes Collection.)

herself, by taking on the middle name "Anima"—the Latin word for soul, a term with vaguely mythic or Gnostic connotations.

Jacob and Susan sent out a formal announcement of their baby's birth, and Salo Baron (who would figure in Jacob's future) responded by sending the gift of a Bible.[5] Though Jacob wrote to numerous correspondents expressing his pride in his new son, it was indicative of his approach to his parental obligations that he left a few weeks after the birth for a trip to the University of Chicago, where he visited with Leo Strauss.

While Strauss's students in Chicago reflected upon the political functions of religion, they were not inclined to investigate actual religious experience in the neighborhoods around their university. Taubes, by contrast, was religiously adept: he had an interest in, taste for, and ability to empathize with a wide range of religious experience. He provided the Straussians with a novel encounter when he suggested that they attend a Sunday service at a local African-American church. The rollicking prayers were followed by a passing of the hat, into which the congregants dropped their contributions. "This we have to take lessons from!" Jacob remarked.[6] He also took the occasion to meet another scholar from central Europe, the liberal economist and philosopher Friedrich Hayek,[7] and tucked away in his mind information about Hayek's current interests in the philosophy of science that he would make use of two decades later.

Between his return from Jerusalem and his trip to Chicago, without a job or source of income, and stuck in the intellectual backwater of Rochester, New York, Jacob did something he was otherwise disinclined to do: he wrote articles for publication, in an attempt to establish an academic track record.

He also hoped to publish his dissertation, *Abendländische Eschatologie*, in English. He procured a translation in Rochester from the son of a cantor of German origin.[8] But the translation—obviously done by someone with no inkling of the subject matter—was so poor as to be unreadable. Though in the years that followed Taubes was to claim that an English language translation was in the works, that remained a pipe dream.

Analyst and Critic of Contemporary Christian Theology

During his year in Rochester, Taubes wrote reviews for academic journals, such as *Philosophy and Phenomenological Research* and *Ethics*, that showcased the range of his learning.[9] He published several more substantial pieces on religious topics, which not only demonstrated his erudition but exhibited real insight. Most of these dealt with the history of Christianity, and especially modern German Protestant theology. But their larger topic was the conditions that stood in the way of developing a plausible theology in the present. Since their arguments are closely related, it makes sense to treat these articles as a group.

Why, Taubes asked, does theology—in the sense of systematic exposition of the nature of God and religious doctrine—exist at all? It is because a change in circumstances and consciousness has rendered the central doctrines, symbols, and myths of a faith less plausible. Much of modern theology was an attempt to make those doctrines, symbols, and myths plausible once again. But there were major stumbling blocks to any such enterprise.

Theology, Taubes posited, arises out of religious crisis, when the "mythical" symbols in canonical texts that express a human encounter with the divine lose their plausibility in their original form.[10] "The hour of theology is come when a mythical configuration breaks down and its symbols that are congealed into a canon come into conflict with a new stage of man's consciousness. When the symbols coined to express man's encounter with the divine at a unique moment of history no longer coincide with his experience, theology tries to interpret the original symbols in order to integrate them within the context of the new situation: what was present in the myth is then only 're-presented' in the theological interpretation." Yet the result of this reinterpretation is paradoxical. For on the one hand, the original symbols are preserved by being reinterpreted. But on the other hand, the reinterpretation means that the original symbols are understood in a new way, befitting the changed stage of consciousness. Then, as culture and consciousness change again, the existing interpretation is once again experienced as inadequate, creating a demand for a *new* theological reinterpretation of the original symbols of the faith. When theology is no longer able to provide an interpretation that is experienced as plausible, the symbols lose their hold and die. That, according to Taubes, was what was happening to Christianity.

Taubes's interpretive framework is historicist and draws upon suggestions by Gershom Scholem[11] and by the late nineteenth-century German New Testament scholar Franz Overbeck—a figure to whom Taubes returned time and again in the decade that followed.

The role of theology in Christianity, Taubes noted, went back to the New Testament itself. That was because the gap between the original symbols and the historical reality manifested themselves almost immediately. The eschatological expectations of the first Christians—of the end of history with Christ's imminent return—were unfulfilled. Thus, "the Christian community was thrown into history against her expectations and against her will, and the hiatus between the eschatological symbols of faith and man's continuing existence in history is as old as the history of the Christian church." The function of Christian theology from then on remained the reinterpretation of the eschatological symbols (such as Christ's incarnation and man's salvation at the end of days) in light of changing historical circumstances. In the process of transforming "an adventistic sect" (that is, a small group of people awaiting the imminent coming of the Messiah and the end of days) into a universal church, Christianity had had to come to terms with the world, to become "secularized." As Taubes formulated the point elsewhere, "Jacob Burckhardt once remarked that all relation to external reality breaks down if you take certain passages of the New Testament in dead earnest; in these, a spirit is reflected that considers the world to be a strange and alien place. Church and theology have done their best, however, to mitigate and obscure this original Christian experience of total alienation from the world; in nineteen centuries they have transformed an originally 'nihilistic' impulse into positive 'social' or 'political' action."[12] That led to a perennial conflict between the canonical texts of the faith (the New Testament) and subsequent theological commentary on it, a "conflict between the eschatological symbols and the brute fact of a continuing history." The main way in which that tension was eased was through the use of allegorical interpretation, the insistence that the Biblical text ought to be understood in a nonliteral way.

But that allegorical tradition of interpretation, Taubes maintained, was no longer viable, for a variety of reasons.

The first was that modern critical scholarship on the Old and New Testaments, which sought to discover the actual history of the texts, was at odds with traditional theological interpretation of the Bible (exegesis). "Does not historical interpretation qua method imply a criticism of all theological exegesis? Whereas theological exegesis must 'transfer'—this is the original meaning of translation—the original symbols by the method of allegorical interpretation into a given situation, the historical analysis interprets the text, the canonic symbols, in their original historical context."[13] Adolf von Harnack (1851–1930), the great liberal Protestant historian of Christianity, resolved this dilemma by interpreting "the essence of Christianity" as the religion of Jesus, while "discarding all Christological doctrine as dead weight." Nietzsche resolved it by concluding that the triumph of historical research had as its implicit premise "the death of the Christian God. Historical research, Nietzsche observed, works only as a post mortem, dissecting the body for the sake of anatomical study and writing an obituary."

Taubes recognized Karl Barth's strategy in the famous second edition of Barth's commentary on Paul's Epistle to the Romans (discussed in chapter 3) as an attempt to circumvent the historical understanding of the Biblical text in favor a direct recovery of its eschatological elements, which seemed resonant in light of the sense of crisis during and after the First World War. Barth's "dialectical theology," Taubes wrote, describes a world so totally bereft of God that it "strangely coincided in its diagnosis with the atheistic interpretation of man's actual situation." But Taubes judged Barth's attempt "a dubious enterprise, combining revolutionary insight into the meaning of the original symbols with an anachronistic exegesis" that smuggled in some typical stereotypes of Protestant orthodoxy. (Taubes probably had in mind Barth's critique of "Pharisees"—a Protestant trope used to stigmatize Catholicism.) Barth's attempt to circumvent historical consciousness was doomed to failure. Taubes criticized Barth's dialectical theology for trying to avoid historical understanding by a naive return to Biblical sources: "Such innocence is illusory and cannot be regained by will or wish."[14]

Taubes agreed with Paul Tillich, the German Protestant radical theologian then teaching at Union Theological Seminary, that all fundamentalist and orthodox theology was no longer plausible. "For the first generation of Christian believers the coming of the Messiah was a reality and not an ontological problem. Many generations did not stumble over the concreteness of central symbols like Father, Lord, or King of Heaven. . . . They could use these symbols naïvely and did not need to develop an allegorical or dialectical interpretation. Anyone who, after two thousand years of Christian history, thinks he can ignore the hiatus of time is the victim of an illusion."[15]

In the essay "Dialectic and Analogy," Taubes explored another barrier to the creation of an adequate contemporary Christian theology. He argued that for most of its history, Christian theology was based on a hierarchical vision of the cosmos, with the earth at its center. In this conception, heaven was really "above," and earthly institutions reflected their heavenly counterparts. Thus in the Middle Ages, "the principle of analogy expresses the basic correspondence between below and above, heaven and earth, the natural and the supernatural." All of that broke down with the Copernican revolution, which revealed that the earth was not in fact at the center of the cosmos, and that it circled the sun. Man was therefore no longer at the center of the cosmos. While the Catholic Church tried to minimize the importance of this discovery, "the Copernican revolution shattered all hierarchical structure, the heavenly as well as the earthly . . . above and below became mere 'metaphors' and not rooted in the external order of the cosmos." Taubes argued that the attempt of modern Catholic thinkers to revive the analogical theology of Thomas Aquinas while abandoning his cosmology was misconceived. That, he thought, was futile—there was no going back.[16] In addition, the decline of monarchy as the dominant form of politics and the rise of democracy left much of the imagery of the traditional liturgy disconnected from contemporary consciousness.[17]

As a result, theistic religion was "forced to retreat to the domain of man's 'inwardness.'"[18] One theological response was to emphasize "dialectic"—the relationship between a distant God and the individual believer, and to stress the individual's inward spirituality.[19] Theology turns from cosmology to "anthropology," focusing on the nature of man and his needs. With ever more to say about man and ever less to say about God, the varieties of "dialectical theology"—whether those of Barth or Tillich—testified to "the eclipse of the divine in our present situation."[20] Among Western intellectuals, in the decade since the Second World War, Marxism had been overshadowed by existentialism. The significance of Tillich's recent writings, Taubes recognized, was in reminding secularists of the religious roots of the characteristic concerns of existentialism—"dread, anxiety, courage, being and non-being."[21]

Taubes suggested that between them, historical consciousness, post-Copernican science, and political democracy had destroyed the traditional techniques of theology. As Christian theologians like Barth gave up on the idea of history as progress and abandoned providentialist accounts that see evidence of God in history in favor of dialectical accounts that stress the gap between God and man, they approached a Gnostic conception of the world as bereft of God, and set the stage for an atheistic theology. "Perhaps the time has come," he speculated in "On the Nature of the Theological Method," "when theology must learn to live without the support of canon and classical authorities and stand in a world without authority." Instead, he suggested, "Theology must remain incognito in the realm of the secular and work incognito for the sanctification of the world."[22] Taubes seems to have borrowed this notion of theology needing to disguise itself in order to attain contemporary influence from Walter Benjamin's "On the Concept of History," a source he would return to time and again in later years.

A decade later, this essay, together with an essay by Susan Taubes on Simone Weil, "The Absent God," would be included in the anthology, *Toward a New Christianity: Readings in the Death of God Theology*, edited by Thomas Altizer, who remarked that "Taubes's essays of the mid-fifties became almost a sacred text to many younger theologians who were being drawn in a radical direction by the very problem which lies at the center of these essays."[23] Taubes had formulated the central dilemmas of contemporary Christian theology with extraordinary acuity.

Religious Ambivalence

Taubes wrote about Judaism as he wrote about Christianity: from the perspective of an external scholarly analyst. He took for granted the results of modern scholarly inquiry that the Pentateuch was comprised of multiple sources composed by multiple authors.[24] Divine Revelation at Sinai, like the Christian doctrine of Incarnation, was a mythic symbol, whose continuous reinterpretation was subject to scholarly analysis. In part of his being, then, Taubes was an academic scholar of religion, with all the intellectual and emotional distance that that implies.

At the same time, he had acquiesced to Susan's desire that their family home remain free of Judaism, to which she was so deeply antipathetic. He wrote to Martin Buber that he was no longer Orthodox—an understatement.[25] Yet Jacob remained conflicted, and a month after Ethan's birth he observed a *pidyon haben* (ceremony of the redemption of the firstborn) for his son, writing to Leo Strauss, "Face to face with the most elementary human circumstances, old rituals gain power and meaning."[26] The battle between Susan and Jacob over Jewish identity and observance continued in the years that followed: in 1956, Jacob confided to Ernst Simon and Hugo Bergmann that there was a "war of religion in the Taubes household."[27]

Yet with part of his being, Jacob longed for Jewish religious practice. Thus on the High Holidays in September 1955, he ventured to the Hasidic enclave of Williamsburg in Brooklyn to pray with his old acquaintance, the Satmar Rebbe, Joel Teitelbaum. As he explained in a letter, "This is the only place where I can pray—I get ill at the modern services. In Williamsburg, life and death is at stake in prayer. Even if I can only participate as an outsider, I am more 'inside' there than where I could belong according to my 'status' (some liberal service)!"[28] Writing to the same correspondent, he reported that while he longed to return to Jerusalem to teach religion at Hebrew University, when it came to the conflict between state and religion in Israel, his sympathies lay with the (ultra-Orthodox and anti-Zionist) Neturai Karta, though his personal connection to religion was very loose. "Is a contradiction of this sort tolerable? Can one live that way? It seems that in me memories live on that act more powerfully than the superstructure of argumentation—a highly dubious way for a philosopher to live."[29]

Judaism and Christianity

Jacob's most striking intellectual intervention came not in an academic journal, but in an article he wrote for *Commentary*, the magazine published by the American Jewish Committee aimed at a broader educated readership. In the years that Jacob had been away in Israel, the magazine had developed into a leading intellectual venue for the discussion not only of Jewish matters but of public affairs more broadly. Its assistant editors included Irving Kristol and Nathan Glazer, both veterans of the Maimonides seminar. Throughout the 1950s and in the decades beyond, *Commentary* became the leading outlet for what were subsequently dubbed the "New York Jewish Intellectuals" (not all of whom were in fact Jewish), especially for its second generation, which included Daniel Bell, Nathan Glazer, Irving Kristol, and Gertrude Himmelfarb. Bell, when he came to chronicle this intellectual network, listed among those individuals who were "close enough at times to be regarded as 'cousins'" Emil Fackenheim, Arthur A. Cohen, Will Herberg—and Jacob Taubes.[30]

One of the aims of the magazine's editor, Elliot Cohen, was to showcase discussion of Jewish religious thought, and he published articles by and about the two most significant German-Jewish theologians of the twentieth century, Martin Buber and Franz Rosenzweig, as well as younger religious thinkers such as Abraham Joshua Heschel and Emil Fackenheim.[31] Another of Cohen's aims was to influence American Jews to come to terms with the fact of their growing success and security in America, and to relinquish their "crippling minority-group defensiveness."[32]

Taubes's article, "The Issue between Judaism and Christianity: Facing Up to the Unresolvable Differences," published in December 1953, is clearer than almost anything else that he published, probably betraying the hand of one of *Commentary*'s editors, who were skilled at converting the work of professors and rabbis into readable prose. The genesis of Taubes's article lay in his own reading of Rosenzweig's *Star of Redemption*, and his dissatisfaction with that book's contention that Jews ought to accord Christianity a favored position in their own theology. For Taubes, that was a provincial, European view that ignored the historical role of Islam, a faith that Rosenzweig had treated as an afterthought.[33]

Like many of Taubes's subsequent articles, the piece was motivated by the desire to call into question some contemporary shibboleth[34]—in this case, the notion of a "Judeo-Christian tradition." The phrase was a recent coinage. It arose during the Second World War to denote the shared values of the West in opposition to fascism. In the aftermath of the war and growing awareness of the Nazi death camps, some Christian theologians found the expression "our Christian civilization" ominously exclusive. The expression developed greater currency during the early years of the Cold War, as "Judeo-Christian" was contrasted to atheistic communism.[35] The term was becoming part of the common sense of liberal public discourse, expressing "the idea that Western values rested on a religious consensus" and having the effect of "pushing Judaism from the margins of American religious life to its very center."[36] But what, in religious terms, did the phrase actually denote? Two frequent contributors to *Commentary* addressed the issue: Will Herberg and Hans-Joachim Schoeps.

Herberg had been a communist activist and theoretician. By the late 1930s, his faith in Marxism had collapsed. His attempt to explain Stalinism led him to the writings of the American Protestant theologian Reinhold Niebuhr, a neo-Augustianian who turned Augustine's pessimistic view of human nature into an argument about the inevitable corruptions of power, yet defended the uses of power in a fallen world. Herberg came to Niebuhr and told him that he was convinced by Niebuhr's argument, but that as a person of Jewish origin, he couldn't see converting to Christianity.[37] Herberg turned toward Judaism and developed an interest in the theology of Franz Rosenzweig, whose work was just starting to become accessible to American Jews, thanks in large part to the labors of Nahum Glatzer, then an editor at the Schocken publishing house in New York.[38]

Glatzer, who had been a close associate of Rosenzweig in Frankfurt, had published an introduction to Rosenzweig's life, which included the story of Rosenzweig's conversations with his friend, Eugen Rosenstock, after which Rosenzweig resolved to convert to Christianity, but only after having first exposed himself to Jewish life. A conversion experience at an Orthodox synagogue on Yom Kippur (so the story went) led him instead to commit himself to Judaism. In the years after the First World War, Rosenzweig developed a radically novel approach to Judaism. He recognized (as Nietzsche had claimed) that the historical approach to Christianity was either based on atheistic premises or led to atheistic conclusions.[39] While he accepted the historicity of the Hebrew Bible—the fact that it was composed by numerous hands—he proclaimed that what interested him was the meaning of the text as it had been redacted. Thus, like Barth (only with a greater degree of historical self-consciousness), Rosenzweig took it upon himself to interpret the Biblical texts, and the Jewish liturgy, in existential religious, rather than historical terms. Like Tillich after him, Rosenzweig began from the experiences and anxieties of the individual, and built his theology from the ground up, so to speak.

Commentary had published excerpts from Rosenzweig's work in 1945 and 1949, and in 1950 published a long and well-informed introduction to his life and thought by Herberg. He called attention to one of Rosenzweig's most striking theological innovations: the fact that he assigned a providential role to Christianity, as "'Judaism for the Gentiles' through which the people of the world are brought to the God of Israel."[40] Herberg went further in an article "Judaism and Christianity: Their Unity and Difference," published in the *Journal of Bible and Religion* in April 1953. Building on his understanding of Rosenzweig, he asserted that "Judaism and Christianity represent one religious reality, Judaism facing *inward* to the Jews and Christianity facing *outward* to the gentiles, who, through it, are brought to the God and under the covenant of Israel, and therefore cease to be gentiles."[41]

The German-Jewish historian of religion Hans Joachim Schoeps echoed Rosenzweig's sentiments in the pages of *Commentary*, contending that "it cannot be a matter of indifference to Jews whether a man is a Christian or non-Christian" and asserting that "I would go so far as to declare that perhaps no Gentile can come to God the Father otherwise than through Jesus Christ." While Jews could not recognize Jesus as the messiah for Israel, Schoeps thought they should be "prepared to recognize that, in some way which we do not understand, a Messianic significance for non-Jewish mankind is attached to the figure of this man."[42]

To all of this, Taubes offered a stinging rebuke.

Much of recent Jewish thought, Taubes contended—with Rosenzweig especially in mind—was overawed by the historical fact of Christianity's dominance. "Jewish thinkers like Hans Joachim Schoeps and Will Herberg have become so spellbound by Christianity's historical success that they try to give it a 'theological' justification." It was ironic that they sought to do so, Taubes thought, because the West was on the threshold of a "post-Christian" era "when Christian symbols and dogmas have begun to look as antiquated as the Old Testament seemed in the Christian era." By contrast, Taubes argued that "the Christian religion in general, and the body of the Christian church in particular, is of no *religious* relevance to the Jewish faith." Indeed, "From the Jewish point of view, the division of the divinity into 'Father" and 'Son' splits the divine essence; it was, and is, regarded by the synagogue quite simply as blasphemy."[43]

Taubes was also critical of the attempt to treat monotheism as the defining element of Judaism, pointing to nonmonotheistic propensities in Kabbalah. No, he insisted; since the time of Ezra, the defining element had been law, halacha: "All theological speculations are secondary to this." The notion that Judaism is "legalistic," the essence of the Pauline critique, is one that many modern Jews have bought into. "Modern Jewish thinking is in large part a prisoner of this antinomianism, which pervades modern thought in general." But, Taubes asserted, "Halacha is a structure in which a considerable variety of religious experience is integrated," from rationalism to mysticism. And he defended the halachic emphasis on "the rational and everyday sobriety of justice" against the fleeting power of love, or the quest for "the ecstasy and delirium of man's soul" (what later came to be called "spirituality").

Moreover, Taubes contended, from the Jewish point of view, Christianity is not exceptional. "Christian history, Jesus's claim to the title of Messiah, and Paul's theology of Christ as the end of the law, are not at all 'unique events' for Judaism, but things that have recurred in the Jewish pattern of religious existence." For "antinomian messianism" is a recurrent phenomenon in Jewish history, Taubes reminded his readers, citing Scholem's work on Sabbatai Zevi. Taubes concluded that modern Jewish thinkers who treat the law as purely external and emphasize instead emotional experience have bought into the antinomian, Pauline critique of the law. "The pseudo-Agadic stress in modern Jewish religious thinking on the 'romance' of Hasidism, or the romance of a mythologized East European Jewry in general, is in the end no obstacle to the Christianizing of the Jewish people"—a jibe, respectively, at Martin Buber's tales of the Hasidim (especially his recently published *Chassidische Botschaft* [*The Message of Hasidism*] [1952]) and Abraham Joshua Heschel's *The Earth Is the Lord's: The Inner World of the Jew in Eastern Europe* (1949).

In the course of describing the Christian view of the Jews, Taubes laid out an interpretation of the message of the Apostle Paul that he would argue decades later with Carl Schmitt and that would reappear in his final lectures on "The Political Theology of Paul." That interpretation was focused on chapters 9–11 of Paul's Epistle to the Romans, in which Paul interpreted "the refusal of the Jewish community to accept Jesus as the Christ as part of the universal drama of redemption: Israel's rejection of Jesus made it possible for salvation to come to the Gentile nations. Israel became an enemy of Jesus Christ, writes Paul to the Christian community in Rome, *'for your sakes—.'*" On this understanding of Paul, "The Jewish synagogue refuses Jesus as the Christ, but this refusal is essential to universal redemption."

Taubes's *Commentary* article was historically and conceptually rich, yet enigmatic. He restated traditional Orthodox Jewish positions, while at the same time indicating that he thought both Christianity and Judaism inadequate. He offered an interpretation of Paul that was far from what most Christians were familiar with. Were one to read this article alone, one might conclude that Taubes was an opponent of antinomianism. In fact, he was attracted to it (both in theory and in practice). But in this case, Taubes's inclinations took second place to the opportunity to challenge reigning opinion.

The article was a brilliant piece by almost any standard. It displayed a remarkable knowledge of the history of Judaism and of Christianity, including modern theology. It offered critiques of both contemporary Christian and Jewish self-understandings. Yet what was Taubes's own position? Where was Taubes coming from religiously? The article provoked letters and article-length responses in *Commentary*. Finally, Taubes responded with a letter of his own, in which he declared, "The theological dispute between Judaism and Christianity, if taken seriously, remains in a perennial stalemate. . . . But if the theological frame of reference is surpassed, do not the premises for a dispute or for a reconciliation between Jewish and Christian doctrine become obsolete?" Taubes went on to observe that in fact there were not many Jews or Christians who took the theological premises of their faith seriously, and that contemporary society was both post-Christian and post-Jewish. He left it at that.[44]

This was a recurrent pattern in Taubes's intellectual engagements: he used his insights into the weak points of any position—religious, philosophical, or political—to criticize it from some opposing position, a position of which he himself was skeptical.

Reaching Out: Rosenstock and Voegelin

In addition to writing articles and reviews at an unprecedented clip, Taubes reached out to émigré scholars, both for intellectual exchange and in search of job prospects. One of them was Eugen Rosenstock-Huessy, a wide-ranging Christian philosopher of history whose books, *Die europäischen Revolutionen* (1931) and *Out of Revolution* (1938), Taubes read in Rochester. The Jewish-born friend of Franz Rosenzweig, Rosenstock had converted to Christianity as a young man, and Rosenzweig developed his own thought in dialogue with Rosenstock. In 1933, Rosenstock left his academic post in Germany and emigrated to the United States, where, after a short sojourn as a lecturer at Harvard, he moved to Dartmouth College in New Hampshire. In Rosenstock, Taubes found an interlocutor who provided a link to interwar German intellectual life, and with whom he could express his own regrets over what he then saw as the definitive end of the German-Jewish relationship. "The German-Jewish marriage was a rare event, and rarely has the Jewish partner courted love as in this instance . . . [but] the Jewish-German marriage has ended in definitive divorce," Taubes wrote.[45]

Their wide-ranging correspondence includes one of Taubes's most striking insights into the difference between the Hebrew Bible and the New Testament, and implicitly, into Judaism as opposed to Christianity. It concerned the significance of progenitivity, and the emphasis on collective versus individual fate:

> In the Old Testament, everything turns on generation [*Geschlecht*], on "from generation to generation." Sarah, Rebecca, Rachael, Hannah—all decisive actors in holy history—are related to the birth of children. All the women plead for a child. That continues up through the beginning of the New Testament: the genealogy of John (and perhaps Jesus). What is striking about Jesus' acts of healing is that never does an infertile wife ask for a son: that is, the recurrent historical theme of the Old

Testament never reoccurs. The illnesses of those who come to Jesus to be cured come from a different zone: the blind, the lepers, the seemingly dead, and so on. In the Pauline epistles, marriage is scorned, sex is treated only as rutting. That is no accusation, only the statement of a difference. In the New Testament man stands on his own, not part of a series of generations—he is an "I," a lonely atom of late antiquity. The philosophy of *Geschlecht* in the double meaning of the term (from generation to generation, and of male and female) has no place in the New Testament scheme of things. From the early Christian communities to monasticism is a straight line.[46]

Taubes's exchange of letters with Rosenstock peaked during the summer of 1953, and continued more sporadically after Taubes's move to Harvard that September.

More consequential was Taubes's epistolary relationship with Eric Voegelin, a learned, iconoclastic conservative thinker whose conception of the history of the West paradoxically shared a good deal with Taubes's radical vision. Voegelin was an intellectual émigré from Nazi Germany, but was neither a leftist nor of Jewish origin.[47] He had come of age intellectually in interwar Vienna, and in the 1930s had written critiques of racist political ideologies and a defense of the authoritarian state as a bulwark against totalitarian political movements. That made him a marked man at the time of the *Anschluss*, when Austria was annexed by Nazi Germany. Like Taubes, Voegelin had a long-standing interest in the intersection of religion and politics, and among the works he published while still in Vienna was a volume on "political religions." He too had a brief sojourn at Harvard, before moving on to a more permanent post at Louisiana State University in Baton Rouge. In 1952, he published *The New Science of Politics*. Reading that book seems to have led Taubes to initiate an active correspondence.

Voegelin contended that modern ideologies could best be understood as attempts to bring about this-worldly salvation, and as an outgrowth (or recurrence) of heretical traditions within Christianity, with their origins in Gnosticism. For Voegelin, these modern ideologies—in which he included communism, Nazism, and liberalism—attempted to divinize the secular sphere, and hence, for him, they represented a deformed version of religious impulses.[48] Citing Taubes's *Abendländische Eschatologie* among other sources, Voegelin described two key historical turning points as the Church's inclusion of the Revelation of St. John in the biblical canon, with its "revolutionary annunciation of the millennium in which Christ would reign with his saints on this earth," and Joachim of Fiore's vision of a new age of the Spirit, beyond the age of the institutionalized church.[49] The congruence of argument between Taubes's dissertation and Voegelin's book was sufficient that Taubes, in a letter to their mutual friend, Carl Friedrich, would claim that several of Voegelin's key theses were already to be found in the earlier work.[50]

In the fall of 1952, on the recommendation of Alfred Schutz (another émigré from Vienna, teaching at the New School in New York), Taubes reached out and introduced himself to Voegelin, asking for advice on the possibility of getting a job in political science (for which Taubes felt qualified based on his knowledge of Hegel, Hans Kelsen, and Carl Schmitt).[51] Voegelin, in turn, approached William Y. Elliott of the Department of Government at Harvard, recommending Taubes as "the author of the brilliant study on *Abendländsiche Eschatologie*, Bern 1947, which traces the history of chiliastic politics from Jewish antiquity to contemporary totalitarian movements." (The latter characterization was Voegelin's gloss.[52]) Taubes and Voegelin shared an intellectual debt to Hans von Balthasar's writings on Gnosticism and apocalypticism, and an interest in the continuities between premodern religious movements and modern radical political ideologies. If the congruence was in their *analysis*, the difference was in their *evaluations*. For Voegelin, the secularization of eschatological hope—what he called "the immanentization of the eschaton"—was the Achilles' heel of modernity. For Taubes, it was the motor of historical progress. After encountering Taubes in person, Voegelin reported, "Today I met a real live Gnostic."[53] Taubes, in turn, wrote to Hannah Arendt, "Eric Voegelin was in town for a few days—rather a harmless version of de Maistre or Donoso Cortes"—two powerful reactionary thinkers of the nineteenth century.[54] But if their differences of temperament and politics kept them from becoming close, it did not get in the way of their intellectual exchange. Voegelin consulted with Taubes while at work on *Israel and Revelation*, the first volume of his series on Order and History, and in the spring of 1956, Taubes was busily reading through and correcting the proofs of Voegelin's book. Their relationship would continue, albeit sporadically, in the decades that followed.

The Elliott Seminar—and Schmitt Again

Taubes first visited Harvard in February 1953. The setting was a seminar presided over by the political scientist William Y. Elliott, whose chief lieutenant was his doctoral student, Henry Kissinger.[55] Taubes spoke on

"Theology and Political Theory"—a wide-ranging talk that presented some of the themes of his recently written but yet unpublished articles. Elliott characterized it as "a very, very brilliant performance." The question and answer session that followed was, if anything, more impressive yet as a display of erudition, as Taubes made reference to contemporary European thinkers then virtually unknown in the United States: Alexandre Kojève's interpretation of Hegel, Henri de Lubac on Proudhon (along with observations on Lubac's troubled relations with his Jesuit order), Carl Schmitt on Donoso Cortes, and Voegelin's just-published *New Science of Politics*, not to speak of Jacob's spontaneous, learned disquisitions on Gnostic passages in the Pauline Epistles, and on Spinoza's *Tractatus* and *Ethics*.[56]

Among those in attendance was a young visiting Fulbright scholar from Germany, Hans-Joachim Arndt, who approached Taubes after the seminar and declared that he was astonished to find a friend of Carl Schmitt at Harvard. It turned out that he was familiar with the letter about Schmitt that Taubes had sent Mohler from Jerusalem, and that Mohler had then passed on to Schmitt, who had dispensed copies to all and sundry. Taubes turned the conversation to a question that preoccupied him in the 1950s and beyond, namely how intellectuals of the caliber of Heidegger and Schmitt could have embraced National Socialism.[57] Arndt became a friend of Jacob's and of Susan, with whom he was much enamored.

Upon discovering that Taubes had not in fact written to Schmitt, Arndt encouraged him to do so. "I cannot yet write to Carl Schmitt. I simply don't know how to begin," Jacob responded. "Should 1933–40 simply be ignored? I don't regard myself as 'authorized' to operate on such wounds. It is a tragedy that the critique of liberalism during the 1920s led to the Nazi-[death] factories—and that Carl Schmitt thus did more than anyone else to rehabilitate liberalism. For against the Nazistic Carl Schmitt, 'even' the liberals were proved right."[58] Schmitt, however, began to send his new works to Taubes, and two years later, Taubes overcame his scruples and responded, consulting with Schmitt about a volume he hoped to edit on the conservative tradition for his book series at Beacon Press.[59]

Taubes and the Frankfurt School

Taubes's greatest affinity was with the intellectuals of the Frankfurt School. At the beginning of 1953, he reported to Hugo Bergmann that he was getting to know two "radical left-Hegelians" in New York, Franz Neumann and Herbert Marcuse, close friends who had been associated with the Institute for Social Research.[60] In the years that followed, Taubes came to identify with the members of what came to be called the Frankfurt School. At the center of the first generation of Frankfurt School thinkers were Max Horkheimer and his close collaborator, Theodor Adorno. Adorno had had an intense friendship with Walter Benjamin (as had Hannah Arendt, and especially Gershom Scholem). After moving to Cambridge, Taubes developed a close relationship with Herbert Marcuse, a slightly younger and more radical member of the Frankfurt circle. In the 1960s and 1970s, Taubes would befriend Jürgen Habermas, the leading figure in the younger generation of the Frankfurt School, with whom he both collaborated and clashed. A man who thrived on tension, both intellectual and personal, Taubes was deeply versed in the contestations among the Frankfurt intellectuals, and indeed played upon them in the decades ahead.

The Frankfurt intellectuals were centered on the Institute for Social Research, an institution founded in the 1920s and funded by Felix Weil, the leftist heir of a successful capitalist entrepreneur who had left his son a small fortune.[61] The Institute was connected to the newly founded University of Frankfurt. In 1930, Horkheimer was named as the Institute's director and appointed to a chair of philosophy at the University. His younger colleague, Theodor Wiesengrund (who later adopted his mother's maiden name, Adorno, as his surname) joined the Institute shortly thereafter, as did Marcuse, who had recently studied with Martin Heidegger. Under Horkheimer's leadership, the Institute aspired to combine an undogmatic Marxist philosophy with empirical research, under the rubric of "Critical Theory."

With Hitler's appointment as chancellor and the subsequent extrusion of Jewish and leftist professors from the universities, the Frankfurt intellectuals—who were decidedly leftist and mostly of Jewish origin—sought shelter abroad. Most wound up in the United States, as the Institute relocated to Columbia University on Morningside Heights in New York City. But, viewing themselves as embodiments of a better German culture that might eventually return to Germany, the Institute continued to publish its journal, the *Zeitschrift für Sozialforschung*, in German. In its pages, Horkheimer, Adorno, Marcuse, and other collaborators—including Walter Benjamin, who was then living in Paris—published a stream of radical social and cultural analysis in the 1930s.

Though clearly on the left, the Frankfurters drew upon a variety of intellectual sources to provide a culturally pessimistic vision of contemporary developments—a pessimism that was only deepened by the ascension of Nazism in Germany. They developed what one might call a re-Hegelianized Marxism. Their intellectual progenitor was Georg Lukács, whose work and personality had impressed Jacob Taubes during his student days in Zurich.

From Lukács, and especially his *History and Class Consciousness* of 1923, the Frankfurters took an emphasis on *Ideologiekritik*—the critique of ideology, intended to unmask contemporary doctrines as witting or unwitting apologies for oppressive hierarchies. Like other Marxists, they assumed that capitalism was fundamentally irrational and oppressive, and that religious, philosophical, and political beliefs had to be ultimately understood by their relationship to changes in the modes of capitalist production. Lukács, however, had focused on the role of consciousness—the beliefs that were held about what was socially possible and what was not. He emphasized what he called "reification" (*Verdinglichung*): the ideological process by which capitalistic social and economic arrangements that were actually the transitory products of historical development came to be regarded as natural, inevitable, and not subject to conscious human action.

Lukács examined works of high culture—novels and social theory— to show how bourgeois writers and theorists remained prisoners of their inability to see that socialism offered the only solution to the alienation brought about by capitalism. He also explored how changes in the means of production, leading to a greater division of labor, tended to rob the working class of insight into the larger process of capitalist oppression. As a result, he argued, the process of capitalist development did not, in itself, produce a revolutionary class consciousness in the working class of the sort that Marxists had long anticipated. For Lukács, the role of the motor of history therefore fell to the Communist Party, which embodied the awareness of the proper, revolutionary direction of history.

The Frankfurters did not agree with Lukács's political conclusion— most of them were not involved with the Communist movement—but they did pick up on his other themes. They went beyond them, by sponsoring empirical research into the actual consciousness of the working class in the early 1930s.

Walter Benjamin expanded the purview of Marxist criticism through his explorations of the popular and high culture of capitalism in nineteenth- and twentieth-century Europe. Unlike Horkheimer or Adorno, Benjamin was drawn to the Soviet Union and the Communist movement, leading to a troubled relationship with the leaders of the Institute, who supported Benjamin financially while trying to rein in what they saw as his sometimes overly materialistic explanations of cultural phenomena. Benjamin was also drawn to secularized invocations of theological motifs, in the manner of Ernst Bloch. After discussing some of Scholem's themes with Hannah Arendt, Benjamin penned a series of reflections called "On the Concept of History," which combined a tragic view of the past and present with a hope for the future, couched in vaguely theological terms.[62] It would become one of Taubes's favorite texts.

Unlike most members of the Institute circle, Benjamin did not survive the war. On the run from Nazi-occupied France in 1940, he escaped over the Pyrenees to Spain, where, fearful of arrest, he took his life. He died as an obscure writer whose essays had appeared scattered in a variety of periodicals. Eventually his legacy would be preserved by his friends Adorno, Arendt, and Scholem, who, spread over three continents, saw to the publication of his essays and correspondence. The essay "On the Concept of History," the manuscript of which Benjamin had entrusted to Arendt, was first published in a hectographed memorial volume assembled by Horkheimer and Adorno, *In Memory of Walter Benjamin* (*Walter Benjamin zum Gedächtnis*), printed in 1942.[63] Benjamin's work became more accessible to a larger public with the publication of a two-volume collection of his essays, edited by Theodor Adorno and his wife Gretel, and published in German by Suhrkamp Verlag in 1955. Publication did not guarantee recognition however, and Benjamin's work went largely unnoticed through the remainder of the decade. It is all the more remarkable, then, that Jacob Taubes evinced a familiarity with Benjamin's works, when, in 1953, he sent the draft of an essay to Hannah Arendt with the comment, "You will perhaps notice the spirit of Walter Benjamin in the final sentences."[64] The essay, probably "Theology and Political Theory," concludes, "A critique of the theological element in political theory rests ultimately on a critique of the principle of power itself"—a reference to Benjamin's essay "Toward the Critique of Violence" ("Zur Kritik der Gewalt").

In their writings of the 1930s and early 1940s, Horkheimer, Adorno, and others affiliated with the Institute continued to seek an explanation for the nonrevolutionary consciousness of the working class and the attraction of so many Germans to Nazism—an attraction that they believed had its parallels in other capitalist societies, including the United States. At the beginning of the Second World War, in an essay entitled "The Jews and Europe," Horkheimer asserted that bourgeois liberalism was helpless in the face of the contradictions of the capitalist economy that had led to the triumph of National Socialism, and that liberalism paved the way for its supersession by fascism.[65]

At the same time, the Frankfurt theorists looked beyond the Marxist tradition, and especially to Freud, for explanations that took into account the role of irrational drives in explaining behavior. Horkheimer and Adorno added an examination of commercial culture as a tool by which the masses were sated through the efforts of "the culture industry." Advertising and commercial mass culture served as means of control, they argued, whether in totalitarian Nazi Germany or in democracies such as the United States.[66]

In 1947, Horkheimer and Adorno published *Dialectic of Enlightenment* (*Dialektik der Aufkärung*), a wide-ranging but fragmentary work of social criticism that ranged from Homer's *Odyssey* to the present. The book was published in German by Querido Verlag, a small press in Amsterdam that published the works of German authors in exile. In the same year, Horkheimer published, in English, his book *The Eclipse of Reason*, based on lectures that he had given at Columbia University in 1944.[67] That book presented many of the key themes of *Dialectic of Enlightenment* in a clearer and more straightforward manner. Neither book was widely read or reviewed at the time of publication.

Horkheimer returned from American exile to the University of Frankfurt in 1950, where, with financial support from liberal American foundations and from the provincial and municipal governments, he founded a new institute and assumed a chair of philosophy. Adorno followed shortly thereafter. But the new institute was distinct from its predecessors in Frankfurt and America. It placed more emphasis on American-style survey research, and its image was far from politically radical.[68] Even before returning to Germany, Horkheimer had omitted some of more overtly anticapitalist passages from the published version of *Dialectic of Enlightenment*. At the new institute, the old *Zeitschrift für Sozialforschung*, with its overtly anticapitalist and antiliberal tone, was literally kept in a locked chest in the basement.[69] Neither *Dialectic of Enlightenment* nor *Eclipse of Reason* were published in Germany, and both remained relatively inaccessible there.[70] This suppression of the Institute's more radical past seems to have reflected prudence on the part of Horkheimer, but also a genuine change of heart, as the prospects of liberal democracy seemed brighter in the *Bundesrepublik*, a prospect to which Horkheimer hoped to contribute through the activities of his Institute. In the course of the 1950s and 1960s, he became ever more explicitly and vehemently anticommunist.

Meanwhile, in classes he taught at Harvard, Taubes was embracing and conveying Horkheimer and Adorno's radical critique of contemporary liberal democratic capitalism, at the very time that Horkheimer and Adorno back in Frankfurt were trying to suppress it.[71] That reflected Taubes's own inclinations, as well as the influence of Marcuse, the member of the Frankfurt group to whom Jacob was closest. Unlike Horkheimer and Adorno, Marcuse had not returned to Germany, and his radicalism remained undiminished.

In *Eclipse of Reason*, Horkheimer had lamented the inability of philosophy to provide substantive criticism of the oppressive qualities of contemporary society. He argued that there was a decline in belief in "objective reason"—the ability of philosophy to provide a well-grounded vision of the good life, which had been a goal of philosophers since Plato. According to Horkheimer, modern thinkers no longer believed in what Hegel had called "objective reason" (*Vernunft*), capable of pointing to ethically superior goals. Belief in the power of philosophy was replaced by belief in the power of science. But science was about the discovery of more effective means, not ends. The quest for objective reason was replaced by an emphasis on what Horkheimer termed "subjective reason" or "functional reason"—a kind of reason oriented to means rather than ends, on the assumption that ultimate ends were a matter of subjective preference, rather than objective goals that could be rationally defended, and in the name of which existing social arrangements could be criticized. In short, what Max Weber had called "functional rationality" had replaced "substantive rationality."[72]

Horkheimer offered a brief historical sketch of the development of the idea of reason. At first, mythology was an attempt to control nature by offering an account of how the world came to be. That was replaced by religion, with its own claim to objective truth. In the early modern period, philosophy began to supplant religion by offering a new rational foundation for objective truth freed from dogmatic authority. But in attacking metaphysics, it abandoned the aim of a single objective truth in favor of a relativistic worldview in which each cultural domain had its own aims and methods. What is "rational" then becomes subjective—a matter of individual preferences—and functional—related to the efficient attainment of goals that are neither socially shared nor philosophically grounded.[73]

Contemporary philosophy, Horkheimer lamented, embraced two rival panaceas, neither of which he thought satisfactory. On the one hand were philosophical trends, such as logical positivism or American pragmatism, that stressed "a scientific or experimental philosophy of life in which all values are tested by their causes and consequences." What this failed to consider, Horkheimer claimed, was that enemies of mankind, such as the Nazis, also put great faith in scientific methods, and that "science can be used to serve the most diabolical social forces, and scientism is no less narrow-minded than militant religion."[74] Another alternative was neo-Thomism—a philosophy embraced by the Catholic Church, but also propagated at the University of Chicago. It was an attempt to recreate a philosophy that offered a coherent vision of the good life, purportedly grounded in human nature itself. The problem with neo-Thomism, in Horkheimer's telling, was that its fundamental assumption that human nature had an intrinsic purpose was prescientific, or rather based upon premises that were regarded as scientific in the Middle Ages, but had been abandoned by modern science.[75] Thus "these philosophers revive authoritarian systems of thought that under modern conditions prove infinitely more naive, arbitrary, and untruthful than they were originally."[76]

The bottom line, for Horkheimer, was that "reason" had become synonymous with instrumental reason, which could and did serve to maintain political domination—which, Horkheimer insinuated, could be eliminated. Contemporary philosophy had ceased to provide a rational perspective from which to criticize—and hence transform—the existing social and economic order. It thus facilitated the conformity and lack of human autonomy that he thought characteristic of contemporary society. But neither in *Eclipse of Reason* nor in subsequent works did Horkheimer present a plausible and well-developed conception of "objective reason" from which social critique could proceed.[77]

Horkheimer and Adorno's vision of the present as an administered world, suppressing autonomy, and rife with suffering and conformity, resonated deeply with Jacob Taubes. For in their own way, and using concepts derived from Marx and Hegel, they offered a secularized version of the Gnostic view of the world as fallen and alienating, a view that had long appealed to Jacob.

Jacob viewed America in good part through the lenses provided by the Frankfurt School. While at Harvard, his friend Stanley Cavell challenged him, asking, "What do you know about America?" "Everything I know about America I learned from Adorno," Taubes answered. To which Cavell responded, "How dare you say that!"[78] Whether influenced by Horkheimer, Adorno, or Marcuse, Jacob's view of the United States was bleak, as was Susan's. Though for a while he wrote articles and reviews for the magazines associated with the New York intellectuals—*Commentary*, *Partisan Review* (where he published an article on Oskar Goldberg), and the *New Leader*—the gap between his views and theirs was ever more palpable.

Toward a Leftist Political Theology:
The History of Heresy Project

Many of the intellectuals whom Taubes admired and corresponded with authored books that told a big, historical story, whether about the West, or the origins of modernity, or some other grand narrative.[79] That included Rosenstock's *Out of Revolution: Autobiography of Western Man* (1938); Löwith's *From Hegel to Nietzsche: The Transformation in Nineteenth-Century Thought* (1941) and *Meaning in History* (1949); Erich Auerbach's *Mimesis: The Representation of Reality in Western Literature* (1946); Arendt's *Origins of Totalitarianism* (1951); Voegelin's *New Science of Politics* (1952); and Leo Strauss's *Natural Right and History* (1953). Each of these books, in their own way, offered some broad account of historical development. They were big thesis books that expressed their author's key interpretive insights. Taubes's *Abendländische Eschatologie* had been an attempt at such a "big book"—though as the product of a precocious twenty-three-year-old, it failed to hit the mark.

Now Taubes resolved to take another crack at a big-thesis book, one that would draw upon some of the material in his doctoral dissertation, but expand and deepen the argument. He sometimes called that book project "Theology and Political Philosophy," and in a sense he worked on it (or didn't work on it) for the rest of his life. From Rochester, he applied for a fellowship from the Rockefeller Foundation to allow him to spend a year at Harvard University to work on the book. His application was supported by Martin Buber, Kurt Riezler, and Paul Weiss.[80] The Foundation turned to Paul Tillich, yet another German intellectual émigré whom Taubes had befriended, for a confidential evaluation.[81] Taubes's application was successful.

Not long after Taubes arrived at Harvard in the fall of 1953, he sent Tillich a memorandum about a project he was developing entitled "Origins of the Free Spirit." It offered a sort of counterhistory of the West, contending that the motor force of historical progress was to be found in Gnostic, antinomian, mystical, and egalitarian religious movements—movements that had often been suppressed and repressed by the dominant religious establishment, but that formed the basis of modern democratic politics. Taubes's sketch was in some ways an expansion and generalization of the patterns that Scholem had limned by suggesting that the motor of Jewish history was the irrational, mystical, heterodox, and messianic, rather than the rational, orthodox, or legal. Influenced by the work of

Rufus M. Jones, an American Quaker historian of religion (especially his *Mysticism and Democracy in the English Commonwealth* [1932]), Taubes traced the lineage of liberal democracy to the mystical and antinomian movements of the medieval and early modern period.

The project was intended to create "a collection of fragments of the heretics concerning the doctrine of the Free Spirit," preceded by a volume of scholarly essays on the "Legacy of the Heretics," and followed by a volume of interpretation of the fragments by theologians, philosophers, sociologists, and psychologists, including Marcuse, Tillich, Reinhold Niebuhr, Scholem, Jonas, Eugen Rosenstock, Erich Fromm, and Carl Jung.

Taubes conceived the text collection as a counterweight to the "Great Books" series then being published under the aegis of the University of Chicago. Describing the project and its rationale to Tillich (who had recently been a visiting professor at Harvard) shortly after Senator McCarthy had chastised the Harvard faculty, Taubes wrote, "We all feel that we should rally around you and break the silence against a growing trend of conformism—and not by 'declarations,' but by concrete work in the limited field where we can operate—in teaching and education. It is no secret that orthodox patterns rule the field—simply by the canon of the 'great books' in all its variations."[82] "A Collection of Texts and Fragments: Origins of the Free Spirit" was intended as an alternative to this. Taubes seems to have planned the project, which they called their *Corpus Hereticorum* (a play on the *Corpus Hermeticum*), with Herbert Marcuse, as a primer of what Marcuse later characterized as the "eschatological distortion, in many heretical movements" of the possibility of the freer, more erotic, more creative civilization he believed was possible.[83]

Taubes developed these ideas into a "Memorandum Concerning a Collection of Texts and Fragments 'Origins of the Free Spirit.'" It reflected Horkheimer's critique of scientism and neo-orthodoxy.

> When one considers the present political and spiritual situation from a large enough perspective one cannot fail to observe that with the close of the Protestant-liberal era, Western society has come to an impasse: either to proceed in the way of atheistic secularism that idolizes the scientific spirit or to find shelter in authoritarian religion that idolizes the spirit of orthodoxy. The positive spirit of scientism and the positive spirit of orthodoxy seem diametrically opposed yet truly complement each other. It is no accident that the rise of the positivistic scientific era has ushered in revivals of positive orthodox religions and led to a decline, even an eclipse of the spirit of liberty.

It is significant that the last classical compilation of the standard literature of the West (organized under the auspices of the University of Chicago) has perpetuated the union between the orthodox spirit and the scientific spirit. The editors of the Great Books series devote the spiritual part of the series predominantly to the official orthodox authorities of the Middle Ages and treat modern times in the perspective of a neutralized scientific spirit as if the modern era had no spiritual religious antecedents that go beyond and even counter to the spirit of medieval orthodoxy.

The spiritual basis of the modern era lies not in the orthodox classical authors of the Middle Ages, but rests on the doctrine of the Free Spirit that developed in the Christian era in the shadow of ruling orthodoxies—be it Jewish, Christian (Catholic and Protestant), or Islamic orthodoxy. The idea of the free spirit was born in the circles of sectarians: spirituals and mystics, apocalyptics and gnostics, and has been incarnated in the principle of liberty that is fundamental in a democratic and libertarian society. The rise of political liberty in modern times cannot be understood except against the background of the doctrine of the free spirit that dominated the scattered sects of the pre-Reformation period and that emerged again in sects of the Reformation when Luther's and Calvin's reform turned into an orthodox authoritarian pattern. The "Brethren of the Free Spirit" [the Joachimites] (and similar sects) discovered the liberty of the Christian man and did not limit his liberty to the ivory tower of his soul, leaving the world in the bonds of the feudal authorities. Liberalism in theology and political theory stems from the sectarian doctrine of the free spirit. The scientific progress of the sixteenth and seventeenth centuries was stimulated by the breakthrough of man's free spirit that endeavored to master the external world in order to guarantee human freedom and independence.

With the neutralization of the scientific spirit into a technical pragmatic tool, liberalism degenerated into an antispiritual "free-thought" that was cut off from the mystical doctrinal of the Free Spirit. A degenerated liberalism and a cynical free-thought, a science reduced to a manipulated technology, gave the opportunity for religious orthodoxies and political tyrannies to move into the spiritual no-man's-land the liberal society left in its wake. . . . Since liberalism in the eighteenth and nineteenth centuries destroyed in an iconoclastic storm the spiritual reserves of its own base and repressed its own chiliastic and charismatic energies, it, ironically enough, called forth a reaction in which the repressed psychic energies broke loose, lending their force to authoritarian religions and tyrannies. [Here was a line of analysis borrowed from Horkheimer and Adorno's *Dialectic of Enlightenment*.]

If man's freedom should be restored it cannot be defended on a technic pragmatic level. . . . It will be necessary to bring into general consciousness the origins of the spirit of freedom. For the origins are not antiquated but must serve as perennial point of reference; the doctrine of the "Free Spirit" comes to the fore in the course of Occidental history in antagonism to orthodoxies that "religiously" stress the realm of order and law, the state of authority, the structure of hierarchy and the form of ceremony. [84]

While the project never came to fruition, its themes were prominent in a course, The History of Heresy, that Taubes taught at Harvard in the autumn of 1954. The opening lecture of the course, "The Gnostic Idea of Man," was transcribed and published in a student journal, *Cambridge Review*.[85] There, Taubes laid out the notion of a community of those alienated from the powers that be. "In the Gnostic perspective the natural order of things was demonized and satanized, and the powers and principalities of the world, the *archontes* became the representation of evil. . . . A new basis for community arose in the Gnostic frame, a new intimacy appeared: men are brothers, because they are all alien to the world. . . . The Gnostic attitude with its image of man and mankind permeated Christianity. Paul's image of man is meaningful only through the general tenets of the Gnostic myth of the fall of the original Man." (Taubes sent an offprint to Joseph Weiss in England, who in turn passed it on to Scholem; it remains among his papers.)

At about the same time, Taubes laid out his theory of the heretical origins of democracy in an article "On the Symbolic Order of Modern Democracy" published in *Confluence*, a journal edited by Henry Kissinger (based on the talk Taubes had given in the seminar of Kissinger's mentor, William Y. Elliott).[86] Together with his published lecture "The Gnostic Idea of Man," it offered the most clear and concise formulation of his conception of Western history. Taubes argued that

democracy flourished not in the orthodox tradition of Christian religions but among the mystical heretics and sectarians of the Middle Ages who renounced the Roman Catholic system of hierarchy, attacked the feudal order of medieval society, and tried to penetrate the entire population with the "egalitarian" message of the Gospel. The heretical sects stressed the equality of church members and insisted that elders and preachers should be elected by the local congregations. The "religious democracies" which came to birth in England in the seventeenth century felt themselves "blessed communities" in the sense that each individual was ennobled through his fellowship with kindred minds, and this same spirit carried over to some degree into the political democracies which grew out of the religious congregations. The democratic principle of church organization which the Anabaptists were the first to put into practice and which came to the fore again in the sects of the English Commonwealth became in the course of time the basic principle of English and American democracy. [87]

These egalitarian movements, Taubes argued, had their roots in Judaism and Christianity:

The principle of congregational association among men in the religious and political realms has a venerable tradition of its own: it is foreshadowed in the message of the Hebrew prophets and in the theology of Paul which prepared the way for a universal "catholic" church recognizing no barrier between Jew and Greek, slave and master. . . . Paul established the religious equality of men "in Christ" but defended the status quo of political inequality in the frame of the Roman Empire. . . . The entire problem of Christian history turns around the fulfillment of the Christian idea of man in the temporal realm. . . . It is a cardinal point of all medieval and modern Free Spirits that the Christian image of man can only be realized and materialized by abandoning the theistic frame of reference—the idea of divine sovereignty, the concept of a divine "Kingship"—this led to the philosophers and ideologists of the French and American revolutions who tried to establish the heavenly city on earth.[88]

In February 1955, while on a visit to New York, Taubes discussed his history of heresy course with Daniel Bell, who was sufficiently intrigued that he set up a meeting between Taubes and Bell's friend, Jason Epstein.[89] (Epstein, a young editor at Doubleday, had recognized that the growing population of college students taking humanities and social science courses created a market for quality paperbacks, a genre he pioneered.) At the meeting, Jacob also tried to interest Epstein in publishing a translation of *Abendländische Eschatologie* and discussed its main themes. "Why don't you bring it up to the Russian Revolution," Epstein asked, "that would be its logical culmination?" "Because of the F.B.I.," Taubes responded—an indication that he was loath to proclaim openly the radical drift of his view of history. Epstein was nevertheless interested in the spirit of heresy book, and Taubes agreed to show him some of the material.[90]

But the project failed to materialize. Perhaps that was because Taubes never produced a manuscript. But it may also have been because someone else did. In 1957, an English historian, Norman Cohn, published *The Pursuit of the Millennium*, an influential study of the tradition of revolutionary millenarianism and mystical anarchism as it developed in Western Europe, stretching back to the Bible but focused on the eleventh to sixteenth centuries, and including a detailed study of the heresy of the "Free Spirit." The book was a sober history, learned and entirely lacking in the radical pathos characteristic of Taubes's *Abendländische Eschatologie* or his history of heresy project. Cohn suggested that these religious movements "can be seen in retrospect to bear a startling resemblance to the great totalitarian movements of our own day."[91] But Cohn, unlike Taubes, characterized these movements as embracing "phantasies" of revolutionary eschatology. In short, what for Taubes were harbingers of modern radicalism were, for Cohn, precursors of modern totalitarianism.

In a sense, Voegelin was right about Taubes. For Taubes, Gnosticism represented the revolutionary potential of religion, which lived on beyond its confessional expressions.[92]

At Harvard

In September 1953, Jacob, Susan, and their infant son moved to Cambridge, Massachusetts. Susan had a Radcliffe fellowship to do graduate work in philosophy, and Jacob, his Rockefeller fellowship to work on his project on theology and politics. They moved into a house at 20 Marie Avenue, a short walk from Harvard Yard. Jacob also had a loose affiliation with the "Department of English and History" at MIT, where he was to give some lectures on "science and scientism."

In Jacob's day, Harvard was more welcoming to Jews than it had been in the interwar era. About a fifth of the undergraduates at Harvard were of Jewish origin. The system of distributing Jews evenly between the various residential houses, in force during the interwar years, had been abandoned.[93] But openness to Jews did not mean openness to Jewish practice, or interest in the academic study of matters Jewish. When Jacob informed a senior member of the Philosophy Department, C. I. Lewis, that he would not be holding class on the Jewish High Holidays, the response was "Jacob, come down from the trees!"[94]

The Department of Philosophy, whose most distinguished member was W.V.O. Quine, was dominated by philosophical pragmatism and by analytic philosophy, which tried to make philosophy more akin to science by limiting its exploration to testable claims and emphasizing precise use of language.[95] The main exception was Harry Austryn Wolfson, an expert on medieval Christian, Jewish, and Islamic philosophy and one of the very few scholars at an elite American university of what would later come to be called "Jewish Studies." But while Wolfson was a scholar of great distinction, he was a solitary spirit, whose presence did not loom large in either his department or the university.[96] He was certainly no model for Jacob Taubes.

Taubes as Teacher

Jacob, who had been a successful lecturer at Hebrew University, was even more popular as a teacher at Harvard. Over the course of his two years there, he taught a section of the humanities sequence of great books (Humanities 3), a course on the philosophy of history, his course on the history of heresy, a lecture course on Hegel, and—at student request—another seminar on the young Hegel. The Hegel lecture, offered in the fall semester of 1954, began with an enrollment of sixty students—already large by the standards of Harvard at the time; but as enrollment grew to over a hundred, it had to be moved into an amphitheater (Sever 11), one of the larger classrooms at the university. The history of heresy course, taught in a lecture hall in Emerson Hall, attracted a slew of auditors, filling the room beyond its seating capacity.[97] In the fall of 1954, a group of undergraduate devotees made a plea to the dean, McGeorge Bundy, for Taubes to teach an additional seminar on the young Hegel during the spring semester, something Taubes was willing to do without emolument. Since that was not permitted, he taught the Hegel seminar in place of his scheduled course on the philosophy of history.[98]

Taubes was often seen strolling along the Charles River, dressed all in black, with twelve young students in tow—rather like Jesus and his disciples.[99] At the beginning of the fall 1954 semester, the student newspaper, the *Harvard Crimson*, touted his courses: "Few want a 9 o'clock class the morning after a weekend, but those who dare have their pick of sparsely filled classrooms and some excellent courses to boot. Dr. Taubes, a visiting professor from Hebrew University in Jerusalem who seems to be giving almost every other course in the catalog this year, will lecture in

Humanities 134, 'Freedom and the Spirit of Heresy.'"[100] A month later, the paper published a faculty profile about him, "Nomad Philosopher," which was as enthusiastic as it was inaccurate—though whether the inaccuracies should be attributed to the faulty reportorial skills of the student reporter or to Jacob's own myth-making is difficult to determine.

> An intense, bushy-haired young professor could frequently be seen ambling through the crowded streets of Jerusalem two years ago, carrying on extended conversations with rabbis and refugees, artists and intellectuals. After searching out the colorful inhabitants of Israel's metropolis, Jacob Taubes felt he had found "deeper wisdom among semi-literates than among many college graduates."
>
> Although Taubes chose to spend his Rockefeller fellowship at Harvard for the past two years primarily because of the library, he insists that his main interest in life is not books, but people. His habit of always meeting a student or colleague for lunch and then talking for hours has caused friends to compare him to the Dostoyevsky characters who carry on coffee-shop dialogues for thirty pages.
>
> His faith in unsophisticated workers was justified, he feels, when he taught an intensive course of adult education in Israel. His students were mainly farmers and artisans, but he found among them a burning interest in fundamental issues. This experience taught him his greatest lesson in teaching—"not to lecture as if students are of the leisure class, for even students have to deal with the most urgent matters."
>
> This sense of urgency fills his lectures, and has made even his course on abstruse nineteenth century philosophy remarkably popular.[101]

Taubes made an impression among graduate students as well, as what was then a rare species at Harvard: a bona fide European intellectual, who could read the various languages that most grad students could not. He was acquainted with contemporary continental philosophy, a subject ignored by most of the philosophy faculty, but of interest to some graduate students, such as Hubert Dreyfus, who went on to become a leading American interpreter of Heidegger.[102] Some graduate and postgraduate students sat in on his courses, such as the philosopher Stanley Cavell, who attended with a young Belgian postgraduate student of literature, Paul de Man. They were impressed by Taubes's intensity, but de Man thought that most of the content was derived from Löwith's book, and came away disappointed.[103]

While visiting Susan in Paris, Jacob had made the acquaintance of Alexandre Kojève. A philosopher of Russian origin who had studied in Germany, Kojève moved to Paris during the 1930s where he offered a seminar on Hegel's *Phenomenology* that interpreted Hegel through Marxist and Heideggerian lenses, turning history into a progressive tale of struggle leading to mutual human recognition in a universal state.[104] Though the lectures were published in French in 1947, Kojève was virtually unknown in the United States. Unknown, that is, except to Leo Strauss—the two had known one another since they were students in the 1920s—and some of Strauss's pupils. Taubes adapted Kojève's interpretation into his Harvard lectures on Hegel—though without noting that the interpretation came from someone other than himself.[105] Here was an example of Taubes as what his friend Victor Gourevitch termed "the most complete sponge," quickly soaking up ideas and then delivering them as if they were his own inspirations.[106]

The emphasis in Taubes's spring 1955 seminar, Introduction to Hegel's Early Theological Writings (which started with Paul and ended with Marx), was on Hegel as a transitional figure in the transformation of Christian faith into philosophic reason, and hence of Christian to post-Christian consciousness. The course started with Paul as articulating a messianic, antinomian view of history, which, Taubes claimed, freed man from the mythical forces ascribed to the cosmos and robbed the earthly powers of divine legitimacy (an interpretation he would repeat three decades later in his *Political Theology of Paul*). Taubes then stressed Hegel's role in the creation of a secular philosophy of history, in which man's ability to negate becomes the basis of freedom in history. Here he made use of Kojève's emphasis on the dialectic of master and slave, in which the slave's struggle for recognition becomes the motive force of the forward movement of history.[107] "If secularization can be defined as the temporalization of the spiritual realm, then Hegel's concept of the Spirit, or even more generally Hegel's philosophy of history, is the radical secularization of the Christian concept of the spirit or more precisely: of Paul's theology of history." The course's exploration of the transition from Hegel to Marx borrowed heavily from Löwith's interpretation (in *From Hegel to Nietzsche* and *Meaning in History*), and from Marcuse's *Reason and Revolution: Hegel and the Rise of Social Theory* (1941). Along the way, Taubes drew on additional themes from *Abendländische Eschatologie*. There was a guest lecture by his friend Krister Stendahl on "Spirit in the New Testament" that stressed the extent to which the New Testament understood itself as fulfilling the promise of the Old. There were also stimulating, critical comments by Taubes on Albert Schweitzer, Karl Barth, Heidegger, and Leo Strauss. The course was attended by Susan Sontag, who took extensive notes, and at times by her husband, Philip Rieff.[108]

A Circle of Friends

In Cambridge, Jacob and Susan developed a new group of friends who provided them with yet wider circles of contacts, personal and institutional. Some of these friendships dissolved in discord, whereas others lasted for decades. The tightest circle was comprised of the quintet of Jacob and Susan Taubes, Philip Rieff and his then wife, Susan Sontag, and Herbert Marcuse.

Susan Taubes met Susan Sontag at Harvard, where both were pursuing graduate work. Susan Taubes began in philosophy, but finding the department's emphasis on analytic philosophy not to her taste, she switched to the Department of the History and Philosophy of Religion, the field in which she eventually took her qualifying exams. By then she had decided to abandon her original dissertation topic of Gnostic motifs in Heidegger in favor of a thesis on Simone Weil. And finding Arthur Nock, a scholar of Gnosticism, too positivistic and unphilosophical for her tastes, she switched thesis readers as well. The dissertation, completed in 1956 when she and Jacob were living in Princeton, had as its readers a professor from the Department of Philosophy, John Wild, and Paul Tillich, a friend of the Taubeses and by then a professor at the Harvard Divinity School.

Among the courses that Susan took were her husband Jacob's course on the history of heresy. Also attending Jacob's courses was another female graduate student in religion, Susan Sontag. The two Susans became fast friends, a friendship that would end a decade and a half later with the death of Susan Taubes, and indeed extend beyond that in Susan Sontag's fiction and her films.

Sontag's husband, Philip Rieff, was a junior professor of sociology. Rieff was a model of self-invention: from the most humble of origins, he transformed himself into a deeply erudite and cultivated persona. While some of his interests converged with Jacob's, their origins and predilections could not have been more different. Born in 1922, a year after his parents arrived in Chicago from Lithuania, Rieff was a year older than Jacob Taubes.[109] His father was a butcher. Rieff's Yiddish-speaking parents did not read or write English: in 1948, when Rieff was already an instructor at the University of Chicago, he taught them each how to write their names in English so that they could sign their citizenship papers. Rieff's parental home was devoid of books and culture. But young Philip took refuge in the local public library, was a brilliant student in high school, and at age eighteen entered the University of Chicago, where he became the editor of the student paper, the *Daily Maroon*. With the outbreak of the War, he left the university after his sophomore year to volunteer for service in the Army Air Force, hoping to fight the Nazis on the battlefield. But when an adjutant to a general discovered that Rieff was a walking encyclopedia, he commandeered Rieff to serve as the general's "Jewboy in the back room." So Rieff spent the war at an air force base in Cairo, Illinois.

After the war, Rieff returned to the University of Chicago as an instructor in sociology—despite the fact that he had never completed his BA—and was at work on a reader in the sociology of politics and religion[110] (a topic close to Jacob's concerns as well). It was there, in November 1949, that Rieff met Sontag, a precocious seventeen-year-old undergraduate, whom Rieff married after a ten-day courtship. The Rieffs moved to Cambridge in 1952 when Philip took up an assistant professorship at the recently founded Brandeis University in nearby Waltham. The University aspired to reach a certain eminence by unconventional hires, including a number of émigré scholars, such as Nahum N. Glatzer—who became the godfather of the Rieffs' son, David.[111]

The Rieffs' marriage was intense intellectually and emotionally, though not sexually. Susan, who was bisexual, later wrote of Philip's "timidity, his sentimentality, his low vitality, his innocence."[112] (After he proposed to her, Susan suggested they should sleep together. "We'll marry first," he responded.[113])

Brash, unsentimental, vital, erotic, and dangerous, Jacob was Rieff's opposite in each of these senses. While there was no American conservative intellectual culture with which Rieff identified, his instincts and predilections were as conservative as Jacob's were radical, stressing the role of cultural codes in restraining man's instincts.[114] Later, while Jacob and Marcuse were mentoring the academic New Left, Rieff would write a penetrating critique of the liberationist impulse in the academy, *Fellow Teachers* (1973).[115] In the interim, Rieff would produce an influential analysis of the contemporary age as characterized by the replacement of "religious man," "political man," and "economic man" by "psychological man," leading to what he called "the triumph of the therapeutic" (the title of his book of 1966).

The two Susans were united by their distance from bourgeois norms, and by their commitment to erudition and intellectual seriousness. Stanley Cavell, who attended a seder at the Taubeses with the Rieffs, recalled a discussion about whether Susan and Susan were damaging themselves by the intensity of their studies, which included reading one hundred pages of Hegel before going to bed at night.[116]

Marcuse was a friend to both the Rieffs and the Taubeses. He had spent most of the decade from 1940 to 1950 as an intelligence analyst for the

American government, first for the new intelligence service, the OSS, and then for the State Department. Thereafter, without an ongoing salary or firm institutional affiliation, he survived on a series of fellowships that his friends procured for him, first at Columbia University (where Franz Neumann was on the faculty), and then at Harvard's Russian Research Center, where he was funded by the Rockefeller Foundation to work on a book on Soviet Marxism. But Marcuse's real interests were in the ways that contemporary capitalism suppressed potentials for greater erotic and creative fulfillment, a theme explored in a book he was writing in his spare time. In 1954–55, commuting from New York to his temporary job at Harvard, and without a home of his own in Cambridge, Marcuse lived at both the Rieff and Taubes households.[117]

There were many shared interests among the five: Jacob Taubes and Marcuse shared an interest in Hegel as a progenitor of radical social theory, and Susan Taubes took a course with Marcuse on the subject. Rieff and Marcuse shared a deep interest in Freud, as did Susan Sontag, who contributed to the book Rieff published in 1959, *Freud: The Mind of the Moralist*. Jacob Taubes and Marcuse, as we've seen, formulated a plan to publish a history of the great antinomian texts of the Western tradition, a sort of counter-Great-Books.

Rieff supplemented his modest Brandeis salary by working as an editor at the Beacon Press. It had recently come under the leadership of Melvin Arnold, who was transforming the press from an outlet for the writings of Unitarian divines into a major force in publishing. Arnold, who had never attended university, hired Rieff to suggest books for the burgeoning academic market.[118] Through Rieff, Jacob Taubes too became acquainted with Arnold, eventually editing a series of his own at Beacon Press.

In the spring of 1954, Philip Rieff helped procure a secure institutional home for Marcuse at Brandeis University. When Rieff brought him to the vice-president of the Brandeis administration, Marcuse was so nervous that he hung on to the desk, since his future seemed to ride on securing a permanent post at Brandeis. The meeting was a success, and Marcuse was appointed a professor of political science and the history of ideas.[119]

A year later he completed *Eros and Civilization*. The book was published with Beacon Press, in a series edited by Jacob Taubes: Marcuse read the proofs on the kitchen table of the Taubes's household.[120] By then the Taubeses had moved to 1 Walker Street Place, around the corner from the Rieffs' home at 29 Chauncy Street.

Both couples were friends with Nahum N. Glatzer, who came to Brandeis as a professor of Jewish Studies in 1950 from his previous post as editor at the Schocken publishing house in New York. In his capacities both as a teacher and editor, Glatzer personified the transmission of the heritage of German-speaking Jewry to the English-speaking world. Jacob made a point of visiting with Glatzer, who thought the younger man quite brilliant. To Glatzer's teenage daughter, Judith, the Taubeses and the Rieffs seemed "a legendary set of couples."[121] Jacob's relationship with both father and daughter would continue in the years to come.

One of Jacob and Susan's most significant new acquaintances was Krister Stendahl. A Swedish Lutheran theologian and scholar of the Old and New Testaments, he arrived at the Harvard Divinity School in the fall of 1954, having been recruited as part of an effort by President Pusey to revive that flagging institution. Stendahl would eventually become dean of the Divinity School, and later bishop of Stockholm and a central figure in ecumenical relations between Christians and Jews.[122] He was one of the first Christian scholars to emphasize the Jewish elements of the Apostle Paul, demonstrating that a careful reading of Romans 7–9 showed that Paul did not advocate the conversion of Jews (which he left to God)—a subject close to Taubes's heart.[123]

Stendahl met Susan Taubes first, when she asked him to do a readings course on Gnosticism, a subject Stendahl had studied. He gave her a stack of books he recommended. She soon came back and said that she couldn't find the Gnostic philosophical concepts that Jacob had talked about. That led them to a discussion of the work of Hans Jonas, to whom Jacob soon introduced Stendahl.

Jacob was the first Jewish scholar whom Stendahl got to know well. Jacob brought Stendahl to his first seder, and later, to his first Simchat Torah celebration. Stendahl found Jacob intellectually vivacious: "everything that was extreme interested Jacob," and talking to him was "an intellectual feast."[124] It was Jacob who urged Stendahl to bring together a seminal volume of essays by scholars of the Dead Sea Scrolls (the subject of Stendahl's dissertation) and paved the way for its publication in 1957.[125] Stendahl and his wife, Brita, would continue to play a role in the life of the Taubes family in the decades to come.

Rounding out the circle of family friends in Cambridge was Elsa First, a younger friend of the two Susans, an undergraduate who seemed to take every course that Jacob offered. She babysat young Ethan, and would go on to play a central role in the life of the Taubes children. Along with her came her then boyfriend, Frederic Rzewski, a pianist and politically radical composer who, like many of their friends, would later fall for Susan Taubes (he appears in *Divorcing* as "Nicholas").[126]

To a remarkable degree, then, while in Rochester and then at Harvard, Jacob moved in circles comprised primarily of intellectuals from German-speaking Europe: Arendt, Friedrich, Glatzer, Marcuse, Rosenstock-Huessy, Stendahl (who had studied in Germany), Tillich, and Voegelin. The contemporaries he took most seriously also came from German-speaking Europe, including Adorno, Buber, Horkheimer, Jonas, Kojève (whose training and influences were German), Löwith, Schmitt, Scholem, and Strauss. To be sure, these thinkers were intellectually and politically diverse. But none were American or British. Jacob and Susan's general attitude toward American culture was one of disdain—and that extended to the academic culture of Harvard. In 1954, Susan wrote to their German friend Hans-Joachim Arndt, "We have experienced the disappointments of Harvard for ourselves although probably not as keenly as you since we found a circle of kindred spirits, most, but not exclusively, continental, who form a strong garrison against the process of moronification."[127]

There were exceptions, of course, American-born friends and acquaintances completing their graduate education whom Jacob would draw upon in the decades to come. Among them were the sociologist Robert Bellah, the linguist Noam Chomsky (then a Junior Fellow at the Harvard Society of Fellows), and the philosopher Stanley Cavell (another Junior Fellow).

Beacon Press

Taubes was excited by the prospect of editing a series for Beacon Press. For here was an opportunity to make use of his wide contacts, especially among émigré intellectuals. And here was the chance to make use of his knowledge of German-language scholarship and to bring it to the attention of an American audience. At first he planned to focus on books that marked the transition from Christian to post-Christian thought—both an interest of his, and perhaps a good fit for a Unitarian publishing house. He had in mind books by Ludwig Feuerbach, Heinrich Heine, Marx's "Economic-Philosophic Manuscripts," and Franz Overbeck's *Christentum und Kultur*, among others.[128] Then he considered focusing the series on "philosophical anthropology," a particularly German genre of philosophizing about the nature of man.[129] He wrote to intellectuals he knew in Germany and the United States, asking Carl Schmitt for advice on what to include in an anthology of conservative thought, or suggesting translations of their works (such as Tillich's *Die Sozialistische Entscheidung*), or new works they might want to write for Beacon. He planned an anthology on historicism, drawing on his own wide-ranging knowledge of German social thought for a volume intended to dispel the disrepute into which the term had fallen as a result of Karl Popper's *The Open Society and Its Enemies*.[130]

The book series that Taubes edited for Beacon, Humanitas: Beacon Studies in Humanities, failed to live up to his hopes for it. In the end, it published only half-a-dozen books: a translation of *Homo Ludens: A Study of the Play-Element in Culture* by the contemporary Dutch historian and philosopher of culture, Johan Huizinga; *Judgments on History and Historians* by the great nineteenth-century Swiss historian Jacob Burckhardt; the American edition of Martin Buber's *Paths in Utopia*, a history of socialism; and an original work, *Spinoza and the Rise of Liberalism*, by the American polymath Lewis S. Feuer. The most important book to appear in the series was Hans Jonas's *The Gnostic Religion*, published in 1958. This was a much more accessible reworking of the interpretation of Gnosticism that Jonas had developed in his earlier, German-language works. It dropped the Heideggerian philosophic jargon and discussions of scholarly controversies, leaving a text aimed at "the general educated reader as well as the scholar."[131] By encouraging Jonas to write and publish it in English in so accessible a form and format, Taubes undoubtedly did a good deal to enhance the influence of Jonas's work in the English-speaking world.[132]

But Taubes's behavior at Beacon Press led to his estrangement from Philip Rieff. While Rieff was working in a back office at the Beacon Press headquarters, Taubes called Arnold to ask for a job as an editor for academic books. Unbeknownst to Taubes, Arnold (who had his suspicions about Taubes) put Rieff on an extension phone. Arnold told Taubes that Rieff was already doing the job that Taubes was proposing for himself. Taubes said, "You don't need Philip. I can do it all. And he's practically a fascist." This act of treachery ended Rieff's relationship with Jacob, without Taubes knowing the reason. He made repeated attempts, unrequited, to renew the relationship, including lengthy letters of self-justification.[133] Within a few years, Rieff and Sontag split up: her relationship with Jacob and Susan would grow closer.

Marcuse's Eros and Civilization

The first book to appear in Jacob's *Humanitas* series was Marcuse's *Eros and Civilization: A Philosophical Inquiry into Freud*. At a time when Marxism was suspect in the United States because of its linkage with communism, Marcuse contrived to write a successor to Lukács's *History and Class Consciousness* that did not mention Marx. Instead, he recast the radical critique of capitalism into the psychoanalytic language favored by American cultural elites of the 1950s. Marcuse was quite uninterested in the empirical validity of Freud's thought or in psychoanalysis as technique. Rather, he latched onto a few key Freudian ideas that had much older roots, and used them to reformulate a radical critique of contemporary capitalism.

Marcuse asserted that although some degree of instinctual repression was necessary for the perpetuation of the species and the preservation of civilization, under capitalism there was more repression of pleasure than was actually necessary. That excess of actual repression over necessary repression he dubbed "surplus repression," playing on the Marxist term "surplus value." Marcuse resurrected Marx's arguments that, in a capitalist society (what Marcuse called "an acquisitive and antagonistic society") production "becomes the more alien the more specialized the division of labor becomes."[134] "For the duration of work, which occupies practically the entire existence of the mature individual, pleasure is 'suspended' and pain prevails."[135] But the potential for a less repressive and more pleasurable existence was gestating in the womb of capitalism, Marcuse claimed, and he hoped to be its midwife. The current level of technology, Marcuse asserted, made it possible to move beyond the conditions of scarcity that had made alienating toil so dominant a feature of existence. If only men saw the light, they would realize that it was possible to live a more pleasurable life, in which work itself would be more creative and hence more fulfilling.

But why were so few people radically dissatisfied with their lives under capitalism? Because, Marcuse answered, the minds of the masses were controlled by the forces of capitalist production through the mass media, which kept people "entertained" while excluding all truly subversive ideas.[136] More perniciously, their consciousness was controlled to make them focus on the choices between consumer goods, between innumerable gadgets, which, according to Marcuse, were all of the same sort. For Marcuse, it was not the empirical, known wishes and consciousness of men and women that was deemed decisive, but what they *ought* to be wishing and thinking. The fact that men and women *feel* happy is the worst symptom of the problem, for "happiness is not in the mere feeling of satisfaction but in the reality of freedom and satisfaction."[137] Though he did not share Taubes's interest in Gnosticism as a historical phenomenon, like the Gnostics, Marcuse's view was that the current world was one of alienation, and that a much better world lay beyond the horizon if men and women only had the right sort of knowledge. It was this line of analysis that struck a chord with Jacob Taubes. Marcuse was to develop it a decade later in his most famous and influential work, *One-Dimensional Man*.

Supporters and Skeptics

Taubes's greatest booster on the Harvard faculty was Carl Joachim Friedrich, a Protestant German émigré scholar who had come to the university in 1926 from Heidelberg. In the 1930s, Friedrich had pioneered cooperation between Harvard and the government bureaucracy. With America's entry into the Second World War, he helped organize the training of diplomats and military officials for the tasks of postwar occupation. During the American occupation of Germany, he traveled to various universities to advise on their role in a democratic, constitutional order, and he played a role in the establishment of the Free University of Berlin, the institution where Taubes would later teach. In 1956, when the University of Heidelberg, with the support of the Rockefeller Foundation, established a chair of political education, Friedrich became its first incumbent, dividing his time between his positions at Harvard and Heidelberg, and helping to train a younger generation of German political theorists.[138]

Unusually for an American academic, Friedrich combined expertise in constitutional law and government administration with interests in political theory and philosophy. In 1949, he edited a collection of Kant's moral and political writings, which was followed by another edited volume, *The Philosophy of Hegel*, completed just before Taubes came to Harvard. Before arriving in Cambridge, Jacob wrote to Friedrich from Rochester, mentioning their shared interest in the political philosophy of Kant and of Hegel.[139] In 1956, Friedrich would edit and provide an introduction to an English-language edition of Hegel's *Philosophy of History*. Discussions about Hegel were thus at the center of their shared concerns. Their relationship grew into friendship, albeit one in which Taubes was the more junior and deferential partner.[140]

While Friedrich became Jacob's greatest supporter at Harvard, there were others on the faculty who valued him and wanted to keep him at the university. They included William Yandell Elliott, the senior figure in the Government Department whom Jacob had so impressed in his seminar in 1953; his junior colleague Louis Hartz (who developed one of the most influential interpretations of American political culture); and George H. Williams, the Acting Dean of the Divinity School.[141] But Taubes was no political scientist. He was part historian of religion, part philosopher. The obstacles to an ongoing position lay in the departments in which he would have to hold his primary appointment.

When Jacob's fellowship year at Harvard came to an end, there were plans for him to teach philosophy at MIT, where he was highly regarded by Warren McCulloch, one of the founders of cybernetics, and the historian of science Giorgio de Santillana. But after the department's plans changed at the last moment, Jacob was offered a lectureship in Harvard's Philosophy Department for 1954–55.[142]

As a teacher, he was even more popular in his second year than in his first—a fact that was resented by some of the more senior members of the department.[143] He was also invited more than once to the home of Harvard's new president, Nathan Pusey, who was interested in religion[144]— invitations that may also have aroused a certain amount of jealousy. Taubes had supporters who sought to find an ongoing position for him at Harvard. But senior members of the two departments in which he might have been appointed, Philosophy and Religion, were more skeptical about his knowledge and character.

Harvard had a chair devoted to the history of religion, occupied by Arthur Darby Nock. Nock was in many respects the anti-Taubes. British by origin and trained at Cambridge, Nock was an enormously erudite expert on Greek, Roman, and Hellenistic religion. He had written on Saint Paul and on Gnosticism—two of Jacob's favorite topics. But their scholarly personae could hardly have been more different. For Nock took "a delight in the discovery, ordering, and establishment of facts," while "the philosophical problems of religion did not much interest him"—making him the opposite of Taubes in both respects.[145] Jacob made an awkward attempt to ingratiate himself with Nock by asking him about some obscure fact in Nock's area of expertise. "Why don't you look it up in the *Encyclopedia Britannica*?" was Nock's reply.[146] Taubes disdained Nock as a "positivist" focused on dry-as-dust facts and lacking imagination.[147] Nock, as we will see, regarded Taubes as less than solid. When, at Friedrich's urging, the Dean of the Faculty of Arts and Sciences, McGeorge Bundy, discussed with Nock the possibility of Taubes's appointment as assistant professor in Nock's field of the history of religion, Nock rejected the idea out of hand.[148]

Jacob's chances of being appointed in the Department of Philosophy were no better. As we have seen, the department was dominated by analytic philosophers, who regarded what Taubes did as bunk. Nor were his religious interests appreciated. To make matters worse, just as he was coming up for consideration during the fall of 1954, Taubes delivered to the Philosophy Club at Harvard a lecture (attended by the faculty), "The

Four Ages of Reason," with its not-so-subtle suggestion that much of what they considered scientific philosophy was a dereliction from their proper duty as critics of the status quo.[149]

Taubes Brings the Frankfurt Critique to Harvard

Taubes's growing affinity with Horkheimer, Adorno, and Marcuse, and his identification with "Critical Theory" was expressed in "Four Ages of Reason," which he published in 1955 with the dedication, "For Max Horkheimer on his sixtieth birthday." The essay closely followed the themes and contentions of Horkheimer and Adorno, citing *Eclipse of Reason* once, and borrowing heavily from it throughout. It assumed that there was such a thing as "universal reason" that could establish accord among the interests of all individuals. Yet, Taubes declared, "the actual split of society into antagonistic groups has brought philosophy or rational discourse into disrepute." In fact, "a society that had staked its future on the progress of reason ended up in barbarism," and technological development had gone together with "the decrease of individual and collective rationality."[150]

Taubes criticized contemporary philosophy for attempting to imitate mathematics in creating a realm of logical relations in which validity was deliberately divorced from human origins and human history. He then offered a brief sketch of the historical stages of reason, which drew upon Horkheimer but added some additional historical nuance.

The first stage was theological. In the Middle Ages, Taubes wrote, "the theological concept of reason interprets man's reason as a reflection of a divine reason revealed in the sacred scriptures of Christianity. . . . The inner agreement between man's reason and the realm of natural things is established by the divine order of creation." That in turn presupposed a hierarchical society, in which "each realm symbolizes by way of analogy the next higher realm." (He had spelled out the theological implications of this theme in another essay from the same period, "Dialectic and Analogy.") It was also based upon a pre-Copernican conception of the universe, in which the earth was planted at the center.[151] Echoing Horkheimer's critique of neo-Thomism, Taubes noted that there was no going back to a theology based on such conceptions.

Next came a stage of reason understood as legal rationality. Here Taubes added a stage not present in Horkheimer's historical sketch, but one derived from Carl Schmitt's *Ex Captivitate Salus*. From Schmitt, as well as from the distinguished medieval historian Ernst Kantorowicz, Taubes took the idea that during the century from 1150 to 1250, the rediscovery of Roman law had led to a science of jurisprudence, based on secular premises, and in tension with the theological claims of the Church. That juridical revolution was based on the primacy of justice, and had its own conception of "immanent necessity," not premised upon the theological assumption of a providential creation or divine intervention through miracles.[152]

The next stage of reason was that of economic and scientific reason. Economic reason abandoned the claims of theology and of justice, and emphasized instead the calculation of economic value, with no criterion beyond that of profit. Taubes grouped it together with scientific reason because both sought to reduce the external world to objects of exploitation. That in turn gave way to the technological conception of reason, in which "the conquest of nature serves as a standard for man to measure the success or the failure of reason." That technological domination of nature was extended to the technological domination of other men. The result, Taubes asserted—for it would be wrong to say that he explained—was the alienation of man from nature and from other men, as Horkheimer had contended. As an alternative to the dominant technical conceptions of reason, Taubes affirmed the need for philosophy to provide a critique of the present order, and hope that would make it possible to "transcend a given situation and anticipate the new that is to come."[153]

Taubes sent the manuscript to Horkheimer with a letter expressing his deep appreciation for the older man's work and as a sign "that your work has borne fruit well beyond the circle of your immediate associates."[154]

"Four Ages of Reason" remained an unknown work. The article was submitted to the journal *Ethics*, and then to another journal, *Philosophy and Phenomenological Research*, where it was placed on a waiting list. Taubes reported to Horkheimer that he had chosen to publish it instead, in English, in the German journal, *Archiv für Rechts- und Sozialphilosophie*, where it finally appeared in October 1956.

Despite its obscure place of publication, the article gives us a sense of what Taubes conveyed to his students and colleagues at Harvard.[155] At a time when academic philosophy at Harvard was dominated by analytic philosophy, Taubes's talk, which linked analytic and scientistic forms of philosophy to the oppressive administrative structure of society, was greeted with outrage and incredulity by much of the philosophy faculty, including such luminaries as Quine and C. I. Lewis. To them, speculative and declarative cultural criticism of this sort was not philosophy at all.[156]

That accounts in part—but only in part—for the vociferous resistance that the Philosophy Department offered to suggestions that Taubes be given an ongoing post at Harvard.

A Legendary Prank

It may have been that lecture, with its wide-ranging and unsubstantiated historical generalizations, that led to perhaps the most famous story about Jacob Taubes—a story that was repeated, in a variety of versions, almost wherever he went. The exact protagonists in the story varied with the telling, but not the substance or import of the tale. The two most likely protagonists (in addition to Jacob) were Henry Aiken and Morton White, who taught successive semesters of Harvard's survey course on the history of Western thought. Both had strong historical interests, albeit in modern British and American philosophy, respectively. Convinced that Jacob pretended to know far more than he actually did, they conspired with Nock and concocted a prank to catch him up. White's skepticism about Jacob seems to have been deepened by his then graduate student, Susan Sontag.[157]

On an occasion when they knew Jacob would be present, Aiken and White began a discussion with Nock about the theory of the soul of Bertram of Hildesheim, a medieval scholastic, whose thought, they suggested, constituted an interesting intermediate form between the Thomistic and Scotist schools. After listening intently for a while, Jacob "spoke brilliantly about Bertram of Hildesheim's psychology and astonished those present with his profound and comprehensive knowledge—until he was informed that no such person existed; he'd been invented for the purpose of the discussion."[158] The story speaks to Jacob's pretensions, of course. But it also reflects his talent for placing a book or thinker in a field of intellectual coordinates, and deducing what the key tenets ought to have been. To pull off the stunt he actually had to know a good deal about Thomism (i.e. the followers of Thomas Aquinas) and Scotism (i.e. the followers of Duns Scotus). It was the sort of feat he had brought off successfully in his doctoral exams, when he had written about Schopenhauer as a transitional figure from German Idealism to European nihilism without having read Schopenhauer. The only difference was that Schopenhauer had indeed existed, while the medieval scholastic was a concoction.

Hans Jonas claimed to have heard the story from Carl Friedrich, who he thought was in on the prank. Aiken and White were more plausibly identified as the organizers by Arnold Band, who was their teaching assistant at the time, and by Daniel Bell. When Bell recounted the story to François Bondy, who had known Jacob in Zurich, Bondy reported that he and another friend had played the same trick on Jacob when he was in high school, posing, even then, as omniscient.[159] Avishai Margalit heard the story about the concocted medieval philosopher from Judith Shklar, who said it had been staged by her and Charles Taylor in a class they had taken with Taubes.[160] In any case, one or another version of the story continued to be told for decades at Harvard and beyond, a story that reinforced the notion that Jacob Taubes was less than solid.

From Harvard to Princeton

For a variety of reasons, then, neither the philosophers nor Nock were interested in having Taubes on their roster. But given the interest in retaining Taubes by the dean of the Divinity School and some members of the government department, Dean Bundy turned to the chairman of the Committee on General Education to see whether that program might adopt him. Alas, Bundy reported to Carl Friedrich, "The Committee feels sufficient concern about the quality of Taubes to be unwilling at this time to assume responsibility for his salary, in light of the refusal of the departments of the Faculty of Arts and Sciences to share his appointment."[161]

Jacob's failure to get an ongoing post at Harvard had many sources. There was the poor fit between Taubes and Nock on the one hand, and between Taubes and the incumbent philosophers on the other. There was Taubes's tendency to boastfulness and display of erudition, some of which was suspect. He was thought by some to be brilliant, and by others to be a fraud. There was his popularity with undergraduates, which aroused suspicion and envy. And then there was his philandering.[162] Taubes, Philip Rieff later recalled with some rhetorical exaggeration, was wont to try to seduce "everyone between five and fifty."[163]

But if Harvard was not interested in hiring Jacob Taubes, others were. One of those who had read Jacob's work and was impressed by him was Walter Kaufmann, a seminal figure in bringing modern German philosophy into the American academy.[164] A few years older than Taubes, Kaufmann had been born in Germany to a Protestant family of Jewish origin. In 1933, at the age of twelve, he decided to convert to Judaism, and in the decades thereafter he remained interested in Jewish thought even as his faith waned. In 1939, he left Germany, attended college in the United States, and then did graduate work in philosophy at Harvard. He began teaching philosophy at Princeton in 1947. At a time when Hegel and Nietzsche were often portrayed as intellectual progenitors of National Socialism, he published an influential critique of that image of Hegel as well as *Nietzsche: Philosopher, Psychologist, Antichrist* (1950), a book-length reinterpretation of Nietzsche that made him more palatable to liberal sensibilities.[165] In the decades that followed, he edited a widely used anthology of existentialist writings, and translated into English works by Goethe, Hegel, Nietzsche, Leo Baeck, and Martin Buber.

Kaufmann had a Fulbright fellowship to spend the 1955–56 academic year at the University of Heidelberg, and Princeton's Department of Philosophy decided to hire Jacob Taubes for the year. The Taubeses moved to Princeton in September 1955. Susan planned to finish her dissertation. Jacob hoped that his one-year position would turn into a tenure-track one.

Scholem-Arendt-Strauss

From Jerusalem, Gershom Scholem's hostility to Jacob Taubes continued, conveyed in letters to friends in the United States such as Leo Strauss and Hannah Arendt. After receiving a critical report on Taubes from Scholem, Leo Strauss wrote back that "I have never experienced such *shameless* ambition. Will anyone be able to instill some manners into him?"[166] Arendt reported to Scholem, "Taubes has naturally turned up, mendacious, impudent and bluffing people with levantine cleverness, as always."[167] A year later, Arendt met Taubes at a lecture at Harvard, and wrote to Scholem, "His methods haven't changed: he is of the opinion that there is no one who cannot be won over by the most vulgar flattery. And of course to a considerable degree he's right."[168]

Strauss adopted his friend Scholem's estimate of Taubes. In October 1955, Strauss learned that Taubes would be visiting the University of Chicago and angling for a position there. He wrote to Scholem, saying that he had heard from "a reliable source" at Harvard that Taubes had passed himself off there as still affiliated with the Hebrew University; that he was teaching a course on the history of heresy that amounted to "philosophical antisemitism"; and that "his other courses in philosophy were, I am told by people in the department, a farce. In short, Harvard was happy to be rid of him"—a half-truth, as we have seen.[169]

While Strauss had become disillusioned with Taubes, Taubes was becoming more skeptical of his old teacher.

In 1953, Strauss published *Natural Right and History*, which offered a critique of historicist understandings and juxtaposed them to the purportedly classical understanding of nature and natural rights. Taubes wrote a critical review of the book, which was to appear in *Political Science Quarterly*. That review noted the esoteric element of the work: for the book began with a warning that the self-understandings of the Declaration of Independence were being eroded, but then proceeded to attack the philosophy of Locke, upon which the Declaration was based.[170] In writing the review, Taubes had assumed that Strauss had given an accurate account of ancient philosophy. But he came to question that assumption, as Carl Friedrich cast doubt upon it, and set his students to checking Strauss's quotations (which were difficult to track down because of the vagueness of Strauss's method of citation). Those doubts were deepened when Taubes gave a lecture on progress, which included a critique of Strauss, at St. John's College, where Strauss was regarded as a "demigod." Taubes was startled to hear from Ludwig Edelstein, a classics scholar at nearby Johns Hopkins University, that he regarded Strauss's interpretation of the classics as "bunk." Taubes then resolved to rewrite his review—but never got around to doing so.[171]

Taubes in the Eyes of His Contemporaries

Among his contemporaries, opinions of Jacob Taubes were divided, not only *among* individuals, but sometimes *within* individuals as well.

In April 1955, Jacob presided over a Passover seder at the Taubes residence, attended by the Rieffs, Krister Stendahl, Stanley Cavell, and Herbert Marcuse. Dressed in a formal rabbinical gown, his head crowned by a silk yarmulke, Jacob conducted the ceremony magnificently. He sang the prayers in a beautiful voice, all the while providing a learned commentary on the text of the *Hagaddah*. It was an occasion sufficiently memorable that some of those in attendance—Cavell and Stendahl—recalled it half a century later.[172]

But some suspected that it was mostly a show for his academic friends: that though he was the only one at the table capable of conducting a seder in this manner, his performance was just that—a performance, without belief and lacking sincerity.[173] The impression that Jacob Taubes was playing a role—or sometimes, a variety of roles—was shared by many of his friends and acquaintances, during his time in Cambridge and after. It was difficult to separate the dancer from the dance.[174]

Forming an accurate estimate of Jacob Taubes's knowledge and achievements was made more difficult by his propensity not only to boastfulness, but to provide misleading information about himself. The 1954 article about him in the *Harvard Crimson*, for example, stated that he had published his dissertation in 1946 at the age of twenty-two (it was actually a year later); that Martin Buber secured him a position as a research fellow at Hebrew University (Buber had nothing to do with it); and that he had returned to the United States in 1952 on a Rockefeller Fellowship (it was actually awarded a year later). A curriculum vitae that Taubes sent to Carl Friedrich in 1954 included on the list of his publications two books, *Apotheosis of History* (Beacon Press, 1955) and *Religion and Political Order: Essays toward an Understanding of Political Philosophy* (Beacon Press, 1955). The first was presumably a translation of his first book, the second a collection of essays on which he had been working. But in fact, neither book existed: they were hopes for books, not publications. On the same document, Taubes gave his date of birth as February 27, 1924.[175] He had actually been born a year earlier. Taubes was used to thinking of himself and presenting himself to others as a wunderkind, but that impression was less plausible the older he grew. A decade later, in 1966, his year of birth moved up to 1926 on the jacket text of a book he edited.[176]

Philip Rieff thought Taubes erudite, even if Taubes didn't know as much as he let on. Rieff found him an interesting personality, fascinated by Gnostic inversion: a world turned upside down, where, because the world itself was evil, one could be duplicitous on principle. He felt entitled to do what he pleased, with no responsibility for anything. "A deeply sinister and evil man," Rieff judged, "the only evil man I've ever known, for whom evil was a principle of existence."[177]

In February 1955, Daniel Bell met Jacob and Susan Taubes in New York. At the time, Bell was the labor reporter for *Fortune* magazine and an adjunct lecturer in sociology at Columbia. He had recently published the book *Marxian Socialism in the United States* (dedicated to Irving and Bea Kristol), and was increasingly involved with the Congress for Cultural Freedom, an international organizations of anticommunist intellectuals, mostly of liberal or socialist persuasion, for whom he would work in Paris the next year. (The organization, it was later revealed, was partly funded by the CIA, as a counterweight to the massive Soviet-backed mobilization of intellectuals in Western Europe and Asia.) There Bell would work with Taubes's old friend, François Bondy.

In two long letters to his wife, Elaine, written a week apart, Bell conveyed his impressions of the Taubeses.

"As always, Jacob was full of interesting talk. He is always stimulating," Bell began. But Bell was troubled by "how little a sense of the concrete they have." "What struck me most, though, was the shallowness of thought and the poverty of experience about America." Susan thought of America as a terrible country, characterized by senseless waste, advertising, and so on. But when the talk turned to foreign affairs, to the Soviet Union and Maoist China, "it became sickening, largely because of the frightening way in which a myth can supersede any emotional grasp of a particular experience. . . . I was taken with the fact that on the level of fact alone they knew so little: Jacob can accept, theoretically, the notion of a totalitarian regime, yet understand nothing about the actual way in which terror operates. There is only the hope that somewhere, someday, 'the spark' may break through and the regime will change. Revolution is a mystique, and so China historically and inevitably is good and Chiang is bad; I couldn't follow the sequiters." The Taubeses, Bell concluded, were "brilliant in many respects," but cut off from concrete historical experience.[178] Jacob proclaimed himself a socialist, and when Bell asked him what that meant, Jacob's answer was "socialism is freedom." But when Bell sought to engage him in discussing what socialism might mean in terms of concrete institutional arrangements, Jacob objected to the terms of the discussion, since for him "some eschatological element was missing . . . [which] we could not pin down, other than the mystique of chiliasm, or revolution, or some transforming power." Jacob was on the side of "history" conceived as progressing toward freedom through human action: "the progress of history is the secularization of messianism and with it anti-nomianism." But, Bell asked, what about the risks of false messianism? "You are too Jewish," Jacob replied. "That is the trouble with Judaism: the messiah is always too far off. . . . When you believe in prophecy you run the risk of false prophets." Bell thought Jacob's radicalism "a mode of thought, both logically and psychologically, to which we were attracted, and which, now, with increasing clarity I find myself rejecting."[179]

Bell recognized in Jacob certain traits of character that he found in himself as well, and thought "not altogether admirable in the way in which they are expressed: the type of ambition, the social climbing, the need to know the famous people; all this, in itself not bad, since often these are the interesting people, and if one is not born into the milieu some striving and contriving is necessary; but at some point a trace of shamelessness or vulgarity becomes evident." These were some of the very qualities that Hannah Arendt and Leo Strauss had found off-putting about Jacob, the qualities conducive to "Making It" in the title phrase of a memoir published a decade later by Taubes's friend, Norman Podhoretz.

Princeton Interlude

While disappointed at his failure to secure an ongoing post at Harvard, Taubes was pleased that Princeton had emerged as an alternative, since, as he explained in a letter to Carl Schmitt, Princeton was, along with

Cambridge, Massachusetts, "one of the very few places where Europeans can live" in the United States.[180] With a salary for the academic year of $5,500, Jacob and Susan were probably better off financially than ever before.[181] They moved into an attic flat in a fine house at 301 Nassau Street, not far from the Princeton campus.[182]

Taubes's hope that his visiting professorship might turn into an ongoing appointment was soon dispelled. For when he arrived, the chairman of the Department of Philosophy, Ledger Wood, make it clear to him that the appointment was for a year only, since, "the appointments on the senior level duplicate your interest." Thus the nerve-racking business of finding a job had to begin again. By now Jacob and Susan were exhausted by their frequent changes of locale, and began to consider looking for a job in Germany—a country Jacob had never visited. Jacob asked Carl Friedrich and Eric Voegelin, each of whom were teaching in Germany for the year, to keep an eye out for positions for him there.[183]

In a campaign to find a permanent post, he gave a lecture at St. John's College in Annapolis, Maryland, and visited Johns Hopkins in Baltimore, where he met (and impressed) Arthur Lovejoy, the founder of the field of the history of ideas. In early December he lectured at the Federated Theological Faculties at the University of Chicago (later renamed the School of Divinity). There was interest in the school in naming him to a chair. The problem, he reported to Carl Friedrich, was that the chair was divided between theology and philosophy, and while the theologians wanted him, "the philosophers refused . . . *a priori* to consider the matter . . . partly, I guess, because of pipelines from Harvard."[184]

Among the courses Taubes taught at Princeton was Philosophy 303, Philosophy of the Nineteenth Century. Judging from the reading list for the course, it was much broader than what would typically have been taught in philosophy courses—closer to a course in intellectual history. This reflected Taubes's conviction that much of what was most philosophically interesting took place beyond the bounds of formal philosophy. Students in the course were expected to read some of Hegel, Kierkegaard, Max Stirner, Marx's *German Ideology*, St. Simon, Comte, Donoso Cortes, Proudon, Dostoyevsky's *The Possessed*, Walter Kaufmann's *The Portable Nietzsche*, as well as Kaufmann's *Nietzsche*, Marcuse's *Reason and Revolution*, and T. G. Masaryk's *The Spirit of Russia*.

Almost from the beginning, Jacob was unhappy in Princeton, an institution that he found far more staid than Harvard.[185] And he was forced to teach a course on Locke, Berkeley, and epistemological matters in which he had little interest.[186] There was less of a student constituency for the sorts of things that interested him than had been the case at Hebrew University or at Harvard.

At least one Princeton undergraduate developed a close relationship with Jacob and Susan Taubes, however. That was Gregory Callimanopulos, the son of a Greek shipping magnate, who took courses with Jacob.[187] In a student body and faculty that was buttoned down and WASPy, Callimanopulos was atypical and European. The couple invited him to their home on Nassau Street, and after a while he felt free to simply drop in. He found Jacob fascinating: a free thinker, constantly shattering stereotypes, intellectually provocative, sometimes pushing conceptions to the point of absurdity. Jacob was unlike the other professors in both his originality and his arrogance. Callimanopulos was also struck by Jacob's manner: his lack of concern for his dress, his stomach paunch and constant pipe-smoking betraying a total lack of interest in physical fitness—in short, a notable lack of couth. Susan, by contrast, was conspicuous for her appearance: dressed in black from head to toe, she conveyed a bohemian elegance. She was more alluring than other faculty wives.

The atmosphere in the Taubes household was one of eroticism and bohemianism. Callimanopulos was clearly attracted to Susan, and she played upon it, engaging in ongoing flirtation. Jacob was excited by the flirtation between Susan and the young man. This was part of the erotic play in the household, which at times led Jacob and Susan to engage in mutual psychological torture, with the young undergraduate as their instrument. That was a pattern that would recur in the future, with other instruments, male and female, and would even be captured on film in fictionalized form.

The spring of 1956 was notable in a number of ways. Jacob was granted American citizenship: the first time in his life he bore a real passport.[188] Susan completed and defended her doctoral thesis at Radcliffe.

In her dissertation, Susan seems to accept, and perhaps endorse, Simone Weil's view of the world as radically evil, including Weil's condemnation of capitalism and the effects of technology. She also conveyed without criticism Weil's antipathy to all particularism, a position that Susan continued to share. These were the elements of Weil's writings that had initially attracted Susan. But what is striking about the dissertation is the extent to which its author was critical of her subject. As the statement and analysis proceeds, Taubes accuses Weil of mystifying human relations. Weil's emphasis on suffering is seen as diverting attention from the *human* and particular historical sources of suffering. Much of the dissertation combines logical analysis of the incompatibility of Weil's arguments with one another, along with a Marxist critique of the ideological nature of Weil's work.[189] The thesis betrays the influence of Marcuse, with whom Susan had taken a course on Marxist Ideology.[190] Susan would adapt portions of her thesis into an article.[191] But by the time she was finished she seems to have been sufficiently critical of Weil to decide that Weil was not really worth writing a book about. Susan's interests in philosophy were waning. She maintained an interest in religion, but now with an emphasis not on theology, but on myth and ritual.

In Princeton as in Cambridge and New York, Jacob and Susan's closest social contacts were with members of the German intellectual diaspora. In Princeton it was with Erich von Kahler, who served as a mentor to Jacob. Von Kahler (1885–1970) exemplified a recurrent pattern among German-speaking Jewry, the transition from *Besitz* to *Bildung*, that is, from wealth to cultural attainment: the sons of successful entrepreneurs were encouraged to pursue careers in cultural professions that were less lucrative, but of higher status among those who valued culture.[192] The scion of an insurance magnate ennobled by the Habsburg emperor, von Kahler was educated in Vienna, but moved to Munich before the First World War, where he became a *Privatgelehrter*, a scholar whose private means obviated the need for a university post. Forced to leave Germany in 1933, von Kahler eventually moved to the United States and settled in Princeton, where he became a member of the Institute for Advanced Study. A cultural historian, philosopher, and polymath, whose circle of friends included Thomas Mann and Albert Einstein, von Kahler was a link between Jacob and the high culture of the Weimar era. On the occasion of Kahler's seventieth birthday, Taubes published an appreciation of the man and his work in *Aufbau*, the German-Jewish newspaper published in New York—an article that served to demonstrate Jacob's knowledge of the range of von Kahler's work.[193]

Brilliant but Risky: Taubes in the Eyes of Senior Scholars

The most important event of that spring was that Jacob got a job. A tenure-track job. At one of the world's foremost universities.

Jacob's job hunt was made more difficult by the fact that he did not fit into any established academic discipline. His doctoral thesis was nominally in the field of sociology. He had published in philosophy journals and taught in philosophy departments, but he had neither the interest nor the talent for engaging in systematic argument about abstract topics. The

focus of his interests was in the no-man's-land between religion, philosophy, social theory, and intellectual history. His intellectual breadth was
part of what made him so attractive; his lack of scholarly focus made him
harder to pigeonhole or to place.

In early 1956, Columbia University put together a committee to consider hiring Jacob Taubes as an assistant professor. It was not unusual
at the time for hiring to be done in this manner. Rather than an open,
public announcement of a position to which anyone could apply (a later
practice), a particular, promising scholar would be considered. Since there
was not yet a formally constituted department of religion, the decision was
made by an ad hoc committee. It was chaired by Salo Baron, who had been
the teacher of Jacob's parents, and had known Jacob since his first arrival
in the United States. The committee's first step was to have the executive officer of the nascent religion department, John A. Hutchison, write
to a number of experts who were acquainted with Taubes, asking them
for their confidential evaluation. Just how the list was assembled remains
uncertain, but many of the names must have been at Taubes's suggestion.

The responses (now in the Salo Baron papers at Stanford University)
are illuminating. Many remarked on Taubes's enthusiasm for teaching and
his success as a teacher at Harvard. They attest to a young scholar that
many senior figures in the fields of religion and philosophy found brilliant
and intellectually vital, while a few raised doubts about his scholarly solidity. Even those who endorsed him enthusiastically tended to note that he
was likely to rub some colleagues the wrong way.

Nahum Glatzer considered Taubes "one of the most genuinely learned
historians of religion today and a profound theological thinker."[194] Abraham Kaplan, a philosopher at UCLA, wrote that in the philosophy of religion Taubes "is the most able and promising young man in his field in the
whole country today."[195]

Fritz Kaufmann, a German-Jewish émigré philosopher of the phenomenological school, then teaching at the University of Buffalo, had maintained an intensive exchange of letters with Taubes for several years on
questions of philosophy and religion. He attested to Taubes's high competence in the philosophy of religion, and developments from Hegel to Marx
to contemporary religious existentialism, including Buber and Rosenzweig, Przywara and Balthasar, Barth and Tillich—that is, of the major
Jewish, Catholic, and Protestant theologians. As to how he would fit into a
department, Kaufmann ventured that "he is a restless, searching, but also
tortured mind, an eschatological nature and hence, I suppose, not always
a comfortable man," and concluded, "If he succeeds in becoming a real

member of your intellectual community, he will certainly be a challenge to both his colleagues and students and a propulsive power in the spiritual enterprise of your Department and Columbia University."[196]

From Paris came positive recommendations from the distinguished philosopher and historian of science, Alexandre Koyré, and from the Hegel scholar Jean Wahl.[197] Most unexpectedly, perhaps, came an endorsement from Lovejoy at Johns Hopkins, who on the basis of "several hours of talk on subjects of interest" concluded that Taubes was "a young man whom it was important, from the point of view of the study of the history of ideas, to retain in this country."[198]

Paul Weiss of Yale, who had known Taubes for years and published his articles in the *Review of Metaphysics*, thought him "a stimulating person; he has a wide range of knowledge in many tongues, he has a vital interest in basic ideas, . . . is lively, engaging, bold and thoughtful. . . . There is no doubt but that he is a gifted person. He has not gone further because he leaves one with the impression of a being a 'wunderkind,' and one doesn't altogether know what to make of him." Weiss declared that "his appointment would be daring and exciting." He recommended appointing him for up to five years "to see how strong in fact he is and how he develops"; during that time, "there is no doubt but he will be the center of student interest, a provoker of genuine thought, a delight, stimulus and perplexity to his colleagues, and a joy to know. The skeptics, e.g. [the philosopher of science Ernst] Nagel, won't care for him, and he will frighten the more staid members of the community. But others will think you have decided brilliantly. So will I."[199]

James Luther Adams, who knew Taubes from Harvard and from his visits to the University of Chicago (where Adams then taught as Professor of Religious Ethics), judged Taubes "one of the most promising scholars of his generation in the field of religious scholarship." He noted not only the range of his linguistic abilities, but the fact that Taubes "appears to have an equal grasp upon Jewish and Christian theological literature and problems," making him potentially "an important liaison figure in American religious life," "able to secure the sort of hearing in the Christian community which Martin Buber has been able to elicit."[200]

Most instructive, perhaps, were the letters from colleagues at Harvard and Princeton, where Taubes had taught. Carl Friedrich was brief but supportive. John Dillenberger of the program on the history and philosophy of religion at Harvard was equivocal. "It is not easy to write about Jacob Taubes, since the picture for me is not clear cut," he began. On the positive side, "He is certainly one of the most brilliant people one could encounter anywhere. His mind is quick and absorbs a broad range of materials. . . . He lives with his subject matter with a great deal of intensity. He also has the requisite technical tools for real scholarly work." On the other hand, Dillenberger noted, "Several of us who got to know him over a period of time had a feeling that his wide reading was not always thorough, and that he succeeded in overwhelming us in the areas where we did not know too much. Taubes's real gift is that he knows something everywhere." He wondered whether Taubes's "exceedingly gifted, scholarly possibilities will actually be brought into some kind of concentrated discipline." He hoped that "some institution will really be able to take on this very gifted man, even though he may be occasionally something of a problem."[201] His colleague, Paul Tillich, seconded this evaluation, adding that "Taubes has such an understanding of philosophical problems that his force should be used by one of the greater institutions in this country."[202] Gregory Vlastos, a senior philosopher in the Princeton department, wrote of Taubes's exceptional erudition, his "quite unusual imaginative power," his ability to make abstract ideas come alive for his students, and "the intensity with which he does philosophy." He too noted that since "the kind of philosophy he does has very little in common with the currently fashionable trends of logical empiricism and linguistic analysis," he was bound to meet with hostility from some philosophers. Vlastos concluded that Taubes was "an exciting, highly gifted man, quite out of the ordinary both as a thinker and as a teacher, but who has still much to learn by way of disciplined performance in scholarship and in the arts of conciliation in getting along with other people."[203]

In short, Taubes was a resource that should not to go unused. If hiring him was something of a risk, the potential payoff was great. And since he would be hired without tenure, Columbia would have ample opportunity to judge.

That seemed to be the conclusion of Harry W. Jones, a professor at Columbia's law faculty whose expertise included legal philosophy, to whom the committee sent a few of Taubes's publications. Jones too was impressed by the range of Taubes's learning, but noted that in the areas in which he had the most competence, "I have some doubt as to the depth of Dr. Taubes' analysis," and that some of Taubes's incidental references to political philosophy and the philosophy of law were "suggestive, perhaps, but too showy and too cryptic to be really illuminating." Yet he too concluded, "Any academic appointment is something of a gamble, and my own bias is in favor of taking a chance on a man of manifest brilliance, however prickly in manner, rather than on a better adjusted man of low ceiling potential."[204]

In April, Jacob received his official letter of appointment to teach the "History and Sociology of Religion" at Columbia.[205] He had heard unofficially a month earlier, and wrote to friends about how pleased he was to be going to Columbia.[206] After a decade of uncertainty about his professional future, he had made it—or so it seemed.

CHAPTER EIGHT

Columbia Years, 1956–66

WHEN JACOB, AGE thirty-three, and Susan, twenty-eight, moved to New York City where Jacob was to teach at Columbia University, the stage seemed set for a permanent home and base of intellectual operations. At Columbia, Jacob was a popular and effective teacher, gathering a coterie of students, some of whom would go on to distinguished careers in intellectual life. Jacob now had scope for his activities as an intellectual entrepreneur, developing seminars that brought together a wide range of scholars to explore issues of religion and culture. Yet within a few years he was dissatisfied with both his marriage and his place at Columbia.

The Taubeses Established

Susan, Jacob, and young Ethan moved to New York in time for the beginning of the fall semester of 1956. During the previous summer, Susan had purchased a motorcycle in Zurich and, with four-year-old Ethan holding onto her waist from behind, toured northern Italy and the south of France.[1] She was an unconventional mother, and an unconventional wife.

After they moved to New York, neither Jacob nor Susan drove a car. Jacob had learned to drive after returning from Jerusalem, but he was not good at it, did not like it, and gave it up once the family moved to Manhattan. His lack of driving ability was characteristic of many central European immigrant intellectuals, whose conceptions of America were limited by their difficulty in moving beyond the metropolitan cities in which they lived.[2] Nor did Jacob resume driving when he moved to Germany.

After living for a year in an apartment on Riverside Drive, the Taubeses acquired their first long-term lease, for an apartment in a Columbia-owned building at 35 Claremont Avenue, two blocks west of the Columbia campus.[3] In August 1957, Susan gave birth to their second child, a daughter they named Tanaquil (Tania). Their home furnishings reflected Susan's highly aesthetic and unconventional sensibility, and included a table, chairs, and bookshelves crafted out of rough-hewn wood—a rare sight in the 1950s.[4] Though hardly well to do, the Taubeses were able to afford a housekeeper/nanny, an African-American woman from nearby Harlem.

Jacob and Susan's parenting style might charitably be characterized as laissez-faire, or less charitably, as negligent. They lacked models of parenthood to imitate. Susan had grown up without a mother. Jacob's mother, Fanny, had been a Jewish *balabusta*, a homemaker devoted to her children, her husband, and her household. But Susan was no *balabusta*. Both Susan and Jacob were too wrapped up in their own process of self-discovery and self-creation to devote much time to the children, who were raised primarily by their housekeeper. Often Jacob was not to be seen in the household during the week. When it came to disciplining his son Ethan, Jacob oscillated between frequent laxity and occasional corporal punishment, using a belt, as his own father had done.[5]

Jacob and Susan were negligent in another way as well: they failed to teach their children the languages that might connect them to the cultures of their parents. Jacob lived primarily in a German-speaking world, and the possibility of moving to German-speaking Europe was very much on his mind. But the children were not taught German. Jacob came from a long line of Jewish scholars—but the children were not taught Hebrew. There were ideological reasons for that.

Columbia University

The Taubeses came to Columbia during the University's heyday. The Cold War had brought a stream of government funding to the University, not only for the development of the sciences, but for the burgeoning field of "area studies" (regions of the world seen as of strategic interest) as well. The university's salaries were among the highest in the nation (ninth to be exact). In order to attract and retain faculty, the University offered them choice apartments near the campus, such as the one on Claremont Avenue, where the Taubeses took up residence.[6]

Part of what made Columbia distinctive—and particularly attractive to Jacob and Susan—was the Core Curriculum of Columbia College, the

University's undergraduate division. Developed after World War I to equip Columbia students for citizenship in the modern world, Contemporary Civilization at first focused on recent history. By the late 1930s there was a move toward teaching all undergraduates some form of "Great Books" as part of the core curriculum.[7] When Taubes arrived at Columbia, all students were required to take a section of Humanities A, a two-semester course intended to expose students to the great works of Western literature and philosophy. It was taught in small classes, largely by senior faculty, and focused on class discussions of classical texts. It was a course in which Jacob Taubes would thrive as a teacher.[8]

Since World War II, Columbia had been a welcoming place for Jewish faculty as well as students, in a way that Princeton was not, and to a degree that was unusual at a time when genteel antisemitism, while declining, was still very much alive in American academic life. Having cast off its own earlier antisemitism, in the two decades after the War, Columbia was in a privileged position to make use of local intellectual talent from among New York's Jews. That advantage would fade by the 1970s, as meritocratic hiring became de rigueur in most of American academia.[9] But while Columbia had many Jewish faculty and students, Orthodox students were few and far between, and religiously observant faculty a rarity.[10]

At the center of Columbia's intellectual life—at least in terms of influence on the larger educated public—were a handful of faculty members: the literary critic Lionel Trilling; Jacques Barzun, a cultural historian; the sociologist Robert K. Merton; Richard Hofstadter, a historian of the United States; and Daniel Bell, who had been appointed to a professorship in sociology.[11] This group was committed to a critical (and self-critical) liberalism. Taubes was very much outside this circle. The only member with whom he was acquainted was Daniel Bell, whose empiricism and political liberalism were alien to Taubes's sensibilities.

The Establishment of the Academic Study of Religion at Columbia: Beyond Christian Apologetics

The field of "religion," in which Jacob was hired to teach at Columbia, was relatively new to the American academy. Though the roots of the scholarly study of religion lay in the Enlightenment, it was only in the mid-nineteenth century that universities across Europe began to create chairs for "the history and philosophy of religion."[12] From its very beginning, the academic study of religion posed a number of challenges to faith. One arose from the historical method, which, as we have seen, threatened to undercut the validity of religious beliefs, for both Christians and Jews. Another challenge came from the comparative method: once Christianity was studied alongside other world religions, and using the same criteria, its claims to unique truth were called into question, if not explicitly, then by implication. Conservative churchmen were therefore wary of the academic study of religion. For their part, advocates of the scientific study of religion were critical of theology. And some secularists were skeptical about whether the study of religion belonged in the university at all.[13]

Until well into the interwar period, the teaching of religion at many American universities was bound up with apologetics; that is, its implicit goal was to contribute to the inspirational aims of mainline Protestantism.[14] Whether and how religion ought to be taught in the academy was a matter of debate in the United States as it had been in Europe, and the origins of the department at Columbia are illustrative of why that was so. At the beginning of the twentieth century, "religion" at Columbia was under the purview of the university chaplain, an Episcopalian clergyman. To make Christianity the subject of academic study within a department of religion was to relativize its claims and to rob it of taken-for-granted authority.

That ethos was at odds with the way in which Protestant Christianity was taught elsewhere on Morningside Heights, namely at Union Theological Seminary, across Broadway from the Columbia campus. To teach Christianity to future clergymen was to assume its truth, however that truth was interpreted, just as to teach Judaism to future rabbis at the nearby Jewish Theological Seminary was to assume *its* truth, subject again to a diversity of interpretation.

On the one hand, therefore, at Columbia as at many other American colleges and universities, there was resistance from believing Christians to religion being taught as an academic subject. On the other hand, there was opposition to the study of religion at Columbia on the grounds that it did not belong in the curriculum of a nondenominational university. When, in 1908, the university approved the university chaplain's request to teach a course on the Bible, it was with the proviso that the course be free from all "denominational bias, so that it could be profitably taken by students without infringement upon their personal religious affiliations."[15] At the time Taubes was hired by Columbia, the university chaplain retained a role in the teaching of religion: the chaplain of the University, James A. Pike, also served as executive officer of the program in religion, and later, when Taubes was already on the faculty, Pike's successor as university chaplain, John M. Krumm, taught courses in the department.[16] By then, religious studies had emerged from the cocoon of the chaplain's office, with the aid of some interested philosophers.[17]

A few members of the Department of Philosophy began to offer courses in religion in the late 1920s. One of them was Horace L. Friess, who, beginning in 1936, served as the editor of the *Review of Religion*, a journal published at Columbia. In 1943, the university decided to offer doctoral degrees in the field of religion, utilizing faculty from a variety of departments, as well as from Union Theological Seminary; most of its students were clergy holding degrees in Divinity.[18] The faculty began to offer a graduate course that Friess coordinated, Critical Introduction to the History and Philosophy of Religion.

After the War, there was increased interest in the study of religion, and by 1954 there were seventeen universities in North America offering doctorates in the field. It was only in the late 1950s and early 1960s that professional societies were established: the Society for the Scientific Study of Religion in 1959, and the American Academy of Religion (a renamed successor to the older National Association of Biblical Instructors).[19] Increasingly, the scholarly study of religion was becoming distinct from the professional training of future clergy.[20] Scholars of religion sought to be scientific humanists: the scholar's own religious commitments (or lack thereof) were to be irrelevant to his scholarly research.[21]

Columbia's program in religion was granted the status of a department in 1961. But it lacked a well-defined undergraduate course of study, and its graduate program lacked a unifying conception.[22]

Jacob's appointment to Columbia was therefore to a vaguely defined discipline, with porous borders. That suited him fine, and in his years at Columbia he taught courses on a wide range of subjects, some centered on religion, some not. In his first year, for example, he taught a course on Religion and Social Change (focused on major early twentieth-century European thinkers Max Weber, Ernst Troeltsch, and Bernard Groethysen), and another on The Interpretation of History, which he called his *Steckenpferd* (hobby-horse), as well as introductory courses in the Humanities core curriculum.[23] During his first three years at Columbia, Taubes also taught courses at the Reform rabbinical seminary in Manhattan, Hebrew Union College-Jewish Institute of Religion.

What made Taubes's courses stand out was that his courses dealt with nineteenth- and twentieth-centuries continental thinkers—Hegel, Freud, and Heidegger—who at the time were barely taught at Columbia, either because they were too modern, or because they fell outside of the academic disciplines as they were then defined. Not long after arriving on campus,

Taubes wrote to Carl Friedrich that "there is no splash of Hegel on campus," which gave Taubes a near monopoly that suited him fine.[24] While Freud was certainly well known and indeed in vogue among literary scholars such as Lionel Trilling, he was not much taught in courses.[25] Heidegger was not taught in the Philosophy Department, a department devoted, like its counterpart at Harvard, to linguistic and conceptual analytic rigor. The work of Max Weber would have been familiar to sociologists; to teach Weber in a Department of Religion, as Taubes did, was uncommon.

Among Taubes's warmest supporters on the Columbia faculty was Horace Friess, with whom he repeatedly taught the introductory graduate course to the study of religion. Of German-Jewish origin, Friess was active in the Ethical Culture Society (founded by a Reform Jewish rabbi who had jettisoned as unnecessary baggage all the elements of Judaism except for ethical monotheism), and was married to the daughter of its founder. Friess was a mediocre teacher, a less than stellar philosopher, and deeply conventional. Yet Friess loved Jacob Taubes, perhaps because Taubes was everything that he was not.[26]

During Jacob's first year at Columbia, Susan occupied the role of "faculty wife," which hardly suited her. With her recent PhD in hand, she looked for a job, and found a position at Columbia as a curator of the Bush Museum, a collection of photographs, slides, and religious ceremonial objects from around the world, begun by Wendell T. Bush, a professor of philosophy and collector.[27] The collection was especially strong in "primitive culture materials," including Navajo artifacts.[28] Her activity there would change the focus of her scholarly interests and lead to books on Native American and African myths and tales. From 1958 to 1962, she taught occasional courses in the Department of Religion, including Introduction to Religion, Religion and the Arts, and in 1961–62 a graduate course, Comparative Mythology.

Taubes as Merchant of Ideas

Taubes lived in the age before the Internet. That fact is obvious when we consider his chronology. But it is worth remembering what that meant in terms of the flow of scholarly information. Information about what had been published, what was being written, and what was being discussed in various scholarly disciplines and national contexts was hard to come by. Acquisition of such information was more dependent on human networks.

In that context, knowing Jacob Taubes was an advantage to his colleagues. For Jacob knew a good deal about what was going on. What was going on in the fields of philosophy, religion, and many of the humanities and social sciences. What was going on in a variety of national contexts—in New York, Chicago, and Cambridge, MA; in Berlin and Frankfurt, as well as in Paris and London. What was going on among Jews, Catholics, and some Protestants. What was going on among intellectuals on the left and on the right. He knew some of this from his reading (a distinctive mode of reading, to which we will return). But he knew much of it from conversations with other intellectuals and scholars, as well as from his students. For more than reading or formal writing, conversation was Jacob's favored mode of communication. Jacob liked to talk to people, especially about ideas—and about intellectuals. He had a quick grasp of ideas,[29] and an insatiable appetite for intellectual gossip.

True, his knowledge was broader than it was deep. And so we find that scholars with whom he talked often assumed that his expertise lay in some field other than their own. But in fact Jacob *did* know more than most about many fields that were not his own. Some of that knowledge was secondhand and some was imperfectly understood. But knowledge it was, and Jacob was eager to share it. Some of that was showing off his erudition, but much of it was an expression of genuine intellectual friendship. To the sociologist Robert Bellah, who was schooled in Durkheim, for example, Taubes exclaimed, "Bob, you've got to read *The King's Two Bodies*"—a recently published work by the medieval historian Ernst Kantorowicz, which was indeed a seminal work exploring the interaction of religion and politics in medieval Europe.[30] The book eventually achieved fame, but it is unlikely that Bellah would have come across it on his own. Jacob's wide-ranging knowledge, fine memory, and ability to make unexpected connections made him a stimulating interlocutor for many who crossed his path. A Columbia colleague, the scholar of German literature Walter Sokel, put it this way: "Before there was Google, there was Taubes." That is, Sokel would ask Taubes about the literature on a topic, and out would come a stream of references. He was capable of presenting differing sides of a question in an undogmatic way.[31] So Taubes was more like Google with charisma. Unlike Google, however, Taubes made unexpected intellectual connections.

He also had a keen sense of humor. In a discussion with the young sociologist of religion, Peter L. Berger, Taubes recounted a dialogue he purported to have had with Leo Strauss. "What, Professor Strauss, is the secret that esotericism seeks to hide?" Taubes asked. Strauss's answer: "That God is dead." To which Taubes replied, "Herr Professor, daß hat sich langsam herumgesprochen"—"Herr Professor, word seems to slowly have

FIGURE 8.1. Martin Buber and Jacob Taubes at Columbia, 1957.
(Ethan and Tania Taubes Collection.)

gotten out." Was the story accurate? Probably not. But from Taubes's perspective, it conveyed a deeper truth, namely that Strauss's esotericism was
anachronistic if not archaic.[32]

Taubes's first foray into intellectual entrepreneurship at Columbia
was organizing the visit of Martin Buber to campus. Buber had visited
the United States once before, in 1951.[33] Taubes arranged for him to visit
Columbia on his second trip, in 1957, with a strategic purpose in mind.

He applied to the University for funds to run a two-week "working group" with Buber on Chassidism and Western Man, which he conceived as the foundation of an ongoing university seminar in religion.[34] Taubes took pains to invite the intellectual luminaries of Morningside Heights, including the theologian Reinhold Niebuhr from Union Theological Seminary, the art historian Meyer Shapiro from Columbia, and Abraham Joshua Heschel from the Jewish Theological Seminary (who seems to have kept his distance). Other faculty and graduate students also attended, including Walter Kaufmann from Princeton (who would go on to translate Buber's best-known work, *I and Thou*, into English); the not-yet-famous scholar of religious myth, Joseph Campbell of Sarah Lawrence College; the prominent jurist Judge Jerome Frank; and Taubes's friend Michael Wyschogrod, who was both an Orthodox Jew and a Heidegger scholar (an extraordinary combination in the 1950s).[35] A vivid exchange took place, with Niebuhr, Frank, and Kaufmann, in sequence, taxing Buber with the question of how the I-Thou relation would make a difference in making political, judicial, and ethical decisions.[36] The Buber seminar, as Taubes had hoped, did become the basis of an ongoing Colloquy on the History of Religions. When Buber visited again in the spring of 1958, Taubes organized a colloquy in his honor, with a panel that included Hans Jonas (then at the New School); John Herman Randall of Columbia, a historian of philosophy; and Benjamin Nelson of Hofstra University, a sociologist with a deep interest in the history of Christianity, who was to become a frequent interlocutor.[37]

Taubes's relationship to Buber was ongoing, and important to the younger man. At a time when Buber's reputation in the United States was swelling—Protestant theologians seemed to regard him as a modern prophet (an image fostered by his beard)—for Taubes to be seen as Buber's impresario could only boost his status. Buber loved flattery, and Taubes laid it on with a trowel.[38] Buber was a frequent visitor to the home of Jacob's parents in Zurich. In a letter written shortly after the death of Fanny Taubes, Jacob wrote to Buber, "I only want to thank you for all the goodness and faithfulness that you have shown us. Consoled by your letter, my mother died reassured about her son. The last printed word that she held in her hands was [Buber's book], *The Way of Man, According to the Teachings of Hasidism*."[39] Taubes contributed an essay to a volume on Buber's thought in the series The Library of Living Philosophers, published in German in 1963, and in English in 1967, by which time Buber was no longer among the living.[40]

The Buber seminar at Columbia set the stage for Jacob's next venture as a merchant of ideas: his leadership of two University Seminars. The

University Seminars were a unique Columbia institution.[41] Organized by Columbia faculty but drawing upon scholars at the many other institutions of higher education in the city, each seminar involved a group of fifteen to twenty professors from a variety of disciplines who shared some common interest and who met periodically to discuss papers, either by members of the seminar or by invited guests. Participation was unremunerated and demanded an ongoing commitment. In 1958, the colloquy on the history of religion was rechristened the University Seminar on Religion and Culture, chaired by Taubes and Friess.

These forums allowed Taubes to hone his skills as a mediator of ideas. His speakers included some Columbia faculty members, but most notably, European immigrant scholars or European professors who were visiting the United States. Before each monthly meeting, Taubes sent a letter of invitation to scholars who he thought might be interested, together with a one-page précis of the talk. Often the letters of invitation included capsule summaries and evaluations of the speaker's career that amounted to small gems of scholarship. Invited speakers during the first year (1957–58) included Friedrich Gogarten, a Protestant theologian who decades earlier had developed "crisis theology" together with Karl Barth; Hans Jonas, who spoke on Gnosticism; Krister Stendahl on Paul's theology; Albert Jacques Cuttat of the École des hautes études in Paris on Indian religion; Mircea Eliade from the University of Chicago on "Shamanistic Initiations in Siberia and Australia"; and Robert Grant, also from Chicago, an expert on Gnosticism.[42]

At the same time, Taubes organized another forum, the Colloquy for Religion and Psychiatry, focused on "the boundaries of psychology and religion." He first invited Paul Ricoeur, professor of philosophy at the Sorbonne, for a series of weekly seminars on the theme of The Sense of Guilt, Its Symbols and Its Myths, that lasted from October through November.[43] Then the colloquy turned to a discussion of the work of the contemporary Swiss analyst, Ludwig Binswanger, a pioneer of the field of existential psychoanalysis. In addition to Taubes's friend Walter Kaufmann, the participants included several figures who were relatively unknown, but would emerge onto the intellectual stage in the decades that followed. Silvano Arieti was an Italian-born physician and psychoanalyst and a professor at New York Medical College. He would go on to write noted books on schizophrenia, depression, and the links between such mental illnesses and creativity—and would play a role in Jacob's later treatment for manic depression. Paul Goodman was a novelist and psychotherapist, who in 1960 would publish *Growing Up Absurd*, which became a widely read work of social criticism. Rollo May was, at the time, the oldest and best-known member of the group: his 1969 book, *Love and Will*, became a bestseller.

For 1959–60, the seminar was organized around a new theme, The Uses of Charisma in Organized Religion. It kicked off with a paper by Taubes, "Dilemmas of a Charismatic Community, a Case Study of Corinth," for which he provided a précis:

> The dissension in the primitive Christian Community at Corinth (which may be reconstructed from Paul's first epistle to the Corinthians) highlights the pneumatic-anarchic implications of the messianic experience . . . Paul's "lyric" song on love, in particular (I. Cor. 13: "Though I speak with the tongues of men and angels, and have no charity . . .") is revealed, upon closer examination, to be a complex polemic against the anarchic solipsistic edge of charismatic experience.[44]

Though the abstract is brief, it reveals a good deal about Taubes's hermeneutic approach. He focused on a famous passage from the New Testament, often read at weddings, funerals, and other ceremonial occasions because of its repeated invocation of the power of love. But when put into its original historical and experiential context, Paul's words take on a very different meaning. What seems to be a hymn to love is in fact a plea for the necessity of love as a tool of forbearance in circumstances when a new, messianic source of charismatic authority leads individuals to see themselves as liberated from the constraints of tradition. Since they lack agreement as to how to live together under the new dispensation, anarchy threatens—leading to Paul's plea for love as tolerance.

In addition to the University Seminars on religion, in 1959 Taubes founded the Columbia University Seminar on Problems of Interpretation (Hermeneutics). Regular attendees, as he told Max Horkheimer when he invited him to address the seminar, included Friess, the historians of philosophy John Herman Randall and Paul Kristeller, and Daniel Bell, as well as "several learned Jesuits, literary critics, and some philosophers from other area universities."[45] Hannah Arendt and Taubes's Columbia colleague the philosopher Sidney Morgenbesser were also among the regular attendees.

Faith and History

Taubes published very little after coming to Columbia, which helps explain why, although he was promoted to associate professor with tenure in 1959, promotion to full professor long eluded him. What little he

produced had nothing to do with Jewish studies until he came to be considered for a chair in that field at the Free University of Berlin in 1961. In
the years that followed, he published only two articles on Jewish themes,
one on Martin Buber's philosophy of history and an article on "Nachman
Krochmal and Modern Historicism," published in the academic journal
Judaism in 1963.[46]

Substantial parts of that article were drawn directly from his Hebrew
chapter (published a decade earlier in an obscure volume) on "Beliefs and
Ideas in Nineteenth Century Theology," which had focused on the challenge of enlightened rationalism and historicism to Jewish religious self-
understanding. Without mentioning Leo Strauss by name, Taubes began
with a not-so-subtle criticism of Strauss's *Natural Right and History*
(1953) by declaring that there was no going back to prehistoricist understandings of natural right or natural law as eternal. Yet the whole rabbinic
tradition, Taubes asserted, is based on the premise of the eternal validity
of the written and oral law, such that the historical process is irrelevant to
the rabbinic mode of thought. Thus, rabbinic Judaism lacks a historical
sense of progress or development. A consciousness of history as a process
is to be found, by contrast, in apocalyptic doctrines, which, Taubes noted,
existed within both the Christian and Jewish traditions. Within rabbinic
Judaism, "The messianic stance was kept in check by the overriding interest to conserve or preserve the law and build a fence around it." Medieval
Jewish philosophy (with the exception of Yehuda Halevi) also tended to be
devoid of historical perspectives. "One could go even further and state that
in the concern for the authority of the law these philosophers responded
to a central theme of primary interest in classical philosophy. The union
between the classic philosophy and the Jewish jurists of the halacha was
not entirely accidental: the categories of the rabbinic jurists are both static
and closed to the historic experience that the apocalyptic mood was able
to articulate."[47] The outbreak of apocalyptic, messianic movements in the
sixteenth and seventeenth centuries (he had in mind Sabbatianism) "left
a trauma that caused an almost complete amnesia of the historical sense
or of historical consciousness in the interpretation of Judaism." Far from
being a bridge to Jewish modernity, as Scholem suggested, the Sabbatian
episode's "failure was a cause for an even more radical suppression of the
historic sense."

Taubes turned again to Krochmal to explore a broader tension between
faith in traditional religion and "the liquidating forces contained in historic consciousness," and between relating to a tradition from inside it
versus an external perspective. "It is often overlooked but nevertheless

fundamental for the understanding of the developments of historic studies since the seventeenth century that the historic consciousness, while
heir to the tradition of the historic religions, Judaism and Christianity,
acts as a critical, even as a liquidating, agent for the tradition of historical
religions," he noted. "Krochmal's philosophy of history constructs an internal history of the spirit seen from the terminal station of the Enlightenment. Krochmal still tries to persuade us of the living meaning of the texts
of scripture and tradition that he himself had put into a definite historic
context. His philosophy of history is on the borderline between a theodicy,
a theology of history evolved inside the circle of a living religion, and a historical investigation developed at a distance from the living tradition." A
generation after Krochmal, "the ideologists of Reform Judaism conceived
the history of the Jewish people as a spiritual history" so that "nothing
remained but a history of a ghost of the prophetic principle or of ethical
ideas. Modern Jewish studies were for generations active in propagating
this idealized image of Jewish history," he charged.[48]

Here was the dilemma to which Taubes pointed. For a person steeped
in modern thought, it was impossible (or intellectually disingenuous) to
think of the key concepts and symbols of Judaism in the ahistorical terms
characteristic of the rabbinic tradition. Yet it was belief in these symbols
that gave legitimacy and cogency to religious language. With the rise of
the historicist sensibility, however, "What were once fixed points in the
constellation become part and parcel of the finite and ephemeral human
historic endeavor." Terms like creation, revelation, and redemption then
lose their psychic hold, the belief that they are binding in an absolute
sense. Thus "the historic sense may also be a disease and danger to our
experience of life: you take life in too easy a fashion if you take it only in
an historical manner." Taubes suggested the need for a "critique of historical reasoning," but acknowledged that "expelled from the paradise of a
transhistorical existence, we cannot regain our innocence except through
the hard and arduous journey on the road of history itself."[49] In short,
historical consciousness dissolved binding faith, leaving the possibility of
what to Taubes seemed an unworthy or unserious existence. But one could
not simply forget history or the modern awareness of the historicity of
religion. That was his dilemma too—and by no means his alone.[50] Here,
Taubes echoed his previous judgment of Karl Barth: that the Protestant
theologian Barth had tried to interpret Christianity in a new way that did
away with the problem of historicism by ignoring it. But Barth too had
failed to offer a plausible approach to a faith tradition by simply refusing
to acknowledge history.

Religious Ambivalence

Jacob's own religious life remained ambivalent.

Susan's adamant opposition to any trace of Jewish religious observance—combined no doubt with Jacob's own doubts—led to a household bereft of even minimal traditional Jewish symbols and practices. There were no Sabbath candles, no kosher food, and no celebration of Jewish holidays: in December there was a Christmas tree.[51]

The Taubeses demonstrated their transformation in dramatic fashion to Jacob's friends Irving Kristol and Gertrude Himmelfarb, who had first encountered him as their guide through Maimonides. They saw him again after his return from Jerusalem: in December 1952, when their son William was born in New York City, they asked Jacob to preside over the ceremony of the redemption of the firstborn (*pidyon haben*) at their home on Riverside Drive. Shortly thereafter, the Kristols moved to London, where Irving went to work as editor of *Encounter*, a magazine published by the Congress for Cultural Freedom. In 1958, the Kristols returned to New York and renewed their friendship with the Taubeses. Jacob invited Irving and Gertrude to a dinner party at his apartment, making a point of the urgent need to arrive promptly on time. When they were seated, he went into the kitchen and emerged bearing a whole suckling pig with an apple in its mouth (the first time the Kristols had seen such a sight, and the last). He did so as a deliberate flouting of the dietary laws of *kashrut*, as if daring God to do something about it. It was a sort of coming out ceremony, a graduation from Jewish observance.[52]

Neither Ethan nor his sister Tania received a Jewish education. When Ethan turned thirteen in 1965, he did not have a bar mitzvah.

Yet Jacob was never fully at peace with this state of affairs. Neither his wife nor his children attended synagogue, but Jacob himself would sometimes attend Sabbath services at the nearby Jewish Theological Seminary. When he did, he sat in the front row with the *gedolim* (the most distinguished members of the faculty, such as Finkelstein and Lieberman), a sign of his own conception of his status, though not one shared by those among whom he sat.[53] On such occasions, he wore a large prayer shawl, and prayed with fervor, sometimes to the point of weeping. He was, it seems, far from certain of his religious choices. From time to time he would venture northward to Yeshiva University to attend lectures by Rabbi Joseph Soloveitchik, the leading light of modern Orthodoxy.[54] Or southward, to Brooklyn, where he would visit with the Satmar Rebbe or attend the mass gatherings (*farbrengen*) of the Rebbe of Lubavitch—rebbes who were prevented by ideological rivalry from visiting with one another—to immerse himself, if only as an observer, in what he regarded as authentic Judaism.[55]

At Columbia, as at Harvard, Jacob did not teach on the High Holy Days, because, as he explained to Carl Friedrich, "these are the three days in the year I retreat from all 'secular' matters. I can't say I retreat into the spiritual sacred realm, but at least into a congregation where many of my forefathers have found the spirit."[56]

Jacob's ambivalence was also expressed in his conversations with Norman Podhoretz, a young literary and social critic who, together with his wife Midge Decter and their children, lived near the Taubeses, at 106th Street and Riverside Drive. Podhoretz had grown up in a Yiddish-speaking home in Brooklyn, and had then taken courses at JTS while attending Columbia University, where he became a protégé of Lionel Trilling.[57] When they would meet on the street, Podhoretz loved to talk with Jacob, and they would kibbitz in Yiddish. Jacob's persona was different when he spoke Yiddish: more ironic, humorous and self-deprecating. (His Yiddish was inflected with German and spoken with a Galician accent.[58]) The two of them would lament the fact that they were not providing their sons with a Jewish education, with Taubes observing, "All *apikorsim* should have only daughters"—because, traditionally, daughters were not thought to require a Jewish education.[59] In 1960, Podhoretz became the editor of *Commentary*, transforming it into a journal more critical of American society: his first major act as editor was to publish excerpts from Paul Goodman's manuscript *Growing Up Absurd* over three issues of the magazine.[60] In 1967, he would publish a debate between Herbert Marcuse and Norman O. Brown (two thinkers that Taubes admired) about Brown's book, *Love's Body* (1966). Later, Podhoretz would become a leading voice of what came to be called "neoconservatism," together with his older mentor, Irving Kristol. But in the late 1950s and 1960s, Podhoretz too was attracted to antinomianism. Paul Goodman was his friend. He published Scholem's essay on Sabbatai Zevi, "Redemption through Sin," in *Commentary*. While Podhoretz saw Jacob Taubes as a deeply corrupt human being, he found him all the more interesting for that very reason. In retrospect, he described Jacob not as what the Jewish liturgy calls a sinner (*choteh*), but as a transgressor (*avaryan*), who transgresses as a deliberate act.[61]

Taubes as Teacher

As a teacher of undergraduates at Columbia, Jacob developed a small but intense following of students, some of whom went on to careers in academia and publishing. Several of them evinced remarkable recall over forty years later of both the content of his courses and the impressions he made upon them. It was not just that his courses covered European thinkers who were rarely discussed elsewhere on the Columbia campus—or discussed in a way that was unusual at the time. It was also because of his charisma, his "magic," as more than one student remembered it.[62] There was his rare ability to make ideas come alive. And there was the antinomian message of so much of his teaching, which anticipated the spirit of revolt characteristic of the decade ahead, a kind of uptown version of what the Beats were doing downtown.[63]

Jacob's most enthusiastic devotees were a quartet of undergraduates who called themselves "the Gnostics," after one of Taubes's favorite themes. They included Morris Dickstein, Marshall Berman, and Richard Locke, each of whom went on to careers as cultural critics. Dickstein, a professor of English at Queens College, would write an influential account of the culture of the 1960s, *Gates of Eden* (1977). Berman would teach political theory at City College and author books of radical cultural analysis, including *The Politics of Authenticity* (1970) and *All That Is Solid Melts into Air: The Experience of Modernity* (1982). Locke became assistant editor of the *New York Times Book Review* and went on to teach writing at Columbia.

Locke and Berman first met Taubes as freshmen in 1958–59, when Taubes taught the Humanities survey.[64] Taubes was informal and seductive. His self-presentation was deliberately enticing: "Is my beard that I grew in Paris scaring you?" he asked his students. He was self-dramatizing and exotic, smoking his pipe and sporting a beret. He was a master of theatrical gestures, stroking his beard pensively, moving his hands outward toward the horizon, and turning his right hand (in a gesture that Susan Sontag called "Turning the celestial screw"[65]). There was about him a certain narcissism in his presentation of self, an endless performance that attracted adulation and communicated a sense of a life lived on the edge. He was a brilliant pedagogue, bringing the students immediately into the midst of the material, with minimal introduction. "What do you know about Homer?" he asked, and "What is myth?"—to which he offered the aperçu: "A myth is a story that never happened but is nevertheless true." His intellectual intensity conveyed the sheer energy and excitement of ideas.

In a broad survey of great books, such as Humanities A, most instructors would teach each work independently. Taubes was unusual in presenting a broad, overarching conception of a trajectory from Homer to Nietzsche, as a history of demythologization. The course included a reading of the *Akedah* (the binding of Isaac in the Book of Genesis), which Taubes (drawing upon Erich Auerbach's interpretation in his book, *Mimesis*) contrasted with Greek modes of storytelling. He offered a close reading of Plato's *Symposium*, stressing the dramatic players and their feelings, and conveying the erotic tension of the dialogue (with frequent use of the word "erotic"). In his exploration of the New Testament, Taubes provided a compelling portrait of Jesus—without in any sense providing a temptation to Christian belief. He stressed the importance of the expectation of Jesus's imminent return (the Parousia). He speculated about the possible link between Judas Iscariot and the radical zealot group, the Sacari, and suggested that perhaps Judas had arranged for Jesus to be killed because of his failure to engage in the political revolution the Zealots favored.

As in his presentation to the University Seminar on Religion, Taubes discussed the Apostle Paul as a revolutionary, betting on the viability of a new charismatic community created by a leap of faith. In that sense, Taubes noted, he was a precursor of modern revolutionary movements, which are also based on a leap of faith that the new community they try to create will have charisma. Taubes evoked the prospect of a new and very different order. But he also presented it as a cautionary tale about the likelihood of failure.[66] Taubes's presentation of religious texts made it possible for secularists to appropriate them and find them relevant. He suggested that because people have similar needs over time, these past models were relevant in the present. He also conveyed what Ernst Bloch had called the "principle of hope"—the need to keep alive the hope for a radically different future. Taubes thus put his students on the lookout for an apocalyptic turn—while also making them aware of the hazards of apocalypticism.[67]

During 1959–60, Locke, Dickstein, and Berman took a course on Hegel and his aftermath, taught by Taubes, assisted by Susan Sontag. The course was scheduled to begin with Hegel's *Phenomenology of Spirit*, then move on to Feuerbach, Marx, Kierkegaard, and Nietzsche. As he had at Harvard, Taubes presented his students with an analysis of Hegel's book focused on the dialectic of master and slave—the interpretation he had picked up from Kojève. By then the semester was half over, and the course took an unexpected turn. Taubes had attended an off-Broadway production of Jean Genet's play *The Balcony*, which is set in a brothel. Taubes thought the play exemplified the dialectic of recognition that Hegel had presented in the *Phenomenology*, and so the class spent some of the remainder of the semester discussing the play in those terms.[68] As in *Abendländische Eschatologie*, Taubes situated Marxism in the longer history of culture, as another link in the chain of transformative movements going back at least as far as Paul. That framing was quite extraordinary at a time when most Marxists presented Marxism as a form of science, and as representing a revolutionary discontinuity from earlier history.[69]

Together with Sontag, Taubes also taught a course that, whatever its title, was effectively about the "erotico-mystical tradition." The class read some essays by Scholem, including "Redemption through Sin" on Sabbatai Zevi and Jacob Frank. Taubes explored the notion of going through evil in order to exhaust it in a way that made it vital to his students. He also took the unusual step of assigning Isaac Bashevis Singer's novel *Satan in Goray*, which recaptures the Sabbatian episode on a local level, and explores the inversion of the social order and social norms—including sexual norms.[70] As he would throughout his teaching career, Taubes was adept at finding contemporary analogies to make historical events more vivid for his students. To illustrate how followers of Jacob Frank subsequently repressed their erstwhile enthusiasm for the pseudo-Messiah, he analogized them to erstwhile communists who during the McCarthy era hid their previous sympathies.[71]

After taking several courses with Taubes, Richard Locke noticed that he was repeating certain stock themes and ideas. Taubes *used* ideas as a form of self-exhibition, Locke realized, and while the individual insights were of interest, there was no coherence or developmental progress in his thought. In each of his classes, Taubes generated an expectation that all of what he was teaching would come together in a new synthesis and a new revelation. But this expectation was inevitably disappointed. (An experience that the Kristols had had earlier.)

Taubes was a magnet for proto-political cultural radicals. To some of Jacob's young devotees, he and Susan seemed the quintessential avant-garde intellectual couple, exemplars of the sort of path they imagined for themselves. As Dickstein recalls,

> Radiating charm, intelligence, and mystery, Taubes drew men and women irresistibly into his orbit. Yet from our lowly viewpoint he also seemed to have the perfect family, a beautiful and brilliant wife, the dark-haired Susan, and two attractive children. On the day of a nuclear air-raid drill, when all of us were supposed to take cover, I saw the four of them standing in mute protest on the steps of Low Library, as if on a windswept English heath.[72]

At least one of the members of the Gnostics, Marshall Berman, though he loved Taubes, also developed a distrust of him. For when Berman introduced his girlfriend to his revered teacher, Taubes began to "cerebrally seduce" her. Berman was aware that other members of the Columbia faculty were suspicious of Taubes. Some regarded him as a cult leader because of his charismatic personality; others as dissolute.[73]

The distrust that Taubes elicited and the suspicion of debauchery that trailed him was connected to his erotic relationships with women. But his relationships with women were not an incidental element of his persona; they were inextricably linked to his transgression of boundaries and his proclivity for risk-taking, precisely the qualities he championed in his lectures and writings on Gnosticism and apocalypticism.

Empathy and Seduction

Jacob Taubes was not only a stimulating conversationalist: he was also a good listener. Many people—men and women, his seniors and his juniors—testified to his ability to understand them, their interests, and their concerns. Some found his ability to penetrate their thoughts after a brief acquaintance as preternatural and even frightening.

Jacob could be treacherous in his relations. But he could also display extraordinary levels of generosity, emotional and even financial.

Take the case of Annette Michelson, who first met Jacob and Susan in 1949, when her friend, Ruth Glazer, took her to their engagement party. Later that year, Michelson moved to Paris, where she remained for the next decade and a half. She had her first intensive discussion with Jacob when he visited her in Paris, en route back from Jerusalem, and declared, "I am an antinomian." Michelson introduced Jacob to a circle of Romanian émigré intellectuals in Paris who were to become his friends, including Emil Cioran and Paul Celan. When Jacob saw her in Paris in the early 1960s, Michelson had just broken up with her longtime lover, was virtually penniless, and was living the most insecure of existences. Jacob spontaneously gave her $300, which tided her over in her time of need. She thought that his own sense of insecurity made him attuned to the insecurity of others.[74] She later returned to New York, helped found the critical arts journals *Artforum* and *October*, and became a professor at New York University. Jacob and Susan remained her friends.

The caring and empathetic side of Jacob is also evident in the case of Jean Houston, who came to know Jacob when she was a junior at Barnard College, majoring in religion, and active in Off-Broadway theater. At a time when she was facing multiple tragedies among members of her family, she suffered a serious concussion when the scenery in a theater production fell on her head. The combination of emotional and physical blows rendered her almost blind, and a crisis of self-confidence brought her close to failing out of the college. It was at that point that, deeply wounded psychologically, she decided to take a course on Job, offered by Jacob Taubes. During the first class, Taubes announced that he would be departing from the course description to focus instead on the implicit dialectic between the Apostle Paul and the work of Friedrich Nietzsche, and in the course of the semester he touched upon Gnosticism, Hegelian philosophy, phenomenology, and existentialism. When she began to ask questions that Taubes regarded as intelligent, he took steps to draw her out.

One day, when she was crossing the campus, she heard his voice calling her name: "Miss Houston, let me walk with you. . . . You know you have a most interesting mind. . . . Your questions are luminous. . . . What do you think is the nature of the transvaluation of values in the apostle Paul and Nietzsche? . . . It is important for my reflections that I have your reflections." His expressed interest and confidence in her allowed Houston to feel confident enough to speculate and expostulate on these questions, and—according to her retrospective account—led to the lifting of her blindness.[75] In her memoir, Houston considered Taubes to be among her most memorable teachers.[76]

What she did not mention was an incident involving Jacob that was related to Ethan Taubes by Houston herself,[77] and recounted in Susan's novel, *Divorcing*, in which Jean Houston appears under the name "Kate Dallas," who, like Houston herself, was over six feet tall. "Once he tried to make a pass at me," Dallas recounts, "I picked him up, put him in an airplane spin and threw him across the floor."

Jean Houston went on to graduate study in religion, then to research on the spiritual uses of LSD, and finally to a career as a founder of the human potential movement. She took to harnessing myth as a tool for personal development.[78] In the 1990s she became a best-selling author in the market for self-help books, and achieved a degree of notoriety when it was revealed that as an advisor to Hillary Clinton, Houston had encouraged the First Lady to envision herself in conversation with Eleanor Roosevelt.[79]

As Jacob's experience with Jean Houston demonstrates, with Jacob there was a fleeting line between empathy and seduction. The empathy may have been sincere enough, but it was often a means to seduction, not necessarily in the physical sense (though there was plenty of that too) but in the sense of craving the attention, approval, and admiration of others. Both men and women who knew Jacob Taubes described him as engaged in an ongoing process of seduction.[80]

Susan Sontag

Susan Sontag would play an important role in the life of both Jacob and Susan Taubes, and they would play a role in hers—not least by providing her with material for her stories, novels, and films.

In the years since their friendship in Cambridge, Sontag had spent time in Oxford and Paris, while her son David was looked after by Philip Rieff's parents. Her French sojourn widened the range of her experience, including the rediscovery and embrace of her erotic preference for women. When she returned to the United States, she informed Philip that their marriage was over. Taking custody of young David, in 1959 she moved to New York, where—thanks to a recommendation from Jacob—she found a job as an assistant editor at *Commentary* magazine. Jacob had long sought to bed Sontag; he now succeeded. She reported in her diary that Jacob was "unexpectedly good + sensitive sexually."[81]

Sontag was looking for other work, and she found it through Jacob Taubes, who helped her to get a job teaching in his department at Columbia, first assisting in his own courses, and then as an instructor with courses of her own.[82] During the spring of 1960, she served as Jacob's assistant in a course on the sociology of religion, which began with Paul's epistles, and she also attended Taubes's seminar on Hegel.[83] In the spring of 1961, they taught a course together that dealt with Nietzsche, Freud, and "Freud in the service of 'Utopian' thinking," focused on recent works by Erich Fromm, Herbert Marcuse, and Norman O. Brown.[84] In the fall of 1961, they taught a course on the problem of love in Western thought, focused on the changing meanings of eros and agape (in Christianity, God's love for man, reflected in human caring love for others), and the question of the costs of repressing or rechanneling eros. The course began with Empedocles and Plato, zeroed in on Paul and Nietzsche, and ended with a discussion of two recent books: Marcuse's *Eros and Civilization* and Norman O. Brown's *Life against Death* (1959).[85] Some of the courses key themes were echoed in a review of Brown's book that Sontag wrote at the time, "Psychoanalysis and Norman O. Brown's *Life against Death*." It was published in the literary supplement to the Columbia student newspaper, a supplement edited by Richard Locke, who participated in the Taubes seminar. The review, with its emphasis on "the revolutionary implications of sexuality in contemporary society," its praise of Brown's focus on the body, and its evocation of the "eschatological aspirations" to end repression, was the complete antithesis of Philip Rieff's recent book, *Freud: The Mind of the Moralist*—the authorship of which Sontag would later claim for herself.[86]

A later course that Taubes taught with Sontag, Biblical Literature and the Western Imagination, initiated a new dynamic in Jacob's style of teaching. Sontag, his assistant, carried the burden of much of the regular instruction in the seminar, running the sections, while Jacob would chime in as the spirit moved him. Sontag too was a brilliant teacher, and like Jacob, she discussed texts spontaneously and in an idiomatic style.[87]

In the years that followed, Sontag taught the freshman Humanities sequence, as well as Introduction to the Old Testament and Theories of Religious Behavior (both in 1963–64). She would have liked to continue teaching at Columbia, but after three years there, the provost, Jacques Barzun, refused to allow her to remain because she did not have a doctorate, and he did not want to set a precedent. It was delegated to Jacob's colleague in the Department of Religion, Harold Stahmer, to convey the message that her contract would not be renewed. She broke down and cried on hearing the news. Stahmer suggested that perhaps her forte was writing rather than teaching.[88] And so it proved to be. For while teaching with Taubes at Columbia, she had begun to publish essays in cultural criticism that were soon to bring her a modicum of fame as a high-brow intellectual in tune with the radical and liberationist sensibilities of the 1960s. Her first collection of essays, published in 1966, *Against Interpretation*, included her review of Norman Brown's *Life against Death*. By 1968, she was back at the Columbia campus, protesting at the university's commencement ceremony against the university's role in the American war effort in Vietnam. Dressed in jeans and sandals, she shouted at Columbia's faculty and administration, whom she referred to, in the avant garde idiom of the day, as "You motherfuckers."[89]

Graduate Students

Half of Taubes's teaching time was devoted to graduate instruction. Together with Friess, he repeatedly taught the course Critical Introduction to the History and Philosophy of Religion. On his own, he taught graduate courses that covered some of the texts and thinkers he had written about in *Abendländische Eschatologie* and had taught at Harvard and Princeton. The Crisis of Religion in Modern Times dealt with Hegel, Feuerbach, Marx, Kierkegaard, Nietzsche, Dostoyevsky, and Heidegger. Humanism and Religion touched upon Greek drama and philosophy, the Old Testament and the New, Augustine, Eckhardt, Nicholas of Cusa, and on to Rousseau. Social Theory and the History of Religions presumably focused on Max Weber and Freud. Toward the end of his time at Columbia, in the spring of 1964, he taught a course on Hegel and Heidegger. Here too there were a number of students who went on to leading academic careers, and whose paths would cross with his in the years to come.

The oldest of these was Jacob Neusner, who was to play a key role in the development of Jewish studies in the United States.[90] Raised in a Reform Jewish household, Neusner had no background in Hebrew before attending Harvard in 1950–53. He was interested in Jewish studies, but his advisor, the yeshiva-trained Harry Wolfson, discouraged him from going into the field on the grounds that he lacked the Talmudic training to handle traditional Jewish texts. Neusner went on nevertheless to study with Saul Liebermann at JTS, spent time in Israel, and was enrolled in both the rabbinics program at JTS and the doctoral program in religion at Columbia. It was there that he met Jacob Taubes, in a course Taubes taught on the history of eschatology in the West. In 1960, Neusner received his rabbinical ordination and his doctorate, with a dissertation on the Talmudic sage Yohanan ben Zakkai. The dissertation was supervised by Morton Smith, an American scholar who had studied with Scholem at the Hebrew University, where he had written his dissertation in Hebrew.[91] Taubes served on Neusner's dissertation committee and thought highly enough of the younger man's abilities to hire him to teach in the Columbia department.

Neusner was a controversial and combative figure in the world of Jewish scholarship, especially in the study of the Jerusalem Talmud. He thought that Lieberman and the other Talmudists at JTS made too little use of critical historical methods in their scholarship on the Talmud, and that their scholarship was erudite but arid. They thought Neusner knew too little Talmud to write about it or translate it with authority. (Lieberman would later conclude his critical review of Neusner's translation of the Jerusalem Talmud, "The right place for his English translation is the wastebasket."[92]) According to Neusner's memoirs, objections to his abilities from the Talmudists at JTS led Columbia to replace him with a more favored candidate.[93] Neusner went on to teach at Dartmouth College, at Brown University, and at the University of South Florida. He also became a critic of Israeli scholarship in Jewish studies, which he thought too bound to textual study and too removed from social scientific methods in the study of religion.[94] Despite his idiosyncratic and cantankerous persona, Neusner became an influential figure in the field of Jewish studies, not only because he was preternaturally prolific in his publications, but because he controlled the Max Richter Foundation (named after his father-in-law, who had funded it), which helped subsidize the publication of his scholarship and that of his students. His contacts with Jacob Taubes would continue for decades.

Taubes brought in David Weiss from JTS to replace Neusner as the instructor for the course Classics of the Jewish Tradition. Weiss (later

Weiss Halivni) had come of age in Sighet, Romania, where as a child he was considered an *ilui* (prodigy) for his remarkable command of the Talmud, aided by a photographic memory. After surviving Auschwitz, he made his way to the United States and to JTS, where he eventually became professor of Talmud, and later yet, professor at Columbia.[95] Taubes prided himself on his ability to spot talent, and Weiss provides a case in point. So too does the man Taubes hired to replace Susan Sontag in teaching the Bible course after her contract ended: Nahum Sarna, then a librarian at JTS, but soon to become one of the greatest Biblical scholars of his generation.

Ismar Schorsch was another student from JTS, but his background and trajectory contrasted with that of Jacob Neusner. Born in Germany in 1935, the son of a rabbi who was a graduate of the Breslau Jewish Theological Seminary, Schorsch left with his family for the United States in December 1938.[96] After graduating from college, Schorsch enrolled in the rabbinical program at JTS, where he was ordained in 1962. He had already begun graduate work at Columbia, which led him to take two seminars with Taubes, including one focused on Hegel's *Phenomenology*. Students were required to write a research paper, and Taubes suggested that Schorsch write on Krochmal's seemingly Hegelian philosophy of history (a subject Taubes had written about in Jerusalem). Schorsch did so, producing a paper on Krochmal and historicism, which he turned into his first scholarly article, published in 1961 in the journal *Judaism*.[97] The experience was significant for both Taubes and Schorsch. For Taubes, it led him back to an interest in Krochmal, about whom he too published the article in *Judaism* discussed earlier. It is instructive to compare the treatment of Krochmal by Schorsch and Taubes: unlike Taubes, Schorsch seemed to concur with Krochmal that a historical understanding of the tradition does *not* undermine its validity.[98] For his doctoral dissertation, Schorsch turned to the political history of German Jewry. But after that he returned to the issue of the Jewish intellectual confrontation with historicism, becoming the leading historian of the development of *Wissenschaft des Judentums*, as well as a professor and eventually the chancellor of JTS.

Another future academic who studied with Taubes was Edith Wyschogrod, the wife of his friend Michael. Taubes pulled her into the philosophy of religion, which was a joint doctoral program between Columbia and Union Theological Seminary. In 1963-64, she took courses with him on Hegel, Freud, and Weber, and on Paul and his interpreters. She would go on to a career in the philosophy of religion, served as president of the American Academy of Religion, and played an ongoing role in Jacob's life.

Perhaps the graduate student closest to Taubes in his later years at Columbia was Gershon Greenberg, who came to the university in 1961, after having studied as an undergraduate with Taubes's old friend Eugen Kuhlmann. When Jacob and Susan separated, Greenberg stayed with him in his apartment on Claremont Avenue. He would follow Taubes to Berlin as an assistant, and then as a lecturer in the program of Judaic studies that Taubes founded there.

A Gnostic Personality

For some graduate students who encountered him at Columbia, there was an extraordinary quality about Jacob Taubes. Berel Lang, then a graduate student in philosophy, described him as "electric" and "magic."[99] But there was also a Gnostic side to Taubes.

The Gnostic elements of Taubes's personality were reflected in his relations with students, colleagues, and lovers. Recall Hans Jonas's description of the Gnostic's way of life as characterized by "cosmic nihilism," a way of life that paradoxically derives its meaning through negation.[100] Those possessed with a consciousness of the true spirit (pneuma) are able to break free of existing society and its norms. Grounded in a purportedly higher knowledge, the Gnostic disdains the world and its "wisdom."[101] The pneumatic, in his own eyes at least, belongs to a privileged aristocracy, a new human type free of the obligations and standards of existing society. The unrestrained use of this freedom becomes a positive injunction, leading to a sanctification of sacrilege. The pneumatic glories in demonstrating his distinction from the rest of society through his actions. Libertinism, in its deliberate flouting of social conventions, is regarded as a sort of declaration of war against the world as it exists.[102]

One element of Jacob's Gnostic personality was his paradoxical combination of egalitarianism in theory and elitism in practice. Upon meeting a student, Jacob would quickly decide whether he or she had "the spark." If yes, he treated them exceedingly well; if not, he was negligent and treated them as worthless. Gershon Greenberg saw Taubes grade the exam books of graduate students by looking at the names on the cover and assigning a grade according to his estimation of the student's worth, without actually opening the book. Seeing Greenberg's startled reaction, Taubes assured him that he planned to read the contents.[103] It was also part of Taubes's elitism that he was much concerned with lineage: the children of intellectually distinguished parents were at a distinct advantage. In 1960, for example, Taubes met Edmund Leites at a party given by Paul Goodman.

Leites was the precocious son of Nathan Leites, a well-known pioneer of political psychology at the University of Chicago. Edmund was a twenty-year-old graduate student in anthropology, having graduated from Yale at the age of nineteen. After talking to him for twenty minutes, Jacob offered him a job as a teaching assistant for a course that Susan was teaching at Columbia.[104] He had the spark. But not all lineage counted: among the students in one of his graduate seminars was a Rockefeller, but that scion did not rate among the elect in Jacob's eyes.[105]

European Connections

Though his body lived in New York City, Jacob's mind remained oriented to Europe in general, and German-speaking Europe in particular. The thinkers who were his stock in trade at Columbia were all from the German cultural realm: Hegel, Marx, Weber, Freud, and Heidegger. Though his contacts and friendships with American scholars were growing, those with whom he felt most at home, and whom he most admired, were also from German-speaking Europe. He kept up a rich correspondence with friends in Germany and Switzerland. And he continued to be fascinated and troubled by what to him was the mystery of how intellectuals of the caliber of Heidegger and Schmitt could have been attracted to National Socialism. In 1958, for example, he read *Social-Psychological Problems of Industrial Society (Soziopsychologische Probleme der Industriegesellschaft)*, a new work on the sources of anomie in modern industrial societies by Arnold Gehlen, a brilliant social theorist who was compromised by his career in the Third Reich. Taubes wondered how the author of what he called this "small masterpiece" could have fallen for the Nazis—a subject he discussed with George Schwab, a Jewish refugee who was writing a doctoral dissertation on Schmitt and was also troubled by the issue.[106]

After a few years at Columbia, the Taubeses were earning a more than respectable income. Jacob's Columbia salary was $11,500, and Susan was earning another $5,000 from her job as curator of the Bush Collection.[107] Now that their income was more substantial they could afford to spend most of every summer in Europe—though not necessarily together. Jacob returned to Switzerland, in part to visit his parents and sister in Zurich, but also to spend time with friends, old and new. He traveled to Zurich in the fall of 1957 for the funeral of his mother, Fanny, who passed away on October 2, 1957, and stayed for several weeks.[108]

Fanny's death was a blow to Jacob, and exacerbated his always fraught relationship with his father, Zwi. When Fanny's friends in Zurich arranged for the publication of a book of her talks on Jewish subjects, Jacob was tasked with writing the foreword. It included a passage that combined critical scholarship with personal confession:

> The various themes [of the book] circle around a single question: What is the position of woman in the religious life of the Jewish community? The history of the Jews has been deeply stamped by the masculine character of the religion of Israel. In its struggle against myth and against the ecstatic cults of the pagan religions, the feminine element was suppressed in Israelite religion and in later Judaism. Women were excluded from the study of Talmud. Even in the language of Jewish mysticism, woman's voice is silent.
>
> Yet woman exerted a subdued but powerful influence on Jewish religious sensibility and piety. This discrepancy between the absence of external representation and the effect on sensibility interested my mother. She saw in Zionism a return to a more natural order. She believed that in the rebirth of the Jewish people the female forces that lay fallow would find their expression. For her, Jewish speech was religious speech. Her son can only testify that for him, everything related to religion is of maternal origin.[109]

The last sentence was bound to be hurtful and insulting to Zwi. For the son of a rabbi and scholar of Judaism to declare that everything religious that mattered to him he had learned from his mother was a twist of the Oedipal rapier.

Despite Jacob's increasingly distant relations with his father (who remarried a year later), Jacob continued to return to Europe each summer. In June 1958, he met with his old friend Armin Mohler for the first time in a decade at Mohler's home in Paris, where he was a correspondent for the newspaper *Die Tat*.[110] For the month of August, Jacob and Susan rented a small house in Cerisy-La-Salle in Normandy.[111] His friend from Harvard days, Hans-Joachim Arndt, visited them there.

By then, neither Jacob nor Susan was content with their lives in New York. To be sure, they thought it was better to live in New York than to be stuck at a college in the Midwest. But, Susan asked, "Why stay in the United States at all?"—a sentiment with which Jacob concurred.[112] In Normandy, Jacob had a conversation with Arndt regarding his doubts about visiting Germany—a country in which he had never set foot. The upshot of their conversation was that Jacob made what was for him the difficult decision to go to Germany to participate in a conference. Not only that, but Jacob asked Arndt to keep a lookout for a position for him "in Europe." "You know that for me, the events of 1933 are of too bloody seriousness to be filed away. But where nowadays are there those who are still concerned with the questions that those events pose to us?"[113] Was this an explanation or a rationalization? Two years later, as Taubes prepared to visit Germany for the first time, he expressed his reservations to Max Horkheimer, who had returned to Germany a decade earlier. Taubes wrote from London to tell Horkheimer that he was going to Germany "with very mixed feelings," but would like to visit with Horkheimer and Adorno in Frankfurt.[114] By early the next year, he had his ear to the ground, listening for possible positions in Germany. In January 1961, he wrote to Horkheimer to say that he had heard that the University of Frankfurt was going to make appointments in philosophy and in *Judaistik* (Judaica), and that he was interested in such a position. He claimed that he lacked for intellectual company at Columbia: "Columbia would be just fine, if only—as God said to Abraham—there were five people to talk to."[115] By then, Jacob's dissatisfactions at Columbia had led him to put out feelers elsewhere in Germany as well.

CHAPTER NINE

Between New York and Berlin, 1961–66

THE YEARS FROM 1961 to 1966 opened a new chapter in Jacob's life. He began a transition from Columbia University to the Free University, from New York to West Berlin, from the United States to West Germany, and from a department of religion to a dual appointment in *Judaistik* (the scholarly study of Judaism) and hermeneutics. Obtaining a position at the Free University involved the coming together of personal contacts from a remarkable range of backgrounds, many of whom would continue to play a role in his life in the decades ahead. After half a decade of oscillating between New York and Berlin, Jacob chose to move permanently to the Free University. By that time, through strenuous efforts he had established himself in the networks of West German intellectual life. During these years, his relationships with women, both erotic and intellectual, became ever more complicated, his religious commitments ever more ambivalent.

Friends Old and New: How Jacob Got His Berlin Job

During the summer of 1959, Jacob returned again to Switzerland. This time he reconnected with a number of friends from his Swiss days at the Fex Valley, a beautiful site in the Upper Engadine near the village of Sils Maria, long valued by hikers, skiers, and academics longing for peace and quiet. For those steeped in intellectual history, the place is inextricably associated with Friedrich Nietzsche, who sojourned there regularly. Among those visiting in Sils was Jacob's friend from Basel, Jean Bollack, who had gone on to a career as a professor of classical literature. He had spent the years from 1955 to 1959 teaching at the Free University in West Berlin and was about to take up a position at the University of Lille. But like many French academics, he and his wife, Mayotte, lived in Paris.[1]

Taubes returned to Europe during the summer of 1960 and again met up with Bollack, who introduced Taubes to Bollack's close friend, Paul Celan.[2] Born Paul Antschel, the son of a Romanian Jewish family living in the city of Czernowitz in Bukovina, Celan was raised with German as his first language. During the war, when Romania was allied with Nazi Germany, the Jews of his town had been rounded up and deported. While Paul survived after spending two years in a forced labor camp, his parents did not. After the War and the Communist takeover of Romania, he moved to Vienna, where he had a love affair with Ingeborg Bachmann, a poet with strong philosophical interests. (She would later figure in Taubes's romantic life.) Celan then moved to Paris, eventually finding work as a lecturer in German at the École normale supérieure. He began to publish his poetry in German, including what was to become his best-known work, "Todesfuge" ("Death Fugue"), which included symbolic evocations of the tortured relationship between Germans and Jews. By the time Taubes met him in 1960, Celan was beginning to achieve literary fame.

Bollack was told by a colleague on the faculty of the Free University that the university was looking to fill a new chair in the study of Judaism (*Lehrstuhl für Judaistik*), and that they preferred to have someone other than a German scholar of the subject. Bollack suggested Jacob Taubes, who he knew was looking for a position in Europe.

The colleague to whom Bollack conveyed that information was Michael Landmann, a professor of philosophy at the Free University who would play a role in bringing Taubes to the FU. Landmann would loom large in Taubes's mind in the decades ahead, first as an ally, then as a foil, and later, after Taubes's mental breakdown, as an object of Taubes's wrath.[3]

Landmann was an identifying Jew, but one with little Jewish background. His mother was a highly educated member of the George-Kreis, the circle of disciples that formed around the German poet Stefan George; his father was an academic economist. Raised in Germany and in Switzerland, Landmann studied philosophy and was one of the first to teach the subject at the FU, beginning as an untenured *außerordentlicher Professor* in 1951, and advancing to ordinary professor in 1959. His lectures were solid but stolid.[4] An insecure speaker, he mostly read his lectures. He was a prolific scholar however, producing not only works of his own, but editing many valuable anthologies, and spearheading the recovery of the works of Georg Simmel, the great German philosopher of culture of the turn of the century. Gentle, industrious, and nonpartisan, Landmann was the polar opposite of Jacob Taubes.

Michael Landmann's wife was Salcia. Born in Galicia just before the First World War, her family had moved during the war to the Swiss town of St. Gallen. Salcia studied in Germany, and then at the University of Basel, where she completed a doctorate in philosophy, and got to know Jacob's friend, Armin Mohler. In 1948, she married Michael Landmann. In 1960 she published *The Jewish Joke* (*Der jüdische Witz*), based upon jokes she had carefully collected from Eastern European Jewish immigrants and refugees. She combined the jokes with some sociology and philosophy about humor as a weapon of the powerless. The book became a bestseller, went through many editions, and paved the way for her successful career as an author.[5] As she was completing the first edition of the book, she and her husband were visited by Taubes at their home in St. Gallen. Taubes explained that he wanted the position in Berlin, and implored her to appeal on his behalf to Heinz Gollwitzer, the Protestant theologian who was a moving force behind the creation of the Jewish studies position—which Salcia proceeded to do.[6]

Landmann also did his best to further Taubes's cause, seeing in him a repository of the Jewish tradition that Landmann himself lacked.[7] It was Landmann himself who extended the formal invitation to Jacob to teach at the FU in the summer of 1961.[8]

A Chair in Jewish Studies in Berlin

Jacob Taubes came to the Free University as a visiting professor in the summer of 1961, and by the end of the summer, arrangements were well underway to have him appointed to a chair in *Judaistik*. It was not the first time that *Judaistik* had been taught in a German university, but it was the first university chair devoted to the subject.[9] For some in the city of West Berlin and at the Free University, it was important both to establish such a chair, and to have it filled by a Jew.

The initiative to create a chair of *Judaistik* at the FU seems to have come jointly from Landmann and Adolf Leschnitzer. Born in 1899, Leschnitzer was a member of the German-Jewish *Bildungsbürgertum* who had managed to emigrate from Berlin in 1938. He eventually found a position teaching German language and literature at New York's City College.[10] At the invitation of students and professors at the FU, he had come to the university's history department (the Friedrich Meinecke Institut) as a visiting professor during the summer of 1952 to teach German-Jewish history and literature. He continued to teach each summer for the next two decades as an *Honorarprofessor*, teaching small seminars of ten to twenty students. But much as Leschnitzer loved teaching students at the FU, it was unthinkable for him to move to Germany permanently, and after his teaching was over each summer, he and his wife took their vacation in Switzerland—a pattern followed by many German-Jewish scholars, even those who, like Horkheimer, had returned to permanent positions in Germany.

The Free University was an unusual institution in an extraordinary metropolis. For when Taubes arrived in Berlin in June of 1961, the city was split into a Western zone and a smaller Eastern zone. The former had been occupied at the end of the Second World War by Britain, France, and the United States, the latter by the Red Army. By 1961, both halves had been remade in the image of their occupiers. East Berlin had been largely Sovietized; West Berlin was for all intents and purposes a Western democracy. It was possible at the time to pass with some difficulty from West to East and from East to West. But in recent years, more and more people—especially skilled and educated people—had voted with their feet by leaving East Germany for West Germany via West Berlin, which was an island surrounded by East Germany. Jacob first taught at the FU from June to July of 1961. On August 13, construction began on the Berlin Wall, intended by the East German government to staunch the flow of human capital. Six days later, the mayor of West Berlin, Willy Brandt, approved a contract appointing Jacob Taubes to the university.[11] West Berlin was a city stamped by the experience of division, with an electorate that was strongly anticommunist, very much including the Social Democratic electorate and its political representatives (such as Brandt himself) who dominated in the city.

The Free University had been founded in 1947–48 in response to the increasing Sovietization of the venerable University of Berlin on Unter den Linden, in what was then the Soviet zone of occupation. When some professors at the University were expelled from the faculty by the Communist authorities, they, together with some of their students, set about founding a new institution free of Communist control, in the Western zone. Soon students began to flow in from both the Western and Eastern zones of the city. The new institution, in the Dahlem neighborhood, was strongly supported by the American high commissioners in Berlin. The then president of Columbia University, Dwight Eisenhower, agreed that his university should "adopt" the FU, and the two institutions were to maintain a special relationship in the decade thereafter. Franz Neumann, Marcuse's close friend, who was then teaching at Columbia, became the liaison between the two universities. Before his death in a car accident in 1954, Neumann arranged for the Ford Foundation to support the FU. It did so massively, contributing over a million dollars to build a new library, student cafeteria, and lecture hall. It also funded an annual faculty exchange between the two universities.[12] An émigré scholar from Columbia, the political scientist Ernst Fraenkel, went from a visiting professorship at the FU to an ongoing appointment, as did Ossip F. Flechtheim, a protégé of Neumann, who returned to Berlin from the United States, and together with Fraenkel helped develop the FU's department of political science, the Otto Suhr Institute, staffed at first in good part by returning émigré scholars.[13]

Unlike the faculty of most other West German universities, the original core of the faculty at the FU was quite free from the taint of National Socialism. The young university tended to draw faculty who might have had a hard time getting positions elsewhere, because they were on the left. The relative liberality of the institution was also reflected in the fact that from its beginnings, the FU had an unusual degree of self-government and of student participation in the university's governance.

Helmut Gollwitzer

In late 1956 and early 1957, Landmann and Leschnitzer cooperated on an initiative to create a chair for the *Wissenschaft des Judentums*, drafting a letter to the dean of the faculty of philosophy.[14] An important supporter of their effort to create such a chair at the FU was Helmut Gollwitzer, who came to the university in 1957 as the first occupant of a chair in Protestant theology in the newly founded Institute for Protestant Theology (Institut für Evangelische Theologie). Most West German universities had schools of theology, sometimes Catholic, sometimes Protestant, and sometimes one of each, in which appointments were traditionally made with clerical approval. The FU, as a new university founded without royal or clerical patronage, had no school of theology. In the course of the 1950s, it was decided to create chairs in Protestant and Catholic theology, and then in *Judaistik* as well.

For Gollwitzer, this was a priority. A Lutheran theologian born in 1908, during the Third Reich Gollwitzer had been active in the Confessing Church (Bekennende Kirche), together with his doctoral adviser, Karl Barth.[15] After the arrest in 1937 of Martin Niemöller, the head of the Confessing Church and pastor of the Sankt-Annen-Kirche in the Dahlem quarter of Berlin, Gollwitzer took over Niemöller's pastoral duties. His contacts with anti-Hitler forces in the army led to his repeated arrest.

Serving as a medic on the Eastern Front during the war, Gollwitzer was taken prisoner by the Soviets and spent years in a Soviet POW camp. After returning to Germany in 1949, he penned an account of his reflections on his captivity that became a bestseller.

In the years thereafter, Gollwitzer became not only a professor of theology, but the most famous political pastor in West Germany. In the mid-1950s, Gollwitzer was a leading figure in the campaign against German remilitarization and participation in NATO, and an active participant in the campaign of 1957–58 against providing nuclear weapons to the Bundeswehr as part of its role in NATO. Though the antiwar movements of the 1960s, '70s, and '80s overshadow it in historical memory, a higher percentage of Germans were mobilized in that campaign, "Struggle against Atomic Death" (Kampf dem Atomtod), than in any cause thereafter. Gollwitzer was not only a public presence. He and his wife Brigitte Freudenberg (who was of Jewish descent) held a weekly open house attended by many religiously and politically engaged students.[16]

For Gollwitzer, overcoming the legacy of Nazism demanded reconciliation between Christian and Jews. That included support for the creation of diplomatic relations between the Federal Republic of Germany and the State of Israel—which the West German government had refrained from establishing, wary of damaging relations with the many governments of the Arab world and in competition with East Germany for recognition. Gollwitzer's support for a chair and institute for *Judaistik*, then, was part of his larger project of national atonement, and of acquainting Germans with a tradition all but extirpated in Germany by the Holocaust. It was to Gollwitzer that Salcia Landmann appealed on behalf of Jacob Taubes.

Between Two Chairs

So it was that in June 1961, Taubes began to teach at the FU as a visiting professor for the summer. He taught a lecture course, Prophesy, Apocalypse and Gnosis: Basic Concepts in the History of Jewish Religion, a seminar on Hegel's Philosophy of Religion, and a seminar on Hasidic literature, focused on Buber's *Legends of Rabbi Nachman*.[17] But arrangements had clearly been made in advance for a more permanent position; for by the end of the month, the senate of the faculty of philosophy had unanimously affirmed ("primo et unico loco") his appointment to a professorship in "the Science of Judaism" (*Ordinariat für die Wissenschaft des Judentums*). He was offered a base salary of 25,932 DM per annum, plus an instructional guarantee (*Unterrichtsgeldgarantie*) of 10,000 DM per annum, for a total of 35,932 DM, or about $9,000—which was somewhat less than his Columbia salary of $11,500. His institute was to have a scholarly assistant (*Wissenschaftliche Assistent*), a secretary, and one or two student aids (*Hilfskräfte*). He was granted 100,000 DM to purchase books over three years, and then a fund of 5,000 DM per year for that purpose. He was guaranteed an annual travel fund for trips "to the USA or to Jerusalem." Already there was talk of the possibility of an additional position as head of a Division of Hermeneutics (Abteilung für Hermeneutik), which would have additional staff. Such were the provisions of the contract approved and signed by Mayor Willy Brandt on August 19, 1961.[18]

The FU wanted Taubes to assume his new position in April or October 1962, but he was uncertain about whether to commit himself to moving to Berlin.[19] Instead, he arranged for a Fulbright fellowship to spend the 1962–63 academic year teaching at the FU. Then, citing the precedent of Carl Friedrich, who moved annually between Harvard and Heidelberg, Taubes discussed with Grayson Kirk, the president of Columbia, the possibility of alternate semesters at Columbia and the FU. Kirk balked, but ultimately agreed to Taubes spending alternate academic years at each institution.[20] Taubes continued to negotiate with the FU, bargaining for a better salary and better conditions.

In the end, the conditions of his appointment were extraordinary favorable. The FU hired Taubes without a *Habilitation*, that is, without him having ever published the second major work that was the usual prerequisite for occupying a university chair. He was hired without German citizenship. German professors were *Beamten*, that is, tenured civil servants, and as such they were ordinarily required to be German citizens. But Taubes—like Horkheimer and some other "returnees"—was absolved from acquiring German citizenship and giving up his American passport because he was Jewish. It was understood by all sides that a Jew would be reluctant to move to Germany without the possibility of leaving again. Another unusual feature of Taubes's employment was that he was made the head of not one but two institutes, each with its own offices and staff. The larger of the two (in terms of personnel, budget, and in its importance in the eyes of the FU administration) was the Institut für Judaistik. But Taubes was also made head of a new Abteilung für Hermeneutik (Division for Hermeneutics),which, as an "interfaculty institute" (*interfakultatives Institut*), was a novel creation.

At Taubes's request, the designation of his chair was changed from the original *Wissenschaft des Judentums* (which connoted *Jewish* scholarship about Judaism) to the more neutral *Judaistik*. He also added "sociology of

Religion" (*Religionssoziologie*) to the designation of the chair—an indication that his remit lay well beyond the teaching of Jewish-related subjects.
His leadership of the new Abteilung für Hermeneutik meant that he could
teach texts of any sort, without disciplinary boundaries.

Among the benefits specified in his contract was that his books would
be obtained *über die kleine Luftbrücke*. That meant that in the island city
of West Berlin, surrounded on all sides by a rival state, he was entitled
to import his books more speedily, by air. (For people, overland travel to
and from West Berlin required a transit visa [*Durchreise-Visum*] from the
East German government.) Last but not least came his salary, which with
a supplement beyond the normal professorial salary, came to 48,000 DM,
which at the current rate of exchange amounted to $12,000—more than
he earned at Columbia.[21]

So it was that Taubes spent the academic years 1962–63 in Berlin,
1963–64 at Columbia, 1964–65 in Berlin, and 1965–66 at Columbia. One
source of his dissatisfaction with Columbia was the fact that the university
refused to promote him to the rank of full professor. It did so partly because
Taubes did not have the requisite publications, and partly because the dean,
Jacques Barzun, ruled that Taubes could not come up for promotion during
a year in which he was not in residence.[22] Taubes used the bait of moving
permanently to Berlin to gain promotion, which came in April 1966.[23]

After several years of rotating between institutions, Taubes was given
an ultimatum by Columbia to decide between New York and Berlin, a
decision over which he would agonize. His indecision was motivated by
factors that pushed him in one direction and pulled him in another.

Berlin: The Social and Cultural Setting

Many factors conspired to push him away from New York and from
Columbia.

One was familial: Jacob's marriage was disintegrating. His infidelity
appears to have been central here, though, since it was not new, it may
have been due to Susan's increasing awareness of his affairs or discom-
fort with them. At any rate, in the year after his first return from Berlin,
Jacob and Susan seemed to be arguing about everything, including what
they would have for dinner. When Susan was especially enraged by Jacob's
behavior, she threatened to tell Gershom Scholem.[24]

Then there was Jacob's dissatisfaction with his position at Columbia.
There he was a minor, peripheral figure in the intellectual life of the university. In the Columbia context, the subjects that interested him—Paul,

eschatology, Christian and Jewish theology, Hegel, Marx, Heidegger—
were exotic. There were relatively few people who shared his intellectual
background and interests. Some prominent members of the faculty suspected that he was less than intellectually solid, and the university refused
his initial quest for promotion to full professor. (Scholem's student Morton
Smith is said to have been among those blocking his promotion.[25]) At the
FU, he would be a full professor—and in a culture in which the status of a
professor was higher than in New York.

Another factor was his position as a Jewish intellectual in New York
compared to Berlin. The scholar has depth in a particular subject or discipline, while the intellectual has broad interests and a willingness to comment upon a wide range of contemporary topics. By that standard, there
were many intellectuals in New York, including some Columbia professors, and many of these intellectuals were Jews—the Upper West Side
abounded in them. By contrast, professors at the FU tended to be scholars
rather than intellectuals. And Jewish intellectuals in West Berlin were virtually nonexistent.[26] As a Jewish intellectual in New York, Taubes was a
small fish in a large pond. In Berlin, by contrast, he was a bigger fish in a
smaller pond.

There were, paradoxically, advantages to being a Jewish intellectual in
West Germany. Most Jews, including Jewish scholars and intellectuals,
were reluctant to *visit* the land that had been responsible for the murder of most of European Jewry. To voluntarily *move* there was unthinkable. There were small communities of Jews in major German cities; but
most were Jews from Eastern Europe who had come as displaced persons
after the War and had settled in Germany, many with a bad conscience for
doing so.[27] There were some scholars and intellectuals of Jewish descent
who had returned to Germany from exile abroad.[28] But they tended to be
of Jewish origin rather than identifying Jews, and even those usually had a
minimum of Jewish knowledge. Jacob Taubes was different: he was a Jew
who actually knew a great deal about Judaism.

The very rarity of Jewish intellectuals in West Germany, and the burden of the recent past that weighed upon their German peers, created a
situation that was potentially fraught. As one of Jacob's non-Jewish colleagues at the FU, who like him held a position in the United States, put it
after a long conversation about Jacob's dilemma, "No one in Germany will
offer real scholarly or personal criticism of a Jew." Thus, he feared, Jacob's
ideas would never be subject to the competition of ideas needed for real
intellectual development.[29] He therefore advised Jacob not to take up the
permanent post in Berlin. But Jacob may have drawn a rather different

conclusion: that in Germany, his ideas and his behavior were beyond criticism. And indeed, as a Jew in West Germany, he had what one of his most long-term acquaintances, Dieter Henrich, called a kind of *Narrenfreiheit*, the special liberty granted to fools: in other words, he was granted a kind of get out of jail free card—forever.[30]

But for Jacob there were disadvantages to moving to Germany as well. The very idea was anathema to his father, Zwi. Of greater weight was the fact that Jacob's children, Ethan and Tania, were American born and bred, and because their mother would not be coming to Berlin, his contact with them would diminish further. Another factor weighing against Berlin was that while he loved being a professor of religion and of hermeneutics, he was not that interested in heading an institute of Jewish studies.[31]

During the years in which Jacob was oscillating and vacillating between New York and West Berlin, the FU was becoming an ever more congenial place for a man of his interests and political orientation. The West German universities were growing rapidly, as the government pursued an educational policy aimed at sending more students into higher education. New universities were being founded, and existing ones such as the FU were expanding. That meant a huge increase in academic appointments at all levels: from 1960 to 1968, the number of professors increased by 63 percent, and the *Mittelbau* (those above the level of students but below the level of professor) by 360 percent.[32] Because the universities were tuition-free and student expenses were subsidized, students could afford to spend years taking courses that interested them or engaging in political activity. Moreover, the nature of the student body at the FU was changing in a more leftist direction. That is because, on the one hand, the construction of the Berlin Wall had staunched the flow of students from East Germany. At the same time, the university saw an influx of students from West Germany proper, some of them men attracted by the fact that the military draft did not apply in West Berlin—and such students tended toward the political left. The sense of being on the front lines of the Cold War heightened the level of anxiety and political activism.[33]

The students flowing into West Berlin after 1961 augmented a nascent intellectual left. Some of it was an outgrowth of the anti-atomic-bomb campaign, with which Gollwitzer had been so closely identified. Another locus was the Sozialistischer Deutscher Studentenbund (Socialist German Student League) (SDS). The SDS had been the youth wing of the mainstream Social Democratic Party, the SPD. In the mid-1950s, the SPD was still Marxist in its official ideology. It aimed at the replacement of capitalism by socialism, looked to the working class as the bedrock of its support, tended toward neutralism between the United States and the Soviet Union, and was antipathetic to religion. But there was a gap between the party's radical rhetorical aims and the more pragmatic policies it had long pursued. In 1959, at a party conference at Bad Godesberg, the SPD adopted a new official program. It abandoned the Marxist theoretical framework of the past; replaced the traditional demand for socializing key industries with an acceptance of private property and competition; and disavowed the policy of military disarmament. The next year, the party accepted the integration of the Federal Republic into the Western alliance.

The politician most identified with this new direction was Willy Brandt. But it was an intellectual, Richard Löwenthal (1908–91), who was an important influence on party's foreign policy. Born into an assimilated Jewish family, Löwenthal had been a Communist during his youth in the 1920s. He left the party at the end of the Weimar Republic to found Neu Beginnen (New Beginning), an organization that tried to bridge the fratricidal rivalry between the Communists and the Social Democrats. With the advent of Hitler, he moved to England, where he engaged in anti-Nazi activities and pursued a career as a journalist. His book *Jenseits des Kapitalismus (Beyond Capitalism)* (1948), published under the pseudonym Paul Sering, made a renewed case for a socialist economy and for neutralism between East and West, while emphasizing the importance of democracy. In the course of the 1950s, Löwenthal became a leading authority on the Soviet Union and the Communist regimes of Eastern Europe, an outspoken anti-Communist, and an advocate of a foreign policy for the SPD strongly committed to the West. In the late 1950s he began to lecture at the FU, where in 1961 he became a professor of international politics. In time, he would shift from a critical supporter of the German New Left to an outspoken critic.

Not all were happy with the SPD's new course. A substantial portion of the membership of the SDS rejected the reformism of the Godesberg program and the Western orientation of the Social Democrats. In 1961, the more moderate members split off into a new organization, the Sozialdemokratischen Hochschulbund (Social Democratic Academic League). The leadership of the Social Democratic Party broke off its relationship with the SDS.[34] Some professors who had supported the SDS in the past expressed their renewed solidarity with the SDS, and formed themselves into the Sozialistische Förderergesellschaft of supporters of the SDS.[35]

One forum for the left-of-the-SPD intelligentsia in Berlin was the magazine *The Argument: A Journal of Politics and Culture (Das Argument: Blätter für Politik und Kultur)*. It grew out of a group of FU students who were opposed to the outfitting of the Bundeswehr with atomic weapons. The editors also founded the Argument-Klub, a venue for political discussion of the undogmatic left. At first, it welcomed criticism of the East German regime. (As we will see, it would become more sympathetic and more dogmatic over time.[36]) Among the key figures around the magazine and the club were Peter Furth and Wolfgang Fritz Haug; among its supporters was a young *Assistentin* in philosophy, Margherita von Brentano.[37] They were part of a distinct leftist intellectual milieu in West Berlin, one in which Jacob Taubes felt at home.[38]

For Jacob Taubes, therefore, Berlin represented a land of opportunities: the chance to be in an environment that was more culturally and politically congenial to him, and the chance to operate as an intellectual entrepreneur on a wider scale.

Interlocutors in Berlin and Beyond

For his colleagues in West Berlin, Taubes's international connections could be vital. Take the case of Dieter Henrich.[39] Born in 1927 (and thus four years younger than Taubes), Henrich was something of a wunderkind: at the age of thirty, he had recently come to the FU as a full professor of philosophy. Early in Taubes's tenure at the FU, Taubes began to attend Henrich's lecture course on the development of German Idealism from Kant to Hegel—a subject on which Henrich was already expert and to which he would return over the course of a long and productive career. Taubes developed a connection with Henrich that would last for decades. For Henrich, as for so many others, Taubes was a novelty and a link to a wider world of scholarship beyond Germany. Taubes was informed about foreign scholarship that was unknown to Henrich, who like most of his cohort was trained in postwar Germany. It was from Taubes that he learned of Marcuse's book on Hegel, *Reason and Revolution*, as well as the key ideas in *Eros and Civilization* and the yet-to-be-published *One-Dimensional Man*.

For Henrich, Taubes represented a breath of cosmopolitanism in a world of German provincialism. When they met, the American academic scene was terra incognita for Henrich. He had heard of Harvard University, but not of Columbia. In 1964, Henrich came to New York for the first time, on a two-week visit sponsored by the FU, to study student housing, and lived with Jacob in his Claremont apartment (Susan was living in Paris). Jacob insisted that Henrich give a lecture to the Columbia Philosophy Department. That lecture led to a recurrent visiting professorship for Henrich, first at Columbia and then at Harvard.[40]

When they first met, Taubes was one of the few Jews that Henrich had ever encountered, and certainly the first *Jewish* Jew. During a semester when both were teaching at Columbia, Taubes took Henrich to Williamsburg (in Brooklyn) to see the ultra-Orthodox Jews there. Taubes also took Henrich to a seder at the home of an Orthodox family, over which Taubes presided. Henrich was moved by a ceremony he had never before witnessed. Yet after they departed, Taubes turned to him and remarked, "Aren't these Orthodox awful!" (*Schrecklich, diese Orthodoxen!*).

Over time, Henrich would conclude that Taubes had both negative and positive qualities as an intellectual and a person. On the one hand, he was intellectually stimulating and his company invigorating, for his mind was explorative and associative, making unexpected connections. But he also had deficiencies of mind and character. His knowledge of the books he discussed was often superficial or flawed. He took pleasure in intrigue and in assuming multiple identities, depending on the circle in which he found himself. He was unreliable in his personal relationships, whether with men or with women. As Henrich once told him, "Dear Taubes, I don't believe a word you say, but it's really great to talk with you" (*Lieber Taubes, ich glaube Ihnen kein Wort, aber mit Ihnen zu reden, ist wirklich gut*).[41] In 1976, after having known Taubes for a decade and a half, Henrich would have a conversation with Victor Gourevitch, who had known Taubes even longer. At the conclusion of their long dialogue about Taubes, his foibles, and his charlatanry, Henrich said, "And yet, we've spent the last hour talking about him!"[42] Despite his flaws, both Henrich and Gourevitch found Taubes an intriguing figure.

Of Jacob's interlocutors in his early years in Berlin, it was Jürgen Habermas who would become the most famous both in Germany and abroad. A politically engaged intellectual, Habermas came to be considered the heir to Horkheimer, Adorno, and Marcuse in the tradition of "Critical Theory." When Jacob first met him, however, all of that was yet to come.

Habermas's background could hardly have been more different from Jacob's.[43] He was born in 1929 into an educated middle-class German family in the Rhineland. His grandfather was a Protestant pastor; his father was an official of the local chamber of commerce, who in 1933 joined the Nazi party, and when war broke out, served in the army. When he was ten, Habermas's parents signed him up for the Nazi organization for boys (Deutsche Jungvolk), and he later graduated to the Hitler Youth. In 1945, he was drafted into the Wehrmacht, but before he could serve, the Rhineland was conquered by American troops, and he was spared.

Habermas went on to study philosophy at a number of German universities. His doctoral dissertation was written at the University of Bonn, where his advisor, Erich Rothacker, was a respected philosopher who had been a supporter of National Socialism. Habermas read the giants of the German intellectual right, including Heidegger and the sociologist Arnold Gehlen. His own political inclinations, however, were decidedly on the left. That was clear from the journalistic pieces that he published in the two years after receiving his doctorate in 1954. Habermas penned critiques of capitalist consumerism. He opposed rearmament, joined the SDS (and later its supporters in the Sozialistische Förderergesellschaft[44]) and became an "anti-anti-Communist." His identity as an intellectual was bound up with his repulsion at the experience of National Socialism, and he sought out intellectual mentors who represented alternative traditions. So it was that in 1956 he came to the Institute of Social Research in Frankfurt to serve as the assistant to Theodor Adorno.

One of Habermas's aims in coming to the Institute was to familiarize himself with empirical social research. For the Institute that Horkheimer had built prided itself on bringing American methods of social investigation to West Germany, which were seen as a contribution to building democracy there.[45] The former Marxism and political radicalism of the Frankfurt Institute was much muted under Horkheimer's leadership. The Institute received substantial funding from American foundations, and Horkheimer maintained his American passport and returned frequently to teach in the United States. Adorno, meanwhile, penned a stream of books of social criticism, lamenting the gap between contemporary institutions and human flourishing, but without a tangible description of what better institutions would look like, and without a hint of political activism. Behind the scenes of German academic life, there was a great deal of tension between those scholars who had opposed National Socialism and gone into exile, and those who had remained and either supported the regime with enthusiasm or made their peace with it. The two main centers of the former camp were the University of Cologne, where Taubes's teacher René König created a center of sociological research, and the Frankfurt Institute. By choosing to go to Frankfurt, Habermas had reason to believe he was entering an atmosphere congenial to his leftist sensibilities. While serving as an assistant to Adorno, Habermas began to read more deeply in the books and articles produced by members of the Institute in their more radical years. He delved into the *Zeitschrift für Sozialforschung*, the journal of Marxist social analysis that the Institute had published during its years in exile.

Habermas came to see his own task as combining a fundamentally (but not fundamentalist) Marxist philosophy of history with the findings of empirical social research. He got to know Herbert Marcuse and was impressed by Marcuse's attempt to combine Freud and Marx into a radical critique of domination in contemporary capitalist society. He published sympathetic accounts of contemporary Marxist thought.[46] In 1959, Adorno asked Habermas to write an introduction to an empirical study of the attitudes of university students to politics. Habermas did so, lamenting the students' lack of political consciousness and advocating the "development from a formal to a material, from a liberal to a social democracy."[47] The implication was that democracy without socialism was no real democracy at all.

All of this did not sit well with Max Horkheimer, who remained the head of the Institute. He found Habermas's radical critique of existing democracy both irresponsible and a slap in the face of the American and German governmental institutions that funded the Institute. He vetoed the publication of Habermas's introduction under the Institute's auspices. And he rejected the idea of Habermas habilitating at Frankfurt.[48] Horkheimer's rejection of Habermas was conveyed in a long letter to Adorno—a letter that remained unknown to Habermas until, decades later, he was sent a copy by none other than Jacob Taubes.

Unable to habilitate in Frankfurt, Habermas turned instead to Wolfgang Abendroth, a Marxist professor of law in Marburg, and at the time one of the few politically active radical professors in the Federal Republic. Habermas soon made a name for himself in the fields of sociology and philosophy. He was appointed as an "extraordinary professor" (a rung below full professor) at Heidelberg. It was at that point, in late 1962 or 1963, that Taubes took the initiative to meet Habermas. He spoke of Habermas as "the next generation of the Frankfurt School"—an as yet unfamiliar designation.

Habermas was astonished by Taubes, who seemed to have come out of nowhere, yet with whom Habermas seemed to have so much in common intellectually. Taubes appeared to know everything about the history of the Frankfurt School, including the tensions among its members. He talked with enthusiasm about Walter Benjamin's writings on theology and the philosophy of history, at a time when Benjamin was little known and this was esoteric knowledge. He was well versed in Marxism and Freud. Though Habermas knew that Taubes had come from the United States, there seemed to be nothing American about him. From conversation, it became clear that he had a remarkable network of intellectual relations, and knew all of the German intellectual émigrés. Nor, at first, did Taubes seem any more Jewish than the Jewish intellectuals that Habermas had encountered during his time in Frankfurt. Habermas was struck, above all, by Taubes's great charm.[49] When Habermas visited New York City during Christmas 1965, he stayed in Taubes's apartment near Columbia.

In 1964, Habermas was appointed to a professorship of philosophy and sociology at the University of Frankfurt—the very chair from which Max Horkheimer had recently retired. In Frankfurt, Habermas came into close contact with Siegfried Unseld, the publisher of Suhrkamp Verlag, who was to play an outsize role in the careers of both Habermas and Taubes.

Taubes and Suhrkamp: The Beginnings

The phrase "the Suhrkamp Culture" was invented in 1973 by George Steiner in an essay in the *Times Literary Supplement*. It was a coinage that the management of Suhrkamp loved to quote. For it captured the image that the press and its publisher, Siegfried Unseld, sought to convey.[50]

Here is how Steiner put it:

> Almost single-handed, by force of cultural-political vision and technical acumen, the publishing firm of Suhrkamp has created a modern philosophic canon. In so far as it has made widely available the most important, demanding, philosophical voices of the age, in so far as it has filled the bookshelves with the presence of that German-Jewish intellectual and nervous genius which Nazism sought to obliterate, the Suhrkamp initiative has been a permanent gain.[51]

Steiner, a name to conjure with in international intellectual life, was himself a Suhrkamp author. He had decided to publish with Suhrkamp, rather than with a rival German publisher, after a conversation with Jacob Taubes.[52]

Taubes's relationship to Siegfried Unseld and his publishing house stretched over two decades, beginning in 1963 and lasting until a few years before his death. As with so many of Taubes's relationships, this one too was marked by intensity, enthusiasm, and disappointment. As an advisor to Unseld, and as an editor of the prestigious Suhrkamp series entitled Theory (Reihe Theorie), he played a role in the formation of the Suhrkamp culture, especially in suggesting foreign works for translation and publication.

The foundations of Suhrkamp Verlag were laid by its founder, Peter Suhrkamp. But it was Unseld, his successor, who built the edifice of the

"Suhrkamp culture." He joined the firm in 1952 and in 1959 succeeded Peter Suhrkamp as publisher. When Unseld arrived at the helm, the press was mainly known for its belles lettres, aimed at a discerning elite readership. In the decade that followed, it would add demanding works of philosophy, of social science, and of cultural criticism to its rapidly expanding list, while reaching a wider circle of readers. In the 1960s and 1970s, the homes of the West German *Bildungsbürgertum* were lined with walls filled with Suhrkamp's books. That educated middle class was swelling thanks to the rapid expansion of the German university system.

Unseld first made his mark by launching a new paperback series, the edition suhrkamp. While at first the emphasis of the series was on literature, the Suhrkamp list increasingly reflected the belief that systematic reflection—"theory"—was an activity in which every educated person (or person who aspired to educated status) ought to be engaged.[53] The series began with Brecht, and in its early years would publish works by Adorno, Benjamin, Bloch, and Marcuse.

In 1962, Unseld visited university towns and concluded that there was a growing demand for fundamental works of philosophy at prices that students could afford.[54] In June 1963, he and his staff editor (*Lektor*), Walter Boehlich, held a meeting with Adorno, Habermas, Hans Heinz Holz, and Wilhelm Weischedel (the senior professor of philosophy at the FU) to discuss the possibility of a wide-ranging philosophical series with the working title LOGOS.[55] Unseld had studied with Weischedel in Tübingen and valued his advice.[56] Weischedel suggested two up-and-coming young men as editors in addition to Habermas, Dieter Henrich and Jacob Taubes.[57] (The inclusion of Holz was vetoed by Habermas on the grounds that he was too Leninist and that his political engagement distorted his scholarly judgment.[58])

Unseld first met Jacob Taubes in New York City in the fall of 1963.[59] In a long conversation, Taubes tried to convince Unseld that the most important forms of contemporary theorizing were going on *outside* of formal philosophy, in fields such as anthropology, sociology, and literary theory.[60] He followed up their conversation with an annotated list of books for Suhrkamp to translate and publish, a list that included some of the most influential recent works in sociology and social psychology (Erving Goffman's *The Presentation of Self in Everyday Life* and *Asylums*, Erik Erikson's *Young Man Luther*, Leon Festinger's *When Prophecy Fails*) and intellectual history (Arthur Lovejoy's *Great Chain of Being*, Frank Manuel's *The Eighteenth Century Confronts the Gods*, Alexandre Koyré's *From the Closed World to the Infinite Universe*). Unseld found that Taubes had a remarkable knowledge of cultural history, and already had some experience in publishing books for the growing market of students and university graduates interested in what was known in the United States as "the humanities." Unseld decided to draw upon that knowledge.[61]

Taubes was politically in tune with the new direction being taken by Unseld and his staff editors (*Lektoren*) at Suhrkamp, such as Karl Markus Michel and Boehlich. Michel, who had studied at the Frankfurt Institute before joining the firm in 1962, was to become an influential figure in West German intellectual life. In 1965, together with Hans-Magnus Enzensberger, he founded a new journal, *Kursbuch*, published by Suhrkamp, which developed into a major theoretical forum for the intellectual left. In a programmatic essay of 1964 on the tasks and challenges of "critical thought" in West Germany entitled "The Freedom of Fools or Straightjacket? The Tasks and Limits of Critical Thought in the Federal Republic," Michel cited Jacob Taubes as a model of the sort of intellectual he sought to promote, together with C. Wright Mills and Enzensberger.[62] Boehlich, who was of half-Jewish origin, was the chief *Lektor* at Suhrkamp. His interests were more literary, his politics Marxist, and in 1968 he would publish a widely read manifesto against "bourgeois" literary criticism and in favor of understanding literature in its economic context.[63] These *Lektoren*, who did much of the day-to-day work of acquiring manuscripts and coordinating the activities of the external editors, were cultural gatekeepers, influencing which books would be published.

The idea at first was for Reihe Theorie to comprise two series: Reihe 1, oriented to texts from the history of philosophy, was to be edited by Habermas and Henrich. Taubes was to be primarily responsible for Reihe 2, a series oriented to works of contemporary social and political thought. But the two series were soon merged, and Reihe Theorie, which began publication at the end of 1966, became a flagship venture for Suhrkamp Verlag, with a reputation for publishing important works by German and foreign authors. In addition to Habermas and Henrich, the philosopher Hans Blumenberg was also brought on board. The series had a decidedly leftist tilt, but not an exclusive one. One role for the series, as Taubes conceived of it, was to convey to a German audience debates that were going on elsewhere, and thus help to overcome "cultural lag."[64]

In an early list of recommendations to the editors, Taubes mentioned recent French books by the anthropologist Claude Lévi-Strauss, the literary critic Roland Barthes, and a book by his friend Lucien Goldmann, *Le dieu caché* (*The Hidden God*), a subtle work of Marxist criticism. He also recommended fashionable new books by left-wing authors, such as

Serge Mallet's *La nouvelle classe ouvrière* (*The New Working Class*) and Lucien Sebag's *Marxisme et structuralisme* (*Marxism and Structuralism*).[65] All of these were names to reckon with in Paris, but little known in Germany at the time. Suhrkamp did indeed go on to publish Levi Strauss, Barthes, and Goldmann. Taubes also recommended that Suhrkamp publish a translation of C. B. Macpherson's *Political Theory of Progressive Individualism*—a recent work on the origins of liberalism (written from a critical perspective), which Suhrkamp published as well. But Taubes's suggestions were by no means confined to leftist authors. He also suggested a translation of the debate between Kojève and Leo Strauss, *On Tyranny*. In 1965, he recommended recent books by Isaiah Berlin, Daniel Bell, and the French historian of science, Alexandre Koyré; books by W. F. Albright on the biblical history of the Jews and by Arthur D. Nock on early Christianity; and books by the British philosopher of science Michael Polanyi, and by Charles Taylor, who, he explained, was "the English Habermas"—a perceptive characterization of the up-and-coming philosopher notable for his wide-ranging interests.[66]

How Taubes Read Books

Taubes provided Suhrkamp with a steady stream of recommendations about books to consider for translation and inclusion in Reihe Theorie. Among his German colleagues, he had a reputation for possessing a remarkable fund of knowledge: of knowing not only what had recently been published, but what intellectuals across much of Europe and America were working on. How did he do it?

Those who knew him well were aware of Taubes's peculiar capacity to ingest the contents of books. He rarely read a book from cover to cover. More typically, he would look at the cover, the table of contents, the index perhaps, and then leaf his way selectively through the book. After this procedure, which might take ten or fifteen minutes, he was prepared to evaluate the book's significance and its key contentions—at least as he construed them. On one occasion, for example, he walked into one of his classes at the Judaica Institute and spotted a student reading a book that aroused his interest. Taubes asked to see the book, spent ten minutes leafing through it, and then offered a compelling critique.[67] He would perform the same procedure in the stacks of libraries and bookstores. It was said that he didn't read books: he appropriated them by laying his hands upon them.[68]

Taubes's talent for ingesting the contents of a book and then conveying them as needed was grounded partly in his intellectual brilliance. But it was also a function of a particular species of cultivation, recently analyzed by Pierre Bayard in *How to Talk about Books You Haven't Read*. "Being culturally literate means being able to get your bearings quickly in a book, which does not require reading the book in its entirely—quite the opposite, in fact. One might even argue that the greater your abilities in this area, the less will it be necessary to read any book in particular." Being cultivated in this sense means being able to locate a book in relation to other books, to know where it fits into a system of books.[69] This was Taubes's great talent: knowing enough about many fields to know what the major lines of controversy were, and hence being able to situate a book's contentions within this larger web of other books.

Taubes also had techniques for ascertaining which books were "hot." He loved to spend time in bookstores, in Paris and elsewhere, inspecting the works most prominently displayed, and watching the customers' reactions. He had a flair for understanding what would interest people and what was current.[70] And he acquired much of his knowledge though conversation with friends and colleagues, gaining information from one and passing it along to another—though at times, as his friend Armin Mohler noted, he would pass along over dessert what he had learned from you over salad.[71]

Of course, Taubes was not always accurate in his estimation of a book's contents or of its significance. Often enough, his verdict depended on how the book related to his own concerns. As one friend put it, the information that Taubes conveyed about a book was more his own midrash (interpretive spin).[72]

But however acquired, Taubes's knowledge of books, and his eagerness to convey what he knew, was a great boon to many of his interlocutors. As Emil Cioran noted, his talks with Taubes spared him the need to read mountains of books.[73] And for the *Lektoren* at Suhrkamp, it meant a flow of recommendations of books to consider: though it also meant extra work, since Taubes's summaries or evaluations might be inaccurate.

It is possible, though, that when it came to judging books, Taubes's brilliance was also his downfall. It allowed him to get away with not reading books carefully or analyzing them precisely.[74] The qualities that made him a stimulating interlocutor in speech and in the classroom were ill-suited to the production of published scholarship in which the veracity of his knowledge was subject to critical scrutiny.[75]

"The Intellectuals and the University"

Of his few writings during these years, Taubes seems to have been proudest of "The Intellectuals and the University," delivered in 1963 at the Universitätstage of the FU, an annual series of lectures open to the entire faculty and student body of the university. The lecture went through several incarnations. It appears to have first been written in English, perhaps for one of the Columbia University Seminars, under the title "The Philosopher in the Marketplace."[76] An expanded German version was the one delivered at the FU and published in its proceedings.[77] Yet another, briefer version was delivered as a radio talk on the West Berlin's *Sender Freies Berlin* under the title "Von der Stellung der Philosophie im technischen Zeitalter" ("On the Position of Philosophy in the Age of Technology").[78] Taubes was sufficiently proud of the piece to send an offprint to the philosopher Hans Blumenberg, who responded that he was grateful to receive one of the rare products of Taubes's pen.

The bulk of the essay dealt with the history of intellectuals from Joachim of Fiore in the Middle Ages through the present, with an emphasis on their changing institutional position and the degree to which they challenged and helped transform existing structures of authority. It was a tour de force, drawing on scholarship in German, English, and French. It then turned to a diagnosis and critique of the present. Taubes argued that in both the Soviet Union and the United States—though in different ways—the intelligentsia had turned from being a source of ideological critique of the powers that be to a technological-organizational stratum that aided the politically dominant forces in each society and served at their pleasure. While in the Soviet Union this subordination of the intellectuals was achieved through violence, in the West, scholarship too was ultimately subordinated to political domination in the form of what Taubes characterized as a totalitarian (*totalitär*) but nonviolent coordination through economic and technological forces. The university too was becoming part of what Adorno had termed an administered world (*verwaltete Welt*), becoming ever more bureaucratized and factory-like. Philosophy now lacked "critical substance": it had abandoned its proper role of seeing through the veil (*Schleier*) of what passed for scientific rationality to reveal the deeper irrationality of contemporary institutions—institutions that robbed the individual of autonomy. The thrust of the lecture was of a piece with Taubes's article "Four Ages of Reason," written a decade earlier in honor of Max Horkheimer. Like that study, it drew upon members of the Frankfurt School, citing recent work by Marcuse (a precursor of his soon-to-be-published *One-Dimensional Man*) and a manuscript by Habermas—the introduction to *University and Society*, which Horkheimer had rejected as too radical. As in Taubes's earlier essay, "The Intellectuals and the University" offered a critique of the purported irrationality and oppressiveness of the institutional status quo without indicating what a more rational society would look like—an absence characteristic of the work of Horkheimer, Adorno, and Marcuse as well.

Fostering Connections

PETER SZONDI

Peter Szondi was among the scholars whom Taubes found congenial to his interests and whom he helped bring to the FU.[79] Born into a Jewish family in Budapest in 1929, as a teenager in 1944 he left Hungary with his parents aboard the Kasztner train, and like its other passengers, he was interned at Bergen-Belsen before the train was allowed to proceed to Switzerland (see chapter 3). Szondi enrolled at the University of Zurich just after Taubes left, and studied literature with Taubes's former teacher, Emil Staiger. Like Taubes, Szondi was influenced by Lukács (primarily his pre-Marxist works) and by Adorno. But Szondi's interests were in modern literary history, and especially the way in which literary forms were a product of history, a history he saw as one of increasing alienation brought about by capitalism. His dissertation on the theory of the modern drama, published by Suhrkamp in 1956, became "a revelatory text" for a younger generation of students.[80] A few years after publishing that study, Szondi met Taubes through their mutual friend, Jean Bollack. In 1961 he habilitated at the FU: his inaugural lecture was on Walter Benjamin, whose combination of moralism with the historical study of culture Szondi echoed in his own work.[81] Five years later, it was Taubes who was most responsible for bringing Szondi back to the FU as a professor and head of the first institute of comparative literature in Germany.[82] Together, Szondi's Institute for Comparative Literature and Taubes's Institute for Hermeneutics would become centers visited by scholars from Germany, France, and beyond. And, for a while at least, Szondi would serve as Taubes's comrade in arms in political battles at the FU.[83]

In 1967, as the wave of political radicalism at the FU was in full swing, Adorno was invited by Szondi to give a talk at his Institute for Comparative Literature. Adorno asked Szondi whether he should also speak at Taubes's Institute for Hermeneutics, to which Szondi responded:

> It's hard for me to advise you as to Taubes. If one is his colleague, one has to live with compromises and reservations. You're not forced to. To be concrete: if I see things correctly, he has a tendency to present his students with guests such as Adorno and Habermas on the one hand, and Gadamer and Henrich on the other; and amidst this back and

forth, to act as if he stood above the two sides, superior to both. Need I say more?[84]

For Szondi, this seemed like evidence of Taubes's lack of ideological reliability. But it testified to another of Taubes's characteristics: his deliberate attempt to foster and maintain connections with a wide range of intellectual circles.

HANS-GEORG GADAMER

Almost from the moment he took up his professorship in Berlin, Taubes scoped out the lay of the landscape in philosophy and related fields in West Germany, and sought to forge links with the major figures in each camp.

One center of philosophy was at the University of Heidelberg, where Hans-Georg Gadamer ruled, as what Taubes jocularly referred to as the "pope" of German philosophy. Gadamer began as a student of Martin Heidegger in the 1920s, trained in both philosophy and classics. After 1933, his lack of support for the new Nazi regime slowed his academic career, but in 1938 he was appointed to a position at the University of Leipzig. His book, *Plato und die Dichter*, published that year, began with a quotation from Goethe that served as an Aesopian wink to the like-minded: "He who philosophizes is not at one with the assumptions of his age" (*Wer philosophiert, ist mit den Vorstellungen seiner Zeit nicht einig*). Many of his students in Leipzig were opponents of National Socialism, including one who later became his wife.

When Leipzig was occupied by the American army in 1945, Gadamer was elected dean of the philosophical faculty, and in early 1946, with the city now occupied by the Red Army, he was elected the university's chancellor. A series of clashes with the new Communist authorities led him to leave Leipzig for the Western zone, and in 1949 he settled in Heidelberg, where he spent the rest of his career.[85] In 1960, he published his most influential work, *Truth and Method* (*Wahrheit und Methode*). There he explored the inevitable necessity of prejudice (in the sense of our pre-judgment), based on being part of a tradition, in making sense of the world. In so doing, he expanded "hermeneutics" from its nineteenth-century sense of the proper reading of texts into a broader philosophy of culture. He showed how the problem of reading texts was related to the problem of reading other people: in each case, it required a merging of our own concerns with those of the other. One element of Gadamer's achievement was to take themes from Heidegger, reformulate them in less idiosyncratic terms, and free them from the antimodern animus that permeated his teacher's work.[86] In the early 1960s, Gadamer turned Heidelberg into a center of German philosophy, attracting up-and-coming younger men such as Habermas and Henrich.

Using flattery to court Gadamer, Taubes wrote to him in 1965 that "Your opus [*Truth and Method*] has given me the confidence to devote my own modest powers to the matter of hermeneutics, and your students, especially Dieter Henrich, whom you have called to Heidelberg, have given me confidence that the grand tradition of philosophy in Germany is not a closed chapter in history."[87] The next year, Taubes invited Gadamer to give a talk at his hermeneutics colloquium in Berlin, which Gadamer did in November 1966, apparently with great success. Indeed, they discussed the possibility that after his retirement from Heidelberg, Gadamer might come to Berlin to be part of Taubes's Institute.[88] But Gadamer did not take up the suggestion.

Taubes shared Gadamer's interest in the interpretation of texts, but not his interest in formulating a systematic philosophy of the challenges of doing so. But Taubes did have a characteristic approach to the texts he taught. He did not approach a text in the manner most typical of philosophy, by trying to reconstruct the larger argument of a book, and then showing how each contention relates to it. His typical approach was instead to begin by putting the work in its historical context. Then he would often focus on the explication of individual passages and paragraphs, and ask about what was *not* said and why—a method he may have picked up from his studies with Leo Strauss. The other key difference between Taubes and Gadamer concerned what they meant by "hermeneutics." Taubes continued to be interested in the interpretation of religious texts. Gadamer, by contrast, was not.[89]

ERIC VOEGELIN AND JOACHIM RITTER

Taubes also maintained his links to Eric Voegelin, who had moved to Germany in 1958 to create an institute of politics at the University of Munich. It was a sign of their mutual regard that Voegelin floated the possibility of Taubes assuming a post at his university.[90] But Voegelin was in fact quite isolated in Munich, not least because his grand philosophical horizons ill comported with the interest of most political scientists in the workings of concrete political institutions. Voegelin returned to the United States in 1969, leaving behind a coterie of students, but no institutional legacy to speak of.[91]

A more influential figure to whom Taubes reached out was Joachim Ritter, a philosopher in Münster, renowned less for his published work than for bringing together scholars from a range of disciplines and generations into fruitful interaction. Among those of the older generation who put in an occasional appearance were radical conservative and former radical conservative intellectuals, including Carl Schmitt, Arnold Gehlen, and Helmut Schelsky. Ritter cultivated in his students a talent for "practical philosophy" that would utilize philosophical ideas to explore contemporary issues, and thus combine the history of philosophy with social engagement. Ritter himself was an influential interpreter of Hegel: his work on Hegel and the French Revolution portrayed Hegel (correctly) as a defender of the ideals of the French Revolution and of the liberal, bourgeois political order it spawned.[92] Ritter's students, as we will see, would become articulate defenders of that order in the face of attacks from the New Left. (See "Politics, Theology, and History: Taubes among the German Philosophers" in chapter 15.)

Joachim Ritter visited with Taubes in 1965, and the next year, after he had decided to remain at the FU permanently, Taubes wrote to Ritter that he hoped to work closely with him and his circle, and perhaps bring some of them to the faculty of the FU.[93] Their relationship was reinforced by the fact that Joachim's son, Henning Ritter, had come to Berlin to study with Taubes and was much enamored with him.[94]

THEODOR ADORNO

While Taubes sought out connections to the leading philosophical figures in Heidelberg, Munich, and Münster—a tribute to his philosophical ecumenicism—his greatest intellectual affinities were with the Institute for Social Research in Frankfurt. As we've seen, ever since his acquaintance with Franz Neumann and Herbert Marcuse a decade earlier, the more radical critiques of liberal, capitalist society developed by various members of the Frankfurt circle had resonated deeply with him, and he incorporated their ideas into his teaching and writing.

In the mid-1960s, the senior figure at the Institute was Theodor Adorno. Taubes had tremendous respect for Adorno, not least for the critique of Heidegger and Heideggerianism that Adorno discussed with Taubes in Sils Maria, as he was completing his book *The Jargon of Authenticity*. "If only this Critique of the Holy Family of our age had appeared a decade earlier, I would have been spared many byways and would have had more courage in my own views,"[95] Taubes wrote. In December 1965, when Taubes was undecided about whether to stay at Columbia or move permanently to Berlin, Adorno tried to convince him to take up the position at the FU.[96]

It seemed that relationship would be strengthened when, at Adorno's initiative, Taubes hired as his *Assistent* Rolf Tiedemann, one of Adorno's students who had recently completed a dissertation on Walter Benjamin. "If Tiedemann comes," Taubes wrote to Adorno, "then he does so as Adorno's pupil and a member of my staff, in order to open a 'branch office' of Frankfurt here."[97] But the relationship between Taubes and Tiedemann was ill-starred. A year later, Tiedemann was concerned that his work for Taubes left him too little time for his own research. Nor was Taubes pleased: he thought that Tiedemann was not doing the work that Taubes expected from him.[98] Tiedemann soon left Taubes's employ, and went on to a career as the editor of the works of Walter Benjamin and then the works of Adorno himself.

A lurking presence in the relationship between Taubes, Adorno, and Tiedemann was Gershom Scholem. Adorno and Scholem worked together in editing for publication the letters of their mutual friend, Walter Benjamin. Taubes rightly suspected that Scholem had impugned his character to Adorno, and at times Taubes expressed his gratitude to Adorno for not allowing Scholem's disparagements of him to cloud their relationship.[99] But at other times, Taubes suspected that Scholem's denunciations influenced the way in which Taubes was seen both by Adorno and Tiedemann.[100] When the University of Frankfurt decided to create its own chair in *Judaistik*, Taubes was eager to be offered the job—a possibility squelched after the university consulted with Scholem.[101] Adorno's final judgment of Taubes was expressed in a letter to Adorno's former student, Elisabeth Lenk, whom Taubes had asked to come to Berlin to replace Tiedemann as his *Assistent*:

> I tend to think that Taubes is a person of good intellectual but bad empirical character; that there is part of him that really wants to do the right thing and that is exceptionally responsive, but that then some hard-to-control impulses get in the way. . . . Certainly Taubes is both a highly talented person, and one whose capacity for productivity is deeply disturbed, and this constellation leaves considerable characterological scars. All things considered, it would be best if you went to Berlin and met with him in order to form an impression for yourself, though to be sure the immediate impression of an extraordinarily quick, intellectual and sensitive man tends to be more favorable than what one eventually experiences.[102]

Yet beneath the surface comity between Taubes and Horkheimer and Adorno lay a deeper source of latent tension. That was because Taubes's own inclinations were far more radical than theirs had become. That was evident in a letter that Taubes sent to Horkheimer in April of 1965. There he quoted with approval a statement that appeared in Horkheimer's article "The Jews and Europe," published in the *Zeitschrift für Sozialforschung* in 1939. Back then, Horkheimer believed that capitalism would lead inevitably to totalitarianism, as it had in Germany. By 1965, given the intervening experience of two decades of relatively stable liberal capitalist democracy in Western Europe and the United States, Horkheimer had long since abandoned that belief. But Taubes still maintained it—or at least purported to. "When I consider what your work has meant to me, I can sum it up, quite raw and in one sentence, through one quote. In 1939 you wrote, 'Today to call upon the liberal mode of thought in the struggle against fascism is to appeal to the very source through which fascism has triumphed.'... What you wrote in 1939 is true in 1965 as well, more than ever."[103] Taubes's disdain for liberalism would soon find an outlet.

By 1966, then, Taubes was well on his way to establishing himself as an intellectual entrepreneur.[104] He made himself into a node that connected diverse intellectual networks, each comprised of members who would otherwise have had limited contact with one another. Or, to put it another way, he functioned as a broker of ideas and information between intellectual circles that for reasons of political orientation or disciplinary boundaries barely overlapped. He could fulfill that function because of his talent and taste for building personal connections. That included his propensity to display different identities in different contexts. He was a would-be entrepreneur of ideas, and a font of potentially creative fertilizations across disciplines and political and national milieus. While he lacked the discipline and fortitude to see most of his projects through to fruition, he sparked new lines of inquiry for many of his interlocutors.

Character and Creed: Taubes and His Women

Taubes was often characterized as a "womanizer" by those who knew him, or even knew of him. But that term does not begin to capture the nature and significance of his erotic relationships. For those relationships not only affected the way in which he was seen by others. They also reflected his larger way of being in the world, or to put it another way, the link between his ideas and his character.

Taubes often taught and wrote about ideas and historical movements—such as Gnosticism and apocalypticism—that were transgressive, deliberately violating accepted institutions and social norms in the name of some higher wisdom. As we've seen, part of the Gnostic worldview (at least as understood by Taubes and the scholars from whom he took his interpretation) was that those with esoteric wisdom formed an elect that was able to penetrate the veil of contemporary institutions.

In his seminars at Columbia, Taubes explored the subject of *eros*—its historical meanings and changing directions. One of his favorite novels, Isaac Bashevis Singer's *Satan in Goray*, dealt with the transgression of erotic boundaries under the influence of Sabbatianism. His favorite artist was Hieronymus Bosch, especially his *The Garden of Earthly Delights*, a panorama of reversals of the natural and erotic order, which Jacob viewed in the Prado Museum on a vacation to Madrid. Taubes was much taken with the belief that Bosch had belonged to a heretical sect, an interpretation offered by Wilhelm Fränger in a book published in 1947. Fränger posited that the painting portrayed the recovery of the joyousness of existence without sin that mankind had experienced before the Fall, a bliss that would be experienced again. At both Columbia and the Free University, Taubes had his students read and discuss Scholem's essay "Redemption through Sin." For him, these were not subjects for the seminar room only.

To describe his erotic relationships is not therefore a diversion or distraction from intellectual history nor a prurient byway. It is to recapture an essential element of the man himself, and of the relationship between theory and practice.

We've examined a few of Jacob's relationships with women: with Myrie Bloch in Zurich, Gerda Seligsohn in New York, Miriam Weiss in Jerusalem, and well as with his wife, Susan. Our focus here is on a number of liaisons that Jacob carried on from 1961 to 1966, the years in which he was moving back and forth between Columbia and the FU.

SUSAN

Jacob's relationship with his then wife was as enigmatic as it was stormy.

Exactly why their marriage reached a crisis point in 1961, when Jacob first went to Berlin, is impossible to know. Jacob had not only been with other women, but took a certain pleasure in telling Susan about it, including his masochistic relationships.[105] She was more baffled than hurt by his recurrent philandering, which she attributed to his need for distraction.[106]

The varieties of transgressive sexual experience were played out in their marriage as well: he adored her purity, while delighting in having her assume obscene positions.[107] We do not know which of Jacob's liaisons proved a bridge too far for Susan—perhaps it was with a close friend, or his deflowering of the babysitter.[108] But the dam broke. They began to discuss the possibility of divorce, but Jacob resisted.[109]

Their quarreling had become even more explosive.[110] In her novel *Divorcing*, Susan portrayed Jacob (Ezra) as eager to argue, and taking a certain pleasure in her verbal and physical attacks on him.[111] He would mock her.[112] Their cohabitation seems to have ended in 1962, when Jacob went to Berlin for the year. At some point, Susan locked Jacob out of the apartment. Jacob pleaded outside the door, until finally Ethan opened it and let him in, incurring Susan's wrath in the process.[113]

Susan continued to teach courses at Barnard College (the women's college of Columbia University) through the spring of 1963. The fruit of her years as curator of the Bush collection were two anthologies, *African Myths and Tales* (1963) and *The Storytelling Stone: Myths and Tales of the American Indians* (1965), which she published under her maiden name, Susan Feldmann. At her initiative and with Jacob's agreement, she went to Paris with the children. They rented an apartment, first on the Quai de la Tournelle, and later on the Boulevard Saint-Germain, which Jacob paid for, and where he stayed when he came each year to Paris, a city he loved.[114]

Susan was intent on finding herself and on developing as a writer. That, plus Jacob's absence and her recurrent depression, led to a decision to put the children in boarding schools, first in France and later in the United States.

From 1962, when Susan moved to Paris, both children were enrolled at the La Coûme boarding school in France. It was a Spartan institution in the French Pyrenees that Taubes apparently chose because it was attended by Luc Bondy, the son of his Zurich friend, François, as well as the children of Hans Magnus Enzensberger, the German author and social critic.[115] Ethan and Tania found the place alienating, and in 1965 they were moved to boarding schools in the United States, Susan being too devoted to her writing projects or too depressed to care for them.[116]

In the fall of 1966, during a trip to speak at Harvard, Jacob planned to visit Ethan and Tania at their boarding school. But he did not have their address, and he wrote in desperation to Susan's father, Sandor Feldmann. The bitterness of Jacob's relationship with Susan in the months before their divorce is reflected in his letter to her father. "I had written you two weeks ago asking for the address of the children. No answer. I grew restless and therefore I cabled yesterday evening. There is a streak of cruelty in Susan's silence. It will not make me better disposed toward her in the negotiations to come. I am baffled since I have tried to be cordial and helpful whenever she requested something from me."[117] In the end, Jacob managed to visit the children at their school near Lake Placid in upstate New York.[118]

Susan had begun work on a novel, completed in 1963, entitled *Lament for Julia*. In 1964, through her friend Susan Sontag, Susan acquired a distinguished literary agent, Georges Borchardt, to represent her. He managed to place two of her stories in literary reviews, but could find no buyer for the novel. Susan found one herself, but the publishing house that acquired it shut down before the novel could be published. She applied for and received support from a number of fellowships in the years from 1965 to 1968, during which she wrote the novel that would become *Divorcing*.[119] While in New York, Susan took part in a women's writers group in which participants shared works in progress. It included Susan Sontag and Elsa First, who played a role in editing the novel.[120]

MARGHERITA

The woman who was to become Jacob's second wife had a great deal of *yichus*, albeit not of a Jewish sort. Christened Margherita Maria Josefa Anna Katherina von Brentano di Tremezzo, she had a remarkable lineage. Her ancestors included poets, philosophers, and social reformers. Her father, Clemens, was the German ambassador to Rome, and Margherita was baptized by the Papal Nuncio to Germany, Eugenio Pacelli, who later became Pope Pius XII. Margherita's uncle Heinrich was the foreign minister in the Christian Democratic government of Konrad Adenauer from 1955 to 1961. But she turned her back on Catholicism and became a radical leftist in her politics, though her affect remained a cross between an aristocrat and a member of the upper bourgeoisie (*Grossbürgertum*).[121]

Born on September 9, 1922, Margherita was a few months older than Jacob. After the Second World War, she studied philosophy with Heidegger in Freiburg, completing her dissertation on Aristotle in 1948. From 1950 to 1956, she produced broadcasts for young people at Southwest radio, where she produced a number of educational programs about the extermination of the Jews—hardly a conventional theme for youth radio at the time. Margherita was an anti-Nazi to the core, and combating antisemitism was central to her self-definition. In 1956, she came to the FU to teach philosophy, as the *Assistentin* to Wilhelm Weischedel. She was active in the anti-atomic-bomb movement, and then in the Sozialistischer Deutscher Studentenbund (SDS). In 1959, she was among the founders of *Das Argument*, and she was among the journal's funders. Together with one of her students, she organized an exhibit about judges who had served during the Third Reich and remained on the bench—a continuity she regarded as a morally scandalous, and evidence of the failure of West German society to break definitively with the legacy of National Socialism.[122] In the midst of a mass demonstration against antisemitism and neo-Nazism in January 1960, she and a small group of SDSers unfurled banners with the names of several active politicians and government officials whose involvement with the Nazi regime was well known. In *Der Spiegel*, she was identified as "the niece of the Minister for Foreign Affairs."[123] In 1964, together with her erstwhile student Peter Furth, she organized a seminar at the FU on Antisemitism and Society, where, among other works, they read Horkheimer's 1939 essay on antisemitism.[124]

Brentano's conception of antisemitism reflected a variety of Marxist interpretation that was to become characteristic of the New Left in the decade ahead. Antisemitism, she maintained, was a "pathology of bourgeois society" (*Pathologie der bürgerlichen Gesellschaft*): that is to say, a product of capitalism. Her view of liberalism was essentially the one that Horkheimer had articulated in 1939 and that Jacob endorsed in 1965, namely that liberalism was an unreliable basis of resistance to fascism.[125] On that understanding, the ultimate way to combat fascism and antisemitism was to replace capitalism with socialism.

They met during Jacob's first summer in Berlin, when Margherita attended a lecture by Michael Landmann, which dealt with the theme of fate (*Schicksal*). After the lecture, she talked to Landmann, and proceeded to quote from Brecht's libretto for the "Lenin Requiem" of Hanns Eisler (the composer who had also written the East German national anthem): "Wo von Schicksal die Rede ist . . ." (When the talk is of fate . . .). From behind her, a male voice completed the sentence: "wird er die Namen nennen" (he will name names). The voice was Jacob's. An intense romantic relationship between the thirty-nine-year-old Margherita and the thirty-eight-year-old Jacob ensued. Margherita asked Jacob whether he was married. No, he said, divorced. That, of course, was not accurate, though Jacob and Susan may have had an informal agreement that left each free to pursue other relationships.[126]

Jacob came back to Berlin in the fall of 1962, renting a furnished room, but living together with Margherita in her apartment. When she returned from a skiing vacation, her neighbors informed her that another woman had been staying with Jacob in the interim. Margherita broke off their relationship, but soon resumed it—a pattern she would repeat time and again in the years that followed. She was quick to anger, but also to reconciliation.[127]

Jacob respected Margherita for her moral seriousness and her resolute anti-Nazism; he was also clearly enamored of the fact that a member of the German nobility was in love with him. Though she had a solid background in philosophy, she was not an original thinker, and lacked Jacob's speculative temperament. The Habermases thought she was fixated on Jacob in an unhealthy way. When he spoke, she was silent. In the early years of their relationship, she was madly in love with him.[128] They were also on the same political wavelength.

JUDITH

Not long after returning to the United States from his first summer at the FU—after the beginning of his love affair with Margherita, and while he was still married to Susan Taubes—Jacob proposed to yet another woman, Judith Glatzer. She was his junior by eighteen years.[129]

Judith had *yichus*—and unlike Margherita, it was of the Jewish sort. Her father, Nahum Glatzer, by then a professor of Jewish studies at Brandeis University, was as we've seen not only among the most respected scholars in that field, but also responsible for making the works of Franz Rosenzweig and Franz Kafka available to English-speaking audiences. Judith was bright, intellectual, aesthetic (she had taken a year off to become a dancer), and innocent. To Jacob, whose marriage to Susan was on the rocks, Judith must have seemed like a new, more Jewish version of the woman he had met and married over a decade earlier.

Judith knew Jacob from his visits to the Glatzer home during his years at Harvard in the mid-1950s. In the spring of 1959, Judith's father invited Jacob to give a lecture at Brandeis, where Jacob spoke on his favorite theme, Gnosticism. Judith found Jacob fascinating, and a friendship ensued. They corresponded when she went to Hebrew University for her junior year in 1960–61. Jacob's letters, as was his wont, mixed intellectual matters with the vicissitudes of his own life. When she returned from Jerusalem and he from Berlin, he began courting her. Not long thereafter, he proposed marriage, and assured her that if she were willing to marry him, he would turn his back on the position in Berlin.

Judith turned him down. True, she found him compelling, brilliant even. She admired the intensity of his engagement with ideas. But she also judged him to be reprobate, if not demonic. In any case, he was conflicted and deeply unhappy. Besides, he was too old for her.

After receiving an MA from Columbia in 1967, Judith went on to study art history at UCLA. She married, moved back to the Boston area, and had a stellar career as a historian of art at Tufts University and as a documentary filmmaker.

INGEBORG

While he was nominally married to Susan, cohabiting with Margherita in Berlin, and conducting at least one affair in New York, Jacob had an extended liaison with Ingeborg Bachmann, among the most powerful German poets of her generation.[130] Born in Klagenfort, Austria, in 1926, she was four years younger than Jacob. In the decades after the war, Bachmann was associated with the "Gruppe 47" of young German writers, and she made a name for herself as a poet, novelist, and literary critic. She shared with Taubes an interest in philosophy, especially that of Heidegger, and in Simone Weil, whose dark view of the world echoed in Bachmann's own sensibilities. By the late 1950s, she had already won prizes for her poetry. Her romantic relationship with the Swiss novelist Max Frisch, which began in 1958, came to an end in 1962, leaving Bachmann emotionally devastated and addicted to pills and alcohol for much of the rest of her life.[131]

Bachmann spent 1963–64 in Berlin, on a fellowship from the Ford Foundation, and it was then, apparently, that her liaison with Jacob began. She attended his seminar in 1964–65 on the prologue to the Gospel of John, and their relationship seems to have lasted into 1966.[132]

In a letter written in 1981, Taubes claimed that together with Bachmann he visited her native town of Klagenfurt, as well as Prague, and Rome, where Bachmann made her home. A recent biographer of Bachmann casts doubt on the veracity of Taubes's claim, attributing it to his nature as a braggart.[133] Taubes was indeed given to braggadocio, and there is no extant evidence that he accompanied Bachmann beyond Berlin. But the thrust of his story checks out. In the letter in question, he refers to the fact that "when we went on our first walk she described ways of torture and death," and we now know that she was working at the time on a project entitled *Todesarten*, which was to encompass several novels. And there are references to Bachmann's relationship with Jacob in poems written at the time but unpublished in their lifetime.[134] A contemporary letter from Margherita von Brentano to Taubes takes note of his affair with

Bachmann.[135] One evening, Jacob was to be picked up after his seminar. Both Bachmann and Brentano showed up and began to argue with one another, almost coming to blows.[136]

The romantic relationship between Jacob and Bachmann seems, then, to have been real. It was intense enough to have helped Bachmann into a period of renewed creativity—though she continued to abuse both alcohol and sleeping pills, including at soirées she attended at the home of Jacob and Margherita.[137] Jacob recalled their relationship as a "revelation" (*gilui*), both in the sense of an experience of the divine (*gilui shechina*) and of erotic transgression (*gilui arayot*). As he had with Myrie Bloch and Gerda Seligsohn, Jacob expressed the intensity of his erotic relationship in terms drawn from Kabbalah. "I understood what it could mean *veshachanti 'betocha'* [to dwell within her], what is said or meant when the patriarchal symbolism of the Jews was forced to open toward a *shechina* [the feminine presence of God], I learned that those symbolic utterances are not just 'words' but dark realities."[138]

JANET

During his final years at Columbia, Jacob carried on a relationship with another young woman, not much older than Judith Glatzer. Her name, then, was Janet Scheindlin.[139] A self-described "nice Ramah girl from Philadelphia" (i.e., a product of a Conservative Jewish milieu), she had attended Barnard and married a rabbi who taught at JTS. By 1963, when she entered graduate studies at Columbia's Department of Religion, her marriage was already in decline. It was then that she met Jacob Taubes.

He was a revelation to her, and their romantic relationship illustrates the carnal and cerebral sides of Jacob's erotic activity. Her account matches many of the characterizations of Jacob in Susan Taubes's novel, *Divorcing*.

At this stage of his life, when he was in his early forties, Jacob's appearance was not conventionally handsome; he was slightly overweight and did no exercise. His hygiene remained deficient. (As Susan put it in her novel, "Your arse hole was the cleanest part of you, if you must know."[140]) Yet his appearance was striking. He dressed in black, with a big black hat. His eyes were incandescent, his facial expressions and hand movements dramatic. He still gave off the vibe of a wunderkind. Everything he said seemed to be on the verge of the sacred. The topics of his discussions and disquisitions were unconventional. He was fascinated by the theme of sacrifice, and by bloody, baroque depictions of Christ crucified by Albrecht Dürer and Matthias Grünewald. He gave Janet books on Hieronymus

Bosch as well. In his graduate seminar, Janet and the other students read Hans Jonas and Eric Voegelin on the subject of Gnostic antinomianism. Taubes recommended to her Scholem's essay "Redemption through Sin." Jacob Frank, whose practices were said to include sexual bedlam, was an important figure for him.

Jacob Taubes was no Jacob Frank, but he was a transgressive figure in his own way. One manifestation of that was his satisfaction in manipulating women of strong religious and moral backgrounds into violating their moral codes. He took Jewish girls from Orthodox or Conservative backgrounds and had them engage in dramatic violations of the law, such as having sex with them on Yom Kippur.

It was not only the occasion of sex that would go beyond the bounds of propriety. It was also the form of sex, the preliminaries of which could include unconventional practices. That included extensive oral sex, a practice rare at the time, at least among the circles in which such women traveled. (In *Divorcing*, there is a woman who meets the Jacob character at the Woman's Interfaith Union in Milton, New Jersey, where he had delivered a lecture on "Agapic and Erotic Theology in Judaism." She declares, "We only spent one evening together but I really enjoyed it. I didn't know about cunnilingus and other Jewish customs before; I believe we Americans have something to learn from all peoples."[141])

Jacob and Janet had a brief affair of a month or two while he was living alone at his home on Claremont Avenue. Sex was only a part, and by no means the predominant part of their relationship: sex with Jacob was usually followed by an intellectual discussion, then going together to the library.

On one occasion, Jacob called Janet and told her to come to his apartment on Claremont Avenue and walk in. When she entered, she was astonished to see together in one bed Jacob, Susan Taubes, and Susan Sontag. He seems to have invited her deliberately to witness the scene— and perhaps to participate. But she fled. (As we'll see, the scene would later be recreated in a film by Susan Sontag.)

The faculty of JTS and their wives tried to speak of Jacob Taubes only when they thought the children were out of earshot. But at least one of those children, Susannah Heschel, recalls their moniker for Jacob Taubes—the *sitra achra*—a kabbalistic designation for one who came from the opposite side of heaven—from the realm of evil.[142]

Yet despite its astonishing and distressing moments, for Janet her relationship with Jacob was a positive one. It exposed her to the existence of forms of behavior beyond the bourgeois Jewish existence she had led heretofore. In its own way, it was—as Jacob had no doubt intended—liberating. They remained in close contact after their erotic liaison was over, until he left New York for Berlin.[143]

EDITH

Jacob's transgressive sexuality—his manipulation of women of strong moral backgrounds into violating their own moral codes—could also take more destructive forms. At the very time of his affair with Janet, he was openly bent upon having sex with Edith Wyschogrod, a graduate student at Columbia and the wife of his Orthodox friend, Michael. To Janet, he expressed his desire with directness and vulgarity. Though it is impossible to know with certainty whether he succeeded, he certainly told those around him that he had—to the tremendous embarrassment of Michael.[144] Taubes took a certain pleasure in destroying marriages, as in other forms of creating chaos around him.[145] The line between degradation and liberation was hard to draw. That was a facet of the demonic side of his character. Yet as we will see, his affairs with married women (purported or real) did not always destroy their marriages, nor did it destroy his friendship with their husbands. A decade later, the Wyschogrods would save him in his time of need.

Family Matters: Mirjam and Zwi

In the meantime, Jacob's ties to his family in Zurich were fraying. In the fall of 1964, on the eve of the holiday of Sukkoth, Jacob's sister, Mirjam, was felled by cancer, not yet forty years of age. Jacob came for the funeral and stayed for the shiva. He was agitated and seemed almost crazed by the loss of his only sibling.[146]

For Jacob's father, Zwi, the death of his daughter was one of a string of disappointments. His second marriage, to a widow from Belgium, was not a happy one. Then there was Jacob, his only son. As Zwi had made clear at Jacob's bar mitzvah, his son represented his hope for the future. Not only was Jacob to carry on the family tradition of Jewish learning and leadership, Zwi had hoped he would reach new heights of Jewish scholarship. But Zwi's relationship with his son was strained by Jacob's decision to take up a position in Berlin, and even more by Jacob's romance with Margherita von Brentano. When Ethan came to visit, Zwi was appalled at his lack of Jewish education and tried to teach him some Hebrew. In 1965, he was heartbroken to learn that his only grandson would not even have a bar mitzvah.[147]

The year before, Zwi had attended a World Zionist Congress in Jerusalem, as a representative of the religious Zionist movement, Mizrachi, in which he was a prominent figure. Now he made plans to retire from the rabbinate and assume a research post in Jerusalem at Mossad Harav Kook, a center of Religious Zionist scholarship. In October 1965, he left Zurich for Jerusalem. But the reality of his situation in Jerusalem did not live up to his expectations. In Zurich, he was a respected and scholarly *Oberrabbiner*. In Jerusalem, there were many rabbis and many scholars. When a former congregant visited him in late December, Zwi expressed his longing for his congregation in Zurich.[148]

Disappointment was piled upon disappointment, and depression set in. On January 11, 1966, Zwi died in Jerusalem, an apparent suicide. His funeral was attended by the president of the State of Israel, Zalman Shazar (a longtime friend), by Yitzhak Nissim, the Sephardic chief rabbi of Israel, and by members of the cabinet.[149] Suicide was a scandalous violation of Jewish law, but sometimes halachically rationalized through the legal fiction that the deceased was temporarily insane at the time of his death. Zwi's son-in-law, Armand Dreyfus, arrived from Zurich and attended the funeral.

Jacob, who was in New York at the time, did not. Louis Finkelstein visited Jacob in his apartment to comfort him and found him in tears, rolling on the rug in his living room.[150] Though from time to time in letters Jacob expressed his intention to visit his father's grave in Jerusalem, it would be over a decade before he returned to the city in which his father was buried and Gershom Scholem lived.

Jacob did, however, take an interest in the publication of the manuscript on which his father had been working for years, and which he had completed just before his death, a compilation of rabbinic sources from the period of the *Geonim* (c. AD 600–1,000) on a tractate of the Talmud. Jacob talked to David Weiss, the Talmud scholar he had hired to teach a course at Columbia, who was about to spend a year in Israel, and Weiss agreed to work on preparing the manuscript for publication. The book, *Otzar ha-geonim le-masekhet Sanhedrin*, was published by Mossad Harav Kook at the end of 1966. After its publication, Jacob reported with satisfaction to the daughter of Rabbi Botschko of the Montreux Yeshiva that the volume was receiving extraordinarily positive reviews in professional journals.[151]

The Decision

Through much of 1965–66, Jacob vacillated and agonized about whether to commit himself to staying in New York or moving permanently to Berlin and marrying Margherita. He discussed the issue with all and sundry, including Paul Celan, Theodor Adorno, and Daniel Bell (who was surprised to find Jacob looking to him for advice on the matter).[152] Jacob's letters are replete with reports of his mental anguish.

Ostensibly at least, his main motivation for staying in the United States was to be closer to his children. He did not regard Susan as a fit mother, and she, in turn, did not regard him as a fit father. Probably they were both right.

Everything else seemed to be pulling toward Berlin: his greater comfort in German and in German academic culture, in which he already had a foothold; the higher status of a professor in Berlin; the opportunities presented by being a Jew in Germany; and not least, Margherita.

In November 1965, Jacob wrote to Margherita from New York, suggesting that she move to New York and marry him. She rejected the idea, arguing that at the age of forty-three, it would be imprudent to give up her tenured position at the FU to move to a country where she had no job and to a culture entirely unfamiliar to her.[153] Nor would they have enough to live comfortably, given his need to support his children, and possibly Susan as well. She could not rely on the permanence of their relationship. "You've emphasized often enough, both in theory and in practice, that a bond like ours ought and must have the freedom for other liaisons."[154] Given his inclinations, that was unlikely to change, she noted, and any of those liaisons might turn into something more permanent. She was well aware that he had other relationships, such as the one with Ingeborg Bachmann. In Berlin, she observed, she could react with anger, sorrow, and even end their relationship without endangering her material existence. But that would be impossible if she moved to New York. Above all, she noted, Jacob was not the sort of person upon whom she could build a life, for he was "absolutely and fundamentally" unreliable. "Your life plans are too chaotic and perhaps totally lacking."[155] She suspected that the real reason for his preference of New York over Berlin was his disinclination toward the field of *Judaistik* that he had been hired to teach at the FU.

Meanwhile, Margherita wrote, Jacob was creating chaos and fostering ill will. He had recently arranged for Tiedemann to come to Berlin from Frankfurt as his *Assistent*. Jacob and Margherita had invested in adjoining homes, an arrangement that made no sense for her unless he returned.[156] Jerked back and forth by Jacob, she felt like a rat in a psychological experiment designed to make her ever more neurotic. It was up to him to decide definitively, she wrote. But if he was going to return to Berlin, he should get the legal status of his marriage in order. The current situation was untenable. Living together in Berlin without being married made them the subject of gossip throughout the university. She thought that the tensions between them—expressed through her yelling at him and throwing him out from time to time—would diminish should he commit himself by deciding for Berlin and for marriage.[157]

In New York, where he was teaching in 1965–66, Jacob had descended into what he described as a "dark night of the soul and mind." He entered psychoanalysis, probably with Silvano Arieti, whom he knew from the Columbia seminar on Religion and Psychiatry. But the experience did not agree with him: when it was over, he told his friends the Wyschogrods that "I am angry at myself that I was ready to listen to the post-Freudian oracle."[158]

One source of his discontent was the fact that Columbia University had not yet decided to elevate him to full professor. Part of his indecision was his hope of using the offer of the Berlin position to get himself promoted at Columbia.[159] He'd published only a few essays since his promotion to associate professor in 1959, though in 1966 he did publish a slim volume he had edited of the autobiographical writings of Franz Overbeck, long a star in his intellectual firmament. Jacob's introduction to the volume, "The Disenchantment of Theology: Toward a Portrait of Overbeck," was in part a self-portrait. Taubes suggested that Overbeck had not simply developed from a professor of theology into an agnostic, as most critics asserted, but rather that his work comprised a "congeries of irreconcilable ideas that give Overbeck's fragments a deep fragility."[160] Whether or not that was an accurate characterization of Overbeck, it fit Taubes quite well.

Taubes's anxiety about professional promotion led him to another small but telling act of treachery. His colleague in the Department of Religion, Harold Stahmer, shared Taubes's interest in twentieth-century German-Jewish thought, and in Franz Rosenzweig in particular. While Taubes was in Berlin, a senior member of the department, Jacob Blau (for whose intellect Taubes had little respect), had given a lecture at Columbia on Rosenzweig. Stahmer reported on the event in a letter to Taubes, writing that "Blau for some ungodly reason gave a lecture on Rosenzweig, though he obviously didn't know shit about Rosenzweig." The next year, when both Stahmer and Taubes were coming up for promotion, Taubes approached Blau, reached into his pocket, and informed Blau that he had a letter, the contents of which would no doubt interest him: he then pulled out Stahmer's letter disparaging Blau. Stahmer learned of the incident years later from a senior colleague who witnessed it.[161] Taubes's behavior toward a colleague whom he viewed as a potential rival echoed his earlier attempt to sabotage Philip Rieff's position at Beacon Press.

In the event, Taubes *was* promoted to full professor, as he was officially informed on April 4, 1966, with a boost in salary to $14,000.[162] He wrote a letter to the President of the FU, Joachim Lieber, saying that he had just informed the dean of the faculty of philosophy that he regretfully was forced to resign. He had hoped to secure the legal guardianship of his children, he explained, but having failed to do so, he felt compelled to stay at Columbia.[163] In June 1966, Jacob sent word to Margharita from Paris that he was sorry, but their relationship was off; he was planning to marry a very rich woman (there is a cryptic reference in Margherita's response to the "Norry millions").[164] But that soon proved a dead end.

There was more Sturm und Drang, and more bargaining. On July 27, he wrote to the chief administrator (*Kurator*) of the FU that he was giving up his Columbia job to become a tenured civil servant (*Beamte auf Lebenszeit*) at the FU—and asking for a raise of both his monthly salary, and of his instructional guarantee to 18,000 DM per annum. The Kurator's response was to indeed raise his pay category (from AH3 to AH6), granting him the desired instructional guarantee along with a monthly salary of 4,020 DM—which meant that Jacob was to earn 66,240 DM per year, a sum he supplemented with his stipend from Suhrkamp.[165] (Jacob later told a friend that "when Derrida meets me, he is jealous of how much I earn."[166]) He now wrote to his dean at Columbia, tendering his resignation as of the end of August.[167] He explained in a letter to a German colleague that he had returned to Berlin with the intention of winding up his affairs there, where it became clear to him that he was indeed committed to Margherita.[168] Perhaps that was the reason. Perhaps he felt unwelcome or too little respected at Columbia. Perhaps it was because Berlin suited him so much better.

Before he could marry Margherita, however, Jacob needed a divorce from Susan.

Divorce

Divorce was still difficult and costly to obtain in New York state. So once Jacob had decided definitively to go to Berlin, Jacob and Susan obtained a legal separation agreement, drawn up on October 31, 1966, and signed in

February 1967.[169] That was followed by a Mexican divorce in Chihuahua on April 8, 1967, in which Susan sued Jacob for divorce on the grounds of incompatibility of temperaments and end of marital cohabitation since 1962. Susan flew to Mexico for the proceedings, while Jacob was represented by a Mexican attorney. The divorce ratified the provisions of their separation agreement. Just how troubled their relationship had become was revealed in the agreement's stipulation that "each party shall be free from interference, authority and control, direct or indirect, by the other as fully as if he or she were unmarried. Neither shall molest the other or compel or endeavor to compel the other to cohabit or dwell with him or her." Strikingly, after eighteen years of legal marriage, there was no marital property to be divided. Neither Jacob nor Susan was rooted to possessions—indeed, they were hardly rooted at all.

Under the financial provisions, Jacob was to pay Susan alimony of $3,600 per annum, plus $2,400 per annum for the support of the children, in addition to their medical expenses. Susan was to have sole custody of the children as long as Jacob lived in Europe, but the children were to spend a month with him each summer. Jacob and Susan agreed to consult with the other regarding the children's education and medical care.

Jacob departed for Berlin, leaving it to his friend Michael Wyschogrod to put his health insurance and life insurance in order, explaining, "On such matters I am utterly incompetent and ignorant. I have not created this complex world and do not know my way about it."[170] He left it to his doctoral student, Gershon Greenberg, to supervise the packing of his books and their shipment to Berlin.[171] Before he left, he borrowed Harold Stahmer's Columbia library card and used it to check out a number of books, which he took with him to Berlin.[172]

With the death of his sister and his father, his divorce from Susan, and his definitive move from New York to Berlin, the ties linking Jacob with his past seemed to be severed. Jacob began a new chapter in his life that revolved around his new home institution. The FU was engulfed in a wave of cultural and political radicalism. In Berlin, history seemed to be marching toward the apocalypse. And Jacob and Margherita would be near the front of the parade.

CHAPTER TEN

Berlin

IMPRESARIO OF THEORY

IN THE FALL OF 1966, Jacob moved to Berlin, leaving behind his post at Columbia and committing himself to the Free University, where he began to build up the institutes of Judaica and of hermeneutics created especially for him. Jacob established himself as a teacher and impresario of ideas, and through his participation in an unprecedented intellectual undertaking—an elite, interdisciplinary seminar of scholars known as Poetics and Hermeneutics—reached out to a broad network of German intellectuals.

Jet-Setting and Vacillation

Though Jacob had made up his mind to move to the FU, he was keen to maintain his contacts in America. Jacob took pleasure in hosting his American friends when they visited in West Berlin. In 1967, Norman Podhoretz and his wife, Midge Decter, visited the city as part of a Ford Foundation group that included Irving Kristol and Gertrude Himmelfarb as well. Jacob got wind of it and took them to the Orthodox synagogue he sometimes attended, comprised largely of older, Eastern European Jews. He also had Podhoretz speak to his class. Podhoretz realized that Jacob was becoming more politically involved and moving to the left, but just how deep and how far he did not know.[1]

In an age when jet travel was still rare among German professors, Jacob was conspicuously on the go.

No sooner had he returned to Berlin than he was invited to participate in a seminar at Harvard on Judaism, Christianity, and Secularization, organized by the sociologist Robert Bellah, together with Jacob's friend, the theologian Krister Stendhal. The audience, Bellah informed Jacob, would include Biblical scholars, theologians, historians, and sociologists. Bellah urged Jacob to take a broad view of the subject, since "your interests are as much Biblical and historical as social scientific."[2]

Jacob sat down to develop a plan that would draw upon his wide-ranging reading to construct a broad historical narrative. He would deal with "Dante (in the light of [Erich] Auerbach's interpretation, but with the accent on his Imperial theology); Spinoza (the destruction of *Heilsgeschichte*); and the Bauer-Marx controversy on the *Judenfrage*." The paper, he told Bellah, would imply "a critique of the current social science analysis, also a critique of its patron saint, Alexis de Tocqueville, who has proved particularly congenial to liberals in the Western world since 1945. I dare say that Marx has more to offer to reveal the riddle of the religious revival in the United States since 1945." The implication was that the ongoing popularity of religion in the United States, rather than a pillar of social integration as Tocqueville had claimed, was a response to the alienation that characterized contemporary American life.[3]

His appearance at Harvard was important to him. Yet once again, Jacob found it difficult to muster the concerted effort required to write. Having left himself too little time to properly prepare, he was almost paralyzed by anxiety. "One waits for years for the 'grand' lecture at Harvard, and when it arrives, one feels such time pressure that it takes one's breath away," he wrote to Miriam Weingort, his Orthodox friend in Montreux.[4] Too anxious to actually write the paper, he dictated it to his graduate student, Gershon Greenberg.[5]

There is some doubt as to the coherence and cogency of the paper he presented. Writing again to Weingort shortly after the Harvard conference, he reported that "the discussion was more successful than the talk itself."[6] In the end, plans to publish it in the *Harvard Theological Review* fell through.[7]

Jacob took the occasion of the conference to attack Gershom Scholem. In his mind, it was a defensive maneuver. He heard from Jacob Fleischmann, a scholar of Judaica who had left Hebrew University for Paris, that Scholem had visited Fleischmann in Paris and harangued him for two hours about Taubes. Scholem had recently published a highly controversial essay, "Against the Myth of the German-Jewish Dialogue," in a festschrift for their mutual friend, Margarete Susman. There, Scholem insisted that the Jewish love affair with German culture was a case of unrequited love, since non-Jewish Germans had no real interest in what the Jews had to say, and were interested at most in insisting upon what the Jews needed to give up rather than what they had to contribute. Thus, Scholem concluded, "When they [German Jews] thought they were speaking to the Germans, they were speaking to themselves."[8] After hearing from Fleischmann about Scholem's denunciation of him, Jacob reported, "I decided to take up the challenge, and in a public discussion I characterized his essay in the Margarete Susman-Festschrift as Jewish fascism." The response was overwhelmingly positive, "even by those from whom one would not have expected it"—or so Jacob claimed.[9]

Jacob reveled in such opportunities to visit at American academic institutions. By April, he was flying back to Harvard to give another talk—it was "a temptation I can't resist."[10]

Jacob's relationship to his children was an ongoing source of concern and anxiety to him. From time to time, the children would come to visit with him in Berlin. They also spent time with him in Europe each summer, sometimes including Susan as well. Particularly troubling for Jacob was his relationship to his fourteen-year-old son, Ethan. After a visit from his son in December 1966, he wrote to Rabbi Moses Botschko of the Montreux Yeshiva that it was difficult in such short periods of time to fashion the sort of trusting relationship between father and son that could only be created by steady care. But, he lamented, he had to confront that reality "without illusion."[11] What Jacob failed to mention (or perhaps notice) was that Ethan was afraid of him, because from the time Ethan was a toddler, Jacob had so frequently resorted to slapping and striking him when Ethan defied his father. That stopped only when, at age fifteen, Ethan told his father, "If you touch me again, I'll kill you!"[12] Their difficult relationship was born of high expectations and low patience on Jacob's part. He frequently importuned male friends in the United States to look in on Ethan and offer him their guidance.[13]

Marriage to Brentano

On December 20, 1967, after six years of an on-and-off relationship—more on than off—Jacob and Margherita married in a civil ceremony in her home, attended by a few friends, with Peter Szondi as their witness.[14] Since Jacob's return to Berlin, they had been living together at Furtwänglerstraße 11 in the Grunewald neighborhood.

Some of Margherita's longtime friends wondered at the pairing. Some thought her more attracted to women than to men.[15] The partners seemed so different. She had a fashion sense that Jacob lacked. She drove a white Alfa Romeo, while after his move to Berlin, Jacob did not drive at all. She was proper and reserved. Jacob was neither. Jacob was ironic, skeptical, and witty; Margherita, more strict and earnest.[16] Jacob had a mind that was explorative and associative, while Margherita did not.[17] She was a dog lover, a not unusual taste among Germans of her background, but foreign to Jacob's. She owned a small house in the Black Forest, to which she withdrew from time to time, a practice Jacob scorned as "Heideggerei." (The philosopher famously had a hut in the Black Forest to which he retreated.) Like Jacob, Margherita smoked. But while he favored a pipe, she smoked cigarettes, more or less constantly. She was by all accounts a nervous type. Margherita would have liked to have children, but Jacob, who had two, was not interested.[18]

Raised in a deeply Catholic milieu, she had turned her back definitively on religion and had no interest in it. Jacob, by contrast, remained interested in religion as a subject of academic study, but also, albeit intermittently, on a personal level. Margherita had no interest in this side of Jacob, indeed was deeply suspicious of it. When Jacob's friend, the Jewish philosopher Michael Wyschogrod, visited with Jacob and Margherita in the years just before their marriage, she was highly antagonistic, suspecting that Wyschogrod had been dispatched by the Jewish elders in New York to rescue Taubes from her clutches. They conducted a three-day-long debate about whether Nazi antisemitism could be explained in Marxist terms: Margherita argued that it could be; Wyschogrod thought not.[19]

The couple had much in common, of course, including a professional interest in philosophy and an interest in Marxism. But Margherita was far more deeply and consistently political than Jacob—and more doctrinaire.[20] What for him was an affinity for the left was for her an object of ongoing engagement and struggle.

At the time of their wedding, Margherita was still an *Akademischer Rat*, the lowest tenured rung on the academic ladder. Her salary was thus substantially below his, though she may have had some additional familial sources of income. Nevertheless, when Jacob would invite others out to dinner at a restaurant after his evening colloquia, once the bill arrived, he would casually ask, "Well Margherita, have you brought your pocketbook along?" She typically paid.[21]

Teacher in Berlin

When Taubes came to Berlin in the early 1960s, he brought with him a wealth of worldly cultural references that he was eager to share with the culturally provincial postwar Germans. He introduced his young students to books and cultural figures that they would not have heard about before. He taught twentieth-century authors such as Freud and Benjamin at a time when few in German academia did so. He discussed the works of scholars in the United States with whom he was acquainted but who were little known in Germany, such as Leo Strauss.[22] But he also raised awareness of figures such as Carl Schmitt, who if known, were generally regarded as beyond the pale by most intellectuals on the left.

Among the handful of friends who attended Jacob's wedding to Margherita was Peter Gente. In February 1965, Gente edited an issue of the magazine *Alternative: Zeitschrift für Literatur und Diskussion*, devoted to contemporary French authors. Impressed with the young man, Taubes hired him to put together a list of books to acquire for the library of the Hermeneutical Institute and to suggest French books for Taubes to pass on to Suhrkamp Verlag for possible inclusion in the Reihe Theorie. When Taubes's books arrived from New York, Gente was tasked with unpacking them. He was astonished to find scores of copies of *Abendländische Eschatologie*, some of which Taubes had clearly pilfered from libraries in an attempt to take his book out of circulation. Gente concluded that Taubes was embarrassed by the book. Gente was also surprised to find books by Carl Schmitt with inscriptions to Taubes. Gente was an engaged, young leftist intellectual, who was a member of the SDS and the Argument Kreis. He admired Taubes and included several selections from Taubes and Brentano in his compendium of the writings of leftist thinkers, *Neuer Roter Katechismus* (*New Red Catechism*) (1968). The volume, which was written under a pseudonym, excerpted the works of contemporary icons of the New Left such as Mao, Adorno, Lukács, Habermas, Sartre, Che Guevera, and Régis Debray.[23] Gente spent a year in Paris learning French so that he could better comprehend the work of Taubes's old friend, the Marxist literary critic Lucien Goldmann.

In his early years at the FU and for some time thereafter, Taubes attracted students like Gente: politically engaged, intellectually curious young men and women who were philosophically inclined, disdainful of disciplinary boundaries, and more attracted to texts and to theories than to empirical investigation. Some, such as Wolfgang Lefèvre, came from the student left and would play key roles in the radicalization of the university. Others, like Henning Ritter, went on to careers in journalism or, like Gente, in publishing. Still others—especially those who were able to maintain a certain intellectual distance from Taubes—went on to successful academic careers, while those who identified most closely with Taubes and chose him as their academic mentor often failed to do so.

Taubes had little time, aptitude, or interest for the more routine demands of his role as an *Ordinarius*. He was a problematic dissertation or habilitation advisor. Rather than providing his advisees with guidelines for limiting their topics, he gave them references and leads for additional material to look at—a useful function, up to a point, but more often a procedure that precluded the student from ever finishing. Thus he was the advisor for many a dissertation that was never completed. That he was uninterested and uninformed about institutional procedures added to the problem.[24]

Like a few other highly charismatic professors at the FU, Taubes had student disciples who studied with him for years on end without submitting papers or passing exams, and often without completing academic degrees. They could do so in part because tuition was free, and they could subsist on earnings from low-paying positions at his institutes, which also provided them with cheap labor. But they could also do so because in an era of rising prosperity in the Federal Republic, their economic future was of little immediate concern; one could study philosophy and related disciplines for years without hearing the word "job." Finding a position seemed unproblematic at a time when ongoing economic growth was taken for granted and when jobs were opening up in the rapidly expanding German university system. Some also saw themselves as working for a common cause, and were loath to leave the nest of the academy.[25] Their leftwing anticapitalist ideology denigrated making a living, and some lived in the expectation of imminent revolution.

Taubes was passionate about ideas, and he conveyed the emotional stakes of intellectual battles, what one former student called the "pathos of theory."[26] In his seminars, he had high intellectual expectations of his students, and sometimes shouted at them when they failed to live up to his standards.[27] He loved drama and had a talent for teaching intellectual debates as dramatic intellectual conflicts—whether it was between Theodor Adorno and Walter Benjamin, or Carl Schmitt and Erik Peterson. At the same time, Taubes had a cavalier attitude toward academic boundaries—both disciplinary boundaries and the boundaries of academic propriety—which he treated with humor and disdain. His skepticism about disciplines, together with his antiauthoritarianism, made him especially attractive to the "generation of 1968," both before and after that date.[28]

When lecturing to large groups of students, Jacob had a dramatic mode of presentation. Speaking without notes, he seemed to be thinking through and experiencing the philosophical issues at hand.[29] He was a dazzler (*Blender*) and in many ways entirely untypical for a German *Ordinarius*. He seemed to be genuinely "present" when he spoke to individual students, looking at them penetratingly and with curiosity—much the same presentation of self that his colleagues at the Jewish Theological Seminary had noticed two decades earlier.[30]

While Taubes taught some lecture courses, for the most part he offered seminars, which were well attended. In 1964–65, he participated in a joint seminar with several rising stars of German philosophy—Dieter Henrich, Michael Theunissen, and Rolf Tiedemann—where Henrich discussed Heidegger, Theunissen taught Buber, and Tiedemann discussed Benjamin. For his part, Taubes explored Freud's *Moses and Monotheism*, and also Marcuse's *Eros and Civilization*. One student participant, Bernhard Lypp, recalled the seminar as chaotic but interesting, with Taubes reveling in the intellectual conflict.[31] Taubes spoke in favor of integrating Marx and Freud (in the characteristic manner of the Frankfurt School), while tying both to a purported tradition of prophetic Judaism. According to one of his students at the time, Thomas Flügge, Taubes told the students, "It is an American tragedy that psychoanalysis there wishes to remain ignorant of Marxism and has separated from it, and that Marxism in America is virtually unknown, since psychoanalysis and Marxism share the same root, that of Jewish, enlightened prophecy. They belong together and can only be meaningful and effective when they complement one another."[32] He explored those themes in a talk he gave on Berlin radio on "Psychoanalysis and Philosophy."[33]

Shortly after his arrival at the FU, Taubes settled on a pattern of teaching that he had begun at Columbia, when Susan Sontag was his teaching assistant. He left much of the preparation for the course, and much of the day-to-day work, in the hands of talented teaching assistants, or colleagues with expertise in texts that Taubes lacked, but that he was interested in exploring. The teaching assistant or colleague would lead the discussion of the text, and Taubes would chime in with suggestive remarks or insights into how the text fit into larger contexts in the intellectual history of the West. In his early years at the FU, he made use of Uta Gerhardt in that capacity, to teach courses on Hegel and on Max Weber. Gerhardt had studied with Adorno in Frankfurt, was active in the SDS, and later went on to a career in sociology. She thought Taubes too lazy or distracted to engage in careful study of the texts they were teaching.[34]

Taubes had a sixth sense for people whose wealth of knowledge he could use, even if their own scholarship was unimaginative, or if they were not productive scholars at all.[35] He would teach courses on Gnosticism with Rudolf Macuch, an Orientalist, and later still with Carsten Colpe, an expert on the subject whom Taubes helped bring to the FU. He taught seminars on medieval texts with his junior colleagues, Wolfgang Hübener of philosophy, and on the Book of Daniel with Friedrich-Wilhelm Marquardt of Protestant theology.[36] They would use their philological erudition to explain the plain meaning of the text. Taubes's contribution was to try to place the text in its political, cultural, and social context, asking what was going on *behind* the words of the text, that is, the deeper concerns and anxieties that motivated the author. He would interject broader observations about the nature and place of the text in the larger sweep of intellectual history, drawing connections to disparate phenomena that would have occurred to few others.[37] He did so without necessarily preparing for class, as a kind of impromptu performance.[38]

Taubes had a talent for using contemporary analogies to bring home to his students the nature and significance of old texts. For example, when teaching about the Dead Sea scrolls, which were thought to have originated as a collection of scrolls maintained by the sect of Essenes and provide a window onto Jewish life in the age of Jesus, Taubes suggested this analogy to his students: "Imagine if contemporary Berlin was destroyed by bombs, and centuries later, someone came across a few articles from the *Extra-Dienst*"—a small, marginal leftist daily, published in West Berlin and read by the student left.[39] It was these interjections and analogies that gave such courses their spice.[40] Taubes's weakness, in his teaching as in his writing, was in systematic explication of concepts. But his talent for concretizing concepts, for making them seem relevant and vital to his students, was unmatched. He could explain Kierkegaard's concept of anxiety (*Angst*) in a more vivid way than an expert on Kierkegaard could.[41]

Taubes's relationship with Rodolphe Gasché, one of his early students at the FU, exemplifies the way in which his intellectual connections benefited his students, and how he made use of his students to expand his own knowledge. Gasché's background and extra-academic involvements illustrate some of the cultural currents in Taubes's Berlin milieu. Gasché arrived at the FU in the fall of 1962, and in the years that followed attended Taubes's lectures on the sociology of religion, on Gnosticism, and on Freud's views on religion. Gasché, who hailed from Luxembourg, was multilingual and had been active in the Situationist International, a fringe group of anarchic, utopian artists and writers who aimed to subvert the capitalist status quo by drawing upon the legacy of surrealism. Their tactics included the use of "constructed situations"—theatrical acts intended to outrage the bourgeoisie and raise the consciousness of the disaffected. Gasché was active in the Situationists West German counterpart, and together with Dieter Kunzelmann, he founded the journal *Subversive*

Aktion.[42] Among the other members in West Berlin were Herbert Nagel, a sociology student interested in social utopias, and Rudi Dutschke, under whose influence the group became politicized. In January 1965, they joined the SDS, promoting the formation within it of "actionist factions" intended to radicalize it from within.[43] But as that organization veered toward Marxist-Leninism, Gasché dropped out. He believed in the power of ideology—what the increasingly dogmatic Marxists scorned as "superstructure"—and took an interest in French structuralism.[44]

Gasché served as a scholarly assistant (*Wissenschaftlicher Hilfsassistent*) at Taubes's Hermeneutic Institute during the academic year 1968–69. (The year before, Herbert Nagel, by then a leading figure in the SDS at the FU, had held the job.) Taubes had a keen interest in current French thought, and was eager to know what was on the cutting edge. Rather than doing the reading himself, he sought out students whom he thought promising and had them explain to him the thinkers they found interesting. Like Gente before him, Taubes had Gasché suggest books to purchase for the library. And he had Gasché write evaluations of French books, such as Michel Foucault's *Les mots et les choses* (*The Order of Things: An Archeology of the Human Sciences*), which Taubes recommended to Suhrkamp for translation into German.[45]

When in July 1968 Taubes invited Jacques Derrida to give some talks in Berlin, he arranged for students, including Gasché, to meet with the rising star of French literary theory. Later, Gasché would translate Derrida's *L'écriture et la différence* into German for Suhrkamp Verlag, and still later, would become a leading interpreter of Derrida's work. Gasché spent the years 1969–71 studying in Paris. Taubes visited with him there, eager to learn from his student about new developments in French theory, and, in keeping with his fascination with conflict and drama, to hear about the latest gossip in French academia and intellectual life.

Inviting Derrida to the Hermeneutic Institute was typical of Taubes's role as an "impresario of theory" in Berlin (the term comes from Gente). He knew the French intellectual and American intellectual scenes and brought up-and-coming intellectuals to Berlin. Among those was his friend Lucien Goldmann, whose reputation in Germany Taubes did much to establish. Taubes had met Michel Foucault at a Nietzsche colloquium in Royaumont, France, in July 1964, where he heard Foucault give a talk on the links between Marx, Freud, and Nietzsche—a talk that marked a turning point in the reception of Nietzsche in French intellectual life.[46] Gente would later bring Foucault to Berlin and founded a publishing house, Merve Verlag, that would publish Foucault in German. Taubes also encouraged a workshop on French structuralism, led by another of his students, Henning Ritter, in which Wolf Lepenies, a rising member of the Department of Sociology, also participated. That workshop led to the publication in 1970 of *Orte des Wilden Denkens*, on the anthropology of Claude Levy-Strauss, in Suhrkamp's Reihe Theorie, a volume edited by Ritter and Lepenies, to which each of them contributed, as did Gasché and Nagel.[47] In 1973, Ritter taught a course (*Übung*) on Foucault.[48] Ritter went on to become a distinguished cultural journalist, as the editor for the humanities at the *Frankfurter Allgemeine Zeitung*, the country's most prestigious daily.

For Taubes, intellectuality was closely linked to sociability. Every two weeks he had a *jour fixe* at a Chinese restaurant on the Kurfürstendamm, where he would gather with Gasché, Ritter, Lepenies, and others. At table, he displayed not only his wit, but his intellectual range, and in an attempt to *épater* not only the bourgeoisie, but the leftist received wisdom, he would defend Carl Schmitt and Ernst Jünger.[49]

Sociologist of Religion

Taubes's approach to the sociology of religion was based not on empirical investigation but rather on his fascination with historical analogies and recurrent historical patterns. He had a single template, which he sought to apply time and again—of antinomian, apocalyptic moments and movements, above all those that drew upon the apocalyptic elements of the Jewish and Christian traditions.

In the mid-1960s, Taubes was much taken by the possible implications of two recent works that seemed to match his template. One was a book by the British anthropologist Peter Worsley, *The Trumpet Shall Sound* (1957), a study of cargo cults in Melanesia and the links between millenarian movements and modern, political nationalism. The second, by the Italian ethnologist of religion Vittorio Lanternari, was entitled *The Religions of the Oppressed: A Study of Modern Messianic Cults* (1963, first published in Italian in 1960). Taubes presented these books as a kind of revelation, as evidence that Third World resistance movements were inspired less by Marxism than by messianism. That was in keeping with his broader contention that "secularization" was an inadequate model for understanding the roles of religion in the modern world. (Later, he added the work of the British sociologist of religion, Bryan Wilson, *Magic and the Millennium: A Sociological Study of Religious Movements among Tribal and Third-World Peoples* [1973].)

In 1966, before leaving Columbia, he wrote up a funding proposal for a project, in which he suggested a working hypothesis that linked social developments to religiously inflected nationalist movements. As he noted in a portion of the draft that he subsequently crossed out, the project was a continuation of themes he had explored in *Abendländische Eschatologie* and subsequent essays.[50] The project proposal was characteristic of his approach to the sociology of religion.

> [T]he rise of messianic cults has been constitutive for the awakening self-consciousness (in the guise of messianic ideologies) in Africa and Asia. . . .
>
> What happened at scores of points of contact between western and native societies was the destruction of the economic substructure of tribal society and ultimately its transformation into an urban and industrial proletariat. Necessarily this resulted in a weakening of traditional religions, beliefs, and habits which were intimately bound up with the ancestral soil. The consequent "conversion" of primitive communities to (a reinterpreted form of) Christianity provided in the first stage a point around which a new sense of community might crystallize. The tribal communities, however, which usually received the Christian (eschatological) message through western missionaries, tend to blend some motifs of the Old and New Testament with traditional beliefs, and so at a second stage the Christian acculturation serves to unleash in these primitive societies dormant revolutionary forces that otherwise would never have come to the fore. The eschatological Christian hopes, which are muted or even suppressed in the institutionalized western churches, thus break through in the primitive context with elemental force: the expectation of an impending destruction and renewal of the world in which the tribe will occupy a privileged position may affirm in an original way the cultural and political autonomy of the primitive society as separate from and superior to the missionaries in particular and western industrial society in general. Causes which were lost and aspirations which were thwarted in the west might, in Asia or Africa, yet be won.

The project was not funded, but Taubes proceeded nevertheless. He tasked a sociology student, Brigitte Luchesi, to assemble the scholarly literature on messianism. Some were astonished that the Judaica library was being stocked with such books. But others found such transdisciplinary stimuli useful and exciting, including Hans G. Kippenberg, who came to the FU in 1969. He arrived at the FU trained in a philological approach to the study of religion. Thanks in part to the influence of Taubes, he left with a far broader perspective, and went on to become a leading historian of religion. Spurred on by Taubes, in 1971, together with two junior faculty members at the Judaica Institute, Kippenberg offered a course on The History of Religion and Social Preconditions of the Bar-Kochba Revolt, a messianic-nationalist Jewish revolt against the Roman empire.[51] In the winter semester of 1973–74, Taubes was scheduled to teach a course on Comparative Sociology of Religion: Chiliasm and Nativism in Late Antiquity and the Third World.[52]

Impresario of Ideas

Some of the qualities that made Taubes a less-than-productive scholar in terms of publications—his inability to maintain solitude, his need for sociability, the speculative and wide-ranging cast of his mind—suited him for the role of impresario of ideas, creating a realm of oral exchange of ideas that was stimulating and energizing. Taubes practiced what Nietzsche had called "die fröhliche Wissenschaft"—free-spirited scholarship. He had a talent for bringing together interesting minds and facilitating intellectual exchange, an activity that gave him great pleasure.

Take the evening colloquium that he convened at his Institute for Hermeneutics, located in a small villa at Auf dem Grat 48. The colloquium would typically begin in the evening, meet formally for two hours, and then continue informally at a local restaurant. Participation was limited to about twenty people, most of them doctoral students and professors, which created an intimate setting for intense conversation. Taubes would choose texts from diverse perspectives to pursue some broad topic. In the fall of 1967, for example, the topic was the potential uses of secularization (*Verweltlichung*) as a perspective on the philosophy of history. As he explained in a letter to Hans-Georg Gadamer inviting him to participate in its deliberations, the colloquium examined the use of the concept by a number of twentieth-century German thinkers, whom Taubes paired into roughly non-Marxist and Marxist perspectives. In the former category were Max Weber, Carl Schmitt, Karl Löwith, and Friedrich Gogarten; in the latter, Walter Benjamin, Ernst Bloch, and Theodor Adorno.[53] Many of these were figures whose writings Taubes had been exploring since his work on his doctoral dissertation. What was unusual—especially at a time when the student left was coming to dominate campus discussion—was the inclusion of Carl Schmitt, and of course the juxtaposition of thinkers from the left, the right, and the center.

Taubes's role as an impresario of ideas was enhanced by the close cooperation between his Hermeneutical Colloquium and the Colloquium on
Comparative Literature, founded by Peter Szondi. Though Taubes was not
much interested in aesthetics, he was attracted by, and attractive to, some
of the intelligent and open-minded students of comparative literature,
many of whom also had philosophical interests.[54]

The Judaica Institute

Before 1933, Judaica (*Judaistik*) had existed within the German university system primarily as an auxiliary field (*Hilfswissenschaft*) for Protestant theology, especially to provide the "Jewish background" for the study
of the New Testament. Jewish scholars of *Wissenschaft des Judentums*
carried out their research and teaching mostly within the confines of institutions for the training of rabbis, such as the Vienna rabbinical seminary
from which Zwi Taubes had graduated.[55] In the United States, the academic study of Jewish matters in the early 1960s was still confined primarily to institutions for rabbinic training, such as the Jewish Theological
Seminary, where Taubes had taught early in his career, and the Jewish
Institute of Religion, also in New York, where he taught some courses during his early years at Columbia University. There were important scholars
of Judaism and Jewish history at a few American universities, such as Salo
Baron at Columbia, Harry Wolfson at Harvard, and Alexander Altmann
and Nahum Glatzer at Brandeis, but "Jewish Studies" as an established
academic field was still in its infancy. Nowhere but at the Hebrew University in Jerusalem was there a secular university with a fully developed
program of Jewish studies, developed in part by Gershom Scholem. It was
left to Jacob Taubes to try to create such a program at the FU. That was
the job for which he had been hired, and his contract had included provisions for building up a Judaica library at the institute, which shared a
building with Catholic and Protestant studies at Bachstelzenweg 29/31.
The building was one of a number of villas in the Dahlem neighborhood,
once owned by Jewish families, and repurposed after World War II for use
by the new university in the American sector of the city.

But there were barriers to carrying out his mandate. Since there were
few Jewish students at the FU (or elsewhere in Germany for that matter),
the audience consisted primarily of students of Christian background with
religiously inspired interests in matters Jewish. Another obstacle was the
fact that Taubes was less interested in teaching Jewish subjects than in
the sorts of courses that he offered in the Department of Philosophy and

the Institute for Hermeneutics—not to speak of the currents of political activism in which he was soon caught up. Margherita, in a letter written in the fall of 1965, noted Taubes's "disinclination toward Jewish Studies," which he did not think of as "his discipline" (*Fach*)—the real source, she thought, of his doubts about moving from Columbia to the FU.[56] When he did make the move, Taubes made a point of having his appointment labeled as *Judaistik und Religionsoziologie*, already extending his range beyond matters Jewish. In addition, he had an appointment as head of the Hermeneutic Institute, stretching the purview of his potential activities much further. In short, fulfilling the responsibilities of his chair in *Judaistik* was, for Taubes, the price to be paid for engaging in the more enticing fields of religion and hermeneutics.

After taking up his permanent position at the FU, Jacob searched for someone who could manage the day-to-day operations of the Judaica Institute, and he hit upon Marianne Awerbuch. Born in Berlin in 1917 (and thus six years older than Jacob), she had emigrated with her husband to Palestine in 1939. Long denied the opportunity of university study, she taught high school in Tel Aviv before enrolling in the newly founded Tel Aviv University in 1961. There she studied history and Bible, and received her MA. Awerbuch was by all accounts highly opinionated, strong-willed, and given to intensity and drama in her relationships with colleagues.[57] Although she was a fine student, her mentor at Tel Aviv University indicated that her argumentative personality made it unlikely that she would get a position there.[58] So, in August 1966, she returned to the city of her birth and enrolled at the FU to pursue a doctoral degree in medieval history, where she eventually wrote a thesis on late medieval Burgundy. Required to do a secondary field (*Nebenfach*), she thought *Judaistik* would be the easiest, and introduced herself to Taubes with that aim in mind. After a brief conversation, he offered her a position as an assistant at his institute. Initially, her job was to supervise the acquisition of books for the library, but her role soon expanded.

Taubes welcomed Awerbuch as someone who would lift the burden of managing the Judaica Institute from his shoulders, allowing him to devote himself to the hermeneutical studies closer to his heart. After taking some courses with him, she concluded that while he was charismatic, intelligent, and highly perceptive, he was also unrealistic, unserious, and not given to working or teaching according to any systematic plan. She never could determine what plans, if any, he had for the Institute. Awerbuch thought his choice of topics—such as "Jewish Gnosticism," Papuan cargo cults, or Max Weber—eccentric and irrelevant. As Taubes plunged ever deeper into the political waters of the university, he delegated issues of instruction in the Judaica Institute to Awerbuch.[59]

Many of those who took her courses were students of Protestant theology. They were philo-Semitic and positively inclined toward Israel, many having participated in Aktion Sühnezeichen (Action Reconciliation), which brought German students to Israel in an effort to atone for what the Germans had done to the Jews. But they lacked a knowledge of Hebrew and of the basics of Jewish history. Having already taught Hebrew as a high-school teacher in Israel, and making use of her previous Bible studies, Awerbuch began to teach these subjects, including the classic medieval Biblical commentary of Rashi, as well as medieval Jewish history.[60]

One of Taubes's early hires at the Judaica Institute was Niko Oswald, a Lutheran who had studied at the Kirchliche Hochschule in Berlin, where there was an Institute for the Church and the Jews (Institut für Kirche und Judentum). He was a product of that tradition of Jewish studies that treated it in relationship to Christianity. His expertise was Aramaic, the language of the Talmud. Some of his students felt that while his linguistic skills were impeccable, compared to Taubes he lacked the intuitive feel for the logic of Talmudic argument cultivated by a yeshiva education—a weakness that Oswald himself acknowledged.[61] He would spend his entire career at the FU, outlasting a series of Institute heads.

Taubes tried to lure his old friend from Basel, the polymath Eugen Kullmann, to come to Berlin from New York, where he was teaching at the New School. At first, Kullmann agreed, and his courses were listed in the course catalogue. But after a rash of highly publicized antisemitic incidents (part of a Soviet campaign of "active measures" designed to blacken the image of the Federal Republic), Kullmann decided not to come to Germany.[62]

Taubes was, however, able to attract promising younger scholars of Jewish studies from German-speaking Europe, the United States, and Israel to teach courses and participate in his graduate seminars.

Johann Maier, a Lutheran scholar who had trained at the University of Vienna, taught at Taubes's institute from 1964 to 1966, before moving to the University of Cologne, where he founded the second institute of Jewish studies at a German university.

Amos Funkenstein was another young scholar associated with the Institute in its early years. Raised in a religious household in Jerusalem, Funkenstein began his university studies there, but in the late 1950s moved to the FU to pursue graduate studies in medieval history. He completed his PhD in 1965 with a dissertation on Christian philosophies of history in the Middle Ages. That same year he participated in Taubes's seminar on Hasidic texts, which focused on the *Tanya*, written in 1797 by Schneur Zalman of Liadi, the founder of Lubavitch Hasidism.[63]

Like Taubes, Funkenstein was the son of an Orthodox scholar, and like him, Funkenstein became an apikores—a heretic deeply versed in the Jewish tradition. Unlike Taubes, however, Funkenstein was not given to ongoing, intermittent observance and belief.[64] The two shared many interests, including the religious origins of modern historical consciousness. Like Taubes, Funkenstein was a man of broad intellectual horizons and synoptic perspectives. The difference was that unlike Taubes, Funkenstein had the patience and fortitude to conduct systematic scholarship, and to fully develop his arguments.[65] At the FU, he taught courses in 1967 on medieval Jewish history and at the Institute on The Problem of Continuity in Jewish History, and another, in 1970, on medieval Jewish and Christian Biblical exegesis. He then left for UCLA, eventually assuming other posts at Stanford and Berkeley.[66]

Taubes repeatedly brought Gershon Greenberg, his former graduate student and teaching assistant at Columbia University, to teach at the Institute and to help in building up the library. Greenberg taught courses on medieval and modern Jewish thought, as well as on American Jewry. In 1971, he returned to the United States and taught philosophy and religion at universities there and in Israel.

It was Taubes's international connections that also brought Paul Flohr (later Mendes-Flohr) to his institute. Flohr was at the time a doctoral student at Brandeis, working on a dissertation on Martin Buber's thought with Nahum Glatzer and Alexander Altmann, among the most distinguished international scholars of Jewish thought. Like Glatzer, Altmann thought highly of Jacob Taubes's abilities: when Taubes was considering his permanent move to Berlin, Altmann met with him in New York and urged him to remain in the United States.[67] Given Flohr's interest in modern German-Jewish thought, Altmann advised him to visit Taubes in Berlin. When they first met there in 1968, Taubes asked the young man, "What do you think of Sabbatai Zevi?" which Flohr later realized was no mere academic question for Taubes. Taubes hired Flohr to teach at the Seminar für Judaistik (as it was then called) in 1969–70. To satisfy student interests, he had Flohr teach a course on the history of Zionism. Flohr, who had some acquaintance with Lubavitch thought, taught a course, in Hebrew, on the *Tanya*.[68] He went on to teach modern Jewish thought at Hebrew University and at the Divinity School of the University of Chicago.

Taubes himself offered an impressive range of Judaica courses in the first years after his permanent move to the FU. There was a lecture course on Jewish historical consciousness since the exile from Spain.[69] It was remembered as spectacularly good by Ruth Geyer, a student from Israel, who would go on to teach Hebrew at the Institute. But he preferred to teach seminars focused on particular topics or texts: on the classic work of Jewish mysticism, the *Zohar*; the Hasidic text *Likutei MaHaran* of Nachman of Breslov, which he had explored with Joseph Weiss; and on Nachman Krochmal's *Guide to the Perplexed of Our Time*, which he had written about in Jerusalem and again while at Columbia. There were topical courses on his favorite subjects: Apocalyptics and Law: On the Eschatology of Early Judaism (1966), Apocalyptics and Politics: On the Sociology of Messianism (1967), and then in 1968 a lecture course, Paul as a Problem in the History of Religion, followed by a seminar, Rabbinic Sources of Basic Concepts of Paul, which required a reading knowledge of Hebrew.[70]

Despite the paucity of students with the linguistic and historical knowledge to participate in advanced courses, in these early years of the Institute it was possible for Taubes to hold advanced seminars, with participants such as Funkenstein, Greenberg, and Flohr. But in the years that followed, his interest in such matters waned. (Though those who passed by the Institute on Sunday might hear Jacob studying Talmud in a traditional sing-song.[71]) Marianne Awerbuch remonstrated with Taubes about the absence of his Judaica courses. In response, he decided to offer a course on Jewish mysticism. It commenced, promisingly enough, with an excellent introductory lecture. After that, the class consisted primarily of weekly student presentations on chapters of Scholem's *Major Trends in Jewish Mysticism*, which required little effort from Taubes himself.[72] By 1973, the only course he taught listed under the rubric of the Institut für Judaistik was History and Theory: Political Theology as Philosophy of History. On the Historical Theory of Carl Schmitt and Walter Benjamin—a daring juxtaposition to be sure, but one that counted as "Jewish," mainly in Taubes's mind.

Not long after Taubes assumed his chair of Judaica at the FU, two other such chairs were established in Germany, one at the University of Cologne, in 1966, and a second at the University of Frankfurt in 1970. The institute in Cologne was headed by Johann Maier. The chair in Frankfurt was occupied by Arnold Maria Goldberg, a convert from Judaism to Catholicism, who wrote primarily about the linguistics of rabbinic literature, and published almost exclusively in a series he himself edited.[73] Goldberg founded a scholarly association, the Verband der Judaisten in der Bundesrepublik Deutschland, devoted to the promotion of Judaic studies, and was cofounder of the European Association for Jewish Studies.[74] Taubes was uninterested in such organizational matters. Nor was he active in international organizations devoted to Jewish studies, in part out of a lack of interest, but also, perhaps, out of an awareness that he was persona non grata among the Jerusalem-centered scholars around Gershom Scholem who dominated the field.

Scholem Again

Marcel Marcus was a Jewish student who had grown up in Berlin, led a leftwing Zionist student group, and attended many of Taubes's classes from 1967 to 1972. Taubes attended his Passover seder. Marcus was keen on pursuing graduate studies in the United States and asked Taubes for a recommendation. "The best recommendation would be to say that you don't know me," Taubes responded.[75] There was more than a grain of truth to that. When Gershon Greenberg went to Jerusalem, he met Jacob Katz, a great historian of modern Jewry, who was part of Scholem's circle. When Greenberg informed Katz that he had studied with Taubes, Katz (an otherwise mild-tempered gentleman) responded, "Young man, to have studied with Jacob Taubes is nothing to be proud of!"[76]

Taubes continued to be haunted by his troubled relationship with Scholem, who, for his part, had not relented in his distaste for his former disciple. Their relationship was complicated by the fact that they had many friends and colleagues in common, including Adorno, Jean and Mayotte Bollack, the journalist George Lichtheim, and Peter Szondi. Whenever Taubes reached out, Scholem responded with disdain compounded by genuine fear. In 1968, Scholem was visiting with the Bollacks at their home in Paris. Taubes appeared unannounced at the door, having somehow divined that Scholem was present. Scholem promptly fled the room and locked himself in the bathroom, swearing he would not set eyes on Taubes again. Only when Taubes left the apartment did Scholem reemerge.[77]

In 1969, Scholem's former student Joseph Weiss committed suicide in London—while facing a photo of Scholem, whom he continued to revere as his master. Weiss's first wife, Miriam, had had an affair with Taubes during his years in Jerusalem. Erna, Weiss's second wife and widow, put Weiss's library of rare Judaica up for sale through Chimen Abramsky, a famed book collector. Taubes arranged for the Judaica Institute to purchase the collection for its library. But when the collection arrived in Berlin, Taubes was astonished to find that the most valuable pieces were missing. It turned out that Weiss had stated in his will that Scholem would have the right to choose a few titles for himself, but Scholem had taken the cream of the collection. Taubes decided to cancel the purchase and return the books to Abramsky in London.[78] He wrote to Mrs. Weiss of his disappointment at the turn of events. He told her he was shocked by the death of Joseph, adding, "Many years ago our ways parted but I continued to esteem him as a person where the erudition of the scholar, the interpretative power of the critic and the metaphysical concern of the theologian came together into a unique, even if uneasy balance." A copy of Taubes's letter reached Scholem, who scrawled in the margin that this characterization was "stolen word for word from the dedication of my book to Walter Benjamin!!!"[79]

Taubes corresponded regularly with George Lichtheim, then living in London, and a friend of both men. (While living in Jerusalem in the 1930s and '40s, Lichtheim had translated Scholem's *Major Trends in Jewish Mysticism* from German into English.) Scholem's latest lectures and essays were a frequent topic in their exchanges. Taubes continued to hear stories of Scholem's denunciations of him. Taubes was reputed to have become an official representative of El-Fatah, or to have converted to Christianity.[80]

Scholem continued to fulminate against Taubes to their mutual acquaintances—including Adorno and Norman Podhoretz—often in tones that his interlocutors found astonishing. In 1973, when Susan Sontag and her son, David Rieff, visited Israel to make a documentary, they had dinner with Scholem. When Sontag mentioned Jacob Taubes, Scholem paled and told them that it was through knowing Jacob Taubes that he had come to know the reality of moral evil in the world. He alluded to a female student whom Taubes had seduced and who then killed herself—probably a reference to Miriam Weiss.[81] Events in the half-decade that followed tended to reinforce Scholem's judgment.

Poetik und Hermeneutik

Jacob's intellectual life extended well beyond Berlin and the FU. He was an early member of Poetik und Hermeneutik (Poetics and Hermeneutics), a novel experiment in academic cooperation in which he participated for almost two decades.

At a time when most West German scholarship was conducted within academic disciplines, Poetik und Hermeneutik was a pioneering effort in interdisciplinary fructification. It brought together some twenty scholars of literature, philosophy, history, theology, and occasionally other academic disciplines as well.[82] They met roughly every two years to explore some topic, and to then publish a volume that would include both the initial contributions and the responses elicited by the discussion. The prestige of the participants, together with the novelty of the enterprise, created widespread interest among scholars in a variety of fields. For Jacob Taubes, it provided yet another important intellectual network.

The initial impetus came from a coterie of literary scholars at the University of Giessen who reached out to colleagues in philosophy with the proposal for a joint endeavor. The initiator and chief organizer was Hans Robert Jauss, a professor of Romance languages, assisted by his colleague in English literature, Wolfgang Iser. What began as a project focused on poetics (literary theory) increasingly morphed into one focused on hermeneutics (the interpretation of texts and works of art). Here Taubes played a role: indeed, the very name of the seminar, originally titled simply "Poetik" was changed at his suggestion to add "Hermeneutik."[83] Jauss was later to achieve international renown as the founder of "reception theory," which emphasized the changing historical contexts and assumptions that readers brought to a text; Iser would soon develop a related theory of reader response.

But it was the philosopher Hans Blumenberg who quickly emerged as the most powerful intellectual force within the group. His contribution to the first colloquium was the idea that "conceptions of reality" (*Wirklichkeitsbegriffe, Wirklichkeitsvorstellungen*) were themselves historical. The red thread that bound the work of the group thereafter was the changing ways in which meaning was constituted over time (*Sinnkonstitution*).[84]

After the first meeting in June 1963 (which focused on the rise of the novel and aesthetic theory in the eighteenth century), the topic of each successive gathering was decided by a core group of members who met on the evening following the final session. Subsequent topics included "the ugly," "the comic," "the nature of myth," and "terror and play." Papers on the topic were solicited from each member of the group, as well as from a few additional guests invited to participate. Over time, new members were co-opted. Rather than being read aloud, the papers were distributed in advance, so that the meeting could be devoted to an open discussion of the topic at hand. These oral interventions were taped, transcribed, and sent to each participant for editing. They were then edited again by two or three of the participants, who were designated as editors for the conference volume. Published by Fink Verlag in Munich, the resulting volumes were reviewed in the prestige press and studied by students, especially in literary studies, who wanted to be up on what was intellectually hot and purportedly exciting. The whole elaborate and expensive enterprise was funded by two leading foundations, Volkswagen and Werner Reimers. Some members oriented their university seminar classes to the forthcoming topic to help prepare themselves—a mark of how seriously they took the enterprise. Taubes did so as well.

Taubes found out about the new initiative through his Berlin colleague Dieter Henrich. Taubes met in Berlin with Jauss and Iser, making clear that he wanted to be invited. And he was. That was in part because Henrich and the others found his company intellectually animating.[85] Then there was the fact that he was a Jew, and one who had come to Germany from New York, a place of longing for German academics at the time.[86] After his participation in the first colloquium, the organizers were sufficiently impressed to make him an ongoing member of the group.[87]

In the decades that followed—an era when scholarship was increasingly being politicized—the seminar was distinguished by the fact that its tone was nonpolitical, though distinctly non-leftist. Taubes played a variety of roles, shifting as he thought the occasion demanded, presenting perspectives and raising questions that departed from any developing consensus.[88] At times he was a theologian, a philosopher of history, an advocate of the need to contextualize texts, and a Marxist. (At the gathering in 1970, at the height of his engagement with the New Left, Taubes said in passing, "I'm not actually a proper Marxist; I don't understand economics at all." To which another participant, Dimitrij Tschiževskij, a professor of Slavic literature, replied, "Mr. Taubes, you are indeed a Marxist"—the implication being that not understanding economics was intrinsic to being a Marxist.[89])

In the years that Taubes attended, most gatherings of Poetik und Hermeneutik were all-male affairs. There was a great display of erudition, as if learning were a peacock's tail, with each participant eager to demonstrate that his stock of knowledge was the largest and most colorful. It was an atmosphere in which Jacob was very much at home.

The seminar brought Taubes together with men of very different life histories.[90] Of the generation that were more or less his own age, most had been drafted as young men into the Wehrmacht, and had then spent months or years in prisoner of war camps (such as the historian Reinhart Koselleck or the philosopher Hermann Lübbe). Robert Jauss had volunteered for the Waffen-SS at the age of seventeen. He reached the rank of *Hauptsturmführer*, serving on the Eastern Front and in the indoctrination of French Waffen-SS volunteers, and after the war was briefly imprisoned by the British—a background unknown to most of his colleagues, which came to light only in the 1990s.[91] He became a left-liberal, identified with the Social Democrats.[92] Werner Krauss, by contrast, an expert on the French

Enlightenment, had been imprisoned by the National Socialist government in 1942 for his association with the Communist Rote Kapelle spy network. After the War, he moved to East Germany and was a member of the East German Akademie der Wissenschaften in East Berlin at the time of his participation in the seminar.[93] The younger members of the group, Dieter Henrich and Wolfgang Iser, had been high-school students during the War.

Hans Blumenberg's background was more complex. He was born into a Catholic family, but since his mother had converted from Judaism to marry his father, Hans was classified during the Third Reich as a "half-Jew" (*Halbjude*). Though a brilliant student at his classically oriented high school (*Gymnasium*) in Lübeck, he was forbidden from enrolling in a public German university, and studied instead at Catholic institutions of higher learning until he was forbidden to re-enroll because of his status as a *Mischling* (part-Jew). He went to work in a private firm in Lübeck that manufactured gas masks and other war materials.[94] When, in October 1944, the provincial government ordered the "de-Judaizing" (*Entjudung*) of all of Schleswig-Holstein, Blumenberg was sent to a labor camp. He escaped and hid with a family, whose daughter he subsequently married.[95]

Blumenberg was one of the scholars whom Taubes valued most highly. He convinced Suhrkamp to publish Blumenberg's magnum opus, *The Legitimacy of the Modern Age* (*Die Legitimität der Neuzeit*), and to bring Blumenberg onto the editorial team of Reihe Theorie. The two shared certain themes and concerns, including the relationship between modernity and secularization, and the relationship of modernity to Gnosticism—though they took different sides on each of these issues (a theme explored in chapter 15). By virtue of their Jewish background (a matter for Blumenberg not of education but of fate), they each regarded erstwhile radical conservative intellectuals like Heidegger, Schmitt, and Arnold Gehlen with a certain degree of suspicion and distance, but with a willingness to engage with their arguments.

Yet in character and inclinations, the two men were a study in contrasts. Blumenberg had the patience and fortitude to engage in meticulous reading of texts, while Taubes did not. From an early age, Blumenberg maintained an elaborate system of index cards to keep track of the gleanings of his reading. Taubes, when he found a scholarly article in a library that he wanted to remember, simply tore it out of the journal. Blumenberg crafted carefully constructed arguments with long chains of evidence, a procedure for which Taubes—who specialized in flashes of insight—had no taste or talent. Blumenberg craved solitude to study, read, and write, and increasingly withdrew from public forums. Taubes could not stand to be alone, and sought out company and attention. Blumenberg spoke and wrote in long, ornate sentences with many internal clauses and qualifications. Taubes was given to shorter, more declarative utterances. Blumenberg leaned toward graphomania: he couldn't stop writing. Taubes's writing was largely confined to his voluminous letters. Blumenberg had an orderly familial life. Taubes didn't. Taubes was inclined toward political radicalism. Blumenberg wasn't.

With his wide-ranging international and interdisciplinary contacts, Jacob played a key role in expanding the geographical horizons of Poetik und Hermeneutik. In 1965, he arranged for Siegfried Kracauer to speak at his Hermeneutic Colloquium at the FU and to participate in the meetings of Poetik und Hermeneutik. Kracauer had been a member of the Frankfurt School and in the 1920s had pioneered the study of popular culture.[96] At Taubes's suggestion, an invitation also went out to Pawel Beylin from Warsaw. Beylin, Taubes reported to Jauss, "is Professor for Aesthetics at the Music Academy and has finished a book on Kitsch that will appear in French next year. He is without a doubt among the smartest philosophical critics of our generation. Without a trace of dogmatic Marxism. On the contrary, he's rather too critical of it for my taste, but just right for yours."[97] Taubes also wanted to invite the poet Ingeborg Bachmann (with whom he had an intense affair), which would have added the first female presence to the colloquium. He also suggested inviting Meyer Schapiro, an art historian from Columbia University, who at the time was well known in the United States but not in Germany.[98] Taubes's seismographic sensitivity to up-and-coming intellectuals at home and abroad was astonishing to his German colleagues.[99]

Nowhere was this more in evidence than in a missive he sent to Hans Blumenberg in September 1966, as planning began for the next meeting of the colloquium, on the topic of religion, myth, and secularization. Taubes provided suggestions of possible participants from abroad, complete with a capsule summary of the background and significance of each scholar, his fluency in German, as well as facts about him that could only have come from personal acquaintance. Among those on his list were the dissident Marxist Leszek Kołakowski from Warsaw, and Taubes's friends Herbert Marcuse from America and Jean Bollack from Paris. Also recommended were three other academics from France: the philosopher Paul Ricouer, the sociologist Pierre Bourdieu, and the polymath Michel Foucault. At the time, these three figures were virtually unknown in Germany, but each would soon acquire an international reputation as a master thinker (*maître de pensée*) of the age.

An even more intriguing suggestion of a foreign participant was E. M. Cioran, part of a circle of intellectuals of Romanian origin whom Taubes had befriended in Paris.[100] An aphorist, essayist, and student of literature and philosophy, Cioran had begun his intellectual career in the 1930s as a sympathizer of the fascistic Iron Guard movement. After studying in Germany, he moved to Paris on the eve of the Second World War, where he remained. A critic not simply of utopianism, but of optimism and belief in progress, he was virtually unknown in Germany in 1966, though his *History of Decay* (*Lehre vom Zerfall*) had been published in German, in a translation by his friend, the poet Paul Celan. In recommending him to Blumenberg, Taubes noted that "Cioran belongs to that very rare species of right-wing intellectuals. . . . I search for right-wing intellectuals of distinction to find a true opponent with the aid of whom one can ascend intellectually. Left to themselves, leftists become vapid and superficial."[101] (Suhrkamp would later publish Cioran's collected works in German.[102])

Taubes was one of the few participants of the Poetik und Hermeneutik colloquia to sometimes attend without submitting a paper in advance—at first a source of frustration to some of the other members, and later a source of scorn. But over the years he did contribute three papers, which are among the handful of article-length publications of his decades at the Free University.

In 1964, for the second gathering of the group, which was devoted to aesthetics, Taubes sent a paper on the subject of surrealism: though in his typical fashion, he contributed only "notes on surrealism" rather than a coherent article. He brought the theme back to his own recurrent concerns, by suggesting that surrealism was a modern recurrence of the nihilistic alienation from the world that had characterized Gnosticism in the era of late antiquity. This allowed him to offer a brief précis of Hans Jonas's book on Gnosticism, a subject he already knew well. He argued that whereas the ancient Gnostics had been able to appeal to a divinity beyond the existing world, in the modern period the dominance of the scientific and materialist worldview made such a transcendent appeal impossible. Thus the surrealist poets of the 1920s could appeal only to poetry itself as a resource for protesting and transcending the determinism characteristic of the scientific worldview.[103] Both Gnosticism and surrealism, Taubes maintained, "freed up revolutionary energies" that pointed beyond the constricting structures of the Roman Empire in the case of Gnosticism and of modern bourgeois society in the case of surrealism by "opening up new forms of human experience."[104]

Discovering these sorts of parallels with past antinomian movements was part of Taubes's stock in trade. He specialized in insights—especially tracing overlooked similarities in different religious and historical contexts. Siegfried Kracauer offered an analysis of Taubes's method that managed to be both critical and complimentary. Taubes's structural comparisons, Kracauer averred, "are as misleading as they are revelatory. They are misleading because they are achieved at a great distance from the given material." Yet, "this same formidable distance from the material, which is responsible for the dubiousness of the structural comparisons . . . also plays a revelatory role. Taken from a great height, they remind one of aerial photographs; like these, they allow one to catch a glimpse of normally invisible configurations of the broader landscape they survey."[105] Blumenberg's response (submitted after the original colloquium but included in the published volume) was more unequivocally critical. He contended that the Gnostics had no tendency to active revolt, and that the attitude toward nature in surrealism was in fact affirmative and hence quite different from the way in which Taubes had portrayed it. In short, Taubes was wrong about the historical facts.[106] (Taubes returned to the topic of Gnosticism in his paper for the 1968 meeting, expanding on the theme of the relationship of Gnosticism to apocalypticism that he had explored in his doctoral dissertation.[107])

For the 1966 meeting of the group, Taubes presented a paper entitled "The Justification of the Ugly in the Early Christian Tradition."[108] Most of the paper had little to do with the announced theme, but rather was an analysis (based upon an obvious immersion in the scholarly literature) of what Nietzsche called the transvaluation of values in Paul's First Letter to the Corinthians, with its message that what the Greeks and Jews called wisdom was foolishness to those who believed in salvation through Christ's crucifixion. Taubes then turned to the theme of the physical ugliness or plainness of Jesus as a recurrent theme in the writings of the Church Fathers. Only at the end of his presentation did he explore how the Cross, once a symbol of the crucifixion and hence of earthly defeat, was transformed into a symbol of Christian triumph, beginning in the age of Constantine, as Christianity became the religion of the Empire. Thus, just as Paul reversed the pre-Christian valuation of wisdom and embraced what the Greeks and Jews thought of as foolishness, the later Church reversed the valuation of beauty, embracing the image of Jesus as physically ugly and the former symbol of ugly death—the cross.

The 1972 meeting had as its theme "Positions of Negativity." Taubes spoke on Heidegger's conception of "nothingness" and its relationship to mystical notions. Here Taubes returned to a subject he had explored before, in this case a paper he had written back in Jerusalem two decades earlier. And once again, after a good deal of to-ing and fro-ing, he concluded, "It remains to be ascertained how the most paradoxical formulations of the mystical insight into God are related to Heidegger's emphasis on the encounter with the Nothing."[109]

Seen in the context of Jacob's career, what is most striking about his prepared contributions to the seminars of Poetik und Hermeneutik is how few he produced and how unoriginal they were. The paucity of his contributions was noticed by the other participants, and none were more perturbed by it than Hans Blumenberg.

Taubes's psychiatric crisis meant that he failed to attend the 1974 or 1976 gatherings. He showed up again in May 1978, where he made some remarks on Paul and the philosophy of history.[110] As was so often the case, the imperative of contesting some reigning argument brought out the best in him. Thus, for example, in a session on theology and interpretation, he reminded Protestant theologians who claimed the historical-critical method of understanding the Bible for the Reformation, that that method had its origins not in the theology of the Reformation, but in Hobbes and Spinoza.[111] In an intervention to a colloquium on "Functions of the Fictive," held in 1979, Taubes offered another insight into the previously unseen connection between disparate phenomena. He noted almost in passing that in the twentieth century, two institutions that were in conflict with one another—the Catholic Church and Communism—had in common their belief in realism—the belief that reality could actually be grasped by the right concepts. They converged in their antipathy to the characteristically modern notion that the nature of the world depends in good part on our *perception* of it, on the changing and always partial categories of thought that we bring to it. Both Catholic Neo-Thomism and Communist dialectical materialism, by contrast, claimed to possess the categories for understanding the world as it really is.[112] That was the last gathering he attended.

Taubes stood out from most members of the seminar by his personality and the nature of his intellectuality. "He was charming and interesting, and always good for a surprise," remembered one member, Harald Weinrich. "One could never anticipate beforehand what he would say, and that remained the case from year to year. He provided spice."[113] He would enliven the atmosphere with his "wonderful, unconventional formulations," remembered another, Renate Lachmann. "He spoke differently from the others, not with long sentences that circled back on themselves, but rather with an informality of expression that led to a general easing of the atmosphere."[114] Hermann Lübbe's description of Taubes's personality and his role in the Poetik und Hermeneutik discussions is echoed by many others who knew Taubes in a variety of contexts in Germany: Taubes possessed a particular genius (*Genie*) for acting as a productive intellectual stimulus to the work of others. He asked hard questions and pointed to lines of inquiry from fields that had not occurred to his interlocutors. What he lacked was the analytic ability to define terms and problems clearly, which was becoming de rigueur in philosophy. Nor could he compete with the wealth of factual and historical knowledge of a Blumenberg (but few could). He was, in short, "a master of insinuating significance," a font of ideas that were suggestive without being fully worked out.[115]

Also quite unique was the way in which Taubes wore his Jewish identity in this circle, in which references to the experience of the Third Reich were carefully avoided.[116] Most of his scholarly colleagues in postwar Germany had little contact with Jews. If they did, it was likely to be with those of Jewish origin who were known to be Jewish but were neither Jewishly knowledgeable nor eager to draw attention to the fact. For all of these reasons, their non-Jewish colleagues (many of whom, one recalls, had belonged to the Hitler Youth or served in the German army during the war) were careful in conversations with Jewish interlocutors not to touch upon the topics of Jews or the experience of the Third Reich with them. Taubes was different. He was a blatant Jew rather than a latent Jew. He made Jewish jokes, and was ironical about his own Jewish identity (where irony expressed a fundamental acceptance of the identity in question). As a result, he created a rare space around him in which his non-Jewish, German counterparts could at least broach subjects that they perceived as otherwise undiscussable with the few Jews with whom they were likely to come into contact. He had, as Hermann Lübbe put it, "the talent of making self-conscious Germans unselfconscious."[117]

Taubes was also unique in a very different sense. He was the only one who brought his girlfriends to the gatherings of Poetik und Hermeneutik.[118]

For some of the members of Poetik und Hermeneutik, such as the distinguished historian of the classical world Christian Meier, Taubes was important in another way as well: as a connecting node between diverse cultural circles. Through his contacts with Siegfried Unseld, Taubes brought Meier to Suhrkamp Verlag.[119] He arranged for Meier to give a lecture on Aeschylus at his Hermeneutic Colloquium in Berlin, which brought Meier to the attention of Dieter Sturm, the dramaturge of the

Schaubühne, a prominent Berlin theater, who was then staging the *Oresteia*. Taubes, that is to say, was not only a merchant of ideas, he was a matchmaker for the talented: a role he could play because of his acknowledged feel for scholarly quality.[120]

Yet by the time of his death, many of Taubes's colleagues in Poetik und Hermeneutik had become disillusioned with him. Asked by Jauss to compose an obituary for the next Poetik und Hermeneutik volume, Hans Blumenberg penned a characterization judged to be too scathing to publish. Instead, Dieter Henrich wrote a brief if ambivalent appreciation. Both noted the gap between Taubes's intellectual pretentions and his actual achievements. But even Blumenberg acknowledged that many members profited from the range of Taubes's contacts in the world of publishing and in international intellectual life.[121]

Building the Faculty

The FU was still a relatively new institution when Jacob assumed his position there, and he was committed to building up the quality of the faculty in the humanities and social sciences. Ever on the lookout for talent, he approached scholars at other institutions whose work he thought impressive (or whom he knew by reputation) and encouraged them to come to the FU. He also campaigned on their behalf, reaching out to respected international intellectuals to vouch for them. Some of those he approached shared his ideological affinities, but that was by no means his major criterion. Breadth of vision or expertise in a field he thought important drew his attention.

One potential appointee whose politics were in keeping with Jacob's own was his friend Herbert Marcuse. In 1965, he began a campaign to bring Marcuse to the FU as an Honorarprofessor—a position outside the regular faculty structure that allowed distinguished visitors to participate in the life of the university by offering lectures and seminars. Taubes's colleague in political science, the committed Social Democrat Richard Löwenthal, objected at first, but then relented. The appointment required three letters of recommendation from foreign scholars. Taubes solicited one from the French philosopher Paul Ricoeur, and another from Lucien Goldmann. The third he requested from his friend Norman Birnbaum, an American sociologist then teaching at Oxford. Though Birnbaum was in fact a very junior academic, himself in search of a permanent post, Taubes gave him explicit instructions to send his letter on paper with a Nuffield College letterhead, and to attest that

Marcuse was among the most important contemporary sociologists.[122] Taubes's campaign was successful, and Marcuse would play a prominent role in the years ahead.

At the same time, Taubes reached out to the historian Ernst Nolte, whose book *Der Faschismus in seiner Epoche* had recently been published to great acclaim (it was translated into English as *Three Faces of Fascism*). Nolte had studied philosophy with Martin Heidegger before turning to history, and his book used a novel phenomenological approach to portray and compare the proto-fascist French Action Française, Italian Fascism, and National Socialism. Nolte characterized their fundamental features as resisting the broad processes of modernity—liberalism, capitalism, communism—that led to the dissolution of a sense of historical particularity. Nolte's book did a great deal to advance the concept of "fascism" as a useful category of historical analysis, even while he insisted that fascism was the product of a particular era and not, for example, an ongoing strategy of bourgeois defense, as Marxists had once argued—and would soon again. When, in 1965, Taubes learned that Nolte had accepted a chair in history at Marburg, he wrote to Nolte that he would gladly have had him as a colleague at the FU.[123] In 1973, after clashes with the radical left at Marburg, Nolte did indeed move to the FU, where he and Taubes were on friendly terms. As we will see, Taubes's championing of Nolte would later lead to a crisis in his relationship with Jürgen Habermas and with Suhrkamp Verlag.

Another historian whom Taubes campaigned to bring to the FU was Thomas Nipperdey, a young scholar (born in 1927) who by the mid-1960s was beginning to display the remarkable range of interests—combining political, intellectual, social, and economic history—that would make him perhaps the greatest historian of Germany of his generation. Nipperdey was teaching at the Technische Hochschule in Karlsruhe, when Taubes learned that he had been offered but had not yet accepted a chair at the new University of Bochum. Taubes urged his colleagues in history to try to appoint Nipperdey, and campaigned successfully on behalf of the appointment. Nipperdey thanked Taubes for his role, and noted that he was disposed to come to the FU to work with philosophers and sociologists, given the interdisciplinary orientation of his work.[124]

Another young scholar, closer to his own fields of interest, whom Taubes brought to the FU was Carsten Colpe.[125] Colpe came to the university in 1969 as a professor of Iranian studies. But his expertise included the history of Gnosticism, New Testament studies, and the history of religion. He would teach seminars on those topics with Taubes in the years ahead.

Taubes invested the most time and energy to bringing the philosopher of science Paul Feyerabend to the FU. By the fall of 1966, Taubes was in a position of unusual authority in the philosophy program. One of the senior philosophers, Hans-Joachim Lieber, had become rector of the university and was thus not actively involved with the department. Then another senior colleague, Dieter Henrich, departed for a position in Heidelberg, leaving an open chair, and Taubes one of the three remaining senior professors charged with finding a replacement.

Taubes was convinced that the philosophy of science was an academically hot field that should be represented in Berlin.[126] He looked around for advice on whom to hire, and Hermann Lübbe suggested the name of Paul Feyerabend, an Austrian-born philosopher of science then teaching at the University of California at Berkeley.[127] Feyerabend had studied with Karl Popper in London, but his work was increasingly critical of Popper's notion that legitimate scientific theories were characterized by falsifiability. In 1970, Feyerabend would publish an essay, "Against Method: Outlines of an Anarchist Theory of Knowledge"—subsequently incorporated into a book of that title—in which he presented his radical critique of the notion of "the scientific method." There *was* no such method, he argued, and far from being grounded in empirical evidence, the history of science showed that the acceptance of scientific theories was influenced by aesthetic criteria, personal preferences, and social factors.[128] Taubes pulled out all the stops of his international connections to convince his colleagues to offer a position to Feyerabend and to make the offer attractive. For letters of evaluation (*Gutachten*), he wrote to Karl Popper, to Rudolf Carnap at UCLA, and to Friedrich Hayek—reminding each that he had visited them in the past.[129] All three were fulsome in their praise. Hayek, then teaching at Freiburg, was himself a critic of "scientism," by which he meant the application of methods and models of the natural sciences to the realm of human behavior. Taubes had met him in Chicago years earlier and somehow knew that he would be a relevant evaluator. Hayek pronounced Feyerabend "the most talented, rich in ideas, and multi-faceted among the younger German-speaking theoreticians of science," and sent Taubes a collection of Feyerabend's articles, which Taubes used to prepare his own memorandum in favor of the hire.[130] To entice Feyerabend to the FU, Taubes secured funds to create a library on the theory of science, and to hire a small army of assistants for the purpose.[131] Feyerabend accepted, on the condition that he also maintain his position at Berkeley. He arrived in Berlin for the summer semester of 1968. Taubes attended all of Feyerabend's lectures, in which he presented some of the ideas that he would later publish in *Against Method* (1975). The lectures were striking for his conception of science as *Spass* (fun), and for his ability to play with texts and ideas.[132]

But what had seemed like such a promising appointment turned out to be a disaster. Feyerabend's behavior at Berkeley had been anarchic: he cancelled many lectures, failed to prepare for others, and insisted on giving all his students A's. Then, after accepting the offer from the FU, he also accepted posts in London and at Yale—while maintaining his position at Berkeley. During his first semester at the FU, he barely showed up for lectures, and during his second semester, he appeared even less.[133] The arrangement quickly came to an end, much to Taubes's chagrin.

Taubes then tried to lure Noam Chomsky, his acquaintance from his years at Harvard, to take up a position as guest professor during the summer of 1969. Chomsky declined, on the grounds that he had no time to do so, given his professional and political activity. The appointment was intended to be as much political as academic.[134] For by then Taubes was riding the radical wave that was sweeping universities in the United States as well as in Germany.

CHAPTER ELEVEN

The Apocalyptic Moment

WITH THE RISE OF THE STUDENT New Left, Taubes and Brentano became the most prominent faculty members to support the movement's attempt to transform their university. The sort of apocalyptic moment that Taubes had written and taught about now seemed at hand.

Taubes and the Radicalization of the FU

A tsunami of protest swept over the universities of the Western world in the 1960s. Nowhere, perhaps, was that radicalization more quickly institutionalized than at the Free University of Berlin. The reasons for that were multiple.

There was a student body, which after the erection of the Berlin Wall was increasingly drawn from West Germany. Since for young men moving to West Berlin (which was legally distinct from West Germany) was a way of avoiding military service, self-selection led to a student body inclined to the radical left. The municipal government of West Berlin had many of the powers of a state (*Land*) government, and was controlled by the Social Democrats, who were eager for the support of young, leftist voters, and more willing to accede to their supposed preferences. That led, after 1969, to a structure of self-governance at the FU that shifted power away from the full professors (*Ordinarien*) and gave unprecedented influence to faculty below the level of full professor (the so-called *Mittelbau*), to students, and even to nonacademic staff. The quest for the "democratization" of the German universities would lead to a transformation of the FU in the years that followed.

In the early 1960s, the professors and students of the philosophical faculty and of the social sciences tended toward the political left, while those in the other faculties were more conservative. In the mid-1960s, enrollments in the faculties of philosophy and in the social sciences were growing. That set the stage for the tensions that followed, which centered at first on three issues: freedom of political speech, opposition to the American role in Vietnam, and the "state of emergency law" (*Notstandsgesetz*) proposed in 1967 by West Germany's governing Christian Democratic-Social Democratic coalition government. A catalyst and complicating factor was the role of the Situationists, that artistic/political movement notable for its use of unorthodox rhetoric and tactics to try to seize public attention. The protests against the American war in Vietnam, which soon developed into antipathy to the American military presence abroad, were particularly explosive in West Berlin. For the city owed its democracy to the American airlift of 1948, was the site of numerous American military installations, and had a voting public that was pro-American and vehemently anti-Communist.

Of the two hundred or so *Ordinarien* at the FU, there were a handful who were highly sympathetic to the rising student left, including Helmut Gollwitzer, Peter Szondi, and (with greater circumspection) Richard Löwenthal.[1] But none were as conspicuous in their support of the student radicals as Jacob Taubes. For a while, Taubes appeared as the *spiritus rector* of the New Left at the FU. He had chiliastic hopes, which he would maintain long after most other professors had given up on them.[2]

Following the example of the Free Speech Movement at the University of California at Berkeley, the Students Council (AStA), under the leadership of Wolfgang Lefèvre, proclaimed the right of students "to hear any person speak in any open area on campus at any time on any subject." They invited the left-wing journalist Erich Kuby to lecture on campus, knowing that Kuby had previously been banned from doing so for what the university administration regarded as his defamation of the FU. The rector refused to allow Kuby to appear, and that led to organized student demonstrations in protest. Shortly thereafter, another *cause célèbre* riled the campus. This time the issue was the rector's treatment of a young political scientist, Ekkehart Krippendorff, who had accused the rector of blocking a campus appearance by the philosopher Karl Jaspers. When Krippendorff discovered that the charge was untrue, he withdrew his accusation, but incurred the rector's wrath. At each stage, the student left distributed leaflets, put up wall placards, and called for demonstrations, involving more and more students in the protests. Together with Gollwitzer, Szondi, and a few other faculty members, Taubes signed a public letter supporting the student protesters.[3]

The first "sit-in" at a German university occurred at the FU on June 22, 1966, when some three thousand students besieged a meeting of the academic senate. The senate was considering a measure to set a limit on the number of years that students could study at state expense (*Studienzeitbegrenzung*).[4] The resolution opposing the measure was drafted by three leading members of the SDS, all of whom were close to Taubes: Rudi Dutschke, Wolfgang Lefèvre, and Johannes Agnoli. For the SDS, the demand for greater student participation in university governance was a prelude to "the abolition of oligarchic domination and the realization of democratic freedom in all realms of social life."[5] In the years that followed, the leadership of the SDS would become ever more insistent that the purpose of its university policy was to use the academy to carry out a struggle for fundamental social transformation.[6]

As the protests continued, a group of radicals influenced by the Situationists who called themselves "Kommune 1" (Commune 1) developed unorthodox strategies to attract public attention. The members of Kommune 1 made a concerted effort to turn the SDS toward tactics based on deliberate provocation, mixed with a touch of humor, in an attempt to demonstrate the irrationality of the existing political and social order. They decided on a "Strolling Protest" (*Spaziergangs-Protest*): on December 17, 1966, the Saturday before Christmas, when stores were open before the holiday, they planned to gather on the main shopping street, the Kurfürstendamm. In order to make their protest difficult for the police to interdict, they would swarm in one location, then dissolve and swarm in another. In the end, the police responded violently, and arrested eighty-six of the protestors, including Jacob Taubes, whose name was prominent in the press coverage of the event.[7] A policeman grabbed him harshly, leaving a mark that Taubes displayed to his colleagues as if it were the stigmata.[8] Taubes published an open letter to the mayor of Berlin, characterizing the actions of the police as brutality against "unprovoking and civil student discussion groups."[9]

The pace of demonstrations at the FU picked up in the spring of 1967. There were more sit-ins, in which students occupied classes and buildings, and "teach-ins," a practice copied from the American student movement, in which speakers would "teach" about the evils of the American war in Vietnam. Many of these took place under the auspices of the AStA, the student council, which was increasingly dominated by activists from the SDS, some of whom had been Taubes's students. In early May, the rector of the university tried to prohibit sit-ins. That led to an assembly on May 6, in which some 1,500 students gathered in the largest auditorium of the

FU, the AudiMax, to protest the rector's decree. Prominent among the speakers defending the students that day were Reverend Gollwitzer and Jacob Taubes, who, to thunderous applause, declared that "a responsible university requires responsible students" (*Das Ziel heißt: der mündige Student in einer mündigen Universität*). The problem, he declared, was broader than the university, for a responsible university was only possible in a responsible society, and today a process of *Entmündigung* (robbing the individual of self-determination as a mature human being) was taking place, to which the proper response was protest and revolt. He defended the sit-ins and teach-ins as a great contribution of American students to this process of becoming responsible.[10]

Later that month, a fire raced through a department store in Brussels, taking the lives of more than three hundred people. Two days later, at the entrance to the FU, the radicals around Kommune 1 distributed a series of pamphlets (*Flugblättern*), headlined "Burn, department store, burn!" advocating the burning down of Berlin department stores as a protest against consumer capitalism and the war in Vietnam.[11] Some claimed the pamphlet was satirical in intent. But the police responded by charging two of the leaders of Kommune 1, Fritz Teufel and Rainer Langhans, with incitement. Both were students at the FU.

In the trial that followed, the accused were defended by Horst Mahler, a radical lawyer who reached out to Taubes to provide a defense of the communards. Taubes complied (as did Szondi), with a learned defense, delivered orally in court and then published in the magazine *Merkur*. It situated the pamphlet's authors in the history of surrealism and of religious sects. "Kommune I is an object for the history of religion and literary scholarship, but not for the public prosecutor and the court," Taubes concluded.[12] The case against the communards was dismissed by the court, not least, Mahler assured Taubes, because of his contribution. "One could see from the faces of the judge and the prosecutor that they had never before heard of the literary movements that you cited. The fact that you managed in your testimony to situate the freely chosen lifestyle of the *Kommune* in the history of the church, led, I believe, to the court's total helplessness."[13]

Taubes, like Mahler, was a member of the Republikaner Club, an association founded in January 1967 which brought together intellectuals from the SPD leftward to debate and socialize. Among its founders were Mahler and another radical lawyer, Otto Schily. Its habitués included intellectuals associated with the New Left, as well as guests from East Berlin. (It was largely funded by the East German secret service, though that was hardly public knowledge at the time.[14]) Marcuse visited whenever he came to Berlin.

Yet while in court Taubes defended their legal innocence, in private he was more skeptical of the Communards' cause. He responded to Mahler that he did not know the members of the Commune personally, nor was he particularly sympathetic to them. In fact, he thought the SDS should distance itself from this minority, who he thought harmed the reputation of all who strove for social change. He also had told the leaders of the AStA that "at the current moment, engagement against the American conduct of the war in Vietnam is implausible as long as it is not coupled with engagement against Nasser and his pseudo-socialistic fascism," and that "those who at that moment look only at Vietnam, while ignoring the more egregious fact that Israel is threatened by the policy of the Arabs, discredit themselves through their inconsistency."[15]

For Taubes, the fate of the state of Israel was a source of anxiety and concern. "For the last ten days my heart has been in Tel-Aviv and Jerusalem," Taubes wrote to Edith Wyschogrod on May 31.[16]

On June 2, the tension in West Berlin escalated. During a mass leftist demonstration against a visit by the Shah of Iran, a demonstrator, Benno Ohnesorg, was shot and killed by a policeman.[17] Among the leaders of the student left, this was interpreted as a sign of the state's willingness to resort to ever-greater levels of violence against their cause. The days that followed were filled with an unprecedented level of political activity. On June 3, four thousand students gathered to protest the police shooting. Gollwitzer, Taubes, and a handful of other faculty members were present as well. The crowd resolved to demand the resignation of the mayor and the chief of police.[18] On June 7, there was an even larger gathering of all students (*Vollversammlung*) in the AudiMax. They protested the decision of the Berlin senate to temporarily forbid demonstrations, and resolved to suspend classes for a week in order to conduct ongoing political discussions. This time, there were two faculty members present and supportive of the decision: Jacob Taubes and Margherita von Brentano. They spoke on "Scholarship and Fascism—The Psychological Preconditions of Fascism." The task at hand, Brentano said, was to begin a discussion of fascism throughout the university, and in the meantime to protest against the police terror and the policies of the Berlin administration.[19]

From Kojève to Marcuse

Amidst the growing turmoil came a visit on June 26 from Alexandre Kojève, who arrived at the FU at Taubes's invitation, en route home to Paris from a visit to Beijing. In the years since publishing his influential interpretation of Hegel and a book-length debate with Leo Strauss, Kojève had become one of the most prominent civil servants in France, his adopted home, working at the Ministry of Finance. On his own time, he wrote a multivolume work on Greek ethics, which Taubes read in manuscript, with enthusiasm.[20] Having concluded that the institutions of modern society were, in their lineaments at least, fated to advance toward a universal state that would guarantee universal human recognition, Kojève devoted himself to the development of its legal institutions and international treaties, which was why he had just come from negotiating with Mao on behalf of the French government. That was the topic of his colloquium at the FU on "The End of History."[21] Taubes had written to him, suggesting that "the students deserve to have you back them up."[22] But when this master thinker appeared and was asked by the students what they ought to do, he advised them, to their astonishment, to study Greek. The implication was that the time for radical action had passed: one might as well understand the process by which history was reaching its fulfillment. Then, he told Taubes, he was off to converse with Carl Schmitt in Schmitt's hometown of Plettenberg.[23]

A few weeks thereafter, Herbert Marcuse came back to Berlin, invited by the SDS. For four days, from July 10 to 13, he lectured to overflowing crowds in the AudiMax, on "The End of Utopia"—intended as a riposte to Kojève's recent talk[24]—and on the problem of the use of violence in opposition. He also participated in a panel on "Morality and Politics in a Society of Superfluity."[25]

In these lectures, Marcuse laid out some of the key theses of his recent book, *One-Dimensional Man*: that modern technology had already developed the means and the knowledge not only to abolish poverty and misery, but through automation, to minimize socially necessary labor and to create a free society with much less of what he called "surplus repression." The imminent possibility of such a society was therefore not "utopian," but realistic. But existing political, economic, and cultural forces were arrayed to prevent this possibility. It remained unclear exactly which forces in Western societies (the "metropole") and the Third World would bring about revolutionary transformation. But, he added, only by attempting a radical transformation could one tell. "It may very well be the case that the realization of a revolutionary project is hindered by counterforces and countertendencies that can be and are overcome precisely in the process of revolution. . . . The social agents of revolution . . . are formed only in the process of the transformation itself, and one cannot count on a situation in which the revolutionary forces are there ready-made, so to speak, when

FIGURE 11.1. At the AudiMax of the Free University, July 1967. L to R, Richard Löwenthal, Jacob Taubes, Herbert Marcuse, Alexander Schwan (Political Science), Dieter Claessens (Sociology). (Granger Historical Picture Archive.)

the revolutionary movement begins."[26] For Marcuse, university students were one such potential oppositional group, and the present task was to foster the consciousness of such radical possibilities.[27]

On the third day, Marcuse was at the center of a public discussion, chaired by Jacob Taubes, and including Richard Löwenthal (the veteran Social Democrat who had been dubious about bringing Marcuse to the FU), Peter Furth (an editor of *Das Argument*), Margherita von Brentano, Wolfgang Lefèvre, and Rudi Dutschke. Taubes set the stage by offering a brief but accurate sketch of the ideas that Marcuse had presented on the previous days—ideas with which Taubes was long acquainted through his friendship with Marcuse. In the discussion that followed, Löwenthal emerged as Marcuse's most powerful and cogent critic. Marcuse's notion of a society free of domination (*Herrschaftslosigkeit*) was at odds with the reality of the need for authority in a modern technological society, Löwenthal declared—a society, he noted, that had brought about a historically unprecedented reduction of poverty. The working class was integrated into that society and hence no longer revolutionary—not, as Marcuse suggested, because it was manipulated into false consciousness, but because it was actually much better off. Marcuse's assertion that Western capitalist societies needed war in order to survive—his explanation for the war in Vietnam—was nonsense. Marcuse advocated tearing down existing institutions with no tangible idea of what to substitute in their place, and Löwenthal warned that "an appeal to the total destruction of existing institutions without a realizable goal of what to replace them with must lead to something that has less to do with Marx than with Bakunin, who characterized the lust for destruction as a creative force." Feeding that destructive urge was not Marcuse's intention, Löwenthal quickly added, but that might indeed be the consequence, as events were already showing.[28] (In the years that followed, Löwenthal sharpened his critique in a series of essays and in a book, *The Romantic Regression*, asserting that beneath the slogans of enlightened, rational critique, the German New Left actually succumbed to a romantic regression, embracing violence in the name of utopia.[29])

The final session devoted to "Vietnam: The Third World and the Opposition in the Metropoles" included Dutschke once again. He invoked Che Guevara and expostulated on the need to overcome the division between the Soviet bloc on the one hand and Communist China and the Third World on the other, in order to combat (American) imperialism. His focus was on Vietnam. Marcuse in turn endorsed collecting funds to provide both medicine and arms to the North Vietnamese and Vietcong.[30]

Marcuse's appearances at the FU were media events. Several were broadcast live on the radio, and a TV crew was onsite, filming material for a documentary. *Der Spiegel*, *Die Zeit*, and other outlets of the prestige press covered the lectures and discussions in detail.[31] *Der Spiegel* quoted Taubes as saying that Marcuse's text "informs the discussion among the students and gives it an intensity that recalls the earnestness with which devotees of the Talmud used to interpret the text of the Torah."[32]

Taubes accompanied Marcuse on a visit to Zurich, where they met with a group of leftist students at the Bel Étage restaurant—Marcuse being a great practitioner of the hedonistic virtues, which he hoped all would eventually be able to enjoy. There, too, they discussed their contention that given the unrevolutionary nature of the working class, radical change depended on changing the consciousness (*Bewusstseinslage*) of the stratum of intellectuals, beginning with students in the universities.[33]

In the months that followed, Taubes sought to influence the student left toward what he believed to be its rational, as opposed to irrational manifestations. "I think that among the students in Berlin a process of differentiation has set in," he wrote to Hans Robert Jauss of the Poetik und Hermeneutik circle.

> The greater portion of the leftist students are committed to a rational line: rational argument and protest with rational goals. To be sure, the SDS is in crisis, having been infiltrated in recent months by Hippie people [the Situationists] who long for romantic, putschist action. While my colleagues are unwilling to dirty their fingers by contact with the SDS, I've taken upon myself the thankless task of purifying the rational elements from relics of romanticism in this circle. I do so without great hope of success. But no stone should be left unturned to save the SDS from the precipitous path of left-wing fascism. . . .
>
> In such actions, one maneuvers along a very narrow ridge. Most of the faculty regards one as a dangerous revolutionary, most of the SDS regards one as a liberal idiot. Every false step threatens to cost me the remainder of my authority, both with the faculty and the leftist students.[34]

In February 1968, Taubes joined Gollwitzer and some other intellectuals in a public declaration of support for a student conference on Vietnam in which Dutschke again figured prominently. In a letter to the Berlin *Morgenpost*, they warned the students against engaging in violence or breaking the law, while calling on the government, the police, and the press not to confuse student actions that degenerated into violence with Nazi terror.[35] The conference, with its anti-American message, appalled the West Berlin senate. It sponsored a huge demonstration of its own on February 21, in which tens of thousands marched under the slogan "Berlin must not become Saigon!" Dutschke was denounced, and some of the marchers attacked young people whom they took to be affiliated with the student left. On March 8, a group of prominent writers and academics published an article in *Die Zeit* in which they denounced the violence of the Berlin police, warned of a threat to free expression in Berlin, and called on the city council to attend to the sources of student unrest. Among the signatories, along with Adorno and Habermas, was Jacob Taubes.[36]

Two months later, on April 11, 1968, Dutschke was the victim of an assassination attempt by a mentally disturbed young man. The attempt failed, but a bullet penetrated Dutschke's brain, leaving him critically wounded and partially disabled. Marcuse flew from Paris to Berlin to lecture again at the FU on May 13, and first visited Dutschke in his hospital room. When Marcuse reported to the student audience that Dutschke was "almost his old self," the students erupted in sustained applause. Marcuse discussed plans for Dutschke to come and study with him at the University of California at San Diego, and Taubes (described by *Der Spiegel* as "Professor Jacob Taubes, the friend of both Marcuse and Dutschke") wrote to the German Academic Exchange Service (Deutsche Akademische Austauschdienst) supporting Dutschke's application for a scholarship to do so.[37] In the end, Dutschke's application for an American visa was turned down, and with his wife and young son, Hosea-Che, he moved to England, and then Denmark before returning to Germany, dying in 1979 from the aftereffects of the assassination attempt.

Marcuse returned to Berlin yet again in May 1968, where he spoke about "History, Transcendence, and Social Change"—a lecture that the increasingly radical students of the SDS found too abstract and removed from concrete action. *Der Spiegel* reported on a small gathering that Marcuse held with Habermas, Taubes, and two others, in which they discussed "the infantile disorders of left radicalism." Marcuse and the radicals of the Berlin SDS were becoming alienated from one another.[38]

Student radical action and violence was on the upswing. At the FU, one seminar after another was disrupted or occupied by students. Professors in the Germanic Seminar had their classes disrupted by students who set off stink-bombs, and the Seminar was taken over and renamed the "Rosa-Luxemburg-Institut," after the German Communist ideologist murdered during the failed revolution of 1918–19.[39] The Philosophy Seminar was occupied by students who demanded a new, more radical structure of governance for the seminar—and locked out scholars who refused their demands. The philosophers Michael Landmann and Wilhelm Weischedel, who had initially been sympathetic to the student left, were increasingly alarmed by such actions. Professors took to moving their precious books out of university offices and into their homes, fearing that the books would be stolen or defaced.[40] When Edith Wyschogrod visited Taubes that year, she found that the seminar room at the FU in which they conversed contained a plaster bust of Kant that had been blackened and inscribed with the legend, "Mao has answered all the questions that I have left open."[41]

Taubes was ignited by this turn of events. Having long written and taught about apocalyptic movements, he was finally experiencing one. "We're now learning at first hand what we had previously only read about: the abdication of the old authorities, their self-surrender and the rise of a new consciousness," he wrote to a colleague.[42] At the same time, his study of apocalyptic movements made him aware that they were fraught with hazards and that they rarely accomplished just what they set out to achieve. Nevertheless, in meetings of the faculty, Taubes defended the student radicals as they began to occupy buildings and interfere with normal instruction, in fiery speeches that combined rhetoric with principled discussions of the issues at hand.[43] He startled friends and liberal colleagues—deliberately, no doubt—by telling them that he regarded himself as a Maoist, that the individualism of the West was a dead end, and that Maoism might present a collectivist alternative, relevant for Western societies.[44] When Peter Schäfer, an aspiring young German scholar of Judaica, met Taubes in 1968, Taubes told Schäfer that his consciousness had been transformed by Marxism and that he no longer did that pedestrian sort of scholarship.[45]

In 1967, Taubes had been invited by Adorno to give a talk on "Culture and Ideology" at the annual conference of German sociologists (*Soziologentag*) to take place the following April in Frankfurt. Typically, by March 13, Taubes had sketched out some ideas for the paper, but not written it.[46] The final paper was a meandering mélange of observations on Marx, on Benjamin's use of Marx, on Adorno's advice to Benjamin in the 1930s, Weber's reflections on modern capitalist institutions as inexorable "fate," and Gehlen's theory of the human need for institutions. But the real thrust of the paper was drawn primarily from Marcuse and to a lesser degree from Foucault, though neither was cited by name. From Marcuse, Taubes took the notion that the development of technology had vanquished the traditional economic problem of scarcity and had diminished class antagonisms. Contemporary political and economic institutions, with their inherent domination (*Herrschaft*), were therefore superfluous, but maintained their hold through regressive ideological appeals. From Foucault, Taubes took the notion that power (Taubes used the term *Gewalt*, which suggested violence as well as power) was now exercised through institutional and bureaucratic structures that disguised domination and led those subjected to it to internalize the institutions' claims to legitimacy.[47] The paper was a standard exercise in the Marxist critique of ideology—according to which non-Marxist thought was a covert defense of the status quo—combined with the Marcusean insinuation that an ill-defined human emancipation might be just around the corner. (Too caught up in contemporary events at the FU to write something new, Taubes repurposed the paper on two later occasions.[48])

During the evening after his talk at the *Soziologentag*, Taubes spent long hours discussing ideas with radical student intellectuals from Frankfurt, including Hans-Jürgen Krahl, a leading figure in the local SDS. Also present was Richard Faber, an activist with the Catholic left. Attracted by what Taubes had to say, Faber came to the FU to pursue his doctoral studies. He stayed until 1973, then returned in 1979 to serve as Taubes's *Assistent*.[49] Faber became a disciple, pursuing research themes suggested by Taubes's own interests.

For Taubes, intellectual and political interests were intertwined. In May 1968, for example, he wrote a long memorandum to Siegfried Unseld and Jürgen Habermas about what he saw as the proper role of Suhrkamp Verlag in channeling the energies of the student generation away from sectarianism and into broader horizons:

> The literary potential of the best of our students (who are actually no longer students in the conventional sense, but rather the younger portion of a free-floating intelligentsia that hangs on to the petticoats of the university out of anxiety about being confronted by reality) is being guided into sectarian channels, and exhausted in word games in the "student journals." I ask myself whether this might present a pedagogic but also political task: to take the best of them and to rescue them from the certainties of their sectarian corner by bringing them into the broader public sphere. I'm aware that there's a risk in that, and I speak from experience. . . . But this is a risk that those of us in publishing and in the university have to assume. Otherwise, we may as well close up shop.[50]

Testimony to Taubes's prominence in the eyes of the student left was a pamphlet distributed at the national conference of the SDS in Hanover in November 1968. A dissident group of female members from Frankfurt, dissatisfied with the organization's failure to address feminist concerns, formed a "women's council." At the Hanover gathering, they distributed a pamphlet entitled "Accountability Report," which included a drawing of a woman with an axe in her hand, and above on the wall, mounted as trophies, the chopped-off penises of six male leaders of the SDS. The pamphlet concluded with a call to "Liberate the Socialist Eminences from Their Bourgeois Dongs!" There followed a long list of these "eminences." And there on the list, a few places below Mao and just above Marx, was "Taubes."[51]

Taubes visited Zurich again in December 1968, invited back by radical students who had been impressed by his appearance with Marcuse the previous year. He suggested as the title of his presentation "The Phantasm of Late-Capitalist Culture"—a nod toward Benjamin. Taubes recommended to his hosts that the talk not be held on a Friday night, in case members of the Jewish bourgeoisie wanted to attend. To that end, he suggested advertising it in the local Jewish newspaper, the *Israelitisches Wochenblatt,* and putting up some placards at the Jewish Community

Center. He was returning to Zurich, he wrote, with some angst as well as great pleasure, "to the very city where I'm known as the son of the Rabbi and am somewhat notorious, having created some headaches for the Jewish bourgeoisie some twenty years ago (it's been that long!)."[52] In the end, he presented the talk he had given earlier in the year to the congress of German sociologists.[53] There is no evidence that the Jewish bourgeoisie of Zurich trembled.

He did, however, forge a friendship with one member of the Zurich Jewish bourgcoisie, when he attended a dramatic reading by Marianne Weinberg of selections from Martin Buber and Franz Rosenzweig's German translation of the Bible. He sat in the front row, and demonstrably leafed through a book while she recited. But afterward he called her and asked her to meet him the next day.

Born in Germany in 1933, Marianne had moved with her Jewish family to Holland shortly thereafter. During the German occupation, she had been interned with other German-Jewish refugees in the Westerbork camp, but survived the war. She later moved to Zurich, where, in a ceremony conducted by Rabbi Taubes, she married Sigi Weinberg, the owner of high-end fashion stores. The family was wealthy and cultured, with original oil paintings by Léger and Max Beckmann on the walls of their home in a Zurich suburb. In her study hung the first version of Paul Klee's *Angelus Novus*. (The second version was the subject of one of Walter Benjamin's reflections, and was bequeathed by him to Gershom Scholem.)

Taubes took Marianne to the city's left-wing bookstore, run by Theo Pinkus, a Jewish communist, and had her purchase books by a number of fashionable leftist authors, presumably as a way of expanding her horizons. Sigi had attended school with Jacob in Zurich and did not care for him. But Marianne found him fascinating, both intellectually and in the almost childlike way he would open up about himself and his travails. Their friendship, despite ups and downs, would last almost until Jacob's death.[54]

Taubes returned to Zurich regularly, not least to visit the grave of his mother. While there, he usually stayed with his friend Ernst Erdös, an engineer and former Trotskyite turned philosopher and scholar of Judaica.

The "Democratization" of the Free University

Most of the handful of professors at the FU who had initially been sympathetic to the student left thought that things would moderate, as they had, for example, at Berkeley. What they failed to take into account was the effect of the new Berlin Higher Education Act.[55]

From its founding in the late 1940s, the FU had an unusual structure of governance, in which full professors, junior faculty, and students played a role in university governance, including the election of the rector. But the functioning of the institutes, in which the actual activity of research and teaching occurred, was entirely the province of the senior faculty (*Lehrstuhlinhaber*).[56]

One of the primary themes of the SDS in the mid-1960s was the critique of the hierarchical structure of authority in West German universities, in which the full professors dominated. A group of young faculty at the FU who identified with the SDS, including Taubes's *Assistentin*, Uta Gerhardt, organized a seminar on the subject, the upshot of which they published in 1965 as *Universities in Democracy* (*Hochschule in der Demokratie*).[57] They argued that the university should be governed equally by professors, *Mittelbau*, and students, in a system of triple parity.

In 1969, the Berlin city government, in an attempt to appeal to university students, adopted a new higher education law (*Hochschulgesetz*) that fundamentally transformed the structure of university governance in the direction long championed by the SDS.[58] The governing Social Democrats and their mayor, Klaus Schütz, sought to divert student radicalism toward the university and away from the streets and plazas of the city.[59] According to the new law, decision-making at each level, including the academic senate, was to be made by representative of four groups: the full professors, the *Mittelbau*, students, and "other service staff" (*andere Dienstkräfte*). While the professors were to have the largest single share of votes, they could be outvoted by the other groups. In practice, the *Mittelbau* and the student representatives tended to be dominated by the more radical leftist groups.

It was under this system that in December 1969, a thirty-one-year-old *Assistent* in sociology who had yet to complete his dissertation, Rolf Kreibich, was elected president of the University. Shortly thereafter, two vice-presidents were elected: Uwe Wesel, a thirty-six-year-old, left-wing jurist and member of the Republikaner Club, and Margherita von Brentano. The university that Kreibich now headed was in the midst of expansion. Student numbers mushroomed as the national government encouraged and subsidized higher education. When Taubes first arrived at the FU in 1961, it numbered some 12,000 students; by 1970, that had grown to 15,000; and by 1980, it had reached 43,000.[60] The number of students grew far faster than the ability of the university to integrate them, leading to student alienation. Some of these students found their social support networks in the web of radical conventicles that sprang up in and around the university.

In the course of 1969, radical students at the FU began to organize themselves by discipline into Red Cells (Rote Zellen). That was soon followed by a plethora of K-Gruppen (Communist groups), divided among Maoists, Trotskyists, plus various groups identified with the East German Communist regime. Among the most important of these were the Action Communities of Democrats and Socialists, an organization run by the Sozialistische Einheitspartei WestBerlins (SEW), the West German wing of the ruling Communist party of East Germany.

One of Kreibich's first pronouncements was that in case of student demonstrations, under no circumstances would he summon the police to the grounds of the university.[61] That policy encouraged disruptive action by the Red Cells.

In the spring of 1969, the Red Cells took to invading university classes demanding that the professors explain the relevance of their classes, and locking out professors who refused to comply. When students terrorized his classes and locked him out, the former rector of the university, Hans-Joachim Lieber, began a disciplinary procedure with an eye to having the disrupters expelled. The student radicals called for additional actions against Lieber, while Taubes cautioned against the use of such tactics, as at odds with the "tradition of social protest."[62] But shortly thereafter, the dean of the Philosophical Faculty, Otto von Simson—a distinguished art historian of Jewish origin who had returned from the United States to Germany to teach at the FU—presented a report on what he saw as the lamentable situation of the university, which he compared to 1933. Taubes responded with a public rebuke, defending student protests as changing the political consciousness of the students and forcing the reform of the university, and charging von Simson with seeking grounds to bring about the use of repressive force.[63] Taubes's colleagues rebuffed his accusation and expressed their solidarity with the dean.[64] A member of the Christian Democratic faction in the Berlin legislature (*Abgeordnetenhaus*), Wolfgang Werth, wrote a stinging letter to the Berlin daily, the *Tagesspiegel*, which cast Taubes as imposing a distortive, American lens on German events.

> Taubes belongs to that group of professors who carry a heavy responsibility for the present catastrophic conditions at many German universities. In the early phase, he already did his all to incite the students against the existing order. As an American citizen, well acquainted with American circumstances, he took the tragic conflict between whites and blacks and the transgressions of the law against the white authorities and tried to carry them over to our country. Yet in post-war Germany,

there have never been abuses in any way comparable [to those suffered by blacks in the US].[65]

Jacob Taubes was becoming the public face of political radicalism at the city's university.

Israel and the New Left: Taubes as Failed Mediator

Though Taubes's attention was focused on developments in Berlin, events in the Middle East weighed upon him.

In the spring of 1967, the Egyptian president, Gamal Abdul Nasser, demanded the evacuation of UN forces from the Sinai Peninsula and the Gaza Strip, forces that had been stationed there in the aftermath of the 1956 Suez campaign. The UN acceded to the request. Following the withdrawal, Egyptian armored units poured into the Sinai Peninsula. On May 23, after his armed forces occupied the strategic site of Sharm-el-Sheikh, Nasser declared a blockade, halting Israeli shipping through the Straits of Tiran. Egyptian propaganda trumpeted the news that Egyptian troops and tanks were massing on the borders with Israel. In Arab capitals, there were marches in support of Nasser, with slogans calling for the elimination of the Jewish state, threats echoed in their national media. The Israeli army ordered a partial mobilization. Having already concluded a military alliance with Syria in November 1966, on May 30, Nasser signed a pact with Jordan, and on June 4, with Iraq. Israeli appeals for support to the Western powers went unheeded. Among the Israeli public and the Jewish Diaspora, there were fears of another Holocaust. Taubes read the Israeli press daily and was distressed by the news from the Middle East.[66]

On June 5, the Israeli army launched a preemptive war, the first step of which was the sudden and complete destruction of the Egyptian air force, quickly followed by the destruction of Syrian and Jordanian air power. Within a few days, the Israeli army had reached the Suez Canal. Jordan had begun shelling across its border with Israel, including in Jerusalem. In the days that followed, Israel conquered East Jerusalem and the West Bank of the Jordan, and then the Golan Heights. The war was over in six days. Public opinion in Israel, marked by high anxiety in May and early June, now crested in a wave of euphoria.[67]

The Israeli victory was interpreted abroad as a victory of the West over the Soviet Union and its allies. The German SDS shared that interpretation. But since it regarded the United States primarily as an imperialistic power at war with the Third World, it categorized Israel as an agent of

American imperialism and as an aggressive and expansionist power. It was now the Palestinians who were seen as righteous victims.[68]

In the months and years after the Six Day War, the demonization of Israel as an expansionist enemy became ever more frequent on the German student left. But that position was contested, including by Taubes's colleague Michael Landmann, a Zionist who at the time sympathized with the left.[69]

In 1968, Landmann, together with Taubes's friend from Zurich Ernst Erdös, composed a "Common Declaration of 20 Representatives of the German Left Regarding the Middle East Conflict," which was signed by Ernst Bloch, Helmut Gollwitzer, and others, including Taubes's teacher René König. It affirmed Israel's right to a safe existence, and challenged the conception of Zionism as neocolonialism.[70] Landmann threw himself into publicistic activity in defense of Israel, penning a pamphlet, "The Pseudo-Israel of the Pseudo-Left" ("Das Israelpseudos der Pseudolinken"), and another, "A Response to Isaac Deutscher," published together in a volume in 1971.[71]

Taubes worried about this anathematization of Israel on the German student left. He took part in a small student seminar on Israel that tried to carry on a more nuanced discussion.[72] But he refused to sign the 1968 declaration, because, he told Landmann, it lacked coherence. He claimed that in London he had worked with George Lichtheim and Eric Hobsbawm on a declaration from the left, but that the Soviet invasion of Czechoslovakia had diverted their attention.[73] (Just what a declaration from Hobsbawm—a lifelong Communist and consistent anti-Zionist—would have looked like is not difficult to imagine.)

By and large, Taubes refrained from addressing the issue of Israel in any public forum. The exception was a talk entitled "As Circumstances Demand," which he gave on the Berlin radio station, Sender Freies Berlin, on December 25, 1969.[74] The circumstances in question were the increasingly vehement and violent attacks on Israel from the German New Left.

The previous June, the Israeli Ambassador, Asher Ben-Natan, had given a lecture at the University of Frankfurt, which was disrupted by members of the SDS, together with supporters of Al Fatah, the General Union of Palestinian Students, and the anti-Zionist Israel Revolutionary Action Committee Abroad. In August, a group of SDS members traveled to Jordan, visited an Al Fatah training camp, and proclaimed their support for "the Palestinian revolutionary struggle." Then, on November 9, 1969 (the anniversary of *Kristallnacht*), a bomb was uncovered at the Jewish Community Center in Berlin. A hitherto unknown group, calling itself the

Tupamaros West Berlin (after a Uruguayan urban guerilla organization), took credit for placing it there. It was comprised of Dieter Kunzelmann, a veteran of the Situationists, Kommune 1, and the Berlin SDS. He published a "Letter from Amman" in *Agit 883*, a Berlin radical magazine, in which he denounced Israel and Zionism, and urged German leftists to get over their neuroses about protecting the Jews.[75]

Taubes's radio address criticized the German New Left's position on Israel, and offered an analysis of the Israeli-Arab conflict. The conflict between Israel and the Palestinian Arabs, Taubes argued, was one of right versus right. The Jewish people had a right to a *Heimstatt* (a collective home) of their own after thousands of years of living as a "guest people" (*Gastvolk*) among others. "Since the catastrophe of European Jewry, the Jewish people grasps for a piece of land in Israel as a drowning man grabbing a plank. And whoever tries to knock this plank away continues—knowingly or unknowingly, wittingly or unwittingly—the Hitlerian fantasy and the methods of the Final Solution." But the Palestinian Arabs had a right, too, to a *Heimstatt* in the land in which they had lived for centuries.

Taubes wanted to approach this seemingly intractable conflict from its implications for what he called "a New Left that reaches from Berkeley to Berlin, and perhaps has awakened in a subterranean way in Warsaw, Prague and Moscow as well," a left beyond the "late capitalism" of the West and the "state socialism" of the East. Its lack of real power allowed it to think about new alternatives, beyond the existing constellations of power, he contended.

Instead, the New Left was losing its credibility by viewing the Israel-Arab conflict through the lenses of the Vietnam conflict, as a black-and-white issue. Here Taubes portrayed himself as treading a middle ground, between insufficiently informed supporters of Israel on the one hand, and an ill-informed New Left on the other. It was absurd, he said, for the New Left to conceive of Israel as the spearhead of Western imperialism, a charge that emanated, he noted, from the Soviet bloc. In fact, Israel was more socialistic than most Western societies, and the proper role of the New Left should be to support such tendencies in Israel itself, and to encourage them in the surrounding Arab countries. The governments of those countries utilized anti-Israeli campaigns to gain mass support for regimes that were based upon military and feudal oligarchies. The New Left, he suggested, ought to encourage the development of socialist forms of organization—Arab kibbutzim—in the occupied West Bank, which would provide an alternative model of social organization. A socialistic Israel and a socialistic Arab society in the West Bank would then have more in common than with the feudal lords of the Arab oil states or the military oligarchies of the Near East. The New Left ought to encourage the Arab freedom fighters to refrain from terror, which would only set off a chain reaction of greater repression, and instead to build an autonomous *Heimstatt* in the West Bank, in which the Palestinians could realize their national identity. Israel, for its part, should strive to overcome its form as a nation-state, and together with the Palestinians develop a state that would comprise "two autonomous and mutually interlocking communities in a single country." The task of the American and European New Left, according to Taubes, was to encourage this "transpolitical concept" in the Near East, one that lay beyond "the nationalistic forces in each camp devoted to states based upon power." That was a utopian vision, he acknowledged, but at a time when the left was harkening back to elements of the socialist tradition that were deemed utopian, such was the proper role of the New Left.

In February 1969, Jacob requested and received a two-year advance on his salary in order to fund the construction of a house for himself and Margherita, at Heydenstraße 15.[76] It was a home built for an adult couple without children. In late July, Ethan and Tania came to Berlin, and from there the family went to Paris.[77]

But no sooner had Jacob and Margherita moved into their new home than their lives were disrupted by a shocking event across the Atlantic Ocean. On November 15, Jacob received a telegram with the news that Susan Taubes had committed suicide.[78]

CHAPTER TWELVE

Deradicalization and Crisis, 1969–75

AS THE FREE UNIVERSITY was transformed by a more democratic structure of governance that empowered the radical left, Jacob emerged as the acting dean of a new unit of the university meant to overcome the disciplinary fragmentation of "bourgeois" scholarship. Margherita became a vice-president of the university. But over time Jacob became disillusioned with what he saw as the ideological rigidity of the academic left and the decline in standards to which it was leading. That was one source of tension with Margherita, as were conflicts over Jacob's children, and Jacob's continuing propensity to engage in a variety of extramarital relationships. When Margherita finally sued for divorce, it precipitated a crisis that triggered full-blown manic depression and drove Jacob into a psychotic state.

Susan's Novel and Suicide

For a time, Susan Taubes and Susan Sontag were a duo. Richard Locke, Jacob's former student at Columbia, spotted them together at the 1967 New York Film Festival, where Sontag was on the selection committee. Dressed in leather, with dark glasses, and male companions who looked like they had walked out of the pages of *European Vogue*, the two Susans projected a kind of staged erotic exhibitionism.[1]

But their fates had taken very different turns. Susan Sontag's essays in cultural criticism, which she began to publish during her time as Jacob's assistant at Columbia, had made a splash, and with the publication of her first essay collection, *Against Interpretation and Other Essays*, her career as a critic took off. She tried her hand as a writer of short stories, as a novelist, and as a filmmaker—with little success. But her essays, which combined a taste for European high theory with analysis of American popular culture, managed to capture the Zeitgeist. She soon became a fixture of the cultural scene, first in New York, and then in Europe. Her intellectual range, her critical brashness, and her striking looks conspired to create a distinctive image. She was also a master of political and intellectual reinvention.

Susan Taubes, by contrast, met with no such success, and was a more fragile person—or weaker, as Sontag saw it, a theme to which she recurred in her diaries, and, as we will see, in her fiction and films.

Since separating from Jacob, Susan had published two collections of myths and folktales under her maiden name. She became involved with the Open Theater, an avant-garde troupe. She tried out her hand at fiction, publishing a number of short stories in literary magazines. A series of fellowships allowed her to focus on her writing. Her agent managed to place one of her novels.[2] Yet Susan's mental health deteriorated. She suffered from insomnia, took sleeping pills to combat it, drank copious cups of coffee to wake up, and then vodka to calm down. Friends who visited her in New York were distressed to see her condition.[3] Her father, the psychoanalyst, talked to her about entering a psychiatric institution.[4] She struggled with depression and thoughts of suicide, and almost stopped eating.[5] Susan Sontag found it ever more difficult to lure her out of the house. Isolated in her apartment, she was lonely.[6]

In the late summer and early fall of 1969, while she was awaiting the publication of her novel, Susan took an extended trip to Hungary to try to establish a sense of herself and perhaps create a coherent narrative of her life. While in Budapest, she had an affair with György Konrád, a dissident social critic and writer. When Susan Sontag met Konrád a few years later, she was startled to see just how much he looked like Jacob.[7] That was more evidence of Susan's inability to escape the shadow of her marriage to Jacob—the main theme of her novel, *Divorcing*.

The book was published by Random House in the fall of 1969, while Susan was in Budapest. Her original title for the novel was *To America and Back in a Coffin*. Her publisher changed it to what was thought to be the more enticing *Divorcing*. The novel's premise is that it is the story of a narrator, Sophie Blind, who is killed in a car accident in Paris, and whose body is to be brought back to the United States. The story is told from the perspective, and in the voice, of its central, deceased character. The book's cover was made up of family photos—Susan's own, minus Jacob. The novel is the story of a disjunctive life, disjunctively told. It is comprised largely of persons and scenes from Susan's life, conveyed in a variety of styles, from realistic to surrealistic, and in a variety of voices, from plaintive to parodic.

As the title indicates, much of the novel is about the difficulty, indeed impossibility, of Sophie divorcing herself from her relationship with her husband, Ezra Blind, a scholar "working on a book that might take all his life to complete, or at least the next twenty years; his work required going to libraries and meeting scholars of different countries."[8] Most of the scenes, characters, and emotions are drawn from Susan's life, sometimes with a directness and precision startling to those familiar with her biography. Names are changed in ways that are sometimes arbitrary, but often evocative and humorous. "Taubes"—with echoes of the German word *taub* (deaf) becomes "Blind"—which also happened to be the maiden name of Jacob's mother. Jean Houston becomes Kate Dallas, Dieter Henrich becomes Heinrich Dieter Uhl, Margherita becomes Renata.

The novel's portrait of Jacob/Ezra was instantly recognizable to those acquainted with its real-life model. Ezra, with his polyglot speech, was "always on stage," and had an unquenchable need for the company of others. "Ezra laughed at decency and propriety" and preached redemption through sin.[9]

There was more that would have been less well-known, such as Ezra's propensity to quarrel with his wife, and the fact that he was "used to being screamed at by his family."[10] His asking his wife to assume obscene positions, including some from Hieronymus Bosch.[11] His constant infidelity, which the heroine Sophie (the stand-in for Susan) attributed to his need for distraction; his various women, some older, some as young as eighteen; his deflowering of the seventeen-year-old baby sitter in New York.[12] The fact that in bed he told her about other women he been with or had just come from, including women with whom he had engaged in sadomasochism.[13] The portrait of Ezra Blind, etched in acid, bore an unmistakable resemblance to Jacob Taubes.

Susan's novel was reviewed in the *New York Times* book review. The review's staff editor was Susan's friend, Richard Locke. He suggested as a reviewer a distinguished scholar of modernist poetry and the modernist novel, Hugh Kenner. Locke let Susan know that a review of her book would be appearing.

What Locke hadn't reckoned with was that Kenner would hate the book. When he read the review that Kenner submitted, Locke was appalled by what he saw as Kenner's misreading of the novel.[14] But he was in no position to stop its publication. The review, published on Sunday, November 2, was a trashing. "This contains mild rewards once you fight down the rising gorge that's coupled to your Sontag-detector," it began. It classed the novel as implausible in a way Kenner thought characteristic of "lady novelists." Though he thought the latter parts of the novel on the narrator's childhood in Budapest compelling, he found the main character of the book's first half, Ezra (Jacob) too implausible: a "stick figure" of a "Superprof," what with his working on a book that would take twenty years of more to complete, visiting libraries and meeting scholars from various countries, and moving between universities on both sides of the Atlantic and as far as Jerusalem. To Kenner's mind, such a character boggled the imagination![15]

Other reviews, published in newspapers in Chicago, Washington, and Los Angeles, were laudatory. But Susan did not know of them, when, on November 6, she took a train to East Hampton, Long Island, ingested a partial bottle of sedatives (barbiturates), and walked into the waves of the ocean, committing suicide. She was forty-one years old. On the beach, she left three letters to friends, explaining that she had been despondent for over a year and did not have the strength to go on. The police summoned Susan Sontag to identify the body.[16] Susan Taubes's plans to kill herself predated the Kenner review of *Divorcing*. An entry in her journal, written in Budapest on October 12, reads "in about two weeks I will drown myself."[17]

Susan's funeral took place at the Riverside Chapel, a funeral home on the Upper West Side. The arrangements were made by Sontag and Elsa First. Jacob returned from Berlin, with Margherita in tow. Elsa picked up Ethan from his boarding school in Weston, Massachusetts. They drove together to Lake Placid, New York, to pick up Tania from her boarding school, and then on to Manhattan.

The memorial service was nondenominational. Krister Stendahl, Susan and Jacob's friend, delivered the eulogy, taking as his text the passage on love from Paul's Letter to the Corinthians. Susan's body was cremated. During the funeral and at the gathering that followed, Jacob wailed that he was not responsible for Susan's death—behavior that mirrored the funeral scene in *Divorcing*. Rather than consoling his children, Jacob spent the days that followed conferring with colleagues in New York.[18]

In her brief suicide note, Susan asked Elsa First to take charge of the children, which she did. She drove Tania back to her boarding school, while Sontag drove Ethan back to his. In the spring, Ethan went to live with the Stendahls. Jacob now found himself, quite unexpectedly, as the parent legally responsible for his children; and Margherita, as the stepmother to two American adolescents. Jacob mooted the idea of the children coming to live with them in Berlin—a possibility that Ethan abhorred. What would become of Ethan and Tania in case of Jacob's death or incapacitation? Jacob turned to perhaps the most reliable, conservative couple that he knew—Irving and Bea Kristol—and asked them to serve as the children's guardians in case of his death. They considered the idea, but politely declined.[19]

Jacob and Susan in the Work of Sontag

Writers, especially novices, are often advised to "write what you know." As Susan Sontag turned her hand to fiction and then to film in the 1960s, she drew heavily upon her own experiences and the people that she knew. Foremost among them were Jacob and Susan Taubes.

A minor figure based in part on Jacob Taubes appears in her first novel, *The Benefactor*, a less-than-successful attempt at modernist fiction published in 1963. The character in question is "Professor Bulgaraux, a scholar whose special field of study was ancient religious sects." Bulgaraux offers classes at the university about a Gnostic-like doctrine, complete with its own mythology, and practices that resemble those attributed to Jacob Frank, the post-Sabbatian false messiah who had long interested Jacob. The novel's hero (or antihero) inquires of Bulgaraux: "It is rumored . . . that you are not content with the vocation of a scholar, but in your private life actually subscribe to the beliefs you study." To which Bulgaraux replies, "Yes, it's true. Or partly . . . I do not believe, alas. But I know how these beliefs truly apply. I am prepared to carry them out, and to teach others how they may be carried out." He expounds "the idea of being liberated through contracting one's settled life and unleashing one's deepest fantasies" by "going through all kinds of experiences," committing "audacities" and performing actions that "critics blushed to name."[20] In a letter of 1969 to his friend George Lichtheim, Taubes recognized elements of himself in the portrait, adding that Bulgaraux's doctrines drew upon the lectures on Gnosticism that Taubes had offered at Harvard and that Sontag had attended.[21]

In 1969, Sontag wrote and directed a film, *Duet for Cannibals*, which she shot in Stockholm in Swedish, on a budget provided by a Swedish government foundation. Lichtheim wrote to Taubes about a rumor circulating in New York that he had heard from Robert Silvers, the editor of the *New York Review of Books*, namely that the lead character in the film, a "mad professor" (*wahnsinniger Professor*) of "demonic character" (*dämonischen Zügen*) was based on Taubes. Lichtheim suspected that the character was a conflation of Taubes and himself.[22] Taubes hadn't seen the film, but conceded in his response that that might be true. For if one looked at the still from the movie that appeared in *Der Spiegel*—an image to be discussed—there could be no doubt that it was Taubes himself.[23] "No one gives us 720,000 DM in our business," Taubes observed laconically. "Let us be grateful that at least we'll achieve some fame through the film."

The published screenplay of *Duet for Cannibals* was dedicated to "Susan Taubes (1928–1969)." And in fact, a character based upon her was equally central to the film. For in large part, *Duet for Cannibals* was a film about the Taubeses. The twists and turns of the plot are less important than the physical and psychological portrait of the couple. The plot focuses upon the relationship between Arthur Bauer, a German radical intellectual living in Swedish exile; his wife, Francesca; Tomas, a male assistant to Bauer; and Tomas's girlfriend, Ingrid, a student in her twenties for whom, at first, Bauer is something of an idol.

Bauer has many of the characteristic habits and traits of Jacob Taubes. To begin with, he is German. He is the author of a book, *The Revolution and Its Enemies* (*Die Revolution und seine Feinde*). (When Ingrid finally asks Bauer "When is the time for the Revolution?" he replies, "It's either too early or too late.") The newspaper he reads is the *Neue Zürcher Zeitung*, Jacob's paper of choice since his student days in Switzerland. Like Jacob, Bauer smokes a pipe and wears a broad-brimmed black hat. Most tellingly, Bauer scoops up food from the table in an unrestrained and unmannered way—just as Jacob Taubes was wont to do. Bauer is charismatic, drawing first Tomas and then Ingrid into his employ and his emotional web.

Bauer's wife, Francesca, is not only closely modeled on Susan Taubes: the actress chosen by Sontag to play the part, Adriana Asti, *looked* a good deal like Susan Taubes. She is beautiful, frail, seductive, and possessed of barely repressed fury. Her husband, Bauer, fears she will commit suicide. Bauer laments to Tomas how much she has changed since they met and married years ago, when she was "so lively and loving."

The relationship between Bauer and Francesca is a sort of kabuki dance of exhibitionistic eroticism—much like the relationship between Jacob and Susan that Gregory Callimanopulos had witnessed during their year in Princeton.[24] Bauer seems to want Tomas to be seduced by Francesca. Later, she does so, while first secreting her husband in the closet where he can watch them have sex. Still later, Bauer makes love with Ingrid, the ingénue, while Francesca looks on. In perhaps the most famous scene of this little-known film, we see the three of them in bed together: Ingrid in the middle, with Bauer and Francesca on either side of their connubial bed, reading. The episode recapitulates the scene presented to Janet

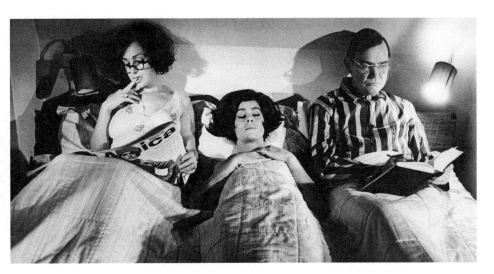

FIGURE 12.1. Still from Sontag's 1969 film *Duet for Cannibals*. L to R,
Francesca, Ingrid, Bauer.

Scheindlin when she walked into Jacob's apartment to find Jacob, Susan
Taubes, and Susan Sontag together in bed.

Here is how the film critic for *Vogue* magazine, Frederic Tuten, characterized the film:

> *Duet for Cannibals* is a witty, bone-dry serio-comedy that fascinates and
> disturbs in turn. . . . Dr. Arthur Bauer, attractive in a swinish way, fifty-
> ish, arch-revolutionary theoretician engaged in writing his memoirs,
> is Sontag's anti- or false revolutionary, an arrogant, self-aggrandizing
> trickster who blurs together revolution and his ego. Francesca, Bauer's
> neurotic, elegantly seductive wife, supports her husband's mystifica-
> tions while composing her own. Tomas, an earnest student revolution-
> ary hired by Bauer to catalogue his documents, and Ingrid, Tomas's
> impressionable girlfriend, are the fodder for the elder couple's psycho-
> logical and sexual feast.[25]

Of course the film is a work of imagination that makes use of elements of
the real Taubes for artistic purposes. Still, it provides a cinematic portrait
that recaptures elements of their relationship, in exaggerated form.

Sontag's film was first screened at the New York Film Festival in September 1969[26] (where Robert Silvers must have seen it), and then for a
week at the theater at Carnegie Hall beginning on November 26. By then,
Susan Taubes was gone.

Duet for Cannibals was not the last time that Sontag drew upon her impressions of Susan Taubes in her fiction. In "Debriefing," a short story published in 1973, Susan Taubes is invoked as "Julia," a friend of the narrator who is wasting away in depression and isolated in her apartment, despite the narrator's attempts to spur her to activity. "Lena," yet another character based on Susan Taubes, appears in Sontag's second (and last) fictional film, *Brother Carl*, shot in 1970 and released in 1972.[27] In that film, Lena is divorced from a choreographer, Martin. The film portrays her spiral of self-destruction as she tries to regain Martin's interest. She tries to make him jealous by having an affair, and when she fails, commits suicide.[28] In the preface to the published screenplay, Sontag noted the continuities between the characters of Bauer in *Cannibals* and Martin in *Brother Carl*: "I recognize in Martin a new version of the psychological fascist in *Duet for Cannibals*. Martin is a Bauer past his prime; a Bauer who has already wreaked the maximum amount of damage; a Bauer who, in a state of exhaustion, revulsion, and weary cynicism, has lost his appetite for playing games and even hopes to behave decently."[29]

Despite these far from flattering cinematic portraits of Jacob Taubes, Sontag and Jacob remained friends in the years that followed, as her international fame continued to swell. Jacob would make a point of visiting with her when he was in New York, and she came to Berlin and spoke at his colloquium on hermeneutics. It was one of the most lasting of Jacob's friendships.

Radicalism Institutionalized: Fachbereich 11

In his most famous speech, delivered in February 1968 at the International Congress on Vietnam in Berlin, Rudi Dutschke argued for a "Long March through the Institutions." This was an allusion to the "Long March" of the Chinese Communists under Mao, in which they retreated to the province of Yunan in an attempt to establish a base from which to conquer the rest of the country. "The aim of the long march," Dutschke explained, "will be to build counter-institutions, liberated zones in bourgeois society." Nowhere was the long march shorter than at the FU, and its Yunan was Fachbereich 11, whose first elected chairman (the equivalent of a dean) was Jacob Taubes.

1970 saw the establishment of a novel academic structure, with new units known as *Fachbereiche* (divisions). Fachbereich 11 (FB11; the number came from its designation in the course catalogue) was made up of philosophy and the social sciences.[30] It was founded to overcome the fragmentation attributed to "bourgeois scholarship," or what Taubes and his students called "the idiocy of academic disciplines" (*Fachidiotentum*). That was a laudable goal in theory; in practice the way in which fragmentation was avoided was through Marxism (and soon, Marxism-Leninism), which was supposed to provide a unified basis for philosophy, sociology, and other social sciences.[31]

Alongside more conventional offerings in philosophy and the social sciences, the Fachbereich offered courses that reflected the ideological propensities of the New Left. In the first semester of its existence, for example, Gollwitzer taught a theology course on Political Implications of the Gospel (Christianity and Socialism), and another on Theology of Revolution. In the Department of Philosophy, Brentano taught a course on Theories of Fascism, while a team of junior faculty taught Karl Marx: Political Economy and Philosophy. Soon there were courses on Logical and Epistemological Inquiries into Karl Marx's *Capital* (taught by Wolfgang Fritz Haug), and ever more esoteric topics such as a seminar on Materialism and Empirio-criticism, for which a knowledge of Marx's work up to *Capital* and Lenin's *Materialism and Empirio-criticism* was a prerequisite.

In short order, Fachbereich 11 became a center of radical leftist teaching and pedagogy at the FU—and a lightning rod for opponents of the university's radicalization, who saw it as a cradle of ideological indoctrination. In a memoir, Wolf Lepenies recalled the ideological milieu: "Today it is hard to conceive the extent to which Marxist beliefs shaped the study of the social sciences in the sixties and well into the seventies, in Berlin and some other places. . . . For us, economics was political economy, . . . history was historical materialism, and dialectical materialism was philosophy."[32]

In 1970, a professor of psychology, Klaus Holzkamp, together with his students, founded an afternoon program for the children of workers (*Arbeiterkinder*) that was supposed to raise the working-class children to be anti-authoritarian and anticapitalist. Word got out to the larger public through the conservative newspaper *Die Welt*.[33] The resulting outcry led the university's psychologists to split into two groups: a pro-Marxist (indeed pro-East German) group around Holzkamp, which remained in Fachbereich 11, and a non-Marxist group that migrated to the division of education. In protest against the university's decision to allow the non-Marxists to split off, Taubes resigned as chair (*Vorsitzender*) of FB11 and Lepenies resigned as assistant chair.[34] They accused the *Senator für Wissenschaft und Kunst* (the Berlin equivalent of a minister of education), Werner Stein, a member of the SPD, of providing aid and comfort to "that party of counter-reform that denounces as a 'red takeover' or 'sell-out of the freedom of scholarship' every attempt to bring socialist orientations into the self-determination process."[35]

In 1971, the governing council (*Fachbereichsrat*) of FB11 tried to appoint the philosopher Hans Heinz Holz to the chair formerly occupied by Paul Feyerabend.[36] A student of Ernst Bloch and a scholar of Leibniz, Holz was not merely a Marxist but a committed Communist. The proposed appointment met public opposition from the Emergency Association for a Free University (Notgemeinschaft für eine Freie Universität), an organization of professors who opposed the radical drift of the university (discussed in a section below). In one of its "Hammer and Sickle" reports, it characterized the Fachbereich's Philosophy Seminar as an "Institute for Marxism-Leninism."[37] The appointment of Holz was also publicly opposed by Iring Fetscher, a professor of political theory and scholar of Marxism in Frankfurt. Wissenschaftssenator Stein, who had ultimate authority over appointments, took exception and refused to appoint Holz.

Taubes emerged as the spokesman for the *Fachbereichsrat*, bombarding Stein with letters and defending the proposed appointment of Holz in the name of methodological pluralism—though as critics pointed out, the Fachbereich was hardly bereft of Marxists.[38] Taubes also published a defense of Holz and a diatribe against his critics in the *EXTRA-Dienst*, the weekly paper that catered to the radical left in West Berlin.[39] (Like the Republikaner Club, it was funded by the East Germans.) Stein's favored candidate was Albrecht Wellmer—a student of Jürgen Habermas, whom Taubes himself had recommended for the post, despite (as he wrote to Senator Stein) the "anti-Frankfurt affect" of some of his colleagues in the Fachbereich and the left-wing students at the FU, for whom scholars associated with the Frankfurt School were far too moderate.[40] Taubes's stance for once put him on the same side as Gershom Scholem, who wrote to the University favoring Holz's appointment.[41] After Senator Stein's rejection of Holz, Taubes traveled to the University of Marburg to campaign on behalf of Holz, who was successfully appointed there.[42]

At the very time he was striving to appoint Holz to a chair of philosophy, Taubes undertook an even more radical initiative. Following a suggestion from his wife, Brentano, Taubes convinced the Fachbereich to extend an invitation for a guest professorship during the summer semester of 1971 to Angela Davis.[43] A former student of Marcuse, Davis had spent two years as a student in Frankfurt studying with Adorno, Habermas, and others. By the time of the invitation from FB11, Davis was not only a declared Communist, but on the FBI's Ten Most Wanted Fugitive List, charged with having purchased the gun used by black militants to kill a judge during an attempted escape from a courtroom in California. (She was later acquitted by a jury.)

Another invitation was extended to Eldridge Cleaver, a leader of the revolutionary Black Panther Party. He was to lecture on a class analysis of the United States and on the educational activities of the Black Panthers. Cleaver, said the Fachbereich, would provide a materialist analysis, and thus correct the "one-sided preference given to bourgeois-positivist scholars from the US."[44]

When news of the invitation to Davis was published in the *Tagesspiegel*, the mayor of West Berlin, an enraged and agitated Klaus Schütz, phoned the FU's president, Kreibich. (The East German-funded *EXTRA*, which reported these events, claimed that Schütz was responding to a request from the American occupation authorities.[45]) The president then declared his willingness to invite Davis, but only after the charges against her had been resolved. Jacob and Margherita protested that the purpose of the invitation had been to demonstrate solidarity with Davis precisely because she was being unjustly prosecuted. In a letter he dashed off to Kreibich, Jacob called into question the president's moral integrity, and likened Kreibich's decision to approve Davis's appointment only *after* her acquittal to a university president during the Nazi era deciding that an invitation to a persecuted academic would be extended only after the prisoner was freed from a concentration camp.[46] Kreibich was dismayed by the comparison and by the aspersions on his moral integrity: he demanded an apology from Jacob, without which, he added, there was no possibility of further cooperation between them.[47] Taubes stood his ground.[48] Queried at a press conference about the invitation to Davis, Kreibich claimed that he had not approved it. Taubes claimed that Kreibich had approved it orally; Kreibich, that he had merely agreed to discuss it.[49] In the end, a formal invitation to Davis was extended, signed by the relevant officer of the university, Vice-President Uwe Wesel, and sent to her care of Herbert Marcuse.[50]

It was, at best, a Pyrrhic victory for Taubes, damaging his relationship with President Kreibich and exposing the university to terrible publicity in the eyes of the mayor. Shortly thereafter, Taubes was criticized by the *Fachbereichsrat* for his "frequent sensationalist actions," and he resigned as acting chair.[51]

Support and Ambivalence: Taubes and Lefèvre

As the student left moved toward ever-greater ideological radicalism, Taubes moved along with it, at least for a time. During the height of the rebellion, the leaflets of the radical student groups were reproduced using the mimeograph machines in the basement of Taubes's Institute for

Hermeneutics.[52] He facilitated the long march through the institutions at the FU—until he reached the point where he rued the very transformations he had helped to bring about.

His support along with his ambivalence was exemplified in Taubes's relationship to Wolfgang Lefèvre, who was among the most prominent figures in the political life of the FU. Lefèvre played an outsize role on the public stage, and Taubes's support for him helped to shine the spotlight on Taubes himself.

In the early 1960s, Lefèvre was a student activist at the FU and a member of the SDS at a time when its membership was still tiny. But the fact that the participation rate in student council (AStA) elections was below 50 percent made it possible for an ideologically motivated minority to exert disproportionate influence, and in 1965, he was elected as head of the student council. Lefèvre was voted out of office later that year, after he signed a petition for peace in Vietnam that originated from a communist group.[53]

Lefèvre was not simply an activist, but a theorist and tactician. As a contributor to the SDS periodical *neue kritik*, he laid out a strategy of escalation, of making demands that could be realized, or rejected by the establishment only by causing an uproar, then going on to the next demand. Demonstrations, he stressed, must be fun.[54]

Lefèvre's politics continued to drift leftward. In the summer of 1968, he attended an international camp in Cuba to school activists in revolutionary methods—an event reported on the front page of *Die Welt*, the flagship newspaper of the conservative Springer newspaper conglomerate.[55] The next year, he led a group of students who stormed a meeting of the philosophical faculty, which led him to be charged with rioting, disturbing the peace, and criminal trespass.[56]

In keeping with his strategy of trying to integrate the young radicals into the culture of the academy, Taubes worked to get Lefèvre a stipend to pursue doctoral research.[57] By the spring of 1970, Lefèvre had completed his dissertation, "On the Historical Character and Historical Function of the Methods of Bourgeois Sociology—A Study of the Work of Max Weber." After reading a draft, Taubes was sufficiently dissatisfied to suggest to Lefèvre that he undertake a fundamental revision of the work. Lefèvre did not follow his advice. By this time, one department after another at the FU was having its classes disrupted and its faculty members threatened by the Red Cells. It was becoming common for radical scholars to be awarded doctorates and even habilitation on the basis of highly ideological works.[58]

During that semester, three positions for tenured assistants (*Assistentenstelle*) of philosophy became available in the recently constituted

Fachbereich 11. As per the new university law, the appointments were to be made by a selection committee (*Auswahlkommission*), comprised on the basis of triple parity. The committee's list of its three top choices was then to be forwarded to the *Wissenschaftssenator*, who had the ultimate decision in such matters. The selection committee drew up its list of the three most qualified candidates. But the Red Cells drew up their counterlist, which included Lefèvre, and threatened a campaign of disruption if the committee did not comply.[59]

At its meeting in June 1970, the selection committee decided to place Lefèvre at the top of its list, together with two other young Marxists drawn from the junior faculty, despite what many saw as Lefèvre's inferior qualifications for the post. That led to an outcry from a number of professors and junior staff. Heinrich Kleiner, the representative of the junior staff (*Vertreter der Wissenschaftlicher Mitarbeiter*) on the committee, sent a letter of protest to the *Fachbereichsrat*, in which he chastised the representatives of the faculty for voting in favor of Lefèvre despite their negative judgment of his scholarly quality. That, Kleiner thought, could only be explained by their fear that a decision against Lefèvre would have unpleasant consequences in terms of university politics.[60] Several of the full professors—including Michael Landmann and Wilhelm Weischedel—also protested, contending that three of the four representatives of the professors on the appointment commission had voted in favor of Lefèvre despite their own best judgment.[61] On November 26, Taubes, in his then capacity as acting chair of the Fachbereich, sent them a hectographed letter (which has not survived) rejecting their letter of protest. Landmann responded four days later, recalling a conversation over the summer in which Taubes had told him that the university ought to reward Lefèvre's activity in the student movement with an assistant position. Landmann thought that Taubes was influenced by the agitation of the Red Cells, with whom he didn't want to come into conflict.[62]

Taubes's formal evaluation of Lefèvre's dissertation stretched for nineteen pages: that is to say, it was the longest of his compositions that year. It was a remarkable document, ambivalent and ambiguous, critical yet conciliatory, or perhaps cowardly. The evaluation raised doubts about the validity of Lefèvre's method, noted that the chain of argument was often unclear, complained of the work's polemical character, its interpretive distortions, and the extent to which its (Marxist) method governed its use of sources, which at one point Taubes deemed "catastrophic." And yet, after eighteen pages of critique, Taubes ultimately praised the work as "imposing and worthy of consideration" and meriting an accolade of "cum laude."

He claimed that "the intellectual energy that has gone into its structure and execution" exceeded that of most dissertations.[63]

Like some other professors at the FU alarmed at the transformation of the university, the opponents of Lefèvre's appointment turned to the local press to air their discontent. On December 29, *Die Welt* ran an article about the affair, headlined "Assistant Post as Reward for Agitation," which quoted from Landmann's letter to Taubes, whom the article characterized as "the professor and Red-Cell-Sympathizer Jacob Taubes."[64]

From there, the story went national, when the liberal weekly magazine *Der Spiegel* published its own article on the controversy. It described the protagonists as "the liberal-conservative philosopher Michael Landmann, 57," "the leftist sociologist of religion and hermeneuticist, Jacob Taubes, 47," and "Wolfgang Lefèvre, erstwhile SDS ideologist and student leader in West Berlin, now an associate of the 'Party-Initiative for a Proletarian Left.'" Taubes was quoted as saying that the left at the FU was being subjected to McCarthyism by the right. On the contrary, Landmann responded, Marxism was "penetrating through every pore," leaving its "bourgeois" opponents with barely room to breathe. *Der Spiegel* noted that Taubes had approved of Lefèvre's dissertation despite his expressed doubts. "The 'Star-Philosopher' (as the ultra-left 'Red Cell Philosophy' calls Taubes) insists that Lefèvre's doctoral work should be judged not only according to scholarly criteria. According to Taubes, the dissertation represents 'an attempt to give voice to the intentions of the student protest movement, which often expresses itself in inarticulate actions. A failure of the university to reward such an attempt would mean a negation of a piece of its history.'" The other four referees (*Gutachtern*) saw the thesis as characterized by "vulgar dogmatism" and requested a new committee, not comprised of Lefèvre's supporters—a move that Taubes pledged to fight with all the legal means at his disposal.[65]

After three hours of discussion, the *Fachbereichsrat* accepted Lefèvre's dissertation.[66] Shortly thereafter, the issue of Taubes's behavior was raised once again in the Berlin senate by a representative from the Christian Democrats.[67]

The Lefèvre dispute dragged on for years. In early 1979, when Lefèvre defended his habilitation, Taubes reported to a colleague that Lefèvre, now firmly established as a faculty member, showed himself to be a "primitiver DDR-nick," that is, a loyal follower of the East German Communist party line.[68] But by then much had changed—including Jacob Taubes.

As Fachbereich 11 attained a well-deserved reputation for ideological radicalism, it became harder and harder to attract distinguished scholars to its ranks. Invitations were extended to a number of leading philosophers to move to the FU, including Taubes's friends Jürgen Habermas and Dieter Henrich. In July of 1970, Taubes sought to attract Habermas to head a new institute.[69] Habermas, along with his wife, visited the FU, met with Lefèvre and Haug among others, and came away thinking that the scene at the FU was crazy (*verrückt*): Lefèvre and Haug told Habermas of their hopes that an attack by the New Left on the American armed forces in West Berlin might lead the Soviets to move in, unfreezing the Cold War.[70] The next year, Dieter Henrich turned down a job offer as well.[71]

Many professors around Taubes found the struggles within FB11 to be exhausting. But not Taubes. He thrived on conflict. He enjoyed not only a good fight, but a bad one.[72]

Co-optation or Confrontation: Taubes vs. Habermas

In August 1969, Taubes journeyed to Frankfurt for the funeral of Theodor Adorno, who had passed away at the age of sixty-five after a series of traumatic confrontations with the student left.[73] Among those in attendance were three senior figures who had influenced Taubes—Ernst Bloch, Max Horkheimer, Gershom Scholem—as well as Jürgen Habermas.[74]

Through much of this tumultuous era, Taubes was in frequent contact with Habermas, who occupied a central but ambiguous role in the political battles of the period. In his books, *Technique and Science as Ideology* (1968), *Protest Movement and University Reform* (1969), and *Theory and Practice* (four editions, from 1963 to 1971), Habermas strove to both update the critique of technological forms of rationality formulated by Horkheimer and Adorno, and to direct and articulate the concerns of the New Left in philosophical and social scientific terms. In *Legitimation Problems of Late Capitalism* (1973), he embraced the term "late capitalism," with its suggestion that capitalism was on its last legs, and (as his critic, Hermann Lübbe noted) thereby helped contribute to its delegitimation. Horkheimer and Adorno had engaged in critique without providing a model of what a better society would look like. Habermas tried to do so in *Toward a Reconstruction of Historical Materialism* (1976), drawing on linguistics and on American pragmatism to formulate a normative criterion of "communicative competence"—essentially, a society, economy, and polity in which all would have an equal ability to participate, and in which claims would be justified based on totally unprejudiced discussion, free from inequalities of power.

At the same time, Habermas emerged as a trenchant and public critic of some of the tactics of the student left.[75] At an SDS conference in Hanover that followed the murder of Ohnesorg in June 1967, Habermas criticized Rudi Dutschke's call for the formation of "action centers" throughout the country to engage in concerted actions.[76] The New Left strategy of using violence to bring out the latent violence in existing institutions (that is the willingness and ability of such institutions to defend themselves) Habermas thought both impractical and dangerous. In 1968, he was skeptical of the "democratization" of the university in the form of triple parity (*Drittelparität*) when it came to matters of scholarship and appointments.[77]

The most direct target of Habermas's criticism was Hans-Jürgen Krahl, the counterpart in the Frankfurt SDS of Rudi Dutschke in Berlin. Like Dutschke, Krahl was a talented agitator and organizer, as well as a theoretician.[78] Krahl had been a doctoral student under Adorno and had served as his teaching assistant.[79]

Krahl and Dutschke had together developed a strained analysis of the economics and politics of the Federal Republic, according to which the forces of capital were increasingly intertwined with the state apparatus, and as the economy entered a period of crisis, the state would become ever more authoritarian. They interpreted the *Notstandsgesetz*—the law proposed by the coalition government in 1967 that provided the government with extraordinary powers in case of an emergency—in this light. The law was vociferously opposed by the SDS and its successor organization, the Extra-Parliamentary Opposition (Ausser-Parliamentarische Opposition or APO). Krahl and Dutschke interpreted the law as evidence of their thesis, and organized a march calling for "resistance" (*Widerstand*) against the "authoritarian state."[80] The assumption of Dutschke and Krahl was that because it was capitalist, West Germany was prone to another round of fascism (it was characteristic of the German New Left in this period that it elided the distinction between fascism and Nazism). Thus the SDS and the APO were to engage in *Widerstand*—the resistance to fascism that had failed to occur during the 1930s.[81] It was this purported parallel between the 1930s and the 1960s that led Dutschke and Krahl to draw upon Max Horkheimer's work of the 1930s analyzing the Nazi regime.

Krahl argued that the scientific and technical intelligentsia—and the university students who aspired to that status—were most sensitive to the psychological immiseration brought about by contemporary capitalism. Hence they had to assume the role of the "collective theoreticians of the proletariat," liberating the working class from false consciousness and convincing it that its real interests lay in overthrowing capitalism. (In short, he linked Marcuse's analysis to Lukács's argument in *History and*

Class Consciousness.[82]) Together with Dutschke, Krahl contended that since the consciousness of the masses was manipulated, parliamentary politics was no longer an effective form of radical transformation. Instead, the APO should transform itself into a decentralized movement of "urban guerrillas"—a concept that would soon serve as the theoretical justification for left-wing terrorism in the 1970s.[83]

Habermas offered a series of withering critiques of the preferred tactics of Dutschke and Krahl—attention-grabbing actions intended to expose the latent violence of the state and raise revolutionary consciousness. He thought their analysis of contemporary circumstances far-fetched, and their emphasis on action tantamount to "left-wing fascism" (*linken Faschismus*)—a term he used in June 1967, and then again in June 1968, when he published "The Pseudo-Revolution and Its Children."[84]

The confrontation between Habermas and Krahl came to a head in January 1969, when the SDS faction headed by Krahl at the University of Frankfurt occupied the Institute for Social Research. Afraid the students would lay waste to the institute and its library, Adorno and Habermas called the police and had the demonstrators forcibly removed. [85] The demonstrators, for their part, characterized Adorno and Habermas as "the bailiffs of the authoritarian state."[86] His lecture disrupted by students, Adorno retreated to Switzerland, where he died that summer. In an elegy for Adorno published in *Die Zeit*, Habermas chastised "one of Adorno's students." The unnamed student had criticized Adorno for continuing to adhere in his life to the very standards of bourgeois individuality that he had criticized in his work, rather than leaving bourgeois conventions behind and supporting the actions of the students.[87] At the end of 1971, after years of disruptions of his seminars and lectures, Habermas left the university altogether, taking up the post of codirector of a new research institute in Starnberg.[88]

Taubes regarded Habermas's open critique of Krahl and company as a tragedy and a strategic error. He dispatched some unsolicited advice to Habermas, counseling him not to give up on Krahl, and to continue discussions.[89] The tension between Habermas and Krahl ended only with the latter's death in an automobile accident, on February 14, 1970. Thereafter, Taubes advised Habermas to be similarly conciliatory to Oskar Negt, an SDS activist and Habermas's erstwhile assistant, who had attacked Habermas for his accusation of "left-wing fascism," an accusation that Negt characterized as evidence of "the disintegration of liberal-bourgeois consciousness."[90]

The fact that Taubes showered Habermas with advice did not mean that Habermas paid it heed. But the contrast in their approach to Lefèvre and to Krahl—encouragement and appeasement in the case of Taubes and Lefèvre; confrontation in the case of Habermas and Krahl—demonstrates the difference in their strategies toward the New Left, and Taubes's greater tolerance for radicalism. For his part, Habermas thought Taubes unreliable.[91] Taubes would continue to hold Habermas's critique of Krahl and of "left-wing fascism" against him.

The Terrorist Connection

Among the aspiring young intellectuals attracted to Taubes was Bernward Vesper. The son of a Nazi poet, Vesper had turned himself into a minor publisher of leftist literature, together with his girlfriend, Gudrun Ensslin, the daughter of a Protestant pastor.[92] In 1964, they moved to the FU, where Vesper chose to work with Taubes on a doctoral dissertation.[93] Taubes got to know Ensslin as well.[94] In 1966, Vesper launched a series of pamphlets and booklets, the "Voltaire Pamphlets," written by spokesmen of the German student left as well as international figures such as Stokely Carmichael. Taubes attended the launch in Berlin, together with Brentano.[95] In a booklet of photos and documents published the next year, *Demonstrations: A Berlin Model*, Vesper reprinted Taubes's open letter to the mayor of Berlin protesting police brutality—requesting Taubes's permission only after the fact.[96] He later approached Taubes and Brentano about writing a critique of the term "left-wing fascism" (*linker Faschismus*), intended to demonstrate the incoherence of that epithet.[97]

By then, Ensslin had left Vesper for her new love, Andreas Baader, a shadowy figure who popped up at the Republikaner Club, meetings of the SDS, and teach-ins at the FU.[98] Together, they undertook to put into practice the suggestion of the Kommune 1 pamphlet that setting fire to a department store would be an effective form of radical protest. Their first attempt at arson, in a Frankfurt department store, failed, and Ensslin and Baader were arrested and put on trial—a trial at which Vesper condemned the German justice system. He then published a defense of Baader and Ensslin. On a trip to Rome to visit Rudi Dutschke, Vesper struck up a friendship with Ulrike Meinhof. She was a radical left-wing journalist who had been involved in the anti-atomic-bomb campaign, had taught courses at the FU, and had apparently studied with Brentano. (Brentano later mentioned this with pride.[99]) Taubes knew her as well.[100] Together with Meinhof, Baader and Ensslin would found the Red Army Faction, a formidable terrorist organization that haunted West German politics in the decade to come.[101] Their lawyer was Horst Mahler, who had called upon Taubes's expertise in his defense of the Kommune 1.[102] When Palestinian terrorists murdered Israeli athletes during the Munich Olympics in September 1972, Meinhof and Mahler hailed "the brave commando action and self-sacrifice of the members of Black September against the Israeli Olympic team."[103]

Vesper took his own life in May 1971. But the shadow of these associations would later fall upon Taubes and Brentano. For several years, plainclothes policemen were stationed outside their home, on the lookout for possible terrorists. At one point they broke in and conducted a surreptitious search of their papers.[104]

Joseph Wulf

One of the qualities that had attracted Jacob Taubes to Margherita von Brentano was her staunch anti-Nazism. As we've seen, in the 1950s she had produced radio programs about the murder of the Jews, and in the early 1960s, she had conducted a seminar on antisemitism at the FU. Yet as a result of the changing political culture of the left in West Germany, she ended up playing a role in squelching the creation of a research institute devoted to the study of the Holocaust, and in that process, threatening the livelihood of one of the few scholars who had made the documentation of the Nazi past his lifework.

One might have thought that the Holocaust would have been a central topic of concern and discussion at Taubes's Judaica Institute. But it was not,[105] perhaps because for different reasons it was embarrassing to both non-Jewish Germans and to Jews. While West German historians had turned their attention to the study of the Third Reich in general, the study of the murder of the Jews was undertaken primarily by scholars elsewhere. While Taubes alluded to the Nazi past and the murder of the Jews in conversations and correspondence, it was not a topic that exercised him at the time.

One of the few to devote themselves to the topic was Joseph Wulf (1912–74).[106] Born in Chemnitz in Saxony and raised in Krakow, during the War, Wulf was imprisoned in the Krakow ghetto and then deported to Auschwitz. But he survived, the only member of his family to do so. After the war he went to Paris, where he founded the first historical commission for research on the murder of the Jews. In the early 1950s, he moved to West Berlin, convinced that the best place to document the evil that had occurred was in the land of the perpetrators and in their language. Together with Léon Poliakov, a historian of antisemitism, Wulf published volume after volume documenting the Holocaust, the role of German civil servants and army officers, and of intellectuals. Much of his scholarship took the form of the publication of original documents, together with commentaries on their significance. Unlike most German historians who wrote about these subjects in vague terms of "devilish powers" and "barbarism," Wulf's volumes named the names of those responsible, from diplomats to Wehrmacht officers to professors of law. The volumes struck a dissonant chord. In a review of one of them, Taubes's right-wing friend Armin Mohler denounced the work as an address book of denazification, lacking in context and scholarly objectivity (*Wissenschaftlichkeit*). Others recognized their invaluable contribution. But as a historian, Wulf was self-taught. He had no academic position, and his work was financed largely by his publisher, who was running out of money.

In January 1970, at the urging of Helmut Gollwitzer, the FU awarded Wulf an honorary doctorate in recognition of his historical work. Jacob Taubes gave the *Laudatio*, the speech praising the recipient.[107] Later that year, Wulf offered a course at the Judaica Institute on "National Socialist Policy toward the Jews."[108] But Wulf was still without regular means of support. Taubes was among those who urged the FU to provide Wulf with a position teaching the history of Eastern European Jewry. But several years passed and no position was offered.[109]

In 1967, Wulf had begun to devote himself to the creation of an archive and memorial museum devoted to the Holocaust, which he intended for the lakeside villa where the infamous Wannsee Conference had taken place. That location proved unavailable—at least in the short term—as it was in use as a boys school. But the mayor of West Berlin, Klaus Schütz, was supportive of Wulf's project. He wanted to find a place at the FU for Wulf and his archive, and was willing to make funds available.[110] The president of the FU convened a commission, headed by Brentano. It met for a year and came to the conclusion that there was no point in such an archive, since the goal should be the struggle against fascism in the present. Her collaborators, Peter Furth, Wolfgang Haug, and Irmingard Staeuble, formulated an elaborate plan for an institute for "Fascism Research."

But by then, Brentano and her collaborators from the *Argument* circle were increasingly committed to a conception of National Socialism as a variety of fascism, and fascism as a form of capitalist defense, always lurking as a possibility in capitalist society. From this perspective, the only real antidote to the poison of fascism was socialism. In this Marxist understanding, the murder of the Jews was incidental to the analysis of Nazism, an analysis now robbed of its historical particularity.[111] That was reflected in their plan for the new institution.

But Mayor Schütz had no interest in such a program: his goal had been to find an institutional home for Wulf. And Wulf, for his part, feared that bringing his project to the FU would involve its political appropriation for an agenda set by the radical left.[112] So in the end, the plan came to naught. The career of the survivor of the Holocaust and chronicler of the Nazi persecution of the Jews had been cut short by academic anti-fascism.

In despair over his inability to secure ongoing support, in 1973 Wulf collapsed physically and psychically. The death of his wife that year was another blow. On October 10, 1974, he leaped to his death from the fourth-story window of his home.

The Counteroffensive of the Professors

The growing influence at the FU of the radical student left—and its pro-fessorial supporters—led to a counterreaction by some of the universi-ty's faculty. Beginning in June 1967, a small group founded the Working Group for the Protection of Freedom and Teaching at the Free University of Berlin, an organization that developed over time into the Emergency Association for a Free University (Notgemeinschaft für eine freie Univer-sität, or NofU for short). Among its founders and most active members was Richard Löwenthal, the Social Democratic foreign policy expert who had returned from exile, as well as Georg N. Knauer, a classical philolo-gist.[113] It issued press releases and more substantial reports, titled "The Free University under Hammer and Sickle," documenting the disruptive actions of the radical left.[114]

In April, 1968, twenty-eight members of the faculty issued a statement in support of wide-ranging student participation in the governance of the university. Among its signatories were Jacob Taubes and the political sci-entists Ossip Flechtheim, Alexander Schwan, and Kurt Sontheimer.[115] In the course of the next few years, Schwan and Sontheimer would change sides. So, eventually, would Taubes. But in the interim, he would emerge as a prominent antagonist of the Notgemeinschaft.

In February, 1970 the newly renamed Notgemeinschaft held its first public meeting, presided over by Thomas Nipperdey—the brilliant his-torian whose appointment to the FU Taubes had welcomed. Among the organization's most prominent members, in addition to Löwenthal, was another political scientist, Ernst Fraenkel, a Social Democrat, and like Löwenthal a Jew who had returned to Germany from exile. Fraenkel's lectures had been disrupted for months on end, leaving him deeply psychically wounded. He confided to a colleague that if he could, he would emigrate again, as in 1933, adding that only the Berlin working class had kept him from total despair.[116]

The strategy of the professors of the Notgemeinschaft was to appeal to public opinion beyond the academy by publicizing what they saw as the destruction of scholarly standards at the university.[117] Löwenthal published an article in the Berlin newspaper, the *Tagesspiegel*, asserting that the FU under the parity system was on the road to rapid decline: soon its degrees would not be recognized by other institutions, faculty of quality were choosing to leave, and the university was unable to attract new distinguished faculty.[118] His analysis was echoed in the more popular *Bildzeitung*, by the historian Hans Herzfeld.[119] And indeed in the year that followed, one prominent figure after another departed from the university, attributing their "exile" to the political atmosphere. In the fall of 1971, Nipperdey left for Munich. In a letter to the *Wissenschaftssenator*, Stein, he complained that instruction at the university was turning into revolutionary and pseudorevolutionary indoctrination. "Examinations are manipulated and hollowed out, the union of the radicals with the lazy and the less talented bears its fruit."[120] Finally, in 1974, Knauer left the FU for a post in the United States, explaining in a public letter that the implementation of the *Hochschulgesetz* had destroyed the basis of professional activity at the university.[121]

The Notgemeinschaft became the model—and most active branch—of a national organization, the Association for Freedom of Scholarship (Bund Freiheit der Wissenschaft, BFdW). Its most prominent members included Hermann Lübbe, Taubes's colleague from the Poetik und Hermeneutik colloquia. Another was Ernst Nolte, then best known as a historian of fascism, whom Taubes had earlier tried to attract to the FU, and whose confrontation with the radical left at the University of Marburg had drawn him into political activism.[122] Some of the most prominent members of the BFdW were longtime members of the SPD, including Löwenthal and Lübbe.[123]

In the course of 1970, some members of the Berlin faculty organized an association to counter the Notgemeinschaft and support the reformed, triple-parity university. The Aktionsgruppe Hochschullehrer (Action Group of University Teachers) included Taubes and Brentano, as well as left-liberal professors such as the political scientist Alexander Schwan. But dissatisfied with the pace of reform, in November 1970, Taubes organized a weekend seminar of radical faculty members devoted to speeding up the pace of change, to which the liberals were not invited.[124] Some of the liberals, including Schwan and Michael Landmann, now formed their own group, the Reformsozialisten (Reform Socialists), to support president Kreibich and to separate him from his radical vice-presidents, Wesel and Brentano.[125] When that strategy failed, many of the liberals joined with Notgemeinschaft.[126]

April 1972 saw the formation of yet another counter-organization of leftist academics, the Union of Democratic Scholars (Bund demokratischer Wissenschaftler). The organization included academics with close ties to the DKP, the West German Communist Party, such as Reinhard Kühnl, a historian from Marburg best known for arguing that fascism should be understood as another form of bourgeois hegemony. Among its founders was Wolfgang Fritz Haug, editor of *Das Argument*, and a junior faculty member at FB11. When one leading member appealed to Margherita for funds, she reached into her wallet and gave him a 1,000 DM bill. Taubes joined as well.[127]

The "Fall Brentano"

In late 1970, Margherita von Brentano became a *cause célèbre*, achieving national attention with articles in *Der Spiegel* and the *Frankfurter Allgemeine Zeitung*, in addition to several Berlin papers. In May of that year, she had been elected a vice-president of the university, responsible for student matters and curricular reform. Her priority, she said, was for reforms that would contribute to social change and democratization.[128]

Addressing a meeting of Young Socialists (Juso) that October, she was reported to have supported a socialist revolution, and praised the Red Cells for their "continuing pressure from below." According to the conservative Berlin daily, *Die Welt*, she advocated that incoming students be politicized, attacked "bourgeois scholarship," and promoted a policy of deliberate hiring of leftists.[129] Similar articles appeared in the *Frankfurter Allgemeine Zeitung*, the *Tagesspiegel*, and other papers.

The newspaper and magazine reports were based on a protocol of Brentano's remarks, prepared, it soon came to light, by Elisabeth Fischer, who had attended the Juso meeting. She was the wife of Wolfram Fischer, a leading economic historian at the FU and active member of the Notgemeinschaft. The Berlin *Wissenschaftssenator* received a copy of the report and sent it to Brentano, requesting her response. She contended that the report was an utter distortion of her remarks. In reality, she said, she advocated not a socialist university, but a pluralistic academy that made space for socialist theory and scholarship; that while the idea of revolution was obsolete, in the interest of social justice and emancipation it was necessary to bring about changes in social structure; and that these were best achieved by bringing about long-term changes in consciousness and through changes in socialization. Such denunciations, she protested, were a form of McCarthyism.[130] Brentano was defended by the president of the FU, Kreibich, and her fellow vice-president, Wesel.[131]

Yet despite her disavowal of the protocol, one could argue that the protocol had merely made explicit what Brentano affirmed in her letter to the senator. She had indeed advocated using the university to transform the consciousness of students, and her plea for theoretical pluralism meant, operationally, the hiring and promotion of more leftist faculty. An inquiry by the Berlin senate, which interviewed a number of witnesses, concluded that the report was unreliable, and the words quoted were either not direct quotations or had a different meaning in context.[132]

The Notgemeinschaft highlighted the affair and reprinted numerous articles about it in its *Pressespiegel*. *Die Zeit* published a long piece defending Brentano, interpreting the senate's inquiry as "symptomatic of the demolition of democratic rules of the game in Berlin."[133] By contrast, one of Brentano's colleagues, the philosopher Norbert Hinske, wrote a letter to *Die Zeit* asserting that the statements attributed to Brentano were in keeping with what he had witnessed in her actions at the university: "time and again she has unashamedly utilized the radical left wing student groups who now comprise the Red Cells as means of pressure to transform scholarship in the direction of ideology and agitation."[134]

At the end of December 1970, Senator Stein, who had fathered the *Hochschulgesetz*, took it upon himself to cancel three Marxist seminars at the FU, on the grounds that they involved political indoctrination.[135] The courses in question, to be offered in the Division of German Studies (*Fachbereich Germanistik*), were to be taught by leftist lecturers (*Dozenten*) and listed in a pamphlet published by the Rote Zellen Germanistik. Their very titles conveyed the East German ideological framing of the assumptions behind them: "Documents on the Struggle of the German Communist Party to Disempower the Monopolists and the Unification of the Working Class in the West Zones," "Literature on the Restoration of Capital in West Germany," "Literature on the Antifascist Order and the Beginning of Socialistic Reconstruction in the German Democratic Republic." Stein's cancellation of the classes led to protest rallies, student strikes in a number of faculties, and more violent actions.[136] When Stein asserted that the state needed to defend itself from instructors who were opposed to its constitution or who followed a party line, Brentano denied that that was the case; she insisted that for Marxism to get a fair hearing at the university, it needed to be taught by Marxist scholars.[137]

During the summer of 1972, another division of the FU, the Division of Economics (*Fachbereich Wirtschaftswissenschaft*), decided to fill an opening with Ernst Mandel, who had been one of the speakers at the Anti-Vietnam Congress in 1968. Born in Germany but a citizen of Belgium, Mandel was a Marxist economist, much respected by the New Left. As a leader of the Trotskyite Fourth International, he was also an activist, and banned from several countries, West and East, for his activities.[138] Once again, Senator Stein decided that such an appointment would be a bridge too far and that someone committed to overthrowing the social system of the Federal Republic could not be regarded as loyal to its constitution—a prerequisite for such a civil service position. He turned down the prospective appointment.[139]

Having been stymied by the government in the cases of Holz, Mandel, and Lefèvre, on February 23, 1972, Brentano resigned in protest from her position as vice-president of the university.[140] That same year, Brentano was habilitated and promoted to full professor, though she had published no monographs of her own. It is possible that she was promoted on the cumulative record of her past articles. Or perhaps it was an act of friendship and loyalty from her colleagues at the FU: one of the so-called "political habilitations" that were a hallmark of the era.

The East European Dissidents

One topic on which Margherita and Jacob cooperated despite growing acrimony was support for Eastern European leftist dissident intellectuals in Czechoslovakia and Hungary.

The first of these was Karel Kosik, a Czech philosopher. Born in 1926, he had been involved in resistance to the German occupation during the Second World War. After the War, he studied in the Soviet Union and became a member in good standing of the Communist Party of Czechoslovakia and a fellow of the Academy of Sciences. By the mid-1950s, however, he had become an internal critic of the Stalinization of his country. In 1963, he published *Dialectics of the Concrete*, which combined elements of Marxism and existentialism into a variety of Marxist humanism that had considerable purchase in Western Europe among the nondogmatic left. During the "Prague Spring" of 1968, Kosik emerged as a voice of democratic socialism. That uprising was suppressed by the armies of the Soviet bloc. In the repression that followed, Kosik lost his job, as did his wife.

Hans Dieter Zimmermann, a young scholar of literature then at the Academy of the Arts (Akademie der Künste) in West Berlin, went to Prague in 1970 and established contact with Kosik and other dissident intellectuals there. In 1972, Taubes wanted to arrange for Kosik to teach as a visiting professor at the FU during the upcoming academic year. Kosik was eager to do so. Taubes and Zimmermann mobilized Günther Grass, who had the ear of the foreign minister, Egon Bahr, then engaged in negotiations with the Soviet Union and the East Bloc. Bahr raised the issue with the Czech government, but it was unbending, and refused to permit Kosik to take up the post in West Berlin.

Together with Brentano, Taubes arranged for Kosik to receive a stipend from the Heinrich Heine Foundation for Philosophy and Critical Scholarship, a foundation recently established by an heiress to support "critical" thought, of which Margherita was an officer. The stipend was sufficient to support Kosik, his wife, and child. The arrangement was entirely legal and continued for almost two decades.[141] In 1977, Taubes raised some money from Hermann Lübbe and others to try to assist others in Prague, funds that would have to be transferred illegally by individuals who would put themselves at risk. What became of those funds remains unclear.[142]

Taubes and Brentano also reached out to assist dissident leftist intellectuals in Hungary, including the philosopher Agnes Heller. She was part of a circle of younger scholars who had studied with Georg Lukács, from whom they imbibed an interest in philosophy and commitment to Marxism, but one that increasingly diverged from Lukács's own. The circle included her husband, Ferenc Feher, the intellectual historian/philosopher György Márkus, and another philosopher, Mihály Vajda, who developed a critique of "real existing socialism."

When Herbert Marcuse declined an invitation from the Department of Philosophy to return to the FU in 1972, the Department turned instead to Heller. She taught at the FU in late 1972—though her classes were disrupted by a general strike of the students—and it was there that she got to know Jacob and Margherita.[143] She visited them frequently in their home and took note of the fact that they were both high-strung, and that their relationship was tense, perhaps because Margherita suspected any woman whom Jacob befriended of having an affair with him—a suspicion borne out by Jacob's actual behavior. Heller found Jacob charming, witty, and funny—by contrast with Margherita, who was cold and strict. But while Margherita was upright and reliable, Jacob was not. She found him self-aggrandizing, puffing up his own importance. He was clearly a man of extremes, who loved and hated, but was rarely neutral.[144]

After Heller's return to Hungary, in 1977 the regime cracked down on the Budapest circle, dismissing them from their jobs and confiscating their passports. They were saved by the fact that Brentano arranged a stipend for them from the Heine Foundation, payable in Budapest. The stipend of 20,000 DM was enough for the three families to live on (frugally) for a year.[145] After 1977, they were allowed to travel again, and they sought employment abroad. Heller met up with Taubes in Paris, where she and her husband were to have dinner with François Erval, the philosophy editor of Gallimard, the distinguished French publishing house. Taubes told them that Erval was a great friend of his, and invited himself to the dinner. When Taubes left at the end of the meal, Erval turned to Heller and asked, "Who was that man?"[146]

Unable to teach in Hungary, in desperation, Heller and her husband moved to Australia, the only place they were offered ongoing employment, and later to New York, where she pursued a productive career as a philosopher. Brentano and Taubes had provided Heller with the temporary lifeline that allowed Heller and her circle to continue their academic careers.

Benjamin and Scholem

For much of the decades of the 1950s and 1960s, Gershom Scholem was a spectral presence, haunting Taubes from afar in letters and conversations with European and American colleagues.

Yet much to Jacob's chagrin, in the course of the decades that followed, Scholem's reputation rose ever higher in the German cultural firmament, fueled by Scholem's relationship to Walter Benjamin.

Before his link to Benjamin came to public attention, Scholem's name was known to a select readership interested in Jewish studies. That began to change in 1966, when Suhrkamp published an edition of Benjamin's letters, which had been collected and edited by Scholem and Adorno. In the decade that followed, Scholem published a number of interpretive essays suggesting that Benjamin was a Jewish thinker whose work was shot through with Jewish and "metaphysical" elements—elements missed by Benjamin's Marxist interpreters.[147] But it was the appearance in the fall of 1975 of Scholem's memoir of his relationship to Benjamin, *Walter Benjamin: Geschichte einer Freundschaft*, that brought Scholem himself to the attention of a broader German public (the book was translated into English in 1981 as *Walter Benjamin: The Story of a Friendship*). The book was widely reviewed in the prestige press, and a year later Scholem was the subject of a full-length interview broadcast on the German television network, ARD.[148] Then, in the fall of 1977, Scholem published a fetching memoir of his youth and his path to Zionism, *From Berlin to Jerusalem: Memoirs of Youth* (*Von Berlin nach Jerusalem: Jugenderinnerungen*). When he turned eighty on December 5, 1977, the occasion was marked in the German press. 1980 saw the publication of Scholem's own exchange of letters with Benjamin from the 1930s, letters that had until recently been sitting in an archive in East Germany.[149]

The enthusiasm with which portions of the young German leftist intelligentsia embraced Walter Benjamin in the later 1960s and 1970s is difficult to overstate. From having been a hot tip in the 1950s and early 1960s, Benjamin became an icon: images of his contemplative visage graced bookstores, and young Marxists took to citing his work as though it were Holy Writ. Debates about how to interpret Benjamin's work increased interest in his letters, and led to heated public disputes in 1967 about how his published correspondence had been selected and edited by Adorno and Scholem.[150] New Leftist critics charged that during the late 1930s, when Benjamin was dependent upon a stipend from the Institute for Social Research, Adorno and Horkheimer had tried to squelch his more Communist effusions, which smacked to them of too mechanical a conception of Marxism. These critics charged Scholem with interpreting Benjamin as more Jewish than was actually the case. They thought that the letters selected for publication by Adorno and Scholem omitted or downplayed two of the figures who most influenced Benjamin, Asja Lacis and Bertolt Brecht, both Communists.[151]

Benjamin was indeed difficult to pigeonhole, which helped to contribute to his cult. He was part literary critic, part cultural historian, part philosopher, and given to employing theological terms of uncertain status. Throughout his life he was open to conflicting personal influences. His writing could be precise, especially when evoking cityscapes in nineteenth-century Paris or early twentieth-century Berlin; or it could be gnomic, as in his "metaphysical" reflections. He had a consistent ideological distaste for capitalism, along with a sometimes exquisite sensitivity for the surfaces and lures of commercial culture. His notion that history as written reflected the perspective and sensibilities of the victors, and that the proper role of the historian whose sympathies lay with the oppressed was therefore to read the sources "against the grain," was a fruitful programmatic statement. His cultural predilection, like those of his contemporaries Georg Lukács and Ernst Bloch, was toward "romantic anticapitalism."[152] Though he never became a member of the Party, Benjamin's political sympathies, at least in the last decade-and-a-half of his life, were decidedly Communist[153]—what Scholem called his "salon Bolshevism." The thrust of his politics, however, is best characterized as apocalyptic.[154] It was an idea that Taubes found deeply attractive.

Taubes referred occasionally to one or another of Benjamin's more substantial works, such as his analysis of the early modern genre of German drama known as the *Trauerspiel*, from which Taubes adopted the notion of a "historical index." By that Benjamin meant that some historical eras had a certain correspondence or parallelism to the present, such that the present era could best be understood by comparison to some historically distant one.[155] But Taubes's main interest was in two of Benjamin's most speculative works. One was the "Political-Theological Fragment" written early in Benjamin's career in the early 1920s; the other was one of Benjamin's last writings, the "Theses on the Philosophy of History" of 1940. (Taubes explored both texts in a seminar on "secularization" in 1968, and from time to time thereafter.[156]) The earlier text is charitably characterized by Benjamin's sympathetic biographers as "one of Benjamin's knottiest little texts."[157] It is so gnomic as to be subject to infinite interpretation. The later text, the "Theses on the Philosophy of History," makes some discernable claims, or at least suggestions. The most important of these—certainly for Taubes—was that "historical materialism" would ultimately be dependent on "the services of theology" if it was to be victorious, by which Benjamin seems to have meant that Marxism had to mobilize sentiments or emotions that were traditionally associated with religion, especially messianism. That struck a chord with Taubes, who had made a similar claim in *Abendländische Eschatologie*, even before he had read Benjamin.

Benjamin also protested against a conception of history as continuous, and of conceiving of the present as a link in the chain of history—a conception that he thought had led the Social Democrats into political passivity in the 1930s. The proper role of the historical materialist, he contended, was to foster an awareness of the present as what he called a *Jetztzeit*, a moment in which history could "explode" to "blast open the continuum of history"—a process he equated with the "messianic."[158] Taubes found this idea highly congenial as well.

When the Adorno and Scholem edition of Benjamin's letters appeared in 1966, Taubes read them with alacrity. He then sent a long letter to Siegfried Unseld of Suhrkamp Verlag with a copy to Adorno, and with the knowledge that Unseld would forward it to Scholem. Taubes pointed out what seemed to be a mistake in the transcription of one of the Benjamin's letters, in which the word *Halbjahr* (half-yearly) appeared, where *Halljahr* (jubilee year) would make more sense. He had indeed come upon what was either a misreading by Scholem, or (as Scholem suggested in a letter to Adorno) a misprint (*Druckfehler*). On its own, pointing out the textual problem would have been a measure of scholarly cooperation. But Taubes's letter was written in a snide tone, suggesting facetiously that perhaps Scholem's knowledge of kabbalistic texts gave him knowledge of the esoteric significance of *Halbjahr*. He also criticized Scholem for leaving out the name of Benjamin's Russian Communist lover, Asja Lacis, in his commentary to one of the letters, an omission that Taubes characterized as *bitterböse* (very wicked) and as reflecting Scholem's censure of Benjamin's relationship.[159] But as Scholem noted in his letter to Adorno, Lacis had already been mentioned several times in the volume, so the insinuation that Scholem was trying to erase her from Benjamin's biography was spurious. To Adorno, Scholem characterized Taubes's letter as "impudent" (*unverschämten*) and "laden with ressentiment" (*ressentimentgeladenen*); "thus does admiration, when it is not reciprocated, turn into hate."[160] Scholem sent Taubes a curt response, noting the misprint (*Druckfehler*), and adding, "I regret that the tone of your commentary and remarks does not permit me to express my thanks in more personal terms."[161]

Almost two years later, in October 1968, Taubes made another overture to Scholem, ruing the tone of his earlier letter, and chastising Scholem for demonstratively avoiding him at the Bollack's home in Paris[162] Scholem responded that the reasons for their estrangement had not diminished, and that "The use that you have made of your great talent stood at the origin of our estrangement and lamentably determines it still. . . . You pursue a path that has nothing to do with what once led you to me."[163]

Working for Suhrkamp

Suhrkamp's Reihe Theorie, edited by Taubes together with Jürgen Habermas, Dieter Henrich, and Hans Blumenberg, made its first appearance on the book market in November 1966, with the publication of Theodor Adorno's *Negative Dialectics* (*Negative Dialektik*), and Blumenberg's critical defense of modernity, *The Legitimacy of the Modern Age* (*Die Legitimität der Neuzeit*). In the decade that followed, it played an important role, not only for Suhrkamp, but in German intellectual life. In the aftermath of the failure of the generation of student radicals to actually bring about revolutionary transformation after 1968, many turned to an ever greater fascination with "theory," systematic and radical questioning of the established order.[164] Stated in terms of the dynamic coined by Taubes in *Occidental*

Eschatology (*Abendländische Eschatologie*) the failure of messianic, apocalyptic hope led to the rise of Gnostic "theory," the secret knowledge of the fallen nature of the world and the potential for escape from it. The Reihe Theorie published not only works by leading German philosophers and social theorists, but translations of what were regarded as important works from abroad, especially works that had a socially critical edge. The series both reflected and helped to shape the Zeitgeist. Though never a major commercial success, the series was a prestige vehicle for Suhrkamp Verlag.

Of the four series editors, Taubes was the most engaged, dispatching a steady stream of recommendations to Unseld and to the *Lektoren* at Suhrkamp, especially from his journeys to Paris, London, and the United States. He described himself to Unseld as a "hunting dog" (*Jagdhund*) for Suhrkamp. Many of his recommendations were based upon discussions with friends, colleagues, and students. Of the series editors, Taubes was probably the most oriented to the changing tastes of the intellectual-political market and the demand for critical studies from a variety of disciplines. He had a talent for scoping out the intellectual landscape beyond Germany, and in his reports to Suhrkamp provided a thumbnail sketch of the cultural, ideological, or disciplinary significance of the books he recommended for translation and publication.[165] Among the books translated and published on his recommendation were *Interaction Ritual*, by Erving Goffman, an eminent American social psychologist, and John Rawls's *Theory of Justice*, a landmark work of political theory.[166]

Taubes's recommendations were by no means confined to what was fashionable, however. He suggested many works of scholarship in the fields of history (Karl Polanyi's *The Great Transformation* and *Primitive, Archaic and Modern Economies*); history of religion (E. R. Dodds's *Pagan and Christian in an Age of Anxiety*; Elaine Pagels's *The Gnostic Gospels*); the history of ideas (books by Isaiah Berlin, Joachim Ritter); and new trends in the philosophy of the natural sciences (Stephen Toulmin's *Foresight and Understanding* and Paul Feyerabend's *Against Method*) and the philosophy of the social sciences (Charles Taylor's *The Explanation of Behavior*). Some of these were published in the Reihe Theorie, others in Suhrkamp's more general list, the "edition suhrkamp."

Taubes was less interested in advancing any particular point of view than in promoting discussion, debate, and disagreement. That was the characteristic feature of his Hermeneutic Colloquium at the FU. It was also characteristic of his personality that he would often advance contrarian and even outlandish points of view, adjusting his position to provide a counterpoint to his interlocutors. In keeping with those propensities, he repeatedly came up with proposals for edited books and journals that would provide a variety of critical perspectives on some hot intellectual topic. In the early stages of Reihe Theorie, at a time when Jean-Paul Sartre was still the dominant figure in French intellectual life, Taubes planned a volume of critical responses to Sartre's *Critique of Dialectical Reason*, a sprawling attempt to reconcile Sartre's existentialism with his Marxism. Taubes reached out to a number of intellectuals, including Hannah Arendt, for responses. But ultimately too few of the potential authors were willing to contribute, and the plan was stillborn.[167]

Early on in his work for Suhrkamp, Taubes floated the idea of a journal of critical thought along the lines of the Frankfurt Institute's *Zeitschrift für Sozialforschung* of the 1930s and '40s, but nothing came of it.[168] In 1971, Taubes laid out a plan for a journal to be published by Suhrkamp, geared to the younger, leftist intelligentsia of the academic *Mittelbau*. Transdisciplinary in nature, it was an attempt to take the innovations arising from the experience of the student revolt, filter it for quality, and channel it into novel scholarship. Taubes and a team of his younger colleagues in Berlin were to edit it, drawing upon like-minded scholars in Paris and London, such as the sociologist Pierre Bourdieu and the historian Eric Hobsbawm.[169] But it was judged to be unviable: perhaps because there were similar journals already on the market, such as *Kursbuch*, perhaps because of a justified skepticism about Taubes's ability to manage such an endeavor. There would be more plans for such projects in the years ahead.

The composition of the editorial board of Reihe Theorie and the roles of its editors changed over time. In 1970, Hans Blumenberg, who felt out of step with the other three editors, left the board after a monetary dispute with Unseld.[170] In the fall of 1972, Unseld created a new line of scholarly paperbacks, suhrkamp taschenbücher-wissenschaft (stw). He now asked Habermas, Henrich, and Taubes to advise the firm well beyond Reihe Theorie, and raised their monthly honoraria from 500 to 1,000 DM—which made it a substantial supplement to their academic incomes.[171] Five years later, it was raised once again, to 1,200 DM.[172]

Taubes's relationship to Suhrkamp was well known among his colleagues and students. His place alongside Habermas and Henrich on the masthead of Reihe Theorie added to his prestige; that he could get one's manuscript published or book translated gave him an air of influence, and added to the sense that he was someone worth knowing.

Deradicalization

In October 1971, Taubes's colleagues were shocked when Peter Szondi, the director of the Institute for Comparative Literature, vanished without a trace. His body was recovered three weeks later in the Halensee; Szondi had drowned himself at the age of forty-one. The campus was rife with rumors that Szondi had committed suicide because of pressure from leftist groups. The rumor was untrue—he had long suffered from depression—but was illustrative of the atmosphere on campus.[173] At the time of his death, Szondi had already decided to leave the FU and had accepted a chair in Zurich—more evidence that scholars of talent were abandoning ship.

Taubes, as we have seen, had been a supporter of the New Left at the FU since its inception in the mid-1960s. Indeed he had done more than perhaps any other chaired professor to bring about the transformation of the university. By 1972, the left within the university—including the students and the junior faculty of the Institute for Philosophy—was becoming ever more intellectually rigid, simplistic, and dogmatic. It became too much for Taubes to swallow. For years, Taubes had invited Herbert Marcuse to spend time at the university each summer as an *Honorarprofessor*. By January 1972, Taubes was privately advising his old friend *not* to come to the university.[174] The students, he explained, were dogmatic, vulgar Leninists eager to dismiss every idea as "superstructure" to be explained by reference to the economic "substructure." (At the time, the German construction workers union had a campaign to urge young men to join the construction industry with the slogan, "Sei schlau: geh zum Bau" [Be smart, come to construction]. Taubes adapted this to his own purposes. "Sei schlau; bleib' beim Überbau," he advised his students: "Be smart: stick to the superstructure."[175])

As an example of the increasing ideological intolerance, Taubes told Marcuse about the case of Fritz Raddatz, a literary critic and scholar who had been invited to a guest professorship at the university. Taubes noted that as an editor at the Rowohlt Verlag, Raddatz had published voices of the antiauthoritarian student movement from its inception, and had edited a three-volume documentary collection on Marxism and literature. In 1971, Raddatz had received his habilitation, and was thus eligible for a professorial post. Yet the invitation to serve as guest professor had been blocked by a boycott organized by an orthodox Communist group, the Activist Community of Democratic and Socialist Germanists

(Aktionsgemeinschaft demokratischer und sozialistischer Germanisten). Taubes feared that an invitation to Marcuse might engender similar opposition within the Philosophy Seminar. "I can't deny that after the success of the student movement, a leftward routinization has set in," Taubes wrote, "which takes the organizational form of conventicles of the SEW [the West Berlin counterpart of the East German Communist party]."[176]

In the early 1970s, the organizations of the student left shifted in style and substance at universities across West Germany. The Red Cells with their emphasis on dramatic, attention-grabbing action, such as disrupting lectures and occupying buildings, were increasingly displaced by more explicitly Marxist-Leninist groups, many of which owed their direction and funding to the East German government. They were interested in systematically developing institutional influence and control.[177]

In the elections of June 1973, to the *Fachbereichsräten* (the governing councils of the Divisions), the Aktionsgemeinschaften won twenty-eight of seventy-four seats.[178] Hans Peter Duerr, a graduate student who at the time was close to Taubes, remembers a seminar at the FU in which the topic of discussion was what to do with the "reactionaries"—among whom were numbered Willy Brandt and Herbert Marcuse—after the coming revolution. Half the seminar participants wanted to deport them to a reeducation camp on the island of Rügen, in the Baltic Sea; the other half thought such efforts fruitless, and favored simple liquidation.[179] Gert Mattenklott, a scholar of comparative literature who also worked with Taubes at the time, recalled that among the conspiratorial, Leninist radicals, Taubes was regarded as a CIA informant.[180]

Thus, while in public Taubes continued to insist that all was well at the FU, he knew it was not. He was appalled by the decline in the intellectual level of the faculty in FB11.[181]

As the politics of the FU heated up in the 1960s, the name of Jacob Taubes began to appear frequently in the Berlin daily, the *Tagesspiegel*, in both the letters pages and in articles about the university. That was a product of Jacob's relationship with Uwe Schlicht, a reporter who covered university affairs. The *Tagesspiegel* was a liberal paper, less conservative than the leading Berlin broadsheet, *Die Welt*, the flagship of the Springer publishing empire. By the 1960s, the *Tagesspiegel* had a readership of about eighty thousand. But to be profitable, it needed one hundred thousand. So, in an effort to attract younger readers, the editors allowed Schlicht to create a beat in higher education, and it soon became the city's leading intellectual newspaper. In the late 1960s, when the only alternative daily was the *Spandauer Postblatt*, a paper linked to the SPD with only local distribution, non-Communist leftists turned to Schlicht to help get their message across to the broader public.

Taubes served as a source for Schlicht. Their relationship, which went on for more than a decade, was based on mutual utility. For Schlicht, Taubes was an inside source on developments at the FU. For Taubes, Schlicht provided access to a public forum, which increased Taubes's ability to be a player (*Spieler*) at the FU, a role he relished.[182]

At the end of 1973, FB11, and especially the Philosophy Seminar within it, remained riven by ideological conflicts that took the form of disputes over new professorial appointments and promotions. Some of those conflicts made their way into the press, particularly into articles written by Schlicht, who was in contact with the senator for education, Werner Stein, as well as with Michael Landmann and Taubes. They were the major protagonists of what his article dubbed "a cultural civil war." When new appointments were to be made, it fell to Stein as the minister responsible for higher education to choose from a list of three candidates presented by the Division Council. For a position in the philosophy of history, the Council listed as its first choices two Marxists already teaching at the university, Friedrich Tomberg and Wolfgang Fritz Haug, both members of the circle around *Das Argument* and critics of "bourgeois scholarship."[183] (In 1979, Tomberg moved to East Germany, where he became a full professor at the University of Jena.[184]) Stein rejected them, both because he was against internal appointments (*Hausberufungen*) and because he feared that the FB was becoming entirely dominated by a single ideology and thus isolated from the larger community of scholarship. He chose instead to appoint the third candidate on the list, a non-Marxist scholar of Hegel, Reinhart Maurer.[185] During the interview that followed, the acting director of the Institute for Philosophy, Peter Furth, discouraged Maurer from coming. He explained that Maurer's scholarship did not fit in with the dominant interests of the institute namely the development of a materialist theory of knowledge, concentrating on the problem of being and consciousness, base and superstructure. Taubes was at the meeting, and when it was over, assured Maurer that he had acquitted himself well.[186] Maurer accepted the position.

With the definitive departure of Feyerabend, the Institute for Philosophy sought to make an appointment in the field of the theory of science. This time they put Haug first on their list of candidates, which would effectively have turned the chair into one focused on historical materialism.

The "liberal" faculty of the FB, including Michael Landmann, saw these attempted appointments as part of a concerted effort by the hard

FIGURE 12.2. Jacob and Margherita at home. (Ethan and Tania Taubes Collection.)

left to establish a dogmatic Marxist hegemony. Whenever a talented non-communist candidate was considered for a position and invited to campus for an interview, they were told in no uncertain terms by Furth and his comrades that they would be unwelcome. In a long memorandum sent to the *Wissenschaftssenator*, Landmann detailed the process by which new appointments to the philosophy seminar had come to be dominated by a faction sympathetic to the East German regime.[187] Not so, said Margherita von Brentano: rather it was based on the conviction that philosophy had to be practiced in combination with history and the social sciences, in order to deal with the objective conditions of philosophy and the vocational needs of the students.

In public, Taubes argued that the FU's philosophy department was being condemned for what ought to be seen as a strength. A West German philosophy department including three or four professors of positivist inclinations would be considered a philosophical school, he noted; but when three or four Marxists were in the same department, it was called a school for the production of communist cadres (*Kaderschule*). (There were, in fact, far more Marxists in the ranks of his department.) However, he urged his leftist colleagues and students to overcome their tendency to sectarianism, and to refrain from their policy of rejecting other scholars of the highest quality.[188]

There was a growing gap between Taubes's public stance and the sentiments he expressed to friends such as Marcuse. By contrast, Brentano's public stance reflected her authentic and ongoing radical commitments. Jacob felt increasingly isolated within FB11. His growing opposition to the radical left and Margherita's continued support was one of the factors leading to a crisis in their marriage.[189]

Family Tensions

In addition to the growing tensions between Jacob and Margherita over university politics, there were also tensions relating to Jacob's children, and to his erotic behavior.

In the spring of 1970, following the death of Susan Taubes, Ethan, who was then a pupil at the Weston School outside of Boston, had gone to live with Krister and Brita Stendahl.[190] Jacob and Margherita wanted to bring the children to Berlin.[191] There was some conflict between Jacob and Elsa First about what to do with Ethan, as the boy was reluctant to join the father he feared, and First sought to protect him.[192]

In the end it was decided that Ethan would continue his education at the Schiller-College, an English-language institution in Berlin, during the academic year 1971–72.[193] Ethan, who had just turned eighteen, lived apart from Jacob and Margherita in a communal apartment. Tania was to continue high school in the United States. "I have been paralyzed in the last weeks due to personal problems," Jacob wrote to a colleague in New York. "After long telephone calls with Krister Stendahl and Tania I reluctantly decided to let Tania continue her senior high school years in the United States. Needless to say that such a decision leaves some scars on my soul."[194]

At Ethan's urging, Tania moved to Berlin in 1972 and lived with Jacob and Margherita at Winklerstraße 14, attending the John F. Kennedy School. Margherita, who had no children of her own, sought to act as Tania's mother. She expected the girl's filial affection, but she lacked a maternal demeanor. Tania took to spending more and more of her time at the home of one of Margherita's friends, Eva Furth (the wife of Peter Furth of *Das Argument*), who had a daughter of Tania's age. Margherita summoned Eva to her house, berated her for alienating Tania from her stepmother, slapped her across the face, and forbade Eva from seeing Tania again.

Raised to be largely dependent upon one another, Ethan and Tania were close, and Ethan often visited his sister and her friends. Margherita interpreted their emotional bond as evidence that Ethan had incestuous designs on his sister and was trying to turn her against Margherita. That only heightened the already tense relations between Jacob and Margherita. Jacob found himself caught between his relationship with his son and with his wife. He longed to have Ethan stay in Berlin. Uncertain of how to square the circle, Jacob turned to Marianne Awerbuch. He asked her to take Ethan under her wing and help maneuver him back into Margherita's good graces. Beginning in January 1973, Marianne met repeatedly with Ethan and Jacob at her home to discuss how the situation might be remedied.

Ethan was living in an apartment with inadequate heating. To help her brother out, Tania found a woven blanket (kilim) in a closet in their home, and gave it to Ethan—without thinking it necessary to tell Margherita. In May, Jacob and Margherita visited Ethan's apartment to celebrate his birthday. There, Margherita saw the blanket—and concluded that Ethan had stolen it. She presented Jacob with an ultimatum: "Either Ethan leaves or I do!"

Still seeking to bring peace to the Taubes household, Awerbuch arranged for Ethan to see a psychoanalyst, Eva Jaeggi, who examined him and wrote a letter attesting to his psychological health. They also arranged for Ethan to write a letter of reconciliation to Margherita. In July, Jacob asked Ethan to come to their home late at night. The plan was for Ethan to sleep in the basement and for Jacob to explain the situation to Margherita and present her with the psychiatrist's report and Ethan's letter. Then, in the morning, Ethan would appear and effect a reconciliation.

When Ethan emerged in the morning, he found Margherita in the kitchen. Upon seeing him, her face went white and she began to rage and scream at Jacob—who had failed to uphold his part of the plan—and at Ethan. Ethan fled the house, resolved to leave for the United States. Jacob pleaded with him to stay, going so far as to get down on his knees. But Ethan thought it essential to put distance between himself and Jacob, to preserve his own sanity. He enrolled at Bennington College and cut off contact with his father.

By the fall of 1974, Jacob and Margherita were fighting constantly, and tensions were at their peak. When Tania got off the school bus to return to their house, Jacob would sometimes urge her not to go home for fear of Margherita's wrath. Tania would then stay at the home of a friend, first for a night and then for weeks at a time. Margherita became even more stressed. She developed psychosomatic asthma to the point of being bedridden.[195]

Divorce and Psychic Breakdown

Jacob's behavior had long evinced the symptoms of hypomania, the mild form of manic depression typical of type-II bipolar disorder in the stage before the onset of full blown illness. The low threshold of boredom, the propensity toward risk-taking, the strong libido, and the violation of social norms—all were classic symptoms that Jacob had long manifested. The more radical stage is typically set off by a trauma in midlife. And Jacob's life was becoming ever more traumatic.

Marriage to Margherita had not diminished Jacob's urge to engage in erotic activity with women. In 1974, when he was fifty-one and Margherita fifty-two, Jacob had an ongoing relationship with a woman of twenty-three. When Margherita and Tania objected, Jacob did not deny the sexual aspect but insisted that it was a metaphysical relationship, and refused to consider it improper.[196]

For Margherita, this was all too much. She concluded that staying with Jacob would be the end of her. She walked out of their house without leaving a forwarding address, resolved to divorce Jacob.[197] Despite the conflicts between them, Jacob knew he needed Margherita. He was accustomed to being cared for and dreaded being alone.

The psychic pressures generated by his involvement in university politics, his calamitous relationship with his son, and Margherita's decision to abandon him combined to throw Jacob into an ever deeper depression and then a psychotic breakdown that launched him into full-blown manic depression. Signs of creeping psychic disorder were evident in Jacob's behavior and in his classes at the university. The last large philosophy course that he taught before his breakdown was in 1973-74, on "The Logic of Historical Knowledge: Hegel and the Aftermath," a course that drew some 300-400 students. At first, his lectures were impressive, conveying the impression of a vast range of knowledge, though without systematic argument. By the spring of 1974, his lectures were wandering. The course was announced again for the next year. But by then Jacob was no longer capable of teaching.[198]

Jacob descended into full psychosis. He was depressed to the point of catatonia. He lay in bed all day without getting up, failed to eat, and was disoriented. He became paranoid. He went out into the yard and began burying books, fearing that he would be persecuted for the books he had taken with him from Columbia on his colleague Stahmer's library card.[199]

In February 1975, he was admitted to the Schlosspark-Klinik, a residential psychiatric institution in Berlin-Charlottenberg. His physician requested that the patient be protected from mail, telephone calls, and visits. That was followed by a lengthy stay in a sanatorium. Tania went to live with a friend of the family.[200]

On May 14, Margherita had Jacob's furniture moved to his new residence at Hirschsprung 63.[201] Their divorce was finalized on May 22, 1975. It was Brentano who had brought the suit. Jacob was found to be the guilty party and had to pay for the cost of the proceedings.[202] That June, Tania left Berlin to pursue her college education in the United States.[203]

Disoriented, Jacob lost control over his institutes.

The Hermeneutic Institute was housed in a villa on Auf dem Grat. The official responsible for the villa's upkeep, Otto Paltian, took Jacob's colleague Reinhart Maurer to the building, where they found the entryway filled with books and papers, soaked in water. Paltian took a shovel and began clearing it away. He explained that Jacob had given the keys to some wild students, and before they departed they opened the water taps and let them run. The typewriters had been stolen.[204] The Hermeneutic Institute was shut down, its library integrated into that of the Institute for Philosophy.[205]

The University suspended Jacob's control over the account of the Judaica Institute.[206] Marianne Awerbuch was promoted to the position of professor (C-4), and took over control of the Institute. Despite Awerbuch's dissatisfaction with Jacob's direction of the Institute, he had confided in her, and she had mothered him.[207] Now Jacob's relationship with Awerbuch soured as well.

By February 1976, Jacob was in the psychiatric clinic of the FU, his status at the FU that of "unfit for service" (*dienstunfähig*). On April 23, he alarmed the secretary of the Institute for Philosophy, Frau Kupferberg, with the news that he intended to hold a class at his home. She asked the university authorities to intercede. Jacob agreed to have the director of the psychiatric clinic, Dr. H. Helmchen, absolved of his professional commitment to secrecy to attest that Jacob was, from a medical perspective, fit to teach.[208] But when the new semester began in September, he was once again unfit for work, back in the psychiatric clinic. The doctors there had limited success in treating him. He descended yet deeper into depression.[209]

Michael Wyschogrod was on his way to visiting the Soviet Union and decided to stop in Berlin to visit Jacob. He found him in the psychiatric clinic and was shocked at what he saw. Jacob seemed to be languishing; the effects of his illness and of his medication left him unable to read and barely able to walk. Wyschogrod took it upon himself to bring Jacob back to New York for treatment.

Treatment in New York

Jacob arrived in New York, psychotic, paranoid, and depressed. Wyschogrod put Jacob up in a hotel and tried to involve some of his old friends in his care, including Arthur Hyman and his wife, Ruth.[210] From September 7 to November 2, Jacob was treated by Silvano Arieti—a psychiatrist well known for his work on depression, and a former member of Taubes's

Columbia seminar on religion and psychiatry. Jacob was given lithium, the only pharmaceutical treatment then available. But that did not help, either because Jacob failed to take the pills, or because he was unresponsive to the medication. Jacob wrote suicide notes to his children, expressing his love for them and telling them not to be burdened by his death, but that the demons were at his heels and throat. Wyschogrod found the notes on a table while Jacob was sleeping and kept them.

Ethan overcame his alienation from his father and took a hand in getting him treatment. He took Jacob to the Payne Whitney Clinic in Manhattan; in the taxi en route to the clinic, Jacob was catatonic. At the clinic, he saw Doctor William Frosch, another expert in manic depression. Frosch told Ethan that as the person legally responsible for his father, he had two options from which to choose: either permanent institutionalization, or electroconvulsive therapy (ECT), popularly known as electroshock treatment. That involved the intentional triggering of generalized seizures by the use of electricity. At the time ECT was popularly stigmatized by the 1975 release of the movie version of Ken Kesey's *One Flew Over the Cuckoo's Nest*.[211] But it was in fact (and remains) the treatment of choice. It involved twelve separate treatment sessions. After consulting with experts, Ethan decided to have the doctors proceed. The procedure was performed by one of its foremost practitioners, Lothar Kalinowsky.

After Jacob's first treatment, he asked Michael Wyschogrod for something to read—the first time he had read in almost a year. Wyschogrod handed him the book he had with him. When they met the next day, Jacob told him that the book had been written to test him, and that it included as Biblical quotations verses that were not in fact in the Bible. Asked to provide an example, Jacob could not. The paranoia lingered, and Jacob cut off contact with Wyschogrod.

Jacob complied sufficiently to undergo eight sessions. The treatments did help, reducing Jacob's depression and, in part, his paranoia. But rather than complete his course of treatment, he left and returned to Berlin, perhaps upset by the temporary memory difficulties characteristic of the procedure.[212] For much of the remaining decade of Jacob's life, he would cycle between mania and depression. Though he spent much of the rest of his life as a peripatetic, he would return to the United States only once—for Ethan's wedding.

CHAPTER THIRTEEN

A Wandering Jew

BERLIN–JERUSALEM–PARIS, 1976–81

JACOB RETURNED TO BERLIN in December 1976, after his uncompleted electroshock therapy. For much of the next decade, he cycled through depression and mania, along with periods of stability, vigor, and vivacity. The cycles could last for weeks, but could also occur within the same conversation.[1] He was in and out of psychiatric clinics in Berlin. At times, he would be brought to the Urbankrankenhaus in Kreuzberg or to the psychiatric clinic at the Wannsee by the police or others who found him disoriented, and so paranoid he would not tell them where he lived.[2]

While the fundaments of his personality were unchanged, in the wake of his manic depressive breakdown, Jacob's persona was marked by greater intensity, volatility, and theatricality. He sometimes had extraordinary energy and forcefulness, and his obsessions could also be a source of fascination to those to whom he poured out his heart.[3] Manic depressives frequently lack self-insight, and are given to machinations and grandiose plans.[4] His illness might account for the ferocity with which Jacob persecuted his academic enemies—a ferocity that alienated some of his longtime friends. It might also account for the obsession with which he pursued women.

Jacob's travel, too, took on new dimensions. During much of this period, he sojourned each year in Berlin, Paris, and Jerusalem, with frequent stops in Frankfurt to visit Suhrkamp Verlag. In Jerusalem and Paris, he moved between wildly divergent cultures.

Jacob remade himself time and again. He took on roles—as Jew, as antinomian, as scholar, as radical—and could move between them in the course of a single conversation.[5] When Victor Gourevitch encountered him at the Center for Interdisciplinary Research in Bielefeld in 1978, Jacob was wearing a *talit katan*—the fringed undergarment worn by Orthodox men in observance of a Biblical commandment—to which he demonstratively called Gourevitch's attention.[6] In Jerusalem, his black cape and broad black hat gave the impression that he might be a Christian cleric.

Finally, Jacob fashioned a new role, as a self-described "Paulinian" at once authentically and primordially Jewish (*Erzjude*), and as antinomian, a liminal figure between Judaism, Christianity, and revolutionary. It was a role that recalled Naphtha, the revolutionary Jewish Jesuit in Thomas Mann's *The Magic Mountain*, who tries to tempt the novel's hero from the path of bourgeois, liberal rationalism and moderation.

Return to Berlin

Worried that Jacob overestimated his own competence, his son, Ethan, contacted Marianne Awerbuch and asked her to help look after Jacob in Berlin, which she at first tried to do. Jacob informed the FU that as of December 8 he was once again fit for work.[7] He was living by himself in Dahlem at Am Hirschsprung 63, not far from the university, but soon moved to Kreuzberg, a more bohemian neighborhood.[8] He was negligent in taking care of himself. His weight ballooned. He looked disheveled, his clothes stained.[9] When his old friend, the philosopher Joseph Agassi, encountered him in Bielefeld in 1978, Jacob appeared to be a has-been, taking copious pills, a once-handsome man turned bloated.[10] For a while, he lived in his Institute at the FU.[11]

But time and again, Jacob managed to bounce back. In 1980, Jacob lived for some months with Christiane Buhmann, a twenty-seven-year-old student, who found Jacob enchanting and was very much in love with him. Their relationship continued for a time after she moved to Paris later that year to pursue her studies, and their friendship would continue through the end of his life.[12]

Jacob returned to the FU to find that as a result of his erratic behavior, followed by his absence, his institutional base—the Division of Hermeneutics of the Department of Philosophy (Abteilung für Hermeneutik)—had been removed from his control. It no longer had a building of its own, and its library had been integrated into that of the Institute for Philosophy. Jacob spent much of the next three years battling fiercely with his colleagues, trying not only to reclaim his academic turf, but to lay his opponents low. He contended—with a good deal of justification—that the faculty of the Institute for Philosophy was now composed of ideologues and mediocrities, and he launched a campaign for its radical reconstruction, amounting to a "refounding."

Jacob bombarded the president of the university with memoranda: complaining of mistreatment, demanding his rights, and proposing an expansion of his control. In July 1977, he dispatched an eleven-page document laying out plans for a separate "Hermeneutic Field," linked to the Institute for Philosophy, but with its own course of studies.[13]

Margherita von Brentano remained his colleague, but not his ally, and a force to be reckoned with. She and Jacob both served on the directorial committee (*Direktorium*) of the Institute for Philosophy, where they would conduct their bitter feuds in public; in the heat of argument, he once exclaimed, "What, are your ears in your asshole?"[14] Their conflicts could go on from morning to early afternoon. Then they would go to their respective homes, get on the phone, and continue the argument for hours.[15] Jacob took to referring to Margherita as Krupskaya (Lenin's wife) or as Anna Pauker, the Romanian Jewish Communist leader who was believed to have denounced her own husband—though he also used that designation for Marianne Awerbuch.[16]

But at the center of Jacob's battle with his colleagues of the Institute for Philosophy was its chairman, Michael Landmann.

The Struggle with Landmann and Other Battles

The antagonism between Taubes and Michael Landmann was as deep as it was tragic.

Landmann, it will be remembered, played a key role in bringing Taubes to the FU to occupy the chair in Judaica.[17] He thought he saw in Jacob Taubes much of what he himself lacked: a scholar with deep training in Jewish matters who was in some sense at least a representative of the Jewish traditions that had been extirpated in Europe by the Nazis. By 1966, however, as Landmann came to know Taubes better, he discovered that Taubes's self-conception was very different, that he longed for what Landmann characterized as an "exodus [from Judaism] into a new reality beyond [existing] religions" that would somehow maintain the best of the Jewish tradition in a transformed manner, free from "the fleshpots of tradition."[18] To Landmann, Taubes's position was tantamount to believing that "the highest task of contemporary Judaism is its self-surrender." That, Landmann thought, was a position too removed from the specific historical reality of the present, which called for putting a premium on the preservation of Judaism and the Jewish people. "We ought not to add to the extermination from outside an indifference from within." The issue was all the more problematic because Landmann accepted that the Enlightenment critique of revealed religion made traditional claims implausible. But in light of the Holocaust, he thought the relevant criterion for judging tradition was not whether it met the standards of reason, but whether it tended toward preservation or further dissolution (*Auflösung*).

Moreover, Landmann thought that Taubes had a symbolic role to play at the FU: not that he should be expected to serve as a model Jew, but that he should not fall into the opposite extreme. "Perhaps you could do that in the USA," he wrote to Jacob, "but vis-a-vis the Germans we ought not to declare our bankruptcy." The source of tension was in the gap between Landmann's conception of Taubes's role and Taubes's inclinations: "We summoned you to Berlin not only as a scholar of Judaica, but as a Jew; while you want to make Berlin a station of your second and more radical Exodus [from Judaism]."[19] So began their distancing from one another.

The next stage of their alienation came with their divergent responses to the New Left's growing antipathy to Israel following the Six Day War. Writing to Taubes in the fall of 1967, Landmann declared, "This summer, for us, a catastrophe occurred—once again—in that those who we regarded as friends revealed themselves to be enemies."[20] Landmann no longer felt at home with the people who congregated at the Republikaner Club, while for Taubes, he thought, "the Left has unlimited credit, which nothing can reduce."[21]

A year later, their alienation was greater yet. Landmann was not only disappointed by Taubes's unwillingness to take a public position on Israel. He was also distressed to find that Taubes seemed to be entirely disengaged from research and publication in the field of Jewish studies, neglecting the implicit duties of his chair.[22]

Landmann had begun as a sympathizer of university reform. But with the political radicalization of the university and Fachbereich 11, he increasingly moved toward resistance. As we've seen, he fought against the appointment of Wolfgang Lefèvre, for whom Taubes had gone to the mat.

After Taubes's return from New York, the conflict between him and Landmann was no longer ideological: if anything, the ideological poles were reversed. Landmann was acting in his institutional capacity, as the chair of the Institute for Philosophy—a unit increasingly comprised of radical leftist faculty whom Landmann thought it his duty to protect. Taubes was now the outsider, attacking Landmann for protecting a department comprised, Taubes claimed, of ideologues and mediocrities, and a department that had marginalized him. Taubes, who only a few years earlier had contested the claim of the Notgemeinschaft für eine freie Universität that FB11 was becoming a training center for political activists (*Kaderschmiede*), now wrote to newspapers contending that the Institute for Philosophy was dominated by "the party of the DDR [East Germany]."

To drive Landmann out of his position of authority, Taubes adopted a deliberate strategy of ridicule. To launch his campaign against Landmann, in January 1977, Taubes wrote a fourteen-page letter to Oskar Negt, by then a professor in Hanover. In it, he recalled a 1962 conversation in Frankfurt, in which Adorno had said that Landmann performed an important function in combating antisemitism by refuting the stereotype that Jews were smart (*gescheit*). Taubes added a series of incidents meant to display that Landmann was not only an intellectual mediocrity, but a Jewish fascist (since he had once referred to a Japanese student of Derrida as an "exotic type"), who by his actions was a cause of antisemitism! He then affixed a copy of the letter to the bulletin board of the Institute for Philosophy for all to read, with the heading "With greetings to the student representatives of the Institute for Philosophy."[23] Taubes would stand outside of Landmann's door during his office hours and tell students, "Don't waste your time with this idiot."[24]

He also worked to ruin Landmann's reputation beyond the university. Landmann had long been an admirer of Ernst Bloch (though they shared little in common philosophically). On the basis of his interviews with the aging philosopher, conducted over two decades, Landmann compiled a volume of Bloch's pronouncements, which he intended to publish. Taubes launched a campaign to torpedo the project. He wrote the literary editor of *Die Zeit*, Fritz Raddatz, informing him that the publication was not authorized by Bloch, and characterized its prospective publication as a scandal.[25] Taubes succeeded. The volume never appeared.[26]

Taubes's behavior alienated him from many of his former friends. In April 1977, Helmut Gollwitzer, who had once been his comrade-in-arms, wrote Taubes a stinging letter about how he had poisoned the atmosphere in committee meetings.[27] Taubes's relationship with Marianne Awerbuch also deteriorated. Now the acting head of the Judaica Institute, she exercised her prerogatives in an authoritarian manner. Taubes planned to give an upper-level seminar on the theme of Gnosticism, Ancient and Modern, which he wanted to cross-list with the Judaica Institute. Awerbuch objected that there was no such thing as Jewish Gnosticism and refused to list the course. Her claim betrayed a lack of familiarity with the scholarly literature, and Taubes was outraged. Their dispute was reported in the pages of the *Tagesspiegel*, and Taubes complained of it bitterly in both his letters to colleagues and in publications.[28]

Taubes now began to persecute Awerbuch as well, declaring, "I've already driven two women to suicide. You will be the third,"[29] and that he would see to it that she would know no rest until her dying day. For a time, Awerbuch would not enter the Judaica Institute for fear of her health.[30] Finally, her husband, Max, journeyed from Israel to Berlin to confront Taubes. He came to the office, grabbed Taubes by the neck, and began to strangle him. The police were called and rescued Jacob.[31] Later, Awerbuch would have the locks of the Judaica Institute changed to keep Taubes from entering the premises.

With Taubes's extrusion from Judaica, the professorship he had occupied was vacant. The FU sought to hire Amos Funkenstein for the post. They negotiated with him for years before he definitively turned down the offer. They then turned to Peter Schäfer, a German Catholic scholar of Talmud and of Jewish mysticism. A student of Arnold Maria Goldberg in Frankfurt, Schäfer had studied in Israel with Ephraim Urbach and Gershom Scholem, and held a chair in Cologne. Schäfer's appointment was controversial because unlike Taubes (or Funkenstein), Schäfer was not Jewish. Awerbuch opposed the appointment. The leadership of the FU asked the head of the Berlin Jewish community, Heinz Galinski, for his opinion. He responded that whether or not the candidate was Jewish was of no concern to the organized Jewish community. The Israeli ambassador favored the appointment, since Schäfer was Hebrew-speaking and had good connections to Israel. Taubes was asked for his view. "Does a professor of mathematics need to be a triangle?" he replied.[32]

During the months when Taubes was being treated in New York, the presidency of the FU had changed. Kreibich was replaced in 1976 by Eberhard Lämmert, a distinguished scholar of German and comparative literature who had previously taught at the FU, and who knew Taubes as a colleague. Less radical than his predecessor, he sought to maneuver among the various political factions that had developed to influence the governance of the university. In the months after Taubes's return, Lämmert found himself bombarded by lengthy letters and memoranda from both Landmann and Taubes.

In April 1977, Taubes applied to take a research leave during the upcoming winter semester. His request was turned down on a technicality by the governing committee of his division (*Fachbereichsrat*)—a sign no doubt of the enmity of his colleagues.[33]

On June 15, Taubes submitted to the president a long memorandum in which he offered a blistering critique of what had become of the Institute for Philosophy, along with a plan for its refounding.[34]

Three days later, Landmann reported to Lämmert that Taubes regularly abused the staff at the Philosophy and Judaica Institutes. Taubes had taken to calling the police over every bagatelle, including thrice in the past week.[35] On June 20, Landmann wrote again to the president, pleading that he do something about Taubes. From fifteen years of experience with Taubes, Landmann wrote, he could attest "that Mr. Taubes has a malevolent nature. Time and again he has sought out a victim, whom he defames and injures mercilessly. . . . Now that his illness makes him unrestrained, there is hardly anyone who can be sure they will not become the object of his attacks, of his vicious slander and injuries."[36] Landmann's letter was buttressed by a memo from the secretary of the Institute for Philosophy, reporting that Taubes had not only insulted and threatened her, but had acted so aggressively against other members of the staff that she had called the police.[37]

A few weeks later, President Lämmert dispatched a long letter to Taubes, for which he demanded Taubes's signature of receipt. He began by noting that despite his numerous discussions with Taubes about his behavior at the Institutes for Philosophy and Judaica, Taubes had failed to improve. To create peace in the institutes, Lämmert decided that Taubes would have his office elsewhere. And despite the fact that the Division Council had turned down Taubes's request for a research leave, "for the sake of peace in the workplace," the president was now granting the request, on the stipulation that Taubes was to spend the semester at the École normale supériere in Paris and at scholarly congresses, but that in any event, he was not to set foot in Berlin. Taubes signed the letter of receipt later that day—"under protest."[38]

Taubes did in fact spend most of the next semester in Jerusalem and in Paris. While he was away, his colleagues tried to further constrain his sphere of activity and initiated actions to have him permanently dismissed. Together with other colleagues, Landmann wrote to President Lämmert, making the case for forcing Taubes into retirement.[39] Landmann, Furth, Awerbuch, and Carsten Colpe met with the president to discuss Landmann's memo. Colpe, the professor of Iranian studies whom Taubes had helped to bring to the FU and who had taught courses with him over the years, opined that he doubted that Taubes was still capable of fulfilling his teaching and research duties. The faculty members described Taubes's persecution of a troubled young philosopher who had subsequently committed suicide, as well as the obscene postcards Taubes had sent Landmann from Paris. They reported that Taubes had retained a lawyer to deal with his relations to the university.[40]

Taubes's egregious behavior was documented in a stream of letters, memoranda, and official notices that circulated between the administrative organs of the FU. These were copied by Landmann and sent to Gershom Scholem, who kept an ever-thickening file about his erstwhile protégé, its contents serving to deepen his antipathy.[41]

While his colleagues were trying to limit his purview, Taubes put forth a proposal to reconstruct the Institute for Philosophy at the FU, addressing it to President Lämmert.[42]

During the semester that he was supposed to remain away from Berlin, Taubes returned repeatedly to the FU, mainly to defend himself from the machinations against him.

On one occasion, while on a visit to Suhrkamp in Frankfurt, he was informed by the administrator of the Institute for Philosophy, Otto Paltian, that the governing committee of the Institute was about to hold a meeting to consider a measure that would threaten Taubes's hermeneutics program. Taubes hopped a train to Berlin and appeared at the meeting. Shocked to see him there, Landmann abandoned the meeting and made his way to the president's office, exclaiming, "Taubes is here!" He then got on his bicycle, drove to his room, packed, and took the train back to his home in St. Gallen, Switzerland. His physician there attested that Landmann could not return to Berlin until Taubes had left.[43]

When Landmann discovered that Taubes was set to publish a piece in honor of Scholem's eightieth birthday in *Die Welt*, he called the cultural editor of the paper and warned him that Taubes was mentally ill (*geisteskrank*). When Taubes learned of this, he was understandably enraged.[44] The piece was published nevertheless.

In the months that followed, Taubes intensified his campaign against Landmann.[45] Close to the age of mandatory retirement, Landmann hoped to get an academic appointment at the University of Haifa, where he had served as a visiting professor. (Lacking a knowledge of Hebrew, he taught in English.) Taubes, who had begun to visit Israel with some regularity, journeyed to Haifa to denounce Landmann to faculty members there. Taubes then went a step further and himself applied for a position at the university. Perhaps Taubes was serious about such a move; more likely, as Landmann suspected, Taubes was trying to torpedo Landmann's own chances.

In January 1978, Landmann reported to his friend at the University of Haifa, the philosopher Michael Strauss, that the president of the FU had initiated a disciplinary procedure against Taubes for having publicly insulted Landmann by comparing him to Idi Amin. In March, Landmann was visiting in Israel and was hospitalized with what his doctors diagnosed as psychosomatic illness, attributed by Landmann's paramour to "that monster, Taubes." Taubes sent Landmann a long, insulting letter ("You yourself know that you are a disgrace for this, indeed for any, university") in which he threatened to destroy Landmann's reputation and initiate a vote of no confidence unless Landmann resigned as chair (*Geschäftsführer*) of the Institute for Philosophy.[46] Landmann chose to resign, and shortly thereafter retired from the FU. In his place, Margharita von Brentano was elected as acting chair. Taubes called on President Lämmert to appoint an outsider (*Staatskommissar*) as chair, lest the Institute be brought to the edge of ruin by "the trench warfare that is to be expected in the near future."[47]

Taubes's persecution of Landmann shocked many of their common friends. Some, like Ernst Simon, stopped corresponding with Taubes, or like Armin Mohler, admonished him for his conduct.[48] When Taubes's daughter, Tania, visited with the Bollack family in Paris, Jean Bollack, who had known both Landmann and Taubes for decades, took her aside and solemnly informed her, "You need to know that your father is the incarnation of evil."[49]

In 1978, Taubes sought to invite the "Pope of German philosophy," Hans-Georg Gadamer, to the Institute for Philosophy as a visiting substitute for one of its unfilled chairs. The governing committee regarded Gadamer as too bourgeois and refused to even consider the proposal.[50] Taubes then hit upon a tactic to demonstrate the ignorance of his colleagues. He proposed that the chair be temporarily filled by Prof. Dr. K. Wojtyla (University of Cracow), whom he described as a distinguished scholar of the work of Max Scheler, and as "well known, well beyond the borders of his country." Taubes noted that "W. speaks German, French, and Italian, almost without an accent. He is known to be active, and with considerable success, beyond his academic activity. . . . I don't believe that the Polish government would object to him teaching at the Free University of Berlin, especially in the Institute for Philosophy, though he cannot be reckoned as belonging to the Marxist camp of Polish philosophers."[51]

This time, the governing committee of the institute approved Taubes's proposal. Only then did he tell them that Prof. Wojtyla was also Pope John Paul II. Taubes thought this hilarious; his colleagues were not amused.

FIGURE 13.1. Jacob in his office, July 1978. Photo by Klaus Mehner.
(Granger Historical Picture Archive.)

The End of FB11 and the Refounding of Philosophy

By the late 1970s, a decade of politicization had reduced FB11 to the edge
of dysfunction and beyond. In the end, Taubes emerged from his battle
victorious, at least on the institutional level. He had a hand in bringing
Fachbereich 11 to an end and in reconstituting the Institute for Philosophy.

Taubes, who had presided over the creation of FB11, now became an
advocate for its dissolution. To the liberal weekly magazine *Der Spiegel*, he
lamented that whole disciplines had become incestuous, ignoring the rest
of the scholarly world and instead promoting (i.e., offering doctorates)
and habilitating from among their own ranks, and then promoting these
hothouse products to professorships. He decried the declining academic
standards within FB11. And he blamed the failure of the FB11 to create a
solid basic course of studies (*Grundstudium*) on "that golden horde of student tutors" who administered the basic courses as if they were a sinecure
(*Pfründe*). "What they created," the magazine quoted him as saying, "was
a sort of mindless Ping-Pong, an abstract competition between Karl Marx
and Max Weber, in which Marx always won by 21–15."[52]

The blatant domination of FB11 by the far left made it an embarrassment to the city's government.[53] The response of the leadership of FB11
to the case of Wolf Biermann was a turning point. Biermann was an East
German singer-songwriter who had become a leading dissident and was
popular in both East and West Germany. (Taubes and Marcuse had met
with him in 1968.[54]) In November 1976, after he gave a sold-out con-
cert at the Sporthalle in Cologne, Biermann was deprived of his citizenship and expelled by the East German Communist regime. The acting
chair (*Stellvertretender Vorsitzender*) of the governing committee of
FB11 was Peter Furth, who had begun as an independent Marxist critical of East German Communism, but had become more favorable toward
the East German regime. He was the leader of a number of like-minded
younger faculty members.

Furth issued a public letter to the East German head of state, Erich
Honecker, on behalf of the governing committee, protesting the expulsion
of Biermann. But the letter was couched in language both obsequious and
saturated in the ideological lingo of the East German Communist Party
(SED) itself, claiming that that expulsion of Biermann would strengthen
those who sought to defend "the inhumanity of the monopolistic capitalist system against the working class movement and against the German
Democratic Republic."[55]

In 1977, Peter Glotz, a young Social Democratic politician, arrived in
Berlin to take over the role of *Wissenschaftssenator*. He befriended the
higher education reporter for the *Tagesspiegel*, Uwe Schlicht, and through
Schlicht came to know Taubes, who was more than eager to offer Glotz his
guidance.[56] Together, they would bring about the transformation of the
Institute for Philosophy, rescuing it from the ideological rut into which it
had fallen, and restoring some of the reputational sheen of the FU.

Glotz was well aware of the sensitive situation in which the FU found
itself. In 1977, the Red Army Faction murdered the Prosecutor General
of West Germany (*Generalbundesanwalt*), Siegfried Buback. A student newspaper at the University of Göttingen published an article that
expressed the author's "quiet joy" on learning of the murder. The article,
signed "Mescalero," was reprinted by a committee that included twelve
faculty members of the FU. It became a touchstone for a wider debate
about the role and extent of sympathizers with the RAF. In an interview
with *Der Spiegel*, Glotz estimate that 15 to 20 percent of university students sympathized with this view.[57]

Glotz was also interested in developing an undergraduate program
that would combine humanities and social sciences, in the manner of

American liberal arts degrees. He decided to visit some leading American universities to see how this might be done. Taubes wrote to Walter Kaufmann at Princeton and to Noam Chomsky at MIT, urging them to meet with Glotz, which they agreed to do.[58] Glotz also met with Eric Voegelin at the Hoover Institution at Stanford, where they discussed the situation at the FU's Institute for Philosophy.[59]

In March 1978, Taubes wrote a long memo to Glotz, "On the Situation and Reconstruction of the Institute for Philosophy," in which he once again characterized the Institute as "an unholy alliance of mediocrity and extremism," the former referring to Landmann, the latter, to the ever more radical Marxists among the instructors. In consultation with Schlicht and Taubes, Glotz decided upon a double strategy. He put an end to internal appointments (*Hausberufungen*), and suspended new appointments. Confronted with the unwillingness of distinguished philosophers to move to the FU, he put together a package deal in which several senior appointments—selected not by the existing faculty, but by a committee of distinguished philosophers from outside the university, chaired by Margherita von Brentano—would be made at the same time, assuring prospective hires that they would be in good company. Glotz's task was made easier by revisions to the Berlin Higher Education Law (*Hochschulgesetz*) in 1978, which gave the government more authority in the running of the universities.

First an offer was made and accepted by the historian of philosophy Karlfried Gründer. Offers were then extended to Michael Theunissen (age forty-six), to Ernst Tugendhat (age forty-nine), and Jürgen Mittelstraß (who turned the FU down). Theunissen and Tugendhat were left-liberal in their politics, but both were respected philosophers, and neither was a Marxist. They were promised not only a new building and library, but that they could bring their existing assistants with them.[60] As part of the deal orchestrated by Glotz, to placate the existing Marxist faction, Wolfgang Fritz Haug was appointed to a tenured, albeit less prestigious professorship.[61]

Theunissen, who had studied at the FU before being appointed elsewhere, was the author of a highly regarded book on the relationship between the self and the other in twentieth-century philosophy, *Der Andere* (1965), and of studies on Hegel. During his student days at the FU, he had been part of the circle around Helmut Gollwitzer, and had also contributed funds to the leftist journal *Das Argument*. His friendship with Taubes went back to the early 1960s, and indeed it was Taubes who convinced him of the relevance of Buber's *I and Thou* to the theme of *Der*

Andere. The FU had tried to lure Theunissen back in 1970, but at that time he found the existing faculty too dogmatic, and the situation too chaotic. Now he agreed to come, but only on the condition that his colleague Tugendhat would join as well.[62]

Taubes had sought to bring Ernst Tugendhat to the FU ever since first meeting him in 1966. Tugendhat was the scion of an enormously rich Jewish family from German-speaking Europe: the family home in Brno, Moravia, the "Villa Tugendhat" was designed by Mies van der Rohe and considered a masterpiece of Bauhaus architecture. With the rise of National Socialism, the family had moved to Switzerland and then to Venezuela, where they owned large estates. There, encouraged by an aunt who had studied with Heidegger, the fifteen-year-old Ernst read *Sein und Zeit*, a book that left an indelible impression upon him and made him eager to study with Heidegger. He went first to Stanford for his undergraduate education, where he was schooled in classics. Then, in 1949, he made his way to Freiburg, only to find that Heidegger was no longer permitted to teach because of his prominent support of Hitler and the Nazi regime. Tugendhat studied instead with some of Heidegger's students, then with Heidegger himself. In the 1960s he spent time in the United States and developed an interest in analytic philosophy.[63] His work was unusual for attempting to use analytic philosophy, focused on the use of language, to explore the large questions characteristic of German philosophy. He was a dean at the University of Heidelberg during the era of the student left, which he had supported. Then he joined Habermas at the Max Planck Institute in Starnberg.[64] When Tugendhat received the offer to come to Berlin, Michael Landmann warned him that Taubes was an evil man, and suggested he refuse the offer. But Tugendhat came nonetheless.[65]

Thus by 1980, FB11 had been dissolved. The study of philosophy at the FU had been transformed by political intervention, with the support of some faculty, but the resentment of others. Among the vociferous defenders of FB11 in its final stage was Marianne Awerbuch, who was serving as its dean.[66] Her defense seems to have been grounded less in any sympathy for the dominant ideology of the Division than in a desire to defend the institution in which she served. Sometimes, where you stand depends on where you sit.

Theunissen and Tugendhat arrived in Berlin in 1980, bringing with them their own assistants and graduate students. With their advent, Taubes's role in the philosophy department was eclipsed.[67] But he had regained his Hermeneutic Institute, which once again had its own offices, in a small villa at Thielallee 43, and a secretary, Ina-Maria Gumbel.

Nolte and Suhrkamp Verlag

Upon his return to Berlin in a mental state that rendered him reckless and unrestrained, Taubes got himself expelled from the editorial quartet of Suhrkamp's Reihe Theorie. The causes of his expulsion were partly ideological, partly a consequence of his behavior. Yet Taubes was ultimately kept on as an advisor by Suhrkamp's publisher, Siegfried Unseld, a testament to the utility of Taubes's wide-ranging knowledge to the firm.

During his long mental crisis, Taubes failed to communicate with Suhrkamp throughout 1975, no longer sending book recommendations or fulfilling his role as editor. At the end of the year, Unseld decided to stop paying him his monthly honorarium, but after a request from Taubes, agreed to continue to pay half the stipend during the period of Taubes's illness.[68] In June 1976, Taubes informed Unseld that he was well again—which was hardly the case—and Unseld raised his monthly honorarium back to its previous level of 1,200 DM. Meanwhile the other editors, Jürgen Habermas and Dieter Henrich, had opted to bring on as an additional editor of the series Niklas Luhmann, a wide-ranging social theorist. Best known for developing a systems-theory approach to contemporary society that stressed the indispensable role of functioning institutions to human well-being, Luhmann had sparred intellectually with Habermas.[69] His addition provided a slightly more conservative voice to the editorial quartet.

Taubes's attempt to add a more radically right-wing author to Suhrkamp's offerings would lead to his expulsion from Reihe Theorie. From his student days on, Taubes had read and associated with right-wing intellectuals, while regarding himself as a man of the left. He had long encouraged his students at the FU to read leading right-wing thinkers, such as Carl Schmitt. In a letter to Unseld of April 1974, he expressed his frustration at the unwillingness of those on the left to confront the critiques of liberal society stemming from the right.[70] Now, returning to active duty as an editor of Reihe Theorie, he pressed his case. He wanted Suhrkamp to publish his controversial colleague, the historian Ernst Nolte.

Taubes had long admired Nolte.[71] In 1973, Nolte arrived at the FU as a professor in the Friedrich-Meinecke Institut, the university's Department of History. He was still best known for his path-breaking book of 1963 on comparative fascism. In his previous appointment at the University of Marburg, Nolte had confronted the powerful radical left on the faculty and among the students, at an institution where the Communist influence was particularly strong. In response, he became a leading member of the anti-New-Left Bund Freiheit der Wissenschaft. With a long-standing interest in Marx, Nolte was one to confront the Marxists on their own terms. But when, during his first year at the FU, he offered a seminar on Marx, the leftist students organized a boycott, and the seminar had no enrollment.

Taubes came to dinner at Nolte's home from time to time, though never with Brentano. Her acquaintance with Nolte went back to their student days during the Second World War, when both had studied with Martin Heidegger in Freiburg. In fact, during a bombing raid in 1944, Nolte lay at Brentano's feet in a university cellar into which they had both gone for protection. But as a staunch woman of the left, she did not consort with the likes of Nolte at the FU. Taubes, by contrast, did, perhaps because both Nolte and Taubes were intellectually intense and unconventional. To Nolte, Taubes seemed a fountain of ideas (*Ideenverstreuer*) and a colorful figure amidst the grey of university life.[72]

Upon his return to Germany from his psychiatric treatment in New York, Taubes read—after his fashion—Nolte's most recent book, *Deutschland und der Kalte Krieg*, published in 1974. The book was a sprawling depiction and analysis of what Nolte regarded as the deep ideological roots of the Cold War. That struggle was grounded, in Nolte's analysis, in the radically different responses to the challenges of modernity offered by modern liberalism, represented by the United States, and communism, centered in the Soviet Union. The division of Germany, in this reading, was a product not so much of contingent events as of deeper historical processes. The book's style of argument was unorthodox, combining wide-ranging but unsystematic historical narrative with philosophical reflection, and empirical history with the philosophy of history. It proceeded by novel if idiosyncratic comparisons, comparisons that tended to leave the reader with the sense that the German experience of National Socialism was no more than a radical version of processes that were ubiquitous. Except for Britain and the United States, every major nation with claims to power, Nolte asserted, had "its own Hitler era, with its own monstrosities and sacrifices."[73] The book devoted many pages to Zionism and Israel, noting the purported similarities between the analysis of the Jewish condition by antisemites and by early Zionists, such as Moses Hess, and suggesting that his Zionist heirs engaged in a "racial struggle" (*Rassenkampf*).[74] "Despite all the differences in their origins and goals, Zionism and National Socialism were far too related for the total opposition between them to be convincing in the long run," he wrote.[75] Nolte had a style that suggested odious parallels, while backing away from their full implications.

Taubes, however, was impressed by Nolte's book—probably by its attempt to combine philosophical reflection with empirical history. Taubes tried to convince Nolte to publish his book in paperback with Suhrkamp, and tried to convince Unseld that Suhrkamp should become Nolte's publisher. Unseld discussed the possibility of bringing Nolte to Suhrkamp with Jürgen Habermas, who had done so much to shape the public image of the imprint. Habermas in turn consulted with his old friend, Hans-Ulrich Wehler (they had been in the Hitler Youth together as teenagers), a champion of the new social history, and a man of impeccable Social Democratic commitments.[76] Wehler apparently advised Habermas that Nolte was too right-wing for Suhrkamp, a judgment that Habermas conveyed in no uncertain terms to Unseld. Habermas called Taubes and chastised him for putting the reputation of Suhrkamp Verlag at risk.[77] This we know from Taubes's letters to Nolte and to Habermas: remarkably enough, Taubes also sent copies of his letters to Nolte to Habermas, and his letters to Habermas to Nolte, which must have impressed upon each recipient Taubes's inability to maintain confidentiality. In a letter to Nolte, he set out reasons that were also intended for Habermas's eyes. "I think that right-wing thought, such as Carl Schmitt and [Reinhart] Koselleck, belongs on our list: 'right-wing' insofar as not fascistic, insofar as it is radical and not lukewarm, has a claim to be heard. Here [in Germany], fascism has discredited everything that is 'right-wing,' 'conservative' etc. and left it speechless, and has thereby led to the neglect of some themes that are authentic questions."[78] This was a genuine divergence between Habermas and Taubes. Habermas seemed to believe that his identity as an anti-fascist man of the left entailed resisting any concession to the legitimacy of right-wing ideas, as opening the door to a return of Nazism. He would shortly edit a collection of essays, *Observations on "The Spiritual Situation of the Age"*, published by Suhrkamp, devoted in good part to a critique of conservative intellectuals. He characterized the contributors to his volume as "those who stand committed to the traditions against which a German regime established itself in 1933"—with the clear implication that their opponents stood *for* the traditions of the regime that established itself in 1933.[79] Taubes, by contrast, was more intellectually tolerant— open to ideas from wherever they came.

In the meantime, a series of misunderstandings and crossed messages poisoned Unseld against Taubes—though only temporarily, as it turned out. Taubes, who was traveling in Paris and Zurich, had given Nolte the impression that Unseld would be calling him about a book contract. Unseld was unwilling to commit himself before consulting with Habermas. When

Unseld did call Nolte he was vague; Nolte seemed puzzled, and Unseld embarrassed. Unseld blamed Taubes for putting himself and Nolte in such an awkward position by promising Nolte a book contract without being authorized to do so. Taubes disputed that he had made such a promise, and eventually Unseld accepted his account—but by then a good deal of damage had been done.[80]

Furious at Habermas for his role in excluding Nolte, Taubes wrote him a long letter in which he revived his accusations against Habermas for his critiques of the New Left. He referred to Habermas and himself as "the heirs of Frankfurt, each of us in our own way: you as the legitimate child, I as the illegitimate son." Startlingly, he attached a copy of the ten-page critique of Habermas that Horkheimer had sent to Adorno in September 1958—the letter in which he vetoed Habermas's habilitation at the Frankfurt Institute on the grounds that Habermas was too radical. It was a letter totally unknown to Habermas, or to almost anyone else for that matter. (In a subsequent letter, Taubes claimed that he had obtained a copy from an archivist at the Heine Foundation; but it may have reached him through Rolf Tiedemann, Adorno's former student and Taubes's former assistant, who edited Adorno's papers.) For Habermas, the content of the letter was bound to be startling. Taubes's aim (aside, perhaps, from unsettling Habermas) was to draw a parallel between Horkheimer's rejection of the young Habermas as too radical during the 1950s, and Habermas's rejection of the radicalism of Dutschke and Krahl in the late 1960s and early 1970s. Habermas, he wrote, was the legitimate heir of Frankfurt, despite the Horkheimer letter: "Abraham slaughters Isaac; Horkheimer, Jürgen Habermas." At the top of the Horkheimer letter, Taubes wrote, "Send back to Taubes for the safe!"[81]

None of this was relevant to the dispute at hand between Taubes and Habermas about whether Suhrkamp ought to publish Nolte. It seems to have been a maneuver by Taubes to throw Habermas off balance—and evidence that Taubes himself was unbalanced at the time. The string of accusations was followed by an invitation that Habermas participate in Taubes's colloquium at the FU on the genealogy of the New Left. Taubes sent a copy of this highly personal letter to Nolte as well.

On March 7, Unseld wrote to Taubes informing him that he was removing Taubes from his position as coeditor (*Mitherausgeber*) of Reihe Theorie. But he would keep Taubes on as an advisor (*Berater*) to the press— though at half of his previous honorarium.[82] Taubes pleaded with him to reconsider, maintaining his innocence in the misunderstanding about whether Suhrkamp would sign up Nolte. He wrote to Habermas and to Dieter Henrich, lamenting his treatment by Suhrkamp during his time of psychic distress, and suggesting that they display their solidarity with him by threatening to resign as editors of the series if Taubes was not reinstated as editor.[83] It was curious of Taubes to speak of solidarity, Habermas responded, as Taubes had shown a lack of solidarity toward him for the last decade, aiming a constant stream of criticism at him.[84] Henrich responded at greater length. He had spent the last decade teaching in Berlin, at Columbia, and at Harvard, retracing in reverse Taubes's own institutional affiliations. He wrote of his affection for Taubes, his gratitude toward him for the early years of their friendship, and for the ongoing stimulation that Taubes offered. But he knew from his own experiences how difficult it was to defend Taubes.

> I have had occasion to act as your defender (literally) hundreds of time. For I've lived and still live—not only through my ties in Berlin, but especially through my ties in America—in circles who know you very well and in which the complaints about you and the hostility toward you are louder and more vehement than against anyone else. You make it difficult for your few friends.[85]

In the end, Unseld conceded that he been wrong about what Taubes had promised Nolte. He remained firm that Taubes would no longer be part of Reihe Theorie. But he agreed to keep Taubes on as a paid advisor to the publishing house on a trial basis—and at the same honorarium (1,200 DM) he had been earning as an editor of Reihe Theorie. Taubes was to visit the Suhrkamp offices in Frankfurt every month to consult with the staff editors (*Lektoren*).[86]

Taubes was eager to display his value to the firm. He resumed sending a stream of suggestions of books for Suhrkamp to publish, including a new edition of Rosenzweig's *Star of Redemption*, and a recent book by his friend, Emil Cioran, for which he suggested another friend, François Bondy, as translator.[87] At the same time, he developed plans for yet another journal, and reached out to Syndikat Verlag—a rival publisher, headed by Karl Markus Michel and Axel Ruetters, two editors who had left Suhrkamp after disputes with Unseld.[88] Unseld warned Taubes in no uncertain terms that he could not stay on at Suhrkamp if he also worked with its competitor.[89] The journal never got off the ground. But in the end, Unseld was satisfied enough with Taubes's input to keep him on, and even to raise his monthly honorarium to 1,300 DM—a sum equal to fifteen percent of his professorial salary.[90]

To Unseld, Taubes lamented the fact that the editors at Suhrkamp were religiously tone deaf, seeing in religion nothing but an illusion.[91] Unseld was sympathetic to this critique, and eager for Jacob to help the firm build its list in the field of religion, above all through its Insel imprint. In 1981, Jacob reached out to Hans Jonas about a German translation of *The Gnostic Religion*—the book that Taubes had commissioned Jonas to write for Beacon Press—to be published by Suhrkamp.[92] (Taubes arranged for a translator. But in the end, Jonas decided to remain with his old publisher. That project fell through, and the book was eventually published by Insel Verlag.[93]) Unseld encouraged Taubes to keep making suggestions about books on the themes of religion and the critique of religion. Taubes obliged with detailed and erudite letters, some of them virtual review articles.[94]

Taubes's relationship with Suhrkamp came to an end in June 1982. Unseld remained satisfied with him. But by then, the firm was incurring huge losses on its scholarly list, and Unseld decided to end his contract with the editors of Reihe Theorie, and with Taubes as well.[95] Unseld's final letter to Jacob expressed his appreciation for the stimulus that Taubes had offered him over the preceding two decades, and for all he had done for the firm.[96]

For Taubes, the link to Unseld and to Suhrkamp had been vital. It provided a substantial supplement to his professorial salary, contacts with key gatekeepers in German intellectual life, an outlet for his intellectual energies, and a penumbra of influence that greased his contacts with intellectuals in Europe and the United States.

Return to Jerusalem

While appalling some of his Berlin colleagues, Taubes was enchanting acquaintances in Jerusalem and Paris.

Taubes had hoped to return to Jerusalem for a visit in the summer of 1964. But the fatal illness of his sister prevented him from doing so. He planned to do so once again in December of that year, and wrote to Martin Buber about visiting with him—but once again decided not to.[97] Another decade and more went by, a decade that included the suicide and burial of his father in Jerusalem. Yet again he put off visiting there.

After his mental breakdown, his return to Berlin, and the behavior that led to his forced leave of absence from the FU, Taubes tried again. Perhaps in an attempt to make a fresh start, or simply because his manic depression had reduced his previous inhibitions, he resolved to visit Jerusalem during Passover of 1977. But before proceeding, he dispatched from Paris a letter of some twenty pages to Gershom Scholem, a letter (as he put it to Arthur A. Cohen), "which I jotted down just before leaving for Israel, creating some psychic space for myself to walk around with my mind and

soul erect in the streets of Jerusalem."[98] The missive was at once plaintive and accusatory, and included a proposal that was as brash as it was
imaginative. Scholem was about to turn eighty in December 1977. The
ostensible reason for Taubes's letter was to propose a "critical festschrift"
for the occasion. The timing was entirely unrealistic. But the proposal provided Taubes with a scaffold on which he could hang the many criticisms
of Scholem's work that he had been accumulating since their last encounter a quarter century ago.

Taubes began by asking to meet with Scholem in Jerusalem to discuss the proposed festschrift. Then he outlined a series of criticisms of
Scholem's work—themes to which Taubes would return in lectures and
articles over the next decade. Scholem had misinterpreted Walter Benjamin's theological position, failing to account for the influence of Carl
Schmitt upon him, and making Benjamin's position out to be more "Jewish" than was in fact the case. Scholem's interpretation of Jewish messianism was faulty. Scholem's assertion of the link between Sabbatianism
and the Enlightenment was implausible, and he had overlooked the role
of the Marranos, such as Spinoza, in "neutralizing" religion by separating
it from the state. Here too, Taubes asserted, Scholem should have paid
more attention to Carl Schmitt, with whom Taubes refused personal contact because of his antisemitic declarations during the Nazi era, but whom
he considered "still today the greatest mind in Germany." Paul, Taubes
asserted, was so much more important in world history than Sabbatai
Zevi, and Scholem ought to have devoted more attention to him. As for
Zionism, it was an illusion to think that the struggle over a land regarded
as holy by Judaism, Christianity, and Islam could find a political solution.
Taubes suggested that Scholem himself respond to his critics in the proposed "Anti-Festschrift."

Taubes concluded by lamenting, "In hindsight, whatever else came
between us belongs to the vanities of academic life," and signed off "with
continuing friendship from your always faithful student."[99]

Taubes dispatched the letter to Scholem, but not to Scholem alone: he
had copies made and sent to some twenty scholars in the fields of Jewish
studies and of philosophy in Europe and the United States.

Scholem's response, dated March 24, was speedy, brief, and biting:

> Esteemed Herr Professor Taubes,
>
> Only today did I receive your detailed airmail letter of
> March 16 (postmarked the eighteenth). You are completely
> mistaken in matters pertaining to me. What has irreparably

separated us for twenty-five years hardly belongs to
the "vanities of academic life," but rather belongs to the
existential decisions of my life (not of my academic life,
but of my moral life, if I may be permitted to use the term),
as well as to the experiences I have had in the course of
my long years of effort to understand Jewish people and
phenomena.

I won't go into the contents of your letter. It's a free
country, and you may write whatever critiques you want
of my propositions, essays or books. But I wish to state
categorically that I will not participate in any book that
deals with me critically, approvingly, or politely in which
you, Herr Taubes, act as editor or contributor. You made
your decisions more than 25 years ago; I made mine and
have no intention of changing them. . . .

> In sad remembrance, and with
> best wishes for your fate,
> Gershom Scholem[100]

Hans Blumenberg, one of the colleagues to whom Taubes sent a copy
of his letter to Scholem, put his finger on the disturbing underlying sentiment. Blumenberg found the letter "frightening" (*erschreckend*), a "deeply
aggressive act" (*eines zutiefst aggressiven Aktes*) encoded in its very vocabulary. "I know this propensity of yours," he wrote, "this strained attempt at
a delicate, brave nature, as dutifully compelled by necessity to mount an
attack, for the sake of some abstract cunning of Reason." As someone who
had labored to publish a body of work, Blumenberg scorned Taubes for
thinking that offering a critique was a substitute for intellectual achievement. "One of the illusions of all those who have elevated 'critique' into
a ubiquitous slogan—also because they themselves have never been the
object of critique since they've not produced a consistent body of work—
one of the illusions of those is that it is only critique that makes life worth-
while and the work worthy of existence."[101]

An international conference on Spinoza, combined with the fact that
his daughter Tania was to spend the academic year at Hebrew University,
finally led Jacob back to Jerusalem in September 1977 for the first time in
a quarter century. Initially reluctant to return to the city from which Scholem had expelled him, Jacob found enough congenial company and intellectual stimulation to keep coming back year after year from 1977 to 1982,

sometimes more than once. During these visits, he moved between cultural and spiritual worlds that most would have viewed as incompatible. He divided his time between the academic intelligentsia around Hebrew University, an extremist Hasidic sect, liberal Orthodox institutions, and Christian settings, especially monasteries. At times he sojourned at the American Colony Hotel, located in East Jerusalem, but moments away from the ultra-Orthodox enclave of Meah She'arim. For Taubes, it was a sanctuary where he could physically distance himself from the intellectual and religious currents of Jewish Jerusalem.

Taubes found the institutions and mundane routines of life in secular, liberal, capitalist, bourgeois society tedious and boring. He identified liberalism with banality, and as one of his friends put it, "banality was the only sin he recognized."[102] One of his objections to secular life was that it lacked passion. His friend Herbert Marcuse had urged his readers to engage in a "Great Refusal" against the institutions of liberal capitalist society. In Jerusalem, Taubes was drawn to a group that practiced a great refusal of its own, the Reb Arele Hasidim.

After his first trip back to Jerusalem, Taubes reported to Arthur A. Cohen that for the first time in years he had begun to really pray in a minyan (quorum). He had been brought "home"—back to Jewish practice— by Rabbi Yosef Sheinberger, the former "foreign minister" of the "Edah Haredit," the representative body of the small, anti-Zionist wing of Israeli ultra-Orthodoxy. Through Sheinberger, Jacob had made a connection with what he called the "subterranean Jerusalem,"[103] and was introduced to the Reb Arele Hasidim, known collectively as the Toldot Aharon (The Descendants of Aharon). The sect was known primarily for its vehement anti-Zionism and its frequent clashes with the secular authorities over religious issues.[104]

Toldot Aharon was a unique phenomenon: the only Hasidic sect founded in the twentieth century. Its founder was Rabbi Aharon (Arele) Roth, who came to Jerusalem from the town of Satmar in the late 1920s. He was not the scion of a Hasidic dynasty, but through his own charisma created a new Hasidic community. When he died in 1947, the community split into two. A minority followed Arele's son, but the majority followed his son-in-law, Avraham Yitzhak Kohn (1914–97), whose background was in Satmar Hasidism. He was the presiding rebbe when Taubes became involved with the community.

The sect, as Taubes encountered it, was thus an offshoot of Satmar Hasidism, but with a uniquely stringent code of observance governing behavior and dress, set out in an eighty-three-page book of regulations.

Members were obliged to live in Jerusalem, and adult males were obligated to spend the entire Sabbath day with the rebbe, a day that was extended by an hour because of the purported halachic uncertainty about when exactly the Sabbath ended.[105] In the interests of female modesty, women were commanded to wear opaque black stockings; married women were obliged not only to shave their scalp, but to cover it with a black kerchief, tightly worn.[106] The community was strict and restrictive even by Hasidic standards: somewhere between a sect and a monastic order. There were some five hundred adult male members, together with their families. This small community was deliberately cut off from the external world and engaged in mutual aid. The rebbe was regarded as holy: on festive occasions, such as Friday night, his followers practiced the Hasidic custom of *chapn shirayim*, diving for leftovers or crumbs from the rebbe's plate.

Because of his long-standing connection to the Satmar Rebbe, extending back to his role in accompanying the Rebbe in Switzerland in 1944–45, Taubes was persona grata in the court of Toldot Aharon. On one occasion, he was strolling through the neighborhood with his friend Paul Mendes-Flohr. They heard music and walked into a wedding celebration. When the Rebbe saw Taubes, he clapped his hands to create total silence. After a brief discussion, he clapped his hands again, and had food brought for his unexpected but honored guests, who watched as a Hasid entertained them by dancing while balancing a bottle on his head.[107]

Jacob spent about two days a week in Meah She'arim. His closest contact in the sect was Raphuel Pappenheim, with whom he visited frequently, especially on the Sabbath. Conversations at the table were in Yiddish. Pappenheim was poor and, like most members of the sect, had a large family, but much of his life was devoted to charitable acts. Jacob regarded him as a tzaddik (saintly person), and he brought Tania, Ethan, and even the Berlin senator for education, Peter Glotz, to meet him.[108]

The milieu of the Reb Arele sect was illiberal, antibourgeois, and anti-Zionist. Self-enclosed, close-knit, devoted to piety, family, and fervent prayer, it embodied a style of life distant from Jacob's own; but it was the milieu in which he chose to pray, precisely because of its combination of authenticity, intensity, and world-negation.

Some two miles southwest of Meah She'arim—but worlds apart—lay the Givat Ram campus of the Hebrew University, built in 1953, just after Taubes's earlier sojourn in the city. It was the focal point of Taubes's second milieu in Jerusalem, that of the secular academic intelligentsia.

Those professors closest to Gershom Scholem regarded Taubes with suspicion, if not contempt. Based upon his reputation, some were afraid to meet him, such as Stéphane Moses, professor of German language and literature at the university.[109] But there were other scholars and intellectuals who were open to Jacob's overtures: Scholem's many enemies, as well as a younger generation not caught up in his battles.

"My trip to Jerusalem was a 'victory march,' in terms of the younger generation, who are not concerned with my struggle with Scholem, and crowded around me," Taubes wrote to Hans Jonas.[110] Taubes was exaggerating, but not by much. The fear and antagonism surrounding Taubes endowed him with an air of mystery and evoked curiosity among the young. Even those aware of his limits and faults were fascinated or stimulated by him. Though Taubes continued to suffer from manic depression, he tended in Jerusalem to be in more manic phases, eager to socialize and given to flights of intellectual exposition. During his frequent sojourns in Jerusalem, Taubes consorted with the crème de la crème of Jerusalem academic life, both established scholars and up-and-coming young men and women. Many were struck by the vividness and beauty of his Hebrew, a Hebrew steeped in references to Jewish texts and liturgy, and stripped of the accretions that had developed in more recent decades.[111]

Taubes befriended Shlomo Pines, a scholar of medieval thought who had succeeded Julius Guttmann to the chair in Jewish philosophy. Born in Paris in 1908, Pines had studied in France and Berlin (where he became friends with Leo Strauss) before moving to Palestine in 1940. From 1952 on, he taught general philosophy as well as Jewish philosophy. Best known in the English-speaking world for his translation of Maimonides's *Guide of the Perplexed*, he was a scholar of remarkable range, studying medieval Muslim, Jewish, and Christian philosophy in Arabic. He maintained, controversially, that Jewish-Christian communities had existed for centuries longer than was conventionally thought (a thesis that Taubes would later adopt); and he also shared Taubes's interest in Spinoza. He was an erudite skeptic.[112]

Scholem had played a role in the appointment of Pines. He had asked Leo Strauss for advice, and Strauss recommended Pines, not only for his scholarly range and insight, but because he fulfilled what Strauss thought should be a requirement for an academic position in Jewish philosophy— that he not be a believer.[113] In the intervening years, however, Scholem and Pines had become estranged. So Pines and Taubes hit it off.

It was at the home of Pines that Taubes met Guy (Gedaliah) and Sarah Stroumsa. Born in France and trained at Hebrew University and Harvard, Guy had recently completed a dissertation on Gnosticism, and been appointed to the Department of Religion at Hebrew University. He was a scholar of the relationship between Judaism, Gnosticism, and early Christianity—themes that had long engaged Taubes. His wife, Sarah, had studied with Pines, and was a student of medieval Arabic philosophy. She too had recently been appointed at Hebrew University, where she would later become rector.

Invited to the Stroumsa home, Jacob spotted a Hebrew University course catalogue lying on the coffee table. He studied it intensely for some ten minutes, asked a question or two of his hosts, and based on the catalogue listings determined the structure of conflicts among the various personalities and departments at the university. Such tensions were grist for his mill. Jacob had a taste for trouble—"he smelled it"—and was happy to stir it up.[114]

In 1981, for example, Guy Stroumsa organized a conference in memory of Hans Yochanan Lewy (1904–45), a distinguished scholar of Hellenic Judaism and close friend of Scholem. It was held in a seminar room at the Israel Academy of Arts and Sciences. Scholem himself gave the introductory talk. Taubes showed up, uninvited, and seated himself at the oblong seminar table, directly across from Scholem. They glared at one another in silence, "like two snakes."[115]

In Germany, Taubes was sometimes characterized as an expert on Gnosticism. But Stroumsa, who really *was* an expert on Gnosticism, found that Jacob did not have a scholarly knowledge of the subject (a view shared by Jacob's colleague in Berlin, Carsten Colpe).[116] Jacob was interested not in the actual history of Gnosticism, but in its purported metaphysical significance, as interpreted by Hans Jonas.[117] Like many of the younger generation of scholars of Gnosticism, Stroumsa was highly skeptical of Jonas's interpretation.[118]

Taubes was no doubt aware of this newer scholarship, but to the degree that it diverged from Jonas's interpretation, it failed to interest him. Ultimately, Stroumsa concluded, Jacob was not interested in historical facts. Avishai Margalit, a philosopher whom Taubes befriended in Jerusalem, reached a similar conclusion. One of Taubes's favorite stories was about Martin Buber, who early in his career wrote a number of highly influential books about Hasidism and its significance for modern man. Decades later, after his own immersion in Hasidic sources, Gershom Scholem informed Buber that he had concluded that Buber's conception of Hasidism was quite mistaken. To which Buber responded, "If what you are now saying is true, my dear Scholem . . . Hasidism does not interest me at all."[119] That was characteristic of Taubes's attitude toward Gnosticism and a range of other intellectual matters: he was less concerned to capture the phenomenon in a way that was scientifically accurate than in a way that was *interesting*.[120]

Avishai Margalit and his wife, Edna Ullman-Margalit, were young philosophers at Hebrew University steeped in analytic philosophy and the philosophy of language when they met Taubes. They found him deeply amusing: a wonderful raconteur (even if his stories were embellished), and a shrewd and perceptive judge of people. Taubes impressed upon Avishai the limits of a rationalist, utilitarian account of human motivation, and emphasized the role of imagination, myth, and the human desire for sacrifice. In that sense, Taubes seems to have influenced Margalit's work, which increasingly attended to the psychological aspects of ideologies, and the relationships between politics and theology. Margalit and others noted that Taubes was profoundly skeptical not only of scientism—the belief that human action can be explained through methods borrowed from the natural sciences—but of science itself.

Moshe Idel was another young academic whom Taubes met at the home of Shlomo Pines.[121] Having heard about Taubes's reputation, Idel did not want to be seen with him at the university, so they usually met in Meah She'arim. Idel too thought that Taubes actually had limited knowledge of his own field of expertise, Kabbalah. Yet he too found Taubes a stimulating interlocutor—cosmopolitan, and a totally free man, independent of all currents of opinion. He also took note of Taubes's urge to fan the embers of disagreement into open conflict. He made Idel out to be the anti-Scholem: that did not comport with Idel's conception of his own work, which in contrast to Scholem's emphasis on mystical concepts and theology, emphasized the experiential elements of mysticism, as well as its practical, magical side.[122]

In addition to Pines and to his new friends drawn from the younger generation of secular Jerusalem academics, Taubes also renewed some friendships from his earlier stay in Jerusalem. One of these was Moshe Barasch (1920–2004), an art historian of remarkable range and international repute, and the founder of the discipline of art history in Israel.[123] Another was Yosef Ben-Shlomo, whom Taubes had taught when Ben-Shlomo was an undergraduate at Hebrew University. In addition to his academic post as head of the Philosophy Department at Tel-Aviv University, Ben-Shlomo became a television host and a public intellectual. He began as a man of the left, but after the refusal of the Arab states to recognize the state of Israel following the Six Day War, he became a leading advocate of the Greater Israel Movement, which aimed to hold on to the territories in the Golan Heights and the West Bank of the Jordan conquered in 1967. In 1977,

Ben-Shlomo was serving as an advisor to Zevulun Hammer, the minister of education in the cabinet of Menachem Begin.[124]

Hammer was a prominent politician of the National Religious Party (NRP), the successor of the Mizrachi movement to which Zwi Taubes had belonged. But the NRP was being transformed by the rising influence of a new, messianic religious Zionism, centered in the movement known as "Gush Emunim" (The Bloc of the Faithful), and supported by Ben-Shlomo.

Until the Six Day War, religious Zionism had largely confined itself to carving out a place for Orthodoxy within political Zionism, a fundamentally secular movement, and securing a place for a non-messianic Zionism within the Orthodox world. On the question of the territorial boundaries of the Jewish state, the NRP was pragmatic.[125] By contrast, Rabbi Avraham Yitzhak Hacohen Kook (1865–1935), a prominent mystic, messianist Orthodox Zionist thinker, famously contended that the secular Zionists were actually instruments of imminent redemption, despite their avowed secularism. They were the "Messiah ben Joseph," the mythical figure in Jewish tradition who would lead the way through crisis to the redemption associated with the Messiah ben David.[126] Kook's conception of redemption as a process of progress and determinist historical evolution applied not only to the Jews, but to the rest of the world as well.

Kook was not a part of Mizrachi and had almost no following among religious Zionists until 1967, and that thanks to the influence of his son, Zwi Yehudah Kook (1891–1981), who politicized his father's ideas. For Zwi Yehudah and his followers, since the State of Israel was part of a divine plan, it was incumbent upon Jews to push the messianic process forward. Precisely because it was a divine process, the normal pragmatic constraints of international relations—including the attitudes and interests of other nations—no longer applied. Among his foremost goals was Jewish rule over the entire Land of Israel. Zwi Yehudah promulgated these ideas as the head (*Rosh Yeshivah*) of Yeshivat Mercaz Harav, the institution founded by his father. But it was only in the aftermath of the Six Day War—a struggle preceded by massive anxiety and followed by a sense of near-miraculous victory—that his ideas came to appeal to a wider audience of young, Orthodox Israelis, many of them graduates of recently founded national-religious yeshivot. After the Yom Kippur War of 1973, they founded Gush Emunim, a movement devoted to the Jewish settlement of the entire West Bank. Hammer was a leader of the young guard of Gush Emunim-influenced politicians who took over leadership of the NRP.

Long interested in the relationship between theology and politics, Taubes was at first fascinated by Gush Emunim, for him another example of a collective great refusal to accept the secular status quo. He came to know some of its young activists, and even sent his son, Ethan, on a Gush Emunim march through Samaria (*Tza'adat HaShomron*) when Ethan visited Israel during Passover 1979.[127] But Jacob soon concluded that Gush Emunim represented a disastrous turn.

Taubes's renewed contact with Ben-Shlomo was short-lived. His connection to David Hartman was more enduring. Hartman was one of Taubes's links to another milieu, that of modern Orthodox intellectuals. He was an Orthodox rabbi from New York, who had been a student of Joseph Soloveitchik, the philosophical eminence of modern American Orthodoxy. Hartman moved to Israel in 1971 and began teaching Jewish thought at Hebrew University. Dissatisfied with the limits of the academic study of Judaism, in 1976 he founded the Shalom Hartman Institute, a pluralist institution intended to address broad issues of Israeli life, to bridge the gap between the academy and a larger public sphere, and to rethink Judaism and Zionism in light of modern democracy. Though he wrote some speeches for Hammer about the role of Jewish education in a pluralistic Israeli society, Hartman had no sympathy for Gush Emunim, or for the messianic strain of Zionism. In Jerusalem, Taubes participated in some of the fledgling institute's activities.

Hartman hoped his institute would supply the intellectual elite for an interdisciplinary integration of Judaism and Western philosophy and democracy—a new vision of Zionism that Hebrew University was originally supposed to produce. The university, by developing along the model of the research university pioneered in Germany, had gone in a different direction. Avishai Margalit and Moshe Idel were among those drawn into the institute's orbit.

Taubes was sympathetic to Hartman's hope for his institute. He thought that the scholarly study of Judaism as conducted within the university, while of intrinsic merit, was not a contribution to the actual practice of Judaism. For a relevant parallel, he pointed to the case of Ignaz Goldziher, the Hungarian Jewish scholar who was the founder of the academic study of Islam in the late nineteenth century. Just as Goldziher's scholarship did nothing for practicing Muslims, Taubes maintained, the scholarly study of Judaism did nothing for the revitalization of Jewish life. To confuse the two was "ruinous for the project of scientific study as well as for religion," as he put it in a letter to Hartman.[128]

Taubes saw Zevulun Hammer as too close to the messianic Zionism of Rav Kook's disciples. By 1982, after repeated visits to Israel, Taubes suggested to Hartman that perhaps the ultra-Orthodox played an indispensable role:

> Consider, maybe <u>because</u> such [messianic] hopes are invested into the State of Israel, hopes we cannot reasonably connect with <u>any</u> modern state, that people become either fanatical or cynical, i.e. are barking up at the wrong tree. Perhaps the non-Zionist Yeshivot are not just recreating an Eastern European ghetto (which they are also), but try to preserve Torah from the Messianic bug. It is a tragic situation: the [National Religious] Yeshivot of Bnei Akiva are the spiritual and physical flower, the elite of Israel today . . . and indeed they are going into a Messianic confrontation with political reality.[129]

Like Taubes, Hartman took pride in bringing together intellectuals from the United States, Europe, and Israel and in stepping beyond academic boundaries. He too was interested in the relationship between religion and politics. But unlike Taubes, Hartman was committed to the revitalization of Judaism in a living relationship with Western liberal thought and institutions.

Like Taubes, Hartman sought to nurture young talent. It was at his home that Taubes met Moshe Halbertal, the youngest of his frequent interlocutors in Jerusalem. Halbertal was nineteen when he met Taubes, had already completed a course of yeshiva study, and was now a fellow in Hartman's Beit Midrash, a program for advanced studies in Talmud. Halbertal's father, like Zwi Taubes, was originally from Galicia, and was active in Mizrachi; his mother stemmed from a distinguished family of Jerusalem rabbis of Lithuanian origin. Jacob recognized the young man's extraordinary talent and promise.[130]

Taubes interjected an antinomian note during his first meeting with Halbertal. There was one thing that he definitely *had* to read, Taubes said, and that was the portion of Nachman of Breslov's *Likutei MaHaran* in which the Hasidic master declares that the source of heresy (*k'fira*) is the moment of *zimzum*, a reference to the kabbalistic notion of God's self-contraction. For Nachman, heresy exists because of the religious man's consciousness not of God's presence, but of his *absence* from the world. This was the deepest moment in Jewish thought, Taubes told Halbertal.[131] In short, to be truly religious was to be on the verge of heresy. This was a passage that had long appealed to Taubes, dating back to his relationship with Joseph Weiss and the essay on nineteenth-century Jewish thought that

Taubes had published at that time.[132] Halbertal was impressed by Taubes's ability to recall such passages in texts he had studied decades earlier.[133]

Taubes was also remarkably knowledgeable about the Jewish world. Once, when Taubes was visiting Halbertal at home, Moshe's father walked in, and seeing Taubes dressed in his typical Jerusalem garb—wide black hat, black clothing, with a white collar, characteristic of a German Protestant pastor—asked Moshe in Yiddish, "What is this priest doing here?" Taubes responded in very fine Galician Yiddish, and proceeded to enter into an extended conversation with Moshe's father in which it became clear that Taubes was acquainted with every corner of Galician Jewish life, including its various Hasidic dynasties.

Max Weber had famously confessed that he was "religiously unmusical," that is, he lacked an intuitive feel for religious practice. Taubes was the opposite: to Halbertal, he seemed to have "perfect pitch" for the religious imagination, a quality that allowed him to empathize fully with the religious sensibilities of those he met, from a variety of religions.

Taubes found the Apostle Paul so congenial, Halbertal thought, because Paul's notion that the will is bound to be sinful accorded with Jacob's own sense that his will was beyond his control. It was in accord with his own religious failures, and his need for grace beyond human will. The cycle of sin, atonement, sacrifice, and redemption was one with which he identified. And Paul's critique of the Law resonated with Taubes's deeply antinomian sensibilities.

Like others who knew him in Jerusalem and beyond, Halbertal was struck by Taubes's dramatic self-presentation. That was in part a reflection of Taubes's deep internal struggles—emotional, religious, and intellectual. But it was also a product of cultivated theatricality, expressed in his dress, his gestures, his shaping of his life as a wanderer between worlds, the air he presented of being about to offer a great revelation—a quality evident to the Kristols decades earlier and still part of Jacob's persona.

A person of great psychological insight, Halbertal concluded that despite his wit and enlivening presence, deep down there was a deep emptiness to Jacob Taubes. He lived in a state of despair and loneliness, which he tried to overcome in a variety of ways, including sexually. He was disappointed in himself and in his inability to achieve his calling as a great thinker. He had no real sense of place—he was always on the move—or of property.

Leon Wieseltier was another young intellectual whom Taubes befriended in Jerusalem, and whom he regarded as a person of great promise.[134] In many ways, Taubes could see himself in Wieseltier, and

Wieseltier in Taubes. Wieseltier came from an Orthodox background and attended a Zionist Orthodox school in Brooklyn. He studied at Columbia University with the literary and social critic Lionel Trilling and the philosopher Dieter Henrich, and then as a postgraduate fellow at Oxford. When Wieseltier met Taubes in 1978, he had already published in prestigious American venues such as the *New York Review of Books*, and was under consideration (ultimately successful) for the Harvard Society of Fellows, where he pursued Jewish studies while writing about broader topics. In 1983, he assumed the role of literary editor of the *New Republic*, which he transformed into perhaps the best review forum in the country. *Kaddish*, his 1998 book dedicated to his father's memory, employed Jewish sources to reflect on issues of death, mourning, the relationship between generations, and his own wrestling with faith and tradition.

Jacob Taubes, Wieseltier came to see, had lost his belief in the Jewish tradition, but not his love for it. He had what Wieseltier characterized as "a narcotic relationship to religion": he couldn't give it up, but neither could he give himself up to it. His antinomian self-conception, paradoxically, demanded an ongoing connection to the tradition. For one cannot rebel against the law unless there is a law to rebel against. The result was a kind of arrested spiritual adolescence, in which one can never stop rebelling, since arriving at a new, positive identity would lead to calm. "Being a bad son was his way of being a son."[135]

Aharon Agus, whom Taubes encountered in Jerusalem, was the closest he came to having a spiritual heir. Born in New York in 1943, Agus was the son of a professor at Yeshiva University, where Agus received his doctorate in the field of Talmud. In 1970, Agus began to teach at Bar-Ilan University, the Orthodox academic institution in Ramat Gan.[136] When Taubes met him in 1978, Agus was living with his wife and children in the Jewish Quarter of the Old City of Jerusalem, while teaching at Bar-Ilan.[137]

Agus was awed by Taubes, who provided an entrée to a larger intellectual world and to intellectual horizons he had not encountered at Yeshiva University or Bar-Ilan. Taubes fanned the antinomian embers of Agus's personality. Under Taubes's tutelage, Agus developed heterodox lines of thought and behavior.[138] His scholarly work moved from traditional textual criticism to topics and approaches influenced by Taubes. He began to find Gnostic themes in the Talmud and explored the relationships between Talmudic themes and the Gospels.[139] He became a devotee of what he called "Jacob Taubes and his way of thinking."[140]

To get a sense of some of the ideas that Taubes conveyed to Agus, we can turn to a long letter Taubes wrote in November 1977 to Arthur A.

Cohen, shortly after his return from Jerusalem.[141] It was written from the Jesuit center at Les Fontaines, near Paris, where Taubes sojourned.

The letter began by referring to a claim by Cohen that there was a significant difference between Jewish critics of Judaism such as Spinoza who were well-versed in Judaism (and hence presumably know of what they speak), and those, like Simone Weil, who were not, and criticize out of ignorance. In response, Taubes's letter first explored the development of "study" into a fundamental category of Judaism. This Taubes connected with the historical transformation of Judaism brought about by the rabbis of the Talmud, who, he claimed, constituted themselves as a dominant caste by valorizing "learning" into a definitive marker of religious piety, and stigmatizing the "am ha-aretz," the unlearned common folk. Thus, in Rabbinic Judaism, "Studying becomes a pneumatic or liturgical activity, a kind of *Ersatz* of living." Thereafter, antinomian, populist revolt and the critique of learning were often interconnected, a combination embodied, Taubes asserted, in the heretical, Gnostic rabbi, Elisha ben Abuyah. The notion that rabbinic Judaism was egalitarian or democratic—as suggested by Louis Finkelstein in his book *The Pharisees*—was therefore an apologetic assertion not born out by the historical record. Jesus's critique of "scribes and Pharisees," as reported in the Gospels, was egalitarian in thrust and latently antinomian.[142] But it was Paul who turned the scandalous death of Jesus (through crucifixion) into an antinomian symbol, and proffered a critique that devalued the "learning" upon which the rabbinic caste was built. Meanwhile, after the definitive destruction of Jewish sovereignty in Palestine, the rabbis created a new form of Jewish life, in which study of the Torah and the Oral Law became a substitute for the real, concrete existence the Jews had previously enjoyed. Much of subsequent Jewish history, from the second through the eighteenth century, Taubes asserted, could be seen as a sequence of struggles between the now-normative rabbinic Judaism and a series of antinomian movements that sought to dethrone the primacy of "learning" and of the rabbinic caste. Early Hasidism was the last of these, until it too was subdued by the values of rabbinic Judaism.

Taubes next questioned whether "study," in the sense of traditional erudition, was truly capable of responding to fundamental contemporary issues. Erudition, he suggested, may be a way of fending off confrontation with ultimate questions. As evidence, he cited Cohen's unsatisfactory experience at the Jewish Theological Seminary, as well as his own. Though Saul Lieberman was the pinnacle of scholarly erudition, whom Louis Finkelstein had idolized, neither was a "guide to the perplexities of the age

of the Moscow trials, of Hitler, of Auschwitz, of Israel." Taubes concluded
by suggesting that Judaic scholarship, as it had developed in the United
States, was vitiated by apologetic assumptions and propensities:

> I am arguing that the whole enterprise of Jewish scholarship, *Wissen-
> schaft des Judentums* à la 3080 Broadway [that is, JTS] and American
> Academy of Jewish Research [an elite institution of Jewish scholar-
> ship, founded by Salo Baron] is a fraud keeping a status quo of the low-
> est common sense philosophy going with some Talmudic quotations
> not asking even a historical question in a radical manner.[143]

Jacob's coterie in Jerusalem also included Orthodox women. One in
particular became his frequent companion. Like Jacob, she came from a
prominent rabbinic family. When they met, she was a wife and mother,
already engaged in Jewish studies and seeking to expand her intellectual
horizons. Jacob provided her with guidance, recognition, and validation.
Their liaison was not kept secret, flouting social and cultural norms. That
was not without its costs: the psychic tensions created by their relationship led for a while to her psychosomatic paralysis.[144]

In addition to the Reb Arele Hasidim of Meah She'arim, to the secu-
lar academics of Hebrew University, and the intellectuals at the Hartman
Institute and beyond, there was another, Christian, locus of Jacob's life in
Jerusalem.

Jacob rented rooms in a number of Christian institutions, most in
close proximity to Meah She'arim. The Albright Institute for Archeological Research on Saladin Street in East Jerusalem was one. The Swedish
Theological Institute (Tabor House) on Hanevi'im Steet in West Jerusalem was another. The Catholic Tantur Ecumenical Institute for Advanced
Theological Studies near Bethlehem was a third. He lived in circumstances that were Spartan, semi-monastic. And he spent a good deal of
time with monks.

Among Jacob's Jerusalem haunts was the École biblique et archéologique
française on the Nablus Road, a fifteen-minute walk from the Swedish Theological Institute, or a ten-minute walk from Meah She'arim. It belonged to
the Dominican Order and was staffed largely by French monks.

Jacob was introduced to the École by Father Paul François Dreyfus,
one of the many Jewish converts to Catholicism with whom Jacob crossed
paths—a reminder to Jacob of a road not taken.[145] A French Jew by birth,
Dreyfus had attended the elite French engineering school, École polytech-
nique, before the Second World War. He spent much of the War in German captivity, and it was there that he converted to Roman Catholicism,

later becoming a Dominican friar. Dreyfus became involved in Jewish-Christian dialogues in Jerusalem, where he met Jacob Taubes. (After the death of Dreyfus's mother, Jacob took him to synagogue to say kaddish for her.) Dreyfus introduced Jacob to Father Marcel Sigrist, a Yale-trained scholar of Assyriology at the École biblique.

When he was in Jerusalem, Jacob would come to dinner at the École every two weeks. After the meal, he would lecture about Paul to a small group of friars—including Dreyfus, Sigrist, and Étienne Nodet, a scholar of Judaism in the Second Temple period. Jacob was convinced that he had found the spiritual center of Paul, and needed an audience to whom to convey it. He offered his listeners the antinomian interpretation of the apostle that would later be published in *The Political Theology of Paul*. His lectures were unbuttoned and had a confessional quality. Characteristically, he mixed his reflections on Paul with talk about his own family, his doctors, as well as politics.

His listeners knew their Paul, and took note of the fact that there were parts of Paul's letters that Jacob ignored or overlooked: rather than confront the evidence at odds with his thesis, Jacob would talk *around* difficult questions. But the Dominicans did not ask him to justify himself: they were there to listen, to learn, perhaps to commiserate, but not to argue. It was clear to them that Jacob did not *believe*, but that he was in awe of Paul as an antinomian. After his postdinner talk, at about 10:00 p.m., he would typically depart for Meah She'arim.

Jacob's visits to the École biblique continued year after year. The monks could not help but notice that he was often accompanied by attractive young women.

Jacob cultivated an air of ambiguity in Jerusalem. His friends and interlocutors knew of the radically divergent milieus in which he circulated. His appearance too was liminal. His dress could make him appear to be a Protestant pastor or a priest. He wore a black beret, but not, ordinarily, a *kippah*. And many of his interlocutors were struck by his almost feminine physiognomy and mannerisms.[146] Jacob Taubes was not easy to pin down. He was a spiritual chameleon: among the Hasidim he could be a Hasid, or a Trappist among Trappists. He was what Moshe Waldoks, one of his young acquaintances, called "polymorphously spiritual."[147]

Jacob was sufficiently enamored of life in Jerusalem that he thought about moving there, and he encouraged his children to consider it as well.[148] While remaining wary of the messianic temptations inherent in Zionism, his attitude toward the Jewish State was one of comfort and concern. Caught between his identities as a German professor and as a Jew,[149] he now leaned increasingly to the Jewish side. As he wrote from Berlin to Werner Hamacher, a young literary scholar active in the Hermeneutic Colloquium, his interest in influencing matters at the FU had waned, because "as a Jew, I am after all is said and done not here with my entire heart, and what happens here was (and is) ultimately a matter of indifference to me."[150]

Jacob's engagement with Israel influenced his intellectual development as well. His encounters with the messianic Zionism of Gush Emunim, the liberal Zionism of many of his academic friends, and the radical anti-Zionism of the Reb Arele Hasidim reinvigorated his long-standing interest in the relationship between theology and politics. He initiated a series of conferences in Germany on the theme of political theology, one of which took "theocracy" as its theme.[151]

Taubes again acted as an intellectual impresario by bringing a number of his Jerusalem interlocutors to the FU, exposing his German colleagues and students to Israeli scholars they would not otherwise have encountered. Shlomo Pines came to the Hermeneutic Colloquium and gave a seminar for four weeks in May 1979, and then again a year later. In 1981 he returned once more to have an honorary doctorate conferred upon him (at Taubes's initiative) by the FU.[152] The art historian Moshe Barasch came as a visiting professor in the winter semester of 1982–83. Avishai Margalit came to the university in 1984–85 intending to teach a course together with Taubes on Maimonides and Spinoza. When the semester began, Taubes informed Margalit that he was too depressed to teach, so Margalit taught the course alone.[153] Taubes's protégé, Aharon Agus, would eventually move from Israel to Germany to take up a chair in Heidelberg.

Taubes took a research leave for the spring of 1981, much of which he spent in Jerusalem. Though he no longer held his chair in Judaica at the FU, he was actually more interested in Judaism, both as a practice and as an object of academic scholarship.

Taubes lived in a hostel on the second floor of the Albright Institute for Archeological Research.[154] In March, he spent a Sabbath with Reb Arele's congregation in Meah She'arim. The roads in Meah Shearim were normally closed to auto traffic to prevent violation of the laws of the Sabbath, but a new road had been constructed to the suburb of Ramot, a road that ran near the ultra-Orthodox quarter. Some young male followers of Reb Arele stoned cars in an attempt to close the road, which led to a violent confrontation between them and the municipal police charged with keeping the road open. As the Sabbath came to a close (the sect maintained an extra hour of Sabbath observance), the police lobbed in tear gas and raided the yeshiva, searching for perpetrators and for bottles and other missiles used against the police.

Taubes was outraged at the behavior of the police. The English-language *Jerusalem Post* wrote an article about the altercation, with a photo of Taubes, who was cited as "a secular authority on religion who has established close ties with the Reb Arele community." The sect's founder, Reb Arele, "gave a new colour to the notion of emuna (faith) which was a response to the cataclysm of the Holocaust and the rapid seculariza-tion of the Jewish community afterwards," Taubes asserted. "They have a disciplined life that makes it possible to live with nobility in spite of their abysmal poverty."[155]

A week later, Taubes wrote a long letter to the editor of the *Post*, in which he described the police raid, including the police's use of tear gas in the midst of a congregation of five hundred adults and four hundred children, gathered for evening prayers. Without referring to the suspected actions of Reb Arele's followers that had led to the altercation, Taubes warned ominously about an atmosphere of "religious civil war [in which] both sides do not recognize the legitimacy of the other and indulge in fan-tasies in which the 'enemy' is liquidated."[156] When he returned to Berlin, Taubes showed the newspaper with his photo to his colleagues, noting, "It usually takes me 4–5 days to produce a scandal, and here I did it in only one day."[157]

Critique of Scholem

During Jacob's frequent visits to Jerusalem, he made contact with many scholars of Judaism, inside the academy and beyond it. His old antagonist, Gershom Scholem, remained a presence. But he was aged, and a new gen-eration of scholars—some of them his students—had risen to prominence. One of those was Joseph Dan, the first incumbent of the Gershom Scholem Chair in Jewish Mysticism at the Hebrew University, who had studied with Scholem and with Scholem's student Isaiah Tishby. Dan was the chair of the steering committee for the eighth World Congress of Jewish Studies, which was to be held in Jerusalem in August 1981. The congress was the major gathering of academic scholars in the field, young and old, who came from around the world to meet colleagues, rub shoulders with the greats in the field, and to present their research. Scholem had been a central figure in the congress since its inception. While he dominated the organization, there were a few scholars who had not been invited to give papers. One was Jacob Taubes. Dan was opposed to this organizational excommunication, and invited Taubes to speak at the congress.[158] Taubes agreed to do so, and submitted as the topic of his paper, "Scholem's Theses on Messianism Reconsidered." The steering committee asked him to use a less provocative title, and he chose "The Price of Messianism."

In August, the time came for Taubes to deliver his presentation. Now eighty-three years of age, Scholem was ailing and unable to attend the congress. Jacob arrived, dressed, as was his custom, in black, sporting the wide-brimmed black hat that suggested he was some kind of priest, pastor, or Hasid. He delivered his talk from notes enfolded in the ultra-Orthodox newspaper that he demonstratively carried to the podium.

David Stern, a recent PhD in Jewish studies from Harvard, was among those present. For Stern, Taubes's name was associated with a certain disrepute and even danger. Back at Harvard, the historian John Clive had told Stern the story about how Taubes had been tricked into expounding about a medieval mystic who never existed. Stern's friend, Arthur A. Cohen, had told him about Taubes's years at JTS, and the air of sexual libertinism around him there. Stern was curious, and he was not alone. A large crowd of two hundred attended, many attracted, no doubt, by Taubes's notoriety in Jewish studies circles.[159]

Taubes began by announcing that while he would lecture in English, he would entertain questions in any language. Then he noted that the original title he had proposed for his talk was "Gershom Scholem's Theses on Messianism Reconsidered," but that the steering committee had asked him to "neutralize" the problem, hence his title "The Price of Messianism"—a title taken from Scholem himself.

"I intend to examine the inner dynamics of the messianic idea in Judaism," he began. "This entails reconsidering Gershom Scholem's theses on messianism."[160] Taubes focused on Scholem's 1959 essay, "Toward an Understanding of the Messianic Idea in Judaism," the lead essay in Scholem's book of 1971, *The Messianic Idea in Judaism.* Taubes took aim, above all, at a distinction that Scholem had made in passing between the nature of messianism in Judaism and in Christianity. In Judaism, Scholem maintained, the coming of the messiah was conceived as an event that occurred in history and in public, transforming the world in some perceptible way. By contrast, after the failure of Jesus to return, Christianity maintained that redemption takes place in an inward transformation, within the soul of individuals.

Taubes argued that this distinction was too sharp, historically inaccurate, and "obfuscates the dynamics inherent in the messianic idea itself." "When prophecy fails" and the messiah fails to appear (or reappear), rather than disintegrating, a messianic community can preserve itself by turning inward and conceiving of redemption as an interior event in the human soul. For Taubes, this marked "a crisis within Jewish eschatology itself—in Pauline Christianity as well as in the Sabbatian movement of the seventeenth century." Taubes's main objection was to Scholem's failure to treat the Pauline experience as paradigmatic of Jewish eschatology.

Some five minutes after Taubes began to speak, Isaiah Tishby rose to voice his dissent. Raving, he had to be accompanied out of the hall by Joseph Dan.

Taubes then proceeded to make a number of disconnected but striking observations. When messianic movements survive after the failure of the initial expectations of redemption, it is not because of the intrinsic nature of the life of the messiah, but because of the *interpretation* of events offered to the community of believers by the would-be messiah's interpreters. That meant Paul of Tarsus in the case of Jesus, Nathan of Gaza in the case of Sabbatai Zevi. The life of Jesus and of Sabbatai Zevi both ended in "scandal": crucifixion in the former case, conversion to Islam in the latter. In each case, it was the *interpretation* of this scandal that mattered.

In cryptic language, Taubes laid out another stimulating thesis about the two major messianic movements in the history of Judaism—Pauline Christianity and Sabbatianism. The first developed "just before rabbinic Judaism had begun to mold the fantasy and reality of the Jewish people," that is, before the destruction of the Second Temple and the creation of rabbinic Judaism—which for Taubes was a spectacular work of creative imagination. Rabbinic Judaism had been consistently opposed to messianic movements, which was why purported messiahs came and went without leaving a trace, until the Sabbatian movement, which came "when rabbinic Judaism in its classical form began to disintegrate."

Taubes offered a direct criticism of Scholem's contention that there was "a 'dialectical' nexus between Sabbatian messianism and the rise of the *Aufklärung* [Jewish Enlightenment]." He agreed with Scholem that the experience of the expulsion from Spain led to the mythical kabbalistic response that Scholem had charted, ending in Sabbatianism. But, Taubes suggested, it also led to an alternative, rationalistic response, by the seventeenth-century offspring of Marranos such as Spinoza. These rationalists were the true precursors of the Jewish Enlightenment, Taubes argued, while the mythical, kabbalistic response had actually delayed the process of Enlightenment, until the failed Sabbatian experience, by taking the mythic response to absurd conclusions, opened the door to Enlightenment.

Taubes then took issue with Scholem's claim, in a famous essay on "The Neutralization of the Messianic Element in Early Hasidism," that Hasidism, with its "unheard-of intensity and intimacy of religious life," had had to "pay dearly for its success. It conquered the realm of inwardness but it abdicated in the realm of messianism," thus robbing messianism of its "apocalyptic fire." But, Taubes asked, since historically messianism had led to "absurd and catastrophic consequences" (he had the Sabbatian and Frankist episodes in mind), was it not *desirable* for Hasidism to have taken this turn inward?

Scholem had contended, "The magnitude of the messianic idea corresponds to the endless powerlessness in Jewish history during all the centuries of exile, when it was unprepared to come forward onto the plane of world history." Taubes took issue with that notion. True, he asserted, rabbinic Judaism had set itself against all messianic movements, and sought an existence outside history, within the symbolic and legal community of halacha. But millenarian movements *beyond* Judaism had indeed influenced history, such as the Puritans who arrived in New England to create a New Zion, and laid the foundation of the United States of America.

Taubes ended by alluding to contemporary trends in Israel. Zionism marked a deliberate turn to history, an attempt by Jews to mold their own historical destiny. But to confuse that with messianism was to court disaster: "every attempt to bring about redemption on the level of history without a transfiguration of the messianic idea leads straight into the abyss," he asserted. The conflation of messianism with Zionism "has allowed wild apocalyptic fantasy to take over political reality in the state of Israel." By setting the record straight, he concluded, the historian "can pose a problem and signal a danger in the present spiritual and political situation of the Jewish people."

Taubes seems to have made the greatest impression at the end of his talk. When it came time for questions, he was like an acrobat—fielding queries in English, Hebrew, German, French, Yiddish, and even Polish.[161]

The Congress held a public reception late that afternoon. Seeing Taubes standing alone and isolated, David Stern approached and introduced himself. Taubes could not have been nicer: he mentioned that he had read some of Stern's pieces in *Commentary* and the *New Republic*, and inquired more deeply about the young scholar's interests. Then he asked, "Do you want to come to Meah She'arim with me?" Taubes proceeded to take him to one of the most poverty-stricken parts of the quarter. Stern was guided into a building and up a flight of stairs into a room where half a dozen Reb Arele Hasidim were seated around a table. They clearly knew Taubes, and inquired in Yiddish what he was doing in town. Taubes replied that he had just given a paper on Gershom Scholem—a name that the Hasidim recognized, to Stern's surprise. They asked about the man who had come with Taubes. "A young scholar from Harvard," Taubes replied. "What is that?" (*Vus iz duz?*), they asked. Taubes explained that Harvard was the Brisk of American universities—Brisk being the most distinguished yeshiva in pre-War Europe. "How can you make such a comparison?" one of the Hasidim exclaimed angrily, distraught at the equation of the great yeshiva with any mere secular institution of learning.

By then, Taubes was hungry. "Is there a wedding nearby?" Taubes inquired. Certainly, he was told, just down the street. Taubes walked down the street with Stern in tow. They looked in a window and spied some five hundred guests dining upon the boiled chicken characteristic of such occasions. Taubes instructed Stern to follow him through an open window and into the hall. He found an open spot at one of the tables, sat himself down, and began to eat his share of chicken. David Stern left. But his encounter with Taubes was one that he remembered decades later, when he himself was a professor of Jewish studies at Harvard. Taubes exuded a frisson of danger, both to himself and others.

Taubes portrayed his presentation at the World Congress of Jewish Studies as a thorough critique of Scholem's key theses. Yet when we compare Taubes's contentions to Scholem's actual views, the contrasts are less dramatic. Taubes was far from alone, or even novel, in warning about the dangers of messianic Zionism in contemporary Israel. Many Israeli intellectuals, such as the historian Jacob Talmon, had been making that argument for years. One of those who had offered such warnings was Gershom Scholem. Indeed, the closer one compares Scholem's work to Taubes's talk, the clearer it becomes that Scholem himself had made most of the points that Taubes offered in his critique.

Scholem's account of Sabbatai Zevi, published in 1957, was in part an examination of Sabbatianism as exemplifying dangers inherent in Zionism.[162] In the preface to the English translation of the book, published in 1973, he characterized the Sabbatian movement as "a movement which shook the House of Israel to its very foundations and has revealed not only the vitality of the Jewish people but also the deep, dangerous, and destructive dialectics inherent in the messianic idea."[163] The essay on "The Messianic Idea in Judaism," first published in 1959, concluded with another such warning.[164] Especially after the rise of Gush Emunim, Scholem referred frequently in public statements to the dangers that messianism posed to the Zionist project itself.[165]

The Pauline experience was never near the center of Scholem's interest as it was for Taubes. But Scholem did indeed refer to it in discussing the history of Jewish messianism, writing, "I naturally would not deny that Paulinism represents a genuine crisis of tradition within Jewish messianism that is analogous to" Sabbatianism. For Scholem, however, this quickly led to "the early Church's exceedingly rapid break from Judaism."[166] He referred to the "far-reaching dialectical and downright antinomian justification" that Paul had developed, "whereby Christ could be proclaimed the 'End of the Law' (Romans 10:4)," where "for the first time the crisis of the tradition is explained out of the inner dynamic of the redemption itself."[167] He devoted many pages of his book on Sabbatai Zevi to the history of Christian chiliastic movements influenced by Jewish messianism—including the Puritans later mentioned by Taubes—before concluding, "The millenarian movements sufficiently illustrate the revolutionary possibilities inherent in precisely those forms of messianism which the church had always suspected of being influenced by Jewish conceptions. These revolutionary tendencies expressed themselves in Christian history at least as much as in Judaism."[168] Scholem returned to that theme in his 1959 essay "Toward an Understanding of the Messianic Idea in Judaism."[169]

In short, what Taubes offered as a *critique* of Scholem's theses on messianism was in many respects either a *restatement* of Scholem's own themes or a *variation* on them. That would not stop later scholars from devoting studies to the purported contrast between their views.[170]

Jacob Neusner, Taubes's former student at Columbia University, was much taken with Taubes's critique of Scholem, with whom Neusner had long been at odds.[171] Taubes was eager to have his critique of Scholem publicized as widely as possible. In addition to the publication in the official proceedings of the Jerusalem conference, he published two other versions, with only slight variations: as "The Price of Messianism," in the *Journal of Jewish Studies*, which Neusner edited; and in *Social Science Information*, a journal published by his Paris friend, Clemens Heller, where it appeared under the title Taubes had originally suggested to the conference organizers, "Scholem's Theses on Messianism Reconsidered."[172]

The specter of Scholem continued to haunt Taubes—and vice-versa. Scholem was now a much-fêted figure in West Germany, the recipient of honorary degrees from universities and scholarly academies. In June 1981, he was inducted into the Orden Pour le Mérite für Wissenschaft und Künste, the apex of the ladder of public honor. At about the same time, he was invited to become part of the first cohort of scholars at the Wissenschaftskolleg zu Berlin. That was an elite institute of advanced study created to bring a measure of intellectual excellence to Berlin in the face of the damage to Berlin's universities wrought by the radical reforms that Taubes had championed a decade earlier.[173] Scholem accepted the invitation—making as a condition of his coming that Taubes would not be allowed on the property.[174]

Scholem arrived at the Wissenschaftskolleg in the Grunewald neighborhood on October 6, 1981, and a month later, he spoke at the institution's formal inauguration. Taubes was not present. But on at least one occasion, they sat at separate tables at the Paris Bar, where Taubes had his regular table, surrounded by friends and disciples, while Scholem had a table of his own, surrounded by his acolytes.[175]

On a visit to Zurich that month, Scholem's friends Marianne and Sigi Weinberg invited him out for dinner along with Elias Canetti, who had just been awarded the Nobel Prize for Literature. In the course of the meal, Canetti inquired about Taubes. At the mention of his name, Scholem turned white as a sheet. When Marianne told Taubes about the incident, he begged her to try to arrange a reconciliation between himself and Scholem. Knowing that such an attempt would be futile, Marianne refused. Taubes was enraged and broke off their relationship. (It would resume later.[176])

Not long thereafter, in early December, Scholem slipped and fell in Berlin, injuring his hip. He returned to Jerusalem on December 17, and passed away there on February 21, 1982, at the age of eighty-four.[177] At the urging of Unseld, Taubes wrote a letter of consolation to Scholem's widow, Fania.[178]

Taubes's obsession with Scholem did not end with the death of his erstwhile teacher. Scholem had deposited his papers, including his massive correspondence, in an archive at the Jewish National Library, on the campus of Hebrew University. At some point, Taubes either visited the archive or had someone do so on his behalf, for among the papers that Taubes left with his children in New York were photocopies of the entire correspondence between him and Scholem, from its inception in 1947.

French Retreats

In addition to Berlin and Jerusalem, Paris was the third geographical node of Jacob's peripatetic existence during the last decade of his life. And as in Jerusalem, Jacob moved among disparate cultural milieus. In France, it was between elite academic institutions in Paris and Jesuit institutions on its periphery, with a sprinkling of Jewish restaurants and synagogues added to the mix.

Jacob had loved Paris ever since first visiting it with Susan in 1952. He had friends of long standing there, including Jean and Mayotte Bollack, François Bondy, and Emil Cioran. But for him, Paris was more of a refuge, where he could think and reflect on his broad interests, distanced from the turmoil at the FU. It was closer and more accessible than Jerusalem, hence easier to escape to for short periods of time.

Jacob's main institutional connection in Paris was the Maison des sciences de l'homme on the Boulevard Raspail. Founded in 1965 at the initiative of the historian Fernand Braudel, it was a center for research in the social sciences. The moving force in the institution, and Jacob's protector there, was its chief administrator, Clemens Heller (1917–2002). Heller was a cultural impresario who played a key role behind the scenes of European intellectual life. An Austrian Jew by birth, he had come to the United States in 1937 and pursued doctoral studies in history at Harvard. In 1947, he was one of the founders of the "Salzburg Seminars," an American outreach effort sometimes known as "the Marshall Plan of the Mind." The Seminars were a center for the exchange of ideas from intellectuals across Europe, and a showcase for American culture. In 1949, Heller moved to Paris to lecture at the École practique des hautes études, headed by Braudel. Later, Heller conceived the Maison des sciences de l'homme and obtained funding for it from the American Ford and Rockefeller foundations. The Maison opened in 1965, headed by Braudel, with Heller as his deputy and administrator. A believer in the intrinsic connection between social science and democracy, Heller devoted himself to creating an alternative to the Marxist—and often Communist—social science dominant in France. He regarded himself as a spotter of talent and had a knack for bringing together intellectuals from different countries and disciplines into fruitful encounter.[179] Heller was fond of Taubes and gave him a small office at the Maison. Among Taubes's contacts there were Pierre Bourdieu, an up-and-coming French sociologist, who also had an office at the Maison; Louis Dumont, an anthropologist then working on a history of individualism;[180] and the British historian Eric Hobsbawm, who characterized the Maison as "the most important international intellectual meeting-point in Europe and perhaps in the world."[181] While there, Taubes lived mainly at the Maison Heinrich Heine, a German cultural institution in the nearby Cité universitaire.

A short walk from the Maison des sciences de l'homme, on the Rue d'Ulm, was the elite French college, the École normale supérieure. Among its most famous faculty members at the time was the philosopher Louis Althusser, a devoted Communist who had developed a conception of

Marxism that he insisted was scientific. Althusser maintained that the recent emphasis on the young, humanistic Marx was misplaced, for in his mature work, Marx had jettisoned those premises in favor of historical materialism, a purportedly scientific understanding of the structures of capitalism and historical development. The truth of "scientific Marxism," Althusser claimed, could only be verified by the praxis of Communist movements.[182] Taubes successfully urged Suhrkamp to publish Althusser's book, *Pour Marx*, in German, though in his own lectures on the subject at the FU in 1973–74, Taubes was dismissive of Althusser's interpretation.[183] But the two men found one another congenial, and Taubes sometimes stayed at Althusser's house.[184] In late 1977 and early 1978, Althusser invited Taubes to the École normale to lecture to his classes on some key Gnostic concepts. Taubes observed that the students seemed to have two concerns: Maoism, and getting good grades on their *agrégation* examinations.[185] Althusser suffered from recurrent bouts of depression—he too had been treated with electroconvulsive therapy—and had missed out on the "revolutionary" events of May 1968 because he was in a psychiatric hospital at the time. In the course of 1978, Althusser's depressions became more frequent and severe, and in November 1980, he strangled his wife, apparently in a fit of madness. Jacob attended the funeral.[186]

Though Jacob's passive and reading knowledge of French was good, he was much less comfortable in spoken French than in German, Hebrew, or English. Many of his closest friends in Paris were German-speaking or bilingual, like the Bollacks. Another was Heinz Wismann, a German philosopher and literary scholar who taught at the École des hautes études en sciences sociales, another elite institution focused on the social sciences and humanities. Wismann, who was a younger collaborator of the Bollacks, first met Taubes when Wismann taught at the FU before moving to Paris. When in Paris, Taubes was an active participant in Wismann's seminars.

To Wismann, Taubes had "a Mephistophelian quality—not Satanic, but more like the lower devils." He seemed to be in several places at the same time: in Berlin, Paris, and Jerusalem. And he would appear unexpectedly and mysteriously, at odd hours and odd places, breaking up the normal flow of experience. After the death of Peter Szondi, for example, Wismann organized a seminar in his memory at the Maison des sciences de l'homme, a seminar to which Taubes was not invited. When it was over, the participants went together to a restaurant—and there was Jacob Taubes, having dinner with a young woman. When Wismann spoke with Taubes about the significance of the Apostle Paul and other religious themes, he never had the sense that Taubes was a believing Jew. Yet an

Orthodox scholar at the Centre nationale de la recherche scientifique with whom Taubes would attend synagogue in Paris reported to Wismann that he had never seen anyone pray with such fervor.[187]

In the course of the late 1970s and 1980s, as Taubes became more religious (after his fashion), such displays of fervent prayer were not confined to the synagogue. In the 1980s, Rudolf von Thadden, a German historian active in promoting German-French academic collaboration, was living in the Maison Heine. Taubes had a room across the hall. Thadden heard loud singing and came over to Taubes's room, where the door had been left open. He found Taubes on the floor, with a cheese on one side, and a Hebrew Bible on the other. Taubes proceeded to talk about the Bible. Thadden suspected that the whole scene had been staged to be provocative.[188]

In Paris, as in Berlin or Zurich, Taubes liked to spend time in bookstores, perusing new publications and watching the customers to get a sense of what was intellectually hot—one source of his intelligence for Suhrkamp. In Paris, his favorite was the famed La Hune on the Boulevard St.-Germain. It was on one such visit in the summer of 1977 that he ran into Arthur A. Cohen. By then Cohen had behind him a successful career as a publisher, and had written a number of works on Jewish topics, including a study of modern Jewish thought, *The Natural and the Supernatural Jew* (1964), and, most recently, a novel, *In the Days of Simon*, steeped in historical allusions to Sabbatai Zevi and his interpreter, Nathan of Gaza. They renewed their friendship, and in the years that followed, Jacob wrote long letters detailing his travels and inner tensions.

If Paris was Taubes's refuge from the tumult of the FU, Les Fontaines, a Jesuit cultural center in Chantilly some forty kilometers outside Paris, was Jacob's refuge from his Paris refuge. Housed in a chateau built by the Rothschilds, it featured a library of half a million books in the fields of theology, philosophy, and history.[189] Since Taubes was living with the Jesuits outside Paris and spending a good deal of time with the Dominicans in Jerusalem, stories began to spread that he had converted to Catholicism. Arthur A. Cohen wrote to him in December 1977, "Rumor circulates that you converted in Jerusalem. . . . As I have told you several times, if it relieves the burdens of your life, gives you sanguinity and focus . . . it's all right with me." So was the alternative chosen by Simone Weil, who was Catholic in all but name but had refused to convert. "Stay outside the church and ring bells if you wish," Cohen advised.[190]

Taubes's interest in Christianity was more than academic: he had, after all, long been fascinated by the Apostle Paul. He knew and respected a number of Jewish contemporaries who had converted to Christianity.

Yet there were limits to Jacob's identification with Christianity. He could never take seriously, for himself at least, the notion of Jesus as the Christ. As we've seen, it was what Paul had managed to make out of Jesus that interested Jacob. Nor could he disengage from the experience of the Holocaust, which took so many of his own relatives, although for much of his radical period in the 1960s and early 1970s, he had downplayed its significance. In the last decade of his life, in the aftermath of his mental breakdown, his turn to greater religiosity, and his re-involvement with Israel, thinking about the Holocaust—"Auschwitz," as he metonymously referred to the event—loomed ever larger in his consciousness.

On March 24, 1978—Good Friday—Jacob returned to Chantilly to be present for the Easter celebrations. Four hundred *lyceé* students, Catholic and Protestant, had come to the monastery for the occasion. He was in attendance on Sunday, when Easter was celebrated. Scripture was quoted and wine drunk from one cup. Then a boy named Robert was baptized. His parents were not there, it was said, "because of Auschwitz"—an indication that Robert was Jewish. The priest pronounced the Pauline dictum "There is neither Greek nor Jew nor slaves," followed by the singing of "Hevenu Shalom Aleichem," ending with the words (not in the original) "Jésus est venu." This was more than Jacob could tolerate. "While I deeply feel that we should be a community of peace etc. etc., I too am unconsolable because of Auschwitz," he wrote to Cohen. He realized that the young Christians around him looked at Jews, especially Jews their own age, as individuals "who have *not yet* reached Christ."[191] Moreover, Jacob did not want to be seen participating in what Jews considered apostasy. He departed from Chantilly, back to the Maison des sciences de l'homme, even though the secular, laicistic, atheistic atmosphere of the place did not accord with his own sensibilities.

Jacob continued to walk a tightrope between Judaism and Christianity. He created his own Pauline perch over an atheistic abyss. In the 1980s, he would become fascinated by Jean-Marie Lustiger, who had actually made the transition from Judaism to Christianity. Born Aaron Lustiger, he stemmed from a Jewish family. Hidden and raised as a Catholic during the Second World War, Lustiger converted to Catholicism at the age of thirteen, but continued to identify as a Jew after his conversion. He was named Archbishop of Paris in 1981 by Pope John Paul II, and Cardinal in 1983. Jacob made a point of meeting Lustiger and attending his sermons at the Notre Dame cathedral.[192]

In Paris, Jacob might spend weekdays at the Maison, while eating at a kosher restaurant in the Marais; attend an Orthodox synagogue on

Saturday; and on Sunday, go to Notre Dame to hear Lustiger preach—going up to greet him after the mass. In between, he attended parties that included the cream of the Parisian academic intellectuals.

The Hermeneutic Institute and Jacob's Berlin Coterie

As part of the deal that reorganized the Institute for Philosophy at the FU, Taubes gave up his claims to teach Judaica and the sociology of religion, but regained his Hermeneutic Institute, which reopened in 1979. The only other faculty member assigned to the Institute was Wolfgang Huebener, an expert in medieval philosophy with whom Jacob had taught, and who now formed a sort of alliance with him. (Like many such alliances, it eventually foundered on Jacob's treatment of Huebener.) The Institute had its own secretary and two assistants.

The central feature of the Institute was the Hermeneutic Colloquium, over which Jacob presided. It once again became an intellectual hub, bringing together senior professors with up-and-coming younger academics, and drawing in scholars from a variety of disciplines—especially comparative literature, philosophy, ethnography, and religion.

From the field of literature came Werner Hamacher and Winfried Menninghaus, scholars with a philosophical bent, in the tradition of Peter Szondi. Menninghaus had studied comparative literature at the FU—he was particularly interested in Walter Benjamin—and became a *Lektor* at Suhrkamp. In 1980, Taubes arranged for him to come back to the FU as a visiting professor, which soon turned into a permanent appointment.[193]

Hamacher had interests in contemporary French deconstructionist thinkers, including Jacques Derrida, who came to the FU under the auspices of the Hermeneutic Institute as well as the Institute for Comparative Literature. Though Taubes knew Derrida from Paris, he had neither much understanding nor much interest in the sort of literary criticism in which Derrida engaged, which was focused on demonstrating the instability of language and the self-contradictory nature of texts. Taubes was interested in texts on the assumption that they said something valuable about the world beyond the text, and was not much drawn to Derrida's claims that they could not do so.[194]

From anthropology came Fritz Kramer (born in 1941), who came to Berlin from Heidelberg, where he had been active in the SDS and then in the K-Gruppen that followed. Kramer helped initiate the "self-reflexive turn" in ethnography, in which practitioners reflected on the history of their discipline and the ways in which the assumptions of Western anthropologists had influenced their accounts of foreign cultures.[195] Another regular participant who came from the student left was Hans Dieter Kittsteiner, whose interests were originally in philosophy. He developed into a wide-ranging thinker on the border between philosophy and history, eventually trying to combine elements of Marx and Heidegger.[196] Other frequent participants were Eberhard Lämmert, professor of comparative literature and president of the FU from 1976 to 1983; Karlfried Gründer, a professor of the history of philosophy; and Gründer's student and successor, Wilhelm Schmidt-Biggemann, who taught some courses together with Taubes.[197]

Renate Schlesier and Gabriele Althaus, two women to whom Taubes had become close, were also among the participants. Althaus (1938–2018) was a left-wing activist who first became acquainted with Taubes and Brentano in the 1960s through the Republikaner Club. She got to know him better during the late 1970s, when she was a representative of the radical junior faculty on the university senate. When Taubes was on his crusade against the FB11 and wrote a long critique of it, which he intended to publish in the conservative *Frankfurter Allgemeine Zeitung*, he showed Althaus the proofs, and she convinced him that it would show more "solidarity" to publish it in the more left-wing *Frankfurter Rundschau*, which he did. He came up with a topic for her habilitation, on the work of Günther Anders, a critic of technology closely associated with the campaign against nuclear weapons, and in 1985–86 co-taught a course with her on Anders's thought.[198] For his part, Taubes took the position that Anders was wrong, an example of "leftist verbiage as nonsense."[199]

Like so many of his students at the FU, Renate Schlesier, born in 1947, was also active in the student left. She took courses with Taubes in the fields of philosophy and religion, and in 1971 completed her MA thesis (*Magisterarbeit*) with him. She edited a number of volumes on ancient and modern conceptions of myth and ultimately became a professor of religion at the FU.

The Hermeneutic Colloquium typically met on Monday evenings from 8 p.m. to 10 p.m. Some of the participants would then join Taubes at the Paris Bar, a restaurant on the Kantstraße in Berlin-Charlottenburg. It was best known not for its food, but as a hangout for artists, show folk, and prominent personalities—a place to see and be seen. There were large windows, and outsiders could peek inside. Taubes made a habit of bringing his coterie with him, along with guests from abroad, such as Susan Sontag. Taubes would sit at a table, surrounded by his assistants and by attractive and well-dressed women.[200] They sat not at the front with the beautiful people, but in a big booth at the back of the restaurant. In this setting, as in his seminars, Taubes's conversational vivacity, humor, and joie de vivre were on display.

Among Taubes's *Assistenten* at the Hermeneutic Institute were Richard Faber—who had begun to study with Taubes before his breakdown—and two younger men, Norbert Bolz and Christoph Schulte.

Bolz wrote his dissertation on Adorno's aesthetics under Taubes's supervision, but Taubes convinced him that Adorno was a less interesting thinker than Walter Benjamin. Together with Richard Faber, Bolz edited two collections of essays on aspects of Benjamin's oeuvre.[201] At a time when Taubes was hellbent on proclaiming the significance of the Carl Schmitt, he told Bolz, "You must get over your childish allergy to counter-revolutionary thinkers."[202] Taubes motivated Bolz to think about radical ideas on the right as well as the left, and Bolz wrote his habilitation thesis, completed the year after Taubes died, on "Philosophical Extremism Between the World Wars."[203] But in contrast to Taubes, Bolz was antipathetic to the antiliberal, antibourgeois ideas he explored, and eventually developed into a conservative liberal thinker, publishing books in defense of capitalism (*The Consumerist Manifesto*) and the bourgeois family, aimed beyond an academic audience.[204] Taubes, Bolz came to realize, lived in a dream world (*Traumwelt*) of ideas. Not only did he lack interest in practical affairs, he was disdainful of economic matters and showed no interest in empirical social research, which he dismissed as "Schmonzes" (trifles).[205]

Schulte arrived in 1980 and stayed until 1983. During that time, he served as Taubes's student assistant, which entailed doing the background research for his courses. In Schulte's case, it involved reading the scholarly literature from the 1960s and 1970s on the Apostle Paul and providing a summary to Taubes of what was most significant. When, as was often the case from 1982 to 1986, Taubes was too unwell to teach, the task would fall to these assistants. Though Taubes wanted him to stay and do a doctorate on Paul that would put Taubes's insights into some more systematic framework, Schulte thought that such a topic would be the kiss of death for a career in philosophy and pursued his doctorate with others.[206] He eventually became a scholar of Jewish studies.

Thus, in the decade after his return from his treatment in New York, Taubes continued to attract and stimulate intellectuals from many fields and political orientations.

CHAPTER FOURTEEN

"Ach, ja, Taubes . . ."

A CHARACTER SKETCH

HOW DID THOSE WHO KNEW JACOB TAUBES in the last decade of his life think of him? What were the most striking elements of his character? The impressions of his friends, colleagues, and family, though diverse, can be combined into a comprehensive portrait.

The Attractions of Taubes

The positive side of Jacob's persona was brilliantly captured by the aphorist and cultural critic Emil Cioran, Jacob's friend of long-standing in Paris, in his contribution to a 1983 festschrift published in honor of Jacob's sixtieth birthday. It is all the more striking coming from a man otherwise given to skepticism, and a pessimism bordering on misanthropy.

> As I'm not a specialist about anything or anyone, least of all about myself, it would be pretentious of me to comment upon the scholarly activity of Jacob Taubes. But what I can talk about are our encounters, which have stretched on for years; encounters that are very enriching for me, for each sojourn of my friend in Paris gives occasion to long monologues about untold subjects, sparkling with life. By that I mean that even if he were evoking Mesopotamia, he would find a way of making a foray into the present. Both a professor and non-professor, Taubes embodies a revulsion against every sort of dreary scholarship. Especially when it comes to matters of religion, he regards erudition for its own sake as senseless. What some heretic has professed is of value only to the degree that his standpoint—or his error—can still evoke an

echo in us. Gnosticism would not be worthy of a moment's notice did it not shake us to our depths; we must confront it precisely because we are its late accomplices and because it lives on in us. Here Taubes's talent is especially in evidence: he makes a past doctrine contemporary, he struggles with [the Gnostic Christian] Marcion as if he would still seduce us and lead us astray. His polemical temperament and his Tertullian impact [a reference to the Church Father known for his striking formulations] has the effect of enlivening everything he talks about. He has saved me the trouble of reading a pile of newly published books, mostly French, the majority of which were significant in content but repellent in style. Why tackle them, why suffer through them, when he has already done so, when he has processed and digested them for us?

To have relations of friendship only makes sense when our friends save us a great expenditure of energy, which our dilettantism or our tedium prevent us from mustering. . . . Only the passionate person, tempered by humor, is a pleasing, welcome guest! That applies to Jacob Taubes. An evening spent together with him leaves one, that rare thing, satisfied with oneself.

For a settled type as I am, the reports that he brings back from his journeys—his exploits in Jerusalem for example, the many-faceted experiences that he accumulated there—are simply unforgettable. His is a spirit that has not been adulterated by his knowledge, who with the same intensity, and at times, with the same detachment, can talk about original sin or the latest headlines.

Cioran's sketch captures an indubitable side of Jacob: his sociability, his intensity, the brilliance of his conversation, the range of his knowledge, and his eagerness to share it.

To those qualities, one should add his wit, his talents as a mimic, and his sense of humor.[1] His jokes were in the service of some insight or generalization. His favorite was about a shipwrecked man who lands on a desert island, where he meets its only inhabitant, a Jew. The Jew begins to show his guest around the island, beginning with the synagogue he has built. Then he shows his visitor the water hole where he fishes, the spot where he gathers mushrooms, and so on. Finally they reach the other end of the island, where the astonished visitor sees a synagogue identical to the first one. "What's that?" he asks. To which the Jew replies, "Ah, that is the synagogue that I *don't* attend." Taubes thought of this story as exemplifying the tendency of Jews to define themselves by negation—by what they are not.[2] He also confessed that it applied to himself.[3] Another such joke with a point: In 1943, two Jews, Aby and Sammy, go to a movie on Fifth Avenue, titled *Mein Kampf.* As they exit the theater, Aby asks Sammy, "Well, what did you think of the film?" To which Sammy replies, "Nu, the film was pretty good, but the book is much better!"[4] The joke is a study in the propensity to intellectual one-upmanship; the humor a vehicle for critique and self-critique.

But there were more sides to Jacob than that, some of them far less humorous or flattering. Those who knew him in the final decade of his life in Berlin, Paris, Zurich, and Jerusalem converged in their portrait of his character. Questioned about the man, they often began with some variation of the exclamation of his Berlin colleague, Wilhelm Schmidt-Biggemann, "Ach, ja, Taubes . . ."

Carnality and Intellectuality

Jacob Taubes lived in the world of ideas to an extent unusual even for an intellectual. Combined with this intellectuality, however, was a striking carnality, an unrestrained appetite for matters of the flesh. That was evident in his eating habits, the almost animal-like way in which he grasped at and devoured food, with a lack of concern for appearances, or for others.[5] At a dinner party at the home of a colleague, the hostess placed a platter of *Parmaschinken* (Prosciutto, dried ham) on the table. Taubes grabbed the platter and proceeded to load the entire serving onto his plate, leaving none for others. Taken aback, his colleague Peter Wapnewski asked, "Taubes, how can you, an Orthodox Jew, eat pork sausages?" "I am an Orthodox Jew," Jacob replied, "but I'm also a great sinner."[6]

Womanizing and Obsessive Behavior

That lack of restraint was increasingly evident in his behavior toward women, which sometimes bordered on the obsessive. He seemed to be constantly trying to seduce, and his erotic organ was his brain. He showed a remarkable disregard for the norms of academic propriety, as when he had a female student who was serving as his secretary provide him visual instruction in Chinese erotic techniques.[7]

Gabriele Althaus's extended experience with Taubes illustrates the extent of his obsessive behavior, but also the complexity of Taubes's relationship with the women he pursued. Althaus was an attractive, politically radical woman when Jacob met her again in 1978, at a time when she was a representative of the junior faculty on the university senate. He inquired about her husband, Klaus, a former student of Jacob's about whom he recalled a great deal, but who had declined into drunkenness. Taubes thus maneuvered his way into her intimate life. For the next three years, he pursued her. As he could not bear to be alone, he spent long hours at her home. At times, he would call her house a dozen times a day. One evening, when she was not home, Jacob spoke to her ten-year-old son on the phone, inquiring into his mother's whereabouts. Told she was at the movies, Jacob waited outside the movie theater where he thought she was likely to be found. When she resisted his advances, Taubes told her, "A woman in your position cannot afford to act this way." Taubes told others that he was in a liaison with Althaus. She continued to resist, and eventually their relationship turned into friendship, devoid of sexual pursuit. Jacob not only came up with a topic for her habilitation—which would be sponsored by Margherita von Brentano—but years later he successfully lobbied the *Wissenschaftssenator* to get her a permanent appointment at the FU.[8]

Renate Schlesier had a similar experience with Taubes. "I have a fondness for intellectual, beautiful women," he told her, and for years in the early 1980s, he tried to get her to sleep with him—indeed, publicly declared his desire to do so. He sat outside her seminar room and accosted her when she emerged. Yet here, too, what began as sexual pursuit resulted in friendship and support, for Jacob genuinely admired her as a scholar. One of his last letters was to the *Wissenschaftssenator*, recommending her as his possible successor.[9]

One of the notable features throughout Taubes's career was his enthusiastic promotion of women scholars, mentoring them through their studies and advancing their professional prospects. That these were often women whom he had tried to bed—successfully or unsuccessfully—demonstrates the complexity of these relations, which were erotic in both a physical and intellectual sense.

Seduction, Abandonment, Betrayal

Jacob's attempts at seduction sometimes had more pernicious effects. He had an eerie ability not only to intuit the deepest vulnerabilities of those he met, but to look them deep in the eyes and open them up to confessional conversation by conveying the sense that he was absolutely "there" for them. Jacob's intense interest gave them the impression that this was the decisive moment in their lives. Once exposed to Jacob's intensity, they craved recognition from him. Yet after a while—sometimes a few minutes, sometimes a few encounters—his interest would turn to boredom. His gaze would lose its intensity, as if a snake-like membrane covered his eye. Sometimes, Jacob would open a wound that seemingly only he could heal. When his attention turned away, it left some of them puzzled or regretful, and others in despair. There were stories in Berlin and in Paris of women Jacob enchanted and then dropped who broke down mentally and had to be institutionalized.[10]

Another source of Jacob's attractiveness to women was the sense he conveyed of helplessness, or of boredom, and the prospect that they—and only they—could rescue him from these discontents.[11]

The memories of many of those who experienced Jacob's sociability and his capacity for friendship were frequently marred by experiences of unreliability or betrayal. To begin with, he had a weakness for indiscretion, or rather took pleasure in passing on information about people he knew to others who had no business knowing it. In fact, one way of conveying information that was nominally secret to a wider audience was to reveal it to Jacob in confidence.[12] To that was added Jacob's tendency not only to turn upon those he had befriended over some intellectual or ideological or personal disagreement, but to do so with a vehemence that left them distraught and bewildered. A number of his colleagues—Carsten Colpe, Wolfgang Hübener, and Karlfried Gründer—went through such a process. In the case of Hübener, the break led to a deep depression. Gründer took to returning Taubes's insulting letters unopened.[13] Of the colleagues with whom he had associated for years in the Poetik und Hermeneutik circle, none were eager to contribute an obituary about him, though Dieter Henrich ultimately took on the task.[14]

Theatricality, Ambiguity, and Ambivalence

Those who knew Jacob well were struck by his theatricality and cultivated ambiguity. He was forever inhabiting roles, one after another, sometimes changing in the course of a day. Edmund Leites, his friend from New York who visited him in Berlin in 1981–82, saw him change in the course of the day from a pious Jew to a religious skeptic and back.[15] In Jerusalem, as we've seen, his dress gave him the appearance of a priest or pastor. "He was always playing a role," noted Leon Wieseltier, who encountered him there. He played on the esoteric, conveying the impression that the most important knowledge was confined to a spiritual elite, entrance to which he could control. In New York, too, Michael Wyschogrod was struck by the many personae that Jacob seemed to inhabit, or that seemed to inhabit him.[16] Add to that the fact that Jacob was perfectly willing to take opposite sides of a debate, to assume a contrarian role, in the interest of being stimulating.[17]

Complicating the *ambiguity* of Jacob's persona was his genuine *ambivalence* on the issues, large and small, of greatest urgency to him. Jacob's religiosity was deeply conflicted. On the one hand, he engaged in and took comfort from traditional Jewish religious practice. But that practice was not reconciled with his other beliefs—including whether or what sense he believed in God. He maintained that after the destruction of the Second Temple, the Jews were faced with two possibilities. The first was a Gnostic rejection of the world (reflected perhaps in Paul); the second was the creation of a new order by an act of will and imagination, which the rabbis accomplished through the Talmud and halacha.[18] Jacob might therefore engage in Orthodox religious practice, including fervent prayer, but since Jacob understood Orthodox Jewish life as a creation of human will and imagination, he could not accept its ultimate truth claims as binding upon himself.

Belief and doubt, Judaism and Christianity, Zionism and ultra-Orthodox rejection thereof, political radicalism and an awareness of its intrinsic dangers, piety and antinomianism—rather than choosing one pole over another, on each of these issues, Jacob continued to embrace both, often at the same time. A questioning mind may not be satisfied with any of the potential answers to the most difficult questions. In that sense, Jacob's ambivalences were a reflection of a mind too questioning and a soul too divided to come down on either side.[19]

But beyond ambiguity, Jacob was also capable of simple deception—indeed, he took a certain delight in it. In the early 1980s, for example, at the Maison de l'homme in Paris, he met Joseph Shatzmiller, a professor of medieval Jewish history and visiting fellow there. Asked what he was doing at the Maison, Jacob claimed to be writing a history of the Manhattan Project as an achievement of Jews.[20] He was of course working on no such project. He also told Shatzmiller that while he regarded Gershom Scholem as a great scholar, he had elected not to continue in Jerusalem because Scholem had chosen another scholar, Zwi Werblowsky, over him—another fabrication, as Shatzmiller realized.

Many of the character traits that Jacob exhibited may well have been linked to his manic depressive condition. It gave him a certain power, energy, and magic: both white magic and black magic.[21] The restlessness and inability to engage in persistent work; the talkativeness and profusion of ideas; the excessive need for social life; the charm in interpersonal encounters together with the ability to uncover vulnerable spots in others and exploit them; the excessive involvement in pleasurable activities, including hypersexuality, combined with an inclination toward risk-taking—all of these qualities are associated with manic depression of the Bipolar II variety. Those qualities, together with Jacob's attraction to conflict, with his propensity to dissimulation and to betrayal, help explain why so many of those who knew him described him as "Mephistophelian"—a term with implications of fostering creativity—or, more critically, as "demonic" or "diabolical."

Loneliness, Melancholy, and the Search for Recognition

Those who knew Jacob well and over a long period of time came to recognize that for all his sociability, for all his animation in conversation, for all his wit, there was about Jacob Taubes a deep loneliness, an ongoing search for human connection. But Jacob's propensities to obsessive behavior, to indiscretion, and to betrayal made it difficult for him to hold on to friends over the long haul. His chronic womanizing led to suspicion among male colleagues, not to speak of poisoning his relationship with Susan and with Margherita.

Alongside this quest for human connection was an ongoing search for recognition. The expectations for Jacob as a scholar and spiritual leader had been high, beginning with his parents, and continued by some of his teachers and by those who hired him. Those expectations were shared by Jacob himself. But there was a gap between his promise and his achievement, between his undeniable talents and what he had made of them, and that gap grew wider the more he aged. For most professors and writers, the quest for recognition is satisfied through research and publications—but Jacob had few of these, and none that would entitle him to the status he had expected to achieve.

One way in which Jacob responded to this unslaked thirst for recognition was by associating himself with the famous, or with their former wives, or with their offspring. He was attracted to men and women of distinguished lineage. He took pleasure in having affairs with the former wives or girlfriends of famous people. In his sixties, he took to bragging to all and sundry about his erstwhile relationship with Ingeborg Bachmann.[22]

Elements of Jacob's personality betray the characteristic features of narcissism, as understood by psychologists and psychotherapists. These include a certain grandiosity of aspiration and self-image—he did, after all, aspire to be another Paul—an excessive desire for admiration and attention, a strong sense of entitlement, and theatricality. All of these, along with the need to consort with the famous and his pleasure in cutting down others were, in part at least, a response to the sense of loneliness, emptiness, despair, and self-doubt that perceptive friends and family noticed in him. Straddling the major dilemmas that faced him made him an acute critic, but also gave him a perch of apparent superiority from which he could criticize the insufficiencies of others.

The persistence with which Jacob pursued an encounter with Carl Schmitt, and then the doggedness with which he returned to that encounter in the last years of his life, cannot be separated from this quest for recognition. For Taubes was convinced that Carl Schmitt was among the great minds of the age. And to be associated with such a figure was itself a path to ongoing fame.

CHAPTER FIFTEEN

Schmitt and Political Theology Revisited, 1982–86

THE FINAL FIVE YEARS of Taubes's life were a rollercoaster of intellectual vitality, depression, a heart attack that drove him to the edge of death, and finally a cancer that would kill him. Much of his intellectual life revolved around issues of religion and its relationship to politics and to modernity, issues that he explored in dialogue with some of the leading German intellectuals of his day. His fascination with the person and ideas of Carl Schmitt deepened. Jacob's path to his direct encounter with Schmitt was neither straight nor straightforward. It was hampered by the gulf of experience and sensibility that separated Taubes from one of the most prestigious legitimizers and defenders of the Nazi regime. For decades, Taubes was reluctant to meet Schmitt face to face. Once he decided to make the attempt, he relied upon a most unconventional acquaintance to do so: Hans-Dietrich Sander, a radical German nationalist, a Schmitt acolyte, and an antisemite to boot. Taubes's teaching at the university increasingly focused on those he saw as apocalyptic thinkers—Schmitt, Benjamin, and Paul. At the end of this period, Taubes would encounter Aleida Assmann, a young scholar and mother with whom he fell in love, and who, together with her husband Jan, would be largely responsible for his posthumous fame.

Schmitt, Sander, and the Benjamin Letter

In the decades after the Second World War, Carl Schmitt devoted much of his efforts to trying to restore his reputation and extend his intellectual influence. He cultivated the image of himself as a "Restrainer" (*Aufhalter*), who had sought to preserve the Weimar Republic from dissolution. Over time, he developed connections to a younger generation of jurists, historians, and political theorists, most of whom did not share his politics or his intellectual radicalism, but drew upon one or another of his ideas or upon intellectual sources he suggested to them.[1] But as a prominent and knowledgeable Jewish intellectual in Germany, Jacob Taubes would play a special role in legitimizing Schmitt.

Taubes's fascination with Carl Schmitt puzzled when it did not appall many of his friends and colleagues. That fascination had several sources. The first was Schmitt's contention that there was some inextricable link between theology and politics, a thesis first presented in his *Politische Theologie* of 1922, and reasserted in the decades thereafter. The links between these realms lay close to the heart of Taubes's concerns as well, going back to the period of his graduate education in Zurich. Then there was Schmitt's erudition: the range of his knowledge in intellectual history, and his willingness to point scholars to forgotten debates of relevance to their own scholarship—in his footnotes, letters, and in person. Thus, while in Jerusalem in 1949, Taubes had turned to Schmitt's *Verfassungslehre* for guidance in early modern philosophy, and a few years later, he wrote to Schmitt for help in editing a proposed volume for Beacon Press on conservatism.

An additional motivation was Taubes's desire to understand why intellectuals of Schmitt's stature had been willing to support the Nazi regime, a subject he had discussed with George Schwab in New York in the late 1950s. Then there was a shared antipathy to liberal, bourgeois normality: Schmitt was fascinated by the "state of exception" (*Ausnahmezustand*), that is, circumstances in which normality broke down, and so was Taubes. Another factor, difficult to evaluate but impossible to overlook, was that in many of the circles in which Taubes traveled (though not all), his professed admiration for Schmitt served to scandalize, thus allowing him to engage in an exhibitionist performance as a bad boy.[2] Last but not least was Taubes's conviction that Schmitt was among the great thinkers of the age, in whose company he was eager to find himself.

Carl Schmitt tended to conceive of modern politics as locked into the iron cage of economic and technical modes of thought, leading to a flaccid existence, devoid of intensity. Taubes and Schmitt also shared a disdain for modern liberalism and for what they took to be the all-too-petty concerns of normal bourgeois life. One of Taubes's favorite sayings was taken from the Russian-Jewish writer, Isaac Babel, a sometime supporter of Bolshevism: "Banality is the counter-revolution."[3] The implication was that radicalism was an escape from banality. In short, Taubes had a lust for extremes, a need to escape from what he saw as the boredom and triviality of life.[4]

For all Schmitt's talk about "political theology," his account of the limits of liberalism and the illuminating role of the "state of exception" require no theological basis. In his usage, "theological" really has nothing to do with the divine, and everything to do with *intensity* of commitment. "The political" and the "state of exception" were antidotes to what Schmitt called the age of neutralizations—i.e., a world marked by technology, economics, and bureaucracy—and the waning of drama that that term implies. Taubes shared that view. Hermann Lübbe, a conservative liberal who knew Schmitt, called him a "Romantic of the exceptional situation," driven by an "intellectual and aesthetic weakness for exceptional political positions."[5] Taubes shared those propensities as well.

Taubes had given a seminar (*Übung*) in the spring of 1973 entitled "History and Theory: Political Theology as Philosophy of History: On Carl Schmitt's and Walter Benjamin's Theories of History."[6] The course began by calling attention to Benjamin's letter to Carl Schmitt of December 9, 1930, which accompanied Benjamin's gift of his recently published book on the German tragic drama (*Trauerspiel*). "To be explored," noted the course description, "is whether Benjamin advocated a 'theological politics' in contrast to Carl Schmitt's 'political theology.'" But in fact the course never got around to discussing any of Schmitt's work, and of Benjamin's, only his "Theses on the Philosophy of History." These were explicated in great detail, along with a discussion of recent controversies about them—drawn mostly from an article by Gerhard Kaiser still to be found in Taubes's file, with his underlining.[7]

In his letter to Scholem of 1977 in which he proposed the anti-festschrift, Taubes had written that he regarded Schmitt as still the most significant mind in Germany. That same year, Hans Blumenberg wrote a letter to Taubes in which he criticized the tendency to refuse to deal seriously and honestly with the work and person of Carl Schmitt, simply on account of the abominable things Schmitt had written half a century before. Blumenberg was opposed to the new censoriousness and censorship of figures like Heidegger, who fell into the same category, even though he had no sympathy for Heidegger as a person or for the substance of his thought. While Blumenberg did not question the right to avoid such contact, he informed Taubes that he, Blumenberg, had been in direct contact with Schmitt since 1971.[8] Taubes now resolved to try to meet with Schmitt, using as his intermediary Hans-Dietrich Sander, among the more outlandish figures whom Taubes would befriend and promote.

The connection came through Armin Mohler, Jacob's right-wing friend since his student days in Switzerland. By the 1970s, Mohler, now the managing director (*Geschäftsführer*) of the Siemens Foundation in Munich, had become an influential figure in West German political culture.[9] He published books and articles intended to promote an unapologetic sense of German national identity. In the 1960s, he critiqued the culture of American-inspired "Re-education" (*Umerziehung*)—intended to convey the mechanisms and virtues of liberal democracy to the Germans—and *Vergangenheitsbewältigung*, that is, coming to terms with the Nazi past, on the grounds that it fostered "national masochism" (*Nationalmasochismus*).[10] Mohler regarded Carl Schmitt as his teacher and master. He kept up an intensive correspondence with Schmitt and worked assiduously to promote Schmitt's ideas and reputation.[11]

It was at a small gathering hosted by Mohler in Munich on May 31, 1977, that Taubes met Sander.

Sander had been born in eastern Germany in 1928. As a young man, he studied at the FU, but after coming under the influence of Brecht, he moved to East Germany in 1952 where he worked in the theater. Then, in 1957, he moved back to West Germany, where, now an anti-Communist, he became a journalist with *Die Welt*.[12]

In 1966, the editor of *Die Welt*, Hans Zehrer, passed away. The new editor, Ernst Cramer, was a German Jew who had been arrested on *Kristallnacht* and imprisoned in Buchenwald, before managing to emigrate to the United States. Cramer returned to Germany as a soldier in the American army and became deputy editor of the *Neue Zeitung*, published by the American occupation authorities. He eventually went to work for the publisher Axel Springer, and together with Springer, helped guide the West German moderate right in a direction that was pro-American, pro-Israeli, and unequivocally opposed to antisemitism.[13] When Cramer ascended to the editorship of *Die Welt*, Sander was pushed out, perhaps, he speculated, because of some derisive remarks he had made over the years about Springer's philo-Semitism.[14]

Sander returned to university studies and began work on a doctoral dissertation on Marxist aesthetics. In 1967, on Mohler's recommendation, Sander began to correspond with Carl Schmitt.[15] Schmitt sent Sander a copy of the December 9, 1930, letter from Benjamin, in which Benjamin stated that his book, *The Origins of the German Tragic Drama* (*Ursprung des deutschen Trauerspiels*) owed a good deal of its discussion of the theory of sovereignty in the seventeenth century to Schmitt's work. In Sander's doctoral dissertation, *Marxist Ideology and Theories of Art*, published in 1970, he included the text of the 1930 letter.[16] Schmitt was grateful to Sander for trying to call attention to Benjamin's debt to Schmitt.[17] But Sander's book found no public or scholarly resonance, and his prospects for a professorial career seemed dashed.[18] He wondered whether he was on some secret boycott list kept by the Jews, but considered that perhaps these conspiracies were figments of his imagination, since even Schmitt's right-wing disciples seemed to lose interest in him.[19]

Inspired by Schmitt's description of Spinoza in his Nazi-era book, *Leviathan in Thomas Hobbes' Theory of the State* (*Der Leviathan in der Staatslehre des Thomas Hobbes*) (1938), Sander traced a link between what he called the deracination (*Entortung*) of the Jews and their attraction to Marxist theory. As Sander contemplated a second edition of his book, Schmitt warned him not to expand it in the direction of "the Jewish problem." That issue, Schmitt wrote, was "deadly" (*tödlich*).[20] But Sander dilated on the subject in the new edition of his book nevertheless.[21]

Sander lamented the fact that Germans were not permitted to cross the Rubicon of "a critical perspective on the Jewish Question."[22] And by and by, he played down the evils of the Nazi regime.[23] By 1975, even some conservative journals were refusing to publish his articles because of his "propensities toward Nazism."[24] In his correspondence with Schmitt, Sander time and again lamented the fact that the "Jewish Question" was taboo in the Federal Republic.[25]

By mid-1976, Sander had lost the minor teaching job he had held at the Technische Universität in Hannover, where faculty and students objected to the critical views put forth in a book he had written about literature in East Germany. By year's end, he and his wife were living in Munich off of government unemployment benefits.[26] Still eager to pursue an academic career by writing a habilitation thesis, he applied to the German Research Foundation (Deutsche Forschungsgemeinschaft) for a stipend, hoping to be habilitated at the University of Munich. But his path there was blocked by Peter Ludz, a professor of political science who was an expert on the East German regime. It was then that Taubes came to his rescue.[27]

When Sander met Taubes at Mohler's party, he showed Taubes his book. Impressed by his perusal of Sander's critique of the Frankfurt School, Taubes invited Sander to meet Herbert Marcuse in the Engadine later that summer. Marcuse did not show up. But Taubes offered to see to Sander's habilitation at the FU, telling him, "You're so extreme that I'm the only one who can afford to sponsor you."

Taubes campaigned to get a visiting post for Sander at the FU's Institute for Philosophy. His proposal was turned down almost unanimously by its faculty. But he managed to get the Institute for Comparative Literature to invite Sander to offer a lecture course on the aesthetic theory of Marx and Engels, and a seminar on Brecht's play *The Measures Taken* (*Maßnahme*).[28]

At first, Taubes involved Sander in a conference he was planning on the subject of political theology. But Sander dropped out, as he informed Schmitt, because it was dominated by leftists and centrists, that is, intellectuals who supported the "juste milieu" of the Federal Republic.[29]

After consulting with Sander, Taubes wrote to Schmitt in 1977, asking for permission to republish a chapter devoted to Spinoza from Schmitt's 1938 book on Hobbes—a chapter on Spinoza as the "first liberal Jew" who undermined the authority of the Hobbesian state by allowing for freedom of conscience. It was to be published in the new journal devoted to "Hermeneutics and the Human Sciences" that Taubes was planning, to be entitled *KASSIBER*. The title, he informed Schmitt, was Rotwelsch (grifters' argot) for a secret message. Taubes's plan was to introduce Schmitt's piece with a reference to Benjamin's 1930 letter to Schmitt.[30] The first issue was to be devoted to Spinoza, and to include an essay from the 1930s by Leo Strauss, together, Taubes hoped, with the excerpt from Schmitt's book.

KASSIBER was to be published by *Syndikat Autoren- und Verlagsgesellschaft*, founded by Karl Markus Michel, who had been an editor at Suhrkamp and left it to found his own publishing house.[31] As Schmitt was aware, the term "Kassiber" was at present most closely associated with the notes surreptitiously smuggled out of the Stammheim prison by the members of the Red Army Faction. (Michel had suggested the title as an allusion to the journal's goal of occupying the terrain "between Starnberg and Stammheim," that is between Jürgen Habermas and Baader-Meinhof.[32])

Sander wrote to Schmitt enthusiastic about the prospect. The coupling of selections from Schmitt with Strauss would go a long way to enhancing Schmitt's reputation, Sander thought. "It might well create a whole new intellectual-historical landscape."[33] A week later, he wrote to Schmitt again, stressing that the publication would break the "boycott" to which he thought Schmitt's works were still subject.[34]

At first Schmitt was amenable. Always eager to burnish his reputation, he told Sander to tell Taubes that in the chapter of his 1938 book in question, he had positively cited a historian by the name of Gerhart Ladner, who was in fact a Jew. (Actually, he had converted to Catholicism in 1933.) Thus did Schmitt seek to portray himself as having resisted antisemitism during the Third Reich.[35] But Hans Blumenberg warned Schmitt off from participating in Taubes's venture, and Schmitt politely declined.[36]

FIGURE 15.1 AND FIGURE 15.2. Two photos of Jacob Taubes, 1980.
(Ethan and Tania Taubes Collection.)

Taubes then suggested that Suhrkamp publish a collection of pieces on "Political Theology" that would include selections from Schmitt's book of 1922, from Erik Peterson's critique, from Schmitt's more recent *Politische Theologie II*, along with a preface by Blumenberg or Taubes himself. He also suggested another volume of Schmitt's essays on literary topics, a collection that he would edit with suggestions from Sander. That, Taubes reckoned, would arouse Habermas's resistance against Suhrkamp publishing the "fascistic intelligentsia" (*faschistische Intelligenz*), but Taubes thought he would prevail. For his part, Unseld was prepared to publish such a volume, and wrote to Schmitt accordingly.[37] But after talking it over with Sander, Schmitt turned down the idea of publishing with Suhrkamp.[38]

Taubes and Schmitt now resolved to meet, and Sander volunteered to accompany Taubes on his first visit to Schmitt's isolated home. But Schmitt made it clear that he did not want Sander to attend: he wanted to meet Taubes alone (*nur unter vier Augen*).[39] Once Taubes began to actually visit Schmitt, there was a falling out between Sander and Schmitt, and then between Sander and Taubes.[40]

Meeting Carl Schmitt

Schmitt invited Taubes to meet with him at his home, and in March 1978, Taubes wrote again to Schmitt informing him of his plans to journey to Plettenberg to meet in person "eye to eye" (*Aug in Aug*)—one of his favorite phrases. He framed their meeting as a potentially historic occasion that would live on into posterity. He planned to conclude his affairs in Berlin and with Suhrkamp in Frankfurt "to be spiritually free for a conversation that, if it succeeds, will leave behind a trace."[41]

By the time of Taubes's visits, Carl Schmitt was ninety years old and feeble, though not lacking in wit: he signed one of his letters to Taubes, "From the intensive-care unit of the World Spirit, your aged Carl Schmitt."[42] The first of their conversations took place several months later, when in September Taubes visited Schmitt at his home for three days. He traveled there together with Martin Kriele, a professor of law with whom he was planning a colloquium on political theology.[43]

Judging by a letter that Taubes dispatched to Schmitt shortly after his visit, their conversation included Schmitt's explanation of "the misadventures of the long life of a jurist"—that is, how he came to support the Nazi regime. Taubes assured him that "precisely as an arch-Jew I hesitate to confront the matter head on." That was because Jews like him had no choice, having been declared by Hitler to be the absolute enemy. And those who had no choice were in no position to judge the others, he claimed. Nevertheless, he needed to try to understand what had happened, the turning point that had led to catastrophe, a catastrophe, as Taubes put it, both for the Jews and the Germans (*unsere und die Ihrige*).

Taubes then launched into a discussion of political theology, specifically of Erik Peterson's 1935 critique of Schmitt's conception of political theology, in which Peterson had insisted that no preferred political form could be deduced from a proper understanding of the Trinity. Taubes wrote as if Schmitt's decision to throw his weight behind the Nazi regime was a product of Schmitt's misunderstanding of Christian political theology. How, Taubes wondered, was it possible for Schmitt to adopt the racist antisemitism of the regime (what he called its "Theo-zoologie")? He then turned to Schmitt's 1938 book on Hobbes: contrary to what Schmitt had asserted there, Taubes wrote, it was not Spinoza as the "first liberal Jew" who had insisted on the limitation of the state when it came to matters religious—it was the Apostle Paul. Taubes ended by suggesting to Schmitt that they meet again to explore Romans 11, "which seems to me the most significant political theology from both a Jewish and Christian point of view."[44]

Taubes journeyed again to Plettenberg on November 23. It was on this occasion, it seems, that he expounded his understanding of Paul's Letter to the Romans and its implications for Christians and Jews, after which, according to Taubes's account, Schmitt said, "You have to tell people about this before you die."[45] It was the interpretation he would repeat in the lectures on "The Political Theology of Paul" that he gave some eight years later, shortly before his death.

The very next day, Schmitt sent Taubes a letter, thanking him for his visit "which was precious for me," and assuring him that the subject matter of their two visits would continue to engage him for the rest of his life— though, Schmitt added, actuarially that was unlikely to be long.[46] In the months that followed, Taubes sent Schmitt letters with updates about the colloquium he was teaching at the FU on Schmitt and Benjamin, and on the colloquium he was organizing on political theology, in which he hoped Schmitt would participate. By then, they were addressing one another as *Vehehrter und lieber* (honored and dear). On the three hundredth anniversary of the death of Thomas Hobbes, Taubes published an article about him in the *Neue Zürcher Zeitung* that relied in good part on Schmitt's interpretation—an article he sent to Schmitt.[47]

In between visits to Israel, Taubes presided over the colloquium "The Prince of This World: Carl Schmitt and His Aftermath" at Bad Homburg. After it ended on February 2, he traveled once again to visit Schmitt in

Plettenberg.[48] They continued to correspond through the end of 1980, by which time Taubes was deeply engaged in his new project on political theology—a project inspired by his reading of Schmitt.

Politics, Theology, and History: Taubes among the German Philosophers

From the mid-1960s through the mid-1980s, Taubes engaged in a series of overlapping debates with three of Germany's most prominent philosophers, whom he came to know through Poetik und Hermeneutik: Hans Blumenberg, Odo Marquard, and Hermann Lübbe. All three were about Taubes's age. Elsewhere, we've examined his relationship with intellectuals on the left and on the far right. Blumenberg, Marquard, and Lübbe, by contrast, were centrists. Despite great differences in style and temperament— Blumenberg preferred the well-documented treatise, Marquard the allusive essay; Lübbe was a public intellectual, Blumenberg a very private one— they all shared a commitment to the modern, liberal, "bourgeois" order of the Federal Republic, an order that Taubes denigrated.

Their debates were partly formulated as contestations and refutations of three intellectuals of the older generation whom we have already encountered: Carl Schmitt, Karl Löwith, and Eric Voegelin. Taubes served at various times as a protagonist, promoter, and foil in these debates. Common to the debates were concerns about the relationship between politics and religion.[49]

DEBATE 1: THE LEGITIMACY OF THE MODERN AGE

In 1966, Hans Blumenberg published *The Legitimacy of the Modern Age* in Suhrkamp's Reihe Theorie—thanks, as we have seen, to Jacob Taubes, who had brought Blumenberg to the press. It was a big book, historically rich and conceptually complex (indeed, sometimes too rich and too complex to make its argument easy to follow). The book took aim at a variety of interpretations of Western history in order to defend, as its title telegraphed, the legitimacy of the modern age.

In what sense was the modern age "illegitimate"? Blumenberg's targets were many and varied: what they had in common was a propensity to interpret the modern world as one of decline (as in Heidegger or Hannah Arendt), or its self-proclaimed novelty as an illusion, or its progress a fundamental continuation of Christianity. One of the implicit addressees of Blumenberg's book was Jacob Taubes. When the book was published,

Blumenberg wrote to Taubes, "I write for a few readers, whose expectations I know, or suppose myself to know . . . it is them whom I address. You may be certain, dear Mr. Taubes, that I wrote many pages in this book with you in mind."[50]

One of Blumenberg's targets was Karl Löwith. Löwith had been forced to leave Germany in 1933 because of his "racially" Jewish origin. In 1952 he returned to Germany, where he taught at the University of Heidelberg, and was very much a presence in the world of German philosophy. Löwith's book *From Hegel to Nietzsche: The Revolution in Nineteenth Century Thought* had influenced the young Jacob Taubes when he was writing *Abendländische Eschatologie*. Taubes's book, in turn, influenced Löwith's next book on the philosophy of history, published in English in 1949 as *Meaning in History* and in German in 1953 as *Weltgeschichte und Heilsgeschehen*. There, Löwith examined the ways in which thinkers in the Western tradition had conceived of history and its direction. Löwith provided a chronologically reverse account, beginning at the end, so to speak, with the nineteenth-century thinkers, Marx, Hegel, and August Comte. He then moved back in time to earlier thinkers, back through the Middle Ages, and ending with the Biblical view of history. Löwith's thesis, in a nutshell, was that the Biblical view of history as having a linear direction and leading to salvation (*Heilsgeschichte*) was a radical break from the Greek conception of history as circular or nonlinear. In all of these claims, he agreed with some of the fundamental assertions of Taubes's *Abendländische Eschatologie*, and he relied on Taubes's account in interpreting Joachim of Fiore as a key point of transition in making the process of redemption an inner-worldly one. Thus on key points of *analysis*, Löwith and Taubes were at one. Where they differed was in their *evaluation*. Taubes thought the development of the Biblical (he didn't distinguish here between Jewish and Christian views) view of history into the modern progressive philosophy of history as represented by Hegel and Marx was a fundamentally positive development, a continuation of an eschatological mentality in a new more secular guise. Löwith, by contrast, thought that the belief that history had a given direction, and that it was fundamentally redemptive, was an illusion, and one with pernicious consequences that lived on as a result of the influence of Christianity in a post-Christian era. His tacit preference was for a pre-Christian, Stoic view of the cosmos. He regarded the modern scientific ideal of the mastery of nature as misguided, and criticized "the secular presumption that we have to transform the world into a better world in the image of man and to save unregenerate nations by Westernization and re-education."[51]

DEBATE 2: GNOSTICISM AND THE MODERN AGE

Eric Voegelin was another object of Blumenberg's critique. He too had returned to Germany from his position in the United States, to become the founding director of an institute of political science at the University of Munich. Voegelin, it will be recalled, regarded Gnosticism as a disruptive force that refused to come to terms with man's real condition. In his *New Science of Politics* and subsequent works, he had developed a critique of modernity as characterized by ideologies that he regarded as a recurrence of Gnosticism. Here again there was an *analytic* overlap with Taubes's view of Gnosticism as a recurrent phenomenon. Where they differed was in their evaluation: for Taubes it was a fundamentally positive force, leading to the negation of the contemporary order and making a better one possible.

DEBATE 3: POLITICS, THEOLOGY, AND HISTORY

Another object of Blumenberg's critique was the contention of Carl Schmitt that had so influenced Taubes, namely that all modern political concepts were secularizations of religious ones. That assertion was first made by Schmitt in his 1922 *Political Theology*. In the decades that followed, Schmitt had returned from time to time to his contention about the relationship between theological and political concepts and symbols. Blumenberg took Schmitt to mean that modern concepts of political sovereignty were in some sense a pale reflection or hollowed-out version of earlier, theological conceptions. (Schmitt later responded that that was not what he had meant to imply.[52] But then the very imprecision of the term was part of what made it so useful to Schmitt and attractive to others.[53]) Schmitt too was a presence in contemporary German intellectual life, albeit one whose influence was felt more behind the scenes.

According to Blumenberg, the rise in late medieval scholasticism of nominalism, which maintained that God could do anything through his will and that the world was not intrinsically ordered, destroyed belief in God as a reliable source of order. That led to the notion that man was dependent on his own resources, and eventually to the belief that he could shape his world. Metaphysics was abandoned, replaced by an emphasis on the use of reason, knowledge, science, and technique. The Gnostic notion of the created world as evil was now replaced with a conception of the world as neither intrinsically good nor evil, but rather subject to human alteration—a process that Blumenberg defended as human "self-assertion" (*Selbstbehauptung*). Thus the modern era, with its conception of the world as malleable through science, had "vanquished" the Gnostic conception of the world as fallen; it was not "Gnostic" as Voegelin maintained; nor was its notion of progress an outcome of Christian eschatology or dependent upon it, as Löwith and Taubes had suggested. And, contra Schmitt, its central concepts were genuinely new, not a reflection, pale or otherwise, of theology. A key element of the novelty of the modern period was the positive value it placed on curiosity (*Neugier*), encouraging open-ended intellectual and technological development as a source of power, in a manner without precedent in the Greek or Christian traditions.

In short (or rather, over hundreds of pages), Blumenberg offered an account on the plane of the history of ideas that he thought explained the intellectual origins of the modern world, while defending the novelty and legitimacy of its achievements.[54] Blumenberg suggested that the legacy of the Christian past was to bequeath vague expectations that institutions are supposed to provide coherent, encompassing answers about the meaningfulness of human life, expectations that tend to overburden and delegitimate the institutions of modern liberal society, leading, as in the case of Heidegger, to the pernicious search for alternatives.[55] The idea that history was to have some ultimate meaning and direction—a holdover of expectations from Christianity—led some modern thinkers (such as Marxists) to formulate elaborate "philosophies of history" and ideas of inevitable progress that would liberate man or free him of alienation.[56] Against these ideas of wholesale, transformative Progress, Blumenberg defended the possibility of partial and piecemeal progress.

The critique of the philosophy of history was picked up and developed in other directions by Odo Marquard and Hermann Lübbe. Both Marquard and Lübbe had studied in Münster after the war with Joachim Ritter, a philosopher renowned less for his published work than for bringing together scholars from a range of disciplines and generations into fruitful interaction (discussed in chapter 9). In the annals of West German intellectual history, the "Ritter School" has gone down as the font of a variety of liberal conservatism that, in the face of the German New Left, set itself the task of the philosophical defense of bourgeois, capitalist, democracy— though the range of political commitments of Ritter's students actually stretched further to the right and to the left.[57]

After having known Taubes for more than fifteen years, Marquard and Lübbe agreed to participate in a series of gatherings that Taubes initiated in 1979, which were meant to examine the relationship between politics and theology, in a setting similar to that of Poetik und Hermeneutik. (Taubes tried to involve both Blumenberg and Carl Schmitt in the endeavor, but both turned him down.[58]) After the initial preliminary meetings, Taubes suffered a series of psychic and medical setbacks. Thus, much of the actual organization of the conferences was done by Martin Kriele and Richard Faber, and the resulting papers were prepared for publication by Taubes's assistant at the time, Norbert Bolz.[59] Funded by Werner Reimers Stiftung, the Working Group on the Theory of Religion and Political Theology met in February 1980. There were subsequent gatherings in 1982 on "Gnosticism and Politics" and then another on the topic of "Theocracy," each of which resulted in published volumes.

Taubes's own contribution to the volume, "The Theory of Religion and Political Theology," consisted of a series of reflections on Hobbes's *Leviathan* (of which he naively took Schmitt to be an accurate interpreter), one of which was of real importance. That was that a great deal of *Leviathan*, and especially its fourth part, is devoted to a critique of theocracy, and more broadly to a critique of the dominance of the state by religion, a central theme of the book often neglected by interpreters.[60]

Of the many contributions to the volume, the essays of Marquard and Lübbe are of particular interest. Marquard's essay, "Is Enlightened Polytheism Also a Form of Political Theology?" recapitulated and expanded upon the claims of one his best-known essays, "In Praise of Polytheism," first delivered a few years earlier. A decade before, in the precincts of Poetik und Hermeneutik, Marquard had remarked that Jacob Taubes "time and again provides one with the opportunity to note with gratitude that the assertion that Marxism is a form of theology . . . is one made by some Marxists, who say it themselves and have long done so."[61] He now began by offering an amusingly condensed summary of the state of play in the debates over politics, theology, and history, along with a biting critique of Taubes's recent politics:

> Biblical-Christian eschatology becomes modernized through its secularization into "political theology" in the form of the modern, revolutionary philosophy of history. Well known representative theses were developed in two books first published in 1947, namely K. Löwith's *Weltgeschichte und Heilsgeschehen* and J. Taubes' *Abendländische Eschatologie*. Löwith negated this secularized event, while Taubes affirmed it. Löwith laments that biblical eschatology was bad; Taubes thinks that the modern revolutionary philosophy of history is good. . . . In matters having to do with the philosophy of history, as a rule Taubes is right, with one exception: one should reverse his evaluation. . . . This new, eschatological "political theology" objectively betrays its position with an immense blindness to

reality in the political realm (through infantilizations) and—as far as I can judge—through diminishing love of one's neighbor in favor of love of those most distant in the religious realm.[62]

Marquard then turned to Schmitt's contention that secularized modernity was an "age of neutralization," marked by the separation of economics and technology from ultimate goals, and lacking the intensity that came with theologically infused conceptions of politics. That was true enough, Marquard responded, but—reversing Schmitt's valuation—that was a *good* thing, for it served to insulate modern societies from the destructive effects of eschatological expectations.[63] The truly modern position, Marquard claimed, would be to abandon the whole notion of a philosophy of history. The notion that history had a discernable, positive direction was, as Taubes and Löwith had argued, a secularized form of monotheistic eschatology, which made the course of history into a single, coherent story. It would be more modern and more sensible to abandon the entire enterprise, Marquard asserted, and embrace instead what he called "enlightened polytheism"—a phrase intended to be provocative. Instead of understanding oneself as a participant in a single history, one should come to terms with the fact that one was part of multiple "stories" or systems of cultural meaning. Part of enlightened polytheism was affirming the fact that modern liberal institutions led to a division of powers—in government, through the market, and in the university. Thus the fact that not all institutions were subordinated to a single source of power that offered to bring salvation or abolish alienation was precisely what thoughtful people ought to embrace, rather than decry in the name of political theology.[64]

Taubes responded in 1983 with "On the Current Trend of Polytheism" ("Zur Konjunktur der Polytheismus"). There (drawing upon the Jewish philosopher Hermann Cohen), he contended that the origins of the Western conception of subjectivity and individual responsibility lay in the prophets Jeremiah and Ezekiel. And, pointing to the recent call by the radical right French philosopher Alain Benoist to create a European identity based on the pre-Christian past, Taubes warned that treating the Biblical story of Creation and the New Testament as myths would lead to a recrudescence of ancient polytheism.[65] But in so doing, he largely ignored what Marquard had meant by "enlightened polytheism," which was not a defense of ancient, mythical polytheism, but rather of cultural pluralism.

Hermann Lübbe was a more politically engaged philosopher, and his critique of political theology was more pointed than that of his friends Blumenberg or Marquard. As Taubes noted, it amounted to "a right-liberal liquidation of the problem of political theology."⁶⁶ Lübbe grouped Taubes together with several contemporary German Christian theologians of radical propensities, such as Dorothee Sölle and Johann Baptist Metz, who were reviving the term "political theology." Their project, Lübbe thought, was actually to selectively take from the Gospels only messages that resonated with their contemporary political ideology, in an attempt to recapture the seriousness (*Ernst*) of religion for political purposes. Taubes's suggestion to try to formulate a new political theology would only make sense, Lübbe thought, if one tried to find political principles that were of exclusively *religious* origin and to create a political theory that was at the same time theological. He was skeptical that it could be done.⁶⁷ Lübbe thus provided a critique that struck at the essence of Taubes's projects, from *Abendländische Eschatologie* to his posthumously published lectures on *The Political Theology of Paul*.

The reaction of Blumenberg, Marquard, and Lübbe to the radical politics of the twentieth century was to try to take the theological drama out of history, as overburdening political action with religious expectations that could only serve to delegitimate existing liberal institutions and efforts at piecemeal reform. Taubes, by contrast, drew on Schmitt in order to heighten the drama by relinking politics to religion, or at least to the intensity that religion inspired.

Taubes had originally hoped that the volumes that emerged out of his political theology project would be published by Suhrkamp Verlag, which had helped to fund the second conference. But Suhrkamp was not interested in doing so. Taubes's assistant, Norbert Bolz, reached out to Raimar Zons, the editor of the Wilhelm Fink Verlag, a smaller and more specialized publishing house. Fink published the three volumes, and thanks to Zons's ongoing interest in Taubes, became the publisher of his posthumous works.⁶⁸ Though their immediate impact was negligible, they would soon play a role in spreading the notion of "political theology" beyond the realm of theologians.

Sander and Amalek

Taubes's relationship to Hans-Dietrich Sander ended in 1980. That was the year that Sander published a collection of his articles, *The National Imperative*, articulating his unrepentant German nationalism. It was part of a still marginal recrudescence of German nationalist thought that included Mohler and Hans-Joachim Arndt, Taubes's longtime acquaintance, now a professor of political science in Heidelberg. For Sander, the

Germans were still under Allied occupation—much as they tried to deny it—and had been reduced to the status of serfs (*Knechtschaft*) and "Helots," albeit prosperous ones.[69] Suffering from imposed and self-imposed guilt over the Third Reich, the West Germans had lost all sense of national belonging and pride. Sander advocated an updating of Fichte's *Lectures to the German Nation* (1807–8), rallying the Germans against their subservient status and calling for their return to international power status. He characterized the Second World War as merely a chapter in "a century-long war of the West against Germany."[70]

Taubes sent a copy of Sander's book to Peter Glotz and to Horst Mahler, recommending Sander as "one of the most independent minds in West Germany."[71]

Yet, after reading an essay that would appear later that year in Sander's book, Taubes wrote Sander a scathing letter, focused on Sander's downplaying of Hitler and of the actions of the Germans during the Third Reich. "With Hitler, a line was crossed that went beyond the normal relations between nations and into the realm of Amalek, who Jews are commanded never to forget—So that you know from where and to where we approach one another in conversation."[72] Sander wrote to Schmitt, and copied most of the text of Taubes's letter for Schmitt's inspection, noting that Taubes seemed to divine exactly the more radical direction in which Sander was moving.[73] In fact, Taubes had already sent Schmitt a copy of his letter to Sander. Schmitt responded that he had been at odds with Sander for some time.[74]

That seems to have ended the relationship between Sander and Taubes—at least during Taubes's lifetime. As we will see, it was Sander who would produce one of the first evaluations of Taubes after his death.

Depression, Festschrift, Heart Attack

In the five years after his mental breakdown and subsequent treatment in New York in 1976, Jacob Taubes continued to have episodes of depression and of mania, during which he seemed to have superhuman energy.[75] On the whole, his mental and emotional condition had been on the upswing. Then, in August 1982, another traumatic event sent him back into deep depression. No sooner had he recovered than he was once again laid low, this time by a heart attack that almost killed him. For much of the time between the summer of 1982 and his death in 1987, he was not a well man.

August 1982 found Jacob in Paris. One of his favorite neighborhoods was the traditional Jewish quarter, the Marais, which still housed many Jewish institutions and establishments. Jacob was in the Marais on August 9, when Chez Jo Goldenberg, a well-known kosher restaurant where he often dined, was attacked by terrorists from the Abu Nidal Organization, a splinter group of El Fatah. Two assailants threw a grenade into the restaurant, then rushed in firing machine guns. Six of those in the restaurant were killed, another twenty-two injured. The attack was a shock to the French public and to Jews around the world. Though he was not at the restaurant when it was attacked, the event sent Jacob into a deep depression.

He returned to Berlin, and on September 22 was hospitalized in the psychiatric unit of the Krankenhaus am Urban in Kreuzberg.[76] He managed to attend the opening in Bad Homberg on October 10 of the conference he had organized, "Gnosticism and Politics" ("Gnosis und Politik"), but collapsed there.[77] By November, he was back in the psychiatric clinic once again.[78] He returned to teaching in January 1983, but soon requested a research leave for the next semester, which was granted.[79] He suffered from a slipped disc and put on weight. Almost an invalid, he lived for a time at the Leo Baeck Heim, a Jewish home for assisted living, where he had an apartment of his own and was able to eat meals in a shared dining room. But the surroundings hardly suited him, and his son Ethan found him an apartment on Heydenstraße, not far from Alexander Haas, a friend who was also a physician.[80] For a time, Jacob moved in with Margherita von Brentano, in her home on Winklerstraße. But his depression recurred, and from September to November, he was once again in and out of psychiatric hospitals. Margherita had taken over handling his financial affairs, since Jacob was no longer capable of doing so, neglecting to answer his mail or simply losing it. When he was living with her, he exhausted her patience: "he insists on my being with him and listen[ing] to him 24 hours a day (or 16, minus sleeping)," she reported to Tania.[81]

Jacob turned sixty on February 25, 1983. Together with Jacob's colleague Wolfgang Hübener, Norbert Bolz edited a festschrift in his honor. Most of the contributions were from Jacob's colleagues in Berlin (including Tugendhat, Karlfried Gründer, Brentano, Dietmar Kamper, and Fritz Kramer), former students, or from younger scholars in his coterie, including Gasché, Kittsteiner, Faber, Hamacher, Menninghaus, and Bolz himself. Two stemmed from Jacob's Israeli colleagues, Moshe Barasch and Avishai Margalit, whom he had brought to the FU as visiting professors. Another was from Edmund Leites, an old friend from New York who had also visited at the FU. Three contributions came from France: from Jacques Derrida, Jean-Luc Nancy (who had also lectured at the FU), and a particularly warm, personal appreciation from Emil Cioran (quoted in chapter 14), which he wrote in French and had translated into German for the festschrift.

Jacob recovered his health once again, at least enough to resume teaching, socializing, and attending lectures. But in December 1984, he suffered a heart attack, which he survived only by being repeatedly defibrillated. He was hospitalized yet again, this time at the University Clinic Steglitz.[82] After this near-death experience, he felt he was living on borrowed time.[83] For a while, he only wanted to speak Hebrew, and passed much of the day reciting Psalms.[84] He spent a few weeks as a patient in a psychiatric clinic on the Wannsee.[85] He gave up smoking, a lifelong habit.

In the wake of his heart attack, Jacob became less given to mood swings, less aggressive, in short, nicer.[86] When the apartment beside Margherita's became available at Winklerstraße 14, Jacob asked her whether he could move into it, and she agreed. Their apartments were separated by a hallway. She looked after him, and Jacob attributed his recovery in good part to her self-sacrificing support (*aufopfernden Bestand*).[87] This arrangement, by which a divorced couple resumed living together, was not unheard of. When he visited Berlin, Joseph Dan of Hebrew University was invited by Jacob and Margherita to a dinner in which all the couples were divorcees who were living together once again.[88]

Of course, for Jacob the arrangement did not entail fidelity.

Teaching in Berlin

In the years from 1979 to 1982, when Taubes was at the FU in Berlin, he taught seminars on topics that had long interested him: Gnosticism, Hobbes, Spinoza, and Benjamin's "Theses on the Philosophy of History." In the summer semester of 1982, together with the sociologist Dietmar Kamper, he offered a seminar on The Aesthetics of the Posthistoire. Aesthetics was not a topic that much interested Taubes, but philosophies of history did. "Posthistoire" referred to the idea that history was for all intents and purposes over, that major transformations had already occurred, and that the present and future should be understood as variations on patterns already established. It was a theme that went back to Hegel and had been articulated—with many variations—in the 1920s by Oswald Spengler, in the 1930s by Alexandre Kojève, and in the 1960s by the German conservative theorist Arnold Gehlen, under the rubric of "crystallization." In the 1970s, a new variation on the theme was developed by the French philosopher Jean François Lyotard, an ex-Communist disillusioned with

Marxism, in his 1979 book, *The Postmodern Condition*. There he argued that all grand historical narratives were exhausted and no longer plausible. Both Lyotard and Derrida made presentations to the seminar.[89]

A manuscript of essays emerged from the seminar, edited by Kamper and Taubes, *After the Modern: Outlines of an "Aesthetic of Posthistoire"* (*Nach der Moderne: Umrisse einer "Äesthetik der Posthistoire"*) in 1986. It was to be published by Suhrkamp, but conflicts with the publisher led the project to fall through.[90] Some of the chapters appeared in print elsewhere. Taubes's contribution, "The Aesthetization of Truth in Posthistoire" ("Ästhetisierung der Wahrheit im Posthistoire"), appeared posthumously in a festschrift for Margherita von Brentano. In it, he claimed that the understanding of the world characteristic of *posthistoire* meant the negation of the Christian and progressive conception of history as having direction and meaning. For Taubes, that took the *seriousness* out of history, leaving a nihilistic conception of life. Truth, meaning, and purpose were understood by the proponents of *posthistoire* not as intrinsic to the world and to history, but as arbitrary, human creations—works of art. He traced the development of this idea from Nietzsche to Heidegger, and to an aesthetic conception of the world that Kojève attributed to the Japanese and saw as a possible future for all.[91]

Also attending the seminar on *posthistoire* were Peter Gente, who in the 1960s had served as Taubes's student assistant at the Hermeneutics Institute, and Gente's partner, Heidi Paris. Together, in 1977, they had founded a small publishing house, Merve Verlag, in Berlin. Marxism was becoming passé, and Merve published radical thinkers who were not (or were no longer) Marxist. It was a shoestring operation that specialized in short books, many of them translations of essays by fashionable French thinkers, including Lyotard, Derrida, and Michel Foucault.[92] On Gente's initiative, it would publish a book by Jacob Taubes.

During the years from 1980 to 1986, when he was well enough to teach—and sometimes, when he was not well enough—Taubes focused his lectures and seminars on three main topics. The first was the Apostle Paul, the historical context of his writings, and their explication. The second was Nietzsche, whose main interest for Taubes lay in his interpretation of Paul's place in the history of the West. The third was Carl Schmitt.

Paul was at the center of the lecture courses that he gave during the summer semester (April–July) of 1981, Paul and the Spirit of Late Antiquity, and during the winter semester of 1982 (October–March), Paul and the "Supercession of Philosophy."[93] In the summer semester of 1986 (April–July), he again lectured on Paul. The thesis this time—described in some detail in the annotated course catalogue—was "the transformation of classical values by Paul, which Nietzsche's hate has illuminated so glaringly" and its replacement by Paul's formula "as though not" (I. Corinthians 7:27–31). That was a reference to the passages "I mean, brothers and sisters, the appointed time has grown short. From now on, let . . . those who deal with the world be as though they had no dealings with it. For the present form of this world is passing away." According to Taubes, Walter Benjamin had quite rightly characterized this approach to world politics as nihilistic.[94]

Taubes's lecture course on Corinthians—like so many of his lectures—was an event, bordering on theater, and filling one of the largest auditoriums at the FU to overflowing. He lectured without notes. According to one of the students who attended, Taubes seemed to be in his own world, holding his head while thinking through the issues at hand in silence, punctuated by moments of creative insight, accompanied by broad gestures with his hands. It was a performance to which his audience listened in awe.[95]

During the winter semester of 1983–84, in addition to a colloquium entitled "Theocracy" related to the conference he was organizing on political theology, he taught Nietzsche's *On the Genealogy of Morals*. During the winter semester of 1984–85, he scheduled a course on Nietzsche's *Antichrist* (though health issues probably kept him away a good deal of the time). Both were seminal texts for the interpretation of Paul he was striving to construct.[96]

Schmitt Seminar at the FU

During the 1985–86 academic year, Taubes taught a seminar on Carl Schmitt, together with Norbert Bolz and Nicolaus Sombart. This too was an event, covered by some Berlin newspapers. That was in part because of the subject matter—Schmitt was still something of a reviled object in official German academic life—and in good part because of the conveners, Taubes and Sombart.

Sombart was a presence on the Berlin cultural scene. The son of the famed economist, Werner Sombart, he had grown up in Berlin with Schmitt, a friend of his father's, as a mentor. Multilingual, he made a career as a cultural bureaucrat for the Council of Europe in Strasbourg. In the fall of 1982, he came back to Berlin to serve as a fellow at the Wissenschaftskolleg for 1982–83 and then decided to stay. In the course of that year, he met some members of Taubes's coterie—Richard Faber, H. D. Kittsteiner, and Wolfgang Fietkau—and was impressed by their erudition. "It's astonishing how much these fellows know (they are almost all students of Taubes)," he noted in his diary.[97] Faber introduced him to Taubes, and in March 1983, Sombart had dinner at the home of Taubes and Brentano (who were living together once again), who promised to get him a teaching post at the FU and the status of an honorary professor (*Honorarprofesseur*).[98]

Sombart moved to Berlin and began to teach courses at the FU under the auspices of Taubes's Hermeneutic Institute. In his ample apartment, Sombart hosted a weekly salon that brought together artists, intellectuals, and media folk. He was a colorful figure, a dandy. At the time of the Schmitt seminar, he had just published a memoir, *Youth in Berlin, 1933–1945*, which included a chapter "Strolls with Carl Schmitt." Later, he would write a book with Schmitt at its center, *The German Men and Their Enemies: Carl Schmitt, a German Fate between Male Bonding and Matriarchal Myth* (1991), in which he traced Schmitt's emphasis on the relationship between friend and enemy to the insecure masculinity that purportedly characterized the German men of his generation.

The focus of the Taubes-Sombart seminar was on Schmitt's *Politische Theologie* of 1922 and his *Politische Theologie II* of 1970, with prominent attention to the Benjamin-Schmitt letter. It was held in a relatively small seminar room, and with forty or more people attending, the space was crowded to overflowing, with students sitting on the windowsills. In the front row sat Saul Friedländer, a distinguished historian of National Socialism, who taught at Tel Aviv University and was spending the year as a fellow at the Wissenschaftskolleg. Elsewhere in the front row sat Ernst Nolte, whom Taubes made a point of acknowledging. Also in attendance was Jürgen Kaube, later the *Feuilleton* editor of the *Frankfurter Allgemeiner Zeitung*.[99] Though visibly ailing, Taubes dominated the seminar, which, to Friedländer's surprise, he conducted with the formality and regalia of a German professor of the old school: beginning each session with a reading of the protocol of the previous session, then asking whether everyone agreed. While Sombart was more amusing, it was Taubes who bestowed depth.[100]

Apocalyptics, Left and Right

Toward the end of the semester, not long after Schmitt's death, Taubes gave a public lecture at the FU, entitled "Carl Schmitt—An Apocalypticist of the Counterrevolution" ("Carl Schmitt—ein Apokalyptiker der

Gegenrevolution") to a packed lecture hall. It was published on July 20, 1985, in *Die Tageszeitung*, the recently founded daily that reflected the sensibilities of the New Left and the counterculture.[101]

Taubes began his lecture by expressing his awe (*Ehrfurcht*) for Schmitt, "despite the fact that as a conscious Jew, I belong to those who he branded as the 'enemy.'" Though as a jurist, Schmitt sought to set limits on the notion that the "enemy" must be destroyed, Taubes asserted, between 1933 and 1938 he made himself into a spokesman for National Socialism, which mythologized the Jew into the destroyer of the Aryan race.[102] Taubes claimed that Schmitt's relationship to the Third Reich went through three stages: first adulation, then betrayal and distancing, and finally connections to groups that sought to overthrow the regime.[103]

There followed a series of biographical anecdotes about Taubes's encounters with Schmitt's works. There was his discovery of *Political Theology* while a student at the University of Zurich. Next, his borrowing of Schmitt's *Constitutional Theory* (*Verfassungslehre*) while at Hebrew University in Jerusalem, discovering that it had been consulted by the minister of justice, and conveying that information to Armin Mohler, who showed it to Schmitt. Then his encounter with Hans-Joachim Arndt at the Harvard seminar presided over by the young Henry Kissinger, and the discovery that Schmitt had circulated his letter. Taubes told the tale of Kojève's assertion in 1967 that he was off to visit Schmitt as the most prominent mind in Germany. Finally, Taubes described his own face-to-face meetings with Schmitt in the late 1970s. Of those encounters in Plettenberg, Taubes reported that he had "the most stormy discussions that I've ever had in German. It was a matter of historiography in a nutshell, compressed into mythical images."[104] This was presumably a reference to Schmitt's exploration of the image of the Leviathan in the work of Thomas Hobbes, the subject of his book of 1938, *The Leviathan in the Political Theory of Thomas Hobbes: The Meaning and Failure of a Political Symbol*.[105] But Taubes revealed nothing about the content of his discussion.

Taubes provided his listeners/readers with some arcane facts about little-known connections in the intellectual world—some real and some spurious. He reported, for example, that in the 1940s, Albert Salomon had published an article in *Social Research*, the journal of the New School, that drew upon Schmitt's chapter on the political theology of counterrevolutionary thought in his book *Political Theology*, and that this article was republished in the proceedings of a conference organized by Louis Finkelstein at the Jewish Theological Seminary. (Actually the article appeared in

1946, four years *after* the conference volume.) From this, Taubes drew the conclusion that "Carl Schmitt's approach to defining the theology of the counterrevolution was adopted as the ideology of a new academic conservatism, propagated throughout America by the institution of Conservative Judaism."[106] A mélange of half-remembered facts ending in a wild claim, believable only to those lacking knowledge of the subject.

Other unexpected associations were more plausible, though not perhaps as earth-shattering as Taubes made them out to be. The 1930 letter of appreciation from Benjamin to Schmitt was cited, along with the assertion that in his "Theses on the Philosophy of History," Benjamin had made use of Schmitt's conception of the state of exception (*Ausnahmezustand*), but had reversed its implications by contending that for the historically oppressed, life was always in a state of exception. Taubes claimed that Schmitt and Benjamin shared a "mystical conception of history" (*mystische Geschichtsauffassung*), at odds with the view of history as one of secularization. Though perhaps defensible, he left the claim hanging in the air.[107]

Taubes's key contention was that Carl Schmitt was "an apocalypticist of the counter-revolution," while, he, Jacob Taubes, was an apocalypticist from the opposite end of the ideological spectrum. "Carl Schmitt thinks apocalyptically, but from above to below, from the point of view of the powers that be; I think from the point of view of those below looking up. But what we have in common is that experience of time as a reprieve, as a stay of execution."[108] Both were interested in the limits of liberalism, in extreme circumstances when the current order threatens to break down. But while Schmitt saw it as his role to preserve existing institutions, by radical measures if need be, Taubes viewed the potential breakdown of existing institutions as an opportunity for radical transformation. Thus Taubes portrayed himself as Schmitt's antiliberal counterpart on the left: Schmitt as the defender of authority; Taubes as the apostle of antiauthoritarianism.

During the course of that year, Jacob had another falling out with Margherita, and came to live with Sombart. Sombart's sexual adventures—mostly paid for—were a recurrent theme in his memoirs of those years. Jacob's were unpaid. They appear to have discussed their sexual life, as Sombart was informed about Jacob's ongoing relationship with a female consort, a psychiatrist, and their role-playing: her as a witch, and Jacob as a warlock. He was astonished at Jacob's habit of bringing home young students to sleep with him, and then ejecting them in the morning. Sombart interpreted Jacob's erotic conquests as a demonstration of power, which he attributed to some deep psychic wound. Their arrangement lasted for just over a week, after which Jacob returned again to Margherita.[109] Sombart later discovered that Jacob had warned the new *Wissenschaftssenator*, Kevenig, against giving Sombart a permanent albeit unpaid appointment. He too came to regard Jacob as an intriguer and a Mephistophelian character.[110]

Saul Friedländer first met Taubes at the Wissenschaftskolleg, an institution that Taubes had opposed as "elitist" when it was first proposed. But after it opened, he frequented the institution as if he were a fellow there, despite the attempts of its rector, Peter Wapnewski, to restrict his participation. In February 1986, Friedländer organized a conference there on memory and the Holocaust in Germany. Brentano and Taubes came as well. The conference was attended by several prominent historians, but Nolte was not among them. The year before, Nolte had published an essay in English, in which he claimed, inter alia, that because in September 1939 the president of the World Zionist Organization, Chaim Weizmann, had stated that in case of war, the Jews of the world would fight against Germany, it was legitimate for Hitler to consider them as enemies and to put them into concentration camps, "as the Americans did with the Japanese." Friedländer knew these and other claims in the essay were absurd, but he agreed to Nolte's invitation to lecture in his seminar at the FU. In June, Nolte invited Friedländer to a dinner at his home, where he reiterated his claim about Weizmann, whom he portrayed as representative of world Jewry (*Weltjudentum*). He then proceeded to repeat some historically dubious claims, which he admitted he had garnered from a neo-Nazi book, *The Auschwitz Myth* (*Der Auschwitz Mythos*). At this point, Friedländer had had enough and left the dinner. Shortly thereafter, he gave an interview to *Die Zeit* in which he mentioned his concern about the views that a well-known historian was peddling. He did not mention Nolte by name. But Nolte announced publicly that he was the historian in question. The event set off what became known as the *Historkerstreit*, a controversy about the appropriate role of comparison in thinking and talking about the Nazi past.[111]

Aleida and Jan Assmann

In the late fall of 1984, Jacob attended a party given by Monika Wapnewski, whose husband, Peter, was the rector of the Wissenschaftskolleg. Though he had recovered from his latest bout of depression, Jacob was not in good health, his appearance ghostly and immobile.[112] Among the guests were Jan Assmann, an Egyptologist from the University of Heidelberg who was spending the academic year as a visiting fellow of the Wissenschaftskolleg, and his wife, Aleida. At age forty-six, Jan was a respected scholar in his field, focused on ancient Egyptian religion. Aleida, thirty-seven, had completed a doctorate in English literature in 1977, and was primarily occupied with raising their five children, the youngest of whom was only a year old. Jan knew of Jacob by reputation, especially his role in Poetik und Hermeneutik, and was eager to meet him. So the couple approached Jacob and introduced themselves.

In the conversation that ensued, Aleida mentioned her father, Günther Bornkamm, a Protestant New Testament scholar and the author of books on Jesus and on Paul. Jacob's attention quickly turned from Jan to Aleida. Here was a young, vital, intellectual woman with *yichus*—the sort to which he was most attracted. He may have seen her, at first, as another potential conquest.

Shortly thereafter, Jacob suffered his heart attack, which left him hospitalized and then in a weakened condition for months. But in the summer of 1985, as the Assmanns' sojourn in Berlin was nearing its end, Jacob visited them at their home. Jacob fell in love with Aleida—and with her family. He began to spend more and more time with them. June 1986 found him in Heidelberg with the Assmanns once again.[113] That summer, he joined them at their summer home near the resort of Bad Ischl—though Jacob, who had little affinity for nature, hated to go to the lake.

During Jacob's periods of residence at the Assmanns' home in Heidelberg, his Jewish religious observance was on full display. He wore a *kippah* in their house, and would sometimes pray in the morning, in *tallith* and *tfillin* (prayer shawl and phylacteries). He would celebrate the Sabbath with them on Friday evening, and bless the children, the traditional Jewish ritual on the Sabbath eve. He took Aleida and her younger children with him to the synagogue on Saturday, where he would pray intensely, as was his habit. "I had to wait 63 years to go to synagogue with a family," he observed, since Susan had been uninterested, not to speak of Margherita. To the Assmanns, this Jewish observance was a strange new world—one they found fascinating. (Later, when after Jacob's death the Assmanns visited in Israel, they celebrated the Sabbath and Jewish holidays as a family.) He gave Aleida works of Rabbi Nachman of Breslov to read.

When Jacob and Aleida were separated and he was working on some intellectual project, he would call her at 2:00 a.m. and pour out his thoughts to her for an hour or more. He had intellectual fits of rapture, which for him were exhilarating, leading to a flood of ideas and concepts.

Since Jacob was no respecter of normal boundaries, he attached his affections not only to Aleida but to her children: indeed, he "adopted" her youngest daughter and invested her with his own meaning, treating her as his own, in a manner uncanny and almost mystical.

Jacob proclaimed his love for Aleida to friends near and far. He brought a photo of her to a faculty meeting and showed it to colleagues.[114] This relationship had a purity, a lack of exploitation that his others had lacked, he told them. Aleida was sent by God: the "Amen" to his prayers.[115]

While Jacob's main attachment was to Aledia, Jan too found Jacob stimulating: his intensity, his ability to present grand intellectual vistas, stretching from the ancients to the moderns, to suggest connections that would not occur to others, but that they might develop. He regaled them both with his theories and insights about Jewish history, and about Paul.

Margherita, for her part, was infuriated by Jacob's relationship with Aleida. She would call up Jan on the telephone and try to work him into a rage, urging him to play the role of the jealous husband, and kick Jacob out of house—and back to Berlin. Perhaps because he saw how much the relationship meant to Aleida, it was not a role that Jan was inclined to play. By providing a supportive familial environment in Heidelberg, removed from the self-created complications of his Berlin milieu, the Assmanns served to nurse Jacob. In Heidelberg, he lived the opposite of his otherwise solitary and peripatetic life. The Assmanns were witness to Jacob's fits of madness, characterized by crying and rushing around. Though his mania, paranoia, and aggression were always in the background, they were never directed at the Assmanns. It would prove to be a fateful relationship, both for Jacob and for Aleida and Jan Assmann.

CHAPTER SIXTEEN

Final Act, 1986–87

NO SOONER DID JACOB CELEBRATE his recovery from his near-fatal heart attack, than he was diagnosed with a deadly cancer. He prepared his children and friends for his imminent demise, intensified his religious observance, and arranged for his final thoughts on Paul to be recorded and preserved. Jacob deepened his relationship with Aleida and Jan Assmann and took steps to create a posthumous legacy.

A Wedding

Jacob returned to New York in late March 1986, together with Margherita. It was the first time he had visited since departing after his electroshock treatment almost a decade earlier. It was the last time he would visit.

The occasion was the wedding of his son, Ethan, to Sally Spitzer. Jacob arrived just before the Jewish holiday of Purim and made his way to Crown Heights in Brooklyn, where he had a brief audience with the Lubavitcher Rebbe, Menachem Schneerson, and stayed for the Purim celebrations. He spent time with Susan Sontag among other old friends. He also tried to meet with Louis Finkelstein, the now-retired chancellor of the Jewish Theological Seminary, but was unable to reach him. So instead he sent Finkelstein a long letter. It began with an expression of respect, but soon proceeded to criticize JTS for its failure to develop philosophers and theologians of note, a not very subtle reference to the fact that it had decided not to keep Jacob Taubes on its faculty.[1]

The wedding ceremony, on April 6, 1986, was conducted by a Reform rabbi, Susan Einbinder, and by Jacob himself. The bride was the daughter of an accountant, and her middle-class family was neither Jewishly nor philosophically learned. To this audience, Jacob gave a long and curious address. It began with a salutation drawn from Paul's First Letter to the Corinthians, "Grace and peace to you." Jacob then went on to speak at length about—himself. He could not legally perform the marriage rite, he explained, because although he had been ordained by two distinguished European rabbis (whom he named),

> I never made use of this ordination I had because very early in my life I went the academic way and became a Professor. I take the distinction between Rabbi and Professor seriously, especially in such permissive times where every amalgam is publicized as a creative innovation. A rabbi can really perform the ritual act, a professor can only tell how the ritual act was or is to be performed. The ritual act itself becomes for the Professor a story. All that remains visible of the Mystery is a tale told by a Professor. We are religiously at the end of a tale, a last link in the chain of tradition. In order to regain the Mystery which is celebrated in the rite of marriage we have to walk the road of narration, start from the story.[2]

He expressed his gratitude to those who had provided assistance during his recent tribulations, who helped deliver him from "the sentence of death," including Ethan and Sally, his daughter, Tania, and Margherita, who, he informed his audience, "came daily to the heart clinic from mid-December 1984 until April 1985." There followed some remarks about Susan's death, and that despite the "disappointments" of their marriage, there were also the "appointments" of Tania and of Ethan, who was now to be sanctified in marriage.

Along the way, Jacob managed to throw in references to the dicta of Rabbi Akiba in the Talmudic tractate *Yoma*; to Plato's discussion in the *Symposium* of the metamorphosis of eros to the love of wisdom; and to Jacob's "passionate discussions at Columbia with Susan Sontag about the mind and the heart of love." There was talk too of Aristotle and Maimonides—along with an admonition that philosophy was a dead end if taken by itself, without love, "Because in love we admit to our fundamental imperfection. We confess that we are not autonomous, but terribly in need for each other."

What was remarkable about Jacob's talk, as noted by Ethan's cousin, Zachary Edelstein, was how much of it was either about Jacob himself, or about the role and limits of philosophy—hardly a subject likely to resonate with most of the assembled guests—with barely a mention of the bride and groom.[3]

Upon returning to Berlin, Jacob threw a party for himself. In an invitation dated June 16, he informed his invitees that he was about to take a

FIGURE 16.1. Jacob Taubes, Clemens Heller, and Heinz Wismann, 1986, before Taubes's
fatal illness. (Ethan and Tania Taubes Collection.)

research leave of absence, and before doing so wanted his friends to join
him in celebrating his recovery from his heart attack and his return to
full academic engagement. "I've also been welcomed back like the Prod-
igal Son in Jerusalem, Frankfurt, and Paris," he reported.[4] The gathering was to take place at the Paris Bar, which had allowed him to reserve
half of the restaurant from 4 p.m. to 7 p.m. Each person, he reminded his
guests, would order for themselves, implying that they would also *pay* for
themselves.

Among those whom Jacob invited was Ernst Nolte. "I very much hope
that you can come," he noted in a handwritten addition to the letter. "I'm
concerned to publicly demonstrate our commonality, at a time when the
Friedländer episode overshadows every other theme in the twaddle of the
Berlin demi-intelligentsia."[5]

After the party at the Paris Bar, there was a smaller dinner gathering at
the Exil restaurant, one of his favorites. Margherita did not attend either
the party or the dinner.[6]

Cancer

Ever since his heart attack, Jacob had prayed more frequently at the
Orthodox synagogue on the Joachimsthaler Straße, the most traditional
service he could find. In September 1986, he had dinner at the Exil in

FIGURE 16.2. Taubes, on the same occasion as above. Note the outfit, and the tallit katan, typically worn under the shirt, but here on full display. (bpk Bildagentur / Maison des sciences de l'homme, Paris / Digne Meller Marcovicz / Art Resource, NY.)

Kreuzberg with Tania and with Gabriele Althaus. Althaus was dressed in a manner befitting the bohemian neighborhood in which they met for dinner, which is to say, immodestly. At the end of the meal, Jacob announced, "Now we're going to the synagogue," which they proceeded to do. It was the season for Slichot, the special prayers for forgiveness that Jews traditionally recite in the weeks leading up to Rosh Hashanah. Gabriele had never before been to a synagogue, and she was astonished to see the fervor with which Jacob—whom she had known up till then as a leftist professor of philosophy—prayed. (Whether the presence of an immodestly clad non-Jewish woman scandalized or merely puzzled the other congregants, we do not know.) Jacob also brought Gabriele with him to a Sabbath dinner at the home of the rabbi.[7]

Jacob spent the High Holidays in Jerusalem, with the Toldot Aharon Hasidim in Meah She'arim. It was there that Saul Friedländer picked him up for dinner at the conclusion of Yom Kippur.[8]

It would be Jacob's last visit to Jerusalem.

Upon his return to Berlin, a large black mole had developed on Jacob's shoulder. It was sent for diagnosis and found to be benign. But the diagnosis was wrong: it was a malignant melanoma, and it metastasized into his lymph nodes, his lungs, and his liver.[9] The doctors informed him that he had four to six months to live.

Jacob continued to visit with Aleida and her family in Heidelberg. Now his state of mind was even more troubled, as he revisited the traumas he had experienced, as well as those he had caused. The Holocaust weighed upon him with ever-greater intensity, and he was overcome with survivor guilt. He looked at Corinna, the youngest Assmann child, whom he had "adopted," and saw reflected in her the souls of the murdered Jewish children. He was convinced that after he died, he would have to account for his sins. Wracked by guilt, he confessed to Aleida his sexual relationship with the wife of Joseph Weiss, which had ultimately led to her demise. He claimed that he was now a "new Jacob," that after a destructive life, he had reached a higher spiritual stage.

Nor was Aleida the only one to whom he confessed his remorse. That same year, he met a young Jewish woman from Munich, Rachel Salamander, at one of Sombart's soirées. He asked about her, and told her about his own background and the fact that his father had been a rabbi. Then he added, "I veered from the proper path," and broke into sobs.[10]

Preparing for the End

Jacob prepared for his death with public equanimity and private *Angst*. In the last months of his life, he arranged for his burial, held numerous send-offs, and laid the basis for his posthumous reputation.

The most pressing task was to secure a grave. Jacob did not care to be laid to rest in Germany. He wanted to be buried next to his mother, Fanny, in the Oberer Friesenberg Jewish cemetery of Zurich. But there were obstacles to Jacob being interred there. Burial in the cemetery was ordinarily available only to members of the Zurich Jewish community, to which Jacob did not belong. The Taubes family owned a plot that adjoined the grave of Jacob's mother, a plot originally intended for her husband. But Zwi had died and been buried in Jerusalem. Jacob's sister, Mirjam, was buried nearby. But since she died as a young woman and had hoped that her husband, Armand, would remarry, she specified that the family not buy a plot next to hers. In the intervening decades since the deaths of Mirjam and Fanny, it was Armand who had paid the maintenance fees on the plot next to Fanny's grave. He had not remarried, and he planned to be buried in the plot for which he had been paying over the years. "Jacob can buy his own grave," was his position.[11] Jacob now accused Armand of stealing a plot that was rightfully his.

To overcome these impediments, Jacob mobilized his connections and persuasive powers. He had Marianne Weinberg, his wealthy and influential friend, intervene with Sigy Feigel, the president of the Jewish Community (*Gemeinde*). She convinced Feigel to permit Jacob to be buried in the cemetery for free—and next to his mother. In the end, his brother-in-law Armand withdrew his objections.[12]

In December, Ethan arrived in Berlin. Jacob now told him about his relationship with Aleida Assmann, whom he was eager for Ethan to meet. But such an encounter had to be hidden from Margherita, for whom Jacob's relationship with Aleida remained scandalous. So Jacob arranged for Aleida, together with Corinna, to meet Jacob and Ethan in Zurich. Jacob's daughter, Tania, who was in medical school, arrived shortly thereafter. Jacob took his children to the cemetery in which he was to be interred and walked them through the burial process, explaining what would occur and what they should expect.[13]

Jacob had not published a book of his own since his doctoral dissertation of 1947. Though he had quite a few essays to his credit, they had appeared over the intervening four decades in widely divergent and sometimes obscure venues, in English and in German. Now he gathered together offprints of what he regarded as the most significant, and gave them to Henning Ritter and Winfried Menninghaus. He asked that they see to their publication, either with Suhrkamp, or with Fink Verlag, whose editor, Reimar Zons, had published the volumes of Jacob's Political Theology project.

Jacob spent much of the time left to him saying his goodbyes to friends and colleagues and orchestrating festivities to mark his imminent departure. In December, he arranged a party for himself on Christmas Eve at the home of Gabriele Althaus. At midnight, the windows were opened to the sound of ringing bells, after which Jacob delivered a spontaneous farewell address in which he took leave of his gathered friends.[14] There was another party, thrown by the female physician with whom he had an ongoing relationship.[15] Margherita hosted a party as well, at her home in Grunewald next door to Jacob's apartment.[16] At one such party a guest who Jacob knew only passingly approached him and remarked, "I've heard that you're bound to die" (*Ich habe gehört Du muss sterben*). To which he replied, "You too!" (*Du auch!*).[17]

In early January 1987, Jacob ventured to Paris for the last time. He had encouraged Christiane Buhmann, who was living there, to have her son baptized; Jacob attended and served as the baby's godfather (another bit of antinomianism by both Christian and Jewish standards). Jacob was eager for her to meet Aleida and Corinna, who came along as well.[18] He took leave of Clemens Heller, his patron at the Maison des sciences de l'homme. "Everyone needs a tree to lean against," Heller responded. "For me, this tree is now being cut."[19] In the street outside, Taubes ran into Heinz Wismann, whom he astonished with the greeting "Oh, Herr Wismann, how nice to see you. By the way, I have cancer."[20] Jacob's friends threw a fête for him at the Maison Heine: among those who attended were Jean and Mayotte Bollack, as well as Luc Ferry, a young philosopher who would later become minister of education.[21]

Jacob showed the Assmanns around his favorite sites in the city. On Saturday morning, he went to synagogue; on Sunday, he took them with to the Cathedral of Notre Dame to hear Cardinal Lustiger. "You have to excuse me," he said. "I can't live in just one world."

In the latter part of January 1987, Jacob's health went into radical decline. During the months that remained to him, he was largely confined to bed.

Margherita had never shown sympathy or understanding for Jacob's religious side. But now, together with Gabriele Althaus, she accompanied him to synagogue on the Joachimsthaler Straße, which he could no longer reach on his own. "Of course I don't believe in all of this, but rituals are useful," Jacob explained to Althaus.[22] Yet he told his daughter, Tania, that one of the things he was most grateful for in his childhood was that he had learned how to pray.[23] And he was deeply anxious lest his son, Ethan, whose Jewish education he had neglected, not be able to properly intone kaddish, the prayer for the dead, after his father's demise. To Aleida Assmann, he confided his anxiety about the fact that he would soon confront God "eye to eye." These conflicting assertions capture some of the inner contradictions of Jacob Taubes—his distanced, skeptical, social scientific perspective on Judaism, and his residual, renewed, faith.

Paul Revisited

In 1947, the twenty-four-year-old Jacob Taubes revealed his aspiration to do for Paul what Heidegger had done for Kierkegaard, "to unchain this Christian content into something universal."[24] Four decades later, in the twilight of his life, Taubes sought to convey what he had found, first in a few lectures and interviews, and then in a weeklong seminar on Paul's Letter to the Romans.

In September 1986, just before the discovery of his cancer, Taubes had lectured in Heidelberg at the Forschungsstätte der Evangelischen Studiengemeinschaft (FEST), a Lutheran interdisciplinary research center. His topic was "Reprieve from the Gallows: The Apocalyptic Experience of Time, Past and Present" ("Galgenfrist. Apokalyptische Zeiterfahrung einst und jetzt"). Taubes had been ruminating upon that theme since his doctoral dissertation, and he had revisited it both in a recent talk at a symposium in Salzburg, and in an interview published in a Suhrkamp volume on contemporary philosophy. As he now formulated it, the Western experience of time was marked by the apocalyptic notion that history was a "reprieve." It was neither eternal, as the ancients had supposed, nor an eternal recurrence, as Nietzsche imagined. Rather, time was experienced as having "urgency." Moreover, contra Nietzsche, there was no innocence to be recovered, for humans are all guilty debtors. "As debtors we have a limited time to repay our debts," he added gnomically. "In the phrase 'The Kingdom of God is near,'" he said, "what is of interest to me is not the question of what the Kingdom of God means, but the plausibility of the notion that it is near." That is, Taubes interpreted Jesus's statement to mean that we ought not to take current institutions too seriously, for sudden transformation is always possible. So too, it was not the theological substance of Paul (in which Taubes did not believe), but Paul's emotional stance toward the world—colored by Gnosticism and apocalypticism—that Taubes valued.[25] These themes inherent in Christianity, Taubes told his audience at a Salzburg symposium, are "mines," capable of exploding existing institutions.[26] He referred to Paul's First Epistle to the Corinthians, in which the apostle famously stated, "The time is short. From now on those who have wives should live as if they had none; those who weep, as if they weep not; those who are joyful, as if they were not; those who make a purchase, as if they had nothing. For the form of this world is passing away. I want you to be free of all concern." Taubes glossed this as demanding "a loosening of one's relations to the world."[27]

In mid-January, Taubes was invited back to the FEST to give a four-day seminar on Paul's Epistle to the Romans at the end of February. To buck up Taubes's spirits, to help him focus his attention, and then to aid him in preparation for the seminar, Monika Wapnewski organized a group of his admirers to hear him discuss the Bible, and especially the Apostle Paul. At first the group met on Saturday afternoons at the Paris Bar. Then it was moved to Sunday and held at the Wapnewski home.[28] The setting was informal. Taubes referred to it as a *Tisch*, his version of a Hasidic gathering in which the rebbe explicates a holy text—except that the texts were drawn mostly from the New Testament, and the audience was comprised of Christian women. He wore a *kippah* as he expounded upon Biblical passages, such as the one in which Moses argues with God about the fate of his people, bringing out the pathos of the Biblical scene—a performance he would repeat in Heidelberg.[29] Margherita found these gatherings unsavory, both because of their religious aura and because of the audience of admiring female devotees.[30]

When the time came for Taubes to give his multiday seminar in Heidelberg, his health had sunk even lower. But he was determined to move ahead with the seminar, to use the occasion to present ideas about Paul that he had been contemplating for years, and indeed for decades. He was driven to Heidelberg by Rudi Thiessen, one of those unorthodox free-spirited intellectuals whom Taubes tended to attract, whose recent dissertation combined interests in religion and in rock and roll.[31] In Heidelberg, Taubes stayed with the Assmanns. He arrived without notes for the seminar, but armed with a document with which to introduce it— his letter to Carl Schmitt of September 1978. Aleida sat him down and helped him organize his thoughts. She had him talk to her about the subjects he planned to discuss, and these she typed up and helped him to arrange in order.

Taubes's deathly condition gave the occasion a particular drama. He held forth on Monday, Tuesday, Thursday, and Friday upon Paul and his legacy in Western thought. He spent Wednesday—his sixty-fourth birthday—in the intensive care unit of a local hospital, and was so ill that it was far from clear that he would return to finish the seminar. A small audience of some forty people listened raptly and asked questions. Aleida had arranged to have the lectures taped. When the lectures were over, Taubes made the Assmanns promise that after his death they would use the tapes to produce a publishable version of what he regarded as his testament.

Taubes began by distributing the letter of September 1978 that he had written to Carl Schmitt after their first meeting, in which Taubes had

FIGURE 16.3. Taubes at the Assmann home in Heidelberg, at the time of his lectures on Paul. (Photo by Aleida Assmann.)

raised the issue of Schmitt's antisemitism and disputed his claims about political theology. Then came a long discussion of his relationship to Schmitt, the upshot of which was that at his meeting with Schmitt, after he had explicated Romans 9–11 in a way that seemed to undercut the anti-Jewish implications of those verses, Schmitt had told him, "Before you die, you have to tell this to people."[32]

Taubes lamented the separation of the field of philosophy from the study of religion. He told his audience that he aspired to fructify them by bringing these fields back into conversation with one another. He also claimed to be speaking as a Jew about Paul.

As Taubes noted, for much of the twentieth century, the tendency among Jewish commentators on Christianity and its relationship to Judaism was to regard Jesus as a "good guy": whether portrayed as a more or less orthodox Jew, he was seen as preaching fundamentally Jewish doctrines. Martin Buber, for example, had claimed Jesus for the Jewish tradition in his *Three Lectures on Judaism* of 1911, and decades later he kept a picture of Jesus on the wall behind his desk in Jerusalem.[33] Jacob's father, Zwi, in his doctoral dissertation, had treated Jesus as firmly within the halachic tradition.

But for almost all Jewish thinkers, Paul was another story: if Jesus remained within the Jewish camp, Paul was regarded as a clear renegade, who not only rejected Jewish law but created the doctrine that with the coming of Christ, the covenant between God and the Jewish people had been superseded.[34] (An important exception was Leo Baeck, whose 1952 lecture "The Faith of Paul," characterized Paul as never ceasing to be a Jew, "whose spiritual, intellectual, and moral world was the Bible."[35]) Taubes, by contrast, was reclaiming Paul for the Jews, describing his enterprise as "bringing the heretic home, because I find him [Paul] to be more Jewish than any Reform or Liberal rabbi that I've encountered, whether in Germany, England, America, or Switzerland; that at least is my personal view."[36]

Taubes reminded his audience that Paul's letters were composed *before* the synoptic Gospels (Matthew, Mark, and Luke), and that at the time he wrote them (c. AD 57–58) there was no such thing as a "Christian"—hence applying that term to Paul was an anachronism.[37] "Jews" and "Christians" were not yet distinct groups in Paul's day, and indeed as Taubes noted— drawing upon what he had learned from Guy Stroumsa and Shlomo Pines—communities of Jewish Christians continued to exist for centuries. Paul was not simply "the apostle to the Gentiles"; he was "the apostle from the Jews to the Gentiles."[38]

Paul, Taubes suggested, saw himself as confronted by the same situation as Moses, when Moses descended from Mount Sinai to find that the Jews had sinned through worship of the Golden Calf. In the account in the Biblical Book of Numbers—and the more elaborate account in the Talmudic tractate *Berachot*, which Taubes quoted at length—God threatens to destroy the Jewish people and create a new nation out of Moses and his descendants. Moses pleads with God to preserve them, and God succumbs to his entreaties. Paul, Taubes claimed, saw himself facing a similar dilemma: how to save the Jewish people from destruction for their sin, this time of failing to recognize Jesus as the Messiah. Paul brings the pagans into the divine Covenant to try to arouse the jealousy of the Jews and win some of them over (Romans 11:13). In an attempt to "outbid" Moses, Paul becomes the founder of a new people, by contending that God's promises apply not only to the Jews—Israel "of the flesh"—but to "all Israel," meaning "Israel of the Spirit," that is, gentile believers in Christ.[39] Taubes instructed his listeners—as he had instructed Carl Schmitt—that in Romans 11:11, Paul declares that Israel is the "enemy" with a view to the Good News (of Christ), but that Jews remain the chosen of God. The Jews are chosen, but it is their refusal to accept Christ that opens the way for the Gentiles to be included in the new, universal covenant of "all Israel"—a dialectic, Taubes asserted, that the Church later forgot.[40] (Later in his lectures, Taubes discussed the case of Marcion, who interpreted Paul as breaking entirely with his Jewish past and with the God of the Old Testament, which Taubes described as a recurrent temptation within Christianity—as had his father, Zwi, in his sermon of 1940.)

To try to elucidate his point about Paul as recapitulating Moses's fear that the Jews might be extinguished, Taubes engaged in an excursion into the Kol Nidre prayer that begins Yom Kippur, the Day of Atonement. The anxiety expressed by Jews on that occasion, Taubes contended, repeated the "primal scene" of God's threatened destruction of Israel.[41] He acknowledged that the Kol Nidre prayer was composed long *after* Paul, but claimed that it recaptured "phenomenologically" "how a Jew experiences this." The implicit assumption was that there was a recurrent "Jewish" experience, felt by Paul, running through medieval Jews, and continued in the person of Jacob Taubes, who was in a position to reveal these truths to his Christian audience.[42]

Indeed, the lectures were replete with examples of contemporary Jewish phenomena with which Taubes was familiar but which were new and exotic for his audience—of young Jewish men from the Diaspora who now came to Jerusalem as returnees to the faith (*ba'alai t'shuva*) for example—phenomena that he analogized (anachronistically) to the experience of Paul.[43]

Taubes's first interpretive move, then, was to emphasize the *Jewishness* of Paul, and to portray Paul's self-conception and mission as taking place *within* a Jewish sensibility, rather than *outside* it. Comparing Paul once again to the Sabbatian experience, Taubes treated him as exemplifying a "paradoxical" "messianic logic": paradoxical because the crucifixion of Jesus, like the conversion of Sabbatai Zevi to Islam, seemingly contradicted the expectations of what a Messiah ought to be.[44]

In much of the Protestant (and especially Lutheran) tradition, Paul's message was interpreted as one of political quietism and respect for constituted authority. Paul was understood as an opponent of "the Law," that is Jewish halacha, but not of secular authority. Taubes's second main thesis was that Paul was in fact antinomian not only in regard to halacha, but in regard to law in general: that included Hellenistic philosophical conceptions of general laws, and the legitimacy of the political authority of the Roman Empire. Here as elsewhere in his lectures, Taubes drew upon Nietzsche's understanding of Paul as engaged in the process of the reversal of values (*Umwertung der Werte*).[45] Agreeing with Nietzsche,

Taubes characterized Paul's stance toward the Roman Empire as one of nihilism.[46]

Here Taubes integrated Walter Benjamin's conception of "the Messianic" as a *Jetztzeit*, a moment in which history could "explode" to "blast open the continuum of history." Paul interpreted the life and crucifixion of Jesus as creating a historical caesura, in which the legitimacy of the Law, Jewish and Roman, was called into question, ushering in a new age. The memory of Paul—or rather, the memory of this *conception* of Paul—was to serve as an ongoing reminder and spur to the possibility of a transformative break from contemporary institutions.

If liberalism rested on a respect for law, Taubes asserted, then Paul was an antiliberal fanatic. "He is thoroughly illiberal, of that I am certain. I've never been taken in by any liberal, whether ancient, medieval, or modern. Rather he is someone who responds entirely differently, namely with protest, with a revaluation of all values. The real ruler is not the law (Nomos), it is the one who has been killed on the Cross by the emperor's authority. Compared to that all the little revolutionaries are insignificant! This revaluation turns the theology of the Jewish-Roman-Hellenistic dominant class on its head." In short, Paul's insistence on the centrality of the Crucified Christ signified "the reversal of all of the values of this world."[47] For Taubes, then, Paul's Epistle to the Romans is "a political theology, a political declaration of war against the Caesars."[48] Paul is a rebel against both the Roman and Jewish status quo—the revolutionary par excellence of Jewish and Christian history.

In explicating Paul, Taubes was fundamentally uninterested in Paul's theological claims. "I do not think theologically," he pronounced. "I work with theological materials, but I think of them in terms of intellectual history and actual history. I inquire into the political potential of theological metaphors."[49] Indeed he insinuated that Paul was more radical, more humanist, and less theological than Jesus. When Paul pronounces in Romans 13 that the sum of the commandments are "you should love your neighbor as yourself," Taubes suggested that this was a highly polemical text, polemical against Jesus. For when, in the Gospels, Jesus is asked about the most important commandments, he responds, "You should love the Lord with all your power, and all your heart and all your soul" and "love your neighbor as yourself." Taubes claimed that Paul's omission of the commandment to love God is deliberate and "an absolutely revolutionary act," for it changes the focus from God to man.[50] The thesis is strained, not least because, as Taubes later acknowledges, the Gospel account was written *after* Paul's Epistle, so Paul may not have known Jesus's formulation as presented there.[51] But it further downplayed the centrality of Paul's *theological* premises to his mission.

There was another apparent difficulty with Taubes's conception of Paul as an antinomian revolutionary. That was a passage in Romans 13:1–2 that had long been at the center of Lutheran thinking about the relationship of theology to politics: "Let every person be subject to the governing authorities; for there is no authority except from God, and those authorities that exist have been instituted by God. Therefore whoever resists authority resists what God has appointed, and those who resist will incur judgment." Taubes tried to reconcile this with his view of Paul by explaining that at the time of this proclamation Paul remained a believer in the imminent apocalypse. Having delegitimated the existing Roman imperial order, he had no need to engage in active political revolution because he believed that that order was already on its way to dissolution.[52] As for other Pauline texts beyond the Epistle to the Romans that counseled acceptance of political authorities, Taubes simply ignored them.[53]

Taubes's interpretive strategy in all of this was to focus upon Paul's critique of the law and of established institutions and hierarchies, while barely noting Paul's *reason* for this stance—his conviction that all had changed with the sacrificial death of Jesus Christ.[54] In Taubes's interpretation, the crucifixion of Jesus provided Paul with an occasion on which to hang a new, radical doctrine and sensibility.

Taubes also explored the significance of Paul for some modern thinkers, above all Nietzsche, from whom, Taubes rightly claims, he had learned the most about Paul.[55] At first, Nietzsche had regarded Platonic rationalism as the source of Western decadence. But as he matured, he came to see Paul as the real culprit. First in *Daybreak* (*Morgenröte*), and then at greater length in *The Anti-Christ*, Nietzsche portrayed Paul as the real founder of Christianity.[56] In Nietzsche's telling, Jesus was a sort of "idiot," an unworldly, unheroic, immature flower-child. Paul, by contrast, was cunning, channeling the ressentiment of the socially and morally inferior into a doctrine that reversed the reverence for wisdom, beauty, and superiority, and instead made these into a source of guilt, undermining a classical worldview premised on human inequality and the value of elites, and substituting an egalitarian doctrine that subverted authority, beauty, and wisdom. Taubes accepted Nietzsche's *analysis* of Paul but reversed his *evaluation*: it was precisely the egalitarian thrust of Paul's doctrine that Taubes valued (in theory, at least).

Taubes also concurred with Nietzsche about the role of unconscious drives, but pointed out that in that respect Nietzsche agreed with Paul that our rational, conscious will is not in real control of our actions. It is not the autonomous self that is in control, but unconscious forces that frustrate that will: "the Ego is profoundly powerless."[57] For Taubes, this doctrine rang true, as did Paul's conception of man as fundamentally guilty and unable to redeem himself by his own efforts. Freud too, Taubes added, saw "that guilt is constitutive of humanity"; and in that respect he went beyond his enlightened, nineteenth-century, scientific identity, such that "his insights are greater than his intentions."[58] Freud too owed a profound debt to Paul, Taubes concluded.

These were the main themes of Taubes's *Political Theology of Paul*, though never presented quite so clearly and plainly. Rather they were cocooned in a remarkably wide-ranging skein of intellectual references, from the Hebrew Bible and the Babylonian Talmud to Marcion, and on to Spinoza, Hegel, Heidegger, Rosenzweig, Adorno, Buber, Baeck, Blumenberg, and of course Benjamin and Schmitt. There were additional references to New Testament scholars, especially his old favorite, the dissident historian of early Christianity, Franz Overbeck. (At the Heidelberg lectures, Taubes distributed an excerpt from Overbeck's posthumously published *Christentum und Kultur*, which did not make it into the published version, probably because of its fragmentary nature.[59]) Taubes had been thinking about Paul since at least the time of his father's 1940 sermon, which prefigured some of Taubes's own themes, and he poured into his Heidelberg lectures nuggets of learning and speculation gathered over a lifetime. It was this range of reference that made the lectures an intellectual feast to some, but a chore to others. Taubes developed his themes in good part through stories about the figures with whom he had discussed Paul over the course of his life: Emil Staiger in Zurich, Scholem in Jerusalem, Stendahl at Harvard, Morton Smith at Columbia, Stroumsa and Pines in Jerusalem. All of which added an air of exoticism and cosmopolitanism to the presentation. It made for an intellectually sparkling brew.

Death and Burial

After completing his Heidelberg lectures, Taubes returned to Berlin and prepared for his end. His deathbed became a sort of court. Jacob called upon friends and colleagues to come to wish him adieu, and many did. Ernst Tugendhat, who visited Jacob a few days before his death, was surprised to see a picture of Susan Taubes hanging on the wall.[60]

Jacob used these deathbed visits to lobby his colleagues Michael Theunissen and Karlfried Gründer to choose Renate Schlesier to succeed him as professor of hermeneutics at the FU.[61] He told Schlesier, Werner Hamacher, and Winfried Menninghaus that he had suggested each of them as his successor. In a letter to the former *Wissenschaftssenator*, Wilhelm Kevenig, he recommended Schlesier, Menninghaus, and Heinz Wismann.[62] To another of these deathbed visitors, his colleague Wilhelm Schmidt-Biggemann, he recommended Hamacher for the post.[63]

Lucid to the end, Jacob continued to crave company and conversation. Tania, who was forbidden by Jacob from breaking off her medical studies in New York, spoke with him daily on the telephone. To her inquiries about how he was doing, his most frequent response was, "Metastatically, not so good; metaphysically, wonderful!"

Looking after Jacob and his constant stream of visitors exhausted Margherita emotionally and financially: in order to help support Jacob, she sold a rare first edition of Marx's *Kapital*, which she had inherited from her ancestor, Lujo Brentano.[64] Margherita was assisted by Gabriele Althaus and Alexander Haas, a physician friend of Ethan's. From time to time, men from Jacob's Orthodox synagogue came by as well.

In mid-March, a week before Jacob's death, Ethan arrived and joined the death watch; Tania flew in a few days later. Jacob longed to return to Jerusalem, and Haas considered renting a private plane to do so, but Margherita objected. Jacob's other wish was to see Aleida and Corinna one last time. Ethan tried to convince Margherita to consent, but she was adamant in her refusal. Caught between the wishes of Jacob and Margherita, Ethan and Gabriele decided to arrange the visit nevertheless, but to do so surreptitiously.

They called Aleida, and she together with Jan and three-year-old Corinna came to Berlin. The plan was for them to sleep elsewhere, then for Aleida and Corinna to visit Jacob early in the morning, before Margherita, a late sleeper, awakened in her adjoining apartment. They arrived at Jacob's apartment and then departed as planned. But Margherita heard the child's voice from next door. Enraged, she confronted Althaus and accused her of violating her trust, exclaiming, "I have a reputation to lose, after all. What will Habermas think of this?"[65] But that evening Ethan called Althaus, told her that Jacob's end was near, and that Margherita was resigned to her return.

One of the last to visit was Rabbi David Weisz of the Orthodox synagogue at which Jacob prayed. He came on Thursday evening. Jacob made sure to have Ethan rehearse the kaddish prayer with the rabbi. On Friday evening, Jacob was groggy from the morphine he was taking to dull his pain. His family members took turns sitting vigil. At 3:30 a.m. on Saturday,

March 21, his breathing changed to a rattling sound, and his family gathered at his bedside, each holding a hand or an arm. Just before 4:00 a.m., Jacob opened his eyes one last time, and then expired. The burial society of Jacob's synagogue was summoned at the end of the Sabbath.

Ethan, Tania, and Margherita placed death notices in the *Tagesspiegel* and the *Tageszeitung*, with instructions that in lieu of flowers, donations should be made to Neve Shalom, a cooperative village of Jews and Arabs in Israel. On Monday, March 23, there was a memorial service (*Trauerfeier*) at the Jüdischer Friedhof am Scholzplatz, at which Rabbi Weisz presided. Jacob's colleague Karlfried Gründer spoke in his capacity as dean of the faculty. Among those who came was Jacob's Jewish colleague, Ernst Tugendhat. He was surprised to see so many Orthodox Jews in attendance: for in all of their years of acquaintance, Jacob had never spoken with him directly about religious issues—another sign of the many facets of Jacob Taubes, and his practice of displaying different faces to different interlocutors.[66]

Following the funeral, there was a large gathering at the Paris Bar, at which Jacob's children, friends, students, colleagues, and lovers (the categories overlapped) celebrated his life. This time, at Jacob's prior instruction, the tab was on him—or rather, on his heirs.

Jacob's body was flown to Zurich and buried the next day in the Jewish cemetery, beside the mother he adored. The *hesped* (eulogy) was given by Rabbi Moderchai Piron, a former chief rabbi of the Israeli Army who had retired to Zurich to serve as community rabbi. Since he had not known Jacob, it was a rote tribute. Among the small group in attendance at the burial of this antinomian, apocalyptic, Pauline professor was Moshe Soloveitchik, an ultra-Orthodox sage who had tutored young Jacob in Talmud.[67]

CHAPTER SEVENTEEN

The Afterlives of Jacob Taubes

The Beginnings of Taubes's Posthumous Reputation

Hans Jonas had known Jacob Taubes since the late 1940s, when Taubes introduced himself to the philosopher and historian of Gnosticism. When Taubes died, Agnes Heller, now a professor at the New School in New York, was at the Jonas home in New Rochelle. Jonas was deeply distressed by the news of Taubes's passing: he praised Taubes's brilliance, while regretting that Taubes had spent his powers in conversation rather than in writing.[1] When Taubes died, it seemed that his reputation and intellectual legacy would die with him. But in fact the decades after his death saw a remarkable proliferation of works by and about him, and a posthumous influence among intellectuals from a variety of countries and fields who had never encountered Taubes in the flesh.

Who, exactly, was Jacob Taubes? Now that he was dead, those who had known him began to give divergent answers.

A week after Taubes's death, the *Tageszeitung* ran a full-page feature, including a photo of Taubes taken at the Heidelberg lectures, and two separate tributes. The first was a well-informed obituary written by Aleida Assmann, but published under the name of her husband, Jan, entitled "Talmud in the Paris-Bar. On the Death of the Jewish Philosopher Jacob Taubes." The emphasis was on Taubes as a *Jewish* philosopher. It gave an accurate account of his biography and rabbinic ancestry, recounted his remarkable memory for books he had read, described his habit of reading in public places (such as the Paris Bar), and his seeming ability to divine a book's contents by simply placing his hands upon it or leafing through it. Assmann repeated Taubes's self-characterization as an "Arch-Jew and Primordial-Christian" (*Erzjude/Urchrist*), for whom Paul represented the quintessential fusion between Judaism and Christianity, a reality that has been systematically neglected by both faith communities and their institutions.[2]

On the next page of the *Tageszeitung* was a second tribute to Taubes, this time by Peter Gäng, who had been a leader of the student left at the FU in the 1960s, then Taubes's last doctoral student (later still he would become an expert on Buddhism, to which he converted). It was entitled "Critical Solidarity. Peter Gäng on the Difficulty of Classifying Taubes Politically." Gäng portrayed Taubes as championing "the truth of the heart" against the claims of autonomous reason, a man who in his last years had become an ever more believing Jew. Taubes, Gäng recounted, frequently used the phrase "I am a foreigner in this country": he was indeed a wanderer between worlds, who did not feel truly at home anywhere. Though to many he appeared to be on the left, Gäng thought him politically unclassifiable, and commented that because Taubes thought politics was more about people than about institutions, his typical mode of political activity was intrigue. Like Assmann, Gäng noted that since learning he was going to die, Taubes longed to visit Jerusalem once again.[3]

Briefer obituaries appeared elsewhere. In the *Frankfurter Allgemeine Zeitung*, Taubes's former student Henning Ritter recalled that Taubes's "access to significant and interesting people, and to the issues that most concerned them, was one of his extraordinary and astonishing talents."[4] In the *Tagesspiegel*, Uwe Schlicht, who had brought Taubes together with Peter Glotz to plot the dissolution of Fachbereich 11, stressed Taubes's role in the changing political struggles of the FU.[5] An unsigned but well-informed obituary in Jacob's hometown newspaper, the *Neue Zürcher Zeitung*, described him as "a man of the spoken word. He developed contradiction and provocation into an art, which did not arouse universal enthusiasm; but his sharpness exerted a fascination, and because it always stemmed from an extraordinarily intellectual presence, it could have a curiously penetrating effect."[6] *Der Spiegel* devoted a short article to Taubes's passing as well.[7] *Die Welt* published a briefer version of Assmann's obituary, entitled "Erzjude und Urchrist."[8] In April, the center-left daily *Frankfurter Rundschau* ran a long excerpt from an interview with Taubes, "Time Is Limited," that was to appear in a forthcoming Suhrkamp volume.[9]

A more substantial portrait came a few months later from Taubes's old friend, Armin Mohler, writing in the conservative magazine *Criticón*. Entitled "The Messianic Will-o'-the-Wisp," the article began by noting that although he had published little since his doctoral dissertation of 1947, "Taubes was a presence in West German intellectual life in a curious way:

Knowing his name was proof that one was intellectually *au courant*, and it was better yet if one knew him personally. Taubes was spoken of with praise or with derisive admiration aimed at his somewhat scurrilous person."[10] One could speak to him without the diffidence (*Befangenheit*) with which most Germans approached Jewish interlocutors, Mohler noted, and recounted his own encounters with Taubes in postwar Switzerland, as an example of Taubes's eagerness to engage in dialogue with those very different from himself. He provided a brief and critical evaluation of *Abendländische Eschatologie* as suffering from overgeneralization and abstraction, which Mohler saw as characteristic of Taubes's impatience with the concrete. He noted Taubes's propensity to charlatanism, and told the tale of his colleagues at Columbia who sought to show up his pretense to learning by inventing a medieval kabbalist about whom Taubes spoke with conviction, only to be told that the figure in question did not exist. The story retold by Mohler—which he had picked up from Michael Landmann's wife, Salcia—had actually occurred years earlier at Harvard, and involved a medieval philosopher, not a kabbalist.[11]

In a "Bio-Bibliographie" about Taubes that followed the main article, Mohler offered a paragraph-long account of Susan Taubes's *Divorcing*:

> Susan Taubes, daughter of a psychoanalyst from Budapest, a scholar of religion and an actress, was married to Jacob Taubes for a decade-and-a-half beginning in 1947. The characterization of the book as a "novel" is deceptive; it consists of autobiographical sketches, using only superficially disguised pseudonyms (Ezra Blind=Jacob Taubes), sketches that veer between surrealistic stylization and stark realism, and may well have been written at different times. Jacob Taubes stands at the center of the book; the two families represented in the marriage, in their span from traditional East European Jewish faith to psychoanalysis, from the ghetto to socio-economic success (both in pre-War Budapest and in the US) are very evocatively rendered. Just after the book's publication, Susan Taubes committed suicide by leaping into the sea.

Mohler's account of *Divorcing* set off a chain reaction that would contribute to the posthumous reputation of both Susan and Jacob.

In 1991, Matthes & Seitz Verlag, a left-leaning publishing house in Munich, brought out a new edition of Taubes's *Abendländische Eschatologie*, a work long out of print, with a brief introduction by Margherita von Brentano. (In an attempt to shape Taubes's posthumous reputation, after his death Margherita had gone through the letters that Taubes kept in his home and destroyed many that she thought were unsavory.[12]) The book's publisher, Axel Matthes, had studied at the FU and seems to have been fascinated with Jacob Taubes. He had been told—probably by Mohler or Sander—that Susan's novel provided "a key to the colorful personality" of Jacob Taubes, and he sought to read it. But the book seemed impossible to find. He learned from Sander that Hans-Joachim Arndt, Jacob and Susan's old acquaintance, now a right-Schmittian professor in Heidelberg, had a copy, and Matthes obtained Arndt's address from Armin Mohler.[13] Arndt agreed to lend the novel to Matthes, noting that the book probably said more about Susan than about Jacob, since it was written from a subjective point of view in order to come to terms with her own problems, and reflected the sensibilities of a female European Jewish emigrant in the United States.[14] Matthes was impressed enough with what he read to publish a German translation of Susan's book, which appeared under the title *Scheiden tut weh* (*Divorcing Hurts*) in 1995.[15] The novel was reviewed in *Der Spiegel*, which ran a photo of Jacob and Susan. The paperback appeared in 1997, published by Piper Verlag, this time with the photo of Jacob and Susan on its cover.

By that time, three more books by Jacob Taubes had appeared in print.

Sander: Taubes as Agent of Chaos

Obituaries aside, the first extended evaluation of Taubes after his death came from none other than Hans-Dietrich Sander, in a curious book that was little read but revealing in a perverse way.[16]

Entitled *The Dissolution of All Things* (*Die Auflösing aller Dinge*) (1988), the book was devoted to "the German-Jewish Question, seen from the perspective of political eschatology."[17] Its main thesis was that modernity was a process of dissolution, for which the Jews were largely responsible. Sander's primary concern was with the Germans and their fate. He had hoped, he wrote, that the book would carry a forward from Jacob Taubes; but since he had passed away, Sander reproduced the letter of 1980 in which Taubes had taken issue with Sander's version of German nationalism and his playing down of the evils of the Third Reich. Sander had so objected to Taubes's letter, he now wrote, that it stimulated him to write his book. While exploring a range of themes, the book turned back time and again to Jacob Taubes.

Sander agreed with Taubes in attributing the disproportion of Jews in modern revolutionary movements to a Jewish affinity with "the apocalyptic soul"—but he reversed Taubes's evaluation.[18] While for Taubes the Jews were agents of radical critique and transformation, for Sander they were agents of dissolution. Sander characterized Taubes as the

"Phenotype of Diasporic thought seeking to hasten the apocalypse," and he repeatedly cited Taubes's assertion in an interview given late in his life that he had "no investment in this world."[19] Sander thus portrayed Taubes as the paradigm of the uprooted Jew, adding character traits that in the case of Taubes had more than a little truth. Taubes, he wrote, "had no fundamental objection to chaos."[20]

Sander's book was too incendiary for any publisher, so he published it himself in his Verlag Castel del Monte. Armin Mohler sent a circular letter (*Rundbrief*) to his friends and acquaintances, recommending the book.[21]

After the fall of Communism and the unification of East and West Germany, Sander founded a journal, *Die Staatsbriefe*, that championed an anti-Western and antiliberal nationalism. In the crazy kaleidoscope of reshuffled intellectual commitments over the decades, its contributors included not only such right-wing nationalist stalwarts as Armin Mohler and Hans-Joachim Arndt, but also Salcia Landmann—who had first recommended Taubes to Gollwitzer for a job at the FU—and Peter Furth, the radical Marxist now turned nationalist critic of bourgeois capitalism![22] Horst Mahler, to whom Taubes had introduced Sander, also contributed to Sander's journal. By 2003, Sander was active in founding the Society for the Rehabilitation of Those Persecuted for Holocaust Denial (Verein zur Rehabilitierung der wegen Bestreitens des Holocaust Verfolgten)[23]—a category that included Mahler himself.

For Sander, Taubes was the perfect Jew of his imagination, in that he really was a nihilist/anarchist of the sort Sander imagined Jews to be. Yet despite Sander's animus, his portrayal of Taubes as a theorist of "apocalyptic chaos," without a commitment to existing institutions, was not implausible. Indeed, it would be embraced by some of Taubes's radical interpreters on the post-Communist left—but with the ideological valuations reversed.

About and against Carl Schmitt

Neither of the two books that became the basis of Taubes's posthumous reputation were actually *written* by him. Both *Ad Carl Schmitt* and *Die politische Theologie des Paulus* were comprised primarily of talks that he had given. Much of their fascination—as well as their limits—derives from the reader's exposure to Taubes's characteristic mode of speaking and lecturing, with its combination of sharply formulated insights, wide-ranging reference, name-dropping, humor, information and misinformation, and an interweaving of matters autobiographical and intellectual.

As we've seen, Taubes had long regarded Carl Schmitt as one of the great minds of the age, a *Meisterdenker*. Late in Taubes's life, Schmitt took on another function for him. Taubes took to describing himself as an "Apocalypticist of Revolution," the counterpart to Schmitt, whom Taubes characterized as the "Apocalypticist of Counterrevolution." That dichotomy had the very intentional effect of elevating Taubes into the category of a *Meisterdenker* as well.

At the time of Schmitt's death in 1985, Taubes had given his lecture on "Carl Schmitt—Apocalypticist of Counterrevolution," which had been published in *Die Tageszeitung*.

The idea of expanding the lecture into a small book originated at the Exil restaurant, where Taubes was dining with Peter Gente, his former assistant, now the publisher of Merve Verlag.[24] Taubes was scheduled to appear on March 19, 1986, at a public debate about Schmitt to be held at the Maison Heinrich Heine, a German cultural institution in Paris. Opposing him would be Kurt Sontheimer, a political scientist and author of *Antidemocratic Thought in the Weimar Republic* (*Antidemokratisches Denken in der Weimarer Republik*), a book that dealt critically and at length with Schmitt's thought, and had gone through several editions since its first publication in 1962. Taubes suggested that Gente come to Paris for the event and tape it. Gente journeyed to Paris for the debate and produced a transcription, which he showed to Taubes.

In his debate with Sontheimer in Paris, Taubes retold many of the anecdotes about his connection to Schmitt over the decades, while adding a few additional points. He defended the utility of Schmitt's invocation of the "state of emergency" during the Weimar Republic. When Sontheimer raised the issue of Schmitt's antisemitism, Taubes responded that he had discussed with Schmitt the antisemitic suggestion in Schmitt's 1938 book on Hobbes that Friedrich Julius Stahl, a convert from Judaism to Lutheranism who became a leading German conservative publicist, was not really a German, since his origins were Jewish. After a meandering comparison of Stahl to Heinrich Heine, who had indeed maintained a Jewish identity despite his nominal conversion to Christianity, Taubes seemed to endorse Schmitt's view that indeed Stahl was ultimately a Jew.[25]

Sontheimer decided that he did not want his part of the exchange published. To help round out the slim volume, Gente reached out to Armin Mohler for a copy of the letter that Taubes had written to him about Schmitt from Jerusalem in 1952—the letter that Schmitt had taken pains to circulate at the time—along with some excerpts from Schmitt's subsequent letters to Mohler about Taubes.

Gente cobbled together a book, composed of the article from the *Tageszeitung*, the letter, and the unpublished transcript of Taubes's remarks on the history of his relationship to Schmitt that Taubes had given at the beginning of his seminar on Paul in Heidelberg, entitled "1948–1978: Thirty Years of Refusal." Once again Taubes formulated the contrast between himself and Schmitt. Schmitt regarded himself (one might say, mythologized himself) as the *Aufhalter* or *Katechon* who holds back chaos and suppresses the unruly forces that come from below. That was not Taubes's sensibility: "I have no spiritual investment in the world as it is [in English in the original], and as an 'apocalypticist' would be happy to see the demise of existing institutions." But, Taubes contended, this shared feeling for the possibility of "apocalypse"—understood as a radical threat to the existing institutional order—allowed Taubes to empathize with Schmitt's stance, even if his own position was quite different.[26]

Days before his death, Taubes suggested as a title something along the lines of "With Carl Schmitt in loving argument" (*Mit Carl Schmitt im liebenden Streit*) and alluded to a passage in Heraclitus for Gente to look up. The passage refers to a productive tension, such as that produced by the string of the bow or of the lyre. At the suggestion of the Assmanns, Gente called the volume *Ad Carl Schmitt. Gegenstrebige Fügung* (roughly, *In the Matter of Carl Schmitt: A Tension of Opposites*, where "Ad" connoted both "about" and "against").

The eighty-page booklet appeared in print a few months after Taubes's death. It was not much reviewed, nor did it sell well. (Merve published a first edition of two thousand; after decades, it eventually sold about three thousand copies.[27]) And yet as one scholar of Schmitt's work has noted, *Ad Carl Schmitt* would eventually become "one of the most influential publications on Schmitt ever written."[28] It made Carl Schmitt kosher for post-Communist leftist intellectuals, just as Taubes's posthumously published lectures on *Die Politische Theologie des Paulus* would make Paul kosher for them.

The Political Theology of Paul

In the months after Jacob's death, Aleida Assmann transcribed the tapes of his Heidelberg lectures, as a work of mourning (*Trauerarbeit*). The lectures were somewhat fragmentary and far from conceptually coherent. And they were filled with allusions to works of modern New Testament scholarship and theology with which the Assmanns were unfamiliar. In trying to track down the references, they were aided by a local prodigy with deep knowledge of nineteenth-century theological controversies, Wolf-Daniel Hartwich, and by Horst Folkers, a staff member at the

FEST who had attended the lectures. They later met Jacob's former student assistant, Christoph Schulte, who had helped Jacob prepare for his courses on Paul. The transcription of the lectures was circulated among these as well as Aharon Agus, Moshe Barasch, and other scholarly friends of Jacob, and through corrections and expansions, edited into a more coherent and readable version. Some of Taubes's insults and tirades were omitted. Parts of the text were moved around in the interests of logical progression. Jan drafted a long afterword, to which Aleida and Hartwich also contributed,[29] that tried to put some of the topics in context and to pull together some of the themes, sometimes with greater conceptual clarity than in the text itself, sometimes by drawing distinctions and coining terms—such as "negative political theology"—that were not Taubes's own.

All of this took time. But there were additional considerations that delayed the publication of the Heidelberg lectures. Margherita von Brentano objected to the entire enterprise, arguing that the publication of work that Taubes had not had the opportunity to revise to his own standards would tarnish his reputation. She accused Aleida of playing the role of Elisabeth Förster-Nietzsche, the philosopher's sister who had edited Friedrich's unpublished work into *The Will to Power*, a book that most scholars regard as a distortion of his thought. Margherita claimed to be Jacob's literary executor, with the right to veto such publications—which was not the case. The Assmanns worked to mollify her concerns, holding off until the republication of Taubes's "finished" work, *Abendländische Eschatologie*. When the Paul lectures were published in 1993, six years after Taubes delivered them, the editors dedicated the volume to Margherita, as well as to Edith Picht-Axenfeld, who had invited Taubes to the FEST.[30]

Jacob's Paris colleague, Heinz Wismann, was unable to attend the Heidelberg lectures. When he read them, he judged them stimulating but ultimately unserious—intended to surprise and astonish, like a magician pulling a rabbit out of a hat. But all too often, he thought, the claims would not stand up to rigorous scrutiny.[31] Wismann was hardly alone among Taubes's friends in his judgment. Yet soon enough *The Political Theology of Paul* would attain international influence and be translated into a dozen or more languages.

The Collected Essays

In the final months of his life, Taubes had discussed with Henning Ritter and Winfried Menninghaus his desire that a collection of his essays be published after his death, and he had given Menninghaus a stack of his published essays and articles with that goal in mind. After Jacob's death, Ritter lost interest in the project. Menninghaus pitched the project to Sigfried Unseld at Suhrkamp, but he turned it down.

The idea for the volume languished until Aleida and Jan Assmann took the initiative. They selected additional essays, had those first published in English translated into German, and with help once again from Wolf-Daniel Hartwich, composed a substantial introduction to the collection of twenty-one articles, published between 1953 and 1984.[32]

The resulting volume, *Vom Kult zur Kultur: Bausteine zu einer Kritik der historischen Vernunft; gesammelte Aufsätze zur Religions- und Geistesgeschichte*, was published by Fink Verlag in Munich, which had in the meantime published *Die Politische Theologie des Paulus*. As the enigmatic title and the two subtitles perhaps indicated, Taubes's work as a whole was difficult to characterize or classify. "Vom Kult zur Kultur" ("From Cult to Culture") was the translated title of a minor essay that Taubes had published in *Partisan Review* in 1954, about the idiosyncratic Jewish thinker Oskar Goldberg. The editors took the phrase to refer, roughly, to the ongoing tension between ancient or traditional religion on the one hand, and philosophy and enlightened culture on the other, a tension that they saw as the red thread running through Taubes's writings. "Contributions toward a Critique of Historical Reason" ("Bausteine zu einer Kritik der historischen Vernunft") was more obscure still. "Collected essays on religious and intellectual history" was closer to the mark. Included were his 1953 *Commentary* article, "The Issue between Judaism and Christianity"; his essays on modern Protestant thinkers published in English in the mid-1950s when he was searching for a job; the portrait of Franz Overbeck that he had written in the early 1960s as the introduction to a small volume of Overbeck's writings; four of his contributions to the Poetik und Hermeneutik conference volumes and two contributions to the series on Political Theology; Taubes's critiques of Buber and Scholem; and some assorted essays on psychoanalysis and intellectuals.

In their introduction, the editors portrayed Taubes's characteristic stance as addressing issues from the margins: "He writes as a philosopher about theological issues and topics in the history of religion; about philosophical matters as a theologian and student of religion; about Christianity as a Jew; about Jewish themes as a Pauline; about cultural and political themes as a Gnostic and Apocalypticist."[33] They stressed that given his restless personality, Taubes's intellectual energy was ignited by his urge to contradict, to object, to dispute some existing position. In light of the character of his works, the editors made it their task to trace the polemical context or polemical target that lay behind many of the essays.[34]

Rival Legatees

In the decade after Taubes's death, there were rival claimants to his legacy among his students, friends, and associates.

In January of 1987, when he was perceptibly ill, Taubes sat for a series of autobiographical interviews with an up-and-coming, unorthodox philosopher, Peter Sloterdijk. They were intended for publication in a series of interviews with contemporary philosophers, funded by a Munich industrialist. But the funding faded, and the interviews were never published.[35] Sloterdijk, however, dedicated his next book, *Eurotaoismus*, to Taubes, whom he characterized as "one of the last great representatives of the Jewish spirit in the German language." His book's account of the Jewish and Christian origins of the philosophy of history drew heavily on *Abendländische Eschatologie*.[36] Shortly thereafter, together with Thomas Macho, a professor of cultural history, Sloterdijk edited a thousand-page sourcebook about Gnosticism, *Weltrevolution der Seele*, clearly inspired by Taubes, and including two of his essays.[37]

With the publication of *Die politische Theologie des Paulus* in 1996, a decade after Taubes's death, there were four books that bore his name as author: the selected essays in *Vom Kult zur Kultur*, the republished *Abendländische Eschatologie*, the booklet on Schmitt, and the lectures on the political theology of Paul. With the exception of the republished doctoral dissertation, Aleida and Jan Assmann had been involved with all of these: they were the moving force behind the Paul lectures and the collected essays, and had played a role in the Carl Schmitt volume as well.

Their devotion to Taubes's memory went beyond publications. In the years after his death, they spent four months in Jerusalem and developed friendships with some of Taubes's associates in Israel, including Moshe Barasch, Guy Stroumsa, and Aharon Agus. With the support of Jan Assmann, Barasch, and Stroumsa, and with funding from the German Minerva Stiftung, Agus founded the Jacob Taubes Minerva Center for Religious Anthropology at Bar-Ilan University. Its mission was to bring together Israeli and German scholars "to study religious phenomena from as wide an academic disciplinary perspective as possible." The intention of the Center's founders was to "concretize their commitment to the intellectual and personal legacy of Jacob Taubes."[38] Initiated in 1993, the Center was short-lived. Just as it was being launched, Agus left Bar-Ilan and moved to Germany to teach at the Hochschule für Jüdische Studien in Heidelberg. Several international conferences were held and the resulting conference volumes published.[39] But the Center ran into difficulties, and in 2000 the Bar-Ilan administration decided to close it down.[40]

Not everyone was pleased with the role the Assmanns had assumed in molding the Taubes legacy.[41] Among the dissatisfied was Eveline Goodman-Thau, who had been close to Taubes in Jerusalem and had since received a doctorate from the University of Kassel. She contacted Richard Faber, Taubes's former *Assistent* and disciple, and together with Thomas Macho, they organized a conference in July 1997 about Taubes and his work. It was focused upon, but not limited to, the themes of *Abendländische Eschatologie*. Some thirty-odd contributions engaged directly with one or another theme in Taubes's work; others compared or contrasted Taubes to figures from the history of philosophy or scholarship; while still others had a very tangential relationship to Taubes.

Some of the essays, particularly by those who had worked closely with Taubes, shed light on the man and his ideas. Carsten Colpe, the expert on Gnosticism who had taught courses together with Taubes on the subject, remarked upon how Taubes made up for his lack of acquaintance with the historical sources through his ability to suggest parallel historical experiences. Christoph Schulte, who had been Taubes's student assistant in the 1980s when he lectured on Paul's Epistle to the Corinthians and Epistle to the Romans, underscored the fact that Taubes had no unified approach and no unified interpretation of Paul's writings. Rather, particular passages in the letters provided Taubes with an anchor for his own, shifting intellectual concerns and confrontations with various thinkers, such as Benjamin or Schmitt.[42]

Though the conference took place in 1997, the volume was only published in 2001. In their foreword, the editors noted that one reason for the heightened interest in Jacob Taubes was the 1995 publication of the German translation of Susan Taubes's novel, *Divorcing*. They hastened to add that it was a mistake to confuse the novel's central character, Ezra Blind, with Jacob Taubes.[43]

The hefty volume edited by Faber, Goodman-Thau, and Macho seems to have gone virtually unreviewed and unnoticed. Its contents were too diffuse, its essays too uneven, its subject matter too abstruse to attract much of an audience. But while interest in Taubes was declining in Germany, it was accelerating abroad. Taubes's work was being appropriated by radical intellectuals in France and Italy, by scholars of early Christianity, and by academics in the field of modern Jewish thought.

Appropriations by the Post-Communist Left

Whether an author's work finds resonance, either while he is alive or after his death, depends not only on what he has written, but on the circumstances under which he is read and interpreted.[44] In ways that would have been hard to predict when Taubes died in 1987, his works would prove remarkably influential on a variety of audiences in Europe and beyond.

Beside the paid death notice for Jacob Taubes in the *Tageszeitung* of March 23, 1987, was a report about a recent incident in which a man from East Berlin had tried to flee to West Berlin and had been shot by the East German Border Police (*DDR Grenzsoldaten*). There were protests from the Allied Commanders of the city, the West Berlin senate, and the government of the Federal Republic.[45] That newspaper report is a reminder that Taubes's entire career in Berlin took place in a divided city and a divided nation in a divided Europe. All of that was soon to end: with the fall of the Berlin Wall in November 1989, the West Berlin of Jacob Taubes was transformed. Communism, an active ideology that had in one form or another been powerful not only in the Soviet sphere, but in France and Italy and even briefly in the precincts of the FU, was definitively discredited. So, more or less, were other radical alternatives to liberal, capitalist, democratic welfare states. "Third-World" anti-colonial movements had largely resulted in repressive autocratic regimes that no one saw as a desirable option. In China, the homeland of Mao and the Cultural Revolution, Maoist Communism had given way under Deng Xiaoping to a more capitalist economy. Already by 1989, and certainly by the 1990s, capitalism—what its opponents were later to christen "neo-liberalism"—seemed to be "the wave of the future."[46]

What were the radical intellectuals who had cut their teeth on the New Left revolts of the 1968 generation to do? After the manifest failure of the apocalyptic phase of the New Left, some turned to Taubes's interpretation of Paul, as providing a Gnostic revolutionary message—secret knowledge of this world's corruption—ready to be activated in the future.

For three prominent intellectuals of the radical left, Alain Badiou, Giorgio Agamben, and Slavoj Žižek, professed atheists all, the invocation of Paul provided a longer, deeper spiritual lineage for a message that was resolutely antiliberal, antibourgeois, and anticapitalist after the failure of their erstwhile Marxist hopes. They took from Taubes the conception of Paul as a radical critic of the existing political and institutional order. What interested them was Paul as a model for the creation of a community free from economic and political domination.[47]

The first to do so was Alain Badiou in his 1997 book, *Saint Paul: Le fondation de l'universalisme*. Badiou had studied with Louis Althusser in the early 1960s and succeeded his teacher as chair of philosophy at the elite École normale supérieure in Paris. By the 1990s, he was among the best-known philosophers in France. For Badiou, the "events" of May 1968 in France were his "fall on the road to Damascus."[48] During the 1970s, he had been a Maoist, a devotee of the Cultural Revolution, and defender of the Khmer Rouge. In the intervening decades, he helped found the small post-Maoist "Organisation Politique," and lost none of his radical anticapitalist and antiliberal zeal. He was particularly perturbed by the rise of identity politics, whether in the form of French nationalism, ethnic identity, or multiculturalism. The ethnic and nationalist identity that most exercised him, however, was that of the Jews.

At the center of Badiou's book is the notion of an "event"—an unexpected, transformative experience that gains its significance from the unwavering faith and commitment of those who believe in it. It is their belief and action that gives meaning to the event, by making it a historical turning point. Hence for Badiou, as for his teacher, Althusser, truth arises through militant action, and is only confirmed retroactively.[49]

For Badiou, Paul's central doctrine of the redemptive force of Christ's resurrection is an "event" of this sort. It is a "fable," invented by Paul, but through the power of belief, able to create a new, more universal "subject" beyond any existing historical or ethnic community.[50] It is not the substance of Paul's doctrine that matters to Badiou, but its form, as a model of radical rupture. Badiou was most exercised by what he saw as the contemporary combination of particular, ethnic identity (as in the notion of a distinctive French identity to be protected) along with capitalist globalization. Badiou portrayed these as complementary processes, though most analysts would see them as in tension. Paul is also important for Badiou for his fundamental challenge to the law: in his case, of the Roman empire. For Badiou, Paul's universalism—as expressed in his statement (in Galatians 3:28) "There is neither Jew nor Greek, there is neither slave nor free, there is neither male nor female"—is all that really matters.[51]

Like Taubes, but with greater detail, Badiou argued that Paul "provoked—entirely alone—a cultural revolution upon which we still depend." Paul did so through his radical critique of law: Jewish religious law, "Greek law as the subordination of destiny to the cosmic order," and Roman, imperial law. The contemporary parallels of this, Badiou contended, were a revolt against capitalism and ethnic particularity. Capitalism, he claimed, subordinates the individual to abstract forces as did the laws of the Romans. And ethnic particularism is what Jewish law is all about.[52]

Badiou failed to cite Taubes's *Political Theology of Paul*—or any other commentary on Paul, for that matter. But Badiou mentioned so many of the texts, events, and figures (such as Marcion, Nietzsche, and Freud) discussed by Taubes that it is obvious that he had not only read Taubes's text, but adopted some of its theses. On one key point, Badiou's account differed radically from Taubes's, however. While Taubes's discussion of the Epistle to the Romans emphasizes Paul's Jewish background and his concern for the Jewish people, Badiou interprets Paul as acknowledging his Jewish lineage and making use of Old Testament texts only in order to bring the Jews into the new, universalist faith.[53] As opposed to the Jewish God, identified with the Christian conception of God the Father, for Badiou it is Paul's "discourse of the son" which creates a real historical rupture, in that it "enjoins us not to put our trust any longer in any discourse laying claim to mastery."[54] In underscoring the absolute break between Paul and the religion of the Hebrew Bible, Badiou's position was neo-Marcionite.

Some of the implications of Badiou's radical universalism were spelled out in his numerous interventions regarding Jews and the State of Israel. He was a vehement opponent of the notion that the Nazi murder of the Jews in any way legitimated Jewish identity or the Jewish state. "That the Nazis and their accomplices exterminated millions of people they called 'Jews' does not to my mind lend any new legitimacy to the identity predicate in question," he wrote. The proper lesson to be learned, he maintained, was that any "communitarian" (i.e. ethnic) identity ultimately leads to disaster. On the premise that "truly contemporary states or countries are always cosmopolitan, perfectly indistinct in their identitarian configuration," he found the very idea of a Jewish state abhorrent. Israel, for Badiou, was simply another colonial state, representing "a form of the oppression of impoverished peoples that is particularly detestable and very rightly obsolete." The only legitimate legacy of Jewish history was represented by those who left Jewish identity behind in the name of universalism, from the Apostle Paul to Trotsky.[55]

Two years after the publication of Badiou's book, another study of Paul appeared, by another purported master of thought, this time in Italian. It originated as a series of seminars at the Collège international de philosophie in Paris, founded by Jacques Derrida, with which Badiou was also affiliated. Its author was Giorgio Agamben, an Italian philosopher who had studied with Heidegger in the 1960s and later became the editor of the Italian edition of the collected works of Walter Benjamin. His book,

The Time That Remains. A Commentary on the Letter to the Romans, was dedicated to Jacob Taubes, and was an erudite—indeed pedantic— exploration of some of the themes and connections suggested by Taubes's *Political Theology of Paul*. (It is hard to disagree with Mark Lilla's characterization of Agamben as "the very model of the baffling post-modernist— obscure, pretentious, humorless."[56])

Agamben had become a figure of international renown (at least in postmodern academic circles), best known for combining multilingual erudition with bombastic generalizations about the contemporary world. Contemporary states, according to Agamben, are fundamentally totalitarian. Their claim to influence the health and safety of their inhabitants— their biological existence—results in totalitarian control, such that the concentration camp is the paradigmatic institution of the current age.[57] For Agamben, the state's law is a form of oppression, which seeks to blot out that which it cannot control.

Agamben took issue with Badiou's characterization of Paul as a universalist.[58] Agamben's interest in Paul was as an exemplar of a strategy that creates a space that escapes "the grasp of power and its laws, without entering into conflict with them yet rendering them inoperative."[59] According to Agamben, for Paul, with Christ's crucifixion, "Messianic time" has already begun, a time characterized by "the inoperativity of the law and the substantial illegitimacy of each and every power."[60] After plunging the reader into the depths of Walter Benjamin's manuscripts, Agamben endorsed Taubes's assertion of the connection between Paul and Benjamin, and characterized Paul's Epistle to the Romans and Benjamin's "Theses on the Philosophy of History" as "the two fundamental messianic texts of our tradition."[61]

The next to turn to Paul as the symbol of radical rejection of the existing order was Slavoj Žižek. Slovenian by origin, attuned to the French intellectual scene, and popular among academic intellectuals in the United States and beyond, Žižek takes a delight in shocking all existing sensibilities, with a style that combines outrageous assertions about the virtues of Stalin and Mao with the sense that he is pulling the reader's leg.[62] In a series of (repetitive) works in the late 1990s and early 2000s, he too turned to Paul. Though without mentioning Taubes directly, Žižek refers to him implicitly when he writes, "One is allowed to praise Paul, if one reinscribes him back into the Jewish legacy—Paul as a radical Jew, an author of Jewish political theology."[63] For Žižek, it is significant that Paul makes almost no reference to the life of Jesus, only the fact of his crucifixion and resurrection—an analysis implicit in Taubes and explicit in Badiou. But for Žižek, as for Badiou, the point of tracing Paul's origins in the Jewish tradition is to emphasize the radicality of his break from it, "the way he undermined the Jewish tradition from within."[64] And following Badiou, the significance of Paul for Žižek lies in his "unconditional universalism," his negation of any form of particular identity.[65]

These writings by Badiou, Agamben, and Žižek have in turn engendered analyses, comparisons, and minor innovations in a still-flowing stream of recursive books.[66] The year 2013 saw the publication of two edited volumes, *Paul in the Grip of the Philosophers*, and *Paul and the Philosophers*, a tome of over six hundred pages, both devoted primarily to the works of Taubes, Badiou, Agamben, and Žižek.[67] Taubes played a central role in an Italian volume that covered some of the same ground, Tiziano Tosolini's *Paolo e i filosofi. Interpretazioni del Cristianesimo da Heidegger a Derrida*. The author was a lecturer at the Pontifical University Gregoriana.[68]

Another vector of influence was via "postcolonial" studies. That was an academic fashion that sought to trace the influence—usually assumed to be malign—of European imperialism upon the nations of Asia and Africa in the decades after decolonization, and said to represent the critical perspectives of the formerly colonized upon the West. In time, this interpretive turn made its way into scholarship on the New Testament, which seized upon Taubes's interpretation of Paul as a radical critic of the legitimacy of the Roman Empire. That interpretive turn, in the words of an expert but skeptical scholar, "reads virtually everything in the New Testament as a coded critique of the Roman Empire."[69] Thus Taubes's portrait could be used to make Paul into a precursor of anti-colonial resistance.

By the 1990s, the process of de-Christianization in Western Europe—in the sense of declining identification with institutionalized Christianity—meant that the market for Christian religious thought was shrinking. The failure of radical leftist projects meant a shrinking audience for radical thought. It was tempting, therefore, for both academic theologians and academic radicals to reach into one another's turf in search of intellectual market share. Some radical academics (and they were all academics) turned their attention to Christianity and to Judaism in search of roots and resonance, without embracing religious belief. Some academics, Christian and Jewish, looked to the radical academics in search of conceptual resources for new interpretations of old texts. Who knows, some seem to have thought, perhaps we can interest secular students and their teachers in Christianity? Hence the appeal of Paul as an antinomian, a political radical, a critic of the empire of his day.

Badiou, Agamben, and Žižek all jettisoned Taubes's emphasis on Paul as a Jewish figure bringing the rest of mankind into the covenant once reserved for the seed of Abraham. But a different stream of intellectuals—scholars of early Christianity—would take from Taubes precisely the emphasis on the Jewishness of Paul.

The Jewish Paul

Paul's statements about the Jews were varied, ambivalent, and some-times contradictory.[70] That may reflect his internal tensions, or the dif-fering occasions, audiences, and purposes of his letters. In the generations after Paul, the early church leaders understood him as marking not only a separation from Judaism but a triumph over it.[71] For much of its history, the Christian tradition extolled the triumph of the Church over the Syna-gogue, and Paul was seen as its origin.

When Jacob Taubes first began to contemplate Paul, that was very much the dominant view among both Christian and Jewish scholars. That view began to change, slowly, in the aftermath of the Holocaust. A major step toward a new interpretation of Paul came from Krister Stendahl, Taubes's friend from his Harvard days, whose essays on Paul and Judaism were collected in 1976 as *Paul among the Jews and Gentiles*. Stendahl, and those who followed him, disputed the image of Paul as the originator of Christian anti-Judaism, and portrayed him as having experienced not a conversion from Judaism but a calling to widen the Covenant. Other scholars, Jewish and non-Jewish, deepened this line of analysis, includ-ing Taubes's friend Michael Wyschogrod.[72] Among the most prominent advocates of this view is John Gager of Princeton University, who makes explicit reference to Taubes, and like other scholars in this interpretive camp, regards Paul as having never left Judaism.[73] Many other scholars have followed in their wake.[74] In 2010, the professional association of aca-demic scholars of the Bible, the Society for Biblical Literature, founded a separate "Paul within Judaism Section," and a developing scholarly trend posits as a working hypothesis "that the apostle Paul should be understood as operating entirely within Judaism."[75]

The term "the parting of the ways" was coined in 1934 by James Parkes, an Anglican priest and author of *The Conflict of the Church and the Syna-gogue: A Study in the Origins of Antisemitism*, which traced the separa-tion of Christianity from Judaism to the end of the first century. More recent scholars have seen Judaism and Christianity as intertwined for much longer, as encapsulated in the title of a recent collection, *The Ways*

That Never Parted: Jews and Christians in Late Antiquity and the Early Middle Ages.[76] In this respect, Taubes was ahead of the scholarly curve. So too was his contention that the Pharisees were a self-created elite, very much a minority during the period of the creation of what became Rabbinic Judaism.[77]

Influence on the Assmanns

To those who knew him in the flesh, Jacob Taubes was a vivid personage. But for those who never met him or knew of him while he was alive, Jacob Taubes could live on mainly through his published works. Their publication, as we have seen, was due primarily to Aleida and Jan Assmann.

If the Assmanns were responsible for Taubes's posthumous reputation, he in turn seems to have had a transformative effect upon them, transmuting Jan from a scholar known primarily to specialists in the rarified discipline of Egyptology, and Aleida from a novice scholar of English literature, into a couple of international fame. Jan's interests had long stretched beyond his academic specialty of ancient Egypt, into the way in which past civilizations were "remembered" in subsequent history. But it was after his encounter with Taubes that he turned to writing books that reached a wider audience, by comparing the religion of ancient Egypt with that of the Jews—a subject of far broader interest—to cast new light on both.[78] In 1997 he published *Moses the Egyptian*, which contrasted the historical memory of the Egyptian monotheistic Pharaoh Akhenaten with that of Moses. The former was more or less forgotten; the latter was remembered as a seminal figure in his people's history.[79]

In that book, Assmann put forward a claim about "the Mosaic distinction" (*die Mosaische Unterscheidung*), which he developed in a series of subsequent works, including one dedicated to the memory of Jacob Taubes,[80] and another, *The Mosaic Distinction, or The Price of Monotheism* (*Die Mosaische Unterscheidung oder der Preis des Monotheismus*), in which the subtitle was an allusion to Taubes's essay "Der Preis des Messianismus," his critique of Gershom Scholem. It referred to the irreconcilable distinction between true and false religion: monotheistic religions, beginning with Biblical Judaism, put forth exclusive claims to the existence of one God, while other deities were defined as false gods. That was in contrast to earlier, polytheistic systems, which maintained that the gods of each group could be translated into one another (Amun, Assur, Zeus, Jupiter).[81] "First the Jews, and then in their wake, the Christians, and then in the wake of both, Islam, did away with this system of inter-cultural translatability [of deities], in that they worshipped a God who refused any correlation with other gods," he wrote.[82] This intolerance toward other faiths implied the possibility of violence as a holy obligation—as in the Israelites' destruction of the Canaanite tribes in the Book of Deuteronomy. This was a prospect from which Judaism, Christianity, and Islam had moved away over time, Assmann noted, but it provides a pretext for violent action that could always be reactivated.[83] Assmann revived an Enlightenment claim (in Hume's *The Natural History of Religion*, for example) about monotheism as a source of intolerance, with polytheism as a more tolerant alternative.[84] Here he took up Jacob Taubes's argument (in his debate with Odo Marquard) on the historically moral role of monotheism, but reversed its implications. Assmann did note, however, "that among the three so-called Abrahamic religions, Judaism is the only one that has never turned the implications of violence and intolerance into historical reality precisely because it has relegated the final universalizing of truth to eschatology and not to history."[85] That is, because Judaism limited its claims upon non-Jews, at least in historical time, it avoided the tendency to use violence to destroy or coerce nonbelievers.[86]

Aleida was called back to academic pursuits by her encounter with Jacob. Together, the Assmanns would write and edit a series of books that, like *Moses the Egyptian*, put the subject of "cultural memory" (*das kulturelle Gedächtnis*)—not the past as it occurred, but as it was remembered—front and center.[87] By the first decade of the twenty-first century, research had exploded on the topic of "cultural memory," which the Assmanns had pioneered.

Translating Taubes

In the two decades after the publication of *Die politische Theologie des Paulus*, Taubes's books began to be translated into other languages. First came Italian, with the translation of *Ad Carl Schmitt* in 1996, *Die Politische Theologie des Paulus* (*PTdP*) and *Abendländische Eschatologie* (*AE*) in 1997, the correspondence between Taubes and Scholem in 2000, and a selection from *Vom Kult zur Kultur* (*KzK*) in 2001. Next came French: *PTdP* was published in 1999 by Edition du Seuil, with the telling subtitle "Schmitt, Benjamin, Nietzsche, Freud"; *Ad Carl Schmitt* in 2003; *"Le Temps Presse": Du culte à la culture*, a translation of *KzK* with some additional articles and interviews, was published, again by Edition du Seuil, in 2009; *AE* (published by Édition de l'Éclat) was published in the same year. In Spain, translations of *KzK* and *PTdP* were both published in 2007 (along with a Catalan edition of *PTdP* in 2005), *AE* in 2010.

The translation of Taubes's books into these Romance languages followed a common pattern. Burgeoning interest in the work of Carl Schmitt (sometimes by leftist writers whose fascination with Benjamin drew their attention to Schmitt) typically led to the translation of *Ad Carl Schmitt* and *PTdP*—both books in which Schmitt and Benjamin figured prominently. The publication of Taubes's other books followed. Thus, Taubes's relationship with Schmitt became a key factor in Taubes's posthumous international reputation. Taubes made Schmitt kosher for a leftist audience, and the relationship to Schmitt turned Taubes into an object of broader attention.

The English-language reception came slightly later: *PTdP* was published in 2004, *AE* in 2009, *KzK* in 2010. All three were published by Stanford University Press in a series founded by Werner Hamacher, Cultural Memory in the Present. The coeditor of the series, Hent de Vries, was a leading figure in writing and editing works devoted to the burgeoning field of "political theology"—a field inspired in good part by Schmitt and Taubes. The English translation of *Ad Carl Schmitt* was published in 2013 by Columbia University Press in the series Insurrections: Critical Studies in Religion, Politics, and Culture, whose editors included Žižek.

One or more of Taubes's works were translated into Hungarian, Polish, and Romanian, and most recently into Chinese and Korean. Thus, three decades after his death, his books had appeared in at least ten languages.

A Great Jewish Thinker?

Part of the interest in Taubes lay in his role as interlocutor of Schmitt, as an exponent of Benjamin, and as an interpreter of Paul. But Taubes also attracted another academic audience: those in search of Jewish thinkers to read and write about. For those without a reading knowledge of Hebrew, but with some training in what had come to be called "continental philosophy," there existed a small canon of twentieth-century Jewish religious thinkers who had written in German (Hermann Cohen, Martin Buber, Franz Rosenzweig) or French (Emmanuel Levinas, or in a conceptual stretch, Jacques Derrida). Jacob Taubes offered some fresh grist for this mill. With the exception of a handful of returning émigrés, German-Jewish thought had seemingly dried up with the expulsion and murder of German Jewry. With the publication of Taubes's works, there appeared to be one more thinker to add to the canon of German-Jewish thought. In 1989,

Peter Sloterdijk had characterized Taubes as "the last of the great represen-tatives of the Jewish spirit in the German language."[88] When Taubes's first book to appear in English, *The Political Theology of Paul*, was published in 2004, he was characterized on the back cover as "the Jewish philosopher of religion Jacob Taubes," and as an "unconventional Jewish intellectual living in post-Holocaust Germany." By the time the translations of *Occidental Eschatology* and *From Cult to Culture* appeared in 2009–10, Jacob Taubes had become "one of the great Jewish intellectuals of the twentieth century." In 2010, *Die Welt* claimed, "Today, Taubes has a reputation as one of the most significant Jewish philosophers of religion of the twentieth century."[89] By 2015, Taubes was described in the *New York Review of Books* as "the noted rabbinic scholar and philosopher Jacob Taubes"—a charac-terization that might surprise many a rabbinic scholar.[90]

In the intervening years, secondary studies of Taubes had begun to appear. Elettra Stimilli, who was responsible for the translation of a num-ber of Taubes's books into Italian, attempted an intellectual biography in 2004, *Jacob Taubes: Sovranità e tempo messianico*, the title of which tele-graphed the emphasis on Taubes's encounters with the work of Schmitt and Benjamin.[91] A stream of articles about Taubes began to appear; a chapter was devoted to him in the 2019 *Palgrave Handbook of Radical Theology*.[92] Then came entire books devoted largely to one or another ele-ment of his thought.[93] There were also conferences devoted to his work or inspired by it.[94]

The translations, inevitably, varied in quality. Translation is necessar-ily a matter of interpretation, since words have various meanings, and choosing the most appropriate one depends on an immersion in the work of the author and in his cultural referents, which, in the case of Taubes, were unusually wide. The secondary scholarship on Taubes faced a dif-ferent challenge: how to make sense of a thinker who could be insight-ful, far-reaching, even brilliant, but eschewed conceptual precision and consistency?

Institutionalization

Interest in Jacob Taubes and scholarship about him were advanced by the Zentrum für Literaturforschung (ZfL) in Berlin. When East and West Ger-many were united in 1990, the issue arose of what to do with academic institutions in the former German Democratic Republic, including its research centers. Among these was the Zentralinstitut für Literaturge-schichte, a center for literary history that had been part of the East German

Academy of Sciences. The Max Planck Society—the umbrella organization of German scientific institutes—supported the refounding of the institute, employing some of its previous staff, as the Zentrum für Literaturforsch-ung (Center for Literary Research), with a wider and more interdisciplin-ary orientation into the history of the humanities. (Its name would later be changed to Zentrum für Literatur- und Kulturforschung.) The center's first director was the former president of the FU, Eberhard Lämmert. In 1999, Sigrid Weigel, a scholar of literature, was appointed to the post.[95] Among Weigel's interests were women in literature, and she had written about Simone Weil.

After encountering the German translation of *Divorcing*, Weigel became curious about Susan Taubes. She sought out some of her essays, which deepened her interest. Weigel contacted Taubes's children in New York, met with them in 1999, and in time convinced them to transfer Susan Taubes's manuscripts and letters to an archive at the ZfL, which Weigel would control. The transfer took place in early 2003. Weigel charged a postdoctoral student, Christina Pareigis, with editing the materials, and arranged with Fink Verlag to publish them.[96]

After Jacob Taubes's death in 1987, his correspondence at the Herme-neutic Institute, which ranged from 1965 to 1985, was packed away into a storeroom. Since Taubes's letters often mixed personal with professional matters, they were far more than mere office correspondence. When the Institute was closed down in 2004, its secretary, Ina-Maria Gumbel, con-tacted his children about the letters, which they decided to donate the ZfL, where their mother's papers were now housed.[97] Martin Treml, who had studied religion at the FU and taken a course with Taubes in his final years, became head of the Jacob Taubes project. He and his collaborators gath-ered additional materials related to Taubes for their research purposes.

In the decade-and-a-half that followed, Treml and his associates pub-lished editions of Jacob Taubes's correspondence with Carl Schmitt and with Hans Blumenberg, drawing upon letters in other archives. Since the letters were by no means self-explanatory, the editors added valu-able annotations, identifying the persons, places, publications, and events alluded to in the letters. And since the letters referred to ideas put forth elsewhere in print, each volume contained supporting materials com-prised of relevant essays, memoranda, and correspondence. So too did the two volumes of correspondence between Susan and Jacob Taubes, covering the years 1950–52, edited by Pareigis, with an informative bio-graphical introduction. Together with Herbert Kopp-Oberstebrink, Treml edited *Apokalypse und Politik*, a collection of Jacob Taubes's previously uncollected articles, reviews, and public interventions. These volumes cast light on Taubes's role in German intellectual life, and signaled his remarkable range of intellectual contacts and interlocutors.

Thus, by an ideologically circuitous route that ran through Hans-Dietrich Sander, Hans-Joachim Arndt, and Armin Mohler, both Susan and Jacob Taubes's papers came to be archived and partially published by the ZfL. And by another circuitous route that included Carl Schmitt, Walter Benjamin, the Apostle Paul, and not least Aleida and Jan Assmann, Jacob Taubes attained a posthumous reputation that few would have imagined on the day his body was laid to rest beside his mother in Zurich.

Conclusion

HOW, THEN, TO THINK about Jacob Taubes, his life and his legacies?

In accounting for Taubes's remarkable afterlife, we must consider not only the conditions that facilitated it, but qualities of his work that made it fit material for ongoing academic exploration. In part, of course, it is the broad historical canvas on which he painted, beginning with his doctoral dissertation. In part it is the range of topics on which he opined, from Marcion to surrealism to *posthistoire*. But another is the combination of radical assertion with ambiguity and even opacity of expression. Armin Mohler described Taubes as a "messianic will-o'-the-wisp," and, indeed, both as a person and as a thinker, he seemed to offer illumination yet was hard to pin down. That, paradoxically, may have added to his posthumous interest, providing grist for the academic mill, to sift, sort, explain, and clarify what Taubes had written and said.

Though some recent scholars have tried to make Taubes into a systematic thinker, with a coherent message stretching across his writings, theirs is a fool's errand. Taubes was interested in being interesting, and in both winning the confidence and challenging the assumptions of whatever audience he confronted. Winning their confidence meant showing them that he knew the erudite rules of their game, while demonstrating that the game might be played to a different conclusion than they had been taught to imagine. In his book on occidental eschatology and in subsequent essays, courses, and encounters, he tried to show secular radicals that their true ancestors were religious, while showing the religiously orthodox the buried subversive elements within their own traditions.

Another way of thinking about Taubes is as a sort of link or bridge from the intellectual radicalism of the post–World War I era through the early decades of the twenty-first century. That included the radical, religious rejection of the world conveyed by the young Karl Barth; the radical anticapitalism of Georg Lukács and Ernst Bloch; and the anticapitalist nihilism of Walter Benjamin. At Harvard in the mid-1950s, it was Taubes who was teaching the most radical critiques developed by Max Horkheimer and Theodor Adorno, at a time when Horkheimer was leaving them behind and Adorno was turning to more aesthetic consolations. At the FU in the early 1960s, Taubes conveyed Marcuse's critique of the purported oppressiveness of one-dimensional society before Marcuse himself appeared on the scene. Taubes embraced Gershom Scholem's project of recuperating historical antinomian movements, and by focusing on Paul rather than Sabbatai Zevi, projected it onto a larger historical canvas. In part through Taubes, these themes reached an audience of the New Left of the 1960s and 1970s. And after the collapse of that seemingly apocalyptic moment, his messages were appropriated and repurposed by a variety of early twenty-first-century radical critics and scholars.

One of the recurrent themes of this book has been the curious way in which Taubes embodied seemingly irreconcilable positions. A historicist understanding of religion in general and Judaism in particular, together with intense—albeit intermittent—Orthodox Jewish observance. Assertions about the centrality of halacha together with neglect or deliberate violation of the law. Fears about the way in which messianism might lead to the abandonment of political prudence in Israel, together with a general suspicion of prudence. Disdain for disciplinary boundaries in academic life, together with an insistence, at times, on maintaining academic procedures and standards.

Given contemporary ideological lenses, Taubes's relentless erotic pursuit of women, together with his high regard for intellectual women, satisfaction in mentoring them, and energetic attention to their professional promotion may seem in tension or irreconcilable. They were not for Jacob Taubes. To repurpose a contemporary mantra, to understand Jacob Taubes, one must embrace his contradictions.

What of the relationship between Taubes's ideas and his life? He personified the longing for apocalyptic transformation, a personality type rare among academics. To the degree that he had a consistent message, it was an antinomian one of challenging rules, boundaries, and conventions— not only as a reflection of his personality, but as a matter of doctrinal conviction. In his own way, he tried to embody Walter Benjamin's conception of the *Jetztzeit*, of the possibility of suddenly breaking out of the expected, the routine, the institutionalized. Readers who have come this far can look back on Jacob's life and decide for themselves about the human benefits and costs of this mode of existence.

Assessing Taubes's life demands reflection upon the relationship between biological or neurological condition and personality. To some degree, Taubes's personality was shaped by his manic depression, first in its milder form, later in its more extreme manifestations. Such neuro-atypical conditions are a two-edged sword. Manic depression made it harder for him to engage in sustained research and scholarship; it could also make him reckless and obsessive in his behavior. But it was the sub-strate of his charisma: of his insight into others; his willingness to take intellectual risks and to make unexpected intellectual connections; his verbal high-flying; the fascination that came from wondering just what he would say, what unexpected perspective he would bring to bear or unan-ticipated avenue of research he would suggest.

Was Jacob Taubes an intellectual charlatan or was he a brilliant thinker? Here, too, the reader will have to judge, and after having plunged into this account of the life of Jacob Taubes, the perspicacious observer is unlikely to render a simple or unequivocal verdict. On the one hand, Taubes did borrow ideas from others without acknowledgment, made assertions not always warranted, and sometimes pretended to know more than he actually did. On the other hand, as we have seen, he really did know a good deal about a remarkable range of subjects, including the his-tory of Judaism, Christianity, and philosophy, and the intellectual and academic scenes in Germany, France, Israel, and the United States. His insights into the internal tensions in contemporary Protestant, Catholic, and Jewish theology were acute. He had a feel and affinity for religious experience, and especially for its more intense manifestations, to a degree rare among academics. The fact that he himself felt the tensions between historical understanding and religious belief, and between scholarly rela-tivism and the intensity of religious commitment, made him particularly sensitive to these dilemmas.

Taubes's modest record of scholarly achievement (as measured by con-ventional standards), set against the stresses and strains of his biography—comedies and dramas, torments undergone and torments inflicted, joys experienced and joys bestowed upon others—may lead one to lose sight of his intellectual insights and creativity.

His own radical affinities allowed him to create a "useable past" for those who combined a personal background in religion with the desire for radical change. And the broad schema suggested in *Occidental Eschatology* and developed in his essays of the 1950s—of religiously inspired egalitarian revolt as a motor force in history—remains a fruitful, if one-sided, framework.

Taubes's fascination with the Apostle to the Gentiles emerged from a unique concatenation of historical circumstances and personal predilections. There was his early immersion in traditional Jewish learning, along with the unusual openness toward Christians and Christianity that emerged from his experiences during the Second World War. To that was added his father's suggestion of Paul as a transformative figure, and Jacob's own aspirations to world-historical status. Taubes never became a second Paul, but he did have a feel for the Jewish elements of Paul and the period of transition between Judaism and Christianity that were decades ahead of the scholarly curve: startling and surprising when he first put them forth in the middle of the twentieth century, yet accepted wisdom among more recent scholars of the period.

Jacob Taubes was a man of the left. To some who shared his political propensities, Taubes's engagement with intellectuals of the right, including the radical right, was evidence of a lack of steadfastness and reliability. He was also a Jew who consorted with antisemites, not ignoring their antisemitism, but confronting it. That was testimony both to an unusual degree of openness on Taubes's part, to his conviction that there were insights to be found in a variety of perspectives, and that it was important to know one's enemy, indeed perhaps to learn from him. That was testimony to Taubes's liberality of character, despite his ideological illiberalism.

Like all of us, but to a heightened degree, Jacob Taubes was an ambivalent and ambiguous figure, marked to a greater degree than most of us by his faults as well as his virtues. Though he was neither an intellectual giant nor moral hero, he was brighter, more talented, more educated, more energetic, more willing to take personal and intellectual risks, more broadly intellectually connected, and more charismatic than most intellectuals. That made him an object of fascination in his day, and his life a window into so many of the intellectual, political, and religious tensions of the twentieth century and beyond.

ACKNOWLEDGMENTS

I MET JACOB TAUBES only once, for less than an hour. It was in Jerusalem, in early 1980, at the home of my brother-in-law, Noam Zion. At the time, I was preparing to write a doctoral dissertation on the intellectuals connected with the Congress for Cultural Freedom, an organization of anticommunist intellectuals, many of whom had undergone a process of deradicalization. Among them were Daniel Bell, Irving Kristol, Gertrude Himmelfarb, and Nathan Glazer. I had read somewhere about the seminar on Maimonides that Taubes conducted with them while he was at the Jewish Theological Seminary after the War. I told Taubes about my project and asked whether he remembered the seminar. He did. Of Irving Kristol and Gertrude Himmelfarb, Taubes remarked that she was the brighter of the two. Kristol would probably have agreed, but it was a startling observation, at a time when Irving was by far the more famous of the two, best known as the Godfather of Neoconservatism. (I can date my encounter with Taubes with some precision only because Taubes refers to it in a letter of March 4, 1980, to Hans-Dietrich Sander—the letter that Sander reproduced in his book, *Die Auflösung aller Dinge*.)

In the end, I wrote my dissertation on a different topic, namely the radicalization and deradicalization of German right-wing intellectuals from the Weimar era through the early decades of the Federal Republic. As I was revising the manuscript for publication, I came across Taubes's recently published book, *Ad Carl Schmitt*. I had trouble making heads or tails of this account by a Jewish, leftist intellectual about his admiration for Schmitt.

For the next fifteen years, Jacob Taubes did not cross my mind. I wrote some books, including an anthology of conservative thought in Europe and the United States, and another, *The Mind and the Market*, on capitalism in modern European thought, published in 2002. I then started work on a new project, on the intersection of the political critique of religion, Biblical criticism, and political criticism from Hobbes and Spinoza through Matthew Arnold and Nietzsche. It was at that point that the encounter with Irving Kristol and Gertrude Himmelfarb recounted in the Introduction set me on the (all too) long road that culminated in this book.

I began to do some research on Taubes, and met with Leon Wieseltier, then the book editor of the *New Republic*, who had known Taubes in

Jerusalem. He encouraged the idea of a book and gave me leads of others who knew Taubes in the United States, Germany, and Israel.

With the prospect of a biography in mind, in the spring of 2004 I reached out to Taubes's son, Ethan, and daughter, Tanaquil (Tania). They did their due diligence about me, and offered to cooperate.

It quickly became clear to me that since Jacob Taubes's impact was less through his writings than through his persona, it was essential for me to interview those who knew him, and since many of those were getting on in years, it was important to interview them as soon as possible. Each interviewee suggested others, and so the chain developed. One of those whom I interviewed early on, Richard Locke, told me that Taubes's life was the stuff of a Saul Bellow novel. I knew that I was no novelist, and that as a historian I was constrained by what I could document. But the challenge of writing about so intense and mercurial a life intrigued me. So did the challenge of writing about the political and intellectual contexts through which Taubes moved in Zurich, the United States, Jerusalem, and West Germany. And because the range of twentieth-century thinkers whom Taubes befriended or with whom he disputed was so large, the book offered the possibility of a sort of mosaic of twentieth-century intellectual life, wrapped around an extraordinary central character.

I conducted several dozen interviews in the United States during the spring of 2004, including the Kristols, Daniel Bell, and Krister Stendahl. The interview with Philip Rieff took place in his bedroom, since he was unable to walk, having undergone an operation for a pulmonary aneurism two weeks earlier. When I called him the day before the interview to confirm, and learned of his recent surgery, I asked whether he'd prefer that I come later in the summer. "Come now," he said, "by then I may be dead."

At first, I planned to record the interviews. I pulled out my small tape recorder for an early interview, with Daniel Bell. He suggested that recording the interview might inhibit the interviewee. He was right, and so from then on, I took quick notes on what was said. After each interview, I would reconstruct the answers based on my notes and my memory, and write them out more fully, a procedure that often took as long as the interview itself. But it had untold benefits in allowing for a more spontaneous flow of conversation, often leading in directions that neither I nor the interviewee had anticipated in advance.

In the summer of 2004, while in Jerusalem, I conducted research in the archives at the Jewish National Library (now renamed the National Library of Israel), consulting the papers of Martin Buber, Ernst Simon, and Gershom Scholem. Few relationships are as important to a historian as those with a veteran archivist. That proved to be the case in Jerusalem, where Margot Cohn, after quizzing me about my intentions, gave me access not only to the files in the Scholem papers marked "Jacob Taubes," which contained their correspondence, but to an additional file, marked "Jacob Taubes. Lo lakahal" (not for the public), which contained the many letters and memoranda *about* Taubes, sent to Scholem by Michael Landmann and others. During that month I also interviewed a number of his Israeli interlocutors, including the Avishai and Edna Margalit, Guy Stroumsa, and Moshe Halbertal. Later that year I also spoke with people who had been Taubes's assistant at various points in his career: Gershon Greenberg at Columbia, and Uta Gerhardt at the FU. Both provided me with additional leads about people to contact. Early in 2005 I met for the first time with Aleida and Jan Assmann, who were then visiting at Yale.

My most intense period of research came during the spring of 2006, spent as a fellow at the American Academy in Berlin. That was invaluable, made all the more so by the Academy's then president, Gary Smith, who was remarkably well connected in German intellectual life. Thanks to a handwritten letter he faxed to Jürgen Habermas, I was invited to the Habermas home in Starnberg, where I spent several productive hours talking to Jürgen and Ute. I also visited others in their homes, including Ernst Nolte in Berlin. Both Habermas and Nolte shared with me their correspondence with and regarding Taubes. Most of all, I profited from research in the collection of Jacob Taubes letters at the Zentrum für Literaturforschung. In addition, I made research trips to archives in other cities, most notably to the Suhrkamp Verlag archive, then located in Frankfurt (the collection, a gold-mine for German intellectual history, has since been moved to the Deutsches Literaturarchiv in Marbach).

I continued to conduct interviews sporadically over the next decade and more, as additional people who had known Jacob Taubes came to my attention. And after I began to publish reviews and essays about him, I was contacted by other scholars, who generously shared with me relevant correspondence that they had come across in their own research. All in all, I reviewed many hundreds of letters from Jacob Taubes, from his correspondence with Myrie Bloch while living in Zurich to letters written in his final months of life.

Other writing projects and professional duties diverted me from working intensively on this book over the decade that followed, though I continued to conduct interviews, collect correspondence, and read up on the relevant secondary literature. Over these many years, I have discussed Jacob Taubes with scores of friends, colleagues, and scholars. Many have offered leads, lines of possible investigation, or interpretive suggestions. Most of all, they have offered encouragement, many by asking the guilt-inducing question, "Are you finished yet?" They have served to bring this project to its conclusion, for which they have my sincere gratitude.

The book in its current form would have been impossible without the cooperation and encouragement of Ethan and Tania Taubes. Over many years, they provided me with materials from their own archives (designated in the endnotes as the "Ethan and Tania Taubes Collection"), and with information about their father and many of his associates. I depended upon them for information about Jacob's psychiatric history, about which Tania, a psychiatrist by training, with a professional knowledge of bipolar disorder, provided additional insights. Both Ethan and Tania read the draft of every chapter, offering corrections, suggestions, and critiques both substantive and stylistic. While we have not always agreed in our judgments about Jacob Taubes, their father and my subject, they have been unstintingly supportive of a project that took longer than any of us anticipated. I dedicate this book to my brother-in-law Noam Zion. It was through Noam that I first became acquainted with Jacob Taubes, and in the intervening decades, he has remained an intellectual interlocutor of the highest order.

I am grateful to the archivists at the archives in Europe, Israel, and the United States listed above. They provide the sinews of historical research.

Over the years, I have given talks related to this project at the American Academy in Berlin, to a conference on "German Intellectuals after 1945" organized by Raphael Gross at the Fritz Bauer Institute in Frankfurt, the Shalom Hartman Institute in Jerusalem, the Department of History at the University of Jena, the Washington Hevrussa and the Washington Jewish History seminar, at a conference in honor of Stephen Whitfield at Brandeis University, at the conference on "Jewish Voices in the German Sixties," organized by John Efron and Michael Brenner at Schloss Elmau, at the Einstein Forum in Berlin at a conference on "Jacob Taubes and Carl Schmitt," as well as at the annual conferences of the Association for Jewish Studies, and the German Studies Association. I am grateful to my hosts, fellow panelists, and interested audiences on each of these occasions.

In addition to those listed as interviewees, I have profited from exchanges about Taubes with Daniel Doneson, John Gager, Michael Gormann-Thelen, Lawrence Kaplan, Gabriel Motzkin, Elliot Neaman, Susan Neiman, Christina Pareigis, Thomas Patteson, Adele Reinhartz, Martin Ritter, Daniel Schwartz, Ilana Silber, Michael Silber, Gary Smith, Thomas Sparr, and Noam Zadoff. A number of scholars shared information or archival sources with me, including Oded Balaban, Wayne Cristaudo, David A. Bell, Marc Shapiro, Eugene Sheppard, Noah Strote, and the late Manfred Voigt. Sarah Brown Ferrario helped me track down and translate some Greek quotations in Taubes's letters, and Peretz Rodman helped me with some particularly difficult rabbinic Hebrew. Early in my preparation for the book, I taught a readings course, Twentieth Century Interpretations of Paul, to Rev. Ben Boswell, a Free Baptist minister who was then a doctoral student at the Catholic University of America. I learned as much from him as he from me, and the course was among the high points of my experience at Catholic University, an institution that served as my academic home for much of my career and to which I remain grateful.

The erudite Harvey Shoolman reached out to me from London midway through my investigations and provided needed encouragement as he read each chapter. So did my mother, Bella Muller.

One of the great pleasures of writing this book came in its penultimate stage, when I circulated a preliminary draft to a number of scholars with varying areas of expertise. Gerald Izenberg and Paul Mendes-Flohr had been my undergraduate teachers, and Stephen Whitfield a friend since my undergraduate days. I had known Noam Zion even longer, since my gap year in Israel during which I fell in love with his sister. Jeffrey Herf, an old friend, kindly volunteered his services. Martin Treml, who has presided over the Jacob Taubes project at the ZfL since its inception and hosted me when I did archival research there near the beginning of my research, kindly agreed to offer his advice as I neared its end. Gershon Greenberg, who had studied with Taubes in New York and Berlin, discussed the draft with me. Liliane Weisberg provided expertise on the German academic scene and much else. Leon Wieseltier, who had urged me to undertake the project, gave the manuscript a careful reading and suggested numerous improvements. The many suggestions for improvement provided by the members of this all-star team improved the analysis, style, and accuracy of the final version, and I am deeply grateful to each of them, as well as to additional anonymous referees who evaluated the book for Princeton University Press.

Fritz Stern, first my doctoral advisor and later my friend, was enthusiastic about the project, and offered insights into hiring practices at Columbia University in the 1950s, when both he and Taubes taught there. He really wanted to read this book, and I regret his passing before its completion.

Fred Appel reached out to acquire the manuscript for Princeton University Press, waited patiently for its completion, and shepherded it through the process of review and publication, aided by his colleague, James Collier; Kathleen Cioffi supervised the transition from manuscript to book; and Hank Southgate proved a conscientious copyeditor. I'm grateful to them and to the entire production team at the press.

My larger support system, intellectual and emotional, includes my wonderful children and children-in-law, who continue to inspire and invigorate me. My grandchildren are my greatest source of joy. Most of them are now able to read, and love seeing their names in print. That means you, Maya, Hannah, Daniel, Nadia, Julia, Benjamin, Aliza, and Naomi. Wait until you're at least twenty-one to read the rest of the book, though.

As for Sharon Muller, my closest companion for most of my lifetime, what can I say? She read and edited the first draft of each chapter, making countless improvements. She urged me onward, while protecting my time and mental energy. For almost two decades, she has shared our house with Jacob Taubes. He's leaving now, so we're truly empty nesters.

Books

ACS. Jacob Taubes, *Ad Carl Schmitt: Gegenstrebige Fügung* (Merve Verlag, 1987)

AE. Jakob Taubes, *Abendländische Eschatologie* (Beiträge zur Soziologie und Sozialphilosophie, Band 3, ed. René König (A. Francke Verlag, 1947)

AuP. Jacob Taubes, *Apokalypse und Politik. Aufsätze, Kritiken und kleinere Schriften*, ed. Herbert Kopp-Oberstebrink and Martin Treml (Wilhelm Fink Verlag, 2017)

Blumenberg-Taubes. Hans Blumenberg, Jacob Taubes, *Briefwechsel 1961-1981 und weitere Materialien*, ed. Herbert Kopp-Oberstebrink and Martin Treml (Suhrkamp Verlag, 2013)

CtC. Jacob Taubes, *From Cult to Culture: Fragments toward a Critique of Historical Reason*, ed. Charlotte Elisheva Fonrobert and Amir Engel (Stanford University Press, 2010)

Divorcing. Susan Taubes, *Divorcing* (Random House, 1969). (A new edition was published by New York Review Books in late 2020, as this study went to press.)

Korrespondenz 1. Susan Taubes, *Die Korrespondenz mit Jacob Taubes, 1950-1951*, ed. Christina Pareigis (Wilhelm Fink Verlag, 2011)

Korrespondenz 2. Susan Taubes, *Die Korrespondenz mit Jacob Taubes, 1952*, ed. Christina Pareigis (Wilhelm Fink Verlag, 2014)

KzK. Jacob Taubes, *Vom Kult zur Kultur: Bausteine zu einer Kritik der historischen Vernunft. Gesammelte Aufsätze zur Religions- und Geistesgeschichte*, ed. Aleida and Jan Assmann, Wolf-Daniel Hartwich, and Winfried Menninghaus (Wilhelm Fink Verlag, 1996)

OE. Jacob Taubes, *Occidental Eschatology*, trans. David Ratmoko (Stanford University Press, 2009)

PdM. Jacob Taubes, *Der Preis des Messianismus. Briefe von Jacob Taubes an Gershom Scholem und andere Materialien*, ed. Elettra Stimilli (Könighausen & Neumann, 2006)

PTdP. Jacob Taubes, *Die Politische Theologie des Paulus. Vorträge, gehalten an der Forschungsstätte der evangelischen Studiengemeinschaft in Heidelberg, 23.-27. Februar 1987. Nach Tonbandaufzeichnungen redigierte Fassung von Aleida Assmann*, ed. Aleida and Jan Assmann (Wilhelm Fink Verlag, 1993; 3rd corrected edition, 2003)

Schmitt-Sander. Carl Schmitt, Hans-Dietrich Sander, *Werkstatt-Discorsi. Briefwechsel 1967-1981*, ed. Erik Lehnert and Günter Maschke (Edition Antaios, 2008)

Taubes-Schmitt. Jacob Taubes, Carl Schmitt, *Briefwechsel mit Materialen*, ed. Herbert Kopp-Oberstebrink, Thorsten Palzhoff, and Matin Treml (Wilhelm Fink Verlag, 2012)

Individuals

FT. Fanny Taubes
JT. Jacob Taubes
MB. Myrie Bloch
MvB. Margherita von Brentano
ST. Susan Taubes

Collections

DLA. Deutsches Literaturarchiv, Marbach
ETT. Ethan and Tanaquil (Tania) Taubes Collection
Hoover. Hoover Institution Archives
IH. Institut für Hermeneutik, Freie Universität Berlin
JTS. Jewish Theological Seminary Archives
NLI. National Library of Israel, Jerusalem
PA. Personalakten Jacob Taubes, Freie Universität Berlin
Suhrkamp. Suhrkamp Archives, now moved to DLA
ZfL. Zentrum für Literatur- und Kulturforschung, Berlin

Introduction: Why Taubes?

1. Interview with Leon Wieseltier.

2. Frederick Goodwin and Kay Redfield Jamison, *Manic-Depressive Illness: Bipolar Disorders and Recurrent Depression*, 2nd ed. (New York, 2007), vol. 1, pp. xxi, 10–11, 32–33, 82.

3. Goodwin and Redfield Jamison, *Manic-Depressive Illness*, p. 402.

4. Goodwin and Redfield Jamison, *Manic-Depressive Illness*, p. 95.

Chapter One. Yichus: Vienna, 1923–36

1. On the Jewish use of Polish, see Piotr Wrobel, "The Jews of Galicia under Austrian-Polish Rule, 1867–1918," *Austrian History Yearbook*, vol. 25 (1994), pp. 97–138; on Edelstein's use of it with Jacob Taubes, interview with Aleida Assmann.

2. See Leora Batnizky, *How Judaism Became a Religion* (Princeton, NJ, 2011).

3. See on this theme Steven E. Aschheim, *Brothers and Strangers: The East European Jew in German and German Jewish Consciousness, 1800–1923* (Madison, WI, 1982).

4. Leo Herzberg-Fränkel, "Die Juden," in *Die österreichisch-ungarische Monarchie in Wort und Bild*, vol. 19, *Galizien* (Vienna, 1898), pp. 475–500, p. 480.

5. Shaul Stampfer, "*Heder* Study, Knowledge of Torah, and the Maintenance of Social Stratification in Traditional East European Jewish Society," *Studies in Jewish Education*, vol. 3 (1988), pp. 271–89, esp. pp. 274–75; Glenn Dynner, *Men of Silk: The Hasidic Conquest of Polish Jewish Society* (New York, 2006), pp. 121ff. On the Taubes-Rashi connection, see *Grosse Jüdische National-Biographie*, vol. 16, s.v. "Taubes" (Czernowitz, 1925).

6. Alexander Beider, *Dictionary of Jewish Surnames from Galicia* (Bergenfeld, NJ, 2004).

7. Herzberg-Fränkel, "Die Juden," p. 486; Dynner, *Men of Silk*, esp. pp. 5–11.

8. *Pinkas Hakehilot: Encyclopedia of Jewish Communities, Poland Vol. II Eastern Galicia* [in Hebrew] (Jerusalem, 1980), pp. 215–16; *Encyclopedia Judaica*, vol. 16 (Jerusalem, 1972), s.v. "Zhidachov"; Meir Wunder, *Encyclopedia of Galician Rabbis and Scholars*, vol. 1, s.v. "Eichenstein, R. Zwi Hirsch" [in Hebrew] (Jerusalem, 1978); *Yivo Encyclopedia of Jews in Eastern Europe* (New Haven, CT, 2008), and online, s.v. "Zhidachov-Komarno Hasidic Dynasty." On Eichenstein and the Zhidachov dynasty, see David Biale et al., *Hasidism: A New History* (Princeton, NJ, 2018), pp. 383–86, and 634–36.

9. "Descendants of Yaakov Taubes," http://familytreemaker.genealogy.com/users/r/a/d/Bob-A-Radcliffe/ODT7-0001.html.

10. *Pinkas Hakehilot*, p. 463.

11. Interview with Zachary Edelstein.

12. J. Krepel, *Juden und Judentum von Heute* (Zurich, 1925), p. 832. On the languages taught in such schools in Galicia, see Moshe Aberbach, *Jewish Education and History*, ed. David Aberbach (New York, 2009), p. 163.

13. *Pinkas Hakehilot*, p. 492.

14. Wunder, *Encyclopedia of Galician Rabbis and Scholars*, vol. 3, s.v. "Taubes, Rabbi Haim Zwi."

15. Interview with Zachary Edelstein.

16. I thank Prof. Rachel Manekin, an expert on Galician Jewry, for the information that this pattern of avoiding civil marriage was typical of Galician Jews at the time.

17. Wunder, *Encyclopedia of Galician Rabbis and Scholars*, vol. 1, s.v. "Zechariah Edelstein"; interview with Zachary Edelstein.

18. *Pinkas Hakehilot*, p. 452; Wrobel, "The Jews of Galicia," table 5.

19. Ismar Schorsch, "The Ethos of Modern Jewish Scholarship," *Leo Baeck Institute Yearbook*, vol. 35 (1990), pp. 55–71, p. 55.

20. On this style of learning, see Shaul Stampfer, *Families, Rabbis and Education: Traditional Jewish Society in Nineteenth-Century Eastern Europe* (Oxford, 2010), p. 245.

21. Schorsch, "Ethos," p. 62.

22. Schorsch, "Ethos," pp. 67–68.

23. Kreppel, *Juden und Judentum*, p. 824.

24. Schorsch, "Ethos," p. 62; and see Susannah Heschel, *Abraham Geiger and the Jewish Jesus* (Chicago, 1998); and Christian Wiese, *Challenging Colonial Discourse: Jewish Studies and Protestant Theology in Wilhelmine Germany* (Leiden, 2005).

25. Marc B. Shapiro, *Between the Yeshiva World and Modern Orthodoxy* (London, 1999), pp. 93ff.

26. Shapiro, *Between the Yeshiva World*, p. 77.

27. Shapiro, *Between the Yeshiva World*, pp. 81ff.

28. On its institutional history, see Peter Landesmann, *Rabbiner aus Wien: Ihre Ausbildung, ihre religiösen und nationalen Konflikte* (Vienna, 1997).

29. "Die Controversen der Schammaiten und Hilleliten. Ein Beitrag zur Entwicklungsgeschichte der Hillelschule," in *Jahresbericht der Israelitisch-Theologischen Lehranstalt* (Vienna, 1893). The names of Zwi Taubes's teachers are drawn from his preface to his doctoral thesis, cited in Wunder, *Encyclopedia of Galician Rabbis*.

30. This paragraph is based on N. M. Ben-Menachem, "Professor Schmuel Krauss," in *Hochmat Yisrael Bemaarav Europa*, ed. Shimon Friedbush (Jerusalem, 1958), vol. 1, pp. 445–50.

31. Samuel Krauss, *Das Leben Jesu nach jüdischen Quellen* (Berlin, 1902).

32. Samuel Krauss, *Torah, Nevi'im u-Khetuvim: 'im perush mada'i / yotse be-hishtatfut lamdanim mumhim 'al yede Avraham Kahana* (Z'itomir, 1902).

33. *Encyclopedia Judaica*, s.v. "Aptowitzer, Victor"; and Meir Waxman, "Professor Avigdor Aptowitzer," in Friedbush, *Hochmat Yisrael Bemaarav Europa*, vol. 1, pp. 25–36. On Aptowitzer's debates with Christian scholars of his time, see Wiese, *Challenging Colonial Discourse*, pp. 378–79, 397.

34. As noted by Raphael Patai, *Apprenticeship in Budapest: Memories of a World That Is No More* (1988; Lanham, MD, 2000).

35. The paragraph that follows draws upon *Encyclopedia Judaica*, s.v. "Chajes, Hirsch (Zwi) Perez"; and Yitzchak Levine, "Harav Zwi Peretz Chajot," in Friedbush, *Hochmat Yisrael Bemaarav Europa*, vol. 1, pp. 241–53. See also Bruria Hutner David, "The Dual Role of Rabbi Zwi Hirsch Chajes: Traditionalist and *Maskil*" (Ph.D. dissertation, Columbia University, 1971).

36. See for example the otherwise valuable Steven Beller, *Vienna and the Jews 1867–1938: A Cultural History* (Cambridge, 1989).

37. Eli Ginzberg, *Louis Ginzberg: Keeper of the Law* (Philadelphia, 1966), p. 192; Levine, "Harav Tzvi Peretz Chajot."

38. George E. Berkley, *Vienna and Its Jews: The Tragedy of Success 1880s–1980s* (Cambridge, MA, 1988), pp. 187–88.

39. Landesmann, *Rabbiner aus Wien*, p. 239.

40. Hirsch Taubes, "Jesus und die Halakah. Dissertation zur Erlangung des philosophischen Doktorgrades vorgelegt der hohen philosophischen Fakultät der Wiener Universität," n.d., ETT.

41. Martin Vahrenhorst, "'Nicht Neues zu lehren, ist mein Beruf . . .': Jesus im Licht der Wissenschaft des Judentums," in *Die Entdeckung des Christentums in der Wissenschaft des Judentums*, ed. Görge K. Hasselhoff (Berlin, 2010), pp. 101–36; Heschel, *Abraham Geiger*, p. 235.

42. Taubes, "Jesus," p. 7.

43. Taubes, "Jesus," pp. 63–64, p. 79. Recent scholars have reached similar conclusions; see Yair Furstenberg, "Defilement Penetrating the Body: A New Understanding of Contamination in Mark 7.15," *New Testament Studies*, vol. 54, no. 2 (1990), pp. 176–200.

44. Taubes, "Jesus," pp. 96–97.

45. Taubes, "Jesus," pp. 108–13.

46. Zwi Taubes, "Die Auflosung des Gelübdes. Ein Beitrag zur Entwicklung der Halacha," *Monatsschrift für Geschichte und Wissenschaft des Judentums*, vol. 73, Neue Folge 37 (1929), pp. 33–46, pp. 328–29.

47. Ruth Beckermann (ed.), *Die Mazzesinsel: Juden in der Wiener Leopoldstadt 1918–1938* (Vienna, 1984), p. 18.

48. On the assimilated Jews of Vienna, see Harriet Pass Freidenreich, *Jewish Politics in Vienna, 1918–1938* (Bloomington, IN, 1991); Berkley, *Vienna and Its Jews*; Frank Stern and Barbara Eichinger (ed.), *Wien und die jüdische Erfahrung 1900–1938* (Vienna, 2009).

49. On the background of Fanny's family, see Wunder, "Zwi Taubes"; and *Zum Andenken an Fanny Taubes-Blind* (Zurich, 1957), p. 6.

50. Jakob Taubes, Geburtsurkunde, Israelitische Kultusgemeinde Wien. On the concentration of Jews in this area, see Freidenreich, *Jewish Politics*, p. 13 and map 2.

51. Eliahu Ashtor, "Viennese Jewry in the 1920s," in *Kurt Grunwald at Eighty*, ed. Nachum Gross (Jerusalem, 1981), p. 13.

52. Such is the indication in Susan Taubes, *Divorcing* (New York, 1969), p. 26.

53. Freidenreich, *Jewish Politics*, p. 12. Kreppel, *Juden und Judentum*, pp. 504–6; Gerald Stourzh, "Ethnic Attribution in Late Imperial Austria: Good Intentions, Evil Consequences," in Stourzh *From Vienna to Chicago and Back* (Chicago, 2007).

54. "Rabbiner Dr. Zwi Taubes," *Die Wahrheit*, October 3, 1930, p. 6.

55. Pierre Geneé, Bob Martens, and Barbara Schedl, "Jüdische Andachtsstätten in Wien vor dem Jahre 1938," in *David: Jüdische Kulturschrift*, online at http://david .juden.at/kulturzeitschrift/57-60/59-Andacht.htm; and Beckermann, *Die Mazzesinsel*, p. 16.

56. See Freidenreich, *Jewish Politics*, p. 119; Evelyn Adunka, "Tempel, Bethäuser, und Rabbiner," in Stern and Eichinger, *Wien und die jüdische Erfahrung 1900-1938*, pp. 131–42.

57. Interviews with Mira Anatot and Naomi Gershoni (Jacob's cousins).

58. Binyamin Shimron, *Das Chajesrealgymnasium in Wien 1919-1938* (Tel Aviv, 1989), privately printed, available online at www.leobaeck.org; Bernard Wasserstein, *On the Eve: The Jews of Europe before the Second World War* (New York, 2012), pp. 327–28; Aberbach, *Jewish Education and History*, pp. 184–85.

59. Stella Klein-Löw, *Erinnerungen* (Vienna, 1980), p. 110.

60. Interviews with Mira Anatot and Naomi Gershoni.

61. JT to Isaac Hepner, n.d., but mid-1950s, in *Jacob Taubes und Oskar Goldberg: Aufsätze, Briefe, Dokumente*, ed. Manfred Voigts (Würzberg, 2011), p. 60.

62. Jacob Taubes, *Berachot Hatefillin. Harzaah Madait* (privately printed, Vienna, 1936). Taubes kept a copy of the cover page of this pamphlet and of his father's speech, printed in Hebrew on the back cover. Before he died, he gave a copy to Martin Ritter, who was kind enough to share it with me.

63. "Barmitzwa Jakob Taubes," *Die Wahrheit*, March 13, 1936, p. 7.

64. See the commentary by Michael Fishbane in his edition of *Haftarot: The JPS Bible Commentary* (Philadelphia, 2002), p. 349.

65. JT to Hugo Bergmann, Bergmann Papers, NLI (n.d., c. 1953).

66. "Barmitzwa Jacob Taubes," *Die Wahrheit*, March 13, 1936, p. 7; and interview with Mira Anatot.

67. On the danger of hindsight, see Michael André Bernstein, *Foregone Conclusions: Against Apocalyptic History* (Berkeley, 1994).

68. Adunka, "Tempel, Bethäuser und Rabbiner." According to Tania Taubes, Zwi was advised to take the Zurich post by the Chief Rabbi of Vienna, who wanted Zwi to succeed him, and regarded that as more likely if Zwi was not an inside candidate.

Chapter Two. Coming of Age in Switzerland, 1936–47

1. The portrait of Zwi and Fanny is based on interviews with Madeleine Dreyfus, Itta Shedletzky, and Marianne Weinberg.

2. René König, *Autobiographische Schriften*, ed. Mario and Oliver König (Opladen, 1999), pp. 399–400; interview with Arthur Hertzberg.

3. *Zum Andenken an Fanny Taubes-Blind.*

4. Fanny Taubes, *Die Sprache des Herzens: Aus Zeiten jüdische Erneuernung* (Zurich, 1959), p. 119.

5. Taubes, *Die Sprache des Herzens*, pp. 34–35.

6. Zwi Taubes to Louis Finkelstein, January 29, 1941–42, JTS IA-26–12, "T, Misc, JTS; Ulrich Bär and Monique R. Siegel (ed.), *Geschichte der Juden im Kanton Zürich* (Zurich, 2005), p. 332.

7. Bär and Siegel, *Geschichte der Juden im Kanton Zürich*, p. 328; Ralph Weingarten, "Jüdisches Leben in Zürich," in *Schtetl Zürich*, ed. Livio Piatti (Zurich, 1997), pp. 7–10.

8. Interview with Madeleine Dreyfus; letters from Mirjam to JT, 1947–49, ETT.

9. Interview with Ethan Taubes.

10. Interview with Gavriel Cohn.

11. Bär and Siegel, *Geschichte der Juden im Kanton Zürich*, p. 357.

12. Jacques Picard, *Die Schweiz und die Juden 1933–1945*, 3rd ed. (Zurich, 1997), p. 61.

13. Picard, *Die Schweiz*, pp. 63–68.

14. On Nansen passports, see Michael R. Marrus, *The Unwanted: European Refugees in the Twentieth Century* (New York, 1985).

15. Picard, *Die Schweiz*, p. 52; Unabhängige Expertenkommission Schweiz, *Die Schweiz und die Flüchtlinge zur Zeit des Nationalsozialismus* (Bern, 1999), p. 47.

16. Bär and Siegel, *Geschichte der Juden im Kanton Zürich*, p. 354.

17. Picard, *Die Schweiz*, p. 82.

18. On Susman, see Hanna Delf von Wolzogen, "Margarete Susman," in *Metzler Lexikon jüdischer Philosophen*, ed. Andreas B. Kilcher and Otfried Fraisse (Stuttgart, 2003), pp. 324–25. On her relationship to Ragaz and to Taubes, see Margarete Susman, *Ich habe viele Leben gelebt: Erinnerungen* (Stuttgart, 1964).

19. Picard, *Die Schweiz*, p. 89.

20. *Die Schweiz und die Flüchtlinge*, pp. 75–88.

21. Picard, *Die Schweiz*, pp. 20–21.

22. Bär and Siegel, *Geschichte der Juden im Kanton Zürich*, p. 333; Stefan Mächler, *Hilfe und Ohnmacht: Der Schweizerische Israelitische Gemeindebund und die nationalsozialistische Verfolgung 1933–1945* (Zurich, 2005), p. 230.

23. Zwi Taubes to Finkelstein, January 29, 1941 in JTS IA-26–12 to 1942, "T, Misc."

24. Interview with Zachary Edelstein; on the death of Zwi's parents, see the forward to Zwi Taubes, *Lebendiges Judentum* (Geneva, 1946), p. 11.

25. Zwi Taubes, "Das gemeinsame in Judentum, Christentum und Islam: Erste Folge einer Vortrags- und Aufsatzreihe," Zurich, February 10, 1940, typescript in Zwi Taubes file, Leo Baeck Institute, NYC.

26. Taubes, "Das gemeinsame in Judentum," p. 5.

27. Taubes, "Das gemeinsame in Judentum," p. 5.

28. Taubes, "Das gemeinsame in Judentum," p. 9.

29. Picard, *Die Schweiz*, p. 368.

30. Picard, *Die Schweiz*, p. 89.

31. Bär and Siegel, *Geschichte der Juden im Kanton Zürich*, p. 366. On these institutions, see also *Die Schweiz und die Flüchtlinge*, pp. 160–75.

32. See on this Mächler, *Hilfe und Ohnmacht*; and the older work by Jenö Lévai, *Abscheu und Grauen vor dem Genocid in aller Welt . . . Diplomaten und Presse als Lebensretter* (New York, 1968).

33. Lévai, *Abscheu und Grauen*, pp. 27–29; Mächler, *Hilfe und Ohnmacht*, p. 377 and passim.

34. Randolph L. Braham, *The Politics of Genocide: The Holocaust in Hungary*, rev. ed (New York, 1994), vol. 2, pp. 1271–72.

35. Mächler, *Hilfe und Ohnmacht*, 378.

36. David Kranzler, *The Man Who Stopped the Trains to Auschwitz: George Mantello, El Salvador, and Switzerland's Finest Hour* (Syracuse, NY, 2000), pp. 106–9.

37. Lévai, *Abscheu und Grauen*, pp. 38–39; Kranzler, *Man Who Stopped the Trains*, p. 114.

38. Lévai, *Abscheu und Grauen*, pp. 40–41, 55; Braham, *Politics of Genocide*, pp. 1226–27.

39. Braham, pp. 1234–35; Kranzler, *Man Who Stopped the Trains*, pp. 105–6.

40. Braham, *Politics of Genocide*, pp. 1232–33.

41. Quotations are from the New Revised Standard Version Bible translation, as found in Amy-Jill Levine and Marc Zwi Brettler (ed.), *The Jewish Annotated New Testament*, 2nd ed. (New York, 2017). I have profited from the commentaries in this volume.

42. See Levine and Brettler, *Jewish Annotated New Testament*, p. 460, on the pseudo-Pauline nature of the text. On the significance of its anti-Jewish claims, see John Connolly, *From Enemy to Brother: The Revolution in Catholic Teaching on the Jews 1933–1965* (Cambridge, MA, 2012), p. 212.

43. Connolly, *From Enemy to Brother*, p. 185.

44. Karl Ludwig Schmidt, *Die Judenfrage im Lichte der Kapitel 9–11 des Römerbriefes: im Text und durch Anmerkungen erweiterter Vortrag gehalten an der fünften Wipkinger Tagung des Schweizerischen evangelischen Hilfswerkes für die bekennende Kirche in Deutschland am 16. November 1942* (Zurich, 1943). It was published in the series Theologische Studien: Eine Schriftenreihe, edited by Karl Barth.

45. On the Swiss "Christlich-Jüdischen Arbeitsgemeinschaft zur Bekämpfung des Antisemitismus," in April 1946, see Zsolt Keller, "Theologie und Politik—Beginn und Konkretisierung des christlich-jüdischen Dialoges in der Schweiz," *Zeitschrift für schweizerische Kirchengeschichte*, vol. 99 (2005), pp. 157–76, esp. pp. 162–66.

46. On the Seelisberg conference and its background, see Christian Rutishauser, "The 1947 Seelisberg Conference: The Foundation of the Jewish-Christian Dialogue," *Studies in Jewish-Christian Relations*, vol. 2, no. 2 (2007), pp. 34–53. On its echoes in subsequent Catholic doctrine, see Connolly, *From Enemy to Brother*.

47. Jacob's longtime friend, Eugen Kuhlmann, was in his English class. JT to Eugen Kuhlmann, n.d., but c. December 1948, ETT.

48. Interview with Sigmund (Sigi) Weinberg.

49. The timing of Taubes's attendance at the yeshiva is based on the curriculum vitae he submitted to the Hebrew University in 1951, translated into German in Christoph Schulte, "PAULUS," in *Abendländische Eschatologie: Ad Jacob Taubes*, ed. Richard Faber et al. (Würzburg, 2001), p. 101.

50. See the description of the grounds by an erstwhile pupil, Raphael Patai, *Apprentice in Budapest*, p. 270.

51. For a fictional, but deeply telling, portrait of the ethos of the Novardok Yeshiva by one of its graduates, see Chaim Grade, *The Yeshiva*, trans. Curt Leviant, 2 vols. (New York, 1977). The account of Rabbi Yehiel Eliahu Botschko and the Montreux Yeshiva is based on the editors' introduction to the collection of Botschko's writings, *Or Hayahadut* (Jerusalem, 2000); S. Schachnowitz, "Drei Erlebnisse," in *Jiskaur . . . Seelenspiegel*, ed. R. E. Botschko (Montreux, 1943), p. 53. Interview with Rabbi Moshe Botschko and Mrs. Helen Botschko, and interview with Eli Holzer, who attended and then taught at the Montreux Yeshiva in the 1980s.

52. For Botschko's Zionist writings, see his book, *Ein Volk ist erwacht* (Montreux, 1950).

53. Editors' introduction to *Or Hayahadut*, p. 17.

54. Interview with Rabbi Moshe Botschko and Mrs. Helen Botschko.

55. References to this in JT to MB, New Years, 1947, ETT; Zwi Taubes to Baron, October 19, 1946, Baron Papers, Stanford; Zwi Taubes to Louis Finkelstein, October 26, 1946, JTS.

56. According to Taubes's speech at the wedding of his son, Ethan, April 6, 1986, ETT.

57. Botschko, *Jiskaur . . . Seelenspiegel*, passim, and especially the "Geleitwort," pp. v–ix; and "Der lebende Leichnam," pp. 104–5; and Botschko, *Der Born Israels* (Montreux, 1944).

58. Joseph Friedenson and David Kranzler, *Heroine of Rescue* (New York, 1984).

59. Susman, *Ich habe viele Leben gelebt*, p. 102.

60. Interview with Jean Bollack.

61. On Teitelbaum's theological anti-Zionism, see Aviezer Ravitzky, *Messianism, Zionism, and Jewish Religious Radicalism* (Chicago, 1996), pp. 44–45 and passim; as well as Zwi Jonathan Kaplan, "Rabbi Joel Teitelbaum, Zionism, and Hungarian Ultra-Orthodoxy," *Modern Judaism*, vol. 24, no. 2 (2004), pp. 165–78.

62. Yehuda Bauer, *Jews for Sale? Nazi-Jewish Negotiations, 1933-1945* (New Haven, CT, 1994), chs. 11–12.

63. Two publications that touch upon Teitelbaum's time in Switzerland are both hagiographic works of limited historical reliability: Hershl Friedman, *Sefer Miafela l'or gadol* [in Yiddish] (Kiryas Yoel, 2001); and Dovid Meisels, *The Rebbe: The Extraordinary Life and Worldview of Rabbeinu Yoel Teitelbaum* (Lakewood, NJ, 2010). According to them, he seems never to have interacted with anyone but ultra-Orthodox Jews. However, individual facts about Teitelbaum's movements seem to be reliable. On Soloveitchik, see Meisels, *Rebbe*, p. 122. On the excision of ideologically inconvenient personages and facts from such accounts, see Marc B. Shapiro, *Changing the Immutable: How Orthodox Judaism Rewrites Its History* (Oxford, 2015).

64. Menachem Keren-Kratz, "Hast Thou Escaped and Also Taken Possession? The Responses of the Satmar Rebbe—Rabbi Yoel Teitelbaum—and His Followers to Criticism of His Conduct during and after the Holocaust," *Dapim: Studies on the Holocaust*, vol. 28, no. 2 (2014), pp. 97–120. The article does not mention Taubes by name.

65. Interview with Moshe Halbertal; interview with Avishai and Edna Margalit.

66. FT to JT, n.d., but spring 1948, ETT.

67. Jacob Taubes, "Kabbala," *Le Monde Religieux*, December 1942, pp. 26–34, reprinted in Voigts, *Jacob Taubes und Oskar Goldberg*, pp. 21–30. The relevant passages from Goldberg, *Maimonides. Kritik der jüdsichen Glaubenslehre* (Vienna, 1935) are reprinted in Voigts, *Jacob Taubes und Oskar Goldberg*, pp. 27–30. See also the letter of JT to Oskar Goldberg, Zurich, February 18, 1946, in Voigts, *Jacob Taubes und Oskar Goldberg*, pp. 31–32.

68. JT to MB, n.d., but between Rosh Hashanah and Yom Kippur, 1946, ETT.

69. JT to MB, n.d., but early 1947; JT to Hans Urs von Balthasar, December 22, 1946; JT, Berlin, to Balthasar, October 25, 1977, Hans Urs von Balthasar Archiv.

70. See Jerry Z. Muller, *The Mind and the Market: Capitalism in Modern European Thought* (New York, 2002), pp. 269–75.

71. JT to MB, n.d., but between Rosh Hashanah and Yom Kippur, 1946, ETT.

72. JT to MB, n.d., but shortly after letter above.

73. On Goldmann, see Mitchell Cohen, *The Wager of Lucien Goldmann: Tragedy, Dialectics, and a Hidden God* (Princeton, NJ, 1994). The information on Zwi and Jacob Taubes's meetings with Goldmann comes from Agnes Heller, *Der Affe auf dem Fahrrad: Eine Lebensgeschichte* (Berlin, 1999), and from a private communication from Mitchell Cohen. On the camp at Gierenbad, see Manes Sperber, *Until My Eyes Are Closed with Shards* (New York, 1994), pp. 208–9.

74. Klaus Harpprecht, "Der Vermittler: François Bondy," *Suddeutsche Zeitung*, September 8, 2003.

75. Interview with Jean Bollack; Jean Bollack, "Durchgänge," in *Zeitenwechsel: Germanistische Literaturwissenschaft vor und nach 1945*, ed. Wilfried Barner and Christoph König (Frankfurt, 1996), pp. 387–403.

76. Jean Bollack, "Texts and Their Interpreters: The Enterprise of Philology," *Sub-Stance*, vol. 22. no. 2/3 (1993), pp. 315–20.

77. Interview with Jean Bollack; Bollack, "Durchgänge."

78. Unless otherwise noted, facts about Mohler are drawn from Karlheinz Weissmann, *Armin Mohler: Eine politische Biographie* (Schnellroda, 2011), a relatively uncritical biography, focused on Mohler's ideas, by an author well-acquainted with the right-wing intellectual scene.

79. Weissmann, *Armin Mohler*, pp. 20–40.

80. Ernst Jünger, "Die totale Mobilmachung," in *Krieg und Krieger*, ed. Jünger (Berlin, 1930), p. 27. One of the better analyses of this current of thought is Leo Strauss's lecture of 1941, "German Nihilism," published in *Interpretation*, vol. 26, no. 3 (1999), pp. 352–78, with corrections by Wiebke Meier, *Interpretation*, vol. 28, no. 2 (2000), pp. 33–34.

81. See the discussion in Jeffrey Herf, *Reactionary Modernism: Technology, Culture, and Politics in Weimar and the Third Reich* (Cambridge, 1984), pp. 101–5.

82. Friedrich Georg Jünger, *Die Perfektion der Technik* (Frankfurt am Main, 1946); English translation: *The Failure of Technology: Perfection without Purpose*, trans. F. D. Wieck (Hinsdale, IL, 1949). On the trajectories of the Jünger brothers, Heidegger, and Mohler, see Daniel Morat, "No Inner Remigration: Martin Heidegger, Ernst Jünger, and the Early Federal Republic of Germany," *Modern Intellectual History*, vol. 9, no. 3 (2012), pp. 661–79.

83. Armin Mohler, *Die Konservative Revolution in Deutschland, 1918-1932: Grundriss ihrer Weltanschauungen* (Stuttgart, 1950).

84. Weissmann, *Armin Mohler*, p. 74. See also Mohler's account, "Eine Promotion in Basel," in his *Tendenzwende für Fortgeschrittene* (Munich, 1978), pp. 175–85.

85. Armin Mohler, "Der messianische Irrwisch: Über Jacob Taubes (1923–1987)," *Criticón*, no. 103 (1987), pp. 219–21. Mohler erroneously gives the date of their first meeting as 1948. But by then, Taubes was already in New York, and their surviving correspondence goes back to 1947. Armin Mohler to JT, Basel, December 6, 1947, ETT.

86. Armin Mohler to Peter Gente, June 30, 1986, Mohler Nachlass, DLA.

87. Weissmann, *Mohler*, pp. 62–75; Neaman, *Ernst Jünger*, p. 72.

88. Interview with Aleida Assmann.

Chapter Three. Intellectual Roots, Grand Themes, 1941–46

1. Interviews with Tania Taubes.

2. Jacob Taubes, "Fragmente," n.d., but early 1947, ETT.

3. Franz Overbeck, *Selbstbekenntnisse, mit einer Einleitung von Jacob Taubes* (Frankfurt, 1966). Taubes's introduction is included in *KzK*. On Overbeck's development, see Karl Löwith, *From Hegel to Nietzsche: The Revolution in Nineteenth-Century Thought*, trans. David E. Green (New York, 1964), pp. 371–88.

4. There is a brilliant characterization of this process in Franz Rosenzweig, "Atheistic Theology" (1914), in Franz Rosenzweig, *Philosophical and Theological Writings*, ed. Paul W. Franks and Michael L. Morgan (Indianapolis, 2000), pp. 10–24.

5. A useful introduction to Harnack's thought is Adolf von Harnack, *Liberal Theology at Its Height*, ed. Martin Rumscheidt (London, 1989).

6. On Barth, I have profited from John Webster, "Introducing Barth," and Christoph Schwöbel, "Theology," in *The Cambridge Companion to Barth*, ed. John Webster (Cambridge, 2000); as well as Gary Dorrien, *The Barthian Revolt in Modern Theology* (Louisville, KY, 1999); Frank Jehle, *Ever against the Stream: The Politics of Karl Barth, 1906–1968*, trans. Richard and Martha Burnett (Grand Rapids, MI, 2002); and the review essay by Rudy Koshar, "Where Is Karl Barth in Modern European History?," *Modern Intellectual History*, vol. 5, no. 2 (2008), pp. 333–62.

7. Karl Barth, *The Epistle to the Romans*, trans. Edwyn C. Hoskyns, from the German 2nd ed. of 1921 (London, 1933), p. 40.

8. Barth, *Epistle*, p. 50.

9. Barth, *Epistle*, pp. 49, 59.

10. Benjamin Lazier, *God Interrupted: Heresy and the European Imagination between the World Wars* (Princeton, NJ, 2008), p. 33 and passim.

11. Barth, "Preface to the Second Edition," *Epistle*, p. 13.

12. Max Schoch, "Brunner, Emil," in *Historisches Lexikon der Schweiz* (online).

13. Emil Brunner, *Christianity and Civilization* (New York, 1948), a book comprised of the Gifford Lectures delivered at the University of St. Andrews in 1947 and 1948.

14. Martin Buber, *Drei Reden über das Judentum* (reprint, Frankfurt, 1920), p. 51.

15. Buber, *Drei Reden*, p. 82.

16. Buber, *Drei Reden*, pp. 89–90.

17. Interview with Judith Buber Agassi. Taubes refers to this meeting in his letter to Martin Buber of Februrary 25, 1948, in Martin Buber, *Briefwechsel aus sieben Jahrzehnten, Band III: 1938–1965*, ed. Grete Schaeder (Heidelberg, 1975), pp. 168–69.

18. On critical evaluations of Buber's work, see Guy G. Stroumsa, "Buber as an Historian of Religion: Presence, not Gnosis," *Archives des sciences sociales des religions*, vol. 101, no. 1 (1998), pp. 87–105.

19. Jacob Taubes, "Martin Buber and the Philosophy of History," in *The Philosophy of Martin Buber*, ed. Paul Arthur Schilpp and Maurice Friedman (La Salle, IL, 1967), pp. 451–68, reprinted in *CtC*.

20. John D. Caputo, "Heidegger and Theology," in *The Cambridge Companion to Heidegger*, 2nd ed., ed. Charles B. Guignon (Cambridge, 2006), pp. 326–44.

21. On Heidegger's development of this theme, see Peter E. Gordon, *Continental Divide: Heidegger, Cassirer, Davos* (Cambridge, MA, 2010), pp. 174ff.; and Michael E. Zimmerman, "Heidegger, Buddhism, and Deep Ecology," in Guignon, *Cambridge Companion to Heidegger*, pp. 293–303.

22. Markus Zürcher, *Unterbrochene Tradition: Die Anfänge der Soziologie in der Schweiz* (Zurich, 1995), pp. 239–42, 256; Peter Atteslander, "Einer, der von aussen kommt," in *René König*, ed. Heine von Alemann and Gerhard Kunz (Opladen, 1992), pp. 170–80.

23. René König to JT, July 27, 1958, König Nachlass; and René König, *Autobiographische Schriften*, ed. Mario König and Oliver König (Opladen, 1999), pp. 399–400.

24. Rolf Ziegler, "In memoriam René König: Für eine Soziologie in moralischer Absicht" (1993), reprinted on the website of the René König-Gesellschaft, http://www.rene-koenig-gesellschaft.de.

25. König, *Autobiographische Schriften*, p. 125. König to Peter Atteslander, November 15, 1971, König Nachlass.

26. M. H. Abrams, *Natural Supernaturalism: Tradition and Revolution in Romantic Literature* (New York, 1971), p. 13.

27. The clearest expression of this view is in Jacob Taubes, "Community—After the Apocalypse," in *Community*, ed. Carl J. Friedrich (New York, 1959), pp. 101–13; German translation in *AuP*.

28. On the suggestiveness and multiple uses of the term "secularization," see Daniel Weidner, "The Rhetoric of Secularization," *New German Critique*, vol. 41, no. 1 (2014), pp. 1–31.

29. Jacob Taubes, "Der Wandel in der Lehre von der Entwicklung des kapitalistischen Arbeitsethos seit Max Weber." A copy of the essay is in the Staatsarchiv Zürich: U 1092.47.

30. Jacob Taubes, *ACS*, pp. 8–10.

31. Carl Schmitt, *Political Theology* (1922), trans. George Schwab (Chicago, 1985), parts 1, 2, 4.

32. Schmitt, *Political Theology*, pp. 36–37.

33. Hans Urs von Balthasar, *Geschichte des eschatologischen Problems in der modernen deutschen Literatur* (Zurich, 1930; new ed., Freiburg, 1998), pp. 13–14.

34. See Balthasar's introduction to Irenäus, *Geduld des Reifens*, ed. and trans. Hans-Urs von Balthasar (Basel, 1945).

35. Luke Timothy Johnson, review of Karen Kilby, *Balthasar: A (Very) Critical Introduction*, *Commonweal*, April 12, 2013, pp. 32–35. Johnson is conveying Kilby's view.

36. *ACS*, p. 8.

37. Löwith, *From Hegel to Nietzsche*, p. 45.

38. Ernst Bloch, *Geist der Utopie* (1918). I have relied upon the analysis in Anson Rabinbach, *In the Shadow of Catastrophe: German Intellectuals between Apocalypse and Enlightenment* (Berkeley, 1997), pp. 44–45; also valuable is the discussion in Paul Mendes-Flohr, "'The Stronger and the Better Jews': Jewish Theological Responses to Political Messianism in the Weimar Republic," in *Jews and Messianism in the Modern Era: Meaning and Metaphor*, ed. Jonathan Frankel, Studies in Contemporary Jewry 7 (New York, 1991), pp. 159–85, pp. 160–62.

39. Ernst Bloch, *Thomas Münzer als Theologe der Revolution* (1921); quoted from Ernst Bloch, *Gesamtausgabe* (Frankfurt, 1969), vol. 2, pp. 228–29.

40. Bloch had called attention to the central role of Joachim's form of historical messianism; see Jeffrey Andrew Barash, "The Sense of History: On the Political Implications of Karl Löwith's Concept of Secularization," *History and Theory*, vol. 37, no. 1 (1998), pp. 69–82, p. 80.

41. On the history of the concept and a skeptical account of its validity, see Karen L. King, *What Is Gnosticism?* (Cambridge, MA, 2003).

42. Lazier, *God Interrupted*, ch. 1.

43. Hans Jonas, *Gnosis und spätantiker Geist, Erster Teil* (Göttingen, 1934), p. 78.

44. Jonas, *Gnosis*, pp. 96–97. For Jonas's own subsequent translation into English, see *The Gnostic Religion* (Boston, 1958), pp. 49–51.

45. Jonas, *Gnosis*, pp. 245–46.

46. Jonas, *Gnosis*, p. 248

47. Jonas, *Gnosis*, pp. 214–15.

48. Jonas, *Gnosis*, pp. 234–35; Jonas, *The Gnostic Religion* (Boston, 1958), pp. 270–74.

49. See Hans Jonas, "Vorwort" to *Gnosis und Spätantiker Geist, Zweiter Teil* (Göttingen, 1954).

50. Jonas, *Gnostic Religion*; Hans Jonas, *Memoirs*, ed. and annotated by Christian Wiese, trans. Krishna Winston (Lebanon, NH, 2008), pp. 168–69.

51. Gershom Scholem, "Redemption through Sin," trans. Hillel Halkin, in *The Messianic Idea in Judaism* (New York, 1971), originally published in Hebrew in *Knesset*, vol. 2 (1937), 347–92.

Chapter Four. Occidental Eschatology and Beyond, 1946–47

1. Jacob Taubes, "Die Begründung des Sozialismus durch Karl Marx," ETT.

2. Taubes, "Die Begründung des Sozialismus," p. 3.

3. Taubes, "Die Begründung des Sozialismus," p. 30.

4. Taubes, "Die Begründung des Sozialismus," p. 33.

5. Taubes, "Die Begründung des Sozialismus," p. 32.

6. Taubes, "Die Begründung des Sozialismus," p. 39.

7. Yuri Slezkine, *The House of Government: A Saga of the Russian Revolution* (Princeton, NJ, 2017), pp. 113ff. and passim.

8. Jacob Taubes, "Apokalyptsche und Marx'sche Geschichtsanschauung. Studien zur Geschichtsanschauung von Karl Marx," draft in ETT.

9. JT to MB, n.d., but c. September 1946, ETT.

10. Hans Barth, *Wahrheit und Ideologie* (1945), translated as *Truth and Ideology*, trans. Frederic Lilge (Berkeley, 1976); the introduction to this edition by Reinhard Bendix provides a useful introduction to Barth's career.

11. Translation from "On the Essence of Truth," adapted from that of John Sallis in Martin Heidegger, *Basic Writings*, rev. ed., ed. David Farrell Krell (New York, 1983), p. 115.

12. Translation adapted from that of David Ratmoko, Jacob Taubes, *Occidental Eschatology* (Stanford, 2009), p. 3.

13. *AE*, pp. 10–13; *OE*, pp. 11–13.

14. Heidegger, *Vom Wesen der Wahrheit* (Frankfurt, 1943), pp. 21–23. *AE*, pp. 257–58; *OE*, pp. 193–94 (the English translation does not convey the extent to which the closing pages are steeped in Heidegger's vocabulary).

15. *AE*, p. 15; *OE*, p. 15.

16. *AE*, pp. 16–19; *OE*, pp. 17–20.

17. *AE*, pp. 21–35; *OE*, pp. 26–40.

18. *AE*, p. 9; *OE*, p. 10. "Die Welt ist das Gegengöttliche und Gott ist das Gegenweltliche. Gott ist in der Welt fremd und unbekannt."

19. *AE*, p. 34; *OE*, p. 34.

20. *AE*, p. 34, *OE*, p. 34.

21. *AE*, p. 35, *OE*, p. 35.

22. *AE*, p. 28; *OE*, pp. 28–29.

23. Lazier, *God Interrupted*, p. 24.

24. *AE*, pp. 46–51; *OE*, pp. 47–52.

25. *AE*, pp. 57–65; *OE*, pp. 58–64.

26. *AE*, p. 67; *OE*, p. 67. On the scholarly sources of Taubes's interpretation of Paul, see the excellent essay of Christoph Schulte, "PAULUS," in Faber et al., *Abendländische Eschatologie. Ad Jacob Taubes*, pp. 93–104.

27. *AE*, p. 70; *OE*, p. 71.

28. *AE*, pp. 71–80; *OE*, pp. 72–80.

29. *AE*, p. 81; *OE*, p. 82.

30. Ernst Bloch, *Erbschaft dieser Zeit* (Zurich, 1935), *Heritage of Our Times* (Cambridge, 1991), pp. 122ff.

31. *AE*, p. 85; *OE*, pp. 85–86.

32. *AE*, p. 119; *OE*, p. 119.

33. *AE*, pp. 86–87.

34. *AE*, pp. 93, 156, 165–66; *OE*, pp. 93, 152, 164–66.

35. *AE*, p. 117; *OE*, pp. 117–18.

36. *AE*, pp. 184–86; *OE*, pp. 184–86.

37. As noted in Romano Pocai, "Die Angst und das Nichts. Überlegungen zu Heideggers 'Was ist Metaphysik?,'" in Faber et al., *Abendländische Eschatologie*, pp. 331–40.

38. Otto Petras, *Post-Christum. Streifzüge durch die geistige Wirklichkeit* (Berlin, 1935), p. 11.

39. *AE*, p. 193; *OE*, p. 193.

40. *AE*, pp. 193–94; *OE*, pp. 193–94.

41. Petras, *Post-Christum*, p. 15.

42. Rudolf G. Zipkes diaries, May 2, 1948 (copy in possession of author); König to Peter Atteslander, November 15, 1971, König Nachlass.

43. Interview with Judith Buber Agassi.

44. Promotionsakte Jacob Taubes—Staatsarchiv Zürich U 1092.47. On the topic of his sociology examination, see JT to MB, n.d., but late December 1946, ETT. On his relationship to Staiger, see Taubes, *Die Politische Theologie des Paulus* (Munich, 2003), p. 11.

45. JT to MB, n.d., but late December 1946, ETT.

46. Hans Barth, untitled Gutachten, December 12, 1946, in Promotionsakte Jacob Taubes, Staatsarchiv Zürich U 1092.47.

47. On MB's lineage, see "Ausschnitt aus dem Stammbaum 'Nachkommen des Michel Bollag,'" in *Geschichte der Juden im Kanton Zürich*, pp. 436–37.

48. Picard, *Die Schweiz*, p. 59; Hans Stutz, *Der Judenmord von Payerne* (Zurich, 2001). There is a slightly fictionalized account by a native of Payerne, who was eight years old when the murder occurred and had met both the victim and his murderers: Jacques Chessex, *Un Juif pour l'exemple* (Paris, 2009), translated into English as *A Jew Must Die* (London, 2010), which mentions the names and dates of birth of MB's daughters.

49. Interview with Madeleine Dreyfus.

50. JT to MB, n.d., but c. early 1946. All correspondence regarding JT and MB are from ETT.

51. JT to MB, n.d., but c. early 1946.

52. JT to MB, News Year's Eve, 1946–47. Jacob notes that in 1946 he received both his rabbinic ordination (*Rabbinerzeugnis*) and doctoral degree (*Doktorhut*).

53. Postcard from JT, Zurich, to MB, in Forest Hills, New York, October 21, 1946.

54. JT to MB, New Year's Eve, 1946–47.

55. JT to MB, n.d.

56. JT to MB, n.d.

57. JT to MB, News Year's Eve, 1946–47.

58. See his first published essay, Taubes, "Kabbala." Now also in *AuP*.

59. Postcard of JT to MB, March 3, 1947.

60. Telegram, JT to MB, October 12, 1946.

61. Postcard from JT to MB, October 14, 1946.

62. JT to MB, n.d., but c. February 16, 1947.

63. JT to MB, n.d., but early 1947.

64. JT to MB, November 6, 1946.

65. JT to MB, n.d., but early March 1947.

66. Western Union telegram from "Taubes to Bloch c/o Bollag in Forest Hills," March 10, 1947.

67. Zwi Taubes, telegram to MB, March 11, 1947.

68. Jacob Taubes, handwritten essay on Richard Beer-Hofmann, c. 1946, ETT.

69. JT to MB, n.d., but c. 1946.

70. Zwi Taubes to Louis Finkelstein [in Hebrew], January 29, 1941, JTS IA-26-12 to 1942, "T, Misc."

71. Zwi Taubes to Louis Finkelstein [in Hebrew], October 26, 1946, JTS IA-26-12 to 1942, "T, Misc."

72. JT to MB, New Year's Eve, 1946–47.

73. JT to MB, n.d., but late 1946.

74. JT to MB, n.d., but December 1946–January 1947; JT to MB, New Year's Eve, 1946–47.

75. JT to MB, n.d., but February 1947.

76. MB, Stampferbachstr., Zurich to JT, c/o Gruber, Villa Monplaisir, St. Moritz, 24 VII, 1947.

77. Letter from MB to JT, n.d., followed by typed letter from Lucie.

78. FT to JT, New York City, November 18, 1947.

79. Telegram from Lilette, Zurich, to JT, New York City, December 6, 1947.

80. FT to JT, New York City, date unclear but probably December 9, 1947.

81. FT to JT, New York City, December 31, 1947.

82. FT to JT, New York City, December 31, 1947.

83. Mirjam Taubes to JT, New York City, January 28, 1948.

84. Letter of JT to Arthur A. Cohen, November 25, 1977, Cohen Papers.

85. Jacob Taubes, "Logos und Telos," *Dialectica*, vol. 1 (1947), pp. 85–90.

86. JT to MB Bloch, undated, 1947, ETT.

87. Otfried Eberz, *Vom Aufgang und Niedergang des männlichen Weltalters: Gedanken über das Zweigeschlechterwesen* (Breslau, 1931). A modern edition, published in the 1970s, was edited by one of Taubes's friends, Annemarie Taeger.

88. JT, untitled sketch, c. 1947, "Fragmente," mid-1947, ETT.

89. "Fragmente," mid-1947, ETT.

90. Taubes, "Kabbala."

91. "Fragmente," mid-1947, ETT.

92. JT to Gonseth, October 3, 1947, ETT.

93. Gonseth to JT, December 23, 1947 (in French), ETT.

94. Gonseth to JT, December 23, 1947.

95. JT to Gonseth, October 3, 1947, ETT.

96. JT to Arthur A. Cohen, November 25, 1977, Cohen Papers,. There is a slightly cleaned-up version of the story (minus the garlic) in *PTdP*, p. 11.

97. For example, in an undated letter to MB, he thanks her for awakening him from what seems to have been a crisis of faith, and says that he has "recognized that it is better to fall into the arms of the living God, for his compassion is great and his grace more powerful than our guilt." JT to MB, n.d., but probably 1946.

98. I owe the formulation of this distinction to Moshe Halbertal.

99. Such would seem to be the thrust of Romans 7:5.

100. JT to Susman, August 22, 1947, Susman Nachlass.

101. On JT's drafting of the document, which he originally gave to Margarete Susman, JT to MB, n.d., but 1947; on the document, see the letter of William W. Simpson of the Council of Christians and Jews, London, September 5, 1947, and "Memorandum zur Palästinafrage," both in ETT. On the Arbeitsgemeinschaft, see Keller, "Theologie und Politik."

102. Regarding letter to Altmann, interview with Paul Mendes-Flohr; Zwi Taubes to Finkelstein, October 26, 1946, JTS; Zwi Taubes to Salo Baron, October 19, 1946, Baron Papers, box 33, folder 1. JT to MB, n.d., but late 1946, ETT.

103. JT to MB, November 28, 1946, ETT.

104. Interview with Morton Leifman. On Niebuhr's trip to Switzerland, where he met with Barth, see Richard Fox, *Reinhold Niebuhr: A Biography* (New York, 1985), p. 231.

105. JT to Gershom Scholem, October 27, 1947, written aboard ship, Scholem Papers, reprinted in *PdM*, p. 93.

106. JT to Gershom Scholem, October 27, 1947, *PdM*, pp. 93–97.

107. On Scholem's life, the best overview is provided by David Biale, *Gershom Scholem: Master of the Kabbalah* (New Haven, CT, 2018). Other relevant information

is in Gershom Scholem, *A Life in Letters, 1914–1982*, ed. and trans. Anthony David Skinner (Cambridge, MA, 2002); Gershom Scholem, *Von Berlin nach Jerusalem* (Frankfurt, 1977), translated as *From Berlin to Jerusalem*, trans. Harry Zohn (New York, 1980); and the lengthy Hebrew audio interview with Scholem conducted by Meir Lamed, "Interview No. (29)38—Scholem, Gershom," at https://www.youtube .com/watch?v=Vc0IxtdodQg.

108. On these elements of Scholem's thought, see Steven Aschheim, "The Metaphysical Psychologist: On the Life and Letters of Gershom Scholem," *Journal of Modern History*, vol. 76, no. 4 (2004), pp. 903–33. On Scholem's thought, see David Biale, *Gershom Scholem: Kabbalah and Counter-History* (Cambridge, MA, 1979); and Shaul Magid, "Gershom Scholem," in *Stanford Encyclopedia of Philosophy* (Fall 2021 edition), ed. Edward N. Zalta.

109. Scholem, "Redemption through Sin," p. 78.

110. Scholem, "Redemption through Sin," p. 84.

111. Scholem, "Redemption through Sin," p. 84.

112. Scholem, "Redemption through Sin," p. 96.

113. Scholem, "Redemption through Sin," pp. 104, 109.

114. Scholem, "Redemption through Sin," p. 113.

115. Scholem, "Redemption through Sin," p. 90.

116. Quoted in Biale, *Gershom Scholem: Kabbalah and Counter-History*, p. 7. Also in Gershom Scholem, *Devarim b'go* (Tel Aviv, 1975); for an English translation, see "Reflections on Modern Jewish Studies," in Gershom Scholem, *On the Possibility of Jewish Mysticism in Our Times and Other Essays*, ed. Avraham Shapira (Philadelphia, 1997).

117. Scholem to Hannah Arendt, December 5/6, 1947, in Hannah Arendt/Gershom Scholem, *Der Briefwechsel*, ed. Marie Luise Knott (Berlin, 2010), pp. 181–82.

118. JT to Gershom Scholem, October 27, 1947, *PdM*, 93–97.

119. Gerhard Scholem, "Offener Brief an Herrn Dr. Siegfried Bernfeld und gegen die Leser dieser Zeitschrift," in *Jerubbal*, vol. 1 (1918–19), pp. 125–30, reprinted in Scholem, *Briefe*, ed. I. Schedletzky (Munich, 1994), vol. 1, pp. 461–66; English translation as "Farewell: An Open Letter to Dr. Seigfried Bernfeld," in Gershom Scholem, *On Jews and Judaism in Crisis: Selected Essays*, ed. Werner Dannhauser (New York, 1976), pp. 54–60.

120. Scholem to JT, December 30, 1947, ZfL.

121. Josef Weiss, "Gershom Scholem—Fünfzig Jahre," *Yedioth hayom*, December 5, 1947, reprinted in Scholem, *Briefe*, vol. 1, pp. 458–60. The article is mentioned by Taubes in his letter to Scholem of January 1, 1948, published in *PdM*, pp. 98–101.

Chapter Five. New York and the Jewish Theological Seminary, 1947–49

1. Lloyd P. Gartner, "Conservative Judaism and Zionism: Scholars, Preachers and Philanthropists," in *Zionism and Religion*, ed. Shmuel Almog, Jehuda Reinharz, and Anita Shapira (Hanover, 1998).

2. On Yeshiva Chaim Berlin in this era, see Richard L. Rubenstein, *Power Struggle: An Autobiographical Confessional* (Boston, 1985), pp. 98ff.

3. Marsha Rosenblitt, "The Seminary during the Holocaust Years," in *Tradition Renewed: A History of the Jewish Theological Seminary of America*, ed. Jack Wertheimer (New York, 1997), vol. 2, p. 286; and Lila Corwin Berman, *Speaking of Jews: Rabbis, Intellectuals, and the Creation of an American Public Identity* (Berkeley, 2009), ch. 4; and Michael B. Greenbaum, "The Finkelstein Era," in Wertheimer, *Tradition Renewed*, vol. 1, pp. 161–232.

4. Berman, *Speaking of Jews*, p. 90.

5. Berman, *Speaking of Jews*, p. 75. See also Mel Scult (ed.), *Communings of the Spirit: The Journals of Mordechai Kaplan*, vol. 3, *1942–1951* (Detroit, 2020), p. 83.

6. Eli Ginzberg, *Keeper of the Law: Louis Ginzberg* (Philadelphia, 1966); on his relationship to Chajes, see pp. 98, 139.

7. Interview with Arthur Hertzberg.

8. Harvey E. Goldberg, "Becoming History: Perspectives on the Seminary Faculty at Mid-Century," in Wertheimer, *Tradition Renewed*, vol. 1, p. 359.

9. Greenbaum, "Finkelstein Era," p. 211.

10. Baila R. Shargel, "The Texture of Seminary Life during the Finkelstein Era," in Wertheimer, *Tradition Renewed*, vol. 1, p. 526; David Ellenson and Lee Bycel, "A Seminary of Sacred Learning: The JTS Rabbinical Curriculum in Historical Perspective," in Wertheimer, *Tradition Renewed*, vol. 2, p. 545.

11. Ellenson and Bycel, "Seminary of Sacred Learning," p. 559.

12. Elijah J. Schochet and Solomon Spiro, *Saul Lieberman: The Man and His Work* (New York, 2005), pp. 51, 71; Ginzberg, *Keeper of the Law*, p. 82.

13. Goldberg, "Becoming History," p. 401; and Naomi W. Cohen, "Diaspora Plus Palestine, Religion Plus Nationalism: The Seminary and Zionism, 1902–1948," in Wertheimer, *Tradition Renewed*, vol. 2, pp. 147ff.; Gartner, "Conservative Judaism and Zionism"; Naomi W. Cohen, *The Americanization of Zionism, 1897–1948* (Hanover, 2003), ch. 8.

14. FT to JT, n.d., but late 1947/early 1948, ETT.

15. Hannah Arendt, "The Jewish State: Fifty Years after, Where Have Herzl's Politics Led?," *Commentary*, May 1946; and Arendt, "To Save the Jewish Homeland," *Commentary*, May 1948, both reprinted in Hannah Arendt, *The Jewish Writings*, ed. Jerome Kohn and Ron H. Feldman (New York, 2007). This was characteristic of *Commentary*'s anti-Zionism during these years; see Benjamin Balint, *Running Commentary: The Contentious Magazine That Transformed the Jewish Left into the Neoconservative Right* (New York, 2010), pp. 36ff.

16. Draft of a translation of the Buber-Magnes appeal against mob violence in Jerusalem, ETT. On the Ichud in this period, see the near contemporaneous account by Ernst Simon, "The Costs of Arab-Jewish Cold War: Ihud's Experiment in Moral Politics," *Commentary*, September 1950, pp. 356–62; and Joseph Heller, *The Birth of Israel, 1945–1949: Ben-Gurion and His Critics* (Gainesville, FL, 2000), pp. 165–80.

17. JT to Scholem, January 28, 1948, *PdM*, p. 98.

18. FT to JT, November 9, 1947, ETT.

19. Mirjam Taubes to JT, November 11, 1947, ETT.

20. Mirjam to JT, November 21, 1947, ETT.

21. Mirjam to JT, December 8, 1948, ETT.

22. Mirjam to JT, March 16, 1948; April 15, 1948, ETT.

23. FT to "Lieber Onkel und Tante," n.d., but on back of Mirjam's wedding announcement, ETT.

24. Mirjam to JT, January 28, 1948, ETT.

25. Mirjam to JT, April 15, 1948, ETT.

26. Paul Tillich to John Marshall, Rockefeller Foundation, February 14, 1953, Tillich Papers. "I have known Mr. Taubes for several years in classes and in many personal conversations. He is extraordinarily gifted."

27. Mentioned in letter of JT to Martin Buber, February 25, 1948, Buber Papers.

28. Erich Fromm to JT, August 14, 1948, ETT.

29. FT to JT, n.d., but spring 1948. On the Satmar settlement in Brooklyn, see Israel Rubin, *Satmar: An Island in the City* (Chicago, 1972), p. 40.

30. JT to Gerda Seligson, from Woodbridge, New York, July 20, 1948, Seligson Papers.

31. JT to Buber, February 25, 1948, Buber Papers.

32. JT, letter to Hans Ornstein, August 11, 1948, ETT.

33. Martin Woessner, *Heidegger in America* (Cambridge, 2011), pp. 20–25.

34. JT to Susman, New York, January 5, 1948, Susman Nachlass.

35. JT, undated manuscript (c. 10 pages), c. 1948, ETT.

36. I am grateful to my Catholic University colleague, Sarah Brown Ferrario, for assistance in identifying and translating these Greek quotations.

37. JT to Buber, February 25, 1948, Buber Papers, NLI.

38. FT to JT, November 18, 1947, ETT.

39. Interview with Ezra Finkelstein.

40. Mirjam to JT, November 21, 1947; and Mirjam to JT, January 28, 1948, ETT.

41. Interview with Morton Leifman.

42. Fanny to JT, November 18, 1947, ETT.

43. JT to Finkelstein [in Hebrew], 1948, JTS.

44. JT to E. W. Beth, Amsterdam, May 10, 1948, ETT. Jacob Taubes, "Notes on the Ontological Interpretation of Theology," *Review of Metaphysics*, vol. 2, no. 8 (1949), pp. 97–104, reprinted in *CtC*.

45. Letter of Zwi to Jacob [in Yiddish], July, 13, 1948, ETT.

46. Letter of FT, Zurich, to her aunt and uncle in New York City, c. May 1948; FT to JT, June 21, 1948, ETT.

47. Zwi Taubes to Finkelstein [in Hebrew], May 4, 1948, JTS.

48. JT to Finkelstein [in Hebrew], spring, 1948, JTS.

49. FT to JT, December 25, 1947, ETT.

50. FT to JT, December 25, 1947, ETT.

51. Jacob's reaction is indicated by the responses of his parents in their letters of this period.

52. Biographical information on Lieberman, and his relationship with Finkelstein, is drawn from Schochet and Spiro, *Saul Lieberman*.

53. Schochet and Spiro, *Saul Lieberman*, pp. 126–27.

54. Schochet and Spiro, *Saul Lieberman*, pp. 22–24.

55. Arthur Hertzberg, *A Jew in America* (New York, 2002), pp. 105–6.

56. Schochet and Spiro, *Saul Lieberman*, p. 51.

57. David Sarna, "Growing Up Conservadox: A Child Grows Up at the Jewish Theological Seminary," online at Academia.edu, p. 18.

58. JT to Arthur A. Cohen, November 3, 1977, Cohen Papers.

59. Goldberg, "Becoming History," pp. 378–79.

60. Leo Strauss to Louis Finkelstein, February 2, 1945, JTS 1C Box 54, Folder 14.

61. Jerry Muller, "Leo Strauss: The Political Philosopher as a Young Zionist," *Jewish Social Studies*, n.s. 17, no.1 (2010), pp. 88–115, and Daniel Tanguay, *Leo Strauss: An Intellectual Biography* (New Haven, CT, 2007; French original, 2003), p. 15.

62. Leo Strauss, *Philosophie und Gesetz* (Berlin, 1935), in Strauss, *Gesammelte Schriften*, Band 2, ed. Heinrich Meier (Stuttgart, 1997).

63. Leo Strauss, "Preface to the English Translation," *Spinoza's Critique of Religion*, trans. E. M. Sinclair (New York, 1965; repr., Chicago, 1997), p. 1.

64. Steven Smith, *Reading Leo Strauss* (Chicago, 2006), pp. 125–28.

65. To the best of my knowledge, Strauss first used the phrase "die mittelälterliche Aufklärung" in his introduction to *Philosophie und Gesetz* (*Gesammelte Schriften Band 2*), p. 27.

66. For a fine (though decidedly non-Straussian) and up-to-date explication of his life and work, see Moshe Halbertal, *Maimonides: Life and Thought* (Princeton, NJ, 2014); along more Straussian lines, Howard Kreisel, *Maimonides' Political Thought: Studies in Ethics, Law, and the Human Ideal* (Albany, 1999), especially the introductory essay, "Maimonides' Political Thought," and Kreisel, "Maimonides' Political Philosophy," in *The Cambridge Companion to Maimonides*, ed. Kenneth Seeskin (New York, 2005); on the history of interpretation of Maimonides's esotericism, Aviezer Ravitzky, "Maimonides: Esotericism and Educational Philosophy," in the same volume.

67. Leo Strauss, "Persecution and the Art of Writing," in *Persecution and the Art of Writing* (1952; repr., Chicago, 1988), pp. 35–36.

68. Leo Strauss, "The Literary Character of *The Guide of the Perplexed*," in *Leo Strauss on Maimonides: The Complete Writings*, ed. Kenneth Hart Green (Chicago, 2013), p. 376.

69. Leo Strauss, "How to Study Medieval Philosophy," in Green, *Leo Strauss on Maimonides*, p. 113.

70. JT to Strauss, February 17, 1949; JT to Strauss, April 5, 1949, Leo Strauss Papers. My thanks to Eugene Sheppard for making copies of these letters available to me.

71. JT to Strauss, April 5, 1949, Leo Strauss Papers.

72. JT, New York, to Gerda Seligsohn, Richmond Surrey, July 28, 1949, Seligson Papers.

73. JT to Mohler, Basel, September 20, 1949, Mohler Nachlass.

74. JT, Zurich, to Scholem, October 2, 1949, *PdM*, p. 105.

75. Zwi Taubes to JT, n.d., but 1949, first page missing, ETT.

76. Joseph Dorman, *Arguing the World: The New York Intellectuals in Their Own Words* (New York, 2000), p. 107.

77. Interviews with Daniel Bell, Irving Kristol, and Gertrude Himmelfarb. The edition they used was almost certainly Moses Maimonides, *The Mishneh Torah, Book 1, edited according to the Bodleian Codex with Introduction, Biblical and Talmudic References, Notes and English Translation by Moses Hyamson* (New York, 1939).

78. Leo Strauss, "Review of *The Mishneh Torah*, Book I," in Green, *Leo Strauss on Maimonides*, p. 338.

79. Kristol in Dorman, *Arguing the World*, p. 108.

80. Rambam seminar protocol, January 23, 1949, ETT. The notes for this session seem to have been prepared by Milton Himmelfarb.

81. Protocol of February 13, 1949, ETT.

82. Protocol of January 31, 1949, ETT.

83. Interviews with Nathan Glazer, Irving Kristol, and Gertrude Himmelfarb.

84. Protocol of February 6, 1949, ETT.

85. Protocol of February 20, 1949, ETT.

86. Protocol of May 1, 1949, ETT.

87. Interview with Irving Kristol and Gertrude Himmelfarb.

88. Protocol of February 27, 1949, ETT.

89. Protocols of February 6, 1949, and February 13, 1949, ETT.

90. Nathan Glazer, "Commentary: The Early Years," in *Commentary in American Life*, ed. Murray Friedman (Philadelphia, 2005), p. 49. Interview with Nathan Glazer.

91. Interview with Irving Kristol.

92. Interview with Nathan Glazer.

93. Interview with Victor Gourevitch.

94. Interview with Daniel Bell.

95. Gertrude Himmelfarb, "The Prophets of the New Conservatism: What Curbs for Presumptuous Democratic Man," *Commentary*, January 1950, pp. 78–85, pp. 84–85.

96. Gertrude Himmelfarb, "Political Thinking: Ancients vs. Moderns," *Commentary*, July 1951, pp. 76–83.

97. Interview with Daniel Bell, and his "Reflections on Jewish Identity: The Risks of Memory," *Commentary*, June 1961, reprinted in Daniel Bell, *The Winding Passage* (Cambridge, MA, 1980), pp. 314–23, including the discussion of the esoteric interpretation of Maimonides.

98. Albert Salomon, "Prophets, Priests, and Social Scientists," *Commentary*, June 1949, pp. 595–600.

99. Biographical information on Cohen is drawn from David Stern's introduction to *An Arthur A. Cohen Reader*, ed. David Stern and Paul Mendes-Flohr (Detroit, 1998).

100. Interview with Richard L. Rubenstein.

101. Interview with Levi Kelman (son of Wolfe Kelman).

102. Interview with Levi Kelman.

103. Interview with Morton Leifman.

104. Interview with Morton Leifman.

105. Interview with Morton Leifman.

106. Interview with Morton Leifman.

107. Interview with Richard L. Rubenstein.

108. Taubes appears in the memoir under the pseudonym "Ezra Band." In an interview with the author, Rubenstein confirmed that he was referring to Taubes.

109. Rubenstein, *Power Struggle*, pp. 93–98.

110. Rubenstein, *Power Struggle*, pp. 105–6.

111. Rubenstein, *Power Struggle*, p. 106.

112. Richard L. Rubenstein, *After Auschwitz* (New York, 1966); *My Brother Paul* (New York, 1972).

113. Interview with Levi Kelman.

114. Goodwin and Redfield Jamison, *Manic Depressive Illness*, p. 402.

115. On Steinberg, see Simon Noveck, "Milton Steinberg," in *The "Other" New York Jewish Intellectuals*, ed. Carole S. Kessner (New York, 1994); Jonathan Steinberg, "Milton Steinberg, American Rabbi," *Jewish Quarterly Review*, vol. 95, no. 3 (2005), pp. 579–600; and Berman, *Speaking of Jews*, pp. 84–90.

116. Interview with Jonathan Steinberg.

117. JT (Chantilly) to Arthur A. Cohen, November 25, 1977, Cohen Papers.

118. Interview with Jonathan Steinberg.

119. Simon Noveck, *Milton Steinberg: Portrait of a Rabbi* (New York, 1978), pp. 211–12, quoted in Steinberg, "Milton Steinberg," pp. 596–97. Quotation from Steinberg's lecture to the Rabbinical Assembly, "Theological Problems of the Hour," *Proceedings of the Rabbinical Assembly*, vol. 13 (1949), pp. 409–28, republished in Milton Steinberg, *The Anatomy of Faith*, ed. Arthur A. Cohen (New York, 1960); for a similar critique of Paul and his legacy written at about the same time, see Milton Steinberg, "Kierkegaard and the Jews," *Menorah Journal*, no. 37 (1949), pp. 163–80, a manuscript of which Steinberg sent to Taubes, ETT.

120. See Carola Dietze, "'Kein Jud' und kein Goi': Konfligierende Selbst- und Fremdwahrnehmungen eines assimilierten 'Halb-Juden' in Exil und Remigration: Das Beispiel Helmuth Plessner," in *"Auch in Deutschland waren wir nicht wirklich zu Hause." Jüdische Remigration nach 1945*, ed. Irmela von der Lühe et al. (Göttingen, 2008), esp. pp. 209ff.

121. Dietze, "'Kein Jud,'" p. 225.

122. Biographical material on Gerda Seligson and her family is based upon the biography on the Leo Baeck Institute website for the "Seligsohn Kroner Family Collection."

123. Todd M. Endelman, *Leaving the Jewish Fold: Conversion and Radical Assimilation in Modern Jewish History* (Princeton, NJ, 2015), p. 104.

124. Alf Christophersen and Friedrich Wilhelm Graf, "Selbstbehauptung des Geistes: Richard Kroner und Paul Tillich—die Korrespondenz," *Zeitschrift für Neure Theologiegeschichte*, vol. 18, no. 2 (2011), pp. 281–339.

125. JT to Seligson, July 14, 1948, Seligson Papers.

126. JT to Seligson, October 9, 1948, Seligson Papers.

127. JT to Seligson, n.d., Seligson Papers.

128. Seligson to JT, November 23, 1948, Seligson Papers. English in original.

129. JT to Seligson, n.d., Seligson Papers.

130. Document in JT's handwriting, n.d., but 1949, Seligson Papers.

131. JT to Seligson, Richmond, Surrey, England, August 1, 1949, Seligson Papers.

132. Letter in *Korrespondenz 1*, p. 42.

133. Interview with Peter Schäfer.

134. Christina Pareigis, "Nachwort," in *Korrespondenz 1*, p. 273.

135. Interview with Annette Michelson. For more on Susan's life, see now Christina Pareigis, *Susan Taubes. Eine intellektuelle Biographie* (Göttingen, 2020).

136. ST to JT, September 27, 1950, *Korrespondenz 1*, p. 27, *Divorcing*, p. 129.

137. Pareigis in *Korrespondenz 1*, p. 27.

138. See the description in *Divorcing*.

139. *Divorcing*, pp. 164–69.

140. Paul Weiss, "Lost in Thought: Alone with Others," in *The Library of Living Philosophers*, vol. 23, *The Philosophy of Paul Weiss*, ed. L. E. Hahn (Chicago, 1995).

141. Pareigis, "Nachwort," in *Korrespondenz 1*, p. 263.

142. ST to Marion Batory, August 25, 1946, quoted in *Korrespondenz 1*, pp. 262–63.

143. Pareigis, *Korrespondenz 1*, p. 274. JT to Ernst Simon, December 14, 1948, Simon Papers.

144. Zwi Taubes to JT, March 3, 1949, ETT.

145. *Divorcing*, p. 129, and JT to Arthur A. Cohen, November 3, 1977, Cohen Papers.

146. As rightly noted by Pareigis, *Korrespondenz 1*, p. 274.

147. *Divorcing*, p. 129.

148. *Divorcing*, pp. 129, 240.

149. JT to Arthur A. Cohen, November 3, 1977, Cohen Papers.

150. On Susan's virginity at the time, see *Divorcing*, pp. 22, 129.

151. *Divorcing*, p. 46.

152. *Divorcing*, p. 113. The six weeks specified in the novel correspond to the period between Easter Sunday and the letters from Jacob's family responding to the news of his engagement.

153. Mirjam to JT, May 3, 1949; letter from Zwi to JT, May 5, 1949; letter in English from Mirjam to Susan and Jacques (i.e., Jacob), May, 8, 1949, ETT.

154. Interview with Annette Michelson.

155. *Divorcing*, p. 128; JT to Arthur A. Cohen, November 3, 1977, Cohen Papers.

156. On Glatzer, letter of ST to JT, October 8, 1950, *Korrespondenz 1*, p. 42; interview with Irving Kristol and Gertrude Himmelfarb; interview with Nathan Glazer.

157. Interview with Judith Buber Agassi.

158. JT to Scholem, January 13, 1949; January 29, 1949; October 22, 1949 (misdated as October 2, 1949, in the published edition), both in *PdM*, pp. 103–6; JT to Strauss, February 17, 1949, March 9, 1949, Leo Strauss Papers.

159. Or at least, so Scholem recalled his conversation with Strauss two decades later. See Scholem to George Lichtheim, October 21, 1948, in Gershom Scholem, *Briefe, Band II 1948-1970*, ed. Thomas Sparr (Munich, 1995), p. 215.

160. On Lieberman and Scholem as the key figures, see Louis Finkelstein to Zwi Taubes, August 3, 1949 (Hebrew), Finkelstein Papers, JTS.

161. H. Rosenthal of Liberaal Joodse Gemeente Amsterdam to Zwi Taubes, February 29, 1949; H. Rosenthal to JT, March 18, 1949, ETT.

162. The contract is in ETT.

163. JT to Joachim Wach, Chicago, n.d., but 1949; Ernst Strauss (Einstein's assistant at the Institute for Advanced Study) to JT, n.d., but 1949, ETT.

164. Mirjam to JT, April 7, 1949.

165. Simon Greenberg to JT, May 20, 1949, JTS.

166. On Scholem and Eranos, see Steven M. Wasserstrom, *Religion after Religion: Gershom Scholem, Mircea Eliade, and Henry Corbin at Eranos* (Princeton, NJ, 1999).

167. FT to JT, n.d., but late summer 1949; Zwi to JT, late summer 1949, ETT.

168. JT to Seligson, Richmond, Surrey, July 23, 1949, LBI.

169. JT to Seligson, Richmond, Surrey, June 29, 1949, LBI.

170. ST to JT, n.d., but summer 1949, *Korrespondenz 1*, pp. 15–16.

171. JT to Gerda Seligson in Richmond, Surrey, England, August 1, 1949, LBI.

172. ST to Gerda Seligson, August 16, 1949, LBI, according to which she had a miscarriage following ten days of bleeding and sickness and bed rest. See also reference to it in *Divorcing*, p. 61.

173. FT to ST, September 12, 1949, ETT Papers.

174. JT to Gerda Seligson, Zurich, n.d., but after September 1, 1949, Seligson Papers. Pareigis, *Susan Taubes*, p. 198.

175. JT to Balthasar, October 3, 1949, Hans Urs von Balthasar Archiv.

176. JT to Scholem, n.d., from "Cunard White Star R.M.S Queen Elizabeth," NLI and *PdM*, p. 107.

Chapter Six. Jerusalem, 1949–52

1. "Seine Frau ist von Israel abgestossen, er fühlt sich besser ein." Zipkes diary, August 17, 1950, copy in possession of author.

2. Dating based largely on Pareigis, "Nachwort," in *Korrespondenz 1*.

3. *Encyclopedia Judaica*, s.v. "Jerusalem."

4. JT, Jerusalem, to Finkelstein, n.d., but January 1950, JTS, IF-90–48 1950, "Jacob Taubes."

5. Walter Laqueur, *Dying for Jerusalem: The Past, Present and Future of the Holiest City* (Naperville, 2006), p. 109.

6. JT to Mohler, April 15, 1950, sent from Beth Caspi, Talpioth, Mohler Nachlass.

7. On the German-Jewish intelligentsia of Rechavia, see Thomas Sparr, *Grunewald im Orient: Das deutsch-jüdische Jerusalem* (Berlin, 2018).

8. Anita Shapira, *Israel: A History* (Waltham, MA, 2012), pp. 222–27.

9. Tom Segev, *1949: The First Israelis* (New York, 1986), p. 78.

10. Shapira, *Israel: A History*, p. 211.

11. Interview with Judith Buber Agassi.

12. Laqueur, *Dying*, p. 124.

13. Joseph Dan, "Gershom Scholem and the Study of Kabbala at Hebrew University" [in Hebrew], in *Toldot Hauniversita Haivrit B'Yerushalayim: Hitbassisut Vetzmicha* [*The History of the Hebrew University of Jerusalem: A Period of Consolidation and Growth*], ed. Hagit Lavsky (Jerusalem, 2005), vol. 1, pp. 199–218, is informative on Scholem's role in the university.

14. Arendt to Scholem, November 21, 1940, in Knott, *Der Briefwechsel*, p. 10.

15. Josef Weiss to FT, January 1949, ZfL.

16. Amos Funkenstein, "Gershom Scholem: Charisma, 'Kairos,' and the Messianic Dialectic," *History and Memory*, vol. 4, no. 1 (1992), pp. 123–40, p. 137.

17. Dan, "Gershom Scholem," pp. 211–16.

18. Scholem to Strauss, January 20, 1950, in Leo Strauss, *Gesammelte Schriften: Band 3* (Stuttgart, 2001), p. 718. On Guttmann, see Yehoyada Amir, "Julius Y. Guttmann: The Discipline of Jewish Philosophy" [in Hebrew], in Lavsky, *History of the Hebrew University*, pp. 219–56.

19. Hebrew University course catalogue for 1950–51.

20. Interview with Arnold Band.

21. Interview with Joseph Ben Shlomo.

22. Neve Gordon and Gabriel Motzkin, "Between Universalism and Particularism: The Origins of the Philosophy Department at Hebrew University and the Zionist Project," *Jewish Social Studies*, vol. 9, no. 2 (2003), pp. 99–122.

23. Carl Djerassi, *Four Jews on Parnassus* (New York, 2008), p. 35. Djerassi's speculation about an affair by Scholem with Fania when he was married to Escha seems unfounded.

24. Steven E. Aschheim, "*Bildung* in Palestine," in his *Beyond the Border: The German-Jewish Legacy Abroad* (Princeton, NJ, 2007), p. 16.

25. Schmuel Hugo Bergmann, *Tagebücher & Briefe*, ed. Miriam Sambursky, vol. 2, *1948–1975* (Königstein, 1985), passim.

26. See William Kluback, "Karl Jaspers and Schmuel Hugo Bergman: Believing Philosophers," in *Karl Jaspers*, ed. Richard Wisser (Würzberg, 1993), pp. 173–85, p. 176.

27. Laqueur, *Dying*; and Heller, *Birth of Israel, 1945–1949*, ch. 6, "The Intellectuals: *Ichud* and the Politics of Binationalism."

28. Simon, "Costs of Arab-Jewish Cold War"; and Aschheim, *Beyond the Border*, pp. 39ff.

29. See, for example, Ernst Simon, "Are We Israelis Still Jews? The Search for Judaism in the New Society," *Commentary*, April 1953.

30. Ernst Simon, "Erziehung zum Frieden in Kriegszeiten: Dargelegt am Beispiel Israel," in his *Entscheidung zum Judentum* (Frankfurt, 1979), pp. 365–66, quoted in Aschheim, *Beyond the Border*, p. 35.

31. Bruce Hoffman, *Anonymous Soldiers: The Struggle for Israel, 1917–1947* (New York, 2015), pp. 101ff.

32. Geula Cohen, *Woman of Violence* (New York, 1966), p. 232.

33. Cohen, *Woman of Violence*, pp. 268–69.

34. JT to Bergmann, n.d., but 1951, Bergmann Papers; cf. Nitzan Lebovic, "The Jerusalem School: Theopolitical Hour," *New German Critique*, vol. 35, no. 3 (2008), pp. 97–120.

35. Interview with Avishai and Edna Margalit.

36. Hebrew University Catalogue for 1951–52.

37. Interview with Ben Shlomo.

38. Interview with Avishai Margalit; interview with Ben Shlomo.

39. Interview with Ben Shlomo.

40. Kobi Selah, "Professor Yosef ben Shlomo Laid to Rest" [in Hebrew], *Arutz7*, April 21, 2007; and "Yosef ben Shlomo" [in Hebrew], Wikipedia.

41. Zwi Taubes to Finkelstein (Hebrew), July 28, 1950, JTS IF-90–48 1950; interview with Ben Shlomo.

42. Derek J. Penslar, "Transmitting Jewish Culture: Radio in Israel," in his *Israel in History: The Jewish State in Comparative Perspective* (New York, 2007).

43. *Korrespondenz 1*, pp. 278–79.

44. Bergmann, *Tagebücher & Briefe*, p. 88.

45. JT to ST, February 12, 1951, in *Korrespondenz 1*, p. 239.

46. Bergmann, *Tagebücher & Briefe*, p. 111.

47. JT to Ernst Simon, April 10, 1949, Simon Papers.

48. JT to Finkelstein, n.d., but January 1950. In quoting from Taubes's English language letters, I have made tiny punctuation and linguistic changes to facilitate their ready comprehension.

49. JT to Simon Greenberg, "Purim, 5710," JTS IF-90–48 1950, "Jacob Taubes."

50. JT to Ernst Simon, n.d., but 1948, Simon Papers.

51. JT to Bergmann, n.d., but 1951, Bergmann Papers.

52. Interview with Joseph Agassi.

53. JT to ST, from Jerusalem, January 7, 1952, *Korrespondenz 2*, pp. 29–30.

54. Mohler to Schmitt, February 14, 1952, quoted in editorial footnotes to *Taubes-Schmitt*, pp. 133–34.

55. Dirk van Laak, *Gespräche in der Sicherheit des Schweigens. Carl Schmitt in der politischen Geistesgeschichte der frühen Bundesrepublik* (Berlin, 1993); Reinhard Mehring, *Carl Schmitt: A Biography* (London, 2014; German original, 2009), ch. 28. For his influence beyond Germany, see Jan-Werner Müller, *A Dangerous Mind: Carl Schmitt in Post-War European Thought* (New Haven, CT, 2003).

56. JT to Mohler, February 14, 1952, in *Taubes-Schmitt*, p. 130.

57. JT to Mohler, February 14, 1952, in *Taubes-Schmitt*, p. 132.

58. JT to Mohler, February 14, 1952, in *Taubes-Schmitt*, p. 130.

59. The timing of Rosen's request fits precisely with Taubes's preparation for a course on early modern European philosophy that he was to offer during the 1951–52 academic year, for which he wanted to consult Schmitt's book. See Claude Klein, "The Right of Return in Israeli Law," November 5, 2015, *Tel Aviv U. Stud. L. 53* (1997), p. 53; available at SSRN: https://ssrn.com/abstract=2686531.

60. Schmitt to Mohler, April 14, 1952, quoted in editorial footnotes, *Taubes-Schmitt*, p. 133.

61. See Schmitt to Mohler, April 14, 1952, quoted in editorial footnotes, *Taubes-Schmitt*, pp. 133–34.

62. For a variety of analyses of these relationships, see Richard Wolin, *Heidegger's Children: Hannah Arendt, Karl Löwith, Hans Jonas, and Herbert Marcuse* (Princeton, NJ, 2001); Samuel Fleischacker (ed.), *Heidegger's Jewish Followers: Essays on Hannah Arendt, Leo Strauss, Hans Jonas, and Emmanuel Levinas* (Pittsburgh, 2008); and most recently and subtly, Daniel M. Herskowitz, *Heidegger and His Jewish Reception* (Cambridge, 2021.)

63. Taubes, "Notes on the Ontological Interpretation of Theology," *Review of Metaphysics*, vol. 2, no. 8 (1949), pp. 97–104, reprinted in *CtC*, to which page numbers refer, p. 219.

64. Taubes, "Notes on the Ontological Interpretation of Theology," pp. 220, 217.

65. Taubes, "Notes on the Ontological Interpretation of Theology," pp. 220–21.

66. Taubes, "Notes on the Ontological Interpretation of Theology," p. 221.

67. JT to Mohler, April 15, 1950, in *Taubes-Schmitt*, p. 125.

68. For a more recent attempt to trace the overlap between Kabbalah and Heidegger, see Elliot R. Wolfson, *Heidegger and Kabbalah: Hidden Gnosis and the Path of Poiēsis* (Bloomington, IN, 2019).

69. Jacob Taubes, "Review of *Symposion: Jahrbuch für Philosophie*, Freiburg, 1949" [in Hebrew], *Iyyun*, vol. 3, no. 1 (1952), pp. 36–40; German translation in *AuP*.

70. Jacob Taubes, "The Development of the Ontological Question in Recent German Philosophy," *Review of Metaphysics*, vol. 6, no. 4 (1952–53), pp. 651–64, p. 661.

71. Jacob Taubes, "Emunot Ve'dayot Be'teologia shel ha'mea ha-19" ["Beliefs and Ideas in Nineteenth Century Theology"], in *Archai Hayahdut (Aspects of Judaism)*, ed. Zwi Adar et al. (Tel Aviv, 1952); German translation as "Glauben und Wissen in der Theologie des 19. Jahrhunderts," in *AuP*.

72. For more on this topic, see Arthur Green, *Tormented Master: A Life of Rabbi Nahman of Bratslav* (Tuskaloosa, 1979), Excursus I, "Faith, Doubt, and Reason"; Funkenstein, "Gershom Scholem," pp. 123–39, citing *Likkutei ha-Moharan* (Jerusalem, 1930), 78a–80a.

73. Daniel B. Schwartz, *The First Modern Jew: Spinoza and the History of an Image* (Princeton, NJ, 2012), pp. 118–53; Steven Nadler, *A Book Forged in Hell: Spinoza's Scandalous Treatise and the Birth of the Secular Age* (Princeton, NJ, 2011), pp. 114–15, 157–59.

74. Schwartz, *First Modern Jew*; and Jan Eike Dunkhase, *Spinoza der Hebräer: Zu einer israelischen Erinnerungsfigur* (Göttingen, 2013), pp. 87–90.

75. Schwartz, *First Modern Jew*, pp. 148–50.

76. Hebrew University Catalogue for 1951–52.

77. JT to Mohler, n.d., but spring 1953, in *Taubes-Schmitt*, p. 141.

78. JT to Hans-Joachim Arndt, February 20, 1953, Arndt Nachlass; the Spinoza translation is also mentioned in JT to Eric Voegelin, May 4, 1953, Voegelin Papers.

79. Baruch Spinoza, *Maamar Teologi-Medini*, trans. Chaim Wirszubski (Jerusalem, 1961).

80. *Divorcing*, p. 77.

81. Interview with Joseph Agassi.

82. ST to JT, November 11, 1950, *Korrespondenz 1*, p. 92.

83. *Divorcing*, pp. 44–45.

84. *Divorcing*, p. 45.

85. JT to ST, January 11, 1951, *Korrespondenz 1*, p. 200.

86. See her self-description in ST to JT, May 1952, *Korrespondenz 2*, p. 229.

87. JT to Finkelstein, September 11, 1950, JTS.

88. See especially ST to JT, January 17–18, 1952, *Korrespondenz 2*, pp. 50–51.

89. ST to JT, November 10, 1950, *Korrespondenz 1*, p. 87.

90. ST to JT, February 19–20, 1952, *Korrespondenz 2*, p. 100.

91. JT to Bergmann, n.d., but about April 1951, referring to a document written a year earlier, Bergmann Papers.

92. These references are scattered through many of Susan's letters: *Korrespondenz 1*, pp. 22, 29, 32, 90.

93. ST to JT, October, 1950, November 3, 1950, November 12, 1950, *Korrespondenz 1*, pp. 43, 77, 96.

94. ST to JT, September 24, 1950, *Korrespondenz 1*, pp. 23, 120, 128, 132; *Korrespondenz 2*, pp. 216, 218.

95. JT to Bergmann, n.d., but likely March 1952, Bergmann Papers.

96. JT to ST, February 1951, *Korrespondenz 1*, p. 244; also pp. 250, 251.

97. ST to JT, November 11, 1950, *Korrespondenz 1*, p. 91.

98. ST to JT, November 28, 1950, *Korrespondenz 1*, p. 122.

99. *Korrespondenz 1*, p. 286; ST to JT, January 2, 1952, *Korrespondenz 2*, p. 18.

100. ST to JT, January 8–9, 1951, *Korrespondenz 1*, p. 189.

101. ST to JT, February 18, 1952, *Korrespondenz 2*, p. 97.

102. *Iyyun 3* (July 1952), pp. 173–75.

103. ST to JT, April 20, 1952, *Korrespondenz 2*, p. 200; ST to JT, April 1952, *Korrespondenz 2*, p. 206.

104. ST to JT, April 8, 1952, *Korrespondenz 2*, pp. 186–88. On Weil and Judaism, see Maud S. Mandel, "Simone Weil (1903–1943): A Jewish Thinker?," in *Makers of Jewish Modernity*, ed. Jacques Picard (Princeton, NJ, 2016), pp. 466–79.

105. ST to JT, March 1952, *Korrespondenz 2*, pp. 126–27.

106. ST to JT, January 24, 1952, *Korrespondenz 2*, pp. 62–63.

107. ST to JT, January 24, 1951, *Korrespondenz 1*, p. 214; ST to JT, January 1952, p. 47; ST to JT, February 1952, p. 94; ST to JT, March 29, 1952, p. 163; ST to JT, May 12, 1952, p. 225, all in *Korrespondenz 2*.

108. ST to JT, May 26/27, 1952, *Korrespondenz 2*, p. 235.

109. ST to JT, December 4, 1950, *Korrespondenz 1*, p. 132.

110. JT to ST, February 23, 1952, *Korrespondenz 2*, p. 107.

111. JT to parents, Erev Pesach, 1952, *Korrespondenz 2*, pp. 181–84.

112. ST to JT, May 1952, *Korrespondenz 2*, p. 228.

113. ST to JT, April 1, 1952, *Korrespondenz 2*, p. 169.

114. ST to JT, April 11, 1952, *Korrespondenz 2*, p. 189.

115. ST to JT, January 17–19, 1952, *Korrespondenz 2*, pp. 50–52.

116. ST to JT, February 26–27, 1952, *Korrespondenz 2*, p. 113.

117. ST to JT, n.d., but January 1952, *Korrespondenz 2*, p. 60; ST to JT, May 1, 1952, p. 213.

118. ST to JT, April–May 1952, *Korrespondenz 2*, p. 211.

119. ST to JT, January 25, 1952, *Korrespondenz 2*, pp. 64–65.

120. JT to ST, March 21, 1952, *Korrespondenz 2*, p. 154.

121. ST to JT, *Korrespondenz 2*, p. 54.

122. ST to JT, January 25, 1952, *Korrespondenz 2*, p. 65.

123. ST to JT, February 8, 1952, *Korrespondenz 2*, p. 84.

124. JT to ST, May 1952, *Korrespondenz 2*, p. 227.

125. JT to ST, April 16, 1952, *Korrespondenz 2*, p. 196.

126. JT to ST, n.d., but April 1952, *Korrespondenz 2*, p. 202.

127. ST to JT, May 1952, *Korrespondenz 2*, pp. 211–13.

128. ST to JT, February 12, 1952, *Korrespondenz 2*, p. 92.

129. ST to JT, February 11, 1952, *Korrespondenz 2*, p. 87.

130. ST to JT, February 22, 1952, *Korrespondenz 2*, 104.

131. ST to JT, April 16, 1952, *Korrespondenz 2*, pp. 197–98.

132. ST to JT, April 21, 1952, *Korrespondenz 2*, p. 205.

133. ST to JT, March 24, 1952, *Korrespondenz 2*, p. 155.

134. ST to JT, April 21, 1952, *Korrespondenz 2*, p. 205.

135. JT to ST, February 19, 1952, *Korrespondenz 2*, p. 99.

136. Abraham P. Socher, *The Radical Enlightenment of Solomon Maimon: Judaism, Heresy and Philosophy* (Stanford, 2006), p. 163.

137. Interview with Annette Michelson.

138. Scholem to Finkelstein, April 16, 1950, JTS IF-89–55 1950, "Gershom Scholem."

139. Finkelstein to Scholem, July 16, 1951, JTS.

140. Interview with Joseph Agassi. ST to JT, February 9, 1951, referring to letters of February 1 and February 3, saying that Scholem and company "did not understand the lecture" (*Korrespondenz 1*, p. 232).

141. Christoph König, "Ungebärdiges Lesen: Laudatio für Jean Bollack," *Lendemains*, vol. 33, no. 129 (2008), pp. 119–27.

142. ST to Scholem, New York, November 8, 1950, reprinted in *PdM*, pp. 125–26.

143. Joseph Dan, "Gershom Scholem."

144. Interviews with Marianne Weinberg and with Jean and Mayotte Bollack, all friends to Gershom and Fania Scholem. For a similar verdict, see Biale, *Gershom Scholem: Master of the Kabbalah*, ch. 3.

145. Interview with Joseph Agassi and Judith Buber Agassi.

146. Interview with Jean and Mayotte Bollack.

147. Biographical information on Weiss is drawn from the introduction by Noam Zadoff to his edited volume, Gershom Scholem and Joseph Weiss, *Correspondence 1948–1964* [in Hebrew] (Jerusalem, 2012), as well as Joseph Dan, "Joseph Weiss Today," in *Studies in East European Jewish Mysticism and Hasidism*, ed. David Goldstein and Joseph Weiss (London, 1997), pp. ix–xx; and Sara Ora Wilensky, "Joseph Weiss: Letters to Ora," in *Hasidism Reappraised*, ed. Ada Rapoport-Albert (London, 1997), pp. 10–31.

148. See in particular "The Beginnings of Hasidism" (in Hebrew with English summary), *Zion*, vol. 16, no. 3–4 (1951), pp. 46–106.

149. Gershom Scholem, "The Neutralization of the Messianic Element in Early Hasidism," in Scholem, *The Messianic Idea in Judaism* (New York, 1971), pp. 176–78.

150. *Korrespondenz 1*, p. 31, n. 10.

151. Based on Jacob's account, late in life, to Aleida Assmann; interview with Aleida Assmann. Also interview with Marianne Weinberg.

152. Weiss to Scholem, November 16, 1950, in *Correspondence 1948–1964*, pp. 53–55.

153. Weiss to Sara Ora Wilensky, March 13, 1951, in *Correspondence 1948–1964*, p. 27.

154. Weiss to Scholem, March 20, 1951, in *Correspondence 1948–1964*, pp. 57–58.

155. Scholem to Weiss, March 27, 1951, in *Correspondence 1948–1964*, pp. 58–59.

156. Interview with Shmaryahu Talmon.

157. Yonina Gerber Talmon to Scholem, June 23, 1951, Scholem Papers.

158. I have used the translation by Anthony David Skinner in Skinner, *Gershom Scholem: A Life in Letters, 1914–1982*, pp. 363–64. German text in Scholem, *Briefe* (Munich, 1995), vol. 2, pp. 25–28, and in *PdM*, pp. 127–29. Here starts my own translation.

159. JT to Scholem, October 11, 1951, in Scholem Papers and *PdM*, pp. 111–13.

160. Bergmann to JT (Rochester), October 8, 1951, Bergmann Papers.

161. JT to Scholem, October 17, 1951, *PdM*, pp. 113–14.

162. JT (Rochester) to Bergmann, October 16, 1951, Bergmann Papers.

163. ST to JT, April 11, 1952, *Korrespondenz 2*, p. 189.

164. JT to ST, January 7, 1952, *Korrespondenz 2*, p. 29.

165. JT to Bergmann, n.d., but late 1951, Hebrew, Bergmann Papers.

166. JT to Bergmann, March 25, 1952, Bergmann papers; and ST to JT, *Korrespondenz 2*, pp. 261ff. Bergmann to "Itzig," i.e., E. I. Poznanski, November 8, 1955 [in Hebrew], Bergmann Papers; JT to ST, March 31, 1952, *Korrespondenz 2*, p. 165.

167. See reference to this in ST to JT, April 26, 1952, *Korrespondenz 2*, p. 210; and JT's comments to Zipkes in Zurich that summer, Zipkes diary, June 25, 1952; shared by Zipkes with the author.

168. JT to Bergmann, n.d., but March 1952, Bergmann Papers.

169. Memo of W. Senator (executive vice-president of Hebrew University) [in Hebrew], March 21, 1952, Bergmann Papers.

170. JT to Bergmann [in Hebrew], n.d., but March 1952, Bergmann Papers.

171. Scholem to Leo Strauss, June 2, 1952, in Scholem, *Briefe*, vol. 2, p. 31.

172. JT to Scholem, September 14, 1952, text in *PdM*, pp. 114–15, and Scholem's handwritten written comments in German and Hebrew on original in Scholem Papers, "Jacob Taubes."

173. JT to Buber, September 16, 1952, Buber Papers.

174. Zipkes diary, June 25, 1952. Shared by Zipkes with the author.

Chapter Seven. Making It? 1952–56

1. ST to JT, June 19, 1952, *Korrespondenz 2*, p. 250.

2. ST to JT, June 19, 1952, *Korrespondenz 2*, p. 251.

3. ST, *Korrespondenz 1*, p. 265, on the timing of trip to London, *Divorcing*, p. 244; the timing of Ethan's birth corresponds precisely to the timeline of the novel.

4. JT to Hans-Joachim Arndt, n.d., but spring 1953, Arndt Nachlass.

5. JT to Salo Baron, n.d., but 1953, Baron Papers.

6. Interview with Victor and Jacqueline Gourevitch.

7. Eric Voegelin to JT, May 15, 1953, Voegelin Papers.

8. Michael Schalit to Susan and Jacob Taubes, Rochester, March 14, 1954; the letter, together with some chapters of the abortive translation, were made available to me by Manfred Voigts.

9. Jacob Taubes, review of *Kafka, pro und contra*, by Guenther Anders, *Philosophy and Phenomenological Research*, vol. 13, no. 4 (1953), pp. 582–83; review of *Philosophical Essays: Ancient, Medieval, and Modern*, by Isaac Husik, *Philosophy and Phenomenological Research*, vol. 14, no. 2 (1953), pp. 267–70; and in the same issue, review of *Symphilosophein*, ed. Helmuth Plessner, pp. 284–85; review of *Religion and the Modern Mind*, by W. T. Stace, *Ethics*, vol. 64, no. 2, part 1 (1954), pp. 137–41. In each case, the author's location is listed as "Rochester, New York."

10. Taubes published two slightly differing versions of the same article, which begins in each case with the same overview of the relationship between religion, theology, and philosophy. The earlier version is "On the Nature of the Theological Method: Some Reflections on the Methodological Principles of Tillich's Theology," *Journal of Religion*, vol. 34 (1954), pp. 12–25, reprinted in *CtC*; the later version is "Theology and the Philosophic Critique of Religion," *CrossCurrents*, vol. 5, no. 4 (1954), pp. 323–30, republished in *Zeitschrift für Religions- und Geistesgeschichte*, vol. 8, no. 2 (1956), pp. 129–38.

11. Cf. Gershom G. Scholem, *Major Trends in Jewish Mysticism* (New York, 1954), pp. 7, 23.

12. Jacob Taubes, "Christian Nihilism," review of *Against the Stream*, by Karl Barth, *Commentary*, September, 1954, pp. 269–72, p. 269.

13. Taubes, "On the Nature of the Theological Method," p. 13.

14. Jacob Taubes, review of *Ausgewählte Reden und Aufsätze*, by Adolf von Harnack, *Ethics*, vol. 64, no. 2 (1954), pp. 150–51.

15. Taubes, "On the Nature of the Theological Method," p. 25.

16. Jacob Taubes, "Dialectic and Analogy," *Journal of Religion*, vol. 34, no. 2 (1954), pp. 111–19, p. 119, reprinted in *CtC*.

17. Jacob Taubes, "On the Symbolic Order of Modern Democracy," *Confluence: An International Forum*, vol. 4, no. 1 (1955), pp. 57–71; similarly, "Theology and Political Theory," *Social Theory*, vol. 22 (1955), pp. 57–68, reprinted in *CtC*. The two essays overlap in content.

18. Taubes, "Dialectic and Analogy," pp. 114–15.

19. Taubes, "Dialectic and Analogy," pp. 116–17.

20. Taubes, "Theology and the Philosophic Critique of Religion."

21. Jacob Taubes, "Nietzsche and Christ," review of *Love, Power and Justice*, by Paul Tillich, *New Leader*, vol. 37, no. 33 (1954), pp. 24–26.

22. Taubes, "On the Nature of the Theological Method," p. 19.

23. Thomas J. J. Altizer (ed.), *Toward a New Christianity: Readings in the Death of God Theology* (New York, 1967), p. 219.

24. Jacob Taubes, "From Cult to Culture," *Partisan Review*, vol. 21 (1954), pp. 387–400, reprinted in *CtC*.

25. JT to Buber, June 7, 1953, Buber Papers.

26. JT to Strauss, June 7, 1954, Leo Strauss Papers.

27. JT to Buber, July 4, 1953, Buber Papers. JT to Bergmann, n.d., postmarked 1956 in Bergmann Papers.

28. JT to Tamara Fuchs, September 24, 1955, in Voigts, *Jacob Taubes und Oskar Goldberg*, p. 68.

29. JT to Tamara Fuchs, n.d., but spring 1955, in Voigts, *Jacob Taubes und Oskar Goldberg*, p. 67.

30. Daniel Bell, "The 'Intelligentsia' in American Society," in Bell, *The Winding Passage: Essays and Sociological Journeys 1960–1980* (Cambridge, MA, 1980), pp. 127–29.

31. Balint, *Running Commentary*, pp. 50ff.

32. The phrase comes from Will Herberg, expressing a sentiment that was Cohen's own. Balint, *Running Commentary*, p. 54.

33. JT to Eugen Rosenstock, May 17, 1953, Rosenstock-Huessy Papers.

34. A point well made by the editors of *KzK*, p. 7.

35. Mark Silk, "Notes on the Judeo-Christian Tradition in America," *American Quarterly*, vol. 36, no. 1 (1984), pp. 65–85, pp. 67–69.

36. Jonathan Sarna, *American Judaism* (New Haven, CT, 2004), p. 267.

37. Silk, "Notes," p. 74; interview with Daniel Bell.

38. Nahum Glatzer, "Franz Rosenzweig," *YIVO Annual*, vol. 1 (1946); Eugene R. Sheppard, "'I am a memory come alive': Nahum Glatzer and the Legacy of German Jewish Thought in America," *Jewish Quarterly Review*, vol. 94, no. 1 (Winter 2004), pp. 123–48; "I Am a Memory Come Alive: Nahum N. Glatzer and the Transmission of German-Jewish Learning," a film by Judith Glatzer Wechsler (2011), https://www.youtube.com/watch?v=PCF7UtsKOAU&t=1s.

39. Franz Rosenzweig, "Atheistic Theology," in Rosenzweig, *Philosophical and Theological Writings*, ed. Paul W. Franks and Michael L. Morgan (Indianapolis, 2000), pp. 10–24.

40. Will Herberg, "Rosenzweig's 'Judaism of Personal Existence': A Third Way between Orthodoxy and Modernism," *Commentary*, December 1950, pp. 541–49, p. 548.

41. Will Herberg, "Judaism and Christianity: Their Unity and Difference," *Journal of Bible and Religion*, vol. 21, no. 2 (1953), pp. 67–78, pp. 71–72.

42. Hans Joachim Schoeps, "A Religious Bridge between Jew and Christian: Shall We Recognize Two Covenants?," *Commentary*, February 1950, pp. 129–32.

43. Jacob Taubes, "The Issue between Judaism and Christianity," *Commentary*, December 1953, pp. 525–33, reprinted in *CtC*.

44. JT, letter to the editor, *Commentary*, October 1954, pp. 371–72.

45. JT to Rosenstock, August 6, 1953, Rosenstock-Huessy Papers.

46. JT to Rosenstock, July 21, 1953. In his final lectures on *Die politische Theologie des Paulus*, Taubes would restate this insight, setting in the context of a class discussion with his student Marshall Berman, at Columbia. See *PTdP*, p. 82, where the name of the interlocutor is misunderstood as "Michael Baermann."

47. Biographical information is drawn from Eric Voegelin, *Autobiographical Reflections*, ed. Ellis Sandoz (Baton Rouge, 1989).

48. Eric Voegelin, *The New Science of Politics: An Introduction* (Chicago, 1952), pp. 107.

49. Voegelin, *New Science*, pp. 107–13.

50. JT to Carl Friedrich, n.d., but 1953, Friedrich Papers, all references are to HUGFP 17.22 Boxes 32 and 33.

51. JT to Eric Voegelin, n.d., but fall 1952, and November 29, 1952, Voegelin Papers, box 37, folder 10. See also Alfred Schütz to Eric Voegelin, November 9, 1952, in Alfred Schütz, Eric Voegelin, *Eine Freundschaft, die ein Leben ausgehalten hat: Briefwechsel 1938–1959*, ed. Gerhard Wagner and Gilbert Weiss (Konstanz, 2004), pp. 448–49.

52. JT to William Y. Elliott, December 3, 1952, Elliott Papers, box 55, Hoover.

53. Quoted in *KzK*, p. 13.

54. JT to Hannah Arendt, n.d., late 1953, Arendt Papers.

55. Niall Ferguson, *Kissinger 1923–1968: The Idealist* (New York, 2015), pp. 272ff.

56. The transcript, Jacob Taubes, "Theology and Political Theory," February 16, 1953, is in the Elliott Papers, box 55, Hoover.

57. This is the account that Taubes offered in *ACS*, p. 23. Arndt later disputed the timing (Arndt to Armin Mohler, May 26, 1987, reprinted in *Taubes-Schmitt*, pp. 205–7), but my reading of the seminar transcript and the Arndt-Taubes correspondence seems to bear out Taubes's account.

58. JT, Rochester, to Hans-Joachim Arndt, February 20, 1953, Arndt Nachlass.

59. JT to Schmitt, August 2, 1955, in *Taubes-Schmitt*, p. 21.

60. JT to Bergmann, January 14, 1953, Bergmann Papers.

61. On the history of the Frankfurt Institute, see Martin Jay, *The Dialectical Imagination: A History of the Frankfurt School and the Institute of Social Research 1923–1950* (Boston, 1973); and Rolf Wiggershaus, *The Frankfurt School: Its History, Theories and Political Significance*, trans. Michael Robertson (Cambridge, MA, 1994; German original, 1986).

62. Howard Eiland and Michael W. Jennings, *Walter Benjamin: A Critical Life* (Cambridge, MA, 2014), pp. 658–62.

63. Uwe Steiner, *Walter Benjamin: An Introduction to His Work and Thought* (Chicago, 2010), p. 174.

64. JT to Hannah Arendt, December 6, 1953, Arendt Papers.

65. On the latter point, see Max Horkheimer, "Die Juden und Europa," *Zeitschrift für Sozialforchung* (1939); English translation in *Critical Theory and Society: A Reader*, ed. Stephen Eric Bonner (New York, 1989).

66. See the discussion in Jay, *Dialectical Imagination*, ch. 6.

67. Max Horkheimer, *The Eclipse of Reason* (New York, 1947; repr., 1974).

68. Günter C. Behrmann, "Zur Publikationsgeschichte der Kritischen Theorie," in *Die intellektuelle Gründung des Bundesrepublik: Eine Wirkungsgeschichte der Frankfurter Schule*, ed. Clemens Albrecht et al. (Frankfurt, 2000), p. 283.

69. Behrmann, "Publikationsgeschichte," p. 264; confirmed in my interview with Jürgen Habermas.

70. Behrmann, "Publikationsgeschichte," p. 252.

71. See Herbert Marcuse to Horkheimer, December 12, 1954, and Horkheimer's response of December 28, 1954, in Max Horkheimer, *Gesammelte Schriften*, vol. 18, *Briefwechsel 1949-1973*, ed. Gunzelin Schmid Noerr (Frankfurt, 1996), pp. 286-87.

72. Horkheimer, *Eclipse of Reason*, pp. 4-10, 58.

73. Horkheimer, *Eclipse of Reason*, pp. 14-41.

74. Horkheimer, *Eclipse of Reason*, pp. 70-71.

75. Horkheimer, *Eclipse of Reason*, p. 64.

76. Horkheimer, *Eclipse of Reason*, p. 61.

77. Martin Jay, *Reason after Its Eclipse: On Late Critical Theory* (Madison, WI, 2016).

78. Interview with Stanley Cavell.

79. The phrase "linke politische Theologie" to characterize his project was used by Taubes in his lecture of 1986 in *ACS*, p. 20.

80. JT to Bergmann, n.d., but 1953, Bergmann Papers.

81. John Marshall, Rockefeller Foundation to Paul Tillich, February 10, 1953, in Tillich Papers, "Taubes."

82. JT, Cambridge, to Tillich, n.d., but November 1953, Tillich Papers, "Taubes."

83. Herbert Marcuse, *Eros and Civilization* (Boston, 1955), p. 126; on the *Corpus Hereticorum*, Barry Katz, *Herbert Marcuse and the Art of Liberation* (London, 1982), p. 154.

84. Jacob Taubes, "Memorandum Concerning a Collection of Texts and Fragments 'Origins of the Free Spirit,'" dated October 24, 1953, Tillich Papers, "Taubes."

85. Jacob Taubes, "The Gnostic Idea of Man," *Cambridge Review*, vol. 1, no. 2 (March 16, 1955), pp. 86-94.

86. Taubes, "On the Symbolic Order of Modern Democracy," pp. 57-71. Some of this argument is repeated in Jacob Taubes, "Virtue and Faith: A Study of Terminology in Western Ethics," in *Philosophy East and West*, vol. 7, no. 1-2 (1957), pp. 27-32.

87. Taubes, "On the Symbolic Order of Modern Democracy," p. 63.

88. Taubes, "On the Symbolic Order of Modern Democracy," p. 71.

89. Daniel Bell to Elaine Bell, February 20, 1955, courtesy of David A. Bell.

90. Daniel Bell to Elaine Bell, February 27, 1955, courtesy of David A. Bell.

91. Norman Cohn, *The Pursuit of the Millennium* (London, 1957), p. xiv and "Conclusion," passim.

92. *KzK*, p. 12.

93. Morton Keller and Phyllis Keller, *Making Harvard Modern: The Rise of America's University* (New York, 2001), p. 51.

94. Interview with Robert Bellah.

95. Keller and Keller, *Making Harvard Modern*, p. 72.

96. On Wolfson, see Paul Ritterband and Harold S. Wechsler, *Jewish Learning in American Universities: The First Century* (Bloomington, 1994), pp. 107-21.

97. Interview with Elsa First.

98. Morton White to JT, December 10, 1954, Philosophy Department Correspondence 1950-55, Harvard University Archives, UAV 687.11.

99. Interview with Nina Holton.

100. "And You Takes Your Choice," *Harvard Crimson*, September 27, 1954.

101. James F. Gilligan, "Nomad Philosopher," *Harvard Crimson*, October 23, 1954.

102. Interviews with Hubert Dreyfus and Robert Wolff.

103. JT to Arndt, on Beacon Press stationary, January 1, 1955, Arndt Nachlass; JT to Tamara Fuchs, September 24, 1955, in Voigts, *Jacob Taubes und Oskar Goldberg*, p. 68; interview with Stanley Cavell.

104. Michael S. Roth, *Knowing and History: Appropriations of Hegel in Twentieth-Century France* (Ithaca, NY, 1988), ch. 2; and Leo Strauss, *On Tyranny: Including the Strauss-Kojève Correspondence*, ed. Victor Gourevitch and Michael S. Roth (New York, 1991), esp. pp. 217ff.

105. Interview with Elsa First; interview with Victor Gourevitch.

106. Interview with Gourevitch; interview with Janet Aviad.

107. Jacob Taubes, Philosophy 286, Spring 1955, "Introduction to Hegel's Early Theological Writings," in Friedrich Papers.

108. Course description in Friedrich Papers. Sontag notes on course "Philosophy 286," n.d., but spring 1955, Susan Sontag Papers, Special Collections, UCLA, box 153, folder 6. Some of the notes seem to be in Rieff's handwriting. The contents of the course are reflected in Jacob Taubes, "Hegel," in *Encyclopedia of Morals*, ed. Vergilius Ferm (New York, 1956), pp. 207–12.

109. Unless otherwise noted, biographical information about Philip Rieff is based on my interview with him.

110. Susan Sontag, *Reborn: Journals and Notebooks 1947–1963*, ed. David Rieff (New York, 2008), p. 56, entry for November 21, 1949.

111. On the early history of Brandeis University, see Stephen J. Whitfield, *Brandeis University: At the Beginning* (Waltham, MA, 2010), which includes information on Glatzer.

112. Sontag, *Reborn*, entry for February 25, 1958, p. 193.

113. Daniel Schreiber, *Susan Sontag: A Biography*, trans. David Dollenmayer (Evanston, IL, 2014), p. 33.

114. On Rieff's thought, see Jerry Z. Muller, "Philip Rieff," in *American Cultural Critics*, ed. David Murray (Exeter, 1995) and the selections in Jerry Z. Muller (ed.), *Conservatism: An Anthology of Social and Political Thought from David Hume to the Present* (Princeton, NJ, 1997), pp. 411ff.

115. For his comments on Marcuse, see Philip Rieff, *Fellow Teachers* (New York, 1973), pp. 108n, 144n, 205–7.

116. Interview with Stanley Cavell.

117. JT to Hugo Bergmann, June 25, 1954, Bergmann Papers.

118. Interview with Philip Rieff; on Arnold, see Alexandra Arnold Lynch, "Melvin Arnold: Publisher, 1913–2000"; Walter Donald Kring, "Beacon Press—The Growth of an Idea," *Christian Register*, April 1956; and Jeannette Hopkins, "Melvin Arnold and Unitarian Publishing"; all at https://www.harvardsquarelibrary.org/biographies/melvin-arnold/.

119. Interview with Philip Rieff; interview with Elsa First. On Marcuse's career at Brandeis, see Stephen J. Whitfield, *Learning on the Left: Political Profiles of Brandeis University* (Waltham, MA, 2020), pp. 164ff.

120. Interview with Elsa First.

121. Interview with Judith Glatzer Wechsler.

122. Will Joyner, "Krister Stendahal: 1921–2008," Harvard Divinity School, April 16, 2008, https://hds.harvard.edu/news/2011/02/07/krister-stendahl-1921 -2008#.

123. Krister Stendahl, *Paul Among Jews and Gentiles and Other Essays* (Philadelphia, 1976); the key essay was first delivered in 1961; George H. Williams, *The "Augustan Age"*, vol. 2, *Divinings: Religion at Harvard* (Göttingen, 2014), pp. 468ff.

124. Interview with Krister Stendahl.

125. See the "New Preface" to *The Scrolls and the New Testament*, ed. Krister Stendahl and James H. Charlesworth (New York, 1992).

126. Interviews with Elsa First and Annette Michelson.

127. ST to Arndt, n.d., but summer/fall 1954, Arndt Papers.

128. JT to Arndt, n.d., but 1955, Arndt Papers.

129. JT to Paul Tillich, June 27, 1955, Tillich Papers.

130. JT to Max Horkheimer, July 7, 1955, MHA V 162, Frankfurt.

131. Hans Jonas, *The Gnostic Religion: The Message of the Alien God and the Beginnings of Christianity* (Boston, 1958), p. xviii.

132. From an edited interview with Hans Jonas, published as Hans Jonas, *Errinnerungen* (Frankfurt, 2003), pp. 272–73; in English as *Memoirs*, edited and annotated by Christian Wiese, trans. Krishna Winston (Waltham, MA, 2008), pp. 168–69.

133. Interview with Philip Rieff.

134. Marcuse, *Eros and Civilization*, pp. 35–45.

135. Marcuse, *Eros and Civilization*, p. 36.

136. Marcuse, *Eros and Civilization*, p. 104.

137. Marcuse, *Eros and Civilization*, p. 102.

138. On Friedrich's biography, see Udi Greenberg, *The Weimar Century: German Émigrés and the Ideological Foundations of the Cold War* (Princeton, NJ, 2014), ch. 1; and Ferguson, *Kissinger 1923–1968*, pp. 228ff.

139. JT to Friedrich, June 14, 1953, Friedrich Papers.

140. JT, Princeton, NJ, to Friedrich, January 19, 1956, Friedrich Papers.

141. Friedrich to McGeorge Bundy, January 12, 1955, Friedrich Papers.

142. ST to Arndt, n.d., but summer/fall 1954, Arndt Papers. Warren C. McCulloch to Albert Balz, June 2, 1954, and attached draft in McCulloch Papers, American Philosophical Society, Philadelphia.

143. Interview with Krister Stendahl.

144. JT to Arndt, Boston, MA, August 20, 1955, Arndt Papers.

145. Crane Brinton et al., "Faculty Minute on the Late Arthur Darby Nock," *Harvard Studies in Classical Philology*, vol. 68 (1964); E. R. Dodds and Henry Chadwick, "Obituary: Arthur Darby Nock," *Journal of Roman Studies*, vol. 53 (1963), pp. 168–69.

146. Interview with Krister Stendahl.

147. JT to Friedrich, January 1, 1956, Friedrich Papers.

148. McGeorge Bundy (Dean) to Friedrich, December 27, 1954, Friedrich Papers.

149. Interview with Hubert Dreyfus.

150. Jacob Taubes, "Four Ages of Reason," cited from *CtC*, p. 268.

151. Taubes, "Dialectic and Analogy."

152. Taubes, "Four Ages of Reason," pp. 271–73.

153. Taubes, "Four Ages of Reason," pp. 278–81.

154. JT, Cambridge, MA, to Horkheimer, April 23, 1955, MHA V 162.

155. Jacob Taubes, "On the Historical Function of Reason," MHA V 162. Both the manuscript and the published versions note in the first footnote that a draft of the paper was first delivered at Harvard and Yale.

156. Interview with Herbert Dreyfus, who was a graduate student in philosophy at Harvard and attended the lecture.

157. From Sontag's journal entry, quoted in Benjamin Moser, *Sontag: Her Life and Work* (New York, 2019), p. 193. The references he gives to her published journal, *Reborn*, do not correspond to the journal entry, however.

158. Jonas, *Errinnerungen*, pp. 272–73; in English as *Memoirs*, p. 168.

159. Interviews with Arnold Band and Daniel Bell. White had indicated his skepticism about Taubes to Susan Sontag, who echoed it; see *Reborn*, p. 244.

160. Interview with Avishai Margalit.

161. Bundy to Friedrich, January 28, 1955, Friedrich Papers.

162. Interview with Nina Holton.

163. Interview with Philip Rieff.

164. Taubes thanks him at the beginning of "Four Ages of Reason."

165. Walter Kaufmann, "The Hegel Myth and Its Method," *Philosophical Review*, vol. 60, no. 4 (1951), pp. 459–86. On Kaufmann and his interpretation of Nietzsche, see Jennifer Ratner-Rosenhagen, *American Nietzsche* (Chicago, 2011), ch. 6.

166. Strauss to Scholem, June 22, 1952, in Strauss, *Gesammelte Schriften*, vol. 3, p. 728.

167. Arendt to Gershom Scholem, New York, April 9, 1953, in *Hannah Arendt-Gershom Scholem: Der Briefwechsel*, ed. Marie Luise Knott (Berlin, 2010), p. 380.

168. Arendt to Scholem, July 8, 1954, in *Hannah Arendt-Gershom Scholem: Der Briefwechsel*, p. 391.

169. Strauss to Scholem, October 27, 1955, in Strauss, *Gesammelte Schriften*, vol. 3, pp. 735–36.

170. The review was read by Victor Gourevitch, to whom Taubes gave a copy; interview with Victor Gourevitch.

171. JT to Carl Friedrich, Princeton, NJ, January 1, 1956, Friedrich Papers.

172. Interviews with Stanley Cavell and Krister Stendahl.

173. Interview with Stanley Cavell.

174. Interviews with Stanley Cavell, Arthur Hyman, and Leon Wieseltier.

175. Jacob Taubes, CV, Friedrich Papers.

176. Franz Overbeck, *Selbstbekenntnisse. Mit einer Einleitung von Jacob Taubes* (Frankurt, 1966).

177. Interview with Philip Rieff.

178. Daniel Bell to Elaine Graham, February 20, 1955, courtesy of David A. Bell.

179. Daniel Bell to Elaine Graham, February 27, 1955, courtesy of David A. Bell.

180. JT to Schmitt, August 2, 1955, in *Taubes-Schmitt*, p. 21.

181. Visiting assistant professor, Princeton University official notice, ETT.

182. JT to Friedrich, September 5, 1955, Friedrich Papers.

183. JT, Princeton, NJ, to Friedrich, September 5, 1955, Friedrich papers; JT to Voegelin, n.d., but fall 1955, Voegelin Papers.

184. JT to Friedrich, January 1, 1956, Friedrich Papers.

185. JT to Tamara Fuchs, September 24, 1955, in Voigts, *Jacob Taubes und Oskar Goldberg*, p. 68.

186. JT to Arndt, Princeton, NJ, March 5, 1956, Arndt Papers.

187. Interview with Gregory Callimanopulos.

188. *Korrespondenz 2*, p. 90.

189. Susan Taubes, "The Absent God: A Study of Simone Weil" (Ph.D. dissertation, Radcliffe College, 1956).

190. The fact that Susan took such a course with Marcuse is noted in Sigrid Weigel, "Between the Philosophy of Religion and Cultural History: Susan Taubes on the Birth of Tragedy and the Negative Theology of Modernity," *Telos*, no. 150 (Spring 2010), pp. 115–35, p. 129.

191. Susan Anima Taubes, "The Absent God," *Journal of Religion*, vol. 35, no. 1 (January 1955), pp. 6–16; for her critique of Weil, see esp. pp. 15–16.

192. George L. Mosse, *German Jews beyond Judaism* (Bloomington, IN, 1985).

193. Jacob Taubes, "Erich von Kahler—70 Jahre," *Aufbau*, December 23, 1955, p. 10, reprinted in *AuP*; JT to Erich von Kahler, December 11, 1955, Nachlass Erich von Kahler, DLA Marbach. On Kahler's background, see Robert E. Lerner, *Ernst Kantorowicz: A Life* (Princeton, NJ, 2017), pp. 41, 44–45; interview with Ethan Taubes.

194. Nahum Glatzer to Hutchison, February 7, 1956, Baron Papers.

195. Abraham Kaplan to Hutchison, February 20, 1956, Baron Papers.

196. Fritz Kaufmann to Hutchison, February 7, 1956, Baron Papers.

197. Alexander Koyré to Hutchison, March 3, 1956; Jean Wahl to Hutchison, February 28, 1956, Baron Papers.

198. Arthur O. Lovejoy to Hutchison, February 7, 1956, Baron Papers.

199. Paul Weiss to Hutchison, February 6, 1956, Baron Papers.

200. James Luther Adams to Hutchison, February 9, 1956, Baron Papers.

201. John Dillenberger to Hutchison, February 8, 1956, Baron Papers.

202. Paul Tillich to Hutchison, February 10, 1956, Baron Papers.

203. Gregory Vlastos to Hutchison, February 16, 1956, Baron Papers.

204. Harry W. Jones to Salo Baron, April 5, 1956, Baron Papers.

205. JT to Voegelin, April 20, 1956, Voegelin Papers.

206. JT to Arndt, Princeton, NJ, March 5, 1956, Arndt Nachlass.

Chapter Eight. Columbia Years, 1956–66

1. JT to Friedrich, October 5, 1956, Friedrich Papers; interview with Ethan Taubes.

2. Walter Laqueur, "The Arendt Cult," in *Arendt in Jerusalem*, ed. Steven Aschheim (Berkeley, 2001), pp. 47–64, pp. 56–57.

3. Their rent at first was $163 per month, rising to $174 in 1958 after some improvements were made. That amounted to about a fifth of Jacob's salary. "Order Adjusting Maximum Rent," March 12, 1956, ETT.

4. Interviews with Irving Kristol and Gertrude Himmelfarb; interview with Joseph and Judith Agassi.

5. Interviews with Ethan and Tania Taubes; interview with David Rieff.

6. Robert A. McCaughey, *Stand Columbia: A History of Columbia University in the City of New York, 1754–2004* (New York, 2003), p. 411.

7. McCaughey, *Stand Columbia*, pp. 290–99.

8. Daniel Bell, *The Reforming of General Education: The Columbia College Experience in Its National Setting* (New York, 1966), p. 224.

9. McCaughey, *Stand Columbia*, p. 390.

10. McCaughey, *Stand Columbia*, pp. 383–87.

11. McCaughey, *Stand Columbia*, p. 386.

12. Thomas Albert Howard, *Protestant Theology and the Making of the Modern German University* (New York, 2006), p. 382.

13. Howard, *Protestant Theology*, pp. 379, 381.

14. D. G. Hart, *The University Gets Religion: Religious Studies in American Higher Education* (Baltimore, 1999), p. 97 and passim.

15. Horace L. Friess, "The Department of Religion," in *A History of Columbia University: The Faculty of Philosophy* (New York, 1957), p. 147.

16. Friess, "Department of Religion," p. 165.

17. On the emergence from campus ministry, see Hart, *University Gets Religion*, pp. 158ff.

18. Friess, "Department of Religion," p. 159.

19. Willard Gurdon Oxtoby, "*Religionswissenschaft* Revisited," in *Religions in Antiquity*, ed. Jacob Neusner (Leiden, 1968), pp. 560–608, p. 593.

20. Oxtoby, "*Religionswissenschaft* Revisited," p. 594.

21. Oxtoby, "*Religionswissenschaft* Revisited," p. 603.

22. Friess, "Department of Religion," pp. 166–67; interview with John J. Gallahue.

23. JT to Arndt, Princeton, NJ, March 5, 1956, Arndt Papers.

24. JT to Carl J. Friedrich, October 5, 1956, Friedrich Papers.

25. Interview with Peter Gay.

26. Interviews with Edmund Leites and John J. Gallahue.

27. ST to Paul Tillich, October 10, 1956, Tillich Papers.

28. Friess, "Department of Religion," p. 153.

29. Interview with Jean Bollack; Mohler, "Der messianische Irrwisch," pp. 219–21.

30. Interview with Robert Bellah.

31. Interview with Walter Sokel.

32. Interview with Peter L. Berger.

33. On Buber's visits to the United States, see Paul Mendes-Flohr, *Martin Buber: A Life of Faith and Dissent* (New Haven, CT, 2019), pp. 291ff.

34. JT to Buber, September 17, 1956, Buber Papers.

35. JT to Buber, November 11, 1956, and January 25, 1957; and the account in Maurice Friedman, *Encounter on the Narrow Ridge: A Life of Martin Buber* (New York, 1991), p. 370.

36. Email account from Berel Lang, July 9, 2017, who as a graduate student attended the seminar.

37. JT to Friedrich, March 17, 1958, Friedrich Papers.

38. Interview with Joseph Agassi.

39. JT to Buber, February 4, 1958, Buber Papers.

40. Jacob Taubes, "Martin Buber und die Geschichtsphilosophie," in *Martin Buber*, ed. Paul Arthur Schilpp and Maurice Feldman (Stuttgart, 1963), reprinted in *KzK*, pp. 50–67; "Martin Buber and the Philosophy of History," in *The Philosophy of Martin Buber*, ed. Paul Arthur Schilpp and Maurice Feldman (La Salle, IL, 1967), reprinted in *CtC*, pp. 10–27.

41. Frank Tannenbaum (ed.), *A Community of Scholars: The University Seminars at Columbia* (New York, 1965); for a valuable discussion, see Paul Goodman, "Columbia's Unorthodox Seminars," *Harper's Magazine*, January 1, 1964, pp. 72–82.

42. JT to "Dear Colleagues," September 5, 1957, Friedrich Papers.

43. JT, "Dear Colleagues," October 6, 1958, ETT.

44. Horace Friess to "Dear Colleagues," October 30, 1959, Friedrich Papers.

45. JT to Horkheimer, October 14 and October 30, 1963, Horkheimer Archiv.

46. Jacob Taubes, "Nachman Krochmal and Modern Historicism," *Judaism*, vol. 12, no. 2 (1963), pp. 150–65, reprinted in *CtC*, pp. 28–44.

47. Taubes, "Nachman Krochmal and Modern Historicism," p. 33.

48. Taubes, "Nachman Krochmal and Modern Historicism," pp. 40–42.

49. Taubes, "Nachman Krochmal and Modern Historicism," p. 44.

50. He expressed these sentiments in discussions with Hugo Bergmann, Martin Buber, Leo Baeck, and Ernst Simon in Jerusalem in May 1951. See Bergmann, *Tagebücher & Briefe*, p. 88.

51. Interviews with Ethan and Tania Taubes.

52. Interview with Irving Kristol and Gertrude Himmelfarb.

53. Interviews with Ismar Schorsch and Janet Aviad.

54. Interview with Michael Wyschogrod.

55. Interview with Michael Wyschogrod.

56. JT to Carl J. Friedrich, October 5, 1956, Friedrich Papers.

57. Norman Podhoretz, *Making It* (New York, 1967); and Thomas J. Jeffers, *Norman Podhoretz: A Biography* (Cambridge, 2010).

58. Interview with Moshe Waldoks.

59. Interview with Midge Decter and Norman Podhoretz.

60. Jeffers, *Norman Podhoretz*, pp. 65–66; and Podhoretz, *Making It*, pp. 297–98.

61. Interview with Norman Podhoretz.

62. Email exchange with Berel Lang.

63. Interview with Richard Locke.

64. The paragraphs that follow are based on my interview with Richard Locke.

65. Susan Sontag, *As Consciousness Is Harnessed to Flesh: Journals and Notebook, 1964–1980*, ed. David Rieff (New York, 2012), p. 480.

66. Interview with Marshall Berman.

67. Interview with Marshall Berman.

68. Morris Dickstein, *Why Not Say What Happened: A Sentimental Education* (New York, 2015), p. 107.

69. Interview with Marshall Berman.

70. Isaac Bashevis Singer, *Satan in Goray* (New York, 1955), esp. ch. 4.

71. Interview with Marshall Berman.

72. Dickstein, *Why Not Say What Happened*, p. 106.

73. Interview with Marshall Berman.

74. Interview with Annette Michelson.

75. Jean Houston, *A Mythic Life: Learning to Live Our Greater Story* (New York, 1996), pp. 263–67.

76. Houston, *Mythic Life*, p. 313.

77. *Divorcing*, pp. 81–82. The story was related to Ethan Taubes by Jean Houston.

78. She appears as "Martha Wooten" in Susan Sontag's story, "Debriefing," in Sontag, *I, Etcetera* (New York, 1977), p. 47.

79. "Jean Houston," Wikipedia.

80. Interviews with Jean Bollack and Annette Michelson.

81. Moser, *Sontag: Her Life and Work*, pp. 172, 176. Taubes's previous designs on Sontag noted in interview with Philip Rieff.

82. Jacob's role in getting Sontag the job, from interview with Harold Stahmer, a member of the Department of Religion at the time.

83. Sontag, *Reborn*, pp. 232, 251.

84. Syllabus for "Religion 94, "The Transition to the Concept of Psychology: Nietzsche," Spring Term 1960–1961, Susan Sontag Papers, UCLA, box 153, folder 10. Taubes gave a talk on Sender Freie Berlin on December 11, 1963, that seems to have grown out of this seminar and the faculty seminar with Ricoeur, "Psychoanalyse und Philosophie: Noten zu einer philosophischen Interpretation der psychoanalytischen Methode," now published in *KzK*, pp. 352–70. A version was delivered at a colloquium organized by his friend Lucien Goldmann, with the École pratique des hautes études (6e section) in Royaumont in December 1965, and published in *Critique sociologique et critique psychanalytique* (Brussels, 1970); Rektor to JT July 9, 1965, PA.

85. Summaries of most of the weekly sessions, and Susan Sontag's notes, are in the Sontag Papers, UCLA, box 152, folder 11.

86. The most detailed analysis of the plausibility of Sontag's claim is Kevin Slack and William Bachelder, "Susan Sontag Was Not the Sole Author of Freud: The Mind of the Moralist," VoegelinView, May 11, 2020, online.

87. Interview with Richard Locke.

88. Interview with Harold Stahmer.

89. Interview with Harold Stahmer.

90. Information on Neusner is drawn from Aaron W. Hughes, *Jacob Neusner: An American Jewish Iconoclast* (New York, 2016), and interview with Jacob Neusner.

91. Morton Smith and Gershom Scholem, *Correspondence 1945–1982*, ed. Guy Stroumsa (Leiden, 2008).

92. Saul Lieberman, "A Tragedy or a Comedy," *Journal of the American Oriental Society*, vol. 104, no. 2 (1984), pp. 315–19.

93. Jacob Neusner and Noam Neusner, *The Price of Excellence: Universities in Conflict during the Cold War Era* (New York, 1995), pp. 112–22.

94. See the correspondence between Neusner and Scholem in the Scholem Papers.

95. Interview with David Weiss Halivni; David Weiss Halivni, *The Book and the Sword* (New York, 1996).

96. On Schorsch's life, see foreword to *Text and Context: Essays in Modern Jewish History in Honor of Ismar Schorsch*, ed. Eli Lederhendler and Jack Wertheimer (New York, 2005), pp. ix–xv; interview with Ismar Schorsch. Many of Schorsch's essays are collected in Ismar Schorsch, *From Text to Context: The Turn to History in Modern Judaism* (Waltham, MA, 1994).

97. Ismar Schorsch, "The Philosophy of History of Nachman Krochmal," *Judaism*, vol. 10 (1961), pp. 237–45.

98. Schorsch, "Philosophy of History," pp. 237–45.

99. Email from Berel Lang.

100. Jonas, *Gnosis*, p. 248.

101. Jonas, *Gnosis*, pp. 214–15.

102. Jonas, *Gnosis*, pp. 234–35; Jonas, *Gnostic Religion*, pp. 270–74.

103. Interview with Gershon Greenberg.

104. Interview with Edmund Leites.

105. Interview with Gershon Greenberg.

106. JT to Arndt, May 12, 1958, Arndt Nachlass.

107. These are the figures for 1961, in Kurator, FU Berlin, August 3, 1961, PA.

108. JT to Arndt, October 25, 1957, Arndt Nachlass.

109. Jacob Taubes, "Vorwort" to *Die Sprache des Herzens: aus Zeiten jüdische Erneuernung*, by Fanny Taubes (Zurich, 1959), pp. 5–6, reprinted in *AuP*, p. 388.

110. JT to Arndt, June 29, 1958, Arndt Nachlass. Entry in Mohler guest book, June 23, 1960, in *Taubes-Schmitt*, p. 267. Weissmann, *Armin Mohler*, p. 95.

111. JT to Arndt, August 17, 1958, Arndt Nachlass.

112. JT to Arndt, January 12, 1958, Arndt Nachlass.

113. JT to Arndt, August 20, 1958, Arndt Nachlass.

114. JT to Horkheimer, January 5, 1960, Horkheimer papers.

115. JT to Horkheimer, January 28, 1961, Horkheimer papers. "Columbia ist ja schon recht, wenn es nur—so sage ich wie Gott zu Abraham—fünf Menschen gäbe, mit denen man ein Gespräch führen könnte."

Chapter Nine. Between New York and Berlin, 1961–66

1. Interview with Jean Bollack.

2. On Celan's life and work, see John Felstiner, *Paul Celan: Poet, Survivor, Jew* (New Haven, CT, 1995).

3. Landmann may have met Taubes when both attended an academic conference in Paris in the summer of 1960. On this possible meeting, see Herbert Kopp-Oberstebrink, "Landmann und Taubes. Historische, wissenschaftspolitische und intellektuelle Kontexte eines akademischen Zerwürfnisses," in *Kulturanthropologie als Philosophie des Schöpferischen. Michael Landmann im Kontext*, ed. Jörn Bohr und Matthias Wunsch (Nordhausen, 2015), p. 182.

4. Norbert Hinske, "Zeit der Enttäuschungen: Errinerungen an Michael Landmann," in *Exzerpt und Prophetie: Gedenkschrift für Michael Landmann (1913–1984)*, ed. Klaus-Jürgen Grundner et al. (Würzburg, 2001), pp. 7–16; and Richard Wisser, "Michael Landmanns Mainzer 'Lehr'-Jahre," in the same volume, pp. 17–22.

5. Valentin Landmann, "Vorwort" to Salcia Landmann, *Der jüdische Witz*, 18th ed. (Ostfildern, 2016); and Manfred Schlapp, "Landman, Salcia," in *Biographisch-Bibliographisches Kirchenlexikon*, vol. 21 (2003).

6. Salcia Landmann to Armin Mohler, June 18, 1987, Mohler Nachlass.

7. Michael Landmann to Eduard Fraenkel, Dekan der Philosophischen Fakultät der FU, August 15, 1960, FU, Universitätsarchiv, PA, cited in Herbert Kopp-Oberstebrink, "Affinitäten, Dissonanzen. Die Korrespondenz zwischen Hans Blumenberg und Jacob Taubes," in *Blumenberg-Taubes*, p. 311, n. 35.

8. According to the editors' note to *Taubes-Schmitt*, p. 27.

9. Peter Schäfer, "Die Entwicklung der Judaistik in der Bundesrepublik Deutschland seit 1945," in *Die sog. Geisteswissenschaften: Innenansichten*, ed. Wolfgang Prinz and Peter Weingart (Frankfurt, 1990), pp. 350–65.

10. Monika Richarz, "Zwischen Berlin und New York: Adolf Leschnitzer—der erste Professor für jüdische Geschichte in der Bundesrepublik," in *Deutsche—Juden—Völkermord. Der Holocaust als Geschichte und Gegenwart*, ed. Klaus-Michael Mallmann und Jürgen Matthäus (Darmstadt, 2006).

11. Kurator (Fritz von Bergmann), July 27, 1961, PA.

12. On the early history of the FU, see Fritz Stern, *Five Germanys I Have Known* (New York, 2006), pp. 206–7; and Siegward Lönnendonker and Tilman Fichter (ed.), *Freie Universität Berlin 1948–1973. Hochschule im Umbruch* (Berlin, 1978).

13. On Flechtheim, see Mario Keßler, *Ossip K. Flechtheim. Politischer Wissenschaftler und Zukunftsdenker (1909–1998)* (Cologne, 2007).

14. Landmann to Leschnitzer, November 26, 1956; and letter to Dekan der Philosophischen Fakultät, dated February 11, 1957, Leschnitzer Papers, LBI.

15. "Helmut Gollwitzer," Wikipedia, last updated February 12, 2021, https://de.wikipedia.org/wiki/Helmut_Gollwitzer.

16. Interview with Michael Theunissen.

17. "Prophetie, Apokalyptik und Gnosis," "Grundbegriffe der jüdischen Religionsgeschichte," "*Legenden des Rabbi Nachman*." "Taubes to Give Lecture Series in Berlin School," *Columbia Spectator*, March 31, 1961; *Blumenberg-Taubes*, editors' note, p. 19.

18. Kurator, August 3, 1961, PA. A public announcement of the appointment appeared in the Berlin newspaper, *Der Tagesspiegel*, September 7, 1961, "Ordinariat für Judaistik an der FU."

19. JT to Carl Friedrich, October 19, 1951, Friedrich Papers.

20. Kurator to JT, August 20, 1962, PA.

21. Kurator to JT, December 13, 1961; August 20, 1962; January 28, 1963; July 4, 1963; October 12, 1964; all in PA.

22. Fliess to JT, June 5, 1965, ZfL.

23. Interview with Gershon Greenberg.

24. Interview with Gershon Greenberg.

25. Interview with Jacob Neusner.

26. Interview with Dieter Henrich.

27. Michael Brenner, *After the Holocaust: Rebuilding Jewish Life in Postwar Germany* (Princeton, NJ, 1997).

28. Irmela von der Lühe et al. (ed.), *"Auch in Deutschland waren wir nicht wirklich zu Hause." Jüdische Remigration nach 1945* (Göttingen, 2008).

29. G. N. Knauer, Princeton, NJ, to JT, March 3, 1966; Notgemeinschaft für eine freie Universität, Box 475, Hoover.

30. Interview with Dieter Henrich.

31. MvB to JT, October 24, 1965, in Margherita von Brentano, *Das Politische und das Persönliche. Eine Collage*, ed. Iris Nachum and Susan Neiman (Göttingen, 2010), p. 463.

32. Hans-Ulrich Wehler, *Deutsche Gesellschaftsgeschichte 1949–1990* (Munich, 2008), p. 381, cited in Julia Amslinger, *Eine neue Form von Akademie: "Poetik und Hermeneutik"—die Anfänge* (Paderborn, 2017), p. 23.

33. Tilman Fichter and Siegward Lönnendonker, *Kleine Geschichte des SDS* (Berlin, 1977), p. 86.

34. For a blow-by-blow account, see Fichter and Lönnendonker, *Kleine Geschichte des SDS*.

35. Fichter and Lönnendonker, *Kleine Geschichte des SDS*, pp. 69–70.

36. On *Das Argument*, see Fichter and Lönnendonker, *Kleine Geschichte des SDS*, p. 177, n. 145.

37. Wolfgang F. Haug, "Erinnerung an Margherita von Brentano," http://www .wolfgangfritzhaug.inkrit.de/documents/BRENTANXX.pdf.

38. Interview with Uta Gerhardt; JT to Karl Michel, February 28, 1966, Suhrkamp.

39. The following is based on an interview with Dieter Henrich, as well as Dieter Henrich, *"Sterbliche Gedanken." Dieter Henrich im Gespräch mit Alexandru Bulucz* (Frankfurt, 2015).

40. Henrich, *Sterbliche Gedanken*, p. 23.

41. Henrich, *Sterbliche Gedanken*, pp. 45–46. See also Dieter Henrich, "In Erinnerung an JACOB TAUBES (1923–1987)," in *Individualität: Poetik und Hermeneutik IX*, ed. Manfred Frank and Anselm Haverkamp (Munich, 1988), p. ix.

42. Interview with Victor Gourevitch.

43. Biographical information on Habermas is drawn mainly from Stefan Müller-Doohm, *Jürgen Habermas: Eine Biographie* (Berlin, 2014); I have also used the English translation, *Habermas: A Biography*, trans. Daniel Steuer (London, 2016), to which page references refer.

44. Matthew G. Specter, *Habermas: An Intellectual Biography* (New York, 2010), p. 37.

45. Müller-Doohm, *Habermas*, p. 72.

46. Müller-Doohm, *Habermas*, p. 83.

47. Müller-Doohm, *Habermas*, p. 87.

48. Müller-Doohm, *Habermas*, pp. 82–88.

49. Interview with Jürgen Habermas.

50. For the history of Suhrkamp Verlag, I have relied upon *Die Bibliographie des Suhrkamp Verlages, 1950–2000*, ed. Wolfgang Jeske (Frankfurt, 2002); Lutz Hagestedt, "Das Glück ist eine Pflicht: Der Suhrkamp Verlag wurde fünfzig Jahre Alt," literaturkrtitik.de, vol. 2, no. 7/8 (July 2000); and conversations with Wolfgang Schopf and Raimund Fellinger of Suhrkamp Verlag.

51. George Steiner, "Adorno: Love and Cognition," *Times Literary Supplement*, March 9, 1973.

52. In a letter from JT to Michel, April 4, 1967 (Suhrkamp Archiv), he reports that he has recently spoken to George Steiner, and urged him to publish with Suhrkamp, rather than with Kieppenhauer. Steiner's first book to be published by Suhrkamp, *Language and Silence* (1967), was published in translation by Suhrkamp in 1969 as *Sprache und Schweigen*, trans. Axel Kaun. In the next decade and a half, Suhrkamp published four other books by Steiner.

53. Raimund Fellinger and Wolfgang Schopf (ed.), *Kleine Geschichte der Edition Suhrkamp* (Frankfurt, 2003), p. 41.

54. Fellinger and Schopf, *Kleine Geschichte der Edition Suhrkamp*, pp. 16–17.

55. Wolfgang Schopf (ed.), *Adorno und seine Frankfurter Verleger* (Frankfurt, 2003), pp. 450–51.

56. Peter Michalzik, *Unseld. Eine Biographie* (Munich, 2002), pp. 57–60.

57. Interviews with Dieter Henrich and Jürgen Habermas.

58. Müller-Doohm, *Habermas*, p. 103.

59. JT to Unseld, November 4, 1963; Unseld to JT, June 30, 1982, Suhrkamp.

60. Similarly, JT to Michel, August 26, 1965, Suhrkamp Archiv.

61. See also Philipp Felsch, *Der lange Sommer der Theorie: Geschichte einer Revolte 1960–1990* (Munich, 2015), p. 58.

62. Karl-Markus Michel, "Narrenfreiheit oder Zwangsjacke? Aufgaben und Grenzen kritischen Denkens in der Bundesrepublik," *Neue Kritik*, vol. 25/26 (1964), pp. 23–29, cited in Albrecht et al., *Die intellektuelle Gründung der Bundesrepublik*, p. 316.

63. Jörg Sundermeier, "Der sträflichst Vergessene. Zum Tod des Publizisten Walter Boehlich," *Jungle World*, April 12, 2006.

64. "Besprechung des Projektes 'Theorie: kritische Beiträge' am 25 Juni 1966," Suhrkamp.

65. "Abschrift Taubes Brief zu Unseld," n.d., but late 1963, Suhrkamp.

66. JT to Michel, November 6, 1965, Suhrkamp.

67. Interview with Marcel Marcus.

68. Henning Ritter, *Verehrte Denker: Porträts nach Begegnungen* (Springe, 2012), p. 40.

69. Pierre Bayard, *How to Talk about Books You Haven't Read* (New York, 2007), p. 14.

70. Interview with Tania Taubes.

71. Mohler, "Messianische Irrwisch"; interview with Peter Gente.

72. Interview with Avishai Margalit.

73. Emile M. Cioran, "Einige Sätze," in *Spiegel und Gleichnis. Festschrift für Jacob Taubes*, ed. Norbert Bolz and Wolfgang Hübener (Würzburg, 1983), p. 422.

74. Interview with Marcel Marcus.

75. Interview with John J. Gallahue.

76. I am grateful to Manfred Voigts for sharing his copy with me.

77. Jacob Taubes, "Die Intellektuellen und die Universität," in *Universitätstage 1963* (Berlin, 1963), pp. 36–55; reprinted in *KzK*, pp. 319–39.

78. A version has now been published in *AuP*, pp. 165–71.

79. Most information on Szondi is drawn from Susanne Zepp (ed.), *Textual Understanding and Historical Experience: On Peter Szondi* (Paderborn, 2015); and the "Zeittafel" in *Paul Celan-Peter Szondi Briefwechsel* (Frankfurt, 2005).

80. Joachim Küpper, "My Encounter with Peter Szondi," in Zepp, *Textual Understanding*, p. 48.

81. On the publication history of that lecture, see Sonja Boos, *Speaking the Unspeakable in Postwar Germany* (Ithaca, NY, 2014), p. 138. Daniel Weidner, "Reading the Wound," in Zepp, *Textual Understanding*, p. 60.

82. Adorno to Scholem, June 22, 1965, in *Adorno-Scholem Briefwechsel 1939–1969*, ed. Asaf Angermann (Berlin, 2015), p. 359.

83. JT to Szondi, September 27, 1966, ZfL.

84. Szondi to Adorno, in Peter Szondi, *Briefe*, ed. Christoph König und Thomas Sparr (Frankfurt, 1993), p. 217.

85. On Gadamer in Leipzig, see Jerry Z. Muller, *The Other God That Failed* (Princeton, NJ, 1987), 317ff.

86. On this theme, see Jürgen Habermas, "Hans Georg Gadamer: Urbanisierung der Heideggerischen Provinz," in Habermas, *Philosophisch-politische Profile*, erweiterte Ausgabe (Frankfurt, 1981).

87. JT to Gadamer, February 10, 1965, ZfL.

88. JT to Gadamer, September 26, 1966, and December 19, 1966, ZfL.

89. Interview with Norbert Bolz. See also JT, "Jacob Taubes," in *Denken, das an der Zeit ist*, ed. Florian Rötzer (Frankfurt, 1987), pp. 305–19.

90. JT to Voegelin, September 1, 1966, ZfL.

91. Hans Maier, "Eric Voegelin and German Political Science," *Review of Politics*, vol. 62, no. 4 (2000), pp. 709–26.

92. See Joachim Ritter, *Metaphysik und Politik: Studien zu Aristoteles und Hegel* (Frankfurt, 1969), partially translated as *Hegel and the French Revolution: Essays on the Philosophy of Right*, trans. Richard Dien Winfield (Cambridge, MA, 1982).

93. JT to Norman Birnbaum, July 2, 1965; JT to Joachim Ritter, July 29, 1966, ZfL.

94. JT to Henning Ritter, December 5, 1966; Henning Ritter to JT, December 17, 1966; Joachim Ritter to JT, February 5, 1968, ZfL.

95. JT to Theodor Adorno, January 12, 1965, ZfL.

96. The conversation is recalled in JT to Adorno, December 18, 1967, ZfL.

97. JT to Adorno, January 18, 1965; similarly, JT to Adorno, February 8, 1965, ZfL.

98. "Errinnerungsprotokoll eines Telephongesprächs zwischen Adorno und Taubes," July 13, 1966, ZfL.

99. JT to Adorno, July 28, 1965, ZfL.

100. "Errinnerungsprotokoll eines Telephongesprächs zwischen Adorno und Taubes," July 13, 1966, ZfL.

101. Adorno to Elisabeth Lenk, September 7, 1967, in *Theodor W. Adorno und Elisabeth Lenk. Briefwechsel 1962–1969*, ed. Elisabeth Lenk (Göttingen, 2001), p. 121.

102. Adorno to Elisabeth Lenk, September 7, 1967.

103. JT to Horkheimer, April 10, 1965, Horkheimer Archiv.

104. This paragraph draws upon concepts in Ronald S. Burt, "The Network Structure of Social Capital," *Research in Organizational Behaviour*, vol. 22 (2000), pp. 345–423.

105. *Divorcing*, pp. 45–46.

106. *Divorcing*, p. 47.

107. *Divorcing*, pp. 47, 129.

108. *Divorcing*, p. 132.

109. *Divorcing*, p. 33.

110. Interview with Krister Stendahl.

111. *Divorcing*, pp. 12–13.

112. *Divorcing*, p. 46.

113. Interview with Ethan Taubes.

114. *Divorcing*, p. 16.

115. Interview with Madeleine Dreyfus.

116. JT to Dietrich Goldschmidt, December 13, 1969, ZfL; interviews with Ethan Taubes, Tania Taubes, and Madeleine Dreyfus.

117. JT to Sandor Feldmann, September 23, 1966, ZfL.

118. JT to Miriam Weingort, November 3, 1966, ZfL.

119. Christina Pareigis, "Die Schriftstellerin Susan Taubes," in Susan Taubes, *Prosaschriften*, ed. Pareigis (Paderborn, 2015), pp. 233–44.

120. Interview with Elsa First.

121. Haug, "Erinnerung an Margherita von Brentano," and "Aristotelikerin: Zum Tode Margherita von Brentanos," *Frankfurter Allgemeine Zeitung*, March 23, 1995.

122. Brentano, *Das Politische und das Persönliche*, pp. 226–27.

123. "Kein Schuß ein Treffer," *Der Spiegel*, February 1960, p. 30; "Verantwortungsvolle Unbotmässigkeit: Zum Tode Margherita von Brentanos," *Neue Zürcher Zeitung*, March, 27, 1995.

124. Brentano, *Das Politische und das Persönliche*, p. 238.

125. Cord Riechelmann, "Joschka minus Machtgehabe: Margherita von Brentano hat sich schon früh mit den personellen Kontinuitäten zwischen Nationalsozialismus und Bundesrepublik beschäftigt," *Jungle World*, no. 44, November 4, 2010. See her essay, "Die Endlösung—Ihre Funktion in Theorie und Praxis," in *Antisemitismus: Zur Pathologie der bürgerlichen Gesellschaft*, ed. Hermann Huss and Andreas Schröder (Frankfurt 1965), pp. 35–76, p. 56.

126. Margherita von Brentano, "Jacob" (1994), in *Das Politische und das Persönliche*, p. 456; and Sibylle Haberditzl interview, pp. 470–71.

127. Brentano, *Das Politische und das Persönlich*, p. 458; and MvB to JT, November 30, 1965, p. 465.

128. Interview with Jürgen and Ute Habermas. See too MvB to JT, July 2, 1964, in *Das Politische und das Persönliche*, p. 459.

129. The account that follows is based largely on interview with Judith Glatzer Wechsler, as well as biographical information on https://judithwechsler.com.

130. See the letter from JT to Arnold Aharon, November 11, 1981, published with accompanying commentary in Sigrid Weigel, "Ingeborg Bachmanns Geist trifft die Geister der Kabbala: Jacob Taubes' Liebesmystik," *Trajekte*, April 2005, pp. 8–16.

131. Ina Hartwig, "Bachmann-Celan: Schuld und Zauber," *Frankfurter Rundschau*, January 29, 2019.

132. On the timing of the colloquium, see JT to Gadamer, February 22, 1966, ZfL. Information about her attendance is in Weigel, "Ingeborg Bachmanns Geist," p. 15, based on information from Jan Assmann.

133. Ina Hartwig, *Wer war Ingeborg Bachmann?* (Frankfurt, 2017).

134. See Weigel's discussion of the poem "Mit einem Dritten sprechen" in Weigel, "Ingeborg Bachmanns Geist," p. 16.

135. MvT to JT, October 24, 1966, in *Das Politische und das Persönliche*, p. 462.

136. Thomas Flügge, *Zeitdienst: Sentimentale Chronik* (Berlin, 1996), p. 142. Flügge was an eyewitness. Interview with Thomas Flügge.

137. Hartwig, *Wer war Ingeborg Bachmann?*

138. JT to Aharon Agus, November 11, 1981, as above.

139. Unless otherwise noted, the paragraphs that follow are based on my interview with Janet Aviad.

140. *Divorcing*, p. 129.

141. *Divorcing*, p. 133.

142. Interview with Susannah Heschel.

143. JT to Janet Scheindlin, September 20, 1966, ZfL.

144. Interview with Daniel Bell.

145. Interview with Janet Aviad. On creating chaos, interview with Avishai Margalit.

146. Interview with Madeleine Dreyfus.

147. Interview with Ethan Taubes.

148. Walter Wreschner, "Rede auf Oberrabiner Dr. Zwi Taubes," copy in Archiv für Zeitgeschichte, ETH Zentrum, Zürich. Interview with Ita Shedletzky.

149. Untitled, *Jüdische Nachrichten*, January 20, 1966, in JUNA Geschäftsarchiv und Dokumentation der Pressestelle des SIG, Archiv für Zeitgeschichte, ETH Zentrum Zürich, JUNA-Archiv 2573; Roger Reiss, "Zum 30. Todestag von Rabbiner Zwi Taubes," *Jüdische Rundschau Maccabi*, January 25, 1996.

150. Interview with Gershon Greenberg.

151. JT to Aebi (probably Avraham) Weingort, August 12, 1966; JT to Miriam Weingort, January 18, 1967, ZfL.

152. JT to Celan, March 18, 1965; JT to Adorno, December 18, 1967, ZfL; interview with Daniel Bell.

153. Brentano, *Das Politische und das Persönliche*, p. 461.

154. Brentano, *Das Politische und das Persönliche*, p. 462.

155. Brentano, *Das Politische und das Persönliche*, pp. 462–63.

156. Brentano, *Das Politische und das Persönliche*, p. 462.

157. MvB to JT, October 30, 1965, in *Das Politische und das Persönliche*, pp. 464–65.

158. MvB to JT, November 5, 1955, in *Das Politische und das Persönliche*, p. 466. See on this also JT to Michael and Edith Wyschogrod, August 16, 1966, ZfL.

159. Interview with Gershon Greenberg.

160. Jacob Taubes, "Entzauberung der Theologie: Zu einem Porträt Overbecks," in Franz Overbeck, *Selbstbekenntnisse. Mit einer Einleitung von Jacob Taubes* (Frankfurt, 1966), p. 10, reprinted in *KzK*.

161. Interview with Harold Stahmer.

162. Jason Kirk to JT, April 4, 1966, ZfL.

163. JT to Joachim Lieber, April 13, 1966, PA.

164. MvB to JT, June 5, 1966, in *Das Politische und das Persönliche*, pp. 468–69. This woman seems to correspond to the character Lily Bodola in *Divorcing*, pp. 131–32.

165. "Kurator, August 22, 1966," PA.

166. Interview with Peter Gente.

167. JT to Dean Ralph S. Halford, August 12, 1966, ZfL.

168. JT to Jauss, July 31, 1966, ZfL.

169. Copies of the separation agreement and the divorce are in ETT, as well as PA.

170. JT to Edith and Michael Wyschogrod, September 14, 1966, ZfL.

171. JT to Gershon Greenberg, September 26, 1966, ZfL.

172. Interview with Harold Stahmer.

Chapter Ten. Berlin: Impresario of Theory

1. Interviews with Norman Podhoretz and Midge Decter.

2. JT to Robert Bellah, September 1, 1966; Robert Bellah to JT, September 8, 1966, ZfL.

3. JT to Bellah, September 21, 1966, ZfL.

4. JT to Miriam Weingort, September 1, 1966, ZfL.

5. Interview with Gershon Greenberg.

6. JT to Miriam Weingort, November 3, 1966, ZfL.

7. *Harvard Theological Review* to JT, December 26, 1967, ZfL.

8. Gershom Scholem, "Wider den Mythos vom deutsch-jüdischen 'Gespräch,'" in *Auf gespaltenem Pfad: Festschrift für Margarete Susman*, ed. Manfred Schlösser (Darmstadt, 1964), translated by Werner Dannhauser as "Against the Myth of the German-Jewish Dialogue," in Scholem, *On Jews and Judaism in Crisis*.

9. JT to Jean Bollack, November 3, 1966, ZfL.

10. JT to Rolf Tiedemann, February 24, 1967, ZfL.

11. JT to Moshe Botschko, January 16, 1967, ZfL.

12. Interview with Ethan Taubes.

13. Interview with John J. Gallahue; JT to Gershon Greenberg, October 11, 1968, ZfL; JT to Raimon Panikkar, November 2, 1969, ZfL.

14. Interview with Peter Gente.

15. Interview with Frigga Haug by Susan Neiman and Iris Nachum, unpublished.

16. Interview with Peter Wapnewski.

17. Dieter Henrich interview with Susan Neiman, unpublished.

18. Interview with Ethan Taubes.

19. Interview with Michael Wyschogrod.

20. Interview with Bernhard Lypp.

21. Interview by Neiman and Nachum with Frigga Haug, unpublished.

22. Henning Ritter, "Jacob Taubes. Verstehen, was da los ist," in Ritter, *Verehrte Denker*, pp. 27–65, pp. 34–35. Altogether a valuable portrait.

23. Interview with Peter Gente; Karl Freydorf (pseudonym), *Neuer Roter Katechismus* (Munich, 1968).

24. Interview with Richard Faber.

25. Interview with Gideon Freudenthal.

26. The term comes from interview with Winfried Menninghaus. Similarly, Rodolphe Gasché to author April 16, 2006.

27. Interview with Henning Ritter; Gasché to author.

28. Interview with Werner Hamacher.

29. Interviews with Tania Taubes and Peter McLaughlin.

30. Interview with Arnulf Conradi.

31. Interview with Bernhard Lypp.

32. Quoted in Flügge, *Zeitdienst*, p. 146.

33. Reprinted in *KzK*.

34. Interview with Uta Gerhardt.

35. Interview with Niko Oswald.

36. Interviews with Uta Gerhardt and Martin Ritter. When Marquardt's Habilitation was called into question, Taubes came to his defense, with a letter to *Die Welt*, "Die 'Pharisäer der kirchlichen Hochschule,'" *Die Welt*, March 3, 1972.

37. Interview with Hans Kippenberg.

38. Interview with Ruth Kahane-Geyer.

39. Interview with Richard Faber.

40. Interview with Martin Ritter.

41. Interview with Bernhard Lypp.

42. On Subversive Aktion, see Wolfgang Kraushaar, *Die blinden Flecken der 68er Bewegung* (Stuttgart, 2018), pp. 348ff.; Fichter and Lönnendonker, *Kleine Geschichte der SDS*, pp. 78–81.

43. Hans Kundnani, *Utopia or Auschwitz: Germany's 1968 Generation and the Holocaust* (New York, 2009), p. 35.

44. Gasché email and interview.

45. Gasché email and interview.

46. Vincent Descombes, "Le moment français de Nietzsche," in *Pourquoi nous ne sommes pas nietzschéens*, ed. Alain Boyer et al. (Paris, 1991), pp. 99–128.

47. Gasché email and interview.

48. FU Vorlesungsverzeichnis.

49. Interview with Wolf Lepenies.

50. Jacob Taubes, "Apocalpyse and Politics. Their Interaction in Transitional Communities," copy in possession of author from M. Voigt Papers. Also published on the website ZfL Blog, and in German translation in *AuP*, pp. 231–35.

51. Interview with Hans Kippenberg.

52. FU Vorlesungsverzeichnis, Winter Semester, 1973–74.

53. JT to Hans-Georg Gadamer, October 24, 1967, ZfL.

54. Interview with Werner Hamacher.

55. Peter Schäfer, "Jüdische Tradition: wesentliches Element unserer Gegenwart," in *Wie die Zukunft Wurzeln schlug: Aus der Forschung der Bundesrepublik Deutschland*, ed. Robert Gerwin (Berlin, 1989), pp. 91–97, p. 91.

56. MvB to JT, November 10, 1965, in *Das Politische und das Persönliche*, p. 463.

57. See the account of her son, Jonathan Awerbuch, "About Marianne: A Son's Perspective," in Marianne Awerbuch, *Erinnerungen aus einem streitbaren Leben* (Berlin, 2007), pp. 497–509.

58. Awerbuch, *Erinnerungen*, p. 421.

59. Awerbuch, *Erinnerungen*, pp. 458–60. Account confirmed by interview with Ruth Kahane-Geyer.

60. Awerbuch, *Erinnerungen*, p. 461.

61. Interviews with Martin Ritter, Marcel Marcus, and Niko Oswald.

62. JT to Eugen Kullmann, Brooklyn, June 16, 1966, ZfL; interview with Gershon Greenberg. On the disinformation campaign, see Thomas Rid, *Active Measures: The Secret History of Disinformation and Political Warfare* (New York, 2020).

63. Interview with Gershon Greenberg.

64. "Renaissance Man Amos Funkenstein Dies at Age 58," *Jewish News of Northern California*, November 17, 1995.

65. For a passing comparison of the two, see Samuel Moyn, "Amos Funkenstein on the Theological Origins of Historicism," *Journal of the History of Ideas* (2004), pp. 639–67, pp. 664–65.

66. See David Biale and Robert S. Westman, introduction to *Thinking Impossibilities: The Intellectual Legacy of Amos Funkenstein* (Toronto, 2008).

67. Interview with Gershon Greenberg.

68. Interview with Paul Mendes-Flohr.

69. "Geschichte und Geschichtsbewußtsein des Judentums seit der spanischen Exilierung."

70. "Apokalyptik und Gesetz: zur Eschatologie des Frühjudentums" (1966); "Apokalyptik und Politik—zur Soziologie des Messianismus" (1967); "Paulus als religionsgeschichtliche Problem," "Rabbinische Quellen Paulinischer Grundbegriffe" (1967).

71. Interview with Marcel Marcus.

72. Interviews with Marcel Marcus and Ruth Kahane-Geyer.

73. Schäfer, "Die Entwicklung der Judaistik in der Bundesrepublik Deutschland seit 1945," pp. 350–65; and "Judaistik—jüdische Wissenschaft in Deutschland heute," *Saeculum*, vol. 42 (1991), pp. 199–216.

74. Rachel Heuberger, "Jüdische Studien in Deutschland," in *Reisen durch das jüdische Deutschland*, ed. Micha Brumlik et al. (Cologne, 2006), pp. 382–91, p. 385.

75. Interview with Marcel Marcus.

76. Interview with Gershon Greenberg.

77. Interview with Jean Bollack. The incident is referred to in a letter of JT to Scholem, October 8, 1968, and Scholem to JT, October 20, 1968, *PdM*, p. 115.

78. Interview with Gershon Greenberg.

79. Scrawled in Hebrew in the margin of JT to Mrs. Weiss, November 3, 1970, in Scholem Papers, "Jacob Taubes." The reference is to *Major Trends in Jewish Mysticism*.

80. JT to George Lichtheim, April 3, 1970, ZfL.

81. Interview with David Rieff. Also Sontag, *As Consciousness Is Harnessed to Flesh*, p. 367.

82. For the institutional history of Poetik und Hermeneutik, I have drawn primarily upon Amslinger, *Eine Neue Form von Akademie*; and Petra Boden and Rüdiger Zill (ed.), *Poetik und Hermeneutik im Rückblick. Interviews mit Beteiligten* (Munich, 2017).

83. Interview with Helga Jauss-Meyer, in Boden and Zill, *Poetik und Hermeneutik im Rückblick*, p. 41.

84. Hans Ulrich Gumbrecht, "Modern Sinnfülle: Vierundzwanzig Jahre 'Poetik und Hermeneutik,'" *Frankfurt Allgemeine Zeitung*, September 16, 1987, pp. 35–36.

85. Henrich, *Sterbliche Gedanken*, p. 45: "Er war . . . im Gespäch mehr auflebend als in der Ausarbeitung"; interview with Hermann Lübbe.

86. Henrich, *Sterbliche Gedanken*, p. 45; also interview with Henrich in Boden and Zill, *Poetik und Hermeneutik im Rückblick*, p. 60.

87. Hans Robert Jauss to JT, October 22, 1963, and March 26, 1964, in Amslinger, *Eine Neue Form von Akademie*, pp. 283–84, 287.

88. Gumbrecht, "Modern Sinnfülle."

89. From the interview with Christian Meier in Boden and Zill, *Poetik und Hermeneutik im Rückblick*, p. 207.

90. Much of the information in this paragraph is from Amslinger, *Neue Form von Akademie*, p. 25.

91. Ahlrich Meyer, "Hermeneutik des Verschweigens," *Neue Zürcher Zeitung*, June 23, 2016; Joachim Güntner, "Akademisches Aushängeschild mit braunen Flecken," *Neue Zürcher Zeitung*, February 26, 2015.

92. Amslinger, *Neue Form von Akademie*, p. 49.

93. Interview with Helga Jauss-Meyer, in Boden and Zill, *Poetik und Hermeneutik im Rückblick*, p. 52.

94. Amslinger, *Neue Form von Akademie*, pp. 93–95.

95. Amslinger, *Neue Form von Akademie*, pp. 102–3.

96. Amslinger, *Neue Form von Akademie*, p. 160.

97. JT to Jauss, March 22, 1965, in Amslinger, *Neue Form von Akademie*, p. 292.

98. Jauss to JT, June 18, 1965, in Amslinger, *Neue Form von Akademie*, p. 294.

99. See for example Jauss, "Wissenschaftsgeschichtliche Memorabilien," in Amslinger, *Neue Form von Akademie*, p. 330.

100. Interview with Annette Michelson.

101. JT to Blumenberg, September 20, 1966, in *Blumenberg-Taubes*, pp. 100–103.

102. "Emil Cioran," Wikipedia, last updated November 30, 2020, https://de.wikipedia.org/wiki/Emil_Cioran.

103. Jacob Taubes, "Noten zum Surrealismus," in *Immanente Ästhetik/Ästhetische Reflexion: Lyrik als Paradigma der Moderne. Kolloquium Köln 1964 Vorlagen und Verhandlungen*, ed. Wolfgang Iser (Munich, 1966), pp. 139–43, reprinted in *KzK*.

104. Taubes in Iser, *Immanente Ästhetik*, p. 433.

105. Iser, *Immanente Ästhetik*, p. 435.

106. Iser, *Immanente Ästhetik*, pp. 437–39.

107. Jacob Taubes, "Der dogmatische Mythos der Gnosis," in *Terror und Spiel: Probleme der Mythenrezeption*, ed. Manfred Fuhrmann (Munich, 1971), pp. 145–57, reprinted in *KzK*.

108. Jacob Taubes, "Die Rechtfertigung des Hässlichen in Urchristlicher Tradition," in *Die Nicht Mehr Schönen Künste: Grenzphänomene des Ästhetischen*, ed. H. R. Jauss (Munich, 1968), pp. 169–86, reprinted in *KzK*.

109. Jacob Taubes, "Vom Adverb 'nichts' zum Substantiv 'das Nichts'. Überlegungen zu Heideggers Frage nach dem Nichts," in *Positionen der Negativität*, ed. Harald Weinrich (Munich, 1975), pp. 141–54, p. 151, reprinted in *KzK*.

110. Jacob Taubes, "Von Fall zu Fall. Erkenntnistheoretische Reflexion zur Geschichte vom Sündenfall," in *Text und Applikation. Theologie, Jurisprudenz und Literaturwissenschaft im Hermeneutischen Gespräch*, ed. Manfred Fuhrmann, Hans Robert Jauss, and Wolfhart Pannenberg (Munich, 1981), pp. 111–16, reprinted in *AuP*.

111. Jacob Taubes, "Zum Problem einer theologischen Methode der Interpretation," in Fuhrmann, Jauss, and Pannenberg, *Text und Applikation*, p. 580, reprinted in *AuP*.

112. Jacob Taubes, "Die Welt als Fiktion und Vorstellung. Konvergenzen der Realismus-Debatte in Wissenschaft und Kunst," in *Funktionen des Fiktiven*, ed. Dieter Henrich und Wolfgang Iser (Munich, 1983), pp. 417–23, reprinted in *AuP*.

113. Interview with Harald Weinrich, in Boden and Zill, *Poetik und Hermeneutik im Rückblick*, p. 141.

114. Interview with Renate Lachmann, in Boden and Zill, *Poetik und Hermeneutik im Rückblick*, p. 289.

115. Interview with Hermann Lübbe; see also the interview with Lübbe in Boden and Zill, *Poetik und Hermeneutik im Rückblick*, p. 165.

116. Interview with Hans Ulrich Gumbrecht, in Boden and Zill, *Poetik und Hermeneutik im Rückblick*, p. 345.

117. Interview with Hermann Lübbe.

118. Interview with Anselm Haverkamp, in Boden and Zill, *Poetik und Hermeneutik im Rückblick*, p. 375.

119. Interview with Christian Meier, in Boden and Zill, *Poetik und Hermeneutik im Rückblick*, p. 223; Christian Meier to JT, September 11, 1969, ZfL.

120. Interview with Christian Meier, in Boden and Zill, *Poetik und Hermeneutik im Rückblick*, p. 224.

121. Interview with Dieter Henrich; Henrich, "In Erinnerung an JACOB TAUBES," in *Individualität*, ed. Manfred Frank and Anselm Haverkamp (Munich, 1988), p. ix. For Blumenberg's rejected obituary, see Hans Blumenberg, "Gedanken zu einem Nachruf auf Jacob Taubes" (1987), published in *Blumenberg-Taubes*, pp. 283–84.

122. JT to Norman Birnbaum, April 26, 1965, ZfL.

123. JT to Ernst Nolte, January 22, 1965, Nolte Papers.

124. JT to Thomas Nipperdey, January 1, 1967; Nipperdey to JT, February 10, 1967, ZfL.

125. JT to Jacob Neusner, December 6, 1967, ZfL; interview with Hans Kippenberg.

126. Gasché email to author.

127. JT to Hans Blumenberg, December 14, 1966, ZfL.

128. For information on Feyerabend, see John Preston, "Paul Feyerabend," in *Stanford Encyclopedia of Philosophy* (Fall 2020 edition), ed. Edward N. Zalta.

129. JT to Karl Popper, November 24, 1966, ZfL.

130. JT to Friedrich A. von Hayek, November 24, 1966; Hayek to JT, November 28, 1966; JT to Hayek, November 29, 1966, ZfL.

131. Gasché email; Paul Feyerabend, *Killing Time* (Chicago, 1995), pp. 131–32.

132. Interview with Renate Schlesier, who attended.

133. Preston, "Paul Feyerabend," p. 40; Gasché email.

134. JT to Noam Chomsky, February 13, 1969; Chomsky to JT, February 24, 1969, ZfL.

Chapter Eleven. The Apocalyptic Moment

1. Peter Szondi, *Über eine "Freie (d.h. freie) Universität": Stellungsnahmen eines Philologen* (Frankfurt, 1973).

2. Interview with Eberhard Lämmert.

3. "Offener Brief von 6 FU-Professoren," *Der Tagesspiegel*, July 28, 1965.

4. Nikolai Wehrs, *Protest der Professoren: Der "Bund Freiheit der Wissenschaft" in den 1970er Jahren* (Göttingen, 2014), p. 53.

5. Quoted in Wehrs, *Protest der Professoren*, p. 54.

6. Wehrs, *Protest der Professoren*, p. 54; Uwe Schlicht, *Vom Burschenschafter bis zum Sponti* (Berlin, 1980), p. 91; Nick Thomas, *Protest Movements in 1960s West Germany* (Oxford, 2003), pp. 62–63. The quotation is from Gretchen Dutschke, *Wir hatten ein barbarisches, schönes Leben. Rudi Dutschke. Eine Biographie* (Cologne, 1996), p. 103.

7. Ulrich Enzensberger, *Die Jahre der Kommune I. Berlin 1967–1969* (Cologne, 2006), pp. 94–95. On the events themselves, see Thomas, *Protest Movements*, pp. 78ff.

8. Hans Blumenberg, "Nachhake(l)n auf einen Nachruf—privatissime" (1987), in *Blumenberg-Taubes*, p. 291.

9. Jacob Taubes, "An den Regierenden Bürgermeister von Berlin, Heinrich Albertz," in *Demonstrationen. Ein Berliner Modell. Entstehung der demokratischen Opposition (Voltaire Flugschrift 10)*, ed. Bernard Larsson (Berlin, 1967), pp. 95–98, reprinted in *AuP*.

10. "Rektor der FU sagte die Teilnahme ab," *Berliner Morgenpost*, May 6, 1967; "Rede von Professor Dr. Jacob Taubes auf der Vollversammlung der Studenten aller Fakultäten am 5.5.1967," in *AuP*, pp. 392–94.

11. Wolfgang Kraushaar, *Die Bombe im Jüdischen Gemeindehaus* (Hamburg, 2005), pp. 269ff.

12. Jacob Taubes, "Surrealistische Provokation. Ein Gutachten zur Anklageschrift in Prozess Langhans-Teufel über die Flugblätter der 'Kommune I,'" *Merkur: Deutsche Zeitschrift für europäisches Denken*, vol. 21 (1967), pp. 1069–79, reprinted in *AuP*.

13. Horst Mahler to JT, July 26, 1967, ZfL.

14. Lönnendonker and Fichter (ed.), *Hochschule im Umbruch: Teil IV: (1964–1967)* (Berlin, 1975), p. 159. Also Keßler, *Ossip K. Flechtheim*, p. 147. On the East German role in funding and steering the Republikaner clubs, see Elliot Neaman, *Free Radicals: Agitators, Hippies, Urban Guerillas, and Germany's Youth Revolt of the 1960s and 1970s* (New York, 2016), ch. 2 and footnote 97 therein.

15. JT to Horst Mahler, July 4, 1967, ZfL.

16. JT to Edith Wyschogrod, May 31, 1967. Similarly JT to Ernst Erdös, May 26, 1967, ZfL.

17. On the Ohnesorg murder and the Stasi affiliations of the policeman who killed him, see Neaman, *Free Radicals*, ch. 2.

18. Siegward Lönnendonker et al. (ed.), *Freie Universität Berlin 1948–1973. Hochschule im Umbruch: Teil V: (1967–1969)* (Berlin, 1975), p. 12.

19. Lönnendonker et al. (ed.), *Freie Universität Berlin 1948–1973. Teil V*, p. 19; Flügge, *Zeitdienst*, pp. 147–49; Dutschke, *Wir hatten ein barbarisches, schönes Leben*, p. 132.

20. Published posthumously as Alexandre Kojève, *Essai d'une histoire raisonée de la philosophie païenne* (Paris, 1969–73).

21. Kojève to Traugott König, May 29, 1967, ZfL.

22. JT to Kojève, June 16, 1967, ZfL.

23. Recounted in *ACS*, p. 69.

24. Marcuse to JT, June 28, 1967, ZfL.

25. https://www.marcuse.org/herbert/pubs/60spubs/67endutopia/67EndUtopiaProbViol.htm.

26. Herbert Marcuse et al., *Das Ende der Utopie* (Berlin, 1967), pp. 14, 16; English translation taken from "The End of Utopia," online as above.

27. Marcuse, *Das Ende der Utopie*, pp. 23, 29.

28. Löwenthal in Marcuse, *Das Ende der Utopie*, pp. 85–88.

29. Richard Löwenthal, *Der romantische Rückfall* (Stuttgart, 1970); see also Kraushaar, *Die blinden Flecken*, p. 42.

30. Marcuse, *Das Ende der Utopie*, pp. 142–47. The SDS had been raising such funds; see Thomas, *Protest Movements*, pp. 84–85.

31. Günter C. Behrmann, "Zwei Monate Kulturrevolution," in Albrecht et al., *Die intellektuelle Gründung der Bundesrepublik*, pp. 335–36.

32. Taubes quoted in "Hilfe von Arbeitslosen," *Der Spiegel*, June 12, 1967.

33. Letter of Rainer Gangl, President, Fortschrittliche Studentenschaft Zürich to JT, April 18, 1968 (recounting a conversation from the previous year), ZfL.

34. JT to Hans Robert Jauss, October 24, 1967, ZfL.

35. Gollwitzer and Taubes, "Öffentliche Erklärung," *Morgenpost*, February 6, 1968.

36. Wolfgang Kraushaar (ed.), *Die 68er-Bewegung International: Eine illustrierte Chronik, 1960-1969*, vol. 3 (Stuttgart, 2018).

37. "Fast der alte," *Der Spiegel*, May 20, 1968.

38. "Entfremdung verspürt," *Der Spiegel*, May 20, 1968.

39. Interview with Peter Wapnewski; Peter Wapnewski, *Mit dem anderen Auge. Erinnerungen 1959-2000* (Berlin, 2006), pp. 60–61. Susanne Leinemann, "Der wilde Sommer der Uni-Revolte," *Berliner Morgenpost*, April 10, 2018.

40. "Professoren besorgt über die weitere Entwicklung," *Die Welt*, December 6, 1968.

41. Edith Wyschogrod, "Religion as Life and Text: Postmodern Re-configurations," in *The Craft of Religious Studies*, ed. Jon R. Stone (New York, 2016), pp. 240–57, p. 256.

42. JT to Ernst Tugendhat, June 9, 1967, ZfL.

43. Interview with Eberhard Lämmert.

44. Interview with John J. Gallahue.

45. Interview with Peter Schäfer.

46. JT to Adorno, March 13, 1968, ZfL.

47. Jacob Taubes, "Kultur und Ideologie," in *Spätkapitalismus oder Industriegesellschaft?*, ed. Theodor Adorno (Stuttgart, 1969), pp. 117–38, reprinted in *KzK*, pp. 283–304, esp. p. 291.

48. Jacob Taubes, "Das Unbehagen an der Institution," in *Das beschädigte Leben*, ed. Alexander Mitscherlich (Grenzach, 1969), pp. 95–107, revised version in *Zur Theorie der Institutionen*, ed. Helmut Schelsky (Düsseldorf, 1970), pp. 68–76.

49. Interview with Richard Faber.

50. JT to Unseld and Habermas, May, 1968, Suhrkamp Archiv.

51. "Rechenschaftsbericht," reprinted in *PROTEST! Literatur um 1968*, ed. Ulrich Ott and Friedlich Pfäfflin (Marbach, 1998), pp. 517–20.

52. JT to B. Beckmann of Fortschrittliche Studentenschaft Zürich, July 1, 1968, ZfL.

53. JT to Fortschrittliche Studentenschaft Zürich, November 21, 1968, ZfL.

54. Interview with Marianne and Sigi Weinberg.

55. Interview with Eberhard Lämmert. The following is drawn primarily from Schlicht, *Vom Burschenschafter bis zum Sponti*, pp. 91ff. and from my interview with Uwe Schlicht.

56. Schlicht, *Vom Burschenschafter bis zum Sponti*, p. 90.

57. Wolfgang Nitsch et al., *Hochschule in der Demokratie* (Berlin, 1965). See also Wehrs, *Protest der Professoren*, p. 53.

58. Schlicht, *Vom Burschenschafter bis zum Sponti*.

59. James F. Tent, *The Free University of Berlin: A Political History* (Bloomington, IN, 1988), p. 406; also, interview with Uwe Schlicht.

60. Tent, *Free University*, p. 423.

61. Wehrs, *Protest der Professoren*, p. 152; Tent, *Free University*, pp. 354–55.

62. "Professor Taubes warnt vor Aussperrung," *Der Tagesspiegel*, April 22, 1969.

63. Jacob Taubes, "Um die Zukunft der FU," *Der Tagesspiegel*, May 4, 1969.

64. "Erklärung der Philosophischen Fakultät der FU: Zur Kontroverse zwischen Professor von Simson und Professor Taubes," *Der Tagesspiegel*, May 8, 1969.

65. Letter of Wolfgang Werth, *Der Tagesspiegel*, May, 1969.

66. JT to Ernst Erdös, May 26, 1967, ZfL.

67. Shapira, *Israel: A History*, pp. 295ff.

68. Kraushaar, *Blinde Flecken*, pp. 102ff.; Kundnani, *Utopia*, pp. 48ff.; Gerd Koenen, "Mythen des 20. Jahrhunderts," in *Neue Antisemitismus?: Eine globale Debatte*, ed. Doron Rabinovici et al. (Frankfurt, 2004), pp. 168–90; and Jeffrey Herf, *Undeclared Wars with Israel: East Germany and the West German Far Left 1967–1989* (Cambridge, 2016).

69. Landmann to JT, September 5, 1967, ZfL.

70. Discussed in Kraushaar, *Blinde Flecken*, p. 106.

71. Michael Landmann, *Das Israelpseudos der Pseudolinken* (Berlin, 1971). A new edition was published in 2013, the topic having lost none of its contemporary relevance.

72. JT to George Lichtheim, April 3, 1970, ZfL.

73. JT to Landmann, October 11, 1968, ZfL.

74. Jacob Taubes, "NOTABENE, Aus gegebenem Anlaß," Sender Freies Berlin, Drittes Programm, Sendung: 25 Dezember, 1969, IH.

75. See Herf, *Undeclared Wars*, pp. 96–107; as well as Kraushaar, *Die Bombe im jüdischen Gemeindehaus*.

76. "Schuldschein," February 13, 1969, PA.

77. JT to Inge and Herbert Marcuse, July 4, 1969, Herbert Marcuse Archiv.

78. Loos to President der FU, November 26, 1969, PA.

Chapter Twelve. Deradicalization and Crisis, 1969–75

1. Interview with Richard Locke.

2. Pareigis, "Die Schriftstellerin Susan Taubes."

3. Interviews with Elsa First, Krister Stendahl, and Nina Holton.

4. *Divorcing*, p. 73.

5. Sontag, *As Consciousness Is Harnessed to Flesh*, pp. 261, 371. See also Pareigis, *Susan Taubes*, pp. 392–93.

6. For a portrait of Susan Taubes in this period, slightly fictionalized as "Julia," see Sontag's story, "Debriefing" (1973), in Sontag, *I, Etcetera*; interview with Nina Holton.

7. Sontag, *As Consciousness Is Harnessed to Flesh*, p. 436.

8. *Divorcing*, p. 9.

9. *Divorcing*, pp. 22, 45, 60, 48, 129.

10. *Divorcing*, p. 12.

11. *Divorcing*, pp. 49, 129.

12. *Divorcing*, pp. 37, 62, 132, 46.

13. *Divorcing*, p. 46.

14. Interview with Richard Locke.

15. Hugh Kenner, review of *Divorcing*, *New York Times*, November 2, 1969.

16. "Certificate of Death for Susan Taubes," ETT; "Suicide Off L.I. Is Identified as a Woman Writer," *New York Times*, November 9, 1969; Lena Zade, "'Ja, ich bin

tot': Zum 40. Todestag der Religionsphilosophin und Schriftstellerin Susan Taubes,"
Jüdische Zeitung, November 2009.

17. Pareigis, *Susan Taubes*, p. 299.

18. Interview with Tania Taubes.

19. Interview with Irving Kristol and Gertrude Himmelfarb.

20. Susan Sontag, *The Benefactor* (New York, 1963), pp. 89, 92–93.

21. JT to George Lichtheim, October 9, 1969, ZfL.

22. Lichtheim to JT, September 27, 1969, ZfL.

23. JT to Lichtheim, October 9, 1969, ZfL.

24. Interview with Gregory Callimanopulos.

25. Susan Sontag, *Duet for Cannibals* (New York, 1970), back cover.

26. Information on the NY Film Festival premiere comes from Schreiber, *Susan Sontag: A Biography*, pp. 115–16.

27. Sontag, *As Consciousness Is Harnessed to Flesh*, p. 336.

28. Schreiber, *Susan Sontag: A Biography*, p. 121.

29. Susan Sontag, *Brother Carl: A Screenplay* (New York, 1974).

30. "Professor Taubes Vorsitzender eines FU-Fachbereichsrats," *Der Tagesspiegel*, June 16, 1970.

31. Wolf Lepenies, "Twenty-Five Years of Social Science and Social Change: A Personal Memoir," in *Schools of Thought: Twenty-Five Years of Interpretive Social Science*, ed. Joan Scott and Debra Keates (Princeton, NJ, 2001), pp. 25–40; and interview with Wolf Lepenies.

32. Lepenies, "Twenty-Five Years of Social Science and Social Change," p. 28.

33. Lönnendonker and Fichter, *Freie Universität Berlin 1948–1973*, vol. 6, pp. 43–45; Tent, *Free University*, p. 368.

34. "Aus Protest zurückgetreten," December 10, 1970 (newspaper clipping, source unclear, press files of the FU); "Linke Professoren sehen Kampagne. Vorsitzende eines FU-Fachbereichsrats zurückgetreten," *Der Tagesspiegel*, December 3, 1970.

35. "Rücktritte im FB 11," FU-Info 14/70, December 8, 1970. Copy in Hoover, Notgemeinschaft 5.8.3/0164 .

36. "Der Senator graut," *Der Spiegel*, March 1, 1971, p. 170.

37. As reported in "Marxisten: Kleine Chance," *Der Spiegel*, February 15, 1971.

38. "Streit über eine Berufung an die Freie Universität Berlin," *Frankfurter Allgemeine Zeitung*, March 3, 1971.

39. Jacob Taubes, "Über einen Handlungsreisenden in Sachen Marxismus," *EXTRA-Dienst*, Nr. 17/V, March 3, 1971, p. 7.

40. JT to Werner Stein, February 24, 1971, IH.

41. Uwe Schlicht, "Hans Heinz Holz wird nicht berufen," *Der Tagesspiegel*, March 27, 1971, p. 9.

42. "Dr. Holz will nach Marburg gehen," *Der Tagesspiegel*, April 24, 1971, p. 9.

43. JT, "An den Fachbereichsrat des Fachbereichs 'Philosophie und Sozialwissenschaften,' Betr: Gasteinladung der Abteilung Hermeneutik für das Sommersemester 1971," January 11, 1971. On Margherita's initiative, see MvB to Kreibich, January 22, 1971; and JT to Marcuse, January 19, 1971, IH.

44. "Widersprüche um FU-Einladung: Fachbererich will Gastprofessuren für Angela Davis und Cleaver," *Der Tagesspiegel*, January 30, 1971.

45. "Angela Davis an die FU: Schütz intervenierte bei Kreibich," *EXTRA-Dienst*, January 16, 1971.

46. MvB to Kreibich, January 22, 1971; JT to Kreibich, January 22, 1971, IH.

47. Kreibich to JT, January 23, 1971, IH.

48. JT to Kreibich, January 26, 1971, IH.

49. "Widersprüche um FU-Einladung."

50. Uwe Wesel to Angela Davis, c/o Herbert Marcuse, February 1, 1971, IH.

51. *Berliner Morgenpost*, April 27, 1971.

52. Interview with Hanns Zischler.

53. Tent, *Free University*, pp. 290–312.

54. Walter Brückmann, "Agitator hinter den Kulissen," *Berliner Morgenpost*, December 6, 1967, p. 7.

55. "Führende SDS-Mitglieder zur Schulung in Cuba," August 2, 1968, *Die Welt*.

56. "Anklage gegen ehemaligen FU-Konventvorsitzenden," DPA July 3, 1969, file, Notgemeinschaft Papers, 5.8.2/ Lefèvre, Hoover.

57. JT to Habermas; JT to Odo Marquard, both September 19, 1968, ZfL.

58. Gerd Koenen, *Das Rote Jahrzehnt: Unsere kleine deutsche Kulturrevolution, 1967–1977* (Cologne, 2001), pp. 198ff.

59. This according to a confidential (*vertraulich*) memorandum of Michael Landmann, "Anamnese zum 'Institut für Philosophie und zum Fachbereich 11,'" part of a letter to Werner Stein, July 14, 1975, in "Berlin-Notgemeinschaft" 5.8.3 (Landmann), Hoover.

60. Heinrich Kleiner, Vertreter der Wiss. Mitarbeiter to Fachbereichsrat, July 6, 1970, copy in Notgemeinschaft, 5.8.3/0161, Hoover.

61. "Der Geschäftsführende Direktor und die unterzeichneten Mitglieder des Lehrkörpers des Philosophischen Seminars," August 7, 1970, in Notgemeinschaft, 5.8.3./0161, Hoover.

62. Landmann to JT (Vorsitzenden des Fachbereichs 11), November 30, 1970, in Notgemeinschaft, Hoover.

63. JT, "Erstgutachten zur Dissertation von Wolfgang Lefèvre," dated October 22, 1970, 20 pages, in Hoover, Notgemeinschaft, 5.8.3./0161.

64. "Assistentenstelle als Prämie für Agitation," *Die Welt*, December 29, 1970.

65. "Yankee am Hof," *Der Spiegel*, January 10, 1971, pp. 51–53.

66. "Fachbereichsrat nimmt Dissertation Lefèvre's an," *Der Tagesspiegel*, January 21, 1971.

67. Landespressedienst Berlin #27, February 9, 1971, in Notgemeinschaft, 5.8.3./0161, Hoover.

68. JT to Mittelstrass, January 26, 1979, ZfL.

69. JT to Habermas, July 22, 1970, ZfL.

70. Interview with Jürgen Habermas.

71. This according to the memorandum of Michael Landmann, "Anamnese zum 'Institut für Philosophie und zum Fachbereich 11,'" cited above.

72. Interview with Wolf Lepenies.

73. Stefan Müller-Doohm, *Adorno: A Biography* (Cambridge, 2005), ch. 19.

74. JT to Peter Szondi, August 17, 1969, Szondi Nachlass, DLA.

75. See Specter, *Habermas: An Intellectual Biography*, pp. 111ff.

76. On the Hanover conference, see Kundnani, *Utopia*, pp. 44–45.

77. Müller-Doohm, *Jürgen Habermas*, pp. 153ff.

78. On Krahl, see Koenen, *Das rote Jahrzehnt*, pp. 141ff.; Koenen, "Der transzendental Obdachlose—Hans-Jürgen Krahl," *Zeitschrift für Ideengeschichte*, vol. 2, no. 3, pp. 5–22; Kundnani, *Utopia*, pp. 57ff.

79. Kundnani, *Utopia*, p. 57.

80. Jens Benicke, *Von Adorno zu Mao* (Freiburg, 2010), p. 40; Kraushaar, *Blinde Flecken*, p. 350.

81. See on this theme Kundnani, *Utopia*, pp. 18–19 and passim; Jan-Werner Müller, "1968 as Event, Milieu, and Ideology," in *German Ideologies since 1945*, ed. Müller (New York, 2003), pp. 117–43.

82. Koenen, *Rote Jahrzehnt*, p. 143; Benicke, *Von Adorno zu Mao*, pp. 54–55.

83. Kundnani, *Utopia*, pp. 59–60.

84. On his speech during the June 1967 congress in Hanover, see Fichter and Lönnendonker, *Kleine Geschichte der SDS*, pp. 106–8. Jürgen Habermas, "Die Scheinrevolution und ihre Kinder—Sechs Thesen über Taktik, Ziele und Situationsanalysen der oppositionellen Jugend," in *Die Linke antwortet Jürgen Habermas*, ed. Oskar Negt (Frankfurt, 1968), pp. 5ff., quoted in Benicke, *Adorno zu Mao*, p. 57.

85. Müller-Doohm, *Jürgen Habermas*, p. 155.

86. Quoted in Benicke, *Von Adorno zu Mao*, p. 64.

87. Jürgen Habermas, "Odyssee der Vernunft in die Natur," *Die Zeit*, September 12, 1969.

88. Müller-Doohm, *Jürgen Habermas*, p. 165.

89. JT to Habermas, September 17, 1969, ZfL.

90. JT to Habermas, April 3, 1970, ZfL. On the background, see Müller-Doohm, *Jürgen Habermas*, pp. 141–54.

91. Interview with Habermas.

92. On Vesper and Ensslin, see Kundnani, *Utopia*, pp. 64–67; Butz Peters, *Tödlicher Irrtum: Die Geschichte der RAF* (Berlin, 2004), pp. 70ff.

93. Vesper to JT, March 20, 1967, ZfL.

94. JT to Arthur A. Cohen, October 2, 1977, Cohen Papers.

95. JT to Traugott König, December 20, 1966, ZfL.

96. Vesper to JT, May 27, 1967, ZfL.

97. Vesper to JT, January 31, 1968, ZfL.

98. Gerd Koenen, *Vesper, Ensslin, Baader: Urszenen des deutschen Terrorismus* (Cologne, 2003), pp. 126–27.

99. Information from Susan Neiman.

100. JT to Arthur A. Cohen, October 2, 1977, Cohen Papers.

101. Koenen, *Vesper, Ensslin, Baader*; Kundnani, *Utopia*, pp. 66–67.

102. On Mahler's ideological development, see George Michael, "The Ideological Evolution of Horst Mahler: The Far Left-Extreme Right Synthesis," *Studies in Conflict and Terrorism*, vol. 32, no. 4 (2009), pp. 346–66.

103. Horst Mahler, "Rede von Gericht," quoted in Wolfgang Kraushaar, "Der Antisemitismus steckt im Antizionismus wie das 'Gewitter in der Wolke': Zur Entstehung der Israelfeindschaft in der radikalen Linken der Bundesrepublik Deutschland," paper presented at the annual meeting of the German Studies Association, Oakland, October 2010.

104. Interview with Tania Taubes.

105. Interviews with Gershon Greenberg, Ruth Kahane-Geyer, and Marcel Marcus.

106. Nicolas Berg, "Ein Außenseiter der Holocaustforschung—Joseph Wulf (1912–1974) im Historikerdiskurs der Bundesrepublik," in *Leipziger Beiträge zur jüdischen Geschichte und Kultur* (Göttingen, 2003), vol. 1, pp. 311–46; and Berg, *Der Holocaust und die westdeutschen Historiker* (Göttingen, 2004), pp. 447ff.

107. Leschnitzer to Wulf, October 15, 1970, Leschnitzer Papers, Leo Baeck Institute, NYC.

108. FU Vorlesungsverzeichnis, Sommersemester, 1970.

109. Klaus Kempter, *Joseph Wulf: Ein Historikerschicksal in Deutschland* (Göttingen, 2013), pp. 362–64.

110. "Gespräch mit Irmingard Staeuble," and "Gespräch mit Eberhard Lämmert," in *Das Politische und das Persönliche*, p. 372–73.

111. See Wolfgang Fritz Haug, "Nachwort zur zweiten Auflage: Das Ende des hilflosen Antifaschismus," in Haug, *Der hilflose Antifaschismus*, 3rd ed. (Frankfurt, 1970); Kraushaar, *Die blinden Flecken*, p. 175ff.; and Berg, *Der Holocaust und die westdeutschen Historiker*, pp. 438ff.

112. See "Der Plan für ein NS-Dokumentationszentrum," *Neue Zürcher Zeitung*, September 12, 1970, reprinted in *Das Politische und das Persönliche*, p. 383.

113. Wehrs, *Protest der Professoren*, pp. 149–50.

114. Wehrs, *Protest der Professoren*, p. 281.

115. Wehrs, *Protest der Professoren*, p. 150.

116. Quoted in Hans Maier, "Als Professor im Jahr 1968," in *Die politische Meinung*, no. 378, May 2001, pp. 17–23, p. 19.

117. Wehrs, *Protest der Professoren*, p. 153.

118. Richard Löwenthal, "Freie Universität auf den schiefen Ebene," *Der Tagesspiegel*, January 30, 1970, cited in Wehrs, *Protest der Professoren*, p. 169.

119. "Professorenflucht aus Berlin," *Bild-Zeitung*, December 5, 1969, quoted in Wehrs, *Protest der Professoren*, p. 283.

120. Nipperdey to Stein, October 31, 1971, quoted in Wehrs, *Protest der Professoren*, p. 284. Stein, a man of many parts, was a professor of biophysics at the FU, and also author of a synoptic historical lexicon.

121. Wehrs, *Protest der Professoren*, pp. 283–84. For a more sympathetic analysis, see Till Kinzel, "Der 'Bund Freiheit der Wissenschaft' und die 'Notgemeinschaft für eine freie Universität' im Widerstand gegen die Achtundsechziger," in *Die 68er und ihre Gegner*, ed. Hartmuth Becker (Graz, 2003), pp. 112–36. For an overview of the publications of the organization, see Bund Freiheit der Wissenschaft, *Notizen zur Geschichte des Bundes Freiheit der Wissenschaft* (Berlin, 2001).

122. Wehrs, *Protest der Professoren*, pp. 168, 227–28, and passim.

123. Jerry Z. Muller, "German Neoconservatism and the History of the Bonn Republic, 1968 to 1985," *German Politics and Society*, vol. 18, no. 1 (Spring 2000), pp. 1–32.

124. Wehrs, *Protest der Professoren*, pp. 312–13. See also "Professor Taubes und Dr. Matakas zur Kontroverse," *Der Tagesspiegel*, November 22, 1970.

125. Wehrs, *Protest der Professoren*, p. 313.

126. Wehrs, *Protest der Professoren*, pp. 316–17.

127. Wehrs, *Protest der Professoren*, pp. 321–22. On Brentano, see unpublished Neiman interview with Michael Theunissen.

128. "Zwei weitere Vizepräsidenten für FU," *Der Tagesspiegel*, May 14, 1970.

129. "Vizepräsidentin der FU Berlin für sozialistische Universität," *Die Welt*, November 13, 1970. For an account from Brentano's supporters in the Aktionsgruppe Hochschullehrer, see "Chronologie eines Skandals," in *Das Politische und das Persönliche*, pp. 384ff.; Wehrs, *Protest der Professoren*, pp. 286–87.

130. *Das Politische und das Persönliche*, pp. 390–91; and "Terrible Nichte," *Der Spiegel*, December 12, 1970.

131. *Das Politische und das Persönliche*, pp. 388ff.

132. "Ermittlung gegen Frau von Brentano eingestellt," *Der Tagesspiegel*, December 24, 1970.

133. Karoll Stein, "Fischer im trüben," *Die Zeit*, December 18, 1970.

134. Norbert Hinske, December 12, 1970, unpublished letter to *Die Zeit*, in Notgemeinschaft, box 5.1.1/0188b, Hoover.

135. "An die Macht," *Der Spiegel*, November 28, 1971, reprinted in *Das Politische und das Persönliche*, pp. 396–99.

136. Uwe Wesel, *Die verspielte Revolution: 1968 und die Folgen* (Munich, 2002), p. 201.

137. "Müssen Professoren staatstreu sein? FU-Vizepräsidentin Margherita von Brentano und Senator Stein diskutieren über Marxisten auf Lehrstühlen," *Der Spiegel*, February 14, 1972, reprinted in *Das Politische und das Persönliche*, pp. 400–407, p. 405.

138. On Mandel and the Trotskyites, see Koenen, *Rote Jahrzehnt*, pp. 276–80.

139. "Alle wegfegen," *Der Spiegel*, February 28, 1972.

140. "Erklärung," in *Das Politische und das Persönliche*, pp. 407–8.

141. Interview with Hans Dieter Zimmermann; Zimmermann to JT, July 13, 1972; JT to Zimmermann, July 26, 1972; JT to Werner Stein, July 27, 1972; "KBS" to Zimmermann, November 20, 1972; Zimmermann to JT, March 20, 1973, all ZfL.

142. JT to Lübbe, February 28, 1977; Lübbe to JT, April 19, 1977; JT to Zürcher Kantonalbank, October 31, 1977; JT to Habermas, February 17, 1977, all ZfL.

143. Heller, *Der Affe auf dem Fahrrad*, pp. 326–27.

144. Interview with Agnes Heller.

145. Heller, *Der Affe auf dem Fahrrad*, p. 371.

146. Interview with Agnes Heller. Taubes refers to the meeting in a letter to György Márkus, July 5, 1977, ZfL.

147. Noam Zadoff, *Gershom Scholem: From Berlin to Jerusalem and Back*, trans. Jeffrey Green (Waltham, MA, 2018), pp. 220–21. Scholem's essays were collected and published as *Walter Benjamin und sein Engel: Vierzehn Aufsätze und kleine Beiträge*, ed. Rolf Tiedemann (Frankfurt, 1983).

148. Zadoff, *Gershom Scholem*, p. 222, 227–28.

149. Walter Benjamin, Gershom Scholem, *Briefwechsel 1933–1940* (Frankfurt, 1980).

150. See Elke Morlok und Frederek Musall, "Die Geschichte *seiner* Freundschaft: Gershom Scholem und die Benjamin-Rezeption in der Bonner Republik," in *Gershom Scholem in Deutschland*, ed. Gerold Necker et al. (Tübingen, 2014), pp. 122, 136.

151. Helmut Heißenbüttels, "Vom Zeugnis des Fortlebens in der Literatur," *Merkur*, March 21, 1967, pp. 232–44; Peter Hamm, "Unter den Neueren der Wichtigste: Walter Benjamins Briefe," *Frankfurter Hefte*, no. 22 (1967), pp. 353–64, cited in Elke Morlok und Frederek Musall, "Die Geschichte *seiner* Freundschaft," p. 126;

and Rosemarie Heise, "Der Benjamin-Nachlaß in Potsdam. Interview von Hildegard Brenner vom 5.10.1967," in *alternative*, no. 56/57 (1967), pp. 186–94. See also the discussion in Behrmann, "Kulturrevolution: Zwei Monate Kulturrevolution." On the history of the reception of Benjamin in Germany, see Thomas Küpper und Timo Skrandies, "Rezeptionsgeschichte," in *Benjamin-Handbuch*, ed. Burkhardt Lindner (Stuttgart, 2006).

152. See Eiland and Jennings, *Walter Benjamin*, p. 127.

153. Eiland and Jennings, *Walter Benjamin*, pp. 3, 322.

154. Eiland and Jennings, *Walter Benjamin*, pp. 132–33. On Benjamin's attraction to violence (at least in theory) and "his constitutional inability to come to terms with the problem of anarchy (spontaneity, intoxication, salvation) and order (programming, reason, and discipline)," see Peter Demetz, introduction to *Walter Benjamin: Reflections*, ed. Demetz (New York, 1978), p. xli.

155. Eiland and Jennings, *Walter Benjamin*, p. 225.

156. JT to Adorno, March 18, 1968, ZfL.

157. Eiland and Jennings, *Walter Benjamin*, p. 129.

158. Walter Benjamin, "Theologico-Political Fragment," sections 14–18, in Demetz, *Walter Benjamin*.

159. JT to Unseld, December 5, 1966, Suhrkamp.

160. Scholem to Adorno, December 9, 1966, with quotations from Taubes's letter to Adorno of December 5, 1966, in *Theodor W. Adorno-Gershom Scholem Briefwechsel 1939-1969*, ed. Asaf Angermann (Berlin, 2015), pp. 393–97.

161. Scholem to JT, n.d., but 1967, ZfL.

162. JT to Scholem, October 8, 1968, ZfL.

163. Scholem to JT, October 20, 1968, ZfL.

164. Felsch, *Der Lange Sommer*, p. 50.

165. Felsch, *Der Lange Sommer*, pp. 57–62.

166. Unseld to JT, December 5, 1972, Suhrkamp.

167. K. H. Michel to Hans Heinz Holz, July 7, 1970, Suhrkamp.

168. JT to Karl Markus Michel, August 12, 1965, Suhrkamp.

169. JT to Unseld, December 6, 1971, Suhrkamp; Felsch, *Der Lange Sommer*, p. 63.

170. JT "Memorandum" to Unseld and Habermas, May 29, 1968, Suhrkamp. See *Blumenberg-Taubes*, pp. 161–62.

171. S. Unseld, "Protokoll eines Gespräches mit den Herren Habermas, Heinrich, Taubes am 16.9.1972," Suhrkamp.

172. Unseld to JT, July 5 and July 6, 1976, Suhrkamp.

173. "FU-Professor Szondi begeht Selbstmord," in *Freie Universität Berlin 1948-1973*, ed. Manfred Görtemaker and Klaus Schroeder, vol. 6, p. 144.

174. JT to Marcuse, January 24, 1972, ZfL.

175. My thanks to Gideon Freudenthal for this information.

176. JT to Marcuse, January 24, 1972, ZfL; and Herbert Marcuse Archiv. See also Tent, *Free University*, pp. 356–69.

177. Wehrs, *Protest der Professoren*, p. 270; and Koenen, *Rote Jahrzehnt*. For a useful overview, see Jürgen Domes and Armin Paul Frank, "The Tribulations of the Free University of Berlin," *Minerva*, vol. 13, no. 2 (1975), pp. 183–99, p. 191.

178. Wehrs, *Protest der Professoren*, pp. 288–89.

179. "Interview Hans Peter Duerr, 09.08.2009," online under "Interviews with German Anthropologists."

180. Gert Mattenklott, "Komm ins Offene, Freund!," in *Zeitschrift für Ideenge-schichte*, vol. 2, no. 3 (2008), p. 5.

181. Interview with Uwe Schlicht.

182. Interview with Uwe Schlicht.

183. Friedrch Tomberg, *Bürgerliche Wissenschaft. Begriff, Geschichte, Kritik* (Frankfurt, 1973).

184. See his apologia, "Korrektur einer Legende," https://www.friedrich-tomberg .com/post/korrektur-einer-legende.

185. This account is based on Uwe Schlicht, "Ein kultureller Bürgerkrieg? Per-sonalpolitik an der FU: das Philosophische Seminar," *Der Tagesspiegel*, Decem-ber 18, 1973.

186. Interview with Reinhard Maurer; JT to Maurer, September 6, 1973, ZfL.

187. Werner Stein to Michael Landmann, November 13, 1973, responding to Landmann's letter and memorandum of July 14, and "Anamnese."

188. Uwe Schlicht, "Ein kultureller Bürgerkrieg?"

189. Interviews with Uwe Schlicht and Richard Faber.

190. Interview with Krister Stendahl.

191. JT to Dietrich Goldschmidt, December 13, 1969, ZfL.

192. JT to Elizabeth and Irving Dworetzsky, June 15, 1970, ZfL; interview with Ethan Taubes.

193. JT to FU President, July 26, 1971, PA.

194. JT to Benjamin Nelson, May, 28, 1971, ZfL.

195. Interviews with Ethan Taubes and Tania Taubes. See also interview with Sib-ylle Haberditzl in *Das Politische und das Persönliche*, p. 472.

196. Interview with Tania Taubes.

197. Interview with Tania Taubes. JT to Edith Wyschogrod, June 26, 1975, ZfL. FU Vorlesungsverzeichnis, Sommersemester, 1975. Moving receipts ETT.

198. Interview with Peter McLaughlin.

199. Interview with Tania Taubes.

200. MvB to John F. Kennedy Schule, February 22, 1975, ETT.

201. Moving receipts, ETT.

202. JT to President, August 11, 1975, PA.

203. JT to President, August 6, 1975, PA.

204. Interview with Reinhard Maurer.

205. Interview with Susan Hechler.

206. President to Hauptkasse der FU, August 29, 1975, PA.

207. Interview with Rachel Freudenthal-Livne.

208. H. Helmchen, Director of Psychiatrische Klinik II to President of FU, May 7, 1976; "Ärtliches Attest," June 1, 1976; "Krankmeldung," September 21, 1976, and Octo-ber 11, 1976, PA.

209. Interview with Tania Taubes.

210. Interviews with Michael Wyschogrod, Ethan Taubes, Tania Taubes. Regard-ing the Hymans, interview with Morton Leifman.

211. Timothy Kneeland and Carol Warren, *Pushbutton Psychiatry: A History of Electroschock in America* (Westport, CT, 2002), pp. 64, 75–76.

212. Interview with William Frosch M.D., who did not recall the specific case, but speculated on the basis of his broader experience.

Chapter Thirteen. A Wandering Jew: Berlin–Jerusalem–Paris, 1976–81

1. Interview with Ethan Taubes.

2. Interview with Gabriele Althaus.

3. Interviews with Richard Faber and with Gabriele Althaus.

4. Interview with Tania Taubes.

5. Interview with Edmund Leites.

6. Interview with Victor Gourevitch.

7. "Gesundemeldung December 17, 1976," PA.

8. JT to Oskar Negt, January 26, 1977, ZfL.

9. Interview with Susan Hechler.

10. Interview with Joseph Agassi.

11. Communication from Christina Buhmann, January 2021.

12. Interview with Christina Buhmann, and communication, January 2021.

13. Jacob Taubes, "Wer hat Angst vor der Philosophie?," July 14, 1977, copy from Nolte Papers.

14. Interview with Susan Hechler.

15. Interview with Reinhard Maurer.

16. JT to Michael Wyschogrod, March 15, 1977, Wyschogrod Papers; interview with Uwe Schlicht; Peter Glotz, "About Jacob Taubes, Who Crossed Frontiers," in *Self, Soul and Body in Religious Experience*, ed. A. I. Baumgarten, J. Assmann, and G. G. Stroumsa (Leiden, 1998), pp. 4–9.

17. See on this also Kopp-Oberstebrink, "Landmann und Taubes."

18. Landmann to JT, July 23, 1966, ZfL.

19. Landmann to JT, July 23, 1966, ZfL.

20. Landmann to JT, September 5, 1967, ZfL.

21. Landmann to JT, September 11, 1967, ZfL.

22. Landmann to JT, October 9, 1968, ZfL.

23. "Mit Grüßen an die Studentenvertreter des Instituts für Philosophie"; JT to Oskar Negt, January 26, 1977. Copy from Peter McLaughlin.

24. Interview with Eberhard Lämmert.

25. Fritz Raddatz to JT, February 3, 1977, ZfL.

26. Klaus-Jürgen Grundner, "Nachwort" to *Exzerpt und Prophetie: Gedenkschrift für Michael Landmann*, ed. Grundner et al. (Würzburg, 2001), p. 305.

27. Gollwitzer to JT, April 3, 1977, ZfL.

28. "Konflikt um Judaistik-Seminar," *Der Tagesspiegel*, April 28, 1977; JT to Ernst Nolte, April 12, 1977, Suhrkamp; Jacob Taubes, "Inmitten des akademischen Taifuns am Fachbereich 'Philosophie und Sozialwissenschaften' der Freien Universität," in *Hochschulreform—und was nun?*, ed. Albert Glazer (Berlin, 1982), pp. 302–20.

29. Interview with Reinhard Maurer.

30. Landmann to President of FU, June 20, 1977 (Eberhard Lämmert), in Scholem Papers, "Jacob Taubes. Lo lakahal."

31. Interviews with Niko Oswald and with Tania Taubes.

32. Interview with Peter Schäfer; Peter Schäfer and Klaus Hermann, "Judaistik an der Freien Universität Berlin," in *Religionswissenschaft, Judaistik, Islamwissenschaft, und Neuere Philologien an der Freien Universität Berlin*, ed. Karol Kubicki und Siegward Lönnendonker (Göttingen, 2012), pp. 53–74.

33. JT to President of FU, April 28, 1977; FB11 to President, June 2, 1977; "Protokoll der Ausserordentlichen Sitzung des Direktoriums der WE.6," May 24, 1977, PA.

34. Jacob Taubes, memorandum "Zur Situation und Rekonstruktion des Instituts für Philosophie," June 15, 1977, PA.

35. Landmann to Lämmert, June 18, 1977, copy in Scholem Papers, "Jacob Taubes. Lo lakahal."

36. Landmann to Lämmert, June 20, 1977, copy in Scholem Papers, "Jacob Taubes. Lo lakahal."

37. "Aktennotiz," June 21, 1977, Scholem Papers, "Jacob Taubes. Lo lakahal."

38. FU President to JT, July 12, 1977, PA.

39. Landmann and others to President Lämmert, July 12, 1977, quoted in Taubes to Glotz, March 1978, in Voegelin Papers.

40. "Protokollnotiz zur 2. Gesprächsrunde beim Präsidenten der FUB zum 'Fall Taubes,'" November 7, 1977, Scholem Papers, "Jacob Taubes. Lo lakahal."

41. Scholem Papers, "Jacob Taubes. Lo lakahal." Landmann to Michael Strauss, Haifa, January 14, 1978, Michael Strauss Papers. I am grateful to Prof. Oded Balaban, Haifa, for making available to me the correspondence between Landmann and Michael Strauss.

42. Jacob Taubes, "Zur Situation und Rekonstruction des Instituts für Philosophie," sent to Lämmert on June 15, 1977. Copy in DLA Marbach, Nachlass Blumenberg, cited in *Blumenberg-Taubes*, p. 181. Portions of this memo are cited in JT, "Memorandum an . . . Peter Glotz," March 1978, copy in Voegelin Papers.

43. This follows the account in Jacob Taubes, "An den Präsidenten der FUB," November 28, 1979, PA. The story is confirmed by interview with Reinhard Maurer. On Taubes's repeated visits to Berlin, see Landmann to Mitglieder der Direktoriums der WE 5 des Fachbereichs 11, January 17, 1978, Scholem Papers, "Jacob Taubes. Lo lakahal."

44. Jacob Taubes, "An den GD der WE5 des FB11 des FUB Herrn M.L.," April 17, 1978, IH.

45. Landmann to Michael Strauss, January 18, 1978; February 5, 1978; February 18, 1978; March 5, 1978, Michael Strauss Papers.

46. Taubes, "An den GD der WE5 des FB11."

47. "Staatskommissar für Philosophisches Institut gefordert," *Der Tagesspiegel*, April 21, 1978.

48. Armin Mohler to JT, March 2, 1978, Mohler Nachlass.

49. Interview with Tania Taubes.

50. Interview with Reinhard Maurer; also recounted in JT to Peter Glotz, 1978, IH.

51. Jacob Taubes, "An den Geschäftsführenden Direktor der WE 5 Frau Prof. Dr. M. v. Brentano. Betr.:Vakanzvertretungen," October 27, 1978, IH.

52. "Ohne Goldene Horde," *Der Spiegel*, May 14, 1979, pp. 231–37.

53. Interview with Susan Hechler, who was at the time a secretary in the philosophy seminar.

54. JT to Marcuse, May 15, 1968, ZfL.

55. "An den Vorsitzenden des Staatsrates der Deutschen Demokratischen Republik Herrn Erich Honecker," signed "Im Auftrage des Fachbereichsrates, Peter Furth," December 2, 1976, reprinted in *Minerva. Blätter für Altertumskunde und Philosophie*, vol. 1 (1987), p. 72.

56. Interview with Uwe Schlicht. In 1977, Schlicht participated in the Hermeneutic Colloquium devoted to the topic "Toward an Archaeology and Genealogy of the New Left." JT to Arthur A. Cohen, July 6, 1977, ZfL. For Glotz's own account, see Glotz, "About Jacob Taubes."

57. "'Jeder fünfte denkt etwas so wie Mescalero': Berlins Wissenschaftssenator Peter Glotz über Sympathisanten und die Situation an den Hochschulen," *Der Spiegel*, October 2, 1977.

58. JT to Walter Kaufmann, March 6, 1978; JT to Noam Chomsky, March 7, 1978; Chomsky to JT, March 18, 1978, ZfL.

59. Voegelin to JT, May 9, 1978, Voegelin Papers.

60. Interview with Uwe Schlicht; "Ohne Goldene Horde," *Der Spiegel*. On von Brentano's role, see JT to Markus, January 24, 1979, ZfL.

61. Interview with Gideon Freudenthal; JT to Blumenberg, August 15, 1979, in *Blumenberg-Taubes*, pp. 199–200.

62. Interview with Michael Theunissen.

63. Interview with Ernst Tugendhat.

64. "Die Zeit des Philosophierens ist vorbei" (interview with Ernst Tugendhat), *Tageszeitung*, July 28, 2007.

65. Interview with Ernst Tugendhat.

66. Uwe Schlicht, "Drei Leben: Zum Tode von Marianne Awerbuch," *Der Tagesspiegel*, June 9, 2004; interview with Eberhard Lämmert.

67. Interview with Peter McLaughlin.

68. Notiz an Unseld, signed by L. Rose, June 26, 1975; JT to Unseld, December 9, 1975; Unseld to JT, January 2, 1976; JT to Unseld, March 25, 1976, Suhrkamp.

69. Unseld to JT, June 1, 1976, Suhrkamp.

70. JT to Unseld, April 12, 1974, Suhrkamp.

71. JT to Nolte, January 20, 1965; and January 22, 1965, Nolte Papers.

72. Interview with Ernst Nolte.

73. Ernst Nolte, *Deutschland und der Kalte Krieg* (Munich, 1974), p. 602.

74. Nolte, *Deutschland und der Kalte Krieg*, pp. 332–37, 607.

75. Nolte, *Deutschland und der Kalte Krieg*, p. 607.

76. Müller-Doohm, *Jürgen Habermas*, pp. 18–19.

77. JT to Habermas, March 3, 1977, Nolte papers; JT to Nolte, March 5, 1977, Nolte Papers; JT to Nolte, March 7, 1977, Habermas Papers.

78. JT to Nolte, March 7, 1977, Habermas Papers.

79. Jürgen Habermas, introduction to *Observations on "The Spiritual Situation of the Age"* (Cambridge, MA, 1984; German original, 1979), p. 3. Wolfgang H. Lorig, *Neokonservatives Denken in der Bundesrepublik Deutschland und in den Vereinigten Staaten von Amerika* (Oplanden, 1988), shows how Habermas time and again mischaracterized the positions of the German neoconservatives.

80. Unseld to Taubes, March 7, 1977; JT to Unseld, May 8, 1977; JT to Unseld, March 30, 1977; JT to Unseld, May 8, 1977; Unseld to JT, June 28, 1977, Suhrkamp Archiv.

81. JT to Habermas, March 3, 1977. Copies in Habermas and Nolte Papers.

82. Unseld to JT, March 7, 1977, Suhrkamp Archiv.

83. JT to Habermas, June 8, 1977, Suhrkamp Archiv.

84. Habermas to JT, with copy to Unseld, July 27, 1977, Suhrkamp Archiv.

85. Henrich to JT, June 20, 1977, ZfL.

86. Unseld to JT, June 28, 1977, Suhrkamp Archiv.

87. Report to Unseld, "Besuch von Jacob Taubes am 24.2.1978 in Verlag," Suhrkamp Archiv.

88. Syndikat Verlag to JT, February 8, 1978, ZfL.

89. Unseld to JT, March 23, 1978, Suhrkamp Archiv.

90. Unseld to JT, January 3, 1979, Suhrkamp Archiv; FU President to JT, March 21, 1979, PA.

91. JT to Unseld, February 6, 1982, Suhrkamp Archiv.

92. JT to Unseld, May 14, 1981, Suhrkamp Archiv.

93. Jonas to JT, January 24, 1978, ZfL; JT to Jonas, August 2, 1982, Jonas Archiv.

94. Unseld to JT, October 13, 1981; JT to Unseld, October 23, 1981; JT to Unseld, February 10, 1982; Unseld to JT, February 2, 1982, Suhrkamp Archiv.

95. Unseld to JT, June 7, 1982, Suhrkamp Archiv.

96. Unseld to JT, June 30, 1982, Suhrkamp Archiv.

97. JT to Martin Buber, December 15, 1964, Buber Papers.

98. JT to Cohen, July 6, 1977, ZfL.

99. JT to Scholem, March 16, 1977, Scholem Papers, and published in *PdM*, pp. 117–23.

100. Scholem to JT, March 24, 1977, Scholem Papers, published in *PdM*, p. 130. I have used but altered the translation in Anthony David Skinner, *Gershom Scholem: A Life in Letters*, p. 468.

101. Blumenberg to JT, May 24, 1977, ZfL, now in *Blumenberg-Taubes*, pp. 171–75.

102. Interview with Avishai and Edna Margalit.

103. JT to Arthur A. Cohen, October 2, 1977, Cohen Papers.

104. Biale et al., *Hasidism: A New History*, pp. 720–21; Abraham Rabinovich, "Praise the Lord and Pass the Ammunition," *Jerusalem Post International Edition*, March 22–28, 1981.

105. Rabinovich, "Praise the Lord."

106. Biale et al., *Hasidism: A New History*, pp. 752–53.

107. Interview with Paul Mendes-Flohr.

108. Interviews with Avishai Margalit, Moshe Halbertal, Tania Taubes, and Ethan Taubes.

109. Interview with Guy Stroumsa.

110. JT to Hans Jonas, December 23, 1977, Jonas Archiv.

111. Interview with Menachem Brinker.

112. Sarah Stroumsa, "Shlomo Pines: The Scholar, The Sage," http://www.shlomopines.org.il/files/articles/stroumsa.doc.

113. Strauss to Scholem, May 10, 1950, in Leo Strauss, *Gesammelte Schriften* (Stuttgart, 2001), vol. 3, pp. 723–24.

114. Interview with Guy and Sarah Stroumsa.

115. Interview with Guy Stroumsa.

116. Carsten Colpe, "'Das eschatologische Widerlager der Politik,' Zu Jacob Taubes' Gnosisbild," in Faber et al., *Abendländische Eschatologie. Ad Jacob Taubes*, pp. 105–30, pp. 119, 128.

117. Interview with Guy and Sarah Stroumsa.

118. Aharon Agus to JT, February 15, 1980, ZfL.

119. Gershom Scholem, "Buber's Conception of Judaism," in Scholem, *On Jews and Judaism in Crisis*, pp. 166–67.

120. Interview with Avishai and Edna Margalit. Similarly, Colpe, "'Das eschatologische Widerlager der Politik.'"

121. Interview with Moshe Idel.

122. On Idel, see H. Tirosh-Samuelson and A. Hughes, *Moshe Idel* (Library of Contemporary Jewish Philosophers) (Leiden, 2015).

123. "Professor Moshe Barasch 1920–2004," https://en.arthistory.huji.ac.il/sites /default/files/arthistoryen/files/barash_english.pdf.

124. JT to President of FU, May 25, 1978; Hartman to JT, American Colony Hotel, May 5, 1978, both in PA.

125. Eliezer Don-Yehiya, "Messianism and Politics: The Ideological Transformation of Religious Zionism," *Israel Studies*, vol. 19, no. 2 (2014), pp. 239–63; Ravitzky, *Messianism, Zionism, and Jewish Religious Radicalism*, ch. 3.

126. Ravitzky, *Messianism, Zionism, and Jewish Religious Radicalism*, pp. 98–99.

127. Interviews with Ze'ev Luria, Menachem Lorberbaum, and Moshe Halbertal.

128. JT to David Hartman, March 1, 1982, ZfL. JT used the same formulation in a letter to Agus, March 1, 1982, ZfL.

129. JT to David Hartman, March 1, 1982, ZfL.

130. Interviews with Moshe Halbertal and with Menachem Lorberbaum.

131. On the significance of this passage, see Shaul Magid, "Through the Void: The Absence of God in R. Naḥman of Bratzlav's 'Likkutei MoHaRan,'" *Harvard Theological Review*, vol. 88, no. 4 (October 1995), pp. 495–519.

132. See chapter 6.

133. Interview with Moshe Halbertal.

134. JT to Arthur A. Cohen, from Jerusalem (American Colony Hotel stationary), August 27, 1978, Cohen Papers.

135. Interview with Leon Wieseltier.

136. Aharon Agus CV, dated January 7, 1979, ZfL.

137. Interview with Naomi Agus, Jerusalem.

138. Interviews with Naomi Agus, Albert Baumgarten, Daniel Tropper, Shlomo Fischer.

139. Aharon Agus, "Some Early Rabbinic Thinking on Gnosticism," *Jewish Quarterly Review*, vol. 71, no. 1 (1980), pp. 18–30; Agus to JT, November 7, 1979, ZfL.

140. Aharon Agus to JT, February 15, 1980, ZfL.

141. For the text of the letter and greater detail, see Jerry Z. Muller, "'I Am Impossible': An Exchange between Jacob Taubes and Arthur A. Cohen," *Jewish Review of Books* (Summer 2017), pp. 42–44.

142. A view borne out in recent scholarship. On rabbinic disdain for the unlearned, see Jeffrey L. Rubinstein, *The Culture of the Babylonian Talmud* (Philadelphia, 2005),

ch. 7; and the discussion in Christine Hayes, "The 'Other' in Rabbinic Literature," in *The Cambridge Companion to the Talmud and Rabbinic Literature*, ed. Charlotte Elisheva Fonrobert and Martin S. Jaffee (Cambridge, 2007).

143. Muller, "'I Am Impossible': An Exchange between Jacob Taubes and Arthur A. Cohen."

144. Interview with Marianne Weinberg.

145. The paragraphs that follow are based on an interview with Marcel Sigrist.

146. Interview with Avishai Margalit.

147. Interview with Moshe Waldoks.

148. A. A. Cohen to JT, October 13, 1977, Cohen Papers.

149. Interview with David Hartman.

150. JT to Werner Hamacher, October 28, 1981, Hamacher private papers.

151. Jacob Taubes and Norbert Bolz, "Vorwort" to *Religionstheorie und politische Theologie: Band 3: Theokratie*, ed. Taubes (Munich, 1987), p. 5.

152. *Taubes-Schmitt*, p. 108.

153. Interview with Avishai Margalit.

154. Interview with Sy Gitin.

155. Rabinovich, "Praise the Lord."

156. JT, letter to the editor, *Jerusalem Post*, April 1, 1981.

157. Interview with Wolf Lepenies.

158. Interview with Joseph Dan.

159. The account of Taubes's talk is based upon an interview with David Stern.

160. "The Price of Messianism," reprinted in *CtC*.

161. Interview with David Stern.

162. Daniel Weidner, *Gershom Scholem: Politisches, esoterisches und historiographisches Schreiben* (Munich, 2003), p. 390.

163. Gershom Scholem, *Sabbatai Sevi: The Mystical Messiah* (Princeton, NJ, 1973), p. xii.

164. Gershom Scholem, "Toward an Understanding of the Messianic Idea in Judaism," in Scholem, *The Messianic Idea in Judaism and Other Essays on Jewish Spirituality* (New York, 1971), p. 36.

165. David Biale, "Gershom Scholem on Nihilism and Anarchism," *Rethinking History*, vol. 19, no. 1 (2015), pp. 61–71, pp. 64ff; Biale, *Gershom Scholem*, pp. 195–96; David Ohana, *Political Theologies in the Holy Land: Israeli Messianism and Its Critics* (London, 2010), ch. 3.

166. Gershom Scholem, "The Crisis of Tradition in Jewish Messianism," in Scholem, *The Messianic Idea in Judaism*, pp. 52–53.

167. Scholem, "Crisis of Tradition," pp. 57–58.

168. Scholem, *Sabbatai Sevi*, pp. 93–102.

169. Scholem, "Toward an Understanding of the Messianic Idea in Judaism," pp. 15–16.

170. See, for example, Elettra Stimilli, "Der Messianismus als politisches Problem," in *PdM*, pp. 131–79; Thomas Macho, "Der intellektuelle Bruch zwischen Gershom Scholem und Jacob Taubes. Zur Frage nach dem Preis des Messianismus," in Faber et al., *Abendländische Eschatologie*, pp. 531–44. By contrast, Willem Styfhals recognizes that Taubes was simply applying Scholem's insights to Paul.

Willem Styfhals, "Deconstructing Orthodoxy: A Failed Dialogue between Gershom Scholem and Jacob Taubes," *New German Critique*, vol. 45, no. 1 (2018), pp. 181–205, p. 192.

171. Neusner to JT, August 19, 1981, ZfL.

172. Taubes, "The Price of Messianism," in *Proceedings of the Eighth World Congress of Jewish Studies* (Jerusalem, 1982), pp. 99–104; "The Price of Messianism," *Journal of Jewish Studies*, vol. 33, no. 1–2 (1982), pp. 595–600; "Scholem's Theses on Messianism Reconsidered," *Social Science Information*, vol. 21, no. 4–5 (1982), pp. 665–75. On the publication history, see *CtC*, pp. 348–49.

173. Zadoff, *Gershom Scholem*, pp. 234–35.

174. According to Gerold Necker, "Gershom Scholems ambivalente Beziehung zu Deutschland," in Necker et al., *Gershom Scholem in Deutschland*, pp. 5–6.

175. Interview with Aleida Assmann.

176. Interview with Marianne and Sigi Weinberg.

177. Zadoff, *Gershom Scholem*, pp. 236–40.

178. JT to Agus, March 1, 1982; JT to Fania Scholem (Hebrew), February 26, 1982, ZfL.

179. "Clemens Heller—Founder of the 'Marshall Plan of the Mind,'" https://www.salzburgglobal.org/about/history/articles/clemens-heller.html; and "Clemens Heller, 85, Founder of Postwar Salzburg Seminar," *New York Times*, September 6, 2002. For additional information, I thank Jean-Louis Fabiani; interview with Joachim Nettelbeck; Wolf Lepenies, "Jongleur im Reich des Geistes. Erinnerungen an Clemens Heller," *Zeitschrift für Ideengeschichte*, vol. 11, no. 4 (2017), pp. 65–82.

180. JT to Louis Dumont, February 16, 1978, Suhrkamp.

181. Quoted in Richard J. Evans, *Eric Hobsbawm: A Life in History* (New York, 2019), p. 502. On Hobsbawm and Heller, see also Eric Hobsbawm, *Interesting Times: A Twentieth-Century Life* (New York, 2005), pp. 326–27.

182. For a full and sympathetic account, see William Lewis, "Louis Althusser," in *Stanford Encyclopedia of Philosophy* (Spring 2018 Edition), ed. Edward N. Zalta. For a more skeptical and analytically acute account, see Roger Scruton, "Nonsense in Paris: Althusser, Lacan and Deleuze," in his *Fools, Frauds and Firebrands: Thinkers of the New Left* (London, 2015), pp. 159–74.

183. "Theorie 2: Vorschläge von Prof. Taubes," n.d., but 1965, Suhrkamp Archiv; interview with Peter McLaughlin.

184. Interview with Avishai Margalit.

185. JT to Cohen, November 25, 1977, Cohen Papers.

186. JT to Marianne Weinberg, November 21, 1980, Weinberg private papers.

187. Interview with Heinz Wismann; email from Wismann, March 29, 2020.

188. Interview with Rudolf von Thadden.

189. JT to Cohen, November 25, 1977, Cohen Papers, *Blumenburg-Taubes*, p. 191, note.

190. Cohen to JT, December 11, 1977, Cohen Papers.

191. JT to Cohen, November 25, 1977, Cohen Papers.

192. Interviews with Christina Buhmann and with Aleida Assmann.

193. Interview with Winfried Menninghaus.

194. Interviews with Werner Hamacher and Norbert Bolz.

195. Hans Peter Duerr, "Proclamation! Next Semesta New Big Darkman Institute Master!," in *Geist, Bild und Narr. Zu einer Ethnologie kultureller Konversionen. Festschrift für Fritz Kramer*, ed. Heike Behrend (Berlin, 2001), pp. 8–11.

196. JT to Koselleck, October 27, 1977, ZfL; interview with Heinz Dieter Kittsteiner; Thomas Assheuer, "Tischgespräch unter Feinden: Heinz Dieter Kittsteiner möchte Karl Marx mit Martin Heidegger versöhnen," *Die Zeit*, July 29, 2004.

197. Interviews with Christoph Schulte and Walter Schmidt-Biggemann.

198. Interview with Gabriele Althaus; FU Vorlesungsverzeichnis.

199. Interview with Christoph Schulte.

200. Interviews with Christoph Schulte, Inka Arroyo, and Renate Schlesier. On the Paris Bar, see Michel Würthle (ed.), *Paris Bar Berlin* (Berlin, 2000); Michael Althen, "Der Sieg der Neuen Mitte," FAZ.NET, November 25, 2004.

201. Norbert Bolz and Richard Faber (ed.), *Walter Benjamin. Profane Erleuchtung und rettende Kritik* (Würzburg, 1985); Bolz and Faber (ed.), *Antike und Moderne. Zu Walter Benjamins "Passagen"* (Würzburg, 1986).

202. Interviews with Norbert Bolz.

203. Norbert Bolz, *Auszug aus der entzauberten Welt. Philosophischer Extremismus zwischen den Weltkriegen* (Munich, 1989).

204. Norbert Bolz, *Das konsumistische Manifest* (Munich, 2002); Bolz, *Die Helden der Familie* (Munich, 2006).

205. Interview with Norberg Bolz.

206. Interview with Christoph Schulte.

Chapter Fourteen. "Ach, ja, Taubes . . .": A Character Sketch

1. Interview with Tania Taubes.

2. Interview with Ruth Kahane-Geyer.

3. Richard Faber, "'Das ist die Synagoge, in die ich nicht gehe': Über Jacob Taubes' politische-religiöse Witze," *Frankfurter Rundschau*, January 20, 1996.

4. Recounted by Hans Ulrich Gumbrecht in Boden and Zill, *Poetik und Hermeneutik im Rückblick*, p. 345.

5. Interviews with Ruth Kahane-Geyer, Avishai Margalit, and Moshe Halbertal.

6. Interview with Peter Wapnewski.

7. Jenny Schon, "Der wahre Jacob. Freundschaft bis zum Totenbett," *Sterz: Zeitschrift für Literatur, Kunst und Kulturpolitik*, no. 107/108 (2013), pp. 8–9.

8. Interview with Gabriele Althaus.

9. Interview with Renate Schlesier; JT to Wilhelm Kewenig, November 21, 1986, ETT.

10. Interviews with Moshe Halbertal and Heinz Wismann.

11. Interviews with Peter Wapneski, Marianne Weinberg, Tania Taubes, Uta Gerhardt, and Heinz Wismann.

12. Interview with Renate Schlesier.

13. Interview with Wilhelm Schmidt-Biggemann.

14. Interview with Dieter Henrich; also Henrich, *Sterbliche Gedanken*, pp. 44–48.

15. Interview with Edmund Leites.

16. Interview with Michael Wyschogrod.

17. Interview with Heinz Wismann.

18. Taubes gave a similar explanation to Daniel Tropper. Interview with Daniel Tropper.

19. I thank Dr. William Frosch, the psychiatrist who treated Taubes in 1976, for this suggestion.

20. Interview with Joseph Schatzmiller.

21. Interview with Richard Faber.

22. Schon, "Der wahre Jacob"; Babette Babich, "Ad Jacob Taubes," *New Nietzsche Studies*, vol. 7, no. 3–4 (2007–8), pp. v–x, p. viii.

Chapter Fifteen. Schmitt and Political Theology Revisited, 1982–86

1. Van Laak, *Gespräche in der Sicherheit des Schweigens*; Reinhard Mehring, "Der esoterische Diskurspartisan: Carl Schmitt in der Bundesrepublik," in *Intellektuelle in der Bundesrpublik Deutschland*, ed. Thomas Kroll and Tilman Reitz (Göttingen, 2013), pp. 232–48; Müller, *Dangerous Mind*.

2. I thank Edmund Leites for this characterization.

3. Interview with Richard Faber.

4. Interview with Norbert Bolz.

5. Hermann Lübbe, "Diskussionsbeitrag," in *Recht und Institution* (Berlin, 1985), p. 99, cited in *Thomas Hobbes and Carl Schmitt*, ed. Johan Tralau (New York, 2011).

6. Based on the protocols preserved by Taubes, and an article in the same file, now in the Manfred Voigt Papers, copy in the author's possession.

7. Gerhard Kaiser, "Walter Benjamins 'Geschichtsphilosophische Thesen.' Zur Kontroverse der Benjamin-Interpreten," *Deutsche Vierteljahresschrift für Literatur- wissenschaft und Geistesgeschichte*, vol. 46, no. 4 (1972), pp. 577–625.

8. Blumenberg to JT, May 24, 1977, ZfL, and in *Blumenberg-Taubes*, p. 174.

9. Weissmann, *Armin Mohler*, p. 119.

10. Weissmann, *Armin Mohler*, pp. 124–36. See Armin Mohler, *Vergangenheitsbe- wältigung oder wie man den Krieg nochmals verliert* (Krefeld, 1980), especially the title essay of 1968.

11. Weissmann, *Armin Mohler*, ch. 9.

12. "Biographische Skizze," in *Grenzgänge—Liber Amicorum für den nationalen Dissidenten Hans-Dietrich Sander*, ed. Heiko Luge (Graz, 2008), pp. 336–42.

13. Mathias Döpner, "Nachruf auf Ernst Cramer," *Die Welt*, January 19, 2010.

14. Weissmann, *Armin Mohler*, p. 156. Sander to Schmitt, June 13, 1972, in *Schmitt-Sander*, pp. 216–17.

15. Sander to Schmitt, May 22, 1967, in *Schmitt-Sander*, p. 2.

16. Schmitt to Sander, May 8, 1968, and May 12, 1968, in *Schmitt-Sander*, pp. 34–35. A version of the letter was first published in Hans-Dietrich Sander, *Marx- istische Ideologie und allgemeine Kunsttheorie* (Basel, 1970), p. 173, n. 79, cited in *Taubes-Schmitt*, p. 30.

17. Schmitt to Sander, July 14, 1972, in *Schmitt-Sander*, p. 221.

18. Sander to Schmitt, December 29, 1971, in *Schmitt-Sander*, p. 187.

19. Sander to Schmitt, June 13, 1972, in *Schmitt-Sander*, pp. 216–17.

20. Schmitt to Sander, June 18, 1975, in *Schmitt-Sander*, p. 313; and Schmitt to Sander, July 1, 1974, in *Schmitt-Sander*, p. 315.

21. Sander to Schmitt, July 30, 1975, in *Schmitt-Sander*, pp. 365–66.

22. Hans-Dietrich Sander, *Marxistische Ideologie und allgemeine Kunsttheorie*, 2nd ed. (Tübingen, 1975), p. 352, n. 150.

23. Sander, *Marxistische Ideologie*, p. 353, n. 152.

24. Sander to Schmitt, August 11, 1975, in *Schmitt-Sander*, p. 367.

25. Sander to Schmitt, November 28, 1975, in *Schmitt-Sander*, p. 377.

26. Sander to Schmitt, June, 1976, in *Schmitt-Sander*, p. 399; Sander to Schmitt, December 21, 1976, in *Schmitt-Sander*, p. 403.

27. Sander to Schmitt, October 31, 1977, in *Schmitt-Sander*, pp. 412–13.

28. Sander to Schmitt, July 8, 1978, in *Schmitt-Sander*, p. 438.

29. Sander to JT, October 9, 1979, ZfL.

30. JT to Schmitt, November 17, 1977, in *Taubes-Schmitt*, pp. 34–35.

31. Editors' note in *Taubes-Schmitt*, p. 35.

32. Taubes, memorandum, March 1978, copy in Cohen Papers.

33. Sander to Schmitt, October 31, 1977, in *Schmitt-Sander*, pp. 412–13, and p. 423, n. 3.; Sander to Schmitt, February 21, 1978, in *Schmitt-Sander*, p. 431.

34. Sander to Schmitt, November 7, 1977, in *Schmitt-Sander*, p. 415.

35. Schmitt to Sander, November 9, 1977, in *Schmitt-Sander*, pp. 415–16.

36. Schmitt to JT, November 29, 1977, in *Taubes-Schmitt*, pp. 36–38; Blumenberg to Schmitt, December 28, 1977, in *Hans Blumenberg-Carl Schmitt. Briefwechsel 1971–1978*, ed. Alexander Schmitz and Marcel Lepper (Frankfurt, 2007), p. 152.

37. Unseld to Schmitt, August 15, 1977, in *Taubes-Schmitt*, p. 171.

38. JT to Schmitt, December 23, 1977, in *Taubes-Schmitt*, pp. 43–46.

39. Sander to Schmitt, January 31, 1978; Schmitt to Sander, February 9, 1978, in *Schmitt-Sander*, pp. 428–29.

40. Sander to Schmitt, October 11, 1979, in *Schmitt-Sander*, p. 450.

41. JT to Schmitt, March 2, 1978, in *Taubes-Schmitt*, pp. 51–52.

42. Schmitt to JT, March 1980, in *Taubes-Schmitt*, p. 106.

43. Editors' note, *Taubes-Schmitt*, p. 61.

44. JT to Schmitt, September 18, 1978, in *Taubes-Schmitt*, pp. 58–61.

45. Jacob Taubes "1948–1978, Dreißig Jahre Verweigerung," in *ACS*, p. 71.

46. Schmitt to JT, November 24, 1978, in *Taubes-Schmitt*, p. 78.

47. JT to Schmitt, November 11, 1979, in *Taubes-Schmitt*, p. 100. Taubes, "Leviathan als sterblicher Gott. Zum 300 Todestag von Thomas Hobbes," *Neue Zürcher Zeitung*, November 30, 1979, reprinted in *AuP*.

48. Editors' note, *Taubes-Schmitt*, p. 105.

49. On these controversies, see Jean-Claude Monod, *La querelle de la sécularisation de Hegel à Blumenberg* (Paris, 2002).

50. Blumenberg to JT, January 9, 1967, ZfL, published in *Blumenberg-Taubes*, p. 120.

51. Karl Löwith, *Meaning in History* (Chicago, 1949), p. 203.

52. Carl Schmitt, *Politische Theologie II: Die Legende von der Erledigung jeder Politischen Theologie* (Berlin, 1970).

53. Heinrich Meier, *Die Lehre Carl Schmitts. Vier Kapitel zur Unterscheidung Politischer Theologie und politischer Philosophie*, 3rd ed. (Stuttgart, 2009), p. 296.

54. Hans Blumenberg, *The Legitimacy of the Modern Age*, trans. Robert M. Wallace (based on the expanded, 1979 edition of *Die Legitimität der Neuzeit*). My understanding of this book has been aided by Franz Josef Wetz, *Hans Blumenberg zur Einführung* (Hamburg, 2004), ch. 3, "Menschliche Selbstbehauptung"; Martin Jay, review of *Legitimacy of the Modern Age*, by Hans Blumenberg, *History and Theory*, vol. 24, no. 2 (1985), pp. 183–96; Robert B. Pippin, "Blumenberg and the Modernity Problem," *Review of Metaphysics*, vol. 40 (1987), pp. 535–57.

55. Blumenberg, *Legitimacy of the Modern Age*, p. 116.

56. See, for example, Blumenberg, *Legitimacy of the Modern Age*, p. 117.

57. On the Ritter Schule and its influence, see Jens Hacke, *Philosophie der Bürgerlichkeit. Die liberalkonservative Begründung der Bundesrepublik* (Göttingen, 2006).

58. *Blumenberg-Schmitt*, p. 172.

59. Jacob Taubes, "Vorwort" to *Religionstheorie und Politische Theologie. Band 1: Der Fürst dieser Welt. Carl Schmitt und die Folgen*, ed. Jacob Taubes (Munich, 1983; 2nd ed., 1985), p. 5.

60. Jacob Taubes, "Statt einer Einleitung: Leviathan als sterblicher Gott," in Taubes, *Der Fürst dieser Welt*, p. 13, reprinted in *AuP*.

61. Odo Marquard, "Die Geschichtsphilosophie und ihre Folgelasten," in *Geschichte—Ereignis und Erzählung*, ed. Reinahrt Koselleck und Wolf-Dieter Stempel (Munich, 1973), p. 464.

62. Odo Marquard, "Aufgeklärter Polytheismus—auch eine politische Theologie?," in Taubes, *Der Fürst dieser Welt*, p. 78.

63. Marquard, "Aufgeklärter Polytheismus," pp. 81–82. Some of these points are spelled out more completely in Odo Marquard, "In Praise of Polytheism (On Monomythical and Polymythical Thinking)," in his *Farewell to Matters of Principle*, trans. Robert M. Wallace (New York, 1989), first published in German in *Philosophie und Mythos. Ein Kolloquium*, ed. Hans Poser (Berlin, 1979), pp. 40–58.

64. Marquard, "Aufgeklärter Polytheismus," pp. 83–84.

65. Jacob Taubes, "Zur Konjunktur des Polytheismus," in *Mythos und Moderne*, ed. Karl Heinz Bohrer (Frankfurt, 1983), pp. 457–70; reprinted in *KzK*.

66. Jacob Taubes, untitled transcript dated January 30, 1980, IH.

67. Hermann Lübbe, "Politische Theologie als Theologie repolitisierter Religion," in Taubes, *Der Fürst dieser Welt*, pp. 45–56, esp. pp. 55–56.

68. Interviews with Richard Faber and Norbert Bolz.

69. Hans-Dietrich Sander, "Von den geistigen Knechtschaft der Deutschen und ihrer möglichen Aufhebung," in *Der nationale Imperative. Ideengänge und Werkstücke zur Wiederherstellung Deutschlands* (Krefeld, 1980), pp. 94–95.

70. Sander, *Der nationale Imperative*, p. 105.

71. Quoted in Luge, *Grenzgänge*, pp. 339–40; JT to Mahler, October 29, 1980; JT to Sander, October 29, 1980, ZfL.

72. JT to Sander, March 4, 1980, ZfL; the letter is reproduced in Hans-Dietrich Sander, *Die Auflösung aller Dinge. Zur geschichtlichen Lage des Judentums in den Metamorphosen der Moderne* (Munich, 1988), pp. 12–17.

73. Sander to Schmitt, *Schmitt-Sander*, pp. 451–52.

74. Schmitt to JT, mid-March 1980, in *Taubes-Schmitt*, p. 106.

75. Interview with Richard Faber.

76. "Dr. Edelmann, Chefarzt of Abt. f. Psychiatrie in Krankenhaus am Urban Kreuzberg, Ärtzliche Bescheinigung," October 14, 1982, PA.

77. Interview with Richard Faber.

78. "Ärtzliche Bescheinigung," October 14, 1982; JT to Personalstelle, January 31, 1983, PA.

79. JT to President, February 4, 1983, PA.

80. Interview with Ethan Taubes.

81. MvB to Tania Taubes, October 23, 1983, ETT.

82. Dr. Christian von Wolff (internist), Uni Klinik Steglitz, December 13, 1984, PA.

83. Interview with Tania Taubes.

84. Interview with Avishai Margalit.

85. Klinik Wannsee, Notiz, PA.

86. Interview with Tania Taubes.

87. JT to Ernst Nolte, June 16, 1986, Nolte Papers.

88. Interview with Joseph Dan.

89. Felsch, *Der lange Sommer der Theorie,* pp. 189–91.

90. Cited in Lutz Niethammer, *Posthistoire: Has History Come to an End?,* trans. Patrick Camiller (London, 1992), p. 22, n. 41; Robert Seyfert, "Streifzüge durch Tausend Milieus," in *Soziologische Denkschulen in der Bundesrepublik Deutschland,* ed. Joachim Fischer and Stephan Mobius (Wiesbaden, 2019), pp. 317–72, p. 355.

91. Jacob Taubes, "Ästhetisierung der Wahrheit im Posthistoire," in *Streitbare Philosophie: Margherita von Brentano zum 65. Geburtstag,* ed. Gabriele Althaus and Irmingard Staeuble (Berlin, 1988), pp. 41–52, reprinted in *AuP.*

92. Interview with Peter Gente; on Merve Verlag, see Felsch, *Lange Sommer der Theorie,* passim.

93. FU Vorlesungverzeichnes, Sommersemester, 1981; FB Philosophie und Sozialwisschenschaft I, Kommentiertes Vorlesungsverzeichnes, Wintersemester, 1981–82.

94. FU, Fachbereich Philosophie und Sozialwissenschaft I, Kommentiertes Vorlesungsverzeichnis, Sommersemester, 1986.

95. Interviews with Inka Arroyo and Tania Taubes.

96. FU, FB Philosophie und Sozialwissenschaft I, Kommentiertes Vorlesungsverzeichnes, Wintersemester, 1984–85.

97. Nicolaus Sombart, *Journal intime 1982/83. Rückkehr nach Berlin* (Berlin, 2003), p. 34.

98. Interview with Richard Faber; Sombart, *Journal intime,* p. 94.

99. Interview with Jürgen Kaube.

100. Interview with Saul Friedländer.

101. *Die Tageszeitung,* July 20, 1985.

102. *ACS,* p. 7.

103. *ACS,* p. 14.

104. *ACS,* p. 25.

105. *ACS,* p. 29.

106. *ACS,* p. 17.

107. *ACS,* p. 28. For an in-depth investigation of this theme, see Susanne Heil, *"Gefährliche Beziehungen." Walter Benjamin und Carl Schmitt* (Stuttgart, 1996), esp. pp. 156–61.

108. *ACS*, p. 22.

109. Interview with Nicolaus Sombart.

110. Interview with Nicolaus Sombart.

111. Interview with Saul Friedländer; Saul Friedländer, *Where Memory Leads. My Life* (New York, 2016), pp. 209–21.

112. Interviews with Aleida and Jan Assmann.

113. JT to Nolte, June 19, 1986, from Heidelberg; Nolte Papers.

114. Interviews with Saul Friedländer and Ernst Tugendhat.

115. Interview with Avishai and Edna Margalit.

Chapter Sixteen. Final Act, 1986–87

1. JT to Louis Finkelstein, March 26, 1986, ETT.

2. Text of Taubes's talk, ETT.

3. Interview with Zachary Edelstein.

4. JT to Nolte, June 16, 1986, Nolte Papers.

5. JT to Nolte, June 16, 1986, Nolte Papers.

6. Interview with Renate Schlesier.

7. Interview with Gabriele Althaus.

8. Interview with Saul Friedländer.

9. JT to Wilhelm Kewenig, November 21, 1986, ETT.

10. Interview with Rachel Salamander.

11. Interviews with Madeleine Dreyfus and Ethan Taubes.

12. Interviews with Madeleine Dreyfus and Marianne Weinberg; JT to Vorstand der Israelitischen Cultusgemeinde Zürich, December 12, 1986, ETT.

13. Interviews with Tania and Ethan Taubes.

14. Interview with Gabriele Althaus.

15. Interview with Peter Gente.

16. Unpublished interview with Sybille Haberditzl by Susan Neiman, who shared it with me.

17. Interview with Tania Taubes.

18. Christina Buhmann to author, March 2, 2006.

19. Information from Aleida Assmann.

20. Interview with Heinz Wismann.

21. Interview with Jean Bollack; communication from Christina Buhmann, 2021.

22. Interview with Gabriele Althaus.

23. Interview with Tania Taubes.

24. JT to Susman, Zurich, August 22, 1947, Susman Nachlass.

25. "Jacob Taubes," in *Denken das an der Zeit ist*, ed. Florian Rötzer (Frankfurt, 1987), pp. 305–19, pp. 316–18, p. 344. The interview was conducted on November 16, 1985.

26. Jacob Taubes, "'Frist' als Form apokalyptischer Zeiterfahrung," in *Wovon werden Wir Morgen geistig leben?*, ed. Oskar Schatz and Hans Spatzenegger (Salzburg, 1986), pp. 89–98, p. 96.

27. Taubes, "'Frist' als Form apokalyptischer Zeiterfahrung," p. 136.

28. Taubes to Wilhelm Kewenig, November 21, 1986, ETT.

29. Interviews with Gabriele Althaus and Ernst Tugendhat.

30. Althaus interview, in *Das Politische und das Persönliche*, p. 478.

31. "Nachruf Rudi Thiessen: Der letze Dandy West-Berlins," *Tageszeitung*, July 29, 2015.

32. *ACS*, p. 71.

33. Paul Mendes-Flohr, *Martin Buber: A Life of Faith and Dissent* (New Haven, CT, 2019), pp. 75, 237–38.

34. Jacob Taubes, *PTdP*, p. 14. On the differing attitudes of Jewish scholars toward Jesus and Paul, see Susannah Heschel, *Abraham Geiger and the Jewish Jesus* (Chicago, 1998), pp. 235–37. For a survey of the attitudes of Jewish scholars toward Paul, see Donald A. Hagner, "Paul in Modern Jewish Thought," in *Pauline Studies*, ed. Hagner (Exeter, 1981), pp. 143–65.

35. Leo Baeck, "The Faith of Paul," based on a lecture delivered in London and first published in the *Journal of Jewish Studies* (1952), and reprinted in Leo Baeck, *Judaism and Christianity* (New York 1970), p. 142.

36. *PTdP*, p. 22.

37. *PTdP*, pp. 33–34.

38. *PTdP*, p. 24.

39. *PTdP*, pp. 54–70.

40. *PTdP*, pp. 71–72.

41. *PTdP*, pp. 47ff.

42. *PTdP*, pp. 66–67. See the critique by Paula Fredriksen of the notion that modern Jews such as Taubes are better able to understand Paul: "There is no natural land bridge, formed by temperament and tradition, into the distant past. In fact, the false familiarity conjured by such claims is a serious impediment to historical thinking." Paula Fredriksen, "Putting Paul in His (Historical) Place," *Journal of the Jesus Movement in Its Jewish Setting*, vol. 5 (2018), 89–110.

43. *PTdP*, p. 39.

44. *PTdP*, pp. 17–22.

45. *PTdP*, p. 40.

46. *PTdP*, p. 100. Taubes may also have drawn here upon the interpretation of Erik Peterson; see Christoph Schmidt, *Die theopolitische Stunde* (Munich, 2009), p. 275, n. 9; p. 282, n. 20.

47. *PTdP*, pp. 37–38.

48. *PTdP*, p. 27.

49. *PTdP*, p. 95.

50. *PTdP*, p. 74.

51. *PTdP*, p. 77.

52. *PTdP*, pp. 73–75.

53. As noted in an astute review by Rémi Brague, "Vous vous appelez bien saint Paul?," *Critique: revue générale des publications françaises et étrangères*, vol. 634 (March 2000), pp. 214–20, pp. 219–20.

54. Of the many commentators on Taubes, one of the few to note this was Christoph Schulte, who helped Taubes to prepare for his classes on Paul. Schulte, "PAULUS," in Faber et al., *Abendländische Eschatologie: Ad Jacob Taubes*, p. 94.

55. *PTdP*, pp. 108–10.

56. *PTdP*, p. 112.

57. *PTdP*, p. 121.

58. *PTdP*, pp. 122–23. Here, Taubes was reiterating a theme he had spelled out decades earlier, in "Religion and the Future of Psychoanalysis," in "Psychoanalysis and the Future: A Century Commemoration of the Birth of Sigmund Freud," special issue, *Psychoanalysis*, vol. 4, no. 45 (1957), pp. 136–42, reprinted in *CtC*.

59. Jacob Taubes, "Die politische Theologie des Paulus. Wörtliche Transkription der in der FEST gehaltenen Vorlesung," p. 18. I thank Aleida Assmann for a copy of this document.

60. Interview with Ernst Tugendhat.

61. Interviews with Michael Theunissen and Renate Schlesier.

62. Interviews with Renate Schlesier, Wilfried Menninghaus, and Werner Hamacher; JT to Wilhelm Kewenig, November 21, 1986, ETT.

63. Interview with Wilhelm Schmidt-Biggemann.

64. Interview with Wilhelm Schmidt-Biggemann.

65. Interviews with Gabriele Althaus and Ethan Taubes.

66. Interview with Ernst Tugendhat.

67. Interview with Marcel Marcus; "Moische Solowiejczyk," https://www.jewiki.net/wiki/Moische_Solowiejczyk.

Chapter Seventeen. The Afterlives of Jacob Taubes

1. Interview with Agnes Heller.

2. Jan Assmann, "Talmud in der Paris-Bar. Zum Tod des jüdischen Philosophen Jacob Taubes (1923–1987)," *Tageszeitung*, March 28, 1987.

3. "Kritische Solidarität. Peter Gäng über die Schwierigkeit, Jacob Taubes politisch einzuordnen," *Tageszeitung*, March 28, 1987.

4. Henning Ritter, "Akosmisch. Zum Tod von Jacob Taubes," *Frankfurter Allgemeine Zeitung*, March 24, 1987. Ritter would later compose a fuller portrait, "Jacob Taubes. Verstehen, was da los ist," in Ritter, *Verehrte Denker*.

5. Uwe Schlicht, "Herausragend als akademischer Lehrer," *Der Tagesspiegel*, March 25, 1987.

6. "Jacob Taubes gestorben," *Neue Zürcher Zeitung*, March 24, 1987.

7. *Der Spiegel*, March 30, 1987, p. 272.

8. Jan Assmann, "Erzjude und Urchrist," *Die Welt*, March 25, 1987.

9. Florian Rötzer, "Zeit heißt: Frist. Interview mit Jacob Taubes," *Frankfurter Rundschau*, April 4, 1987.

10. Mohler, "Der messianische Irrwisch," pp. 219–21.

11. Mohler, "Der messianische Irrwisch," pp. 219–21.

12. Interview with Peter McLaughlin; Iris Nachum in unpublished interview with Susan Neiman and Dieter Henrich.

13. Axel Matthes to Hans-Joachim Arndt, April 26, 1991, Arndt Nachlass.

14. Hans-Joachim Arndt to Axel Matthes, May 2, 1991, Arndt Nachlass.

15. Axel Matthes to Hans-Joachim Arndt, January 31, 1995, Arndt Nachlass.

16. Sander, *Die Auflösung aller Dinge*.

17. Sander, *Die Auflösung aller Dinge*, p. 7.

18. Sander, *Die Auflösung aller Dinge*, p. 26.

19. Sander, *Die Auflösung aller Dinge*, p. 95.

20. Sander, *Die Auflösung aller Dinge*, p. 159.

21. Weissmann, *Armin Mohler*, p. 281, n. 43.

22. *Grenzgänge*, p. 341. Furth was among the contributors to this tribute volume. On Mohler, see Weissmann, *Armin Mohler*, p. 230.

23. "Ursula Haverbeck," Wikipedia, last updated January 17, 2021, https://en .wikipedia.org/wiki/Ursula_Haverbeck#cite_note-NVSB-2.

24. Interview with Peter Gente.

25. *ACS*, p. 6.

26. *ACS*, p. 73. Of the seemingly endless historical literature on Carl Schmitt, the best biographical treatment is by Reinhard Mehring, *Carl Schmitt* (Munich, 2009; English translation, Cambridge, 2014); for an incisive, essay-length critical exploration of Schmitt's thought, career, and the fascination he exerted, see Lutz Niethammer, "Die politische Anstrengung des Begriffs. Über die exemplarische Faszination Carl Schmitts," in *Nationalsozialismus in den Kulturwissenschaften. Band 2. Leitbegriffe— Deutungsmuster—Paradigmenkämpfe Erfahrungen und Transformationen im Exil*, ed. Hartmut Lehmann and Otto Gerhard Oexle (Göttingen, 2004), pp. 41–82.

27. Interview with Peter Gente.

28. Horst Bredekamp, "Walter Benjamin's Esteem for Carl Schmitt," in *The Oxford Handbook of Carl Schmitt*, ed. Hens Meierhenich and Oliver Simons (New York, 2019), p. 682.

29. Interview with Jan Assmann.

30. Aleida Assmann, "Vorwort" and "Editorische Notiz" to *PTdP*, and interview with Aleida Assmann.

31. Interview with Heinz Wismann.

32. Interviews with Jan Assmann, Aleida Assmann, and Winfried Menninghaus.

33. Aleida Assmann, Jan Assmann, Wolf-Daniel Hartwich, and Winfried Menninghaus, "Einleitung" to *KzK*, p. 8.

34. Assmann et al., "Einleitung" to *KzK*, p. 7.

35. Interview with Thomas Macho.

36. Peter Sloterdijk, *Eurotaoismus. Zur Kritik der politischen Kinetik* (Frankfurt, 1989), p. 15, pp. 277ff.

37. Peter Sloterdijk and Thomas Macho (ed.), *Weltrevolution der Seele. Eine Lese- und Arbeitsbuch der Gnosis von der Spätantike bis zur Gegenwart* (Zurich, 1991).

38. Jan Assmann, introduction to *Self, Soul and Body in Religious Experience*, ed. A. I. Baumgarten, J. Assmann, and G. G. Stroumsa (Leiden, 1998), pp. 1–3.

39. Assmann, introduction.

40. Interview with Albert Baumgarten.

41. Interview with Thomas Macho; Richard Faber, Eveline Goodman-Thau, and Thomas Macho, "Vorwort" to Faber et al., *Abendländische Eschatologie. Ad Jacob Taubes*.

42. Schulte, "PAULUS," in Faber et al., *Abendländische Eschatologie: Ad Jacob Taubes*, p. 95.

43. Faber et al., "Vorwort" to *Abendländische Eschatologie*, pp. 23–24.

44. Niethammer, "Die politische Anstrengung des Begriffs," pp. 60–67.

45. "Unannehmbare Praktiken," *Tageszeitung*, March 23, 1987, p. 20.

46. Jerry Z. Muller, "Capitalism: The Wave of the Future," *Commentary*, December 1988, pp. 21–26.

47. See Paul J. Griffiths, "Christ and Critical Theory," *First Things*, August–September 2004, pp. 46–55.

48. Alain Badiou, interview in *Le Monde*, May 3, 2008, quoted in Mark Lilla, "From Mao to Saint Paul," in Lilla, *The Shipwrecked Mind: On Political Reaction* (New York, 2016), p. 92.

49. Alain Badiou, *Saint Paul: The Foundation of Universalism*, trans. Ray Brassier (Stanford, 2003; French, 1998), p. 109. The parallel to Althusser is noted by Žižek, "Paul and the Truth Event," in John Milbank, Slavoj Žižek, and Creston Davis, *Paul's New Moment: Continental Philosophy and the Future of Christian Theology* (Grand Rapids, MI, 2010), p. 88. A valuable, skeptical study of Badiou is Scruton, "The Kraken Wakes: Badiou and Žižek," in his *Fools, Frauds, and Firebrands: Thinkers of the New Left*.

50. Badiou, *Saint Paul*, pp. 4–6.

51. Badiou, *Saint Paul*, pp. 7–11.

52. Badiou, *Saint Paul*, pp. 14–15.

53. Badiou, *Saint Paul*, p. 102.

54. Badiou, *Saint Paul*, p. 43.

55. Alain Badiou, "Part Two: Uses of the Word 'Jew,'" in Badiou, *Polemics*, trans. Steve Corcoran (London, 2006), pp. 161–63, translated from Badiou, *Circonstances 3* (Paris, 2005). See also Sarah Hammerschlag, "Bad Jews, Authentic Jews, Figural Jews: Badiou and the Politics of Exemplarity," in *Judaism, Liberalism, and Political Theology*, ed. Randi Rashkover and Martin Kavka (Bloomington, IN, 2013), pp. 221–40.

56. Mark Lilla, "A New, Political Saint Paul?," *New York Review of Books*, October 23, 2008.

57. Daniel Binswanger, "Prediger des Profanen," *Die Welt*, March 8, 2005.

58. Georgio Agamben, *The Time That Remains: A Commentary on the Letter to the Romans*, trans. Patricia Dailey (Stanford, 2005; Italian, 2000), pp. 51–52.

59. Agamben, *Time That Remains*, p. 27.

60. Agamben, *Time That Remains*, p. 111.

61. Agamben, *Time That Remains*, p. 145.

62. On the fascinations and frustrations of Žižek's style, see Scruton, "Kraken Wakes: Badiou and Žižek."

63. Slavoj Žižek, *The Puppet and the Dwarf: The Perverse Core of Christianity* (Cambridge, MA, 2003), p. 9.

64. Žižek, *Puppet and the Dwarf*, p. 10.

65. Žižek, *Puppet and the Dwarf*, p. 130.

66. See, for example, Ward Blanton, *A Materialism for the Masses. Saint Paul and the Philosophy of Undying Life* (New York, 2014).

67. Ward Blanton and Hent de Vries (ed.), *Paul and the Philosophers* (New York, 2013); Peter Frick (ed.), *Paul in the Grip of the Philosophers. The Apostle and Contemporary Continental Philosophy* (Minneapolis, 2013).

68. Tiziano Tosolini, *Paolo e i filosofi. Interpretazioni del Cristianesimo da Heidegger a Derrida* (Bologna, 2019). On the growing interest in Taubes in Italian theological circles, see Giuseppe Cagnata, "Osservatorio paolino," *Eco dei Barnabiti*, no. 1 (2020), pp. 29–34.

69. Luke Timothy Johnson, "Reading Romans," *Christian Century*, January 15, 2008, pp. 32–36, p. 35. For examples, see R. S. Sugirtharajah and Fernando F. Segovia (ed.),

A Postcolonial Commentary on the New Testament Writings (London, 2009); part of the series The Bible and Postcolonialism, ed. R. S. Sugirtharajah.

70. For a fine overview of the issue, see David Nirenberg, *Anti-Judaism: The Western Tradition* (New York, 2013), ch. 2.

71. John G. Gager, *Who Made Early Christianity?: The Jewish Lives of the Apostle Paul* (New York, 2015), p. 14.

72. Gager, *Who Made Early Christianity?*, pp. 49–51.

73. Gager, *Who Made Early Christianity?*, pp. 29–30; and more broadly, John G. Gager, *Reinventing Paul* (New York, 2000).

74. Paula Fredriksen, *Paul: The Pagan's Apostle* (New Haven, CT, 2017), pp. 175–77.

75. Matthew N. Novenson, "Whither the Paul within Judaism *Schule*?," *Journal of the Jesus Movement in its Jewish Setting*, vol. 5 (2018), pp. 79–88, p. 79. For current literature on the topic, see "Theology," Paul within Judaism, https://www.paulwithinjudaism.com/theology.

76. Annette Yoshiko Reid and A. H. Becker (ed.), *The Ways That Never Parted: Jews and Christians in Late Antiquity and the Early Middle Ages* (Tübingen, 2003).

77. See, for example, Seth Schwartz, *Imperialism and Jewish Society, 200 B.C.E. to 640 C.E.* (Princeton, NJ, 2001), pp. 12–13; Rubinstein, *Culture of the Babylonian Talmud*, ch. 7; Hayes, "'Other' in Rabbinic Literature."

78. Jan Assmann, "Die übersetzten Götter. Ein Gespräch mit Elisabetta Colagrossi," *Zeitschrift für Ideengeschichte*, vol. 12, no. 4 (2018), pp. 75–90, p. 79.

79. Jan Assmann, *Moses the Egyptian* (Cambridge, MA, 1997).

80. Jan Assmann, *Herrschaft und Heil. Politische Theologie in Altägyptien, Israel und Europa* (Munich, 2000), dedicated to the memory of Jacob Taubes; *Die Mosaische Unterscheidung oder der Preis des Monotheismus* (Munich, 2003), English translation, *The Price of Monotheism* (Stanford, 2009); and *Of God and Gods: Egypt, Israel, and the Rise of Monotheism* (Madison, WI, 2008).

81. Assmann, "Die übersetzten Götter," pp. 84–85.

82. Assmann, "Die übersetzten Götter," p. 86.

83. Assmann, "Die übersetzten Götter," p. 88; Assmann, *Die Mosaische Unterscheidung*. See also the chapter "No God but God: Exclusive Monotheism and the Language of Violence," in Assmann, *Of God and Gods*.

84. Assmann mentions Hume in *Of God and Gods*, p. 109.

85. Assmann, *Of God and Gods*, p. 111; similarly, *Die Mosaische Unterscheidung*, pp. 30–31.

86. For a brief but useful overview of Assmann's claims, see Robert Erlewine, "Reason within the Bounds of Religion: Assmann, Cohen, and the Possibilities of Monotheism," in Rashkover and Kavka, *Judaism, Liberalism, and Political Theology*, pp. 269–88.

87. See for example, see Aleida Assmann, *Erinnerungsräume: Formen und Wandlungen des kulturellen Gedächtnisses* (Munich, 1999).

88. Sloterdijk, *Eurotaoismus*, p. 15.

89. Jacques Schuster, "Ein Leben in Finsternis," *Die Welt*, June 26, 2010.

90. G. W. Bowersock, "Who Was Saint Paul?," *New York Review of Books* (November 5, 2015), p. 22.

91. Elettra Stimilli, *Jacob Taubes: Sovranità e tempo messianico* (Brescia, 2004).

92. Bruce Rosenstock, "Jacob Taubes," in *The Palgrave Handbook of Radical Theology*, ed. Christopher Rodkey and Jordan E. Miller (London, 2018), pp. 381–97.

93. Willem Styfhals, *No Spiritual Investment in the World: Gnosticism and Postwar German Philosophy* (Ithaca, NY, 2019); Ole Jacob Løland, *Pauline Ugliness: Jacob Taubes and the Turn to Paul* (New York, 2020).

94. "Thirty Years after: Jacob Taubes between Politics, Philosophy and Religion," Zurich, October 20–21, 2017, https://www.zfl-berlin.org/event/thirty-years-after-jacob-taubes-between-politics-philosophy-and-religion.html.

95. "About Us," Leinbniz-Zentrum für Literatur- und Kulturforschung, https://www.zfl-berlin.org/the-zfl.html.

96. Sigrid Weigel, "Zur Edition der *Schriften* und zum Nachlass von Susan Taubes," in *Korrespondenz 1*, pp. 7–10.

97. Martin Treml, "Reinventing the Canonical: The Radical Thinking of Jacob Taubes," in *"Escape to Life": German Intellectuals in New York. A Compendium on Exile after 1933*, ed. Eckart Goebel and Sigrid Weigel (Berlin, 2012), pp. 457–78, p. 459; and "Vorbermerkung der Herausgeber," in *Taubes-Schmitt*, p. 8.

Archival Collections

(The terms collection, papers, and Nachlass are used interchangeably)
Archiv für Zeitgeschichte, ETH Zentrum, Zürich
Hannah Arendt, Arendt Papers, Library of Congress
Hans-Joachim Arndt, Nachlass, courtesy of Volker Beismann, Burchsal
Hans Urs von Balthasar, Hans Urs von Balthasar Archiv, Basel
Salo W. Baron, Stanford University
Daniel Bell, courtesy of David A. Bell
Samuel Hugo Bergmann, NLI
Martin Buber, NLI
Arthur A. Cohen, Beinecke Library, Yale University
William Y. Elliott, Elliott Collection, Hoover Institution Archives
Jürgen Habermas, personal collection
Hermeneutische Institut Files, Freie Universität Berlin (HI)
Max Horkheimer, Stadt- und Universitätsbibliothek, Frankfurt
Carl J. Friedrich, Harvard University Archives
Hans Jonas, Philosophisches Archiv der Universität Konstanz
Erich von Kahler, DLA Marbach
René König, Historisches Archiv der Stadt Köln
Adolf Leschnitzer, Leo Baeck Institute, New York City
Herbert Marcuse, Stadt- und Universitätsbibliothek, Frankfurt
Warren C. McCulloch, American Philosophical Society, Philadelphia
Armin Mohler, DLA Marbach
Ernst Nolte, personal collection
Notgemeinschaft für eine freie Universität; Bund Freiheit der Wissenschaft, Hoover
    Institution Archives
Philosophy Department Correspondence 1950–55, Harvard University Archives,
    UAV 687.11
Eugen Rosenstock-Huessy, Dartmouth College
Gershom Scholem, NLI
Gerda Seligson, Leo Baeck Institute, New York City
Ernst (Akiba) Simon, NLI
Susan Sontag Papers, Special Collections, UCLA
Leo Strauss, Special Collections Research Center, University of Chicago Library
Michael Strauss, Haifa, courtesy of Oded Balaban
Suhrkamp Archiv, used at the Literaturarchiv der Universität Frankfurt am Main,
    since transferred to DLA, Marbach as Siegfried Unseld Archiv
Margarete Susman, DLA Marbach
Peter Szondi, DLA Marbach
Jacob Taubes, Ethan and Tania Taubes Collection (ETT)

Jacob Taubes, Personalakten, Universitätsarchiv, Freie Universität Berlin (PA)
Jacob Taubes, Promotionsakte Jacob Taubes, Staatsarchiv Zürich: U 1092.47
Jacob Taubes, Zentrum für Literatur- und Kulturforschung, Berlin (ZfL)
Paul Tillich, Harvard University
Eric Voegelin, Hoover Institution Archives
Michael Wyschogrod, personal collection

Interviews

Agassi, Joseph and Judith Buber Agassi—phone interview, August 24, 2004
Agus, Naomi—phone interview, June 16, 2005
Althaus, Gabriele—Berlin, March 31, 2006
Anatot, Mira—phone interview, January 11, 2006
Arroyo, Inka—Jerusalem, June 20, 2005
Assmann, Aleida—New Haven, CT, March 4, 2005; Berlin, February 11, 2006
Assmann, Jan—New Haven, CT, March 4, 2005; Berlin, February 11, 2006
Aviad, Janet—Jerusalem, August 20, 2004
Band, Arnold—phone interview, 2004
Baumgarten, Albert—phone interview, April 30, 2004
Bell, Daniel—Cambridge, MA, March 26, 2004
Bellah, Robert—phone interview, August 2, 2004
Ben Shlomo, Joseph—phone interview, August 25, 2004
Berger, Peter L.—Washington, DC, 2006
Berman, Marshall—New York City, June 30, 2004
Bollack, Jean and Mayotte—Paris, May 26, 2007
Bolz, Norbert—Berlin, May 11, 2006; November 20, 2019
Botschko, Moshe and Helen—Kochav Ya'akov, June 22, 2005
Brinker, Menachem—Jerusalem, August 20, 2004
Buhmann, Christina (Tina)—Berlin, April 9, 2006
Callimanopulos, Gregory—phone interview, January 7, 2009
Cavell, Stanley—phone interview, August 2, 2004
Cohn, Gavriel—phone interview, May 18, 2009
Conradi, Arnulf—Berlin, January 17, 2006
Dan, Joseph—Jerusalem, August 24, 2004
Decter, Midge—phone interview, December 10, 2004
Dreyfus, Hubert—phone interview, March 27, 2005
Dreyfus, Madeleine—Zurich, May 5, 2006
Edelstein, Zachary—New York City, December 27, 2005
Faber, Richard—Berlin, April 8, 2006
Finkelstein, Ezra—phone interview, 2005
First, Elsa—New York City, November 24, 2004
Fischer, Shlomo—phone interview, January 22, 2020
Freudenthal, Gideon—phone interview, January 26, 2005
Freudenthal-Livne, Rachel—phone interview, June 17, 2005
Friedländer, Saul—phone interview, December, 2005
Frosch, William—phone interview, August 16, 2013

Flügge, Thomas—Berlin, March 27, 2006

Gallahue, John J.—New York City, November 23, 2004

Gasché, Rodolphe—Buffalo, April 16, 2006

Gay, Peter—phone interview, 2008

Gente, Peter—Berlin, May 11, 2006

Gerhardt, Uta—Washington, DC, April, 2004

Gershoni, Naomi—phone interview, January 11, 2006

Gitin, Seymour (Sy)—phone interview, 2005

Glazer, Nathan—phone interview, 2004

Gourevitch, Victor and Jacqueline—New York City, November 23, 2004

Greenberg, Gershon—Washington, DC, March 2004; June 10, 2020

Habermas, Jürgen and Ute—Starnberg, April 20, 2006

Halbertal, Moshe—Jerusalem, August 18, 2004

Hamacher, Werner—Frankfurt, April 21, 2006

Hartman, David—phone interview, March 20, 2008

Hechler, Susan—Berlin, February 22, 2006

Heller, Agnes—Berlin, May 18, 2006

Henrich, Dieter—Stuttgart, March 12, 2006

Hertzberg, Arthur—Englewood, NJ, May 19, 2004

Heschel, Susannah—Waltham, MA, March 25, 2004

Himmelfarb, Gertrude—Washington, DC, May 20, 2004

Holton, Nina—phone interview, December 29, 2005

Holzer, Eli—Jerusalem, June 20, 2005

Hyman, Arthur—phone interview, 2004

Idel, Moshe—Jerusalem, August 19, 2004

Kahane-Geyer, Ruth—Lisbon, October 28, 2004

Kaube, Jürgen—Berlin, March 5, 2006

Kelman, Levi—Jerusalem, June 22, 2005

Kippenberg, Hans—phone interview, March 4, 2006

Kittsteiner, Hans Dieter—Berlin, March 31, 2006

Klausner, Magda—phone interview, December 29, 2008

Kristol, Irving—Washington, DC, May 20, 2004

Lämmert, Eberhard—Berlin, 2006

Lang, Berel—email, July 9, 2017

Leifman, Morton—phone interview, June 6, 2005

Leites, Edmund—New York City, June 30, 2004

Lepenies, Wolf—Berlin, April 25, 2006

Locke, Richard—New York City, October 25, 2006

Lorberbaum, Menachem—phone interview, January 6, 2020

Lübbe, Hermann—Havixbeck, May 28, 2007

Lypp, Bernhard—Munich, April 20, 2006

Luria, Ze'ev—Jerusalem, June 19, 2005

Macho, Thomas—Berlin, March 4, 2006

Marcus, Marcel—Jerusalem, August 18, 2004

Margalit, Avishai and Edna—Jerusalem, August 19, 2004

Maurer, Reinhard—Berlin, April 7, 2006

McLaughlin, Peter—Arlington, Virginia, August 3, 2005

Mendes-Flohr, Paul—Jerusalem, March 29, 2004; June 6, 2017

Menninghaus, Winfried—Berlin, April 26, 2006

Michelson, Annette—New York City, March 3, 2005

Nettelback, Joachim—Berlin, April 25, 2006

Neusner, Jacob—phone interview, 2005

Nolte, Ernst—Berlin, March 24, 2006

Oswald, Niko—Berlin, April 26, 2006

Podhoretz, Norman—phone interview, December 15, 2004

Rieff, David—New York City, December 27, 2005

Rieff, Philip—Philadelphia, May 5, 2004

Ritter, Henning—Frankfurt, April 21, 2006

Ritter, Martin—Berlin, January 20, 2006

Rubenstein, Richard L.—Fairfield, CT, March 4, 2005

Salamander, Rachel—Schloss Elmau, June 28, 2011

Schäfer, Peter—Princeton, NJ, March 1, 2005

Schatzmiller, Joseph—Durham, NC, March 3, 2004

Schlesier, Renate—Berlin, April 7, 2006

Schlicht, Uwe—Berlin, March 8, 2006

Schmidt-Biggemann, Wilhelm—Princeton, NJ, January 9, 2006

Schorsch, Ismar—phone interview, July 25, 2004

Schulte, Christoph—Berlin, February 10, 2006

Shedletzky, Itta—Jerusalem, August 16, 2004

Shiman, Leon—Brookline, MA, September 22, 2005

Sigrist, Marcel—Jerusalem, March 22, 2006

Sokel, Walter H.—phone interview, August 2, 2004

Stahmer, Harold—phone interview, 2004

Steinberg, Jonathan—phone interview, May 19, 2009

Stendahl, Krister—phone interview, August 3, 2004

Stern, David—phone interview, August 28, 2017

Stroumsa, Guy and Sarah—Jerusalem, August 22, 2004

Szony, Lily—phone interview, February 28, 2005

Talmon, Shmaryahu—phone interview, February 26, 2009

Taubes, Ethan—phone, email, and interviews, 2004–20

Taubes, Tanaquil (Tania)—phone, email, and interviews, 2004–20

Thadden, Rudolf von—phone interview, April 6, 2006

Theunissen, Michael—Berlin, May 20, 2006

Tropper, Daniel—phone interview, June 20, 2005

Tugendhat, Ernst—Tübingen, March 13, 2006

Waldoks, Moshe—phone interview, August 8, 2005

Wapnewski, Peter—Berlin, March 27, 2006

Wechsler, Judith (Glatzer)—phone interview, September 4, 2005

Weinberg, Marianne and Sigbert (Sigi)—Zurich, March 28, 2009

Weiss Halivni, David—phone interview, May 3, 2004

Wieseltier, Leon—Washington, DC, March 19, 2004

Wismann, Heinz—Paris, May 25, 2007

Wolff, Robert—phone interview, May 10, 2004
Wyschogrod, Edith—New York City, March 3, 2005
Wyschogrod, Michael—New York City, March 3, 2005
Zischler, Hanns—Berlin, 2006
Zimmermann, Hans Dieter—phone interview, May 2006

Figures are denoted by page numbers in italics

A NOTE ON THE TYPE

THIS BOOK has been composed in Miller, a Scotch Roman typeface designed by Matthew Carter and first released by Font Bureau in 1997. It resembles Monticello, the typeface developed for The Papers of Thomas Jefferson in the 1940s by C. H. Griffith and P. J. Conkwright and reinterpreted in digital form by Carter in 2003.

Pleasant Jefferson ("P. J.") Conkwright (1905–1986) was Typographer at Princeton University Press from 1939 to 1970. He was an acclaimed book designer and AIGA Medalist.